Contents

FEMALE AND MALE
Psychological Perspectives

Rhoda K. Unger
MONTCLAIR STATE COLLEGE

HARPER & ROW, PUBLISHERS
New York   Hagerstown   Philadelphia   San Francisco   London

*To Burt, Laurel, and Rachel and all my friends and colleagues—
who shared both the joy of discovery and the labor of putting it
all together.*

Sponsoring Editor: George A. Middendorf
Project Editor: Joyce Marshall
Senior Production Manager: Kewal K. Sharma
Compositor: Bi-Comp Incorporated
Printer and Binder: Halliday Lithograph Corporation
Art Studio: Vantage Art Inc.

Female and Male: Psychological Perspectives

Library of Congress Cataloging in Publication Data

Unger, Rhoda Kesler.
  Female and male.

  Bibliography: p.
  Includes index.
  1. Sex role. 2. Sex differences (Psychology)
I. Title. [DNLM: 1. Sex characteristics. BF692 U57f]
HQ1075.U53   301.41   79-13233
ISBN 0-06-046727-4

Preface

Although in recent years increasing attention has been paid to the effect of sex on individual and group behavior, and even to the particular experiences of females as females (rather than as a subspecies of males), there has been little agreement on how to define what is being studied. The number of books being produced in the field seems to be increasing at an explosive rate; the amount of data being generated by researchers seems to be increasing even more rapidly; and like the characters in *Through the Looking Glass* we are all running (and writing) as fast as we can to keep up. Thus a perfectly reasonable question for the reader to ask is "Why another book?" or "What will this book tell me about the behavior of women (and men) that cannot be acquired from already available sources?"

Although this book clearly focuses on women, I have deliberately avoided the use of the word *women* in the title. Instead, the book may be characterized as taking a feminist approach to issues involving sex and gender. Among the characteristics of this position are the following: (1) It is absurd to assume that one can examine women in isolation from the rest of humanity; indeed, a critique of an identical assumption for men was one of the bases from which this field of study evolved. (2) It is questionable whether we have only two sexes to study. The factors that define sex do not vary dichotomously but are often seen to vary in a continuous manner. This is because sex is not a unidimensional but a multidimensional characteristic. (3) It is questionable whether sex provides a valid explanation of most psychological phenomena. The term *sex*, as it is usually used, merely provides us with a convenient means of describing various individuals. (4) It is unfair as well as unscientific to assume that there are psychological processes that are unique to women (with the possible exception of the psychophysiology of reproduction). We can learn a great deal about the processes that mediate sex-related behaviors by examining individuals with characteristics that are suposely appropriate to the other sex(es).

The position of this book is that sex can be more appropriately investigated as a stimulus variable than as a subject variable. Its focus is on what people believe sex controls as well as what it actually does control. It views many sex-related effects from a cognitive perception framework—what people believe greatly affects what they perceive in the social world around them. The role of society in the maintenance of sex roles will be examined, as well as more traditional biological explanations of sex differences.

The organization of the book is based on a feminist framework for the study of sex and gender. First, several chapters are devoted to a definition of the field and a demonstration that sex as a stimulus variable—what people perceive about what people do—affects a wide variety of everyday behaviors. Second, we consider what sex differences—behavioral and biological—can be shown to exist. In these chapters we are concerned with the social and scientific construction of particular sexes and gender identities and roles. Third, we move to environments that foster sex and gender differentiation. Here particular attention is paid to the role of other individuals, the kinds of information available to them (and to oneself), and attributions based on this information. Fourth, we are concerned with adult sex roles—particularly those that are considered gender-specific, such as the marital roles of women and men, parenthood, and the world of achievement. Later chapters are concerned with the effects of nonconformity with sex roles as they have traditionally been constructed. Personal deviance is viewed in terms of mental-health issues, whereas societal mechanisms that define and penalize deviance are considered as a separate issue. Sexism is viewed from a sociocultural perspective as well as in terms of a series of interpersonal transactions. Finally, I would rashly like to suggest directions in which the field is moving. Specific comments are provided for students, educators, counselors, researchers, and professional people. Perhaps each of us is all of these things, but some specificity may be helpful.

This book is designed to serve as a textbook for undergraduate and graduate courses in the psychology of women and the psychology of sex roles, as well as the courses in sex roles taught in many sociology departments. It is somewhat more difficult than an introductory textbook, but this is a result of a definite commitment. During the past few years I have become more and more aware of the need for an advanced textbook in this area—something to bridge the gap between the professional literature and the textbooks that simply make people aware that there is a body of scholarship in this area. I have found that students are not willing to stop at the introductory level but will buy books in other disciplines to gain more information—even books that appear to be aimed toward medical practitioners and researchers. Of all the courses I have taught, moreover, I find that in this subject alone students are willing to "stretch," to work to understand conceptualizations and methodologies that they would label "too hard" in other areas. They continually offer practical demonstrations of the importance of motivation for learning.

Since I have chosen to label this book as feminist in approach, I have been particularly careful to document my points as fully as possible. Feminist scholarship can be as objective as any other scholarship with a particular theoretical bias. It only appears polemical because a "masculinist" bias underlies much research in the area of sex and gender. The reference section of this book lists more than 1000 books and articles. Indeed, much information has been omitted in order to bring this book down to a manageable size. All of the information that has been retained is connected in some way to the area as a whole. As we will see, a number of themes run through the study of sex and gender, no matter what content area is being examined.

A major issue is the question of what information to consider important, not just now but in the future. And how can we tell what is important? I have tried to avoid the pitfalls of applying my own yardstick too extensively or relying on what the "old-girl network" is circulating today. The major determinants of what information to include were two: Does it fit a space in the jigsaw puzzle, or does it open up a new boundary into which the puzzle can be expanded? I am also partial to information that helps integrate the psychology of women with psychology as a whole.

I would like to add a word on the equation of "feminist" with "polemical" or "anti-male." While this book focuses on the psychology of women, it can be useful to men as well. Just as females have not acquired an inferior status through choice, the higher status of males in our society is not necessarily a reflection of greater freedom of choice for men. Many mechanisms that produce sex-specific effects operate without our awareness and are destructive to the personal growth of all of us. Knowledge of such mechanisms may help destroy them and create a sex-free or sex-blind environment that would be advantageous to all of us—whatever our sex.

ACKNOWLEDGMENTS

I want to give special thanks to the many people who helped make this book possible. They generously shared ideas, unpublished papers, and were kind enough to react to mine. I have tried to give them credit for their work throughout the body of this book, but some of the ideas came as the result of intensive seminars, discussions, or late-night rap sessions. I apologize for any omissions. Colleagues in this area have been outstandingly cooperative. I hope their style as well as their content may serve as a model for the field of psychology as a whole.

Specifically, I would like to thank Judith Alpert, Georgia Babladelis, Pauline Bart, Robert Brannon, Sandra Bem, Phyllis Berman, Annette Brodsky, Florence Denmark, Barbara Dohrenwend, Alice Eagly, Linda Fidell, Laurel Furomoto, Jo-Ann Gardner, Philip Goldberg, Kathleen Grady, Nancy Henley, Susan Herman, Lois Hoffman, Arnold Kahn, Judy Long Laws, Jacqueline Macaulay, Jean Marecek, Wendy McKenna, Martha Mednick, Virginia O'Leary, Helen Olive, Mary Parlee, Joseph Pleck, Lenore Radloff, Estelle Ramey, Mary Sue Richardson, Nancy Russo, Carolyn Sherif, Julia Sherman, Janet Spence, Sandra Tangri, Ethel Tobach, Reesa Vaughter, Lenore Walker, Barbara Wallston, and Judith Waters—all of whom took time from busy schedules to teach me something. Any mistakes I have made are not their fault.

I would also like to thank the people at Montclair State: Mary Bredemeier, Katherine Ellison, Marsha Flint, Margarita Garcia, Laura Gordon, Moira Lemay, George and Naomi Rotter, and Roland Siiter who took time to read materials and/or to help me clarify them. I would especially like to thank Agnes O'Connell who lent me her expertise in the area of personality and contributed a vital chapter to this book. Also, I would like to thank my students in the psychology of women who listened to all my latest findings with enthusiasm and patience; and I would like to especially thank Nancy Rosenfeld, who cheerfully typed a seemingly endless manuscript.

Lastly, I would like to thank Kay Deaux and Michele Wittig who read through earlier drafts of the entire manuscript and were extremely helpful in bringing it to its final form. And, I would like to thank my editors at Harper & Row for helping bring it all about.

RHODA K. UNGER

Chapter 1
An Introduction and a
Review

The study of sex and gender represents a case study of an area that is in a state of intellectual ferment. Although social scientists have examined sex differences for many years, recent critics have argued that we know little about the effects of sex. There is even disagreement about what the field should be named as well as about what its subject matter ought to be. This book represents a personal attempt to synthesize a framework for examination of the field. The framework rests on the following points: (1) Research on sex differences is distinct from examination of sex as a variable. (2) A new focus on sex derives from the greater visibility and legitimacy of women in social science. (3) Conceptualization of sex as a social variable leads to fundamentally different research than does conceptualization of sex as a biological variable. (4) Predictions presumably based on sex are often predictions based on sex roles as prescribed and controlled by social processes.

The title of this book was conceived in an effort to focus attention on these points. Each of them will be considered in this chapter and will reappear in subsequent chapters.

THE HISTORY OF THE STUDY OF WOMEN

Research on Sex Differences

It cannot be argued that psychology has totally ignored women. Women have been considered as a special group by psychologists since the mid-nineteenth century (Shields, 1974). For example, some researchers were convinced that they could distinguish between male and female brains in terms of differences in gross structure. They disagreed only on where such differences were to be found. The location of the differences varied according to the theoretical framework that was in vogue at the time. When it was believed that the frontal lobe was the repository of the highest mental capacities, the male frontal lobe was seen as larger (Shields, 1975a). When, however, the parietal lobes came to be seen as being more important, a bit of historical revisionism occurred. Females were now seen as having equal or larger frontal lobes, but smaller parietal lobes, than males.

When size differences in neural structures became difficult to document, a heated debate began over differences between female and male variability. Beginning with Darwin, it was noted that males had greater variability—an advantageous characteristic, since variability enabled species to evolve (Shields, 1974). This "variability hypothesis," first formalized by Havelock Ellis, was used to explain why there were so many more men than women with high intelligence (of course it also predicted a higher incidence of mental deficiency among males, a fact that was virtually ignored). Implications about sex differences in perceptual–motor abilities and emotionality were also derived from this hypothesis. The great danger of such hypotheses lay not in their possible validity but in the educational and social policies that they implied. "If this tendency to mediocrity was natural to the 'fair' sex, as the variability hypothesis would hold true, then it would be wasteful of public and private resources to train or encourage women to high levels of achievement" (Shields, 1974, p. 6). Thus the tendency to use scientific information about women to formulate a social policy that would be detrimental to them is evident in the earliest instances of the study of women as individuals separate from men. "When issues faded in importance, it was not because they were resolved but because they ceased to serve as viable scientific 'myths' in the changing social and scientific milieu" (Shields, 1975a, p. 740).

What Does a Sex Difference Mean?

Much of the history of the psychology of women has consisted of the study of sex differences. Psychologists study sex differences because they believe that they can more effectively understand or predict a behavior if they know the sex of the organism. Sex differences are a form of variable that is known as *organismic*. Other organismic variables are age, race, blood type, and the like. These variables cannot be directly manipulated by the experimenter, but he or she can select individuals who possess the particular trait desired. All such characteristics are often studied under the heading "individual differences."

Individual differences have predictive but not explanatory value. In other words, we can project a person's test score more accurately if we know the category to which he or she is assigned than we could if we had no information about that person's psychological label. However, we do *not*, necessarily understand why this is so. Predictions are often made simply on the basis of past experience with members of the group in question. An analogy for differentiating between prediction and explanation may be drawn from medieval astronomy. Medieval astronomers were able to predict the positions of the planets and stars—information needed for navigation, agriculture, and other practical purposes. Yet Galileo was condemned as a heretic for offering the correct explanation of these phenomena because his explanation involved displacing the earth from its "central" position in the universe.

Research on individual differences has, in fact, been largely applied rather than theoretical—and has been geared toward predicting social-policy needs. For example, Binet invented the IQ test in order to determine which students would profit most from the school system of nineteenth century France.

Throughout this book we will ask whether assigning individuals to groups by sex is any more meaningful in terms of explaining behavior than assigning them at random. At this point, however, it must be noted that the selection of what organismic variable to study is not made at random. From the large number of organismic variables by which humans can be grouped, only a few—such as race or sex—are usually chosen. It is also noteworthy that the traits that tend to characterize groups other than white males are less positive and socially desirable than the traits attributed to the so-called reference group. There seem to be no "separate-but-equal" classification schemes available.

Bias in Research on Sex Differences

Interestingly, sex differences have not always been investigated with subjects of different sexes. Research conclusions may be affected by systematic biases in terms of what gets investigated and with whom. One survey of 314 experimental studies on aggression conducted between 1967 and 1974 (Frodi, Macaulay, & Thome, 1977) found that 54 percent were concerned only with men, 24 percent with both sexes, and 8 percent only with women; 14 percent either did not specify the sex of their subjects or analyze for sex differences. Another survey of studies reported in the professional psychological literature (McKenna & Kessler, 1977) found that when females were used as subjects in aggression studies they were less likely than males to experience an active treatment designed to arouse their emotions. Moreover, female "aggression" was more likely to be evaluated by means of paper-and-pencil manipulation whereas male "aggression" was more likely to be evaluated by means of an active behavioral measure such as the number or strength of the electric shocks one subject is willing to give another. The same survey also showed that the area of research also biased the choice of subjects in terms of sex. Many more studies of aggression are done with males, whereas many more studies of attraction, cooperation, and compliance are done with females. A minority of studies appear to utilize the same procedures with subjects of both sexes.

Surveys revealing sex bias are limited to examination of studies that have actually been published in the scientific literature. However, biases about what work gets reported as well as what work is done also exist. Professional journals are often unwilling to accept "negative" results. Hence, reports about sex differences are more likely to be published than reports about sex similarities. Inability to publish material showing sex similarities may be particularly deleterious to a young field that is interested in "revising" psychological "truth."

In addition, many psychologists are interested in sex only as a peripheral variable. They do not use sex as a major or only hypothesis (Grady, 1975). It is tacked onto investigations of other, "more major" variables; thus, while sex has been related tangentially to every conceivable psychological phenomenon, no *theoretical explanation* has ever been provided. There is also no theoretical basis for a literature on sex similarities. Hence, materials related to sex differences tend to be scattered and disorganized. They are also more subject to covert individual biases than areas with a more distinctive theoretical framework.

Failure to report the sex of subjects or to analyze for sex differences appears to be more common in the psychological literature than one would readily believe. Male experimenters are more apt to omit the sex of their subjects than female experimenters. The position that "male = human" may be just as confusing for the psychology of men as it is for the psychology of women. However, researchers have been less reluctant to make generalizations about human behavior from all-male research than from all-female research (Holmes & Jorgenson, 1971).

The Critique of Sex Bias

Much of the history of the psychology of women, as distinct from the study of sex differences, emanates from objections to largely unsupported hypotheses about psychological differences between women and men. In addition to biases in the areas examined with females and males as subjects, women were frequently ignored altogether as subjects of research (Carlson & Carlson, 1961). Since the sex of subjects was not regarded as being of particular importance, it should not be surprising that the sex of the researcher was also assumed to have no effect. It seems to have come as a surprise to some people that the sex of the experimenter or other evaluator of the subject's performance could affect that performance (Harris, 1971). In a review of studies using a wide variety of projective and objective tests, Harris showed that there was sometimes an interaction between the sex of the subject and the sex of the person administering the test. Even with such an "objective" instrument as the quantitative component of the Wechsler intelligence test, children performed best for examiners who were members of their own sex (Pedersen, Shinedling, & Johnson, 1968). These effects parellel those involving the race of the tester and subject, discovered at about the same time. The objectivity of the testing instrument is not being questioned in this context. Sex biases may occur because of implicit sex biases in our social processes. A more recent survey of sex effects in behavioral research (Rumenik, Capasso, & Hendrick, 1977) suggests that the sex of the experimenter is a particularly potent source of effects in studies of children and in those involving person perception.

More overt bias may occur in the interpretation of testing instruments. For example, Naomi Weisstein (1968) points out that there is little evidence to support the notion that women have different personalities than men. She recounts an attempt by a Harvard graduate seminar to distinguish between the TAT (thematic apperception test) protocols of men and women. Only 4 out of 20 students were able to identify correctly which protocols belonged to which sex (after one and a half months of intensively studying the differences between the sexes). A similar study has documented the inability of professionals to distinguish between the protocols of male homosexuals and heterosexuals in three widely used projective tests (Hooker, 1957). Of course most evaluations are not done in a sex-blind manner and people have no difficulty demonstrating that their subjects' personalities contain "sex-typed" components.

Covert bias may underlie investigators' reluctance to examine so-called sex differences using the same procedures for both males and females. Researchers in the area of aggression have been interviewed about their choice of subjects and variables (Prescott & Foster, 1974). Their responses are indicative of a sexist pattern of beliefs that may be prevalent among male researchers:

1. "Females are more likely to refuse to receive or administer shocks than males."
2. "Most physical aggression in our society has been male–male."
3. "I manipulated anxiety and frankly I couldn't bring myself to do this with college girls."
4. "I often do not obtain significant results with females because they are more variable in their responses."
5. "Cultural values regarding sex roles make it easier to expose males to aversive stimulation."
6. "Prior research in this area indicated that I did not understand some of the important motivations of female subjects."

These answers both reflect and perpetuate sex-biased assumptions. Researchers make no attempt to disconfirm these assumptions because they are only peripherally aware of them at all. They are more a part of the male psychologist's sociocultural framework than of his theoretical one. Hence, he feels no need to question them. (It also says something about the ethics of research with human subjects if some manipulations are regarded as too "inhumane" for some humans.)

It is likely that aggression is a greater social problem in males than in females in our society. Most empirical research of the nature just discussed, purports to be objective. It is implied in this research that the problems, variables, and subjects chosen are selected on the basis of scholarly merit rather than for their value in social policy.

Many social critics, however, are beginning to recognize that research is never value free and to incorporate this into a feminist critique of science.

Is Science Value Free?

Recent feminist critiques go beyond the relatively simple position that sex biases exist in science in terms of choice of subjects (with the relative omission of females), what content areas are investigated, and what questions are asked. They now ask, To what extent do scholars share the assumptions of the larger community and how do these assumptions affect their work? For example, throughout the nineteenth century and most of the twentieth century, estrogen was known as the female hormone despite the fact that the richest source of this hormone was the urine of stallions (Hall, 1977).

We will probably never know how many feminist researchers of the past spent their lives disproving hypotheses that are no longer part of official psychological history. Leta Hollingsworth and Helen Montague, two feminist psychologists of the early twentieth century, exhaustively examined the hospital records of 2000 newborns (1000 of each sex) for birth weight and length in order to test the hypothesis of greater male variability (Shields, 1975b). Other early feminist psychologists struggled to empirically validate beliefs about "superior" male variability in brain size (measured by head circumference), intelligence, or other more "psychological" characteristics. They all found few or no differences. Hollingsworth not only didn't believe in superior male variability but didn't believe it could matter or account for the phenomena she was examining. She and other women spent their professional lives rigorously and carefully gathering data to refute hypotheses most of us have never heard of.

Mary Payer (1977), a philosopher of science, points out that what facts are regarded as scientifically valid depends on the institutional framework in which the science is done. She suggests that scholarship itself fits the definition of a social institution: (1) It has an established organization recognized within and across groups. (2) It has a specific purpose. (3) It involves particular roles with responsibilities and privileges attached to them. (4) Institutional vocabularies are created that condition our attitudes toward those who use them (for example, the idea that the language of science is unbiased and value free). Scholarship carries with it a legitimizing function—it defines what is to be taken as knowledge. And it is implied, moreover, that this knowledge, so defined, transcends institutional or personal interests.

Table 1.1 THE HISTORY OF PSYCHOLOGY: SOME LITTLE KNOWN FACTS

TEST YOURSELF (No Peeking):

Q1. Who were the first persons to use the term *projective technique* in print?

Q2. Who was the first person to develop child analysis through play?

Q3. Who developed the Cattell Infant Intelligence Test Scale?

Q4. What do the following have in common?
Bender-Gestalt Test (Bender, 1938); Taylor Manifest Anxiety Scale (Taylor, 1953); Kent-Rosanoff Word Association Test (Kent & Rosanoff, 1910); Thematic Apperception Test (Morgan & Murray, 1935); Sentence Completion Method (Rohde, 1946).

Q5. The following are the last names of individuals who have contributed to the scientific study of human behavior. What else do these names have in common?
Ausubel, Bellak, Brunswick, Buhler, Dennis, Gardner, Gibson, Glueck, Harlow, Hartley, Hoffman, Horowitz, Jones, Kendler, Koch, Lacey, Luchins, Lynd, Murphy, Premack, Rossi, Sears, Sherif, Spence, Staats, Stendler, Whiting, Yarrow.

NOW FOR THE ANSWERS:

A1. Lois Murphy and Ruth Horowitz (1938).

A2. Hermine von Hug-Hellmuth (1921).

A3. Psyche Cattell (1947).

A4. A woman is either the senior author or the sole author of each work.

A5. They are the surnames of female social scientists.

SOURCE: From M. D. Bernstein and N. F. Russo, "The History of Psychology Revisited: Or, Up with Our Foremothers," *American Psychologist,* 1974, 29, 130–134. Copyright 1974 by the American Psychological Association. Reprinted by permission.

Scholarship has a wide variety of techniques for dealing with dissident scholars. They were banished in ancient Greece and called heretics in medieval Europe. College faculties in the United States were slow to appoint Darwinists, and notable German universities apparently were able to reconcile Nazi book burning with scholarship. Omission seems to be the technique of choice in dealing with feminist scholarship. Little is known about the research of early feminist psychologists because they dealt with questions in which psychology is no longer "interested." This may be a consequence of the fact that their "answers" were a response to someone else's "questions."

The contribution of women to psychology in general has been largely ignored. Women psychologists have no official history. Since reference information is identified by means of initials, even their identity as women seems to become lost over the years. A quiz devised by Maxine Bernstein and Nancy Russo in 1974 (see Table 1.1) dramatically documents the extent to which women's contributions have been forgotten. One could suggest that information about the sex of the researcher is irrelevant if it were not for the message conveyed to beginning students: "After all, women just drop out or go on to get married and waste their education. . . . What have women ever contributed to psychology anyway!" (Bernstein & Russo, 1974, p. 130).

Science as an institution tends to reduce knowledge to a particular set of "truths." Knowledge once acquired, however, is neither ageless nor unchangeable (Payer, 1977). Knowledge is a result of interaction with one's community. Feminist scholarship is rooted in a community different from that which has traditionally been of concern to science. It will not be surprising, therefore, if it provides some new and different "truths" to the field.

The "New" Feminist Psychology

Focus on a particular content area is nothing new to psychologists. From time to time psychologists have preoccupied themselves with individual differences, small-group interactions, the brain, or the behavior of the white rat (Babladelis, 1977). Attention to women parallels the recent focus on the behavior of newborns, the aged, and "regular" or middle-aged adults. More unique to feminist psychology is the perspective rather than the content area. There are some proponents of feminist scholarship (Parlee, 1975) who feel that we cannot define a psychology *of* women but only a psychology *for* or *against* them. Psychology against women is represented in the kind of research discussed earlier (e.g., research with implicit and explicit sex biases in subject selection, choice of variables, and overgeneralization of findings). Of course the worst kind of psychology against women is that which is used to construct a second, inferior sex and leads to policy applications that maintain the societal status quo.

Many such hypotheses are based on interpretation of data rather than on the data themselves. For example, it has been argued that reading is a simple rather than a complex cognitive skill (Broverman, Klaiber, Kobayashi, & Vogel, 1968) on no other apparent basis than the fact that girls find it easier to do than boys. The hypothetical earlier maturation of the female brain has been used to their disadvantage in arguments that suggest that the male nervous system, having more time to develop, is ultimately able to reach a higher level. Even female superiority in verbal skills is used in arguing that males should continue to appear more often than females in elementary school textbooks. Facts have little to do with these arguments.

Psychology of women, on the other hand, involves (1) reinterpretation of traditional notions (e.g., women are less aggressive than men; they have less need for achievement; they have an instinct for motherhood, etc.), (2) the discovery of new phenomena (e.g., both sexes may be prejudiced against women), (3) the use of general psychological theory to explain effects that are supposedly unique to women. While there is some disagreement over exactly what term to use, those who are interested in the area agree that one important function of research is to show how psychological phenomena operate in society to keep women "down" (Mednick, 1976).

What all this research has in common is an emphasis on the social mechanisms that foster and, perhaps, produce sex differences. Sex differences per se are of less concern than social mechanisms. For the moment, biological explanations have been minimized. I for one am especially delighted when I can find a psychological phenomenon that has been largely explored in women—such as fear of success—but can be used to explain men as well. As will be discussed in subsequent chapters, androgyny and learned helplessness, as well as attributions about skill versus luck, represent areas in which sex role may explain behavior better than biological sex does. In fact a recent development in this area is the attempt to redefine what is meant by some of our traditional definitions of sex and sex roles.

SOME DEFINITIONS OF TERMS

Sex as Reproductive Functionalism

Who are the sexes? At first glance the answer to this question appears perfectly obvious. The sexes are male and female, and if one wants to be finicky about definitions there are a few ambiguous cases who might be termed *hermaphrodites*—individuals who have a mixture of anatomical and physiological characteristics that cannot be defined as exclusively female or male. Perhaps, however, I am asking the question in terms of behavioral sex. In that case males might be those who carry out the reproductive functions characteristic of males: the production of sperm, the anatomical means of conveying it to the female, and the behaviors required to convey it. In terms of this kind of definition, females are those who have the anatomical and physiological capacity to develop and nurture fertile eggs and the behaviors required for fertilization to take place. However, there are some difficulties with this kind of definition. Can sterile individuals be categorized as male or female? What about organisms who appear to be physiologically normal but do not engage in reproductive behaviors? Does the ability to remain celibate really raise questions about someone's sexual category?

Originally biologists viewed sex in just this way. Sex was viewed as an economical means of rearranging genetic systems faster than would be the case in a system of random mutation. Separate sexes do not exist in lower organisms, and even among relatively advanced organisms "male" and "female" functions are present in the same individual. Oysters and snails, for example, are functional hermaphrodites, although they do not fertilize themselves. Some vertebrates—certain fish and birds—practice a kind of serial hermaphrodism in which they change sex owing to the absence of individuals of the "opposite" sex or damage to one gonad. Fortunately for our definitions, however, mammals seem to have lost this degree of reproductive plasticity.

Viewing sex in terms of reproductive functionalism does not solve our problem of definition. Individuals can engage in reproductive activities with other individuals and still produce no offspring. Of course we are now talking about reproductive activities with members of one's own sex. Homosexual behavior is not a unique characteristic of humans. In fact males and females of all mammalian species studied so far engage in a full range of reproductive behaviors, including those that supposedly are only in the repertoire of the "other" sex. No behavior appears to be uniquely the property of one sex (Bermant & Davidson, 1974). Animals do show variation in the degree to which they engage in same-sex reproductive behavior, but this variation is affected by their position within the dominance hierarchy as well as by their biological sex.

The Labeling of Sex

No one would seriously state that the object of one's sexual preference determines one's sex. Perhaps we should ask people what sex they are. However, there are difficulties involved in this apparently simple solution too. First, we have moved from a definition of sex—physiological, anatomical, and behavioral mechanisms that function in one of two ways to produce offspring—to a definition of sexual identity. Second, this kind of technique cannot be used to categorize either animals or infants who are too young to tell us who they think they are. Again, we would not seriously suggest that children have no sex until they think they do—but perhaps this suggestion is not as absurd as it first appears.

Reproductive functionalism does not seem to be a useful criterion for sexual categorizing because of the difficulties I have enumerated. Separating people into two categories is made even more difficult by the existence of a relatively high percentage of individuals for whom the correlation between genetic, hormonal, anatomical, and behavioral determinants is not complete (Money & Ehrhardt, 1972). If all the different kinds of sexual "anomalies" are taken into account, they might characterize as much as 5 to 10 percent of the human population. Why don't we notice such a large number of people? It may be argued that sex is largely a matter of societal definition rather than biological or psychological characteristics. In Western society at least, two sexes are socially defined, and thus, for the purposes of society, only two sexes really exist. When an infant is born, the individuals around him or her engage in a kind of "construct-a-sex" game.

Of course gender is not assigned at random. People base their assumptions on the anatomical structures with which the infant comes equipped. Little or no allowance is made for ambiguity—the child can be surgically reconstructed to appear more "normally" male or female. Indeed, if the sex of rearing is unambiguous for the first two years of life, the child appears to accept the gender identity with which it has been labeled even in the presence of enormous physical evidence to the contrary, which may develop at adolescence (Money & Ehrhardt, 1972). Thus we may define sex or gender identity as the label the individual applies to herself or himself on the basis of information acquired during the early years of life. This information can on occasion be at variance with the genetic or hormonal programing of the individual. We do not know exactly in what form the individual acquires this information, but it can become so enormously important to some people's sense of themselves that they will undergo massive psychological and surgical trauma in order to create a body structure that is compatible with their inner view of themselves. Transsexuals like Jan Morris and Renée Richards can be viewed as exemplifying the tremendous importance of sexual dichotomies in our culture in that these people seem to feel that they must drastically change their bodies in order to conform to their psychological persona.

The Social Function of Sex Labels

Sex roles may be defined as the behaviors that are considered to be appropriate to an individual on the basis of social definitions of his or her sex. Sex roles vary widely within our culture, between cultures, and over relatively brief time periods. We tend to forget, for example, that the notion of a limited nuclear family with a mother who is almost solely responsible for childrearing as well as childbearing is a relatively recent American invention. Sex roles mark the limits of permissible behavior for individuals who have been categorized as members of a given sex. The limits to which they may be transgressed not only varies culturally and chronologically but also probably changes during the life span of the individual. Thus it appears that during early and middle childhood females are permitted to engage in "male" behaviors. We have even institutionalized the category of "tomboy." Permission to deviate begins to be withdrawn at puberty in the guise of concern with the girl's development of "proper" affiliative relationships with boys. Competition in male-defined spheres is a major cause of social sanctioning of adult females. Males, on the other hand, are permitted less latitude in the early years, when sexual identity is supposedly "set."

Sex role development seems to be a result of these processes of sex typing and sex role socialization. The former refers to a generalized social judgment process—of which we as individuals are only partially aware—that states that some characteristics are more appropriate to or even purely the property of one sex or the other. Sex role stereotypes reflect the nature of prevailing social judgments about the characteristics of some sexual categories. They share with ethnic and racial stereotypes the properties of rigidity, inaccuracy, and universality. They seem almost to be a property of a group consciousness rather than of individual attitudes (Goldberg, 1974).

Individuals become sex typed through the process of sex role socialization. The environment contains many sources of sex role information (Busby, 1975). People acquire from interactions with it the personality characteristics and behaviors that they and others perceive to be appropriate to members of the category to which they belong. There is ample evidence, however, that individuals are less sex typed than they believe others to be (Unger & Siiter, 1975; Spence, Helmreich, & Stapp, 1975). In general, people's self-evaluation of their own personality and behaviors contain more intermingling of supposed male and female characteristics than one would suppose. There is even evidence that androgynous individuals—those with both strongly masculine and strongly feminine characteristics, whatever "sex" they may be—are more functionally adaptive than individuals who are more traditionally sex typed (Bem, 1975). Since we cannot do personality tests historically, it is difficult to know whether this has been true all along or whether it represents a development associated with the recent resurgence of feminism.

While androgyny may be defined as an individual personality characteristic, feminism may be defined as a sociopolitical attitude.

There seems to be as many definitions of feminism as there are feminists. Broadly, it may be defined as the belief that people should be treated as human beings independent of categorical judgments. Roles are viewed as a product of individual choice rather than mandatory pigeonholes. Thus a man can be a homemaker if he so chooses and a woman a doctor without the prefix "lady." An obvious correlate of this position is that income be based on performance and not on membership in some group or other. Sexism, on the other hand, may be loosely defined as the belief that some characteristics and roles are the prerogative of one sex. Individuals who have a sexist viewpoint usually assume that the social system will be greatly upset if gender roles are abolished.

Just as one does not have to be male or female to be androgynous, one does not have to be a male or a female to be a feminist or a sexist. Assumptions about what is desirable and normal probably play a role in the development of such attitudes, just as they play a role in the development of any personality characteristic. The value of the concept of androgyny is the separation of sex role from sex— the idea that important components of sexual categories may be independent of each other.

WHAT KIND OF VARIABLE IS SEX?

This point brings us back to the original question. If we cannot define who the sexes are, is it possible to define what sex is? What kind of variable are we studying? Strangely enough, this question appears to be easier to answer than the first one. In a sense this is because there is really no single definition encompassing all the ways we use the term *sex*. Who belongs in what category varies, depending on how the categories are constructed. It is possible, however, to get a handle on how we construct and use various definitions. Such an analysis may provide us with considerable information about what we are actually studying.

Sex as an Independent Variable

There are a number of ways in which one can conceptualize the study of sex. Sex may be viewed as an independent or dependent variable (Unger & Denmark, 1975). As an independent variable, sex is viewed as built into the organism by his or her chromosomes, genes, and hormones. According to this view, the individual comes into the world with an unambiguous sex and this sex predisposes him or her to acquire certain personality characteristics that are considered gender specific if not gender exclusive. Personality characteristics in combination with undefined neural and physiological factors are then presumed to make certain people more comfortable in certain roles. In this view maternal behavior is regarded as more a product of biology than of socialization, and some adult behaviors are predictable from the moment of birth.

Bem and Bem (1970) have illustrated this point very effectively in terms of a little quiz. Suppose you were told that an infant had just been born and were asked to predict what that person would be doing twenty-five years from today. Of course you would say that you had too little information to answer the question. If, on the other hand, one small piece of information was added—the fact that the newborn child was female—you would probably confidently predict that she would be a wife and mother in twenty-five years. The point of this exercise is that individual variability in personality traits, intelligence, racial or socioeconomic identity, and so forth become less important in determining the future of this individual than her sexual category. We recognize that there is much greater room for variability in making assumptions about newborn males.

Predictability: Sex or Sex Role?

This matter of predictability is a crucial one for the examination of the psychology of sex and gender. Maccoby and Jacklin (1974) have provided us with an important point in this regard:

> We invite the reader to imagine a situation in which all psychological researchers routinely divide their subjects into two groups at random, and perform their data analyses separately for the two halves of the sample. Whenever a difference in findings emerges between the two groups (and this would of course sometimes happen by chance even when no difference exists that would replicate with further samples), our imaginary researcher tests the difference for significance, and any significant differences are included in the published report of the study. If we are not told that the original subdivision has been made at random, we might misspend a great deal of time attempting to explain the differences. [pp. 3–4]

The conclusion of their evaluation of the research literature on sex differences seems to suggest that assigning variables to groups by sex is somewhat more meaningful than assigning them at random. However, this assessment appears valid only for a few behaviors, such as aggressiveness and spatial and mathematical analysis. Assigning variables by gender or internalized sex roles would probably greatly increase our predictability. No one, however, would get very excited over the idea that masculine and feminine people are different from each other.

Even if we increase our predictability by assigning people to categories according to sex, we have not necessarily increased our ability to explain their behavior by doing so. Assignment to groups by sex is not random the way we randomly assign people to conditions if we wish to examine the effects on learning of the noise level in a room. Males and females may be different in some ways, just as blonds probably differ in some ways from redheads, tall people from short ones, and people with type O blood from those with type A. Individuals reflect the sum total of the environmental and social experiences they have been exposed to and bring this "baggage" with them to any given situation. Even if the particular situation investigated is "sex blind," we have ample evidence that the previous environment was not. The predictability we gain from an individual's group membership is as likely to derive from the similarity of experiences acquired from membership in that group as it is from assumed biological similarities. Because sex, like race, is to some extent an organismic variable, however, explanations of sex differences have been assumed to be due to processes that occur in some as yet undiscovered spot(s) within the brain or endocrine system. Psychological theory still implies a direct hookup between the gonads and the brain. If we can't find the spot in the brain we are looking for, we can always move to another one.

THE LIMITS OF BIOLOGICAL EXPLANATIONS

Are Environments Ever Sex Blind?

Biologically deterministic hypotheses carry with them the implication of relatively equal social environments. Such hypotheses reduce the probability that we will examine how factors in the environment affect behaviors that are defined as having a large biological component. Nevertheless environmental characteristics may play a larger role than we usually suppose. In a recent study (Mossip & Unger, 1977), we examined spatial lateralization in girls and boys aged 3 through 11 by means of asymmetrical cartoon figures. (See Figure 1.1.) We found that girls tended to focus on one side of the cartoon figures at an earlier age than boys, but this initial degree of lateralization did not change significantly as they got older. Boys, on the other hand, were less lateralized initially, but their degree of lateralization increased with age until by the age of 9 they surpassed girls. This information could be interpreted as indicative of a biological or maturational process if we had not simultaneously gathered data on the kinds of toys possessed by each child. At every age boys had significantly more spatial toys (vehicles, sports

Figure 1.1. Examples of asymmetrical faces. The two figures below are made from the left and right halves of the figure above. The subject chooses the face that most resembles the original. (C. Mossip & R. K. Unger, unpublished)

equipment, construction sets, and the like—the kinds of toys that appear to foster hand–eye coordination) than girls. We found that the number of such toys possessed by the child was increasingly positively correlated with spatial lateralization in boys as they grew older. No such effect was apparent for girls.

There are several possible interpretations of these data. Children's play preferences may reflect their developing laterality as much as they may cause them. Or girls may not have enough "biological" potential for spatial lateralization to permit the environment to have an effect. We do know, however, that differential toy selection for boys and girls begins as early as the second year of life (Rheingold & Cook, 1975). Thus we are certainly not justified in assuming a psychologically equivalent environment in which purely biological effects can manifest themselves. Self-labels may also affect presumably biological processes. For example, Sharon Nash (1975) has shown that sex differences in spatial visualization in children are found only between boys and girls who prefer the sex role that is appropriate to their own sex. Boys who would prefer to be girls (very few) and girls who would prefer to be boys show no sex differences in this behavior.

The Issue of Irreversibility

Concentration on biological variables also implies irreversibility. Recently there has been evidence that effects induced by much more major treatments than those usually associated with differential treatment of the sexes appear to be reversed later in life. For example, Jerome Kagan (1976) notes that the cognitive development of "normal" South American Indian children who have been malnourished and socially isolated during the first few years of life appears to reach the level of American children by age 18. A number of studies (Hoffman & Maier, 1966; Witkin, 1949 cited by Parlee, 1976) have indicated "improvements" in female problem solving and perceptual faculties in the direction of the male following short-term practice or instruction procedures. The evidence that sex differences do not usually decrease but, rather, increase with further socialization experiences would suggest that biological explanations are masking more important (because they are more explanatory) social ones.

Explaining the Status Quo

Before making biologically causative assumptions it is necessary to be able to spell out the biological–psychological mechanisms involved. Recent sociobiological theorizing, for example, has sought to explain maternal behavior by the amount of investment made by the female in producing and incubating her eggs and rearing their product (Wilson, 1975). Males are conceived of as having less of a stake in any particular offspring because they are able to produce sperm in abundance. Male behavior, therefore, is explained by their "need" to be reproductively prolific. A variety of human social behaviors ranging from promiscuity to rape can be "explained" in this manner. But exactly what have we explained? I will admit that we have described the status quo as currently defined by our society. Scientific explanation, however, requires that one provide a means of disproving one's hypothesis. How can we demonstrate that any female organism does not have a larger biological investment in her egg than the male has in his sperm? How do we explain how genetic processes operate through the organism's behavior? And how do we explain the wide variety of childrearing practices (including infanticide) in many cultures?

Sociobiological explanations are seductive because they are simple and have a kind of face validity—they tell us why things are the way they are now. They are not useful in explaining how sex or gender affect behavior because they separate the world into two distinct categories: male and female. They do not tell us at what point—genes, hormones, and/or neurons—gender-exclusive information is programed. As yet, we cannot a priori define what we mean by *male* and *female* without some ambiguous statements such as "Chromosomally I'm male, hormonally I'm female, and genitally it's too early to tell" (Grady, 1975). At present, therefore, it may be more useful to assume that sex and gender are programed in a multidimensional way, with room for more than two categories in each dimension. Although there is evidence that the first two years of life are critical in the first definition of gender, there is also evidence that gender-related characteristics can be altered in later life. We cannot expect to find a simple answer to our questions. "It is possible that genetic–endocrine–experiential contributions will be found to be species-specific, sex-specific, and even behavior specific" (Unger & Denmark, 1975, p. 443).

ALTERNATIVE WAYS OF CONCEPTUALIZING SEX

Sex as a Stimulus Variable

It has become increasingly clear in recent years that males and females are most alike in their perception of their own differences. The most interesting psychological phenomenon may be in the discrepancy between actual similarities between the sexes and the belief in sex differences. Kathleen Grady (1977) has recently provided some empirical research on the illusion of sex differences. She notes that people cannot behaviorally express an evaluative bias against women unless they first decide that the target is a woman. In other words, translation of prejudicial attitudes into discrimination requires identification of the proper stimulus cue. Thus Grady asked questions such as "Do people always notice the sex of another person?" or "Can they ignore sex in favor of a rational assessment of the requirements for the task at hand?"

In her first field demonstration Grady chose a situation in which sex did not appear to have any functional value for the perceiver. People who were waiting at a subway station were approached and asked whether they had just purchased a token. If they had, they were told that a study on eyewitness reports was being conducted and would they please describe the token seller by listing characteristics for purposes of identification. Of the characteristics mentioned, the sex of the token seller, which in this case was female, was always included. It was given as a first or second characteristic 100 percent of the time. In fact it was given first 75 percent of the time and was displaced to second position only by race, which in this case was black. "And they never varied—all respondents agreed on female for each of the token sellers. As if to underscore the prominence of sex as a characteristic, the one respondent who couldn't offer any description said, 'I can't even remember whether it was a man or a woman'" (Grady, 1977, p. 4).

Grady's subjects apparently thought that sex was a very important characteristic to mention for purposes of identification. Of course it isn't important in any statistical sense. By naming the sex of a target person one distinguishes that individual from about 50 percent of the population. Most people have many more discriminating characteristics—glasses, blond hair, freckles, and so forth. Thus Grady asked another question that could be tested by means of a laboratory game: Do people use statistical rules at all in distinguishing a target person from other people in a group? And do they violate this strategy for a characteristic like sex? She devised a game in which people had to describe one person to their partners, choosing from a group of 10 pictures of people's faces in front of them. They were supposed to do this with as few cues as possible. The clues they could use were distributed systematically across the pictures—for example, there were 1 blond and 9 brunettes; 2 had hats on and 8 didn't; 3 had light clothing and 7 dark; 4 wore glasses and 6 did not; and 5 were female and 5 male. Although subjects generally chose cues in order of their statistical distinctiveness, they used sex for the first cue 60 percent of the time. This is three times more likely than would be predicted by chance and twice as likely as would be predicted by rules of statistical distinctiveness. Subjects attend to sex not only when it is irrelevant but also when it is actually counterproductive in terms of their goals.

Grady suggests that sex as a characteristic of oneself is treated differently from other organismic characteristics such as handedness or eye color. When she told people they would do well on a particular task because of the latter two variables, they were not affected by these instructions. In fact they laughed when they were debriefed. Sex, on the other hand, produced effects based on instructions even when expectancies were manipulated in a counterstereotypic direction.

Using no stimulus materials other than the label "male" or "female," other investigators have found that sex controls the evaluation of "goodness" or "badness" of performance (Pheterson, Kiesler, & Goldberg, 1971) and leads to differential assumptions about the causes of one's own or someone else's behavior (Deaux, 1976). Sex differences are especially likely to be found in studies that use self-evaluations as the measure of behavior in which the investigators are interested (Frodi, Macaulay, & Thome, 1977). Behaviors are consistently dichotomized by sex, even though females and males usually form two overlapping distributions with a minority of people of either sex at the extreme. Moreover, even though some behaviors have been found to be sex related, none that are sex exclusive have been found.

A Biosocial Explanation of Sex Effects

Perhaps because people seem to prefer biological explanations of sex differences over social ones, we may have greatly underestimated the effects of social judgments on psychological states. Psychological states that are considered unique to women may be particularly important in maintaining a dichotomy. In a recent novel experiment in this regard, Taylor and Langer (1977) found that both men and women (although men more than women) stand farther away from a pregnant woman, although they may stare at her more. Subjects also indicated that they liked a pregnant woman more when she was passive than when she was assertive. At the same time, they rejected the pregnant woman as a companion. Social expectations about passivity could be as important in maintaining behaviors during pregnancy as any direct effects on the brain of high levels of female hormones.

Recent studies of attributions about the menstrual cycle (Koeske & Koeske, 1975) also indicate that moods are readily attributed to biological causes. In fact there is suggestive evidence that people are more ready to assume biological causality in general for females than for males (Hansen, O'Leary, & Stonner, 1976). External characteristics other than male or female secondary sexual characteristics may also play a role in such differential attributions. For example, we know that females are generally smaller than males, but until recently we have virtually ignored the role of size variables in assumptions about aggressiveness, social status and power, and so forth (Unger, 1976, 1978). The fact that transsexuals can be readily accepted as the "sex" they choose to be indicates that a large portion of sex-related characteristics are socially defined.

Sex as a Social Variable

Viewing sex in terms of social definition leads to a wide variety of questions that are yet to be answered by researchers. For example, will sex predict more or less of a person's behavior depending on how important it is to that person? A number of experiments by Sandra Bem (Bem, 1975; Bem & Lenney, 1976; Bem, Martyna, & Watson, 1976) indicate that androgynous people of both biological sexes are more like each other than sex-typed individuals are. We do not know whether sex is less important to the self-definition of such androgynous individuals, although there is suggestive evidence that cross-sex behavior is less problematic for them (Bem & Lenney, 1976).

Another question yet to be explored is that of the uniqueness of phenomena related to sex. If we find equivalent phenomena in terms of race, ethnicity, and the like, how do we go about finding out what explanatory variables account for the similarities? A related question is that of what reinforces biological interpretations of sex differences. What sorts of rewards do individuals or society provide for maintaining exaggerated perceptions of differences between relatively similar groups? Here it is important to focus on areas in which biological processes exist that are supposedly unique to women. A recent study in this regard (Schilling & Jacobi, 1977), for example, noted that someone is less likely to be blamed for disagreeable behavior when she or he has a cold, just as there is less likelihood of blame when a person is "premenstrual."

Other questions involve the equivalence of social environments. Can males and females ever engage in identical behaviors? Or does the way we construct reality in terms of sex make it impossible to ever talk about gender equivalence? An issue related to this one is that of "actuarial expectancy" (Kiesler, 1975). Since adult sex differences do exist in some areas, expectations about differential behaviors for women and men will be correct some of the time.

Thus, sex role stereotypes could be viewed as a form of cognitive economy. Of course it is neither economical nor advantageous for the individuals being prejudged. How do we develop learning strategies to offset this kind of intellectual shortcut?

Sex as a Relational Variable

One area that is beginning to be explored is the role of the social environment in judgments about social behavior. Men and women make different judgments when they are alone than when they are together (Starer & Denmark, 1974). Their behavior is also different when they function in mixed-sex rather than same-sex groups (Ruble & Higgins, 1976, Kidder, Bellettirie, & Cohn, 1977). It is noteworthy that more dramatic illustrations of sex-discriminatory effects seem to be obtained in field than in laboratory studies. Is this a result of norms about "sex-blind" conduct in formal situations? To what degree is misogyny in our society masked by the desire to appear to behave in a socially appropriate manner? Goldberg (1974), for example, notes that misogyny is well-nigh universal in our culture and that it is more difficult to find people in whom it is absent than people in whom it is present. How can we measure the actual level of sexism in our society?

Sex as a Self-Fulfilling Prophecy

Probably some of the most exciting developments in the field are findings that indicate that socially engendered expectations produce the behaviors that are regarded as resulting from long-term socialization processes. Thus women defer to more dominant males (Weitz, 1976) or behave in a more socially responsive manner when the males with whom they are interacting are told (unbeknownst to the females) that they are physically attractive (Snyder, Tanke, & Berscheid, 1977). This line of research stresses that people are what other people around them expect them to be. One can argue that it has emerged as a serious object of concern for social scientists partly owing to the spread of a feminist theoretical perspective.

THE VALUE OF ADVOCACY

Social scientists concentrated on the biological view of sex because they were largely unaware that sex as a stimulus variable is a pervasive aspect of our culture—so universal that we do not even notice that it is there. Political feminism led social scientists to pay new attention to sex as a variable, and since the most obvious targets of sexism have been women, women as researchers and women as the subject of research have been the most obvious results. Nevertheless feminism, sexism, and the psychology of women are by no means identical.

Those who study the psychology of women have often actually been concerned with the social effects of sex. They are also concerned with gender—the responses learned by individuals as a function of these social processes. Those who study the area may be male or female, may use male or female subjects, and may or may not be feminists.

A feminist perspective in psychology reflects concern about the societal implications of one's work. It is not necessary to distort one's data—sexist effects are widespread and easy to measure. In fact one of the greatest difficulties in the area may be to get beyond the relatively obvious demonstrations of individual and societal sexism. Feminist psychology implies a commitment to a theoretical reorganization of the field in order to explore relationships relevant to both sexes that have been obscured by the limitation of research to one sex. Sex, not the sexes, is a major object of study. Reesa Vaughter's (1976) definition of the psychology of women actually defines a feminist psychology:

> concerned with the construction of a psychology that is relevant to women, as well as men; that studies women, as well as men; that employs methodology that is appropriate, meaningful and congruent with the lives of women, as well as men's; that develops theories that predict female, as well as male, behaviors; and that studies questions that are of interest to women, as well as men. In brief, the goal of the psychology of women is the development of a nonsexist science, a psychology of human behavior. [p. 120]

WHAT'S IN A NAME?

We will probably be arguing for a long time about whether the field about which this book is written should properly be called the psychology of women, the psychology of gender, feminist psychology, psychology for women, the psychology of female–male comparisons, and so on. The argument is really a friendly and healthy one. This point is probably most beautifully illustrated by an analogy provided by Judith Alpert (1977) at a recent meeting of the Eastern Psychological Association during which the question of what was being studied was debated:

> It is helpful to distinguish between birth names and nicknames. Birth names are names given at birth by parents. Usually, birth names, or at

least first birth names, are not changed. Nicknames are names given at various developmental stages by various people. They frequently change as the named one changes. To better understand nicknames, a personal example might be helpful. Before my daughter was born we named her "Ivanya." Somehow, at birth, her bald and squealing presence did not fit the name. She would grow into the name, we thought. So at birth time, we nicknamed her "Peanut." At two, "Soldier" seemed like the most appropriate nickname. Now, at age five, we think "Princess" describes the way she expects us to treat her. . . .

While I call her Princess and her best friends call her Jan, her worst enemies call her Shrimp, because she is sensitive about her petite size and the name hurts her feelings. From the perspective of her mother, her best friends, and her worst enemies, these three nicknames, Princess, Jan, and Shrimp, describe Ivanya at age five. What becomes clear is that people who know Ivanya do not all see her the same way. The interaction between Ivanya and her world is complicated enough to deserve at least three nicknames. [pp. 3–5]

As she points out, while we may not all agree on the developmental nicknames for the subject whose birth name is the psychology of women, or on the sequence of nicknames chosen, we can all agree that the interaction between the field and each of us is complicated enough to deserve several nicknames at any point in time. Just as the birth of the psychology of women affected the development of the psychology of sex differences and sex roles, our different perspectives, as evidenced by the different terms we use, will affect the development of the psychology of women. And the field is the richer for its ability to tolerate differences in scope, focus, and orientation. After all, wasn't it complaints about premature strictures that started all this in the first place?

Chapter 2
Proving the Obvious: Sex Role Stereotyping from Womb to Tomb

Although the phrase "You can't judge a book by its cover" has become a cliché, in the area of sex and gender such prejudgments take place all the time. How well people are judged to perform and why we think they performed as they did is greatly affected by an apparently irrelevant characteristic—the sex of that individual. In this chapter we will review the phenomenon of sex role stereotyping and its implications for a psychology of women. Two themes—(1) actions are considered more appropriate in judgments about males than in judgments about females and (2) there are no separate but equal social judgments—recur frequently in this area. Sex role stereotypes show us many of the mechanisms by which gender is defined in our society.

WHAT IS A STEREOTYPE?

The term *stereotype* was not invented by a psychologist or sociologist. It is derived from printing and was first applied to humans over fifty years ago, in 1922, by Walter Lippman. Lippman defined stereotypes as mainly culturally determined pictures that impinge between an individual's cognitive faculties and his or her perceptions of the world. Although the term *stereotype* was first used in the investigation of attitudes toward religious, racial, or ethnic groups, it would seem to apply to sex as well. A sex role stereotype may be defined as an attitudinal or behavioral bias against individuals in identical situations engaged in identical behaviors because of their membership in some specific sexual group. Sex role stereotypes also fulfill one or more of the following criteria:

1. There is little agreement between the composite picture of the group and the actual characteristics of members of that group.
2. Groups that are commonly the targets of stereotypes are relatively easily identified and relatively powerless.
3. Individuals who hold the stereotype do not perceive themselves as possessing the characteristics in question.
4. The misperception is a product of overgeneralization or some other form of faulty reasoning.
5. The misperception is difficult to modify, even though the people who hold the stereotype have encountered numerous disconfirming examples.
6. Stereotypes imply at least a covert comparison between groups, to the disadvantage of the stereotyped group.
7. Stereotypes are characterized by relatively little variability between individuals in terms of what characteristics they judge to be appropriate to the group in question.

The lack of variability between different people in applying stereotypic labels and the great agreement across age groups, social strata, different times and places, and sexes are the most outstanding features of stereotypes. In fact it is this general agreement that defines stereotyping. In many ways stereotypes function more like societal norms than like individual attitudes. They form a covert body of information, a convenient societal pigeonhole, that people may or may not use. Only most of the time people are unaware that they possess this conceptual framework at all.

THE STIMULI FOR SEX ROLE STEREOTYPES

Stereotyping of Infants and Young Children

Stereotyping on the basis of sex begins before birth. Parents attribute different sexes to their unborn infants on the basis of their prenatal behavioral characteristics. An active, kicking fetus is presumed to be male, while a quiet, passive one is presumed to be female. The parents of newborn infants engage in similar sex-specific attribution of characteristics. Rubin, Provenzano, and Luria (1974) interviewed 30 parents during the 24-hour period following the birth of their first child. Half the newborns were girls and half were boys. Although male and female infants did not differ in birth length, weight, or neonatal activity scores, daughters were significantly more likely than sons to be described as little, beautiful, pretty, and cute. Sons were seen as firmer, more alert, and stronger. Fathers made more extreme and stereotyped judgments of their newborns than mothers did. Subjects other than parents (e.g., college students) are also willing to differentiate their responses according to the supposed sex label of young infants (Seavey, Katz, & Zalk, 1975). It is apparently impossible to find an age below which sex role stereotyping does not take place.

Consistent with this pattern of early labeling of children's characteristics on the basis of their sex, more men than women rate the behaviors of toddlers as young as 18 months of age as sex typed (Fagot, 1973). Although both sexes agree that most of the behaviors in which toddlers engage are neutral with respect to sex, certain behaviors are regarded, especially by men, as more masculine or feminine. Roughhouse play, play with transportation toys, and aggressive behavior are rated as masculine while play with dolls, dressing up, and looking in the mirror are seen as feminine.

These 20-year-old students had not had much contact with children. However, even people who have had extensive contact with them (e.g., teachers) tend to engage in sex role stereotyping. When asked to evaluate the behavior of a hypothetical girl or boy who was described as engaging in either dependent, aggressive, or achievement behavior, teachers liked dependent girls more than aggressive girls; no such differentiation was found for boys (Levitin & Chananie, 1972). An achieving girl was liked more but not approved of more than an achieving boy.

Although adults with varying degrees of contact with children tend to characterize them in terms of stable traits, there is no evidence that children behave consistently in terms of their sex role identities. Maccoby and Jacklin (1974), after summarizing a large number of studies from the developmental literature, find few consistent sex differences in behavior. In fact preschool children rated in a variety of classroom situations (alone, with others, in group activities with teacher leadership, in test-taking situations, etc.) showed little behavioral stability across situations (Rose, Blank, & Spalter, 1975). When children were observed in the same type of situation they showed stable patterns of behavior even after a four-month interval. In different situations, however, their behavior was poorly predicted even from day to day.

Sex Role Stereotypes and School-Age Children

Elementary school children stereotype themselves. Black and white first- and third-grade girls showed differential perceptions about the size and strength, power and intelligence of boys and girls their own age (Gold & St. Ange, 1974). Adults also stereotype boys and girls of this age group. Grade school teachers given vignettes about a hypothetical 9-year-old child labeled either male or female rated boys as displaying more leadership and being more active, more gregarious, and more accepted by their peers than girls (Rotter, 1967). Boys were also rated as dirtier. There is also evidence that mothers report the behaviors of their children in terms of sex role stereotypes. However, we do not know the relationship between the mother's perception and the child's actual behavior.

Sex Role Stereotypes and the College Student

By far the most popular subject of study in this as well as many other areas has been the college student. The most frequently cited studies in this area were done by Inge Broverman and her associates (Rosenkrantz, Vogel, Bee, Broverman, & Broverman, 1968; Vogel, Broverman, Broverman, Clarkson, & Rosenkrantz, 1970; Broverman, Vogel, Broverman, Clarkson, & Rosenkrantz, 1972). They conceived of stereotypes in terms of the degree to which men and women are perceived to possess any specific trait. Their questionnaire was set up as a series of bipolar pairs: passive–active, sneaky–direct, dependent–not dependent, and so forth. Subjects were asked to indicate the extent to which each item characterized a normal male, a normal female, and themselves. Only items on which at least 75 percent of individuals of each sex agreed as to which pole was more descriptive of the average man or woman were termed stereotypic. Even with this relatively conservative definition, the researchers found high agreement about the differing characteristics of men and women that was independent of the age, sex, religion, education level, or marital status of the subject. (See Table 2.1.)

A recent study by a colleague and myself (Unger & Siiter, 1975), using an entirely different rank ordering method, also confirmed the widespread existence of sex role stereotypes among college students. Although males and females do not describe themselves as different from each other in terms of the values with which

Table 2.1 STEREOTYPIC SEX ROLE ITEMS
(RESPONSES FROM 74 COLLEGE MEN AND 80 COLLEGE WOMEN)

COMPETENCY CLUSTER: MASCULINE POLE IS MORE DESIRABLE

FEMININE	MASCULINE
Not at all aggressive	Very aggressive
Not at all independent	Very independent
Very emotional	Not at all emotional
Does not hide emotions at all	Almost always hides emotions
Very subjective	Very objective
Very easily influenced	Not at all easily influenced
Very submissive	Very dominant
Dislikes math and science very much	Likes math and science very much
Very excitable in a minor crisis	Not at all excitable in a minor crisis
Very passive	Very active
Not at all competitive	Very competitive
Very illogical	Very logical
Very home oriented	Very worldly
Not at all skilled in business	Very skilled in business
Very sneaky	Very direct
Does not know the way of the world	Knows the way of the world
Feelings easily hurt	Feelings not easily hurt
Not at all adventurous	Very adventurous
Has difficulty making decisions	Can make decisions easily
Cries very easily	Never cries
Almost never acts as a leader	Almost always acts as a leader
Not at all self-confident	Very self-confident
Very uncomfortable about being aggressive	Not at all uncomfortable about being aggressive
Not at all ambitious	Very ambitious
Unable to separate feelings from ideas	Easily able to separate feelings from ideas
Very dependent	Not at all dependent
Very conceited about appearance	Never conceited about appearance
Thinks women are always superior to men	Thinks men are always superior to women
Does not talk freely about sex with men	Talks freely about sex with men

they guide their lives, they stereotype the values that they believe to be important to members of the opposite sex. The perceived importance that males give to achievement-oriented values is exaggerated by females to the same degree that the perceived importance that females give to nurturant-oriented values is exaggerated by males. If self-values are considered to reflect reality, there is little relationship between the perceived and actual differences between the sexes. In another study Spence, Helmreich, and Stapp (1974) found there was no relationship between the way subjects described themselves in terms of sex-typed characteristics and the extent to which they stereotyped the characteristics of others.

Table 2.1 *Continued*

WARMTH-EXPRESSIVENESS CLUSTER: FEMININE POLE IS MORE DESIRABLE	
FEMININE	MASCULINE
Doesn't use harsh language at all	Uses very harsh language
Very talkative	Not at all talkative
Very tactful	Very blunt
Very gentle	Very rough
Very aware of feelings of others	Not at all aware of feelings of others
Very religious	Not at all religious
Very interested in own appearance	Not at all interested in own appearance
Very neat in habits	Very sloppy in habits
Very quiet	Very loud
Very strong need for security	Very little need for security
Enjoys art and literature	Does not enjoy art and literature at all
Easily expresses tender feelings	Does not express tender feelings at all easily

SOURCE: From I. K. Broverman et al., "Sex-Role Stereotypes: A Current Appraisal," *Journal of Social Issues,* 1972, 28, 59–78. Copyright 1972 by the Society for the Psychological Study of Social Issues. Reprinted by permission.

Adults and Sex Role Stereotypes

There have been few attempts to examine the stereotypes of individuals who function outside of some sort of institutional framework such as the educational establishment. Partly this is a matter of simple convenience, partly it occurs because noninstitutionalized individuals' attitudes cannot be studied unobtrusively, and partly it is because their rate of willingness to cooperate in such surveys is relatively poor. We do not know whether people who are willing to participate in psychological studies are idiosyncratic in other ways too. Nevertheless it is important to find out whether misunderstandings about the characteristics possessed by another individual because of her or his membership in a particular sexual category increase or decrease as a person leaves "the learning environment." It is important to keep in mind, however, that people outside of school may differ from people in school in a variety of other ways (e.g., socioeconomic status, political ideology, age, etc.). It is also important to remember that people of different ages differ in other characteristics as well. In particular, they may have grown up in a different sociocultural milieu. And it is questionable whether one can do a psychological survey historically.

Surveys of general adult populations have found sex role stereotypes similar to those found among college students (Siiter & Unger, 1978). In fact there are more of them, and those that exist in both populations are exaggerated among the adults. (See Table 2.2.) In the adult population males and females also differ in how they

Table 2.2 (a) COLLEGE STUDENTS' RANK ORDERING OF VALUES THAT MADE SIGNIFICANT DIFFERENCES[a]

VALUES	MALES RANK SELF	FEMALES RANK SELF	MALES RANK FEMALES	FEMALES RANK MALES
Imaginative[b]	16 (11.7)	8 (8.9)	10 (10.0)	13 (11.5)
Clean[c]	17 (13.7)	17 (14.6)	6 (8.3)	17 (13.8)
Broad-minded[c,d]	3 (6.5)	2 (5.8)	9 (9.8)	9 (8.6)
Polite[c]	15 (11.1)	16 (12.9)	11 (10.0)	16 (12.4)
Independent[c,d]	8 (9.1)	7 (8.2)	12 (10.5)	1 (5.1)
Courageous[c,d]	12 (10.6)	9 (9.0)	16 (11.7)	8 (8.3)
Ambitious[d]	9 (9.6)	13 (10.4)	15 (11.3)	3 (6.7)
Intellectual[d]	13 (10.7)	10 (9.3)	14 (11.1)	7 (8.0)
Forgiving[d]	5 (7.5)	5 (7.5)	5 (8.2)	11 (11.1)
Cheerful[d]	10 (9.6)	12 (9.6)	4 (7.7)	14 (11.6)
Helpful[d]	6 (8.3)	6 (8.0)	8 (9.8)	15 (11.6)

SOURCE: From R. Siiter and R. K. Unger, "Sex role Stereotypes, Sex Typing, and Self-Typing: Some Considerations about Reference Groups." Manuscript submitted for publication, 1978.
[a] Numbers in parentheses are mean rankings from 40 subjects. All comparisons used Duncan's Multiple Range Test, $p < .05$.
[b] Males and females differed in their ranking for self on this value.
[c] Males' ranking for females differed from female self-rankings.
[d] Females' ranking for males differed from male self-rankings.

Table 2.2 (b) NONCOLLEGE ADULTS' RANK ORDERING OF VALUES THAT MADE SIGNIFICANT DIFFERENCES[a]

VALUES	MALES RANK SELF	FEMALES RANK SELF	MALES RANK FEMALES	FEMALES RANK MALES
Independent[b]	1 (6.9)	6 (9.0)	9 (10.0)	3 (6.6)
Capable[b]	3 (7.0)	11 (10.1)	10 (10.2)	4 (6.8)
Ambitious[b]	5 (7.8)	9 (9.7)	14 (10.9)	2 (5.8)
Self-controlled[b]	7 (8.3)	14 (11.0)	13 (10.9)	11 (9.9)
Loving[b]	10 (9.5)	1 (4.9)	1 (3.9)	8 (8.8)
Logical[b]	11 (9.7)	17 (12.2)	16 (11.3)	9 (8.9)
Forgiving[b]	13 (11.0)	7 (9.1)	6 (8.8)	14 (11.7)
Helpful[b]	14 (11.1)	4 (8.6)	4 (7.6)	16 (12.1)
Clean[c]	17 (12.3)	16 (11.1)	5 (8.0)	12 (10.4)
Courageous[c]	12 (10.0)	12 (10.3)	17 (12.2)	7 (8.8)
Responsible[d]	4 (7.3)	3 (7.0)	3 (7.6)	1 (5.0)
Imaginative[d]	9 (.0)	13 (10.7)	12 (10.4)	13 (11.5)

SOURCE: From R. Siiter and R. K. Unger, "Sex role Stereotypes, Sex Typing, and Self-Typing: Some Considerations about Reference Groups." Manuscript submitted for publication, 1978.
[a] Numbers in parentheses are mean rankings from 40 subjects. All comparisons used Duncan's Multiple Range Test, $p < .05$.
[b] Males and females differed in their ranking for self on this value.
[c] Males' ranking for females differed from female self-rankings.
[d] Females' ranking for males differed from male self-rankings.

rank values for themselves. To a degree they show a sex typing of values that resembles the sex role stereotyping of the values of others. Their judgments about others, however, are always much more extreme than the differences between the sexes when ranking for themselves.

Sex role stereotypes persist into old age. Both male and female college students view males as more effective and autonomous than females until age 75 (O'Connell & Rotter, 1977). Females were perceived as more personally acceptable throughout their life span. There does not appear to be a period during a person's life during which he or she is immune from the effects of sex role stereotyping.

NEGATIVE ATTITUDES TOWARD WOMEN—A BRIEF HISTORY

Studies of attitudes toward women are not a new phenomenon, despite the widespread interest the subject has received in the past few years. The first psychological scale in this area seems to have been constructed by Kirkpatrick in 1936. It included items like:

> Women are too nervous and high strung to make good surgeons.
> A husband has the right to expect that his wife will be obliging and dutiful at all times.
> One should never trust a woman's account of another woman.
> Women should not be permitted to hold political offices that involve great responsibility.

Kitay (1940) and Fernberger (1948) did work in this area in the 1940's, and Sheriffs and his associates (McKee & Sheriffs, 1957, 1959; Sheriffs & Jarrett, 1953; Sheriffs & McKee, 1957) contributed an extensive body of research in the 1950's. These studies seem to show that stereotypes about gender, defined as consensual beliefs about the differing characteristics of men and women, are widely held, persistent, and highly traditional. Despite the apparent fluidity of sex role definition in today's society, stereotypes similar to those found forty years ago exist in contemporary society. Goldberg (1974) has concluded that "sexism approaches being a culturally fixed and almost universal attitude. . . . It would seem that final explanations of the phenomenon are not profitably to be looked for at the level of individual psychology. Indeed, neither explanation nor solution is likely located there, although the price of sexism is paid for person by person" (p. 62).

WHO ISN'T PREJUDICED?

As can be seen from the studies cited earlier, men and women in our society, old and young, appear to share assumptions about the

characteristics that are appropriate to men and women to a remarkable extent. In fact men and women are most alike in their beliefs
about the differences between them. It appears to be simpler to
determine the properties of those who do not share these widespread cultural stereotypes than to delimit the characteristics of
those who have negative attitudes toward women. In an extensive
study designed to find correlations between prejudice toward
women and other personality characteristics such as authoritarianism and self-esteem, few personality differences were found
between those who were misogynist and those who were not
(Goldberg, 1974). It seemed that the likelihood of finding people
who were not prejudiced was smaller than the margin of error of the
measuring device used to find them. Others have found, however,
that men who opposed the women's-rights movement had lower
self-esteem than those who did not (Miller, 1974). College students
whose mothers worked outside the home appear to have fewer sex
role stereotypes than those whose mothers did not (Vogel et al.,
1970).

A more depressing finding is that mental-health practitioners
share the assumptions of college students about the appropriate
characteristics of males and females (Broverman, Broverman,
Clarkson, Rosenkrantz, & Vogel, 1970). Seventy-nine practicing
mental-health clinicians—clinical psychologists, psychiatrists, and
psychiatric social workers—completed a sex role questionnaire on
the characteristics of a mature, healthy, socially competent adult
man, woman, or person (sex unspecified). Both men and women
agreed that competence was more characteristic of the healthy male
than of the healthy female. The clinicians suggested that healthy
women differ from healthy men by being more submissive, less
independent, less adventurous, less objective, more easily influenced, less aggressive, less competitive, more excitable in minor
crises, more emotional, more conceited about their appearance, and
more prone to having their feelings hurt. Moreover, the clinicians'
ratings of the healthy male and the healthy adult did not differ from
each other. Thus a double standard of mental health exists for men
and women. Adult women are in a double bind: They cannot be
both adult *and* feminine. Healthy women are perceived as less
adult by clinical standards.

As might be expected, feminists are a little less prone to stereotype women than nonfeminists (Nielsen & Doyle, 1975). Feminists
see the ideal woman as higher in dominance and boastfulness than
nonfeminists do. These traits are usually seen as positive in a male.
College women who believe in women's liberation have a higher
evaluation of women in general and a slightly more positive self-
concept.

A number of recent studies indicate that there is less sex role stereotyping among blacks in the United States than among whites. Black grade school girls gave fewer stereotyped responses to questions about adults than white girls did (Gold & St. Ange, 1974). Studies by O'Leary and Harrison (1975) and Siiter and Unger (1975) also failed to confirm the existence of typical sex role stereotypes in black adult males and females. In fact Siiter and Unger found a tendency for gender stereotypes to be reversed in this group. A recent intriguing finding tends to behaviorally validate these findings about racial differences in gender-specific attitudes. Large numbers of black and white heterosexual couples on the streets of New York City and Washington, D.C., were observed to see who preceded whom (Miransky, Mulvey, & Grady, 1976). Leading someone down the street may be considered an unobtrusive nonverbal gesture of dominance. Although among white couples the man walked in front of the woman significantly more often, no such difference was found among black couples. These data rule out an anatomical explanation of the "man-in-front" phenomenon and, in conjunction with cross-racial attitudinal data, may represent racial differences in sex role ideology.

A CONTENT ANALYSIS OF SEX ROLE STEREOTYPES

Content analysis of studies of sex role stereotypes done over many years, in many places, and with many different populations indicates that the characteristics that are considered appropriate to the male possess the dimension of instrumentality. Men are expected to do, to be active, and to relate to the world around them in an objective manner. They are presumed to be independent, aggressive, direct, worldly, unemotional, dominant, and above all, television situation comedies notwithstanding, competent. The characteristics that are considered appropriate to the female, on the other hand, revolve around an affective dimension. Women are presumed to be warm, expressive, concerned about other individuals more than about themselves, concerned more with people than with things, and to be nurturant in all ways.

In sex as in race, "separate but equal" does not appear to be a viable condition. Although males and females are perceived to possess different qualities, these qualities are not generally viewed as being of equivalent value to society. Men and masculine characteristics are more highly valued than women and feminine characteristics. Male characteristics are considered to be more socially desirable by members of both sexes. In fact male properties appear to form the referent point for personhood in our society. When individuals are requested to indicate that point on each item of a bipolar

Table 2.3 DISTRIBUTION OF SUBJECTS CLASSIFIED BY SCORES
ABOVE OR BELOW THE MEDIAN ON MALE–VALUED AND
FEMALE–VALUED SELF SCALES

SUBJECTS	CATEGORY 1: LOW MASCU-LINE–LOW FEMALE	CATEGORY 2: LOW MASCU-LINE–HIGH FEMALE	CATEGORY 3: HIGH MASCU-LINE–LOW FEMALE	CATEGORY 4: HIGH MASCU-LINE–HIGH FEMALE
MALES				
n	72	30	64	68
%	30.8	12.8	27.4	29.1
Mean self-esteem[a]	66.82	74.55	87.02	93.73
FEMALES				
n	56	104	30	80
%	20.7	38.5	11.1	29.6
Mean self-esteem[a]	69.66	75.41	92.17	98.73

SOURCE: From J. T. Spence et al., "Ratings of Self and Peers on Sex Role Attitudes
and Their Relation to Self-esteem and Conceptions of Masculinity and Femininity,"
Journal of Personality and Social Psychology, 1975, 32, 29–39. Copyright 1975 by
the American Psychological Association. Reprinted by permission.
[a] One-way analysis of variance, $p < .001$.

scale of personality characteristics that they consider most desirable
for an adult, sex unspecified, they choose points closer to the masculine pole much more frequently than they choose points closer to
the feminine pole (Rosenkrantz et al., 1968).

Even studies using the newer concept of ability to possess both
masculine and feminine traits simultaneously—androgyny—do not
contradict the notion that male traits are deemed more valuable by
both sexes. Both males and females who were above the median in
the possession of male-valued traits (as judged by self-rating) had
higher self-esteem than individuals who rated themselves low in
male-valued traits (Spence, Helmreich, & Stapp, 1975; see Table
2.3). In fact women who judged themselves to be high in male-
valued traits had greater self-esteem than comparable men.

THE EFFECT OF STEREOTYPES ON EVALUATION OF OTHERS

Are Women Prejudiced Against Women?

What effect does the notion that males are competent while females
are loving have on our judgments of others? One of the strongest
sex-specific effects that has been investigated is that which shows
systematic devaluation of the products of women's work. The classic
study in this area, done by Goldberg (1968), was simple but elegant.
Goldberg presented female undergraduates with booklets contain-

ing excerpts of actual articles printed in professional journals in the areas of law and city planning (fields previously found to be strongly associated with men), elementary school teaching and dietetics (strongly associated with women), and linguistics and art history (not strongly associated with either sex). The articles were combined into two equal sets of booklets; however, the same article had a male author's name in one set and a female author's name in the other. After reading each article the women were asked to rate its value, persuasiveness, and profundity and to rate the author's writing style, professional competence, professional status, and ability to sway the reader. On all nine questions, regardless of occupational field, the subjects consistently found an article more valuable and its author more competent when it was associated with a male author's name. Even in traditionally feminine fields women were perceived to be inferior to men. Men were even considered more effective as elementary school teachers and dietitians.

In subsequent studies it was found that women tended to evaluate abstract paintings attributed to male artists as better than the same paintings credited to female artists. If, however, the work was designated as having won an art contest instead of merely being entered in one, the same work was evaluated similarly regardless of whether it was thought to be by a man or a woman. Only if her performance has received some form of social sanction was a woman's work considered as good as a man's (Pheterson, Kiesler, & Goldberg, 1971).

Evaluation Bias in Causal Attributions

Another form of evaluation bias related to gender labels has come from studies on causal attribution. This theory suggests that in analyzing the behavior of another person individuals use explanations based on internal or external causes. Internal explanations rely on the inferred properties and characteristics of the individual, such as his or her intelligence or motivation. External explanations rely on properties of the situation, such as whether or not chance was operating. Thus one might blame the failure of an individual to get into medical school on lack of ability (internal cause) or on some aspect of the situation—perhaps the exam was particularly hard at that time (external cause). Of course our knowledge of and assumptions about the characteristics of others will affect what types of attributions we use to explain their behavior. Equally obviously, attributions about the behaviors of males and females in equivalent situations should be affected by our preconceptions about their attributes—or, in other words, by our sex role stereotypes.

Under identical circumstances, and when they are engaged in identical behaviors, the performance of males and females is attributed to different sources (Deaux & Emswiller, 1974). For example, male and female college students were given the purported results of an object identification task that varied in sex appropriateness. The task involved identifying a series of familiar objects from a confusing background. The feminine task used household objects such as mops while the masculine task used mechanical objects such as tire jacks or wrenches. Both tasks were pretested so that they would be equally difficult. Either a male or a female stimulus person was heard to perform in an above-average manner in either the male- or the female-"appropriate" task. Good performance by a male on a "masculine" task was likely to be attributed to skill, whereas the same performance by a female on the same task was seen as more likely to have been influenced by luck. The opposite was not true for a "feminine" task. Overall, males were seen as more skillful than females by both men and women. To amplify this biasing effect, performance on the masculine task was seen as better by subjects, despite the fact that the tasks had been pretested and shown to be equivalent. These results support the conception that masculine accomplishments are better accomplishments in terms of both the task and the performer.

Bias in evaluating the performance of women does not appear to be easily overcome by objective evidence of good performance. In a pen-and-pencil examination of this issue college students were asked to attribute causes for the success of Dr. Mark or Marcia Greer, who had successfully completed medical school and had set up a surgical practice (Feldman-Summers & Kiesler, 1974). Male subjects in particular attributed more ability to the male physician. They suggested that the female physician had been successful because she had had an easier task and because she had tried harder. In fact the authors entitled their paper "Those Who Are Number Two Try Harder." The women in this study agreed that the female physician had tried harder, but thought that her task had been harder than that of a comparable male. Medicine may be a particularly sex-linked occupation. Recently, in an Australian girls' school, it was shown that a woman's success in medical school was more likely to be seen as due to good luck, an easy course, and cheating on exams than a man's success (Feather & Simon, 1975). The man's success was attributed, of course, to ability.

The Practical Effects of Evaluation Bias

Unfortunately these effects are not simply interesting laboratory demonstrations. In a widely cited and probably unrepeatable study, descriptions of individuals who had supposedly received a Ph.D. in psychology five years before were sent to a large number of departments of psychology all over the United States (Fidell, 1970). The descriptions varied in terms of competence and personal characteristics, and Fidell suggested to the departmental chairmen (all but two were male) that she wished to examine the criteria that determined who would be hired and at what rank and salary. As usual, half the departments received a given description with a male name attached and half received the identical description with a female name. Fidell found that, for a given stimulus person, males were preferred over females. They would have been hired at higher ranks and with larger salaries. In fact for these relatively inexperienced individuals the modal rank that would have been offered to the males was that of associate professor while the modal rank for equivalent females was that of assistant professor.

Even when subjects are not willing to make differential attributions about the performance of males and females, they are still unwilling to offer a woman the full reward for her labors. In a recent study in which male and female bookkeepers were portrayed, it was found that although male and female subjects agreed that the female was as competent, hardworking, and valuable an employee as the male, the male still deserved to receive more money (Rotter, 1976). The researcher is still trying to find out the causal basis for this wage differential.

Attributional Biases Harm Males Too

If success is a male attribute for which females are penalized, one would expect that males will be penalized for failure. This assumption was tested using audio tapes of students who were supposed to be candidates for a prestigious scholarship (Deaux and Taynor, 1973). Students who did well in the interview received higher evaluations when they were male than when they were female. If the interview was a failure, however, the males were censured more than the females. A pervasive tendency for female subjects to downgrade unsuccessful males as contrasted to successful males and to downgrade successful females in relation to unsuccessful females has also been found (Feather & Simon, 1975). Fully 70 percent of the measures of interaction between sex and outcome were significant, and attributions ranged from global judgments about the individuals involved to rather trivial assumptions about their behavior following success or failure. For example, males were rated as more likely to throw a wild party after success and females as more likely to do so after failure. Several anthologies on "the psychology of men" that have appeared recently (Pleck & Sawyer,

1974; David & Brannon, 1976) suggest that the unwillingness of society to accept emotion in males has been as much of a tragedy for men as the unwillingness of society to accept competence in females has been for women.

SOURCES OF INFORMATION ABOUT STEREOTYPES IN OUR SOCIETY

Language Itself

A number of recent studies have shown that the English language contains an abundant number of gender-differentiating terms that imply sex role stereotypes. Analyses of English have been done in terms of the content of its vocabulary (i.e., the number of words referring to females versus males); the denotative (dictionary) definition of words that are supposedly complementary (e.g., *bachelor* versus *spinster*); the historical development of gender-specific terms (*hussy* derives from the old English *huswif* or housewife and originally meant the female head of the house); and the slang vocabulary referring to males and females. In addition to these various forms of analysis involving word usage, studies have been made of gender-specific linguistic styles and even intonation patterns.

Content analyses of English have shown a consistent pattern of derogation of words having to do with females in comparison to similar words referring to males. Various forms of debasement that have occurred in female-gender words in English have been traced by M. R. Schultz (1975). The mildest form appears to be democratic leveling whereby a word that was previously reserved for people in high places comes to refer to people at any level of society. For example, the word *lord* still refers to the deity and a few Englishmen, while anyone may call herself a lady. A governor is still one who exerts authority; however, a governess is little more than an educated nursemaid. Other word pairs in which a similar process has taken place are *sir–dame* and *master–mistress*.

Terms of endearment addressed to females have also undergone derogation. Dolly, Kitty, and Polly all began as pet names derived from nicknames and eventually acquired the meaning of mistress or prostitute. A tart was originally a small pie or pastry, then a term of endearment, then a term applied first to young women who were sexually desirable and later to those who were careless of their morals, and finally a word meaning women of the street. Words denoting boys and young men have failed to undergo the debasement that has commonly occurred in terms associated with girls and women. The words *boy, youth, stripling, lad,* or *fellow* do not appear to be associated with any particular negative or sexual content.

Metaphors and labels are likely to have wide reference when applied to men and to be narrower, with sexual connotations, when applied to women (Lakoff, 1975). For example, if one states that a man is a professional, one is suggesting that he is a practitioner of a respected occupation. If one calls a woman a professional, one implies that she is practicing "the oldest profession." Other terms of the same sort include *tramp* (a male drifter but a female prostitute) and *game* (a male dupe but a female who is seducible).

Terms referring to women resemble those referring to children to a surprising extent. Excluding any negative connotations, words like *doll, honey, pussycat,* and *baby* can apply equally well to women or children (particularly girl children). Our language, like our culture, equates adulthood with manhood (Graham, 1975). There is a clear demarcation between the words *boy* and *man* that does not exist between *girl* and *woman*. In fact a boy greatly increases his status when he becomes a man, while a girl loses status and bargaining power when her youth is lost. Language echoes our gender stereotypes when it encourages females to cling to girlhood as long as possible.

Male–female power relationships may also be explored in terms of gender-specific slang vocabulary. College-age males listed a far larger total number of sex-related slang expressions than comparable females did (Kutner & Brogan, 1974). They used many more words equating woman with "sexual objects" than comparable women did. Very few words were given by either sex that equated the male with either a sexual actor or an object. In fact the score for female- versus male-related terms referring to sex was 79 versus 5. Males also listed many slang expressions for sexual intercourse that denoted male dominance over the female. Females were much more likely to use euphemisms for these terms. If one tunes into CB radio one is given no indication that this usage is changing. *Beaver* is the most frequent name for a female sender, but no comparable term appears to be used for males.

A number of socialization mechanisms that seem to operate in the linguistic distortion of gender-specific words have been suggested (Graham, 1975):

1. Labeling of what is considered to be an exception to the rule—*woman doctor, male nurse, career girl.* The term *feminine logic* is a particularly sexist example of this method.
2. Trivializing female gender forms—*poetess, suffragette,* and more recently, *libber.*

3. "His virtue is her vice"—*mannish attire* or *aggressive female*.
4. "Praise him/blame her"—*father* is still sometimes applied to God whereas *mother* . . . has quite a different meaning in some places.
5. Exclusion, which may be the most pervasive mechanism of all—the use of *man* in its extended sense, as in *mankind* or "the youth is father to the man," may be one of the major sources of the lack of relationship between our perceptions of females and our perception of adults.

The Effects of Sexist Language

Although researchers have conjectured that the use of sexist language increases the probability of sex role stereotypes and sex-biased behaviors, it is difficult to test these assumptions directly. One recent study offered students chapter headings for a potential sociology textbook and asked them to select pictures that would appropriately illustrate the themes of these chapters (Schneider & Hacker, 1973). Half the students received headings such as "Social Man," "Industrial Man," and "Political Man," while the other half were given corresponding headings such as "Society," "Industrial Life," and "Political Behavior." They found that titles using *man* resulted in the filtering out of photos that illustrated people of both sexes participating in these major areas of life. Moreover, using *man* in the chapter titles evoked images of power and dominance. For example, the theme "Political Man" was illustrated with pictures of Nixon or other politicians making speeches to mixed audiences. "Political Behavior" was also illustrated with portraits of prominent politicians, but it contained more instances of people, including women and minority males, engaging in political protest. In response to "Industrial Man," students submitted photos of heavy machinery and men doing heavy or dirty work. "Industrial Life" resulted in more photos of inside craft work or scientific and technical work.

Stereotypes in the Communications Media

So many studies have documented the existence of stereotypes about male and female sex roles in the various media—children's picture books, textbooks, children's TV programs, movies, adult TV (especially commercials), magazine fiction, and so on—that one is hardly excited when a new one appears. These studies document the implicit as well as the explicit content of what is being communicated. The presence of gender asymmetries rather than gender differences seems to be their major message.

Representation of the Sexes in Children's Books

Sex role stereotypes are present in materials created for children from the earliest age on. The contents of all picture books that have won the Caldecott Medal since 1938 have been analyzed (Weitzman, Eifler, Hokada, & Ross, 1972). An even more intense analysis of the 18 winners and runners-up for the 5 years preceding the study was performed. In the more recent prize winners and runners-up, 11 males were counted for every female. Boys were portrayed as active while girls were portrayed as passive; boys led and rescued others while girls followed and served others. Men were portrayed as engaging in a wide variety of occupations while women usually served as wives and mothers. The average picture book for children probably contains many more stereotypes than the winners. In a similar analysis of 36 randomly chosen books for 4- to 7-year olds, a disproportionately higher number of male than female characters has been found (Walstedt, 1975). In fact the majority of female central characters were animals, as opposed to the majority of male central characters, who were human beings. A number of books with no females were found, but no books with no male characters. A picture of the composite male and the composite female as portrayed in these books is presented in Table 2.4.

Textbooks for children also present this kind of sexist image. An extensive investigation of 134 children's readers from 12 different publishers was conducted by Women on Words and Images, a task force of the National Organization for Women (NOW) in Princeton and published as a monograph entitled "Dick and Jane as Victims" (1972). It documented 2760 stories and found that the ratio of boy-centered to girl-centered stories was 5 to 2, the ratio of adult male characters to adult female characters 3 to 1, and the ratio of biographies of males to biographies of females 6 to 1. Clever boys appeared 131 times, clever girls 33 times. Boys built and created things, showed initiative, and were brave and strong. When girls mastered an adult skill, it was usually a domestic one. Boys were competitive and independent; girls were usually smaller, less ambitious, and more fearful than boys.

In another analysis of first-, second-, and third-grade readers (Saario, Jacklin, & Tittle, 1973), boys were portrayed as displaying more aggression, physical exertion, and problem solving. Girls were portrayed as engaging in fantasy, carrying out directions, and talking about themselves. Particularly crucial in terms of data on differ-

Table 2.4 THE COMPOSITE FEMALE AND THE COMPOSITE MALE AS PORTRAYED IN CHILDREN'S PICTURE BOOKS

COMPOSITE FEMALE	COMPOSITE MALE
Animal	Human
Small	Large
Does routine, domestic work at home	Does skilled work outside the home
Timid, never undertakes risky activities	Brave, undertakes risky activities
Stays on the sidelines	Actively participates
Obeys orders but never gives them, powerless	Gives orders but rarely obeys them, powerful
Gives permission but must often seek it, not own boss	Gives permission but rarely seeks it, own boss
Kind, good	Important, valuable
Foolish, inept, and gives up easily	Clever, resourceful, and persistent
Loving, warm	Loving, warm
Usually surrounded by other characters but has few friendships, disinterested parents	Often alone, often with friends of own sex, sometimes with doting parent figure
Makes limited use of objects in the environment	Actively uses the objects in the environment
Initiates few activities, has few adventures	Initiates many activities, has many adventures
Meets obstacles but rarely overcomes them by herself	Meets many obstacles and often overcomes them by himself
Rarely rehearses for adult role	Often rehearses for adult role
Unemotional, sometimes expresses distress–anxiety or happiness–joy	Wide range of emotions with interest–excitement predominating
Unable to express angry feelings or get interested or excited	Able to express angry feelings or become joyous or distressed
Inferior, invisible, and discriminated against	Superior, highly visible, and not discriminated against

SOURCE: From J. J. Walstedt, "A Content Analysis of Sexual Discrimination in Children's Literature," 1973, in R. K. Unger ed., *Sex Role Stereotypes Revisited* (New York: Harper & Row, 1975), p. 38.

ences in attitudes toward each sex's ability to get things done is the finding that young male characters were shown significantly more often as receiving positive outcomes as a result of *their own actions* while girls were shown as receiving positive outcomes as a result of circumstances.

These books also portray different images of adult males and females. Adult males are shown as jobholders *and* fathers. Adult females are jobholders *or* mothers. In fact women in roles outside the domestic sphere are rarely present in children's textbooks. Despite the preponderance of man and boy in textbooks, the word *mother* occurs much more frequently than the word *father* and the word *wife* is used three times as often as the word *husband* (Graham, 1975). In the world of elementary school textbooks women function in supporting roles in relation to men and children. This discrepancy between the roles of mother and father is not simply because the mother is portrayed as the chief parent in these years. When the number of times the words *son* and *daughter* appear are counted, four times as many sons as daughters appear as children of their male parent. Mothers are also more likely to be the parents of sons than of daughters, while four out of every five fathers mentioned are the parents of sons. Even uncles appear twice as often as aunts.

Adult males are seen as engaging more often in constructive and productive behaviors, physical activity, and problem solving (Saario et al., 1973). Adult females are presented as conforming and are usually found in home and school settings. In fact the presentation of women has sometimes been referred to as the "cult of the apron" because of the preponderance of this article of attire in illustrations of women in children's textbooks.

Sex role stereotyping in children's readers is not limited to the differential number of males and females who appear or even to the different activities in which they are shown to engage. Parallel constructions that are not really parallel may be particularly harmful. What is the child supposed to perceive after reading "He was the manliest of his sex and she was the loveliest of hers" or "The men are strong, virile, and graceful, and the girls often beauties" (Graham 1975, p. 59)? You may note the inappropriate contrasts as well as the different number of modifiers applied to each sex in the second sentence. The pronoun *he* also predominates in these textbooks, only partly because males are the referent for most descriptions of humans. The pronoun he is also overwhelmingly present because most of the humans who are portrayed are indeed males.

What harm is produced by the limited concept of gender roles presented by elementary school readers?

> The real world is more varied than the one depicted in elementary readers. Boys and girls, and men and women, are fat and skinny, short and tall. Boys and men are sometimes gentle, sometimes dreamers. Artists, doctors, lawyers, and college professors are sometimes mothers as well. Rather than limiting possibilities, elementary texts should seek to maximize individual development and self-esteem by presenting a wide range of models and activities. If the average is the only model presented to a child and therefore assumed to be the child's goal, most children—and most adults—would probably be unable to match the model. [Saario et al., 1973, p. 399]

Sex and Children's Television

As might be expected, the portrayal of men and women on children's television is similar to their portrayal in children's books. The nature of the male and female role models presented on ten popular commercially produced children's TV programs has been analyzed (Sternglanz & Serbin, 1974). As expected, there were twice as many male as female roles. Males were more often portrayed as aggressive and constructive, while females were diffident. Interestingly, the consequences of male and female behavior were portrayed as different. Males were much more often rewarded for their behavior, while females were shown as receiving no consequences. The only exception to the latter observation was that females were shown being punished for high levels of activity more often than males.

An unexpected result of this research was the finding that the use of "magic" was limited almost entirely to females. Four of the five female title role stars were witches of some kind. These included such characters as a genie (in "I Dream of Jeannie") and the witches who star in "Bewitched" and "Sabrina the Teenage Witch." These programs seem to indicate to children that the only way to be a successful human being if you are female is through the use of magic. "By using magic, one may manipulate others without their being aware of it, and may manipulate them effectively. One may imagine the shock to the little girls at the age of ten or so when they realize that witchcraft is not really a viable career" (Sternglanz & Serbin, 1974, p. 714). The use of indirect power as a peculiarly feminine characteristic will be discussed in the next chapter.

Recently the NOW task force that analyzed stereotyping in children's textbooks performed a similar analysis of children's television programs (Women on Words and Images, 1975). They found the sorts of sex-specific images that have already been discussed. Plot summaries of various serials demonstrate that women are usually treated as domestic adjuncts, incompetents, or sex objects. Commercials only make the sexist message more explicit. Here are some examples:

> "He touched me, and suddenly nothing is the same"—
> Chantilly.
> "Tide was designed with mothers in mind."
> [Father and son racing on motorcycles, eating Wheaties; male voice over] "He knows he's a man."

The locale also differs depending on whether a male or a female is being featured in the commercial (Lee, 1974 cited by Thorne & Henley, 1975). Home is the setting for females 71 percent of the time, but for males only 34 percent of the time. More males are pictured in faraway places. With these role models it is not surprising that domestic activities are the main features in the fantasy play of young girls, whereas play in unusual locations is a prominant characteristic in the fantasy play of young boys (Mathews, 1975).

The Effect of Media Stereotypes on Children

In order to understand the mechanisms by which stereotypical sex roles produce negative effects on children it appears necessary to show that (1) children are aware of sex roles in the media, (2) children formulate ideas about their roles in society from media content, and (3) sex has a direct effect on the way the child uses the media and on what he or she will remember of its content. Research findings are available in all three of these areas.

Two recent studies (Deutsch, 1975; Jennings, 1975) show that even preschool children are aware of sex roles in stories. The children were better able to identify affective and intrapersonal responses (emotions and motivations) in stories with characters of the same sex as themselves (Deutsch, 1975). They performed better on same-sex than on cross-sex stories regardless of age and mental ability. Another study presented thirty-two preschool children with two stories—one about a character of their own sex and one about a character of the opposite sex (Jennings, 1975). The main character engaged in behavior that was either sex appropriate or sex inappropriate (e.g., the girls listened to stories about girls who wanted to be a ballerina or a mail carrier, the boys listened to stories about boys who wanted to be a male dancer or a mail carrier). A significant number of the children preferred stories in which the character displayed behavior that was appropriate for his or her sex. They remembered the stories with the reversed sex role longer and in greater detail—presumably because of their novelty. A large majority of boys from low-income, one-parent homes showed intense disapproval of the story about a male dancer. They labeled it "stupid" and even refused to listen to it. The boys showed clear-cut preference patterns earlier than the girls.

There is also evidence that children learn about their roles in society from media content. One extensive study analyzed the working world as it appeared on TV for a six-month period during the hours of heaviest viewing by children in the Midwest (DeFleur, 1964). It found that nearly one-third of the televised work force was involved with enforcement of or administration of the law. Professional workers were also substantially overrepresented. When children were asked to select the job characteristics that were most desirable, most of the children aged 6–13 selected a job that lets you boss other people. Jobs that enable one to make a lot of money, that bring one respect, that enable one to travel, and that enable one to help others were ranked below jobs that bring one power, in descending order. This ranking held for rural and urban children, males and females, dull and bright children, and younger and older children. Occupations were preferred according to the degree of power associated with them, as defined by how often the occupant gave or received an order, gave or received permission, and/or received or used a title of respect.

TV appears to represent an important source of incidental learning for children. Yet women are portrayed in less than 20 percent of the roles involving definite occupational activity. More recent analyses of television programing (Gerbner, 1972) also show that women have as few as 25 percent of the major roles on TV, and as in other forms of communication directed at children, women tend to be portrayed as some male's wife, mother, girlfriend, daughter, grandmother, or other female adjunct.

Since traditional sex typing appears in most TV programs, as well as in commercials, it has been hypothesized that the amount of time children spend watching television should be related to their degree of traditional sex role acceptance (Frueh & McGhee, 1975). Researchers studied children from several elementary school grades, divided into high (25 or more hours per week) and low (less than 10 hours per week) television watchers. They found that strong traditional sex role development was associated with high TV watching. There was an equal effect for boys and girls that did not change with increasing age. Although high TV watchers can differ from low TV watchers in other ways besides degree of exposure to sex role stereotypes, this study presents the first relatively direct evidence that children conform to the roles they see modeled in this medium.

An extensive literature exists that demonstrates that children model both the aggressive and prosocial behaviors that they see portrayed in a television context (videotape). Much of these data are not gender specific and will not be discussed here. One recent study, however, shows that children may model different aspects of the TV experience depending on their sex (Friedrich & Stein, 1975). Verbal labeling was found to be particularly effective in enhancing the helping behavior of kindergarten girls, while role-playing training was more effective for boys. Again, we find that males are more likely to focus on the active elements of a model's behavior whereas females are more easily controlled verbally. We do not know to what extent the selection of what behavioral components to model is af-

Figure 2.1. Cartoon illustrating sexual stereotypes (e.g., women are cleaner than men). (Reprinted by permission of United Feature Syndicate.)

fected by stereotypic attributions fostered by the communications media to which the children are exposed.

The Adult Media—or More of the Same

It will come as no surprise that the media that are specifically directed toward adults contain the same kind of sex role stereotypes as have already been discussed. (See Figure 2.1 for an example of these stereotypes.) In fact the distinction between children's and adult media is somewhat blurred, since many children's programs originated as situation comedies for an adult audience. Humor may be a particularly subtle way of "keeping her in her place," since people are not supposed to take offense at "harmless" jokes. Feminists in particular have been accused of being humorless. Nevertheless it has been shown that even in the late 1960s, 10 percent of the humor in *Reader's Digest* involved negative female stereotypes and there was an unfavorable ratio of anti-female to anti-male jokes (Zimbardo & Meadow, 1974). A rank ordering of the kinds of negative traits attributed to women in this "humor" showed that the stupid, incompetent, and foolish woman was the most frequent category.

A number of analyses of the content of women's-magazine fiction have been made, of which the one by Franzwa (1975) may serve as a representative sample. In women's magazines from 1940 through 1970, the following themes were stressed: Marriage is inevitable for every normal female; to catch a man you must be less competent than he; married women do not work; being a housewife–mother is the best career of all; the childless woman has wasted her life. The widow–divorcee is portrayed as being hopelessly incompetent without a man. Spinsters are portrayed as lonely, useless creatures even when they hold relatively high-status jobs. Their work is portrayed as dull, meaningless, and unimportant in comparison with having a man. Television has also largely failed to portray many women who are satisfied and happy in their careers, and there would seem to be no adequate, mature, adult, independent roles for women in the movies unless they are over fifty years of age.

Even though soap operas have introduced such controversial subjects as extramarital affairs and abortion to daytime television, their characters are still being portrayed as responding in traditionally stereotyped ways. Women appear more often in home settings and men in office situations (Finz & Waters, 1976). When the conversation involves a male–female interaction it is likely to take place in the home. This finding is particularly interesting in view of the fact that many of the leading serials use hospitals as a major location and have a number of leading characters who are nurses and doctors by profession and, as such, could be expected to spend more time in the employment situation.

The Future of Research on Stereotypes in the Media

The vast majority of studies in this area have been content analyses of the forms in which sex role stereotypes appear in various communications media. The same general conclusions appear to be reached irrespective of the particular area of focus [It would be advisable to look at Busby's (1975) compendium of research in this area for additional specific details.] It is likely that more such work will be done in relatively neglected areas such as newspapers and pulp novels. People will also be looking for more subtle forms of stereotyping, such as the locale of the interaction, how effective interpersonal transactions are, and whether males and females are offered different rewards for their behaviors.

SEX ROLE STEREOTYPES: AN OVERVIEW

Sex role stereotypes may be characterized as stable constructs that reappear in every context, in all age groups, and across a wide variety of situations. In this chapter I stressed the content of such stereotypes and the role that language and the communication media play in conveying these stereotypes. The underlying assumption of the stereotypes seems to be that to be a female is somehow less human than to be a male. Another underlying assumption appears to be that people cannot encompass certain "masculine" and "feminine" characteristics at the same time—that one cannot be both nurturant and achieving, assertive and dependent, objective and subjective, and so forth. In part these contradictions may be a result of the way stereotypes are usually measured—by means of a bipolar scale, with one end being the "opposite" of the other. Similar sex stereotypes appear, however, when other techniques, such as rank ordering of values, are used. Apparent contradictions about "male" and "female" characteristics may also be due to limitations in our language. However, evidence showing that blacks in our society seem to have fewer sexist assumptions than whites makes this conjecture unlikely.

It is more likely that stereotypes are a component of a larger conceptual process involving how we view the causes of our own and others' behavior. We are likely to give ourselves the benefit of the doubt but to assume that the behavior of others is more a product of internal predispositions. The tendency to stereotype may be related to how well we can put ourselves into another's place. There is ample evidence in later chapters that communication between males and females is limited at best, and limited communication could explain the pattern of cross-sex stereotyping. Unfortunately it is more difficult to explain the pattern of within-sex stereotyping, which leads to women devaluing the work of other women. Further study will be needed to explain why and how women incorporate the "male-equals-human" model.

Another focus of future study will be the personal and social needs that are served by sex role stereotypes. Many social institutions other than language or the communications media have implicit and explicit sexist assumptions. Since these assumptions are not usually considered to be stereotypes, they will be examined in the context of the various institutions—marriage, parenthood, the occupational world, and so forth. It appears that stereotypes serve to maintain the status quo. It is important to find out, however, to what extent stereotypes are derived from social systems and to what extent they create them. While this area is the province of the sociologist rather than the psychologist, the psychologist can provide important information by examining the attitudes of people who are exposed to rapidly changing social systems.

Why are sexist misperceptions maintained? There is ample evidence that people "select" information to support their conceptual systems. Among the questions that remain to be answered are the following: At what point will the weight of contrary evidence break down a cognitive system? Is the maintenance of stereotypes more important for some individuals or groups than others? How are attitudes that are presumably destructive to one's personal growth maintained? Since we all engage in sex-inappropriate behavior, why doesn't this change our assumptions about certain behaviors being more appropriate to members of one sex? How important are stereotypic attitudes in the maintenance of sex-asymmetrical or sex-prejudiced behavior? Issues relating to the existence of such asymmetries will be discussed in the next chapter.

Chapter 3
The Politics of Gender

We cannot dismiss sex role stereotypes as individual idiosyncracies similar to attitudes toward redheads, people with a Brooklyn accent, or Texans. Instead we must examine what stereotypes tell us about power. Not every group is a subject of stereotypes. Stereotyped characteristics, moreover, usually reflect negative judgments about the group to which they are applied. In this chapter we will examine the relationship between the social power of particular behaviors and the sex of the people who usually manifest such behaviors. Maleness, independent of "masculine" behaviors, confers more social status and power. It may be these variables rather than sex as such that control many of the behaviors that are considered more common to one sex than the other. In this chapter we will examine relationships among and between the sexes in terms of status relationships. In other words, we will examine the extent to which sex typing is actually power typing.

DEFINITIONS OF TERMS

This area has been termed *the politics of gender* because it focuses on the way power affects how males and females treat each other. In this sense "power" has been removed from the political sphere in order to show how it influences the daily behavior of all of us. The concept of power most frequently dealt with by psychologists is individual social power—how a person or group influences or controls some aspect of another person or group. Behaviorally, *social power* can be defined as the relative effectiveness of attempts to influence others over time (Sherif & Sherif, 1969). It differs from *influence* in that it implies some form of coercive control. Since, however, it is often difficult to determine what sorts of implicit rewards and punishments are operating in a relationship, power and influence are often used interchangeably by social scientists. Unless otherwise noted, the two terms will also be used interchangeably in this chapter.

Social scientists who are concerned with the operation of relationships involving the use of social power are also concerned with the attributes of people who possess different degrees of social power. The term *status* is used to refer to a person's potential ability to influence others, as opposed to *social power*, which reflects actual influence. Status may be defined as an individual's position in a hierarchy of power relations within a social unit as measured by his or her relative effectiveness in the control of interpersonal behaviors and in group decision making (Sherif & Sherif, 1969). Sociologists usually recognize two kinds of status: ascribed and achieved. *Achieved status* is based on the role one performs within an organization or family, for example, boss versus secretary, father versus mother, professor versus student, and so forth. How well one performs one's role is also a component of achieved status, although this is often difficult to determine since many roles have no explicit criteria by which to evaluate the individual. Good students are fairly easy to distinguish from poor students, but within the general range of "normality" how does one distinguish "good" fathers from "poor" ones?

A more interesting form of status for those who are interested in relationships having to do with power is ascribed status. *Ascribed status* is based on the possession of characteristics with which an individual is born. The degree of status conferred because of a particular characteristic depends on how valuable society defines it to be. Determinants of ascribed status in the United States include age, race, social class, and sex. Although these characteristics can change, it is difficult or impossible for them to do so as a result of the individual's efforts. While achieved status is usually described in terms of the functional differences required by different roles, ascribed status is usually described in scalar terms—more or less. Status in this scalar sense is often used to predict relationships between individuals in terms of the rewards, benefits, or compliance they give each other—in other words, to predict who has the power in a relationship.

POWER, STATUS, AND GENDER: A THEORETICAL MODEL

It can be argued that women almost always have a lower ascriptive status than men. Thus sex differences in power exist automatically. Those who are interested in the politics of gender argue that male–female relationships are essentially similar to relationships between individuals varying in other dimensions of ascribed status, such as social class, race, or age (Hacker, 1951; Henley, 1973; Unger, 1978). Sexual equality may actually be an exception. In almost every behavioral interaction between the sexes the male is more powerful. Male dominance appears to be due to the almost uniform and universal ascription of higher status to maleness than to femaleness. Independent of behaviors typed as appropriate for each sex, such as achievement-related traits for males and affective–nurturant traits for females, sex conveys information about status.

Since this status asymmetry between the sexes is based on ascribed rather than achieved status, it cannot easily be changed by the performance capabilities of particular individuals. It also extends throughout a large range of environments and situations in which relative status would not appear to be relevant. Because status is so highly correlated with sex, the effects of status differences may have been confused with the effects of sex differences. This view may be termed a status/gender identity model of sex differences (Unger, 1978). It permits a different perspective on the relationship between the individual and society. For example, if women lack power because of their roles as childbearers, childrearers, and the like, they will gain power as a result of changing their roles. If, however, their relative lack of power is a result of who they are, they will continue to lack power even in "male" roles. An understanding of the bases of ascriptive categories and their use in society will be necessary before any real change in the relationships between the sexes can take place.

EVIDENCE THAT THE SEXES POSSESS DIFFERENT DEGREES OF STATUS

Nonverbal Cues to Status: Gestures of Dominance and Submission

Nancy Henley (1973) did some of the pioneering work on the relationship between status variables and the behaviors of men and women. On the basis of a large-scale observational study of touching in public, she argues that touch privilege is a correlate of status. Individuals with higher status initiate touching more frequently and reciprocate touching more. Males were more likely to touch females than vice versa, and they would reciprocate a touch initiated by a female more frequently. Henley argues that failure to reciprocate touching connotes an acceptance of the legitimacy of the touch and that reciprocation indicates a reassertion of power.

In a similar vein, touching is used to communicate asymmetry of power relations in terms of age and socioeconomic status. In the same study it was found that young people and those of presumed lower economic status (on the basis of attire) were more likely to be the recipients of touching and less likely to reciprocate it.

It has been argued that touching connotes intimacy, but Henley points out that there is no necessary contradiction between a gesture being used to communicate power and the same gesture being used to communicate closeness. An analogy is made to the verbal gesture of calling another person by his or her first name. Used reciprocally, first names connote friendship; used nonreciprocally, they connote status (Brown & Gilman, 1960). In both verbal and nonverbal cases movement toward greater intimacy is usually initiated by the persons with the higher status.

Females behave in a manner similar to males with low status and are treated by others as though they possess such status in many aspects of nonverbal behavior. Gender-related behavior having to do with territoriality has received considerable attention recently. Females require a smaller envelope of personal space than males (Lott & Sommer, 1967). Outside the laboratory, such as on a beach, single females or all-female groups claim less space than single males or all-male groups (Edney & Jordan-Edney, 1974). Dominant males require a larger envelope of personal space surrounding them than nondominant males (Sommer, 1969). The degree of personal space required may be a function of level of aggression. For example, prisoners convicted of a violent crime require a larger envelope of personal space than other male prisoners (Kinzel, 1970).

Sex differences in the amount of personal space required appear at a very early age. Among normal middle-class 3- to 5-year-old children, boys spend more time playing outdoors than girls and use about one and one-half times as much space (Harper & Sanders, 1975). The amount of time the girls spent playing outdoors was not affected by whether they habitually dressed in jeans or dresses. From the age of 6 upward male pairs interact at greater distances than female pairs (Aiello & Aiello, 1974). Males also confront each other at less direct body orientations than females.

Females are approached more closely than males. Subjects of

both sexes are more willing to intrude upon a woman than upon a man (Leibman, 1970; Nesbitt & Steven, 1974). Mixed-sex pairs are also more likely to be intruded upon than same-sex pairs (Walker & Borden, 1976). The probability of intrusion upon a mixed-sex dyad was decreased only when a high-status male (as indicated by attire) was present.

Although the personal space of women is more likely to be intruded upon, they are less likely to respond to the invasion by fleeing the scene. When female confederates invaded the personal space of men and women by seating themselves directly across from, adjacent to, or quite far from them in a college library, male subjects tended to leave the situation while females decreased rather than increased their motor behavior (Mahoney, 1974). Their behavior became more constricted and immobile, making them more easily encroached upon.

The amount of personal space required and the effect of invasion of that space appears to serve a major social function. Who invades and who is invaded denotes status in our society. Preschool children of both sexes approach a female experimenter more closely than a male experimenter (Eberts & Lepper, 1975). Although this behavior may be a result of their willingness to engage in more intimacy with a female than with a male, once more we find a confusion between a gesture connoting closeness and one connoting status. By the time children have reached the age at which their physical proximity makes adults uncomfortable they have already formed the habit of getting closer to females.

Adults are sensitive to the invasion of their personal space by children. One investigation examined the effect of such invasions on adults standing on line in a theater (Fry & Willis, 1971). Five-year-old children generally received positive reactions to their invasions; 8-year-olds were generally ignored, and 10-year-olds received negative reactions similar to those received by an adult invader in a similar situation. Adults tended to move or lean away from the 10-year-old invaders. They also rocked or shifted their weight more frequently. Males tended to interpose barriers (coats or parcels) between themselves and 10-year-old invaders of either sex, while females were more likely to shift their weight without moving from their place. The form of the response of males and females to invasion by a near-adult appears to be consistent with the response to invasion for female college students. In either case the responses would not appear to be due to fear.

Female nonverbal behaviors are more consonant with gestures of submission than with those of dominance. One of the more widely noted examples of differences between the sexes is the frequency with which they smile. Smiling may have different motivational bases for women and men. In women, smiling seems to correlate with feelings of social anxiety, discomfort, deference, and abasement (Beekman, 1974). In men, smiling is associated with feelings of affiliation and sociability. Children seem to be aware of this dissociation of affect and facial expression in adult women (Bugental, Love, & Gianetto, 1971). They tend to discount female smiling when it is accompanied by a conflicting verbal message, but to respond to male smiling in a similar context. Ethologists have suggested that smiling or slight baring of the teeth is associated with placatory gestures by low-dominance primates when they are menaced by high-status males.

Eye contact is another gesture that may be used to communicate either affiliation or power. Women engage in mutual visual interaction more than men (Exline, 1963; Exline, Gray, & Schuette, 1965); however, they seem to back down when looking becomes staring, that is, a gesture of dominance. Reciprocation of eye contact seems to be related to dominance in both sexes. High-dominance males and females were more likely to reciprocate the eye contact of a confederate than low-dominance males and females (Fromme & Beam, 1974). In general, males were more likely to reciprocate than females. Males also used amount of eye contact as a cue for approach to the confederate. A high degree of eye contact led to a faster and closer approach when the subject was dominant but produced a slower approach with a greater final interpersonal distance when he was low in dominance.

Eye contact appears to be a cue that can either enhance or inhibit aggression. It appears to both communicate and manipulate relative status. Ethologists have noted that gaze aversion is a common gesture of submission among many primates whereas staring is a gesture of dominance. It is possible that interpretation of the gesture may depend on other clues to relative status. Thus in one study in which college students were permitted to "shock" accomplices, victims with pupils that had been enlarged chemically were shocked significantly less than victims with constricted pupils (Kidd, 1975). Subjects were less willing to look into the line of regard of victims with dilated pupils. It would be interesting to know how pupil size would be perceived if it were manipulated for the individuals in the higher-status rather than the lower-status position. (Table 3.1 presents a summary of information conveyed nonverbally which relate to status differences between the sexes.)

Nonverbal Cues in Interpersonal Transactions

If cross-sexual situations are more threatening to females than to males, one would expect that females would make more use of

Table 3.1 SUMMARY OF BEHAVIORAL SITUATIONS IN WHICH WOMEN
APPEAR LESS POWERFUL THAN MEN

SITUATION	DESCRIPTION OF BEHAVIOR	RESEARCHER(S)
Touching in public	Women touched more frequently	Henley, 1973
	Men reciprocate a touch more often.	
Personal space	Boys interact at a greater distance.	Aiello & Aiello, 1974
	Boys use more space in outdoor play.	Harper & Sanders, 1975
	Women require less personal space.	Lott & Sommer, 1967
	Women claim less territory on a beach.	Edney & Jordan-Edney, 1974
Intrusion	Preschool children approach an adult female more closely.	Eberts & Lepper, 1975
	Women are intruded upon more often.	Leibman, 1970
		Nesbitt & Steven, 1974
Response to intrusion	Women freeze more.	Mahoney, 1974
Eye contact	Men reciprocate eye contact more.	Fromme & Beam, 1974
Attention to status cues	Women remember more about people's clothing, hair styles, and expressions.	Kanter, 1977
	Girls use proximity cues more accurately.	Post & Hetherington, 1974
Body posture	Women maintain a tenser posture at rest.	Mehrabian, 1968
Helping	Women are usually helped more.	Krebs, 1970
	Men usually help more.	
	Women are helped more in situations involving danger or personal inconvenience.	Howard & Crano, 1974
	Women are more likely to have dropped pencils picked up, doors opened, permission to go ahead in lines.	Latané & Dabbs, 1975
		Walum, 1974
		Unger et al., 1974
Imitation and influence	People are more willing to sign a petition presented by a man.	Keasey & Tomlinson-Keasey, 1971
	Boys' toys are preferred.	Rosenberg & Sutton-Smith, 1960
	Men are perceived as more likely to send direct power messages.	Johnson, 1974
	Women are less likely to be chosen as leaders of small groups.	Piliavin, 1976

nonverbal cues in such encounters. Females do appear to be more sensitive to photographic cues involving facial expressions or articles of attire than males are (Kanter, 1977). At age 6 only girls are accurate in using proximity cues in judging how well people like each other (Post & Hetherington, 1974). They are also more accurate than boys in using eye contact cues to judge affiliation.

Other studies of nonverbal behavior indicate that women may find social situations more stressful than men do. Males customarily occupy more space than females at rest, even allowing for their larger body size. Women usually hold their limbs closer to the body and their legs crossed or closer together than men do. A greater degree of body tension and vigilance is characteristic of individuals communicating an intense degree of dislike for another person (Mehrabian, 1968). Males, however, assume a very relaxed position when addressing an intensely disliked female. These data may be interpreted to mean that threat evokes body tension. Females, of course, do not threaten. One could also interpret these data to indicate that females are under greater stress than males even under supposedly relaxed conditions. This interpretation is consistent with the suggestion that they customarily occupy a lower place in the dominance hierarchy than males.

The role of nonverbal cues in cross-sex interactions may be both more pervasive and more subtle than was previously believed. In one rather sophisticated laboratory study encounters between male and female graduate students and members of the same and opposite sexes were videotaped (Weitz, 1976). The nonverbal aspects of these encounters were evaluated by raters who did not have available to them any information about the sex of the person with whom the interaction was taking place (the two participants were taped in separate frames). Raters also did not have available to them any information about the personality characteristics of the participants, although information about them was obtained by means of questionnaires.

Liberalness in sex role attitudes in men was found to be correlated with raters' evaluation of degree of nonverbal warmth. The finding supports the idea that rigid sex typing inhibits the expression of positive affect in men in their interactions with either women or other men. Sex role attitudes were not related to the rating of nonverbal affect for women.

The most interesting aspect of the women's nonverbal behavior was their adjustment of their interpersonal style to the personality characteristics of a man with whom they were conversing even in the first few minutes of an initial encounter with him. Raters evaluated the women as being more nonverbally submissive with a more dominant male partner and more nonverbally dominant with a more submissive partner. The male nonverbal scores did *not* relate significantly to any measured aspect of the female partner's personality. The women also did not similarly attune themselves to the personality characteristics of female partners.

During initial interactions female partners elicited ratings of greater warmth in both men and women who interacted with them. In a later interaction (in the context of a political discussion about Watergate), male partners seemed to generate greater anxiety in people of both sexes. The personality characteristics of the men also molded the nonverbal reactions of their female partners. They focused more on their partner's face when he was highly dominant than on the face of a less dominant partner.

This study reveals how the microprocesses of interpersonal transactions reflect the macrostructure of sex roles. Women elicit more warmth during initial encounters than men—they may be approached more readily without posing a threat. Men produce more anxiety—they put others more "on guard" and need to be taken more seriously. Women appear to respond more closely to social cues only in interaction with a man. These nonverbal social cues appear to be clear enough to be perceived by an outside observer seeing only half the interaction (and hearing nothing of it at all). Leaving aside questions as to why only the female appears to feel that she needs to adjust her behavior to the personality of her partner and why she so adjusts it only for males, one may also ask whether she performs such adjustments at the expense of her own contributions to the interaction. Because these behaviors are nonverbal and may even be unconscious, they may be particularly difficult to deal with.

Sex Differences in the Interpretation of the Physical and Social Milieu

Even under conditions in which no stress appears to be involved, females and males seem to interpret "identical" physical or social environments differently. Thus increasing group density in heterosexual groups produces different emotional responses in male and female college students (Schettino & Borden, 1976). Males responded to crowding primarily by reporting increased feelings of aggressiveness. Females reported increased nervousness.

Being crowded can have different implications for males and females. Males preferred mixed-sex groups regardless of size or density (Marshall & Heslin, 1975). Females preferred mixed-sex groups only when they were large and preferred same-sex groups when crowded in smaller groups. Crowding in small groups may increase a woman's feelings of being vulnerable to unwanted advances. Crowded conditions inevitably increase intimacy between the sexes. Men have more social permission to express affection in public toward people they do not know well. Women may neither reciprocate that affection nor feel that they have social permission to do so. Rejection of another person, however, may be more difficult and conflict producing in a small group than in a large one. In a large group a woman may be more anonymous and less subject to social penalties for her actions. Therefore women may feel comfortable about crowded conditions involving men only when they perceive themselves to be somewhat protected by the deindividualization produced by such conditions.

Invasions of an individual's personal space by a male is perceived as more negative than a similar invasion by a female (Fisher & Byrne, 1975). Male subjects were more negatively affected by an invader who sat across from them in a college library whereas female subjects were more upset by an invader who sat next to them. Men who are alone in the library tend to erect barriers against face-to-face invasion while women erect barriers against adjacent invasions. Research (Norum, Russo, & Sommer, 1967) suggests that people generally sit face to face in competitive situations and adjacent in cooperative ones. It is possible that an uninvited stranger sitting across from a male is seen as presenting a threatening, competitive challenge while a similar stranger sitting next to a female is seen as issuing an unwarranted demand for affiliation.

These studies suggest that women and men make assumptions about the implicit motives and consequences of the behaviors of those whom they do not know that affect the meaning they attach to these encounters. It is what the individual perceives rather than what the stranger really means that will shape her or his response to the situation. For example, when female or male college students seated alone outdoors on a college campus were approached by a same-sex invader who either did or did not ask permission before invading their personal space, women left more quickly if permission was asked whereas men left more rapidly when confronted with a silent invader (Sundstrom & Sundstrom, 1977). For males, an invasion may be perceived as a threat or show of dominance that is alleviated by the other male's showing subordination by asking permission. For females, invasion may be seen as a gesture of affiliation. The subsequent silence of the invader may be seen as some sort of threat.

Some laboratory studies also indicate that interpersonal distance has different meanings for males and females. When male or female confederates sat either close to or far from male and female students, males showed *greater* liking for the near female than in any other condition while females showed *less* liking for the far male than in any other condition (Kahn & McGaughey, 1977). Since males are usually the initiators in cross-sex encounters, males sitting near and females sitting far may be seen as normative and noninformative. A far-sitting male, on the other hand, may imply rejection and dislike to the female and a close-sitting female a comparable degree of liking and acceptance for the male. Thus even when proximity cues are made clear and unambiguous, individuals may derive differential attributions based on such cues. These attributions would appear to be based on two sources: sex role stereotypes about male and female characteristics and behaviors and the asymmetry of cross-sex relationships in which males are expected to take the lead.

SEX DIFFERENCES IN AGGRESSION AND CONFORMITY AS A FUNCTION OF POWER DIFFERENCES

Many so-called sex differences in motivation or personality may also be due to attributional processes. In these cases attributions would involve expectations about one's own properties as well as about the meanings of the actions of others. For example, males are usually found to be more aggressive and females to be more conforming or cooperative. It is noteworthy that the studies that find maximal differences in these areas tend to be those that measure differences in self-perception rather than in actual behavior (Maccoby & Jacklin, 1974; Frodi et al., 1977). In other words, differences are most likely to be found under conditions in which people are giving information about what they have social permission to do or be rather than about how they may actually behave.

Conformity as a Status-Related Behavior

The sex differences in aggression and conformity that may actually exist are consistent with the interpretation that males have more status and power than females. Low-status individuals tend to conform more in group situations than high-status individuals or leaders. It is interesting that a recent survey of a vast amount of literature on conformity, persuadability, and influenceability indicates that women are not as compliant in group situations as they are usually portrayed as being (Eagly, 1978). They are, however, more likely to conform than men when tasks involve male "expertise" or when their behavior is being evaluated in the presence of a male expert. These data are consistent with the idea that males possess greater status in a group context. Females also do not differ from males in conformity when relatively abstract tasks are used. In general, people appear to conform less when the task is more salient to them. And most early studies of conformity utilized male-oriented tasks.

Since achievement-related tasks are stereotypically masculine in our society, it would not be surprising if children are socialized to respond to complex cognitive decision-making tasks within groups in terms of appropriate sex roles. Males, for example, may be trained to resist conforming to the demands of the group. In a large-scale developmental study of conformity and independence, unanimous peer pressure produced decreasing conformity in boys from the first through tenth grades (Allen & Newtson, 1972). Girls, in contrast, showed only slight decreases in conformity with increasing age. A similar effect has been reported for boys and girls in accommodative versus exploitative strategies in a competitive board game (Vinacke & Gullickson, 1964). Groups of three males playing such a game show increasing amounts of exploitation of one individual from primary school through college age. Female triads of every age worked out arrangements by which each individual gained equally.

The relationships between conformity, cooperation, and competition are not at all clearly understood. It may be that they are not related at all, but appear to be because they appear in individuals who are subjected to similar kinds of socialization pressures. Of course these socialization practices are related to sex by way of status and power. We also do not know whether cooperation and competition are necessarily the inverse of each other or whether this relationship is a product of how we construct our games and our society. We do know, however, that competition appears to be particularly salient for males in our society.

Competition as a Status-Related Behavior

Males appear to treat games as competitions in which individual gain is salient and a win must be gained at any cost. Females may be more interested in treating a game as a social-interaction situation in which equitable outcomes are sought. Since females do not tend to view games in the context of competition, it is not surprising to find that they are less accurate in assessing their opponent's strategy (Pilisuk, Skolnick, & Overstreet, 1968). However, they appear to adopt the same strategies as men when placed in a clearly competitive situation in which outcomes are subject to risk (Lirtzman &

Wahba, 1972). A similar idea is suggested by a finding that while women may cooperate more than men in the early trials of a competitive game, sex differences in strategies disappear as the logic of the conflict situation becomes compelling to the subjects (Tedeschi, Lesnick, & Gahagan, 1968). Thus sex differences in laboratory games may be a reflection of sex differences in the meaning of an experience with competitive situations.

Probably the most interesting studies in terms of our understanding of the politics of gender are games involving cross-sex or cross-status interactions. Several studies suggest that women and men play out "appropriate" sex roles in the context of a gamelike situation. As has been noted before, maleness is associated with power and femaleness with powerlessness. When men and women participate in games against simulated opponents of the same sex, they exploit powerful opponents less than they do weak ones (Black & Higbee, 1973). Males, however, appear to be more responsive to the threat of retaliation as related to actual power to retaliate. When subjects were informed that their opponents could retaliate and cause them losses in a competitive game, females decreased their exploitation of all opponents regardless of their degree of power. Males, in contrast, exploited their weak opponents more than their more powerful ones when retaliation was possible. They also exploited an unconditionally cooperative opponent more when he was powerful than when he was weak. The nonuse of available resources became a cue suggesting weakness·to males and appeared to invite them to become exploitive. Women are less willing to antagonize others through excessive exploitation, especially if the other person has more power than they do or appears to be able to threaten them.

One intriguing study provides some understanding of the covert assumptions underlying behavior in competitive games. Male and female subjects played games in which the sex of the partner varied as well as the level of verbal and nonverbal communication permitted between opponents (Wiley, 1973). No difference between the sexes in the degree of cooperative behavior was found when no verbal communication was allowed. Traditional sex-related patterns of behavior appeared, however, when the subjects were allowed verbal communication with a partner of the opposite sex. In all but one case the male made the first suggestion of a cooperative strategy—one that ensured equity. These responses were suggestive of a "chivalrous" attitude on the part of the men. The percentage of cooperative choices for men in mixed-sex games was almost 17 percent greater than for men playing against another man. The degree of cooperative choices by women increased only 5 percent over their cooperative choices when playing against another woman. The presence of sex-related differences only in mixed-sex interactions suggests cross-sex reinforcement of traditional power patterns.

The Relationship Between Competition and Aggression

Among children competition seems to increase aggression. Surprisingly, at least one finding has noted that, among third- to fifth-grade boys, winning a competition led to an increase in aggression (Perry & Perry, 1976). High competition has been fostered in young boys by limiting the supply of resources (blocks in a tower-building task) and by offering high rewards (Rocha & Rogers, 1976). The increased aggression took the form of verbal threats, taking of the opponent's blocks, and outright physical attacks. Also surprisingly, competition appears to be related to high self-esteem in children. Pairs of 8- to 12-year-old children with high self-esteem were more competitive than pairs in which only one child had high self-esteem or in pairs of children with low self-esteem (Vance & Richmond, 1975). White children were significantly more competitive than black children. In this study no sex differences were found.

Failure in adult males has been found to be associated with reduced aggression during competition (Dengerink & Myers, 1977). Aggression was particularly likely to be inhibited if the individual was already depressed.

Factors that foster competition are related to sex via status in our society. In a later chapter I will show that females are offered more limited rewards than males. Low self-esteem is also more common among females, as is depression. Of course this is a circular phenomenon, since withdrawal from competition limits access to rewards. There is some evidence that by the high school years competitiveness is associated with involvement in learning activities and a feeling of personal worth as a student (Johnson & Ahlegren, 1976). These are activities that would permit one to acquire more status.

Aggression and the Threat of Retaliation

Females may be more cooperative or less aggressive because they are less competitive than males, but female aggressive behavior may also be inhibited by the threat of male retaliation. In some "safe" laboratory settings females may react as aggressively as males. In one study (Taylor & Epstein, 1967) females were unaggressive toward female opponents but reacted to male provocation in a highly aggressive manner. They increased the intensity of the electric shocks they delivered to their opponents more sharply than their opponents increased theirs. A unique aspect of this experimental situation was the equal ability of the two sexes to inflict pain. There was no other way to communicate, and hence any appeal to helplessness was useless. When, on the other hand, individuals are given a choice of options about how to respond in an aggressive encounter, females may choose less destructive alternatives (Frodi et al., 1977). This more limited aggression may be a result of a lower drive for aggression in females or may occur because they perceive that retaliation would be socially undesirable for them. Taylor and Epstein, for example, point out that individuals of both sexes expressed amazement that a woman could shock them so severely. Women may be more willing to appear aggressive in the presence of a female experimenter than in the presence of a male experimenter (Larwood, O'Neal, & Brennan, 1977). Practice at angry role play did, however, seem to disinhibit the expression of aggression in the presence of a male.

How males retaliate to female aggression seems to reflect their attitudes about sexual equality. In one study a series of encounters was staged between female confederates and male subjects who either had traditional views on women's roles or were in favor of women's liberation, using Bataca (pillow) clubs with sensors that relayed information about the frequency and intensity of the blows (Young, Beier, Beier, & Barton, 1975). Two 90-second bouts were staged. During the first bout the woman maintained a defensive style. In the second bout she attacked at a fixed rate. Pro-liberation males used blows of greater average intensity than anti-liberation males in both bouts. Both groups increased the intensity of their blows when they were attacked, but the anti-liberation males increased them much more than the pro-liberation males. The most authoritarian males (who were also least likely to favor women's liberation) were most resistant toward aggression against a female in the first bout. They made remarks such as "Can't you get me a guy?" and "I can't hit *her!*" The pro-liberation males seem to have regarded a woman as a more worthy or equal opponent.

Children appear to be socialized to inhibit aggressive retaliatory responses to aggression instigated by someone who is less powerful than themselves (Kirchner, 1974). Thus assertions of lack of power by a female may inhibit aggression toward them. At the same time, aggression may be inhibited by females because they are not completely assured that aggression will be withheld under all circumstances. Social norms such as chivalry institutionalize power-related behaviors for the two sexes. After a while they cease to be aware that their behavior is not a reflection of their own choices.

SEX DIFFERENCES IN HELPING AND COOPERATION AS A FUNCTION OF POWER DIFFERENCES

Although helping seems to be quite the opposite of aggression, there is a lot of information indicating that both behaviors are influenced by similar variables. Sometimes, in fact, aggression appears to be the withholding of help and help the withholding of aggression. Social norms exist that stress that one should not harm someone who is more helpless than oneself. These are the same individuals for whom social norms mandate assistance. Helping may be reserved for dependent others. In an interesting experiment contrasting sex, dependency, and helping, the most important determinant of whether or not an individual was helped was whether or not his or her dependency was recognized (Gruder & Cook, 1971). Dependent females were helped more than nondependent females. Nondependent females received marginally more help than dependent males. Dependency did not appear to affect the degree to which men were helped. This may be because the concept of a dependent male may violate our assumptions about the social normality of the situation.

Although there are many situations in which no differences between the levels of help offered to females and males are found, where differences do exist it is the female who is more likely to be helped (Krebs, 1970). Men are much more likely to help women than women are to help men, especially under naturalistic field conditions in which some danger or personal inconvenience might be involved (Howard & Crano, 1974). Women are more likely to be regarded as dependent than men if no other information is available. A large-scale field study that was recently performed in various parts of the United States illustrates the effect of regional norms on the extent to which women and men are helped in a similar situation (Latané & Dabbs, 1975): 145 experimenters "accidentally" dropped a handful of pencils or coins on 1497 occasions before a total of 4813 bystanders in elevators in Columbus, Ohio; Seattle, Washington; and Athens, Georgia. In picking up the objects females received more help than males and males gave more help than females. (See Table 3.2.) Trends involving helping and being helped operated in a complementary basis in terms of sex. As helping for females went up, helping for males went down; as the willingness of males to help increased, the willingness of females to help decreased. These effects were particularly striking in Atlanta. The notion of tradi-

Table 3.2   PERCENTAGES OF BYSTANDERS GIVING HELP
(N's IN PARENTHESES)

	COLUMBUS	SEATTLE	ATLANTA
FEMALE BYSTANDERS:			
Helping males	23%	16%	7%
	(715)	(338)	(389)
Helping females	23%	26%	26%
	(588)	(207)	(180)
MALE BYSTANDERS:			
Helping males	25%	32%	12%
	(815)	(322)	(448)
Helping females	32%	39%	70%
	(505)	(141)	(165)

SOURCE: From B. Latané and J. M. Dabbs, Jr., "Sex, Group Size and Helping in Three Cities," *Sociometry*, 1975, 38, 180–194. Copyright 1975 by the American Sociological Association. Reprinted by permission.

tional sex differences—helpless ladies and courtly gentlemen—seems more potent in the South. Helpfulness and helplessness are channeled by differential sex role definitions.

It has been suggested (Walum, 1974) that helping encounters between males and females involve more than empty gestures of courtesy or chivalry. Using door opening as her behavioral measure, Walum investigated what happens when customary norms are violated. When women opened the doors for men, deference confrontations occurred. The amount of emotion and discussion generated by this apparently slight deviation from routine indicates that more than a violation of the tenets of Emily Post was occurring. Walum compares sex differences in door opening to similar encounters between individuals possessing differing amounts of authority: "The doctor ushers in his patient, the mother—her children, and the Dean—his faculty, the young and able facilitate the old and infirm. Even reference to the 'gatekeepers of knowledge' symbolically acknowledge the role of authority vested in those responsible for the door" (1974, p. 509). She suggests that opening a door is a political act, one that affirms patriarchal ideology.

THE EFFECT OF SOCIAL DEVIANCE ON INTERPERSONAL TRANSACTIONS BETWEEN THE SEXES

If helpfulness and aggression between the sexes are largely mediated by social norms, it should not be surprising that when individuals remove themselves from the normative social structure they interfere with the customary between- and within-sex relationships. The easiest way for the psychologist to manipulate social deviance is by means of attire. A number of studies indicate that the degree to which women are helped by men is decreased by nontraditional clothing. Women who request help in a supermarket are helped less when they are dressed in slacks than when they are dressed in skirts or dresses (Harris & Bays, 1973). Doors are also opened more readily for women who are dressed in "feminine" apparel (Renne & Allen, 1976). "Hippie" women are less frequently permitted to go ahead in line in a supermarket than women who are more conventionally attired (Unger, Raymond, & Levine, 1974). Males in deviant dress are also less likely to be helped than those who are dressed conventionally (Raymond & Unger, 1972).

The effect of deviant attire may be to remove people from the normal status hierarchy. Other behaviors that are known to be affected by status variables also show an interaction with sex and with attire. For example, people are more willing to sign a petition if it is tendered by a male than if it is tendered by a female (Keasey & Tomlinson-Keasey, 1971). They are also more likely to sign a petition if they are urged to do so by a conventionally dressed individual than if they are asked to do so by a person in hippie garb. This phenomenon was made use of during the 1968 presidential election campaign and was termed the "get clean for Gene" procedure. College students who volunteered to work for the election of Eugene McCarthy (an anti-Vietnam war candidate) cut their hair, shaved their beards, and took to wearing suits or skirts. These practices—which appeared to heighten their effectiveness with the general electorate—may be among the few examples of direct application of psychological knowledge to the American political process.

The way helping shades into aggression may be illustrated by means of a procedure known as the stalled-car situation (Doob & Gross, 1968). In this procedure an automobile stops at an intersection with a traffic signal and waits 15 seconds after the light has changed from red to green before starting. The dependent variable measured here is, of course, how long it takes for the driver behind the stalled car to honk her or his horn. In the original study it was found that people are more ready to honk at an apparently stalled Rambler than at a Cadillac in a similar predicament. People are also more willing to honk at an apparently stalled car driven by a woman than at one driven by a man (Deaux, 1971). In a large-scale study of the interrelationships between sex, attire, and situations requiring help (or at least the inhibition of aggression), we found that both sexes were especially likely to honk at a woman driver if she was driving a car adorned with "Flower Power" (Unger, Raymond, &

Levine, 1974). An apparently irrelevant aggressive cue (a "Drop Dead" T-shirt) can also increase actual aggressive responses when the confederate cuts in line in front of the subject (Harris, 1976). Cues connoting dependency, such as a crutch, inhibit aggression.

Situations in which women are not helped more than men may involve the women's violation of social expectations about their dependency. One can point to the widespread humor involving the woman driver, which is completely unsupported by traffic statistics. It is noteworthy that when typewriters were first invented and considered to be complex mechanical devices only males were considered fit to be typists. Now, of course, typing is "women's work" and carries with it little prestige or status. Humor may be one way of dealing with the violation of social expectancies—male "clerks" (e.g., Dagwood) are now regarded as a little bit funny.

Women who aspire to power may be particularly likely to be regarded as unfeminine or unattractive. In an interesting study of this possibility college students were presented with thirty photographs of randomly selected college-age women (Goldberg, Gottesdiener, & Abramson, 1975). They were informed that half the women belonged to women's-liberation groups while the other half did not. (See Figure 3.1.) Both men and women selected less attractive women as members of those groups, although in fact there was no difference in attractiveness, on the average, between those who belonged and those who did not, as judged by people who had no information about the possible politics of the women in the stimulus photographs. The attractiveness of the women in the stimulus photographs was also unrelated to their actual degree of belief in women's liberation.

THE SEX TYPING OF POWER

Power is sex typed to the extent that desire for power in women is regarded as somewhat of a deviant characteristic. Women politicians are freaks to some people. They are often subject to devaluation of their femininity. It still comes as a big surprise to everyone that Bella Abzug has a happy marriage and likes to dance.

Laboratory studies indicate that it is somewhat simplistic to assume that power and influence are perceived as global characteristics whose possession is limited to only one sex. Different forms of power may be separated out and judgments about the appropriateness of their use by males and females examined (Johnson, 1974). In a sense what are being investigated here are stereotypes about power roles rather than sex roles. These studies use a typology of the social bases of power developed by French and Raven (1959).

Figure 3.1. Which of these women is a feminist? These are some of the photos used in a study showing that less attractive women are perceived as more likely to be feminists. (Reprinted with the permission of P. A. Goldberg.)

The model states that the major bases of power in our society are legitimacy, information or expertise, belonging to one or another reference group to which others also belong, and helplessness. *Expert power* is based on possession of some needed skill or competence that is not possessed by another person, for example, medical knowledge. *Informational power* is based on possession of information that is needed by another person, for example, the knowledge possessed by teachers. Gossips have this kind of power until they give their information away. The reason so many individuals find it difficult to keep a secret if it is of any interest to others is that they have a degree of power while the information is being conveyed. *Legitimate power* is based on position, for example, the position of boss. *Referent power* is based on the need to belong to a group and to further its goals, and may be seen in the husband–wife relationship or the relationships among members of a fraternal organization.

Recently Raven (1974) has suggested that society has legitimated another form of power—helplessness. He argues that dependency represents a legitimate channel through which help can be requested. The helpless person acquires this power because of the existence of strong social norms. Infants, schizophrenics, and blind people are members of groups that possess this kind of power. They are to be helped because they cannot help themselves. To a limited extent women possess this kind of helpless power too. For example, the female motorist wrestling with a flat tire is seen as needing assistance more than a comparable male. It is also seen as more appropriate that females should require assistance in understanding mathematics, world affairs, or national politics.

Other social bases of power are also influenced by gender. Paula Johnson gave subjects of both sexes an opportunity to select one of six power messages in an experimental situation in which they were the leaders in a task requiring group cooperation. (See Table 3.3.) In an independent study she also requested subjects to indicate which messages they thought had been sent by males and which by females. Subjects tended to perceive that messages communicating referent, helpless, and indirect power had been sent by a female and that messages communicating expert, legitimate, and informational power had been sent by a male. Perhaps more interestingly, individuals tended to choose which messages to send to others on the basis of their own gender. The largest effects were a strong rejection of expert power by females (although males frequently chose such a message) and a strong rejection of helpless power by males (although females frequently chose this message). The use of any form of power except helplessness raised the self-esteem of the user. Those who used helpless power showed a reduc-

Table 3.3 POWER BASE MESSAGES

MESSAGE	POWER TYPE
Please sort faster. I think our group can be one of the best. Let's all try to sort very fast.	Referent
Please sort faster. I know it's possible to go faster because I've worked on this sort of thing before and you can really go fast.	Expert
Help. Please sort faster. I'm really depending on you.	Helpless
As your supervisor, I'd like to ask you to please sort faster.	Legitimate
I overheard someone say we can make the most points and get done sooner by sorting very fast.	Indirect
Please sort faster. We can make the most points and get done sooner if we sort very fast.	Informational

SOURCE: From P. Johnson, "Social Power and Sex Role Stereotypes," paper presented at the meeting of the Western Psychological Association, San Francisco, 1974. Reprinted by permission.

tion in self-esteem. Although this effect has not yet been reproduced, it has many implications for the psychology of women. What must be evaluated is not just whether someone has an effect on surrounding individuals but the personal cost of having that effect. The relationship between helplessness, the perception of powerlessness, and depression in women will be discussed in a later chapter.

Using a more subjective self-report technique, "How I Get My Way," Falbo (1976) reports data on power typing and gender similar to Johnson's. She finds that twice as many males as females report using assertiveness to get their way, while many more females than males report the use of tears and ingratiation. Many more females than males also report the use of reasoning. However, it is difficult to determine how this relates to other types of social power without further investigation.

POWER AND PERCEPTIONS OF LEADERSHIP

In another part of her study Johnson (1974) investigated people's perceptions about the users of various forms of power. She found that users of male power were seen as becoming more powerful, aggressive, cold, and competent than users of female power. If the sex of the user was inconsistent with the stereotypic gender of the message, women were penalized even more. Female users of male power, especially expert and legitimate power, were seen as colder and more aggressive as well as more powerful than comparable males. However, they were not seen as becoming more competent.

In sum, data on power typing seem to indicate another "double bind" for women. If they operate according to "appropriate" feminine tactics, they may suffer a loss in self-esteem (in addition to the fact that such indirect tactics may actually be less effective than direct methods). If, however, they use more direct, male-typed forms of power, they are likely to be labeled as less feminine and suffer penalties for their social "deviance."

Legitimate and expert power, which are considered appropriate for males, are also characteristics that are considered appropriate for those we choose to be our leaders. Thus it should be no surprise that males are preferred over females as leaders of groups. What is unclear, however, is whether it is the characteristics of males that are preferred or the status of maleness. Obviously, most of the time male characteristics and male gender are highly related to each other but it may be possible to separate them. The evidence seems to indicate that sex affects perceptions about performance more than the performance itself.

Some people in groups always communicate much more than others. The distribution is usually J-shaped, with the majority of members saying nothing (Argyle, 1969). The more unequal the status or competence of the members of the group, the more unequal the rates of communication. The people who say the most are also addressed the most. It seems likely that people communicate as much as the rest of the group wants or permits them to.

Very few individuals appear to be endowed with a general personal quality of leadership such that they become leaders of different groups having different objectives. Other things being equal, dominance in a group will be asserted by the person whose formal status assigns him or her to leadership. Status characteristics such as sex, age, race, and occupational prestige determine the distribution of participation, influence, and prestige among members of groups. This effect may be independent of any prior cultural belief in the relevance of the status characteristic to the task at hand (Berger, Cohen, & Zelditch, 1972). Status characteristics may be relevant for all situations except when they are explicitly known to be irrelevant.

Status relationships within a group may actually hinder their problem-solving effectiveness. Hoffman (1965), for example, cites a study by Torrance on problem solving in Air Force crews that showed that the lowest-ranking member was least likely to influence the group's decision even when he was correct. When communication patterns in different kinds of restricted networks are explored, it is found that when the status of the occupant of a central position in the network was discrepant with peripheral members' expectations, the efficiency of communication within the group was decreased (Moore, Johnson, & Arnold, 1972). These peripheral members were also more dissatisfied with the group process than peripheral members of status-congruent groups. Information appears to flow upward in a status hierarchy. More information is sent by other members of a group to high-status individuals than to those with lower status (Alkire, Collum, Kaswan, & Love, 1968). It is unclear, however, whether high-status people make demands for information or in any way use their power to affect the flow of information.

Perceived competence is not independent of the status of the participants. The contributions of high-status members of groups tends to be overrated compared to that of low-status members (Hurwitz, Zander, & Hymovitch, 1968). High-status members of a group are also liked more than those with low status. High-status individuals like low-status individuals less than other high-status individuals and much less than low-status members like each other. Those with high status also tend to overestimate their performance and those with low status to underestimate it (Harvey, 1953). Even estimates of a male group member's height varies with his status within the group (Koslin, Haarlow, Karlins, & Pargament, 1968). These investigators found a correlation of .51 between the observed status of a man in a group and overestimation of his height, and a correlation of .66 between sociometric rating by the individual of his status within the group and estimation of height. The greatest effects were found for individuals at the top and bottom of the status hierarchy.

ACHIEVED VS. ASCRIBED STATUS IN SMALL GROUPS

It has been suggested that with continued association with a group the relative competence of the individuals in skills that are important to the objectives of the group should weigh more heavily so that status variables should become less important with time. Thus if a woman group member possesses skills that are important for the group, her degree of dominance within it should increase. Even ignoring the evidence (discussed in Chapter 13) that there are different standards of evaluation depending on sex, the assumption that groups reevaluate dominance hierarchies on the basis of individual performance may not always be true.

One study of the effects of individual expertise on how people gain social power within a group examined the effect on the group's decision-making process of different degrees of expertise shown by various subjects within the group (Richardson, Dugan, Gray, & Mayhew, 1973). Since either all-male or all-female groups were used, there is no direct information on the effect of sex on influence. However, it was found that very little variation (about 20 percent) in the group's compliance with a particular member's solution to a problem was related to that person's degree of success in previous solutions as measured objectively. The number of solutions suggested by an individual were a much stronger predictor of the extent of his or her influence on the group. Judgments by group members of the demonstrated expertise of each participant were based on differential contributions rather than on demonstrable expertise.

The position of women in mixed-sex groups is strikingly similar to the position of low-status males in all-male groups. They consistently devaluate their potential performance in comparison to that of reference males (Piliavin, 1976). When they speak as frequently as males, their performance is less likely to be recognized. Even in groups interacting on "feminine" topics, in which females are significantly more active and instrumental during brainstorming than males, they are ranked as equal contributors (Jens, 1976). In female-led groups in which there were no sex differences in activity, instrumentality, or influence on decision making, males were ranked as more influential than females by participants of both sexes.

Perceived differences in performance are more important than actual sex differences in performance within a group. One serendipitous finding illustrates the way power is sex typed. Leadership behavior of males was less effectively manipulated by an experimenter labeled as "female" than by the same experimenter with a "male" label, although all manipulations were actually performed mechanically and out of sight of the subjects (Piliavin, 1976). The manipulations of the "female" experimenter were not taken seriously by some of the all-male groups.

A woman who shows a high degree of competence or leadership within a group is operating against prescribed sex role norms. Not only is her activity unlikely to be noticed, but she may fear penalties if it is indeed noted. In one study (Fallon & Hollander, 1976) in which subjects were given feedback about their performance on a leadership task, female leaders actually decreased in influence following feedback while male leaders maintained their influence. In this study sex stereotypic assumptions about how females should behave may actually have impaired the performance of women in out-of-role positions.

The high premium on being liked that may reduce women's participation in groups probably has some basis in objective reality. Studies of small groups suggest that active participants who are typically rated as highest for "good ideas" are not always liked as much as people who are rated less high in frequency of participation (Bales, 1965). The most active talkers tended to be disliked more frequently. Specific sanctions against women who are active in heavily male groups will be discussed in Chapter 15. Women with a high internal locus of control—who perceive themselves to be in control of the consequences of their behaviors—prefer low-power positions within a group, in contrast to men with a high locus of control, who prefer high-power positions (Hrycenko & Minton, 1974). These women prefer a dependent position consistent with the culturally defined stereotypic female role.

Good performance within a group may be less salient to the self-image of some women. In one study female subjects were informed that the social-judgment task in which they were performing badly was or was not related to their level of mental health and intelligence (Tessler & Schwartz, 1972). They were also informed that guidelines were available to help them. Task difficulty was varied by telling some that 60 percent of the subjects needed to consult the guidelines, and telling others that 10 percent needed to do so. The subjects sought help more frequently when it was reasonable to assume that the responsibility for their failure was external to themselves (the task was too difficult for most subjects). Those with high self-esteem were willing to seek help only when the social-judgment task was not portrayed as central to their self-concept, whereas those with low self-esteem sought help even when it reflected on their intelligence and mental health. Subjects with low achievement motivation were also more likely to seek help than those with high achievement motivation. Thus it appears that help seeking by women is associated with such "feminine" characteristics as low self-esteem and low achievement motivation.

Perceptions about their own low status and a reluctance to display the so-called masculine qualities of competence and drive could lead women to behave in ways that are incompatible with the ability to influence a group. Women may put out nonverbal signals that they are not interested in leadership. For example, a male confederate who chooses the head seat at a table is more able to influence a group, even from a very deviant position, than either a confederate who chooses a side seat or one who is placed at the head seat (Nemeth & Wachtler, 1974). Although the confederate was not liked, he was considered by others in the group to have stability and strength. These, of course, are also characteristics that are not considered stereotypically appropriate to the female role. Informal surveys also indicate that women are less apt to interrupt others, maintain more eye contact with a speaker (which makes it likely that she or he will continue speaking), and dominate less space within the group situation. These nonverbal gestures of subordination may condition perceptions about their performance even when it is objectively equivalent to that of males.

What we are reviewing here is a complex interactive process. Beginning in early childhood, females are socialized to engage in low-status behaviors and males in high-status behaviors. Nonverbal gestures as well as more overt behaviors involving conformity and aggression stress the power differences between the sexes. Perceptions about differential behavior are fueled by these different social signals even when there is objective evidence that task performance by the sexes is identical. High-status behaviors, socialized as male, lead to self-attributions about power and competence. They are more likely to lead to successful outcomes, which makes further striving and aggression more likely. Females are less likely to be rewarded for assertive behavior and therefore may realistically assume that such behaviors are less meaningful to them. Institutionalized cross-sex transactions, such as who helps and who is helped, reinforce assumptions about relative power. These effects are more insidious because we are largely unaware of them.

POWER RELATIONSHIPS IN THE LABORATORY AND IN THE FIELD

It is clear that power relations between the sexes may operate even under conditions in which it is not clearly apparent that any power is being exerted at all. Since power relationships operate largely without the awareness of the participants, it should not be surprising that a large variety of effects having to do with the politics of gender are based on nonverbal measures. Just because we are unaware of these processes does not mean that they do not exist. It just means that they will be more difficult to study and to change.

Many more sex-specific effects seem to appear in the "real world" than under the controlled conditions of the laboratory experiment. One question that can be raised, therefore, is that of whether these effects are any "more" or "less" real because they are not easily examined in the laboratory. The fact that the extent of effects related to sex differs depending on where such effects are examined may illustrate some of the special properties of sex as a variable. For example, it is not regarded as socially acceptable to admit to prejudice on the basis of sex. Moreover, we are sometimes quite unaware of how our behavior reflects our sexual prejudgments. Unobtrusive measures may tell us more about how people act than questions about their attitudes. A good example of how difficult it is to obtain information about critical subjects by means of attitude measures was the pollsters' inability to predict the results of the vote on the Equal Rights Amendment in New Jersey in 1975. Although a poll conducted by an extremely reputable group of political scientists, the Eagleton Institute of Rutgers University, only a few days before the ballot indicated that ERA would win handily, it lost by a considerable margin. People were more willing to admit to potential sexism in the privacy of the polling booth than in public. It has been estimated that nonverbal cues convey three times as much information as verbal cues (Argyle, 1969). In sensitive areas such as sexism or racism it is probably well to "listen to what people do rather than what they say."

Since power relations seem to be based on relative ascribed status more than on relative performance, it is difficult to regulate the social assumptions that people bring with them to situations. Even elaborate attempts to eliminate the high status of maleness from experiments do not always succeed. In a classic study by Bandura, Ross, and Ross (1963b), the effect of the sex of the reward giver on children's imitation was investigated. Male and female adults either dispensed rewards, stood by while they were dispensed, or, like the children, consumed them. Despite these manipulations designed to establish differential power and status among the various adults involved, a number of children actually attributed rewarding power to the ignored or reward-consuming adult male bystander. They were firmly convinced that only a male could possess resources and that a female can only be an intermediate for the male: "He's the daddy so it's his, but he shares nice with the mommy . . ."; "He's the man and it's all his because he's a daddy"; "Mommy never really has things belong to her . . ."; "He's the man and the man always really has the money and he lets ladies play too . . ."

Sex effects also demonstrate how strongly situational variables control behavior. When we control our subjects in the laboratory, we may lead them to try to disregard social rules that operate in everyday life. Effects may be more dramatically illustrated by the interpersonal transactions involving the task to be performed rather than in the performance of the task itself. In some ways the laboratory method is a strength because it tells us that many behaviors are organized around roles rather than around sex. When roles are controlled or at least ignored, sex differences tend to be minimal too. Status and gender or sex role are highly correlated, however, and changes in sex roles will not necessarily eliminate sexism. Institutional processes that control sexist effects will be discussed further in Chapter 15. Who has power in society as well as in person is obviously relevant to issues in the politics of gender.

Chapter 4
Sex Differences:
Subjectivity and Objectivity
in Many Dimensions

The question of what sex differences exist is central to the psychology of women. Obviously, the number of similarities and differences that can be found defines the domain of the field. Historically the study of sex differences greatly predates the focus on the female sex. Nevertheless the psychology of women does not directly derive from the study of sex differences and is not conceptually equivalent to half of it. Sex difference research tends to carry with it an implied standard—male. Deviations from this standard are assumed to warrant differential educational and social policies with respect to each sex. In this view differences between the behavior of men and women are assumed to reflect actual differences in their characteristics. In studies of ethnic and racial prejudice this is known as the "grain of truth" hypothesis. It is analogous to the proverb "Where there's smoke, there's fire."

In this chapter we will examine some of the areas in which sex difference research is carried out. Since the study of sex differences evolved from the study of individual differences in general, it is not surprising that much of the work in the area has concentrated on differences in the performance of tasks involving academic or intellectual skills. It is usually assumed that such skills can be measured objectively. As we will see, however, subjective decisions about what will be examined as well as how it will be studied exist throughout the field. Interpretations of data are also subject to personal bias.

PROBLEMS WITH THE STUDY OF SEX DIFFERENCES

There are probably a number of reasons why the study of sex differences seems to be more susceptible to methodological and conceptual biases than many other areas of psychology. First, while it is obviously important to reach conclusions about the areas in which females and males differ and those in which they are essentially similar, no theoretical framework that explains either sex differences or sex similarities exists. Since most researchers have not been interested in using sex as either the only or the primary variable, results tend to be scattered and disorganized. "Sex" effects may be related tangentially to every conceivable psychological phenomenon, but they are to be found tacked onto investigations of other, more "major" variables. It also is not clear, moreover, whether the sex effects that appear in the psychological literature are the only ones that exist. Covert biases about what work gets reported as well as what work is done also exist. Professional journals are often unwilling to accept "negative" results. Hence, reports about sex differences are more likely to be published than reports about sex similarities. Indeed, we do not always have the information to decide whether a sex similarity or difference does or does not exist, since a small but significant minority of psychological studies do not even publish the sex of their subjects.

Second, an unconscious theoretical framework seems to pervade the sex difference literature. Aside from the assumption that the standard sex is male, there exists the assumption that male behaviors are characteristically more objective than female behaviors, which are correspondingly more subjective that the behaviors of males. This objective–subjective dichotomy is similar to the one found in the masculine–feminine stereotype and is probably related to it. An example of this kind of thinking is the apparent presumption that language skills are less complex cognitively than mathematical ones. Thus when researchers talk about the relative deficits of females in the restructuring of stimulus materials they are able to ignore the fact that no sex difference in the ability to do anagrams has been found (Mendelsohn, Griswald, & Anderson, 1966).

Third, sex differences are rarely viewed as just differences. Distinctions are used to make or explain social and educational policies that facilitate male control of social systems outside the home. In other words, traditional sex difference research tends to support the traditional status quo in sex roles. The assumption that underlies this support of societal structures is that many sex differences are biological in origin. Social explanations of sex differences have been virtually ignored. Yet as we will see in this chapter, sex role differences may predict effects more consistently than biological sex does.

Although conclusions are important in this area, few conclusions can yet be agreed upon. It is even possible to argue that one should not study sex differences at all. Many reasons can be cited for this position:

1. There is such an infinite number of behaviors that if one wants to find a sex difference one can probably do so.
2. Sex differences are often investigated as a result of someone else's questions. Finding out that a given difference is or is not present does not elucidate the mechanisms that create the differences.
3. Many psychologists have spent a great deal of time trying to prove the null hypothesis, which is impossible and, moreover, just shifts the argument to another ground.
4. Sex differences are used to justify the asymmetries in attitudes toward and treatment of males and females, and those who are concerned with sex and gender should spend their time dealing with this kind of issue rather than with the degree to which such treatment is justified. In fact differential treatment based on sex is never justified, since individual potential is still a far better predictor of behavior than membership in any particular racial, ethnic, or sexual group.
5. Examination of sex differences obscures the examination of sex similarities. In fact the sexes are similar in far more ways than they are different, but this is not considered startling psychological news.
6. Even on a given trait males and females form two overlapping distributions, with a minority of people of either sex at the extremes. It might be more valuable for the understanding of psychological processes to examine the individuals who are high and low on a particular trait within a sex rather than looking at trait differences between groups.
7. Analyses based on sex differences tend to imply a "trait" view of psychology, which obscures the situational deter-

minants of behavior. This is particularly important, since many social psychologists believe that the constraints of the situation play a larger role in determining the individual's behavior in that context than the psychological characteristics he or she brings to that situation.

8. Particular variables, although they are measured the same way, may not have the same implications for males and females. For example, Frodi and her associates (1977) found that face-to-face insults cause more anxiety in females than in males. There is also, of course, the classic situation of high need-for-achievement measures that predicted competitive behavior in males but were not able to predict female behavior consistently (Horner, 1972). For a long time, therefore, females were simply not used in such studies, since they only created confusion for the theorist. We were faced with the strange situation of a psychological variable that correctly predicted the behavior of Indian and Japanese males (McClelland, 1961) but not American women.

9. Studies of sex differences do not examine behaviors in which the rate is virtually zero for one sex. Thus we do not find studies on sex differences in rape, and until recently there has been no comparison of male and female periodic cycles. In a sense, therefore, studies of sex differences concentrate on the areas in which men and women are least different.

Nevertheless it is probably not a good idea to throw the baby out with the bathwater. Science builds on past research. How, however, do we discriminate between studies that are questionable and those whose data seem reasonable? A one-word answer is "Cautiously." We cannot base our acceptance or rejection of a particular result on our politics. Recently, concerned researchers have begun to reanalyze the vast body of sex difference literature. It would be foolish to ignore it, and it would be equally foolish not to make use of the labors of those who are engaged in the reanalysis of these data. Some sex differences undoubtedly exist. What we do not know is why they exist. Conclusions in this area (probably as in most other areas in which biases cannot be so clearly illustrated) should be interpreted as interim ones—dependent on the contextual framework in which questions are asked.

WHAT SEX DIFFERENCES EXIST?

Most reviews of sex differences involve studying the results of all available research in a given area or areas. The latest and most noteworthy attempt to do so appears in a book entitled *The Psychology of Sex Differences* by Eleanor Maccoby and Carol Jacklin (1974). Depending on how one orders their categories, Maccoby and Jacklin have reviewed the psychological literature in over fifty areas in which it has been suggested that sex differences exist. They conclude that an essentially "null hypothesis" position about sex differences may be accepted. That is, except in a relatively few areas, which we will discuss shortly, researchers have demonstrated few consistent differences between the behaviors of females and males.

While a feminist position would urge one to seize upon the evidence that differences between the sexes are largely illusory, the conclusions of Maccoby and Jacklin's prestigious book have not gone unchallenged. First, we must look at the way sex difference research is surveyed. Maccoby and Jacklin's large-scale search of the professional literature involved a "box score" approach. In this approach an area is surveyed and the number of studies showing that "females score higher than males," "males score higher than females," or "no sex differences are reported" are counted. If studies in the area show an effect "in favor of" one sex and an equal number show an effect "in favor of" the other, it is concluded that no sex differences have been found. Inconsistency in the direction of sex differences is *not* logically the same thing as no sex differences. Such inconsistencies should not make us discard the question but should lead us to look for underlying mechanisms that explain the inconsistencies.

Recently Jeanne Block, a noted developmental psychologist, has criticized Maccoby and Jacklin's conclusions and has pointed out some of the mechanisms by which inconsistent findings about a given sex-related effect could be produced (Block, 1976). She notes that many studies in which no sex differences are found consist of samples of forty subjects or less. When such "small" studies are excluded from the sample, she counts many more sex differences in Maccoby and Jacklin's survey than they themselves note. Aside from demonstrating that conclusions depend on what information one takes into account, her procedure may also demonstrate that many sex differences are small in degree and can be shown only with a large number of subjects. Of course one may question whether effects that are this small are of any great conceptual importance.

Block also notes that sex differences emerge with greater consistency as the age of the subjects increases. Many studies of sex differences are done on preschool children—the group that shows the fewest such differences. When Block sorted studies according to the ages of the participants, she found that significant sex differences were found in 37 percent of the studies of young children, in 47 percent of the studies of older children, and in more than half (55%) of the studies of teenagers and adults. Again, whether or not one concludes that one has a sex difference depends on how one counts. It is probably no accident that the sex differences that are most frequently discussed—that is, differences in personality and achievement—are those that must be demonstrated in older children and adults.

"Box score" approaches imply acceptance of the data base. This puts psychologists who wish to "reconstruct" some aspect of the field in something of a dilemma. In order to criticize something adequately, one must know as much about it as possible. Whether or not a given sex difference "exists," however, depends on how one evaluates the available data. There are also serious difficulties as to whether the available data are all that might be available. Sins of omission and commission seem to be particularly common in the study of sex differences. They limit the extent to which one can use any sort of box score approach.

SOME CONCLUSIONS ABOUT SEX DIFFERENCES

It is both illuminating and disheartening to see the number of psychological dimensions that have been examined for sex differences. In *The Psychology of Sex Differences* over 1600 studies published mostly between 1966 and 1973 have been surveyed. Table 4.1 summarizes some of the topics included. The content areas have been simplified, and the only attempt to indicate the relative importance of each area for psychologists is a simple count of the number of studies in each as cited in Maccoby and Jacklin's various tables. The interested reader should consult this important reference work for more specific information.

Maccoby and Jacklin conclude that sex differences can clearly be demonstrated to exist in only four areas: (1) Girls have greater verbal ability than boys; (2) boys excel in visual–spatial ability; (3) boys excel in mathematical ability; (4) males are more aggressive. Other areas in which they find suggestive, but ambiguous evidence of sex differences are the following: (1) Girls have greater tactile sensitivity; (2) males are more active, especially in the company of others; (3) girls are more likely or willing to report fear, timidity, or anxious behavior; (4) males are more competitive; (5) males are more dominant; (6) girls tend to be more compliant. While the bases on which these researchers decide whether a sex difference exists have been challenged (Block, 1976), their conclusions provide a good stepping-off point from which to view particular sex differences. In this chapter we will discuss the differences that appear to be most closely related to stereotypic conceptions of male objectivity and female subjectivity. They seem for the most part to involve relative performance on different kinds of tasks. These differences are also the ones that have most often been used to justify differential treatment of males and females.

Developmental trends in the data, critical analyses of the factors that affect these behaviors, and interpretations of findings will also be taken into account. It should be reemphasized that data are subject to a number of different interpretations and that scientific truths are a form of consensual agreement about interpretation. Part of the purpose of studying sex differences, therefore, is to raise the question of alternate interpretations. This is not to say that new "truths" are necessarily better than old ones—just that they are different.

SEX DIFFERENCES AND THE SOCIAL WORLD

One of the classic stereotypes of the behavior of males and females is that males are objective and females are subjective (Broverman et al., 1972). This hypothesis can take many forms. For example, it has been suggested that female infants are more responsive to social stimuli (e.g., faces and voices) than male infants are. The measures used may be either those that estimate preference for a particular kind of stimulation or those that estimate the amount of emotional arousal produced by it. In older children and adults one can study memory for social stimuli versus memory for stimuli featuring characteristics of the objective world—these may be nonpatterned versus patterned stimuli or just people versus objects. Significant differences are sometimes found for one sex, sometimes for the other, and sometimes not at all. Although interest in complex stimuli, including faces, increases with an infants' age, this increase does not appear to be sex specific.

Some sex differences in infant sensitivity have been found, but it is difficult to figure out what implications they have for later development. A rather amusing example of this kind of study is one that used the size of the aperture in the nipple and the amount of sugar in the formula to estimate the amount of effort that newborns are willing to exert for a more or less pleasurable stimulus (Nisbett & Gurwitz, 1970). The experimenters found that newborn girls are more responsive to sweet tastes than males, but less willing to exert effort to obtain them. However, there are no sex differences in the percentages of infants who are overweight.

Maccoby and Jacklin cite some evidence that illustrates the

Table 4.1 SOME OF THE TOPICS SURVEYED BY MACCOBY AND JACKLIN WHICH ARE RELEVANT TO AN OBJECTIVITY-SUBJECTIVITY DICHOTOMY

TABLE NUMBER IN MACCOBY & JACKLIN	MAJOR CONTENT AREA	SPECIFIC CHARACTERISTIC	HYPOTHESIS	NUMBER OF STUDIES CITED
2.1	sensation	tactile sensitivity	girls > boys[a]	9 (4+)
2.2	sensation	tactile perception	girls > boys	11 (2+)
2.3	sensation	auditory sensitivity or attentiveness	females > males	19 (6+, 2−)
2.4	sensation	habituation to visual stimuli	boys > girls	12 (5+, 2−)
2.6	sensation	vision in first year of life	girls > boys	33 (9+, 9−)
2.7	sensation	vision, second year to adulthood	females > males	28 (2+, 3−)
2.9	responsiveness	social vs. nonsocial responsiveness (first year)	girls > boys	10 (7+, 6−)[b]
2.20	memory	verbal memory	females > males[a]	19 (10+)[c]
2.21	memory	memory for objects and digits	males > females	23 (2+, 1−)
2.23	memory	social memory	females > males	5 (0)
3.1	intelligence	general intellectual ability	males > females	46 (3+, 15−)

88

TABLE NUMBER IN MACCOBY & JACKLIN	MAJOR CONTENT AREA	SPECIFIC CHARACTERISTIC	HYPOTHESIS	NUMBER OF STUDIES CITED
3.2	verbal ability	spontaneous vocal and verbal ability	females > males	25 (8+, 2−)
3.3	verbal ability	tested verbal ability	females > males[a]	98 (37+, 14−)
3.5	quantitative ability	tested quantitative ability	males > females[a]	27 (16+, 4−)[c]
3.7	spatial ability	visual–spatial ability	males > females[a]	30 (9+, 2−)[c]
3.8	spatial ability	disembedding	males > females[a]	47 (26+, 3−)[c]
3.10	cognitive ability	anagrams	males > females	8 (0+, 4−)
3.11	cognitive ability	Piagetian level	males > females	45 (5+, 4−)
3.12	cognitive ability	reasoning	males > females	29 (7+, 5−)
3.13	creativity	verbal creativity	females > males[a]	21 (11+, 5−)[c]
3.14	creativity	nonverbal creativity	males > females	9 (8+, 8−)[b]
3.15	social judgment	moral judgment	females > males	27 (10+, 5−)
4.6	social judgment	sensitivity to social reinforcement	females > males	23 (1+, 2−)

NOTE: The figures in parentheses following the number of studies cited refer to the number of times the hypothesis was supported or not supported (any additional studies found no significant sex difference).

[a] Hypotheses in which Maccoby and Jacklin believe a sex difference is likely.

[b] Some studies found more than one effect.

[c] In these areas sex differences appear consistently near or after adolescence.

difficulty of trying to generalize across studies in the "same" area. Newborn females are assumed to have a greater amount of tactile sensitivity than newborn males. They show more movement after a covering blanket is removed and have higher skin conductance. However, these effects are not always found. Moreover, there appears to be no relationship between tactile sensitivity and the soothability of an infant. One researcher waited for newborn infants to cry and then wrapped them in either a synthetic fur or a soft, smooth cotton blanket. The fur quieted infants of both sexes more effectively. It is also reported that a similar procedure produces no sex differences in children aged 3½ months. Thus the evidence on which we base assertions that females are more responsive than males is not clear. As can be seen from the preceding discussion, even tactile responsiveness is much too global a concept.

Sex differences in social responsiveness also appear to be minimal. The sexes are equally interested in social as compared with nonsocial stimuli; in childhood girls are no more dependent on their caretakers than are boys; and both sexes appear to be equally responsive to social reinforcement. Boys, in fact, appear to spend more time with their playmates, at least at certain ages, than girls do. There is no consistent evidence that infants of either sex vocalize or smile more, although there may be sex differences if the kind of stimulus is taken into account. Similarities appear to be far more salient than differences, although the sexes are subject to rather large and consistent differences in the amount of social stimuli they receive. It may be concluded that young children are manifesting very subtle differences in their behavior that have been missed in most empirical studies. Or, differential parent and, later, teacher behavior is a reflection of perceived rather than real behavioral differences between the sexes, at least for variables that involve interaction with a subjective world.

You may note that the argument appears to have shifted from subjectivity versus objectivity to the question of whether males and females are differentially sensitive to social stimuli. Studies in sex differences have a way of doing this, since they tend to imply masculine and feminine poles of behavior that are somehow opposite to each other. Surprisingly enough, however, no one ever considers alternate tendencies in the same study or with the same subjects. We do not know whether a given child, of either sex, who is particularly responsive to social stimuli will be particularly irresponsive to things as opposed to people. The only children for whom such opposing tendencies have been found are autistic ones. In fact it would appear that interest in both the objective environment and the subjective environment is highly adaptive, since both boys and girls with cross-sex preferences and interests tend to have higher IQs than those who are more sex typed (Kagan & Moss, 1962). Studies of toy preferences tend to show sex differences on a subjective–objective dimension; however, these studies are so confounded with differential opportunities to play with various kinds of toys, the social prestige of various kinds of toys, pressures to behave according to appropriate sex role, and social-desirability effects (performing the way one thinks the observer expects one to) that it is impossible to evaluate them. The most conservative assumption seems to be that no important or consistent sex differences in objectivity–subjectivity exist.

SEX DIFFERENCES AND INTELLECTUAL ACHIEVEMENT

Language: Quantitative and Qualitative Aspects

It is possible that assertions about sex differences in social awareness are based on sex differences in the development and use of language. Maccoby and Jacklin suggest that it is probably true that girls' verbal ability matures somewhat faster in early life, although there are a number of studies of this subject in which sex differences have not been found. From the preschool years through early adolescence males and females have very similar verbal ability. At about age 11 the sexes start to diverge, with females showing increasing superiority in tasks involving receptive and productive language, verbal comprehension, and ability to understand verbal analogies, as well as tasks involving verbal fluency and the creative use of language.

Girls also show somewhat better memory of verbal materials. More than half of the studies Maccoby and Jacklin cite have found no sex differences. However, whenever such differences are found girls have higher scores. The superiority of girls in verbal memory is especially clear after the age of 7. In contrast, no consistent sex differences have been found in memory for objects or digits. In one study contrasting memory of both verbal and nonverbal materials, boys remembered material performed by a model better than verbalized material while girls did equally well in both tasks (Grusec, 1972). Adult females appear to do better at recalling pictures when verbal labels are allowed, while males do better when no labels are present (Koen, 1966). Each sex may be more ready to respond to certain kinds of inputs from the environment, or the sexes may be different in what each finds easier to learn, but there is no evidence that the content of the materials presented has any effect.

We might argue that females are more socially responsive only in the sense that they appear to make more effective use of language than males. There is a large amount of cross-cultural data indicating that female superiority in the use of language is not limited to the United States (Trudgill, 1972; Haugen, 1974; cited in Thorne & Henley, 1975). In general, females tend to use more standard, high-prestige forms of language than males do. This fact would seem to contradict notions about the relative subordination of females in most societies. However, there is evidence that greater care about one's behavior accompanies subordination. Goffman (1956), for example, reports that doctors at staff meetings are more apt to engage in swearing and undignified expressions than attendants are. Although the use of slang by young children does not appear to have been systematically investigated, I can provide some anecdotal evidence in this regard. My daughters' 7- and 5-year-old male classmates were far more likely to use such words as *tit* and *shit* even in a classroom situation. The sex difference appears to be in productive speech rather than in comprehension. Giggles from the girls lead me to believe that they were quite clear about the meanings of the words. Nonstandard speech may be taken as a sign of masculinity and used to signal group solidarity (Trudgill, 1972). Interestingly, deviants from all-male peer groups are also more likely to use standard forms of speech (Labov, 1973).

In other words, although female superiority in the use of language may be a result of biological factors, it can equally well be argued that it is a result of differential socialization. Given equal access to language in the early years, children may select and develop components of behavior in order to signal their appropriate sex role. Since the male and female sex roles are inherently asymmetric, language too can be made to serve and promote asymmetries between the sexes. Robin Lakoff (1975), in an intriguingly argued little book, *Language and Woman's Place,* notes that little girls, even in the United States, are trained to speak a kind of "woman's language." Elements of female language include the following.

1. Lexical disparities—only women and other deviants use and understand such words as *mauve*.
2. Differential use of expletives—"oh dear" or "oh fudge" versus "oh shit."
3. Differential use of adjectives denoting approbation or admiration rather than being merely descriptive—*adorable, charming, sweet, lovely,* and the like.
4. Syntactic disparities—differential use of tag questions such as "Looks like rain, doesn't it?" or "Sure is hot in here, isn't

it?" Questions like these do not really require an answer, but they do suggest lack of confidence on the part of the speaker.

5. Sex differences in intonational patterns—for example, in response to the question "When will dinner be ready?," the reply "Oh . . . around six o'clock . . . ?" Such a response would seem to demand confirmation from the questioner.

Lakoff suggests that while at first both sexes learn to talk "properly," girls are more likely to be scolded, ostracized, or made fun of for "talking roughly" in the school-age years. "So a girl is damned if she does, damned if she doesn't. If she refuses to talk like a lady, she is ridiculed and subjected to criticism as unfeminine; if she does learn, she is ridiculed as unable to think clearly, unable to take part in a serious discussion: in some sense as less than fully human" (1975, p. 6).

Sex differences in the use of language may be a manifestation of power differences between the sexes. Linguistic competence as a function of low status may be the implicit basis for little boys' conviction that English and reading are girls' subjects (Levy, 1974). In this area, as in many others, we have not yet separated the effects of asymmetric sex roles from the biological foundations of behavior. It is noteworthy that sex differences in verbal ability are most manifest during the period of greatest societal differentiation of the sexes—the adolescent years. A major area yet to be researched is how and why this sex differentiation develops. It might be interesting to focus on the exceptions for a change—what are the origins and characteristics of nonverbal girls and verbal boys?

Cognitive Processes: Mathematical or Spatial Ability

Another basis for the assumption that males are objective and females subjective may be sex differences in mathematical ability. Even more than linguistic skills, such sex differences are difficult to document until the school-age years. It is noteworthy, therefore, that sex differences in conservation, object constancy, numerical correspondence, and other Piagetian tasks that have been considered to relate to the ability to form concepts have not been found (Maccoby & Jacklin, 1974). Like the female linguistic advantage, the male advantage in mathematics does not appear consistently until adolescence.

One of the most consistent findings of those who are interested in cognitive differences between males and females may not be a cognitive difference at all but a perceptual one. A large number of

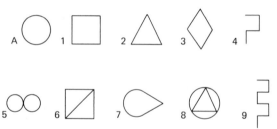

Figure 4.1. An example of the spatial patterns that boys and girls walk through in a qualitatively different manner. (From B. K. Keogh, "Pattern Copying Under Three Conditions of an Expanded Spatial Field," *Developmental Psychology*, 4 (1971): 25–31. Copyright 1971 by the American Psychological Association. Reprinted by permission.)

studies show that males may have an advantage in the ability to visualize space. This characteristic is difficult to define except in terms of the tasks used to measure it. For example, children have been asked to copy geometric configurations by either drawing them or walking them on sand (Keogh, 1971). Nine-year-old boys showed a significant qualitative and quantitative advantage in ability to walk simple patterns. (See Figure 4.1.) Boys made more precise angles and corners, were more accurate in their starting and stopping points, and indicated clearly when a pattern was incomplete. However, such sex differences have been found only in pattern walking, not in pattern drawing, so it is difficult to interpret these findings completely.

Females are thought generally to have more difficulty than males in abstracting stimuli from the context in which they appear. The tasks that are most commonly used to demonstrate these sorts of sex differences are those that involve embedded figures and the rod-and-frame test (Witkin, Dyk, Faterson, Goodenough, & Karp, 1962). The latter test involves being able to detect the deviation of a rod from a vertical orientation when it is framed by a rectangle that varies itself. (See Figure 4.2.) Sometimes the subject sits on a chair that is also more or less tilted.

From information on these tests Witkin and his associates have devised the terms *field dependent* and *field independent* to describe individuals. Field-dependent individuals are most affected by the context of the situation, while field-independent individuals have little difficulty ignoring irrelevant cues in their surroundings. Of course females are much more likely to be field dependent than males.

Feminist researchers have attacked the description of females as field dependent on many grounds. First, the term is much too

Figure 4.2. The rod-and-frame task. Subjects are required to report how much the rod deviates from the vertical. The frame may also deviate; subjects may be seated in a tilted chair; and other perceptual cues are minimized by having the task performed in a darkened room. (Reprinted by permission of H. A. Witkin.)

global a description. No difference between the ability of males and females to "disembed" nonvisual stimuli has been found (Sherman, 1967). Females are just as capable as males of removing stimuli in an auditory context (Maccoby, 1969) and may even have an advantage when the situation involves manipulation of verbal materials, for example, anagrams. Witkin and his colleagues (1968) themselves report no sex differences when the embedded-figure task is translated by means of matchsticks into a tactile framework. Thus field independence–dependence may simply reflect sex differences in ability to visualize.

A second criticism of the use of field independent–dependence to characterize the cognitive abilities of subjects is the irreversibility that appears to be built into the definition. Even Witkin (1949) himself found that largely didactic training significantly decreased the visual dependence of a group of women on a spatial-orientation task. He never followed up this preliminary study because the subjects reported that the correct response still seemed "wrong" and, thus, did not presumably reflect a change in their cognitive style. Many researchers, however, would prefer to believe what subjects do rather than what they say about what they do.

The practice effect in tasks involving stimulus embedding seems to have been largely ignored. Performance on the embedded-figures task improves with practice, and although significant sex differences were found on the first block of ten trials, they had disappeared by the last ten trials (Goldstein & Chance, 1965). It is interesting to note how great a theoretical framework has been built around a phenomenon in which sex differences may disappear in as few as 68 experiences.

Field dependence–independence has been lifted out of its original perceptual framework and used as a manifestation of a more general dimension of psychological functioning. Witkin (1967) uses performance on embedded-figures tasks and the rod-and-frame test as an indicator of an individual's cognitive functioning. McClelland (1964) even uses sex differences in field dependence to explain why women go into nursing and social work while men enter occupations that "express their assertive interests, like selling, soldiering, engineering . . . and law." (p. 175). Mary Parlee (unpublished), in her careful review of this area, notes that "descriptions of field dependency—whether in perception or cognition or personality— sound remarkably like stereotypic conceptions of femininity and those of field independence like masculinity . . ." (p. 16).

The term *field dependent* can also be objected to because of its value-laden nature. A term like *field sensitivity* would have very different connotations. Field sensitivity would imply a positive value for the ability to attend to one's surroundings as opposed to a negative disregard of one's environment. Attentiveness to a central cue versus its surround or to different aspects of the environment may have adaptive value, depending on the circumstances. Sometimes rigid attention to one cue and the ability to screen out irrelevant ones may be valuable. Sometimes the ability to modify responses on the basis of varying features of the environment may be valuable. It seems unwise to characterize perceptual phenomena in terms of personality styles. Conclusions are overgeneralized and easily misapplied.

It is interesting that a recent study demonstrates one situation in which females are less "field dependent" than males. The study involves a so-called Ames room in which subjects view an apparently normal room (Figure 4.3) within which two people appear to vary widely in size. In reality the rear of the room is not parallel to the front, so that the stimulus persons are actually at very different

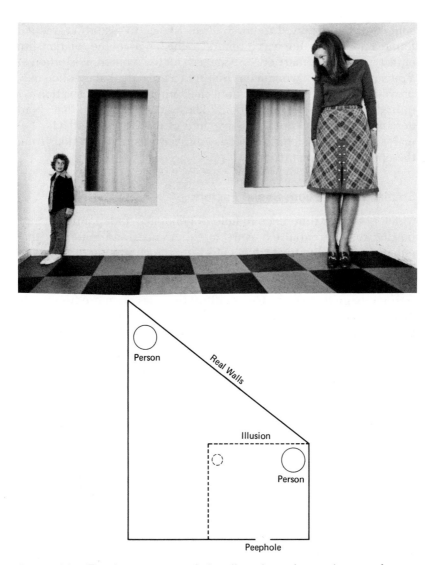

Figure 4.3.   The Ames room and size distortions. As can be seen from the diagram in the lower left, size and distance cues are confused. One of the stimulus persons is actually standing much farther from the subject than the other. (Photograph from Wolman Woodfin Camp.)

distances from the viewer. The researchers found that only women with a high positive cathexis to their male partner (they loved, like, and trusted him) resisted the distorting effects of the room on that partner (Dion & Dion, 1976). They perceived a stranger as significantly more distorted than their partner when they viewed him in the context of the distorted room. Such resistance to distortion was not found among men, nor was it related to the length of the relationship or its type (dating, married, or engaged) for the women. Distortion of a person in whom a woman has invested a great deal of emotion may provoke a high degree of anxiety that provides the motivation required to resist the distortion. These data suggest that field dependence–independence is not free of motivational effects. Females may usually feel less need to separate their perceptions from the environmental surround.

Spatial Visualization: Social Factors

Much of the sex difference in field dependence–independence may be due to differential exposure to experiences and materials that enhance the ability to abstract cues from the environment. Boys are given toys such as vehicles, which may cause them to make more use of movement and space as compared to dolls, which are more frequently given to girls. Cross-culturally, boys are more frequently given tasks that enable them to leave their home environment (Whiting & Edwards, 1973). "Very few girls are found in the high school classes of mechanical drawing, analytical geometry, and shop. Spare-time activities of tinkering with the car, sports, model building, driving a car, direction findings, and map-reading are sex-typed and might also be sources of differential practice" (Sherman, 1967).

Unfortunately there have to date been no studies on the direct relationship between differential experience and the various tasks relating to field dependence–independence. There is some suggestive evidence, however, about the effect of social variables upon such tasks. One intriguing and yet unexplained finding showed that while 12- and 13-year-old girls from normal family situations were significantly more cue dependent than comparable boys, opposite effects were found with orphaned girls and boys (Sherman and Smith, 1967). Orphaned girls were less cue dependent than girls from intact families, while orphaned boys were more cue dependent than boys from intact families. In fact orphaned boys were more cue dependent than orphaned girls.

These data indicate the extent to which parental models influence the development of cue dependence. A recent study (Nash, 1975) illustrates the relationship between social role and sex differences in spatial visualization. Nash finds that male gender preference is positively related to spatial performance in both sexes in both sixth and ninth grades. Sixth-grade boys who prefer to be boys score higher on the Differential Aptitude Test (a space relations test) than boys who prefer to be girls (there were no ninth-grade boys who preferred to be girls). Boys who prefer to be boys score higher than girls who prefer to be girls, while girls who prefer to be boys score significantly higher than girls who prefer to be girls. There were no sex differences in scores among children of either sex who preferred to be boys. There was also no difference in overall intelligence between girls who preferred to be boys and those who preferred to be girls. Table 4.2 shows the relationship between preference for male gender and spatial relations scores for boys and girls in the sixth and ninth grades. It also shows the relative difference in cross-sex preference between boys and girls.

There were more girls of both ages who preferred to be boys than there were boys who preferred to be girls. More younger girls than older girls preferred to be boys. Children who preferred to be male explained their choices in terms of society's preference for the male role ("I like to get paid for working"), the desirability of male activities (especially sports), and the high value afforded "machismo" characteristics such as strength, roughness, the protector–provider role, and so forth. One older girl who preferred to be a boy pointed out that "males can do a lot of things females cannot do. If a wife wants to help her husband's business, most people think she's bossy and interfering. But if a husband helps his wife do housework, we think he's a very kind man" (Nash, 1975, p. 27). Girls who preferred to be girls valued "positive" feminine attributes such as attractiveness, liked being dependent, or shunned male obligations. Girls with cross-sex preferences did not perceive themselves as more masculine than others; they just thought it would be better to be a male.

This study establishes a relationship between gender preference and intellectual functioning, just as the study by Spence, Helmreich, and Stapp (1975) discussed in Chapter 2 establishes a relationship between gender role and self-esteem. In both studies masculine attributes in either sex appear to predict performance in "male appropriate" arenas more than sex itself does. Perhaps we should relabel these behaviors as sex role or gender differences rather than sex differences.

Mathematical Ability: Nature vs. Nurture—Again!

Sex differences in mathematical ability appear to be fairly well established, especially by the adolescent years. Mathematical superiority in males has been linked to their greater ability to visualize spatial relationships. This particular aspect of sex differences is more closely associated with biological explanations than any

Table 4.2 MEAN SPATIAL REASONING PERFORMANCE (±SD) ON THE DIFFERENTIAL APTITUDES SPACE RELATIONS TEST AS A FUNCTION OF GENDER PREFERENCE (OPEN FORMAT)

6th-grade boys who prefer to be boys (N = 32)	9th-grade boys who prefer to be boys (N = 25)	6th-grade boys who prefer to be girls (N = 4)	9th-grade boys who prefer to be girls (N = 0)	6th-grade girls who prefer to be girls (N = 32)	9th-grade girls who prefer to be girls (N = 41)	6th-grade girls who prefer to be boys (N = 23)	9th-grade girls who prefer to be boys (N = 7)
22.96 (15.21)	42.26 (19.87)	6.75 (12.20)	None	12.91 (13.07)	29.04 (18.59)	21.75 (10.59)	44.19 (17.36)

SOURCE: From S. Nash, "The Relationship Among Sex-Role Stereotyping, Sex-Role Preference, and the Sex Difference in Spatial Visualization," *Sex Roles*, 1975, *1*, 15–32. Copyright 1975 by Plenum Press. Reprinted by permission.

other intellectual or social difference between the sexes. Most of the biological theorizing concerns the existence of a recessive gene conferring visualization ability that is carried on the X chromosome.

Data in support of such a hypothesis are offered in terms of findings that girls' scores in spatial visualization tasks appear to be more closely correlated to that of their fathers (a father gives his only X to his daughters) while boys' scores are correlated with their mothers' scores but not with their fathers' (boys receive an X chromosome only from their mothers) (Stafford, 1961). If an important recessive gene for spatial visualization is carried on the X chromosome, all males who receive the gene will express it phenotypically. Females, on the other hand, will show the effects of the gene only if they receive it from both parents. It has been calculated that the ratio of males to females showing a high degree of ability to visualize is 2 : 1 (Bock & Kolakowski, 1973).

More recent large-scale, cross-cultural studies on so-called X-linkage for spatial abilities have failed to reproduce the predicted pattern of within-family correlations (Vandenberg & Kuse, 1978). An additional difficulty with this kind of genetic explanation is that it assumes no interaction with the environment in the expression of the trait. Given the gene or genes, the behavior must inevitably occur. Even in more clearly understood genetic traits such as diabetes, however, we know that the environment can make it more or less likely that the trait will appear in a person who has the genetic predisposition for it (e.g., notably effects of high carbohydrate intake, weight gain, and other physiological stressors). Environmental interaction that affects the relative probability of phenotypic expression seems even more likely in psychological characteristics.

Social Factors in the Development of Mathematical Abilities

Evidence exists for the presence of sex role stereotypes involving mathematical and scientific achievement. This evidence must be examined before any hypothesis about biological sex differences can be seriously evaluated. For example, children of all ages tend to stereotype math and science as masculine (Dwyer, 1973). Presumably they are responding to the relative absence of girls and of problems relating to female interests in most grade school math and science textbooks. Even when problems mention children of both sexes, they often include such comments as "Susan could not figure out how to . . ." or "Jim showed her how . . ." (Federbush, 1974). There are occasional explanations that put the stereotype into words: " 'I guess girls are just no good in math,' said Joe" (Federbush, 1974, p. 180). These sins of omission and commission appear in textbooks for every level right up through the college years. A recent report indicates that college-level statistics textbooks have more examples concerning males and continue to refer to males and females as engaging in sex-stereotyped activities (Alpert & Gibbons, 1976).

In addition, children are more likely to be exposed to live male role models when learning about math and science than they are when learning about history and literature. A majority of math and science teachers are male, especially at the junior high and high school levels, where consistently lower scores in mathematical skills begin to appear in females. Surprisingly, there have been relatively few studies examining the effect of the sex of the teacher on children's performance in these areas. In fourth-graders the quantitative performance of males improved under male teachers (Shinedling and Pedersen, 1970). However, female performance did not improve under the tutelage of female mathematics teachers. That these effects may have been mediated by sex role stereotypes is suggested by findings (in the same study) that boys performed significantly more poorly in verbal skills with female teachers.

The same researchers (Pedersen, Shinedling, & Johnson, 1968) have found sex-of-examiner effects on children's performance on quantitative tasks. In a rather complicated design children were tested on various arithmetic subtests of the WISC by each of three male and three female examiners. They found that third-graders of either sex performed best for examiners of their own sex. Despite the fact that the components of this widely used IQ scale for children are supposed to be relatively insensitive to extraneous variables, rather impressive experimenter bias effects related to sex were found. Some of the differences in mathematical and verbal abilities between males and females in our society might be accounted for by the greater percentages of male mathematics teachers and female English teachers.

There is evidence that differential practice with mathematics can also account for some of the sex differences in this area. By high school girls choose fewer advanced math and science courses than boys, since they have been socialized to believe that such careers are not appropriate to females. Engineering students—mostly male—gained almost one standard deviation in scores on space relations tests following a year of engineering study (Blade & Watson, 1955). When one controls for equivalency of education of adult males and females, most sex differences on the Wechsler IQ tests disappear (Levinson, 1963). Even relative short-term learning experiences may have an effect. Hoffman and Maier (1966) attempted to reduce the female disadvantage in problem solving by manipulating a number of variables such as the sex of the examiner, motivation, and the masculine or feminine content of the problem. Although not all of their procedures worked, females' performance improved on some problems when they were examined by another female. Interestingly, when the problems were given a female orientation both sexes found them more difficult. In fact male performance on the feminine problems was reduced to the level of female performance on the masculine problems. The authors suggest that since attitudes that inhibit competent female performance in problem solving are a result of eighteen or more years of socialization, perhaps we should feel encouraged that sex differences could be reduced even to this minor extent by such simple manipulations.

THE MEANING OF SEX DIFFERENCES: SOCIETAL BIAS IN PSYCHOLOGY

When one examines sex differences it is difficult to avoid the "nature–nurture" controversy. Although there is much evidence that various fields of endeavor have different implications for males and females, that there is differential access to information and training for males and females, and that gender role appears to be a better predictor in this area than physiological sex, arguments that females are genetically less well suited to intellectual achievement still appear in respectable learned journals. In one case (Lehrke, 1972) the pretext was the argument about greater male variability discussed in Chapter 1. Rather than repeating the arguments and evidence against this hypothesis here, it might be more valuable to discuss the relationship between science and value systems. Lehrke's arguments bear a striking relationship to those of Jensen (1969) on the heritability of IQ and its implications for racial differences. The major counterargument in regard to sex is that we can show that the performance of males and females varies tremendously as a result of different situational and motivational determinants. "Only when we are willing to allow boys and girls equal opportunity to express their individual genetic predispositions, independently of the child's sex, will we begin to have a clearer idea of how much of a difference genes really do make in determining psychological sex differences in intellectual functioning" (Wittig, 1976, p. 73). Wittig also points out that what is dangerous about such biological hypotheses about group differences is not just that they may be factually untrue but that they can be used to derogate members of groups and to justify unequal treatment of them. Parlee (1975) makes a similar point about the uses and abuses of scientific information when she characterizes aspects of psychology as being "for" or "against" women.

For example, even assuming that spatial visualization is genetically determined, the sex difference is one of degree rather than kind. A conservative estimate suggests that 25 percent of all women possess the trait in question. There appear to be rather few modern occupations that are largely dependent on the ability to visualize in three dimensions. If, however, we assume that architecture, engineering, and orthodontics are among those that involve this ability, the percentage of women in these occupations is still far lower than the percentage of women who presumably possess the required ability.

Sex differences seem to lead to different social and educational recommendations depending on what sex the difference appears to "favor." Thus instead of female superiority in verbal skills being considered an asset for them, it is used to argue for the continued large percentage of males (and concomitant invisibility of females) in elementary school textbooks. After all, it is the boys who have trouble learning to read! Similar arguments do not appear to have been advanced for increasing the number of females or female-oriented content in science or math textbooks. Reading also has been classified as a simple rather than a complex cognitive skill on no other apparent basis than that girls find it easier to do than boys (Broverman et al., 1968). Of course the ability to do math is accorded higher prestige in our society than the ability to read well.

Sex difference issues are particularly difficult to deal with, since they depend on interpretation of the evidence more than on the evidence itself. The practice of drawing implications and making policy decisions on the basis of these data introduce further dangers of subjective bias. Exploring the mechanisms of sex differences rather than enumerating them may provide more conclusive findings.

Chapter 5
Biological Bases of Sex and Gender

In earlier chapters we have considered some of the perceived and actual differences between the sexes. In this chapter we will consider some of the biological mechanisms by which such differences may develop. Biological factors will be defined broadly and will include genetic, hormonal, and structural factors. "Anomalous" development will be examined in terms of what it can tell us about so-called normal sexual differentiation.

Two issues will be raised in this chapter. First, are there any other biologically based variables that are relatively unexplored but may be used to predict behavior at least as nonrandomly as sex differences? Second, what is the evidence to support the contention that distributing sex dichotomously—male and female—is too simplistic even on a biological level? It is the second point that will be considered first.

WHAT ARE THE SEXUAL UNIVERSALS?

Despite the fact that everyone talks about sex, very few investigators attempt to define it. Examination of a number of articles and books on the subject leads me to conclude that the authors feel that sex is either too self-evident to require an explanation or so complicated that they feel justified in devoting an entire book to the subject. The most simple satisfactory definition seems to be one by Bermant and Davidson (1974):

> Sex is separateness: a division of reproductive labor into specialized cells, organs, and organisms. The sexes of a species are the classes of reproductively incomplete individuals. In order for a sex member to contribute to the physical foundations of its species, to reproduce part of itself into the next generation, it must remedy its incompleteness. The remedy is found in the union of incomplete parts from complementary complete organisms: egg and sperm unite. [p. 9]

Most evolutionary biologists feel that the sexes evolved to increase the variability of characteristics within a species. However, they have not explained how species that reproduce asexually have been able to survive, nor why fusion of incomplete individuals is limited to two components. Theoretically, one could hypothesize the existence of several different sexes, each contributing to the next generation.

Because sex is usually considered in terms of mammalian physiology, the characteristics of the egg producer—female—and the sperm producer—male—are often thought of as fixed and universal. Nevertheless many invertebrate organisms (e.g., earthworms and oysters) are hermaphroditic in the sense that individuals of the species have both kinds of gonads, either concurrently or sequentially. Even among vertebrates some fish and birds can be made to change sex and produce viable eggs or sperm after a period of maturity during which they produced the form of germ cells characteristic of their chromosomal sex (Yamamoto, 1969; van Tienhoven, 1961). One Red Sea fish that has been studied recently changes from fertile female to fertile male form spontaneously in the absence of any males of the species (Fishelson, 1970). This differentiation will be inhibited by the sight of a male even if he cannot be reached by any of the females.

Aside from being interesting curiosities, these phenomena demonstrate that sex roles should not be viewed solely as a reflection of evolutionarily fixed functions resulting from inherited structures (Tobach, 1971). The variety of reproductive behavior patterns between and within an animal species suggests that there is no necessary relationship between even the most specifically sex-related behaviors—those involving reproduction—and biological sex. Our understanding of the biological mechanisms that mediate sexual differentiation is also complicated by the question of which biological dimension we are using to define biological sex.

Biological sex is not a unidemensional variable. At least five separate biological categories may be distinguished: chromosomal sex, gonadal sex, hormonal sex, sex of the internal accessory organs, and sex as determined by the appearance and function of the external genitalia (Bermant & Davidson, 1974). In human beings we must also consider sociocultural variables: the sex to which the individual is assigned and the gender role with which the individual identifies. Although under normal circumstances all of these biological and psychological variables are highly correlated with one another, disorders in prenatal and postnatal development suggest that considering sex as a dichotomous variable may be extremely misleading.

NORMAL SEX DIFFERENTIATION

It is a striking fact that all vertebrate embryos, whatever their sex chromosome constitution, originally develop the basis of both male and female sex organs (Mittwoch, 1973). Immediately after being formed, the gonads pass through an apparently undifferentiated state and contain the forerunners of both ovarian and testicular tissue. Each embryo also starts off with a pair of male and female accessory organs—the Wolffian (male) and Mullerian (female) ducts. It has been suggested that the process of sex differentiation may be regarded as originating in the hermaphroditic condition and consisting of the progressive development of the organs of one sex at the expense of the other.

Two principal regions can be distinguished in the embryonic gonad: an outer cortex or skin and an inner medulla. The cortex is potentially capable of developing into an ovary, while the medulla can develop into a testis. The normal development of the gonad depends on the sex chromosomes that are present. In mammals, if two X chromosomes are present, the cortex develops while the medulla regresses; if an X and a Y chromosome are present, the medulla develops at the expense of the cortex. In the human embryo two sets of gonadal ducts also persist side by side until the eighth week of development. Differential development appears first in the male embryo. The Mullerian duct begins to regress and then disappear. (See Figure 5.1). This is followed by the formation of the buds of the future prostate gland. Each Wolffian duct develops into a vas deferens, which at its caudal end forms the seminal vesicles. The urethra terminates in the genital tubercle, which becomes the penis. In female embryos the Wolffian ducts gradually disappear while the Mullerian ducts form the Fallopian tubes and the uterus. In humans the ducts fuse at the base to form a uterus.

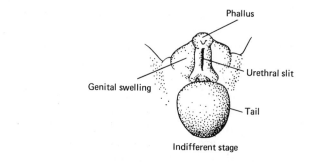

Indifferent stage

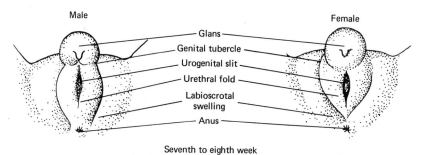

Seventh to eighth week

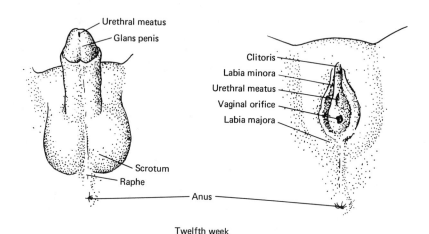

Twelfth week

Figure 5.1. Prenatal differentiation of male and female genitalia. From a relatively undifferentiated state, development proceeds by means of the relative enlargement of structures that have analogs in members of the other sex.

In mammals, differentiation of the male phenotype is dependent on a hormone secreted by the embryonic testis. If the gonads are removed from male rabbits after the testis has differentiated but before the genital tract is distinguishable as male, the embryos develop female characteristics independently of chromosomal sex (Jost, 1970). The Wolffian ducts diappear; the Mullerian ducts develop into Fallopian tubes and uterus; and the external genitalia are indistinguishable from those of females. The embryonic ovary, on the other hand, does not appear to be necessary for the development of the female phenotype, which develops spontaneously in the absence of either fetal gonad.

The embryonic testis secretes a second, unknown substance that inhibits the development of the Mullerian ducts. The Wolffian ducts, however, must remain in the presence of some source of androgen in order to develop completely. In mammals, therefore it is the Y chromosome that is the principal determinant of sexual differentiation. If a Y chromosome is present, the gonad becomes a testis, with subsequent male phenotypic development. In the absence of a Y, an ovary is produced, with subsequent female phenotypic development. The number of X chromosomes present does not appear to be important in this context.

Interestingly, in birds it is the females who are heterogametic (XY) and the males who are homogametic (XX). And in birds it is the ovary that is the dominant embryonic differentiator. If the gonads of male bird embryos are removed, the male phenotype continues to be produced, except for the persistence of the Mullerian ducts (Wolff & Wolff, 1951). It has been suggested that the differences between the mechanisms of gonadal differentiation in birds and mammals are due to their reproductive physiology. A certain amount of female sex hormones can be expected to pass through the mammalian placenta and enter the embryo. It would be maladaptive to have as important chemical triggers for dimorphic development substances that are present in the prenatal environment of both male and female mammals.

Nevertheless it is instructive that the chromosomal and hormonal bases for sexual differentiation are by no means universal—not even among vertebrates. Since sex-characteristic behaviors such as nurturance and dominance are often discussed across species and since these behaviors are widely considered to have a genetic basis, it is noteworthy that even the somatic substrata of sexual dimorphism do *not* have the same biological base across rather closely related species. Perhaps we are unfortunate in that the genetically popular superstar, the fruit fly (Drosophila), has some aspects of chromosomal sex determination that are similar to those of mammals (e.g., male fruit flies are XY and females are XX). Nevertheless they are different from mammals in that the number of X's and Y's present and the ratio of sex chromosomes to autosomes present play a role in sexual differentiation. To paraphrase an old song in terms of the normal biological bases for becoming a male or a female, "Birds do it, bees do it," but not the same way humans "do it."

It is still not clear what causes the apparently bipotential mammalian gonad to develop into a testis when a Y chromosome is present. Testicular differentiation does not appear to be influenced by either androgens or antiandrogens (Mittwoch, 1973). Mittwoch suggests that the presence of a Y increases the number of mitotic divisions of cells in the embryonic gonad. Incipient testes grow faster than incipient ovaries. The larger size of the future testis is evident before any cellular differences between it and an embryonic ovary are discernible. She hypothesizes that the sex chromosomes function by regulating the growth of the gonadal rudiment. In birds, whose heterogametic sex is female, it is ovarian differentiation that is accompanied by a faster growth rate. Differential growth as a basis of sexual dimorphism will be discussed again later in this chapter.

SEX CHROMOSOMES AND SEX

There are two major ways of understanding the relationship between biological factors, such as chromosomes and hormones, and sex differentiation. One way, which we have already discussed, is to do comparative-development studies between species, particularly species that differ in cause–effect relationships. These studies lead us to conclude that although sexual dimorphism appears to be universal among higher organisms, determinants of such dimorphism appear to vary widely across species. It may be premature to base our thinking about behavioral "universals" on the biological determinants noted in the study of a select sample of animals. Accordingly, many students of sex differentiation in humans have concentrated on clinical abnormalities involving the chromosomal determinants of sex. These abnormalities usually involve deletions of or excessive numbers of sex chromosomes.

Under normal circumstances humans possess 46 chromosomes. These chromosomes are found in matched pairs in the female but not in the male. While both males and females have 22 pairs of chromosomes that appear to have little to do with sex differentiation (the autosomes), one pair—the sex chromosomes—differs greatly between males and females. In females the sex chromosomes are a matched set (XX) similar to the autosomes. Males have one X chromosome and a much smaller matching one (Y). Even in females, however, the two X chromosomes are not similar to a matched set of autosomes. For many years geneticists have divided chromosomal material into two parts, euchromatin and heterocromatin (on the basis of their staining properties during certain stages of division) and have suggested that active functioning genes are found in the euchromatic portions of the chromosomes. Although probably all chromosomes have heterochromatic regions, the sex chromosomes appear to be out of phase with the rest of the chromosomes during cell division. The darkly staining body found in the cell nuclei of normal females (the Barr body) but not in normal males appears to originate from one of the two X chromosomes (McKusick, 1964). At least two X chromosomes must be present for one Barr body to be formed, and if more than two X chromosomes are present more than one Barr body may be formed. Along with several other cytological differences, the presence or absence of Barr bodies and their number form the bases of the chromosomal determination of sex in individuals when other information is ambiguous or contradictory.

Turner's Syndrome

One of the most intensively studied chromosomal abnormalities in humans is Turner's syndrome. Individuals with this disorder usually have only one unmatched X chromosome, although sometimes a fragmented or structurally abnormal second X chromosome is found. It has been found to occur in fewer than one in 1000 live births, although many more individuals with this chromosomal abnormality are found in examinations of aborted and stillborn fetuses. Although there is considerable variability in phenotypic expression, individuals with Turner's syndrome are of unusually short stature (rarely reaching more than 4½ feet as adults) and have a short and/or webbed neck and a broad chest with widely spaced nipples (McKusick, 1964). Although the missing chromosome could have been either an X or a Y (individuals with Turner's syndrome are usually classified as XO), these individuals are always classified as "female" on the basis of their external genitalia, which are completely female. Their internal reproductive structures, however, are rudimentary, with ovaries represented only by fibrous streaks of tissue. Breast development does not occur at puberty unless hormonal treatment is instituted. These individuals do not menstruate and of course are completely sterile.

Individuals with Turner's syndrome are particularly interesting because they represent a form of development occurring in the absence of any endogenous gonadal hormones. They offer evidence that supports the results of animal experimentation: In the absence of any gonadal influences differentiation will take a female direction. A number of studies have been done comparing their psychological and behavioral responses to those of normal females (Money & Ehrhardt, 1972). Individuals with Turner's syndrome have often been described as being slightly retarded. However, Money (1969) found that in an unbiased sample of 38 individuals the Wechsler verbal intelligence quotient approximated a normal curve. Individual IQs ranged from below 70 to above 130. Nonverbal IQs in the same individuals, in contrast, were significantly below normal. Only one had a nonverbal IQ above 110. The discrepancy seems to derive from the relative inability of individuals with Turner's syndrome to make conceptualizations involving space–form relationships. Money has termed this disability *space–form blindness.* To a lesser extent, XO individuals have difficulty orienting themselves in terms of direction and performing numerical calculations.

Some researchers have compared the difficulties of individuals with Turner's syndrome to "similar" difficulties found in normal females. We have already discussed field dependency and related perceptual phenomena. What must be emphasized here is that individuals with Turner's syndrome are *not* aberrant females. (See Figure 5.2.) They are essentially neuter individuals whose external genitalia are similar to those of females. They are defined as female simply because of the inadequacy of our dichotomous classification system for sex.

Presumably on the basis of their external genitalia (in the absence of any evidence that their central nervous systems are subject to any gonadal hormone effects other than those to which all mammals are subject during gestation), individuals with Turner's syndrome tend to identify themselves as female (Money & Ehrhardt, 1972). As a group they are similar to normal females. As children they appear even more feminine than female controls. They manifest less interest and skill in athletics, fight less, and have a greater interest in personal adornment.

> Despite the handicap of their stature and infertility which all the older Turner girls knew about, all but one explicitly hoped to get married one day. They all reported daydreams and fantasies of being pregnant and wanting to have a baby to care for one day. All but one had played with dolls exclusively, and the one preferred dolls even though she played with boys' toys occasionally. [p. 107]

These data suggest that a feminine gender identity can differentiate very effectively without any help from prenatal gonadal hormones that might influence the brain.

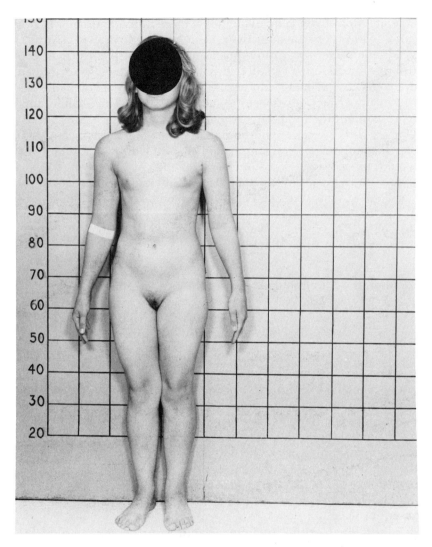

Figure 5.2.   Individual (age 21) with Turner's syndrome (XO). Note the short height and lack of secondary sexual characteristics. (From J. Money and A. Ehrhardt, *Man and Woman, Boy and Girl* (Baltimore: Johns Hopkins Press, 1972). Copyright 1972 by the Johns Hopkins Press. Reprinted by permission.)

Do we need to bring in gonadal hormones to explain these results? The only obvious physical difference, and sometimes the only external sign, of XO individuals is their small size. Other aspects of their physical immaturity do not become obvious until adolescence. It is clear that they will not be reinforced for their skill at athletics or fighting. Later, when we discuss size as a status variable, it will be even more evident that these individuals are likely to possess low status among their peers. Individuals with Turner's syndrome score lower in enthusiasm and impulsiveness than control ninth-grade girls (Shaffer, 1963). They also score lower in generalized activity, energy, and masculinity on temperment scales and higher in personal relationships and cooperativeness. Shaffer found more uniformity in these estimates of "feminine" traits among women with Turner's syndrome than among normative women. In fact the degree of overcompliance that XO individuals manifest would be considered a clinical problem among chromosomally normal individuals. What remains to be elucidated is whether the personality, and even the cognitive functions, of individuals with Turner's syndrome is a result of their unique chromosomal constitution or a response to their body image and the social pressures brought to bear upon them because of it.

Klinefelter's Syndrome

More common chromosomal abnormalities involve people with more than two sex chromosomes. The most common of these is Klinefelter's syndrome (XXY). It is found in about one in 500 "male" births (Hsia, 1968). Individuals with this chromosome constitution actually have both the normal male and the normal female chromosomal determinants present simultaneously. Consistent with the experiments on animals by Jost, XXY individuals appear to be phenotypically male. (See Figure 5.3.) Their external genitalia are male, but the penis and testes are smaller than normal and body hair is sparse (McKusick, 1964). Although their height is equal to that of normal males, there is often some breast development (gynecomastia), and some widening of the pelvic girdle may be found. They tend to be unusually long legged. Their sex drive is absent or weak.

Individuals with Klinefelter's syndrome are often retarded, but many are reported to be intellectually normal or occasionally gifted (Money, 1969). No disparity between verbal and nonverbal IQ has been reported. Reports tend to concentrate on the greater potentiality for social and sexual maladjustment of these individuals (Money & Ehrhardt, 1972), but do not note any relationship to IQ. Since Klinefelter's syndrome is the most common chromosomal aberration found in humans, the dearth of research on the psychosexual development of XXY individuals with normal or near-normal IQs is surprising. At least one researcher (Forssman, 1970) seems to suggest that the passive–aggressive personality supposedly characteristic of XXY individuals is a result of their "excess" X chromosome.

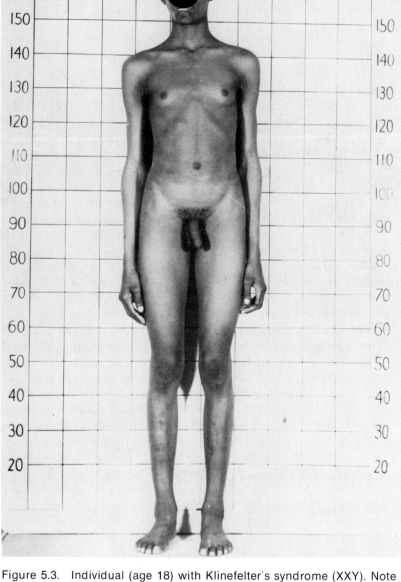

Figure 5.3. Individual (age 18) with Klinefelter's syndrome (XXY). Note feminization of hips, breast development, small penis and testes. (From J. Money and A. Ehrhardt, *Man and Woman, Boy and Girl* (Baltimore: Johns Hopkins Press, 1972). Copyright 1972 by the Johns Hopkins Press. Reprinted by permission.)

The increased risk of psychosexual pathology in Klinefelter "males" may be a result of deviance and ambiguity in their primary and secondary sex characteristics rather than a direct effect of their chromosomes on their brains. The social mediation of biologically based variables must be ruled out before we discuss the biological causality of personality characteristics.

The XYY Male

An interesting example of initial assumptions about biological causality that needed to be reconsidered is the case of the XYY male. These individuals were first reported among the inmates of institutions for violent, dangerous, and aggressive patients (Jacobs, Brenton, Melville, Brittain, & McClemont, 1965). No physical abnormality was reported except for unusual height. Recently, however, the link between aggressive behavior and an extra Y chromosome became less clear-cut when large-scale screening of newborns for chromosomal abnormalities found that the XYY condition may exist in as many as one in 700 newborn males (Ratcliffe, Stewart, Melville, Jacobs, & Keay, 1970). Such males may appear as frequently on basketball teams as they do as inmates in institutions for the criminally insane. So far the fate of the large majority of XYY males is unknown. They appear to reproduce successfully and probably rarely come to the attention of the clinical investigator.

This example illustrates the problem with analyzing abnormalities among humans as a way of explaining normal psychosexual development. The population that is studied may be highly biased. It is self-selected in the sense that only the more severe physical and psychological manifestations of the disorder may come to the attention of the clinician. The rest of the people with the same chromosomal abnormality may blithely glide through life unaware that something is "wrong." We also must not confuse potentiality or predisposition with biological determinism. There is some evidence that individuals with the XYY syndrome have a stormy adolescence with severe acne and unusual timing and length of the adolescent growth spurt. This may cause severe psychological problems for all of these individuals, but only those with other attendant difficulties such as an unstable family life will be permanently affected. Although some violent murderers have been reported to be XYYs, it would be erroneous to label it, as the media did, a "criminality syndrome."

Selection of the most severely affected individuals probably limits the explanatory value of chromosomal aberrations for normal development. For example, XXX individuals appear to occur in one

Table 5.1   HEIGHT AND NUMERICAL ANOMALIES OF SEX
CHROMOSOMES WITHOUT MOSAICISM

TYPE	NUMBER OF INDIVIDUALS	MEAN HEIGHT (cm)	STANDARD ERROR
45,X	128	141.80	0.56
46XX	Normal population of females	162.20	
47XXX	30	163.07	1.49
46XY	Normal population of males	174.70	
47XXY	118	175.69	0.77
48XXYY	22	180.52	2.12
47XYY	19	182.95	1.67

SOURCE: Adapted from P. Polani, "Chromosome Phenotypes—Sex Chromosomes,"
in F. C. Fraser and V. A. McKusick, eds., *Congenital Malformations* (Amsterdam:
Excepta Medica, 1970). Reprinted by permission.

in 1000 female births (Hsia, 1968). Although there is a slight tendency for such individuals to appear in above-chance numbers in
institutions for the retarded, most of these women are phenotypically normal. In fact they have normal or near-normal fertility and
appear to be indistinguishable from normal adult females. Their
relative normality may be explained by inactivation of their excess
X chromosome (Lyon, 1961). Certainly there are no human "super-
females" such as are found among fruit flies.

Sex Chromosomes and Size

One of the most neglected forms of sexual dimorphism in human
beings is the difference in relative size between males and females.
There is considerable evidence that both the X and Y chromosome,
but especially the Y, contribute to height. The most dramatic illustration of the effect of the sex chromosomes upon adult height is a
table (Polani, 1970) showing the relationship between height in
centimeters and numerical anomalies of the sex chromosomes. (See
Table 5.1.) You may notice that once more than one X chromosome
is present, extra X's appear to contribute little to ultimate size.

Even the Y chromosome probably contains a number of genes,
so it may be simplistic to view the contributions of the sex chromosomes to sexual dimorphism in a holistic way. For example, about 10
percent of the individuals who are diagnosed as having Turner's
syndrome have a partially rather than completely absent second X
chromosome. If the deletion involves the short arm of the X, they
tend to show the classical Turner stigmata (Hsia, 1968). If, however,
it is the long arm of the X that is deleted, the patients are found to
have streak gonads but are otherwise phenotypically normal. In par-

ticular, they do not have the short stature characteristic of XO individuals. These data would suggest that information about height is carried on the short arm of the X chromosome and is somewhat independent of whatever genes control the development of the gonads. Thus although chromosomal sex is one component of the "what is the sex" equation, it cannot be said to make a unitary contribution in all situations.

PRENATAL HORMONES AND SEX DIFFERENTIATION

Presumably the sex chromosomes operate by telling the embryonic cells what hormones and other inducer substances to produce, leading first to the production of a particular fetal gonad, which in turn leads to the production of a particular set of accessory organs. Although it is difficult to produce the kind of chromosome changes one wants on demand, even prenatal hormonal manipulation is relatively easy. There is a large body of experimental literature relating to the morphological and psychological effects of prenatal administration of estrogens, androgens, and antiandrogens in various species, including humans. In this section we will concentrate on the effects of prenatal sex hormones on the differentiation of various bodily structures.

A Summary of Animal Studies: Hermaphrodism

The presence of a male gonad usually ensures that the male hormone, testosterone, will also be present. Whether or not a mammalian embryo will develop as a male or a female is not solely dependent on the presence or absence of testosterone. The primary sex difference—the nature of the gonads—is unaffected by testosterone. At least two substances appear to be necessary for the development of the male genital apparatus. Testosterone appears to cause the development of the Wolffian ducts, while another, unknown substance suppresses female development (Jost, Jones, & Scott, 1969). It appears that the female pattern is basic. In the absence of any gonadal influences at all, a uterus and Fallopian tubes will develop.

Gonadal differentiation precedes duct regression and development in human beings, as in other mammals. The external genitalia differentiate at about the same time that duct formation takes place and will differentiate as male if testosterone is present in the bloodstream. As in the case of the gonads, male–female differentiation of the genitalia is a result of differential growth of various parts of an originally undifferentiated structure, and as we will see shortly, various degrees of ambiguity can occur.

Since gonad formation, duct development, and the differentiation of the external genitalia take place at different times and in response to somewhat different cues, the various structures can produce contradictory information in terms of sex. Experimental production of such anomalies in animals and clinical investigations of them in humans are important steps toward the understanding of the relationship between hormones and sex. Organisms who possess contradictory characteristics with respect to sex are sometimes referred to as *hermaphrodites*. This word is derived from the mythical Greek god–goddess who had attributes of both sexes. Technically, a hermaphrodite should have functioning organs of both sexes (either simultaneously or sequentially, as is the case in many invertebrates), but this is a vanishingly small occurrence in more highly organized mammals. Now the term seems to apply to any organism in whom there is a discrepancy between the various components of sexual anatomy and physiology, that is, in whom chromosomal sex, gonadal sex, hormonal sex, and/or external genitalia are not consonant. Money and Ehrhardt (1972) use the term almost interchangeably with the terms *intersexuality* or *improperly differentiated*. Depending on the stage of development at which interference occurs, organisms with varying degrees and kinds of disparities are produced.

Hermaphrodites are of particular interest to psychologists because of the question of whether there is such a thing as "central-nervous-system sex." Do the hormones that produce dimorphic anatomical differentiation also produce differences in the brain? Are we predisposed to particular kinds of behavior because of the influence hormones have had on our developing brains? As with gonadal structures and external genitalia, is there a critical period during which neural sex can be interfered with? And what are the implications of these data for the origin of various psychosexual abnormalities in human beings?

The Testicular Feminizing Syndrome

One of the most interesting forms of discrepancy among the various indicators of sexuality found in humans is the testicular feminizing or androgen insensitivity syndrome. Individuals with this disorder are chromosomally normal genetic males (XY). As a result of a recessive autosomal gene defect, however, it is thought that their tissues are insensitive to the action of testosterone (Stempfel, 1969). Their internal reproductive apparatus is similar to that of a normal male in appearance, although the testis contains unusual cells. Combined with this male internal structure are the external genitalia of a normal female. In fact these individuals are usually unquestioningly classified as female at birth and diagnosed as having the testicular feminizing syndrome only after the discovery of a hernia that turns out to be a testis. These individuals appear to be totally unresponsive to testosterone, while estrogen produces breast development and feminine contours. Since there is a high probability that the testes will become malignant, they are usually removed when they are discovered and the person is unambigously reared as a female. Since a blind vagina is present, little or no plastic surgery is necessary in order to assist the individual to function cosmetically as a female. Of course such individuals, having no uterus, do not menstruate and are sterile.

Since this is a rare disorder, there have been relatively few studies of the behavior of such individuals. Money and Ehrhardt (1972) surveyed the clinical data on ten such subjects who had reached puberty and reported that these individuals show a high preference for the feminine role. Eighty percent preferred the role of homemaker over an outside job; 100 percent reported having dreams and fantasies of raising a family; 80 percent reported playing primarily with dolls and other girls' toys. They rated themselves as high in affectionateness and fully content with the female role. It is the impression of some geneticists who are familiar with the clinical literature on individuals with this syndrome (Krooth, personal communication) that they tend to be found in occupations that put a high premium on an attractive female appearance and feminine behavior (e.g., modeling, acting, and prostitution).

It has been suggested that individuals with this syndrome present an unusually attractive appearance. It should be noted that even externally they are not phenotypically identical to normal females. The Y chromosome carries information that is not completely mediated by testosterone. Thus such individuals tend to have male height and the longer, more symmetrical legs of males. Their breast development is normal and appears to result from the action of estrogens produced by the testes (if they are still present) and the adrenal glands. Pubic and auxillary hair tends to be sparse or absent in these individuals. (See Figure 5.4.) It is disconcerting to find that the most attractive female body may be that of a genetic male. In any case the socially mediated effects of personal attractiveness must be considered before we attribute the feminine identity of these individuals to the lack of testosterone influence on their central nervous system.

It is also unfortunate that no studies of the cognitive functions of individuals with the testicular feminizing syndrome appear to be available. Certainly no retardation has been mentioned in the literature, but it is important to know something about these individuals'

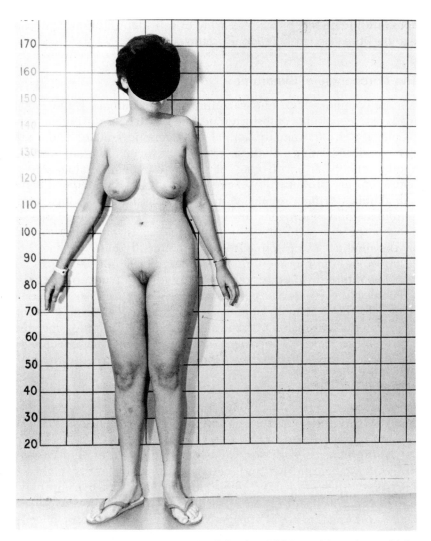

Figure 5.4. Adult with testicular feminization (XY, but with an insensitivity to androgen). These individuals are usually taller than the average female and tend to have a very attractive "female" physique. (From J. Money and A. Ehrhardt, *Man and Woman, Boy and Girl* (Baltimore: Johns Hopkins Press, 1972). Copyright 1972 by the Johns Hopkins Press. Reprinted by permission.)

ability to perceive space–form relationships in order to understand something about the relative contribution of genes and hormones to this supposedly sexually dimorphic mental faculty. A breed of mice with a high propensity for testicular feminization has been reported in the literature and could also provide test subjects without the confounding effects of sex of rearing or self-identification. Unfortunately, little has yet been done in this area.

The Adrenogenital Syndrome

A more common cause of hermaphroditism in humans is the action of excessive amounts of testosterone-like substances during the gestation of a chromosomally normal (XX) genetic female. There are two possible sources of these excess androgens, which produce similar effects at birth. One of these sources is endogenous—androgens are produced by excessive activity of the mother's adrenal glands during pregnancy (the adrenal glands produce both estrogens and androgens in both sexes). The other source is exogenous—masculinization of female fetuses is sometimes caused by the medical use of progesterone (chemically closely related to testosterone) or other steroids to prevent abortion of the fetus.

The internal structures of these individuals do not appear to be affected, but the external genitalia bear varying degrees of resemblance to those of male infants. A completely male configuration never occurs in females with the adrenogenital syndrome, since the ovaries never descend and there are never scrotal gonads (Schlegel & Gardner, 1969). Ordinarily a penis of normal structure and dimensions is not produced. There is usually an enlarged clitoris and a fusion of the labioscrotal folds, producing a picture of ambiguous gender. (See Figure 5.5.) Some individuals, however, have complete closure of the urethral groove and a penis that is capable of becoming erect.

Until rather recently sex was assigned on the basis of inspection of the genitalia, and two individuals with equivalent ambiguities might have been classified differently. Thus sex of rearing might have been consonant or disconsonant with genetic sex. More recently, information about gonadal structure and chromosomal composition has been acquired, and most females with the adrenal genital syndrome are now reared as females. Since their internal structures tend to be normally female and many of them are fertile, a relatively small amount of cosmetic surgery is all that is required to make their external appearance consonant with the other components of their sexual identity. Those for whom excessive androgens are due to overactivity of their own adrenal glands must also be regulated with cortisone to prevent early virilization or masculinization at puberty. (See Figure 5.6.)

Money and Ehrhardt (1972) recently reported on an extensive study of 25 such fetally androgenized girls (10 due to exogenous causes and 15 to endogenous causes) who had been treated since

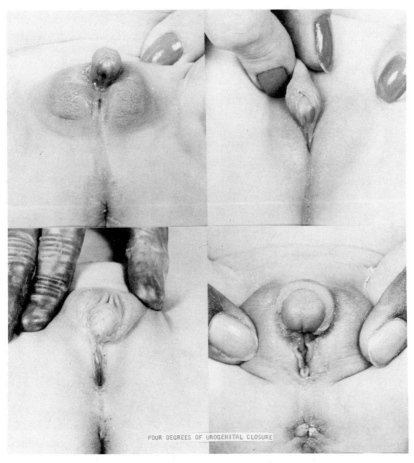

Figure 5.5.   Ambiguous appearance at birth of the genitalia of individuals with the adrenogenital syndrome (XX, but with excessive androgen during prenatal differentiation). (From J. Money and A. Ehrhardt, *Man and Woman, Boy and Girl* (Baltimore: Johns Hopkins Press, 1972). Copyright 1972 by the Johns Hopkins Press. Reprinted by permission.)

infancy and reared as girls. They ranged in age from 4 to 16 and were compared with a sample of normal girls, who were matched with them on the basis of age, IQ, socioeconomic background, and race. Since the two diagnostic groups did not appear to differ from each other, they were compared as a group with the normal population.

Twenty of the 25 girls with the adrenogenital syndrome claimed to be tomboys. Their mothers and playmates agreed with this label. Only a few of the girls in the normative sample claimed to

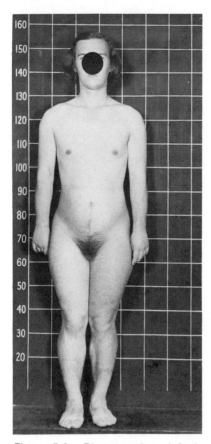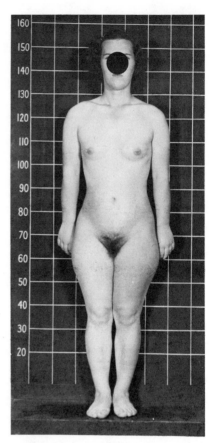

Figure 5.6. Photograph on left shows the masculinized body contours of a female with untreated adrenogenital syndrome. Photograph on the right shows the beginning of feminization induced by treatment. (From J. Money and A. Ehrhardt, *Man and Woman, Boy and Girl* (Baltimore: Johns Hopkins Press, 1972). Copyright 1972 by the Johns Hopkins Press. Reprinted by permission.)

be tomboys, and then only to a limited extent. The patient population was significantly more dissatisfied with being female than the normal sample, although none of the patients stated that she would actually like to change her sex. The patients preferred energetic and athletic play but were not more aggressive than the control population. These girls also preferred functional and utilitarian clothing and chose shorts, slacks, or skirts more often than dresses. They preferred traditionally male toys such as cars and trucks over doll play. They also indicated a preference for a career over marriage, or at least indicated that they saw occupational and marital status as equally important. Marriage was the most important goal of the majority of the control girls.

The IQ distribution curve of these girls tended to be skewed in favor of above-average IQs (Money, 1969). No difference was found between verbal and nonverbal IQ. However, the IQs of the affected group were not shown to be significantly higher than those of their nonaffected siblings, so it is unclear what this enhancement of IQ in adrenogenital girls compared with their controls means. A similar enhancement of IQ has been found in both males and females with idiopathic (due to the physiology of the individual, but of unknown cause) sexual precocity. Their IQ advantage is maintained long after the early period of somatic maturation has been controlled. Money suggests that there is some unspecified relationship between intelligence and the mechanism that initiates early puberty. It would be premature to speculate on any such relationship, but it is noteworthy that, once again, data point to a linkage between a behavior that has been considered to be related to sex and factors that are related to growth and development.

Hormones and Behavior: Data from Animal Experiments

Prenatal masculinization of female mammals is a relatively simple procedure, and numerous experiments have been done on rats, guinea pigs, and monkeys. In rats, the potentiality to manifest both male and female reproductive behaviors seems to coexist in the same animal at the same time (Bermant & Davidson, 1974). The main effects of prenatal androgen seems to be the suppression of the future potential for female sexual behavior and the production of external genitalia like those of males. It has not yet been demonstrated that male behavior patterns that are directly related to reproduction are enhanced by the presence of prenatal androgen, even in lower mammals.

In fact it is possible that the presence of male reproductive behaviors is due to the presence of a functional penis rather than to predetermination within the central nervous system. Studies of the prenatal feminization of genetically male mammals (by means of chemicals that antagonize the action of testosterone) indicate that feminized rats and guinea pigs will show fully male patterns of behavior only if they possess a fully developed phallic structure (Bermant & Davidson, 1974). Mounting and other male reproductive behaviors in these mammals appears to be maintained by the sensory response accompanying these behaviors (Beach, 1968).

Because the scientific study of sexual function and dysfunction in humans has until recently been taboo, we know little about how various chromosomal, genetic, and hormonal abnormalities affect penile sensitivity. We also lack information on how body image in terms of the size and structure of the external genitalia affects sexual behavior in both males and females. What we need are studies of genitally normal males with a history of prenatal androgen deficit. Such individuals are important because they tell us whether the central nervous system mediates sexually dimorphic behaviors independent of other physical differences between males and females.

There is evidence that the prenatal feminization of male rats affects both their behavior and their genital structure (Ward, 1972). The male offspring of rats who were intensely stressed during pregnancy were found to be deficient in mating behavior as adults when tested with receptive females. The vast amounts of adrenal hormones produced by the mothers in response to intense stress could have interfered with the organizing effects of androgens within the fetal brain. The deficiency in male behavior may not have been induced solely by effects within the central nervous system, since these males also showed decreased testicular size and penis length in comparison with the male offspring of unstressed females.

A Critical Reappraisal of the Results of Animal Studies

There exist major unresolved questions about what constitutes a "male" versus a "female" reproductive behavior even in lower mammals. The most commonly used measure of male behavior—the mounting of other animals—is not unusual behavior in females of many species (Bermant & Davidson, 1974). Although lordosis—presentation of the genital area in response to mounting—is not present in normal males and seems to be suppressed by the action of testosterone, recent evidence suggests that male and female behaviors cannot be ordered on a simple continuum. When androstenedione (the second most important androgen produced by the testes) is injected into neonatally castrated male rats, neither is lordosis behavior suppressed nor is the development of male reproductive behaviors prevented (Goldfoot, Feder, & Goy, 1969; Stern, 1969). Males were produced who showed normal male behaviors upon contact with receptive females but typical female mating patterns when paired with vigorous males. In other words, these animals were "normally" bisexual. Although such animals are clearly anomalies produced by careful manipulation of various hormonal organizers during critical periods of development, they illustrate that the potentiality to manifest both male and female reproductive patterns can coexist in the same animal at the same time.

Sexually dimorphic behaviors other than those that are directly related to reproduction may also be affected by prenatal androgens. A number of studies of prenatally androgenized female rhesus monkeys indicate that their levels of rough-and-tumble play, aggression, and grooming appear to be intermediate between the levels found in normal males and normal females (Goy, 1970). However, no one behavior is found exclusively in one sex or the other. It is the quantitative extent of a given behavior that is altered, not its qualitative form. Reports about the behavior of these masculinized female monkeys parallel reports about the behavior of androgenized "tomboy" human females to a surprising degree.

We do not yet know what role the external genitalia play in the maintenance of sexually dimorphic behaviors that are not directly related to reproduction. There is some evidence that they are not related to each other. If testosterone is injected into the female embryo between the critical period for genital differentiation and that for the assumed differentiation of the central nervous system, it is possible to produce female monkeys with somewhat masculinized behavior and little or no masculinization of the external genitalia. No relationship between degree of genital masculinization and extent of behavioral effects has been noted in humans with the adrenogenital syndrome.

The extent to which the central nervous system, and especially the higher parts of that system (the neocortex) is involved with sexual behavior apparently varies from one species to another. It appears to be more important for male sexual behavior than for female sexual behavior and to increase in importance as one ascends the phylogenetic scale (Beach, 1947). At the same time that dependence on hormonal influences decreases, the role of experiential factors increases. However, these generalizations may hold only for the physical and perhaps the sensory aspects of reproductive behavior. Less is known about the central nervous system's involvement in sexually dimorphic nonreproductive behavior patterns or in gender identity.

Nevertheless the data seem to indicate that exposure to various sex hormones during critical periods of development can produce characteristic behavioral predispositions in all mammals. Such behaviors can be regarded as typical of members of the same sex or of those of the opposite sex, but are *not* mutually exclusive. Hormonal influences may not be limited to direct effects on adult reproductive behavior. Studies of higher mammals and humans stress effects on sexually dimorphic characteristics such as grooming and rough-and-tumble play. The presence or absence of testosterone appears to be particularly important in the development of "male" behaviors, just as it is in the development of the male reproductive apparatus. However, I cannot overemphasize the fact that there are more similarities than differences between the behaviors of males and females. Unfortunately the similarities are less interesting to most investigators than the differences.

In the next section we will discuss the possible mechanisms regulating such differences and the effect of social and environmental factors on sexually dimorphic behavior. I will take the position that (for most species) hormonal events during fetal development potentiate the development of homotypical behaviors but are not causal in an absolutely determinist way. It appears that such influences may be mediated by the central nervous system independently of genital differentiation, but that genital structure and function play a major role in sexual behavior even among lower mammals. Lastly, we will consider the way sexually dimorphic behaviors can be molded by experiences during early life.

EARLY POSTNATAL INFLUENCES ON SEXUALLY DIMORPHIC BEHAVIORS

Once we begin to talk about the animal after birth, we are no longer able to limit ourselves to purely biological contributions to behavior. Whether or not an organism brings predispositions toward certain kinds of behavior to his or her social environment, the form of the organism as a whole and of his or her accessory organs can certainly alter the kinds of environmental interactions possible. Nevertheless we will attempt to separate the effects of the biological environment of the organism from the social interaction it induces, bearing in mind that this is, in fact, logically impossible.

There appears to be little difference between the hormonal environments of male and female mammals during the early period of postnatal life. In fact sex hormones appear to be present minimally if at all. Nevertheless differences between the sexes in social-behavior patterns appear during this period of minimal hormonal activity. In rhesus monkeys castration or ovariectomy on the day of birth affects the level at which sexually dimorphic behaviors are emitted by genetically male or female monkeys as compared with intact juvenile controls, but does not prevent their existence (Goy, 1970). In fact according to Goy's figures castrated males are the most likely of all the animals studied to engage in a high degree of threatening and rough-and-tumble behaviors. Thus genetic and prenatal hormonal influences may be more important than the postnatal hormonal environment. Data like these suggest that hormonal influences on the central nervous system are not limited to changing

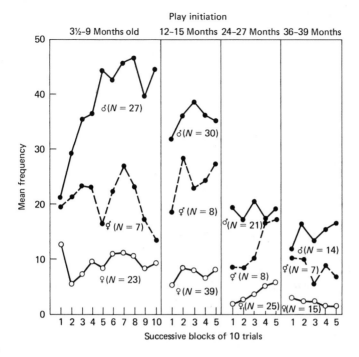

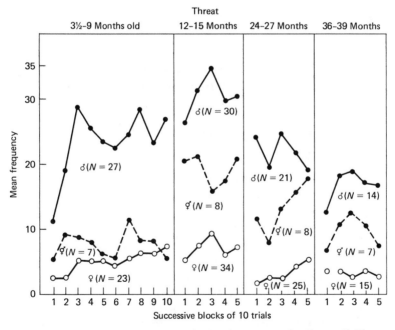

Figure 5.7. The levels of various kinds of nonreproductive activities shown by male (♂), female (♀), and prenatally masculinized (♀) monkeys during the first three and a half years of life. (From R. W. Goy, "Early Hormonal Influences on the Development of Sexual and Sex-Related Behavior" in F. O. Schmitt, (ed.), *The Neurosciences: Second Study Program* (New York: Rockefeller University Press, 1970). Reprinted by permission.)

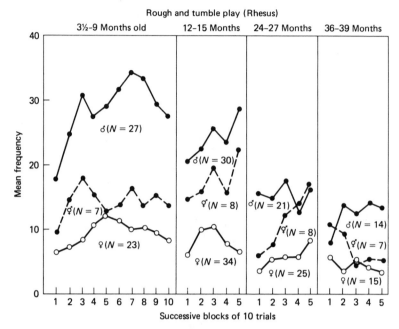

Rough and tumble play (Rhesus)

Figure 5.7 *Continued*

the level of neural sensitivity to estrogens and androgens, since behavior is altered in the apparent absence of such hormonal influences. (See Figure 5.7.)

Although there are physiological and morphological differences between human males and females before puberty, which we will discuss shortly, there is no evidence that the levels of circulating androgens and estrogens are different in boys and girls. In children of both sexes very few adrenal androgens are found before age 7 (Tanner, 1969). After this age there is a gradual rise, until just before puberty a level equivalent to about one-third of that of a young adult is reached. There is also a low and roughly constant excretion of estrogenic substances by both boys and girls from age 3 to age 7, with a gradual rise in both sexes until adolescence. Only after puberty is testosterone produced in the male body (Tanner, 1969). Hence, any behavioral differences between the sexes during childhood must be attributed either to prenatal biochemical influences or to environmental influences. The basic question thus becomes, To what extent are environmental factors modified by the psychological predisposition versus the body structure of the child?

UNIQUELY HUMAN: BODY IMAGE AND PSYCHOSEXUAL IDENTITY

One of the more obvious, but frequently ignored, truisms in the study of the biological bases of sex and gender is that one cannot remove the organism from his or her environment. What is often ignored, however, is that the organism's body structure forms part of that environment. Social and physical environments do not act in a vacuum. What components come into play are probably conditioned by the form of the organism. This point is well known to students of animal behavior in terms of the special capabilities of particular sense organs in various species that determine how much detail we see in the environment, the optimal level and frequency of illumination, whether or not we are able to make color distinctions, and so forth. However, except in cases of special pathologies of the external genitalia, we have tended to ignore the potential role of the individual's body structure in determining behaviors that are considered to be characteristic of one sex or the other.

Studies of animals, discussed earlier, indicate that a complete range of male reproductive behavior is elicited from males only in the presence of an intact, functional penis. At this point we will focus on studies of humans that also stress the primacy of the penis as a stimulus for characteristic male behaviors. However, we must focus not only on a particular body structure but also on the social attitudes and cultural factors that seem to mediate behaviors based on the possession or absence of such a structure. We have discussed in other contexts stereotypic concepts about males and females— that is, individuals who do or do not possess a penis—and psychoanalytic notions about the psychology of such individuals. Here we would like to concentrate on evidence showing that the possession or absence of a penis and concomitant attitudes about sex-appropriate or -inappropriate behaviors can mediate gender identity in humans independent of other biological determinants of sex (e.g., chromosomes, genes, hormones, etc.).

Scientific studies of how humans establish gender identity are unfortunately rare. There is considerable evidence that children can label themselves as boys or girls without adopting other characteristics of a particular gender role. In fact some theorists have attempted to separate behavioral components in terms of sex role identification (one's implicit body image), sex role preference (what one would prefer to be), and sex role adoption (behaving in a manner consistent with one gender whether or not one feels oneself or prefers to be of that gender) (Lynn, 1959). One's object of sexual preference may also be independent of any of these measures. Certainly data on various forms of human sexual "dysfunctions" such as homosexuality, transsexualism, fetishism, and the like indicate that various components of sex that we think of as being highly unitary can take highly divergent paths. We will discuss the implications of such information shortly.

Although few studies have concentrated on the bases on which children establish their gender labels, there is some evidence for the primacy of the penis (Kessler &McKenna, 1978). These researchers developed a series of transparencies that could be overlaid upon featureless bodies either alone or in combination. They found that when the figure possessed a penis, no matter what other contradictory physical (breasts) or social information (clothing or hair style and length) was conveyed, 96 percent of their subjects labeled the figure "male." A vagina alone produced no such agreement. In order to reach such a level of agreement on a label of "female," the figure had to possess breasts and long hair as well as a female vaginal opening.

One could argue that children are not given access to much information about the genital structure of individuals other than themselves. However, informal observations of 3- and 4-year-old children in nursery school toilets (which recently seem to have become sexually liberated) indicates considerable interest in others' anatomy. This interest does not appear to be limited to boys or girls or to members of one's own or the opposite sex. One could also argue that it is this very lack of intimate access that underlies our culture's insistence on sexual dimorphism in attire, hair length, and preferred behaviors. Children's gender label is their main descriptor at birth and one of the earliest labels they are taught. Chris and Terry are not told that they are tall or short, fat or thin, black or white, Catholic or atheist, rich or poor nearly as repeatedly as their sex is labeled for and to them. In fact we are vaguely embarrassed by many of the other labels and may even request children not to use them.

Clinical investigations of disorders in sex and gender development also indicate the importance of genital anatomy and the social response to it in the development of human psychosexual identity. John Money and his associates, in particular, have stressed the need for lack of ambiguity in sexual assignment during the first few years of life. On the basis of studies of matched pairs of congenital hermaphrodites with the same apparent external genitalia at birth, but with different sexes of assignment (Money, Hampson, & Hampson, 1957), it was concluded that psychosexual identity is established more in accordance with the sex of rearing than on the basis of such

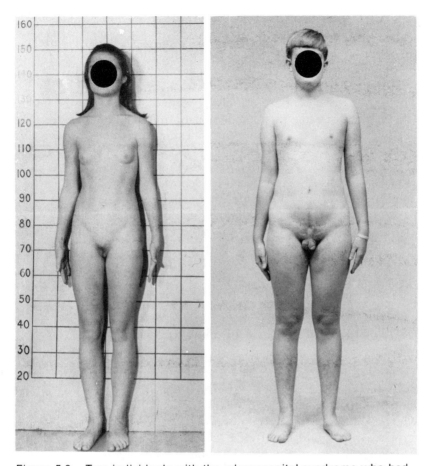

Figure 5.8. Two individuals with the adrenogenital syndrome who had equivalent genital structures at birth, but were identified as different sexes and reared and given different surgical and hormonal treatment accordingly. The ages when photographed were 14½ years for the girl and 15 years for the boy. (From J. Money and A. Ehrhardt, *Man and Woman, Boy and Girl* (Baltimore: Johns Hopkins Press, 1972). Copyright 1972 by the Johns Hopkins Press. Reprinted by permission.)

biological determinants as chromosomes or hormonal sex (Figure 5.8). Requests for sex reassignment have been rare (Money, 1971). In fact Money (1971) asserts that the conformity of most human hermaphrodites to their early sex of assignment is so strong that it can withstand even ugly virilization in a "girl" at puberty or breast development and erectile inadequacy in a "boy." Money and Ehrhardt (1972) discuss such individuals extensively in their book *Man and Woman, Boy and Girl*. They conclude that the human central nervous system is so amenable to the effects of learning that biological contributions to psychosexual identity can be molded and even reversed by the social influences of early childhood.

The conclusions that Money reaches on the basis of his clinical investigations have been criticized by a number of investigators. The most cogent of these criticisms seem to be those of Diamond (1965; 1968). He suggests that demonstrating that human beings are flexible in their psychosexual identification does not disprove that "built-in biases" must be overcome. In particular, he stresses that Money's subjects have tended to be "hermaphroditic," that is, individuals who have been exposed to inconsistencies between various determinants of sex and gender that usually work together. On the basis of their external genitalia they could be either "male" or "female," which is why Money was able to establish matched pairs who were physiologically and morphologically consonant but were disconsonant in terms of sex of rearing. Showing that individuals of ambiguous sex are flexible in their psychosexual orientation does not establish that the same is true for "normal" human beings.

CROSS-SEX REARING IN A PRENATALLY NORMAL MALE

To resolve the controversy over whether the sex of rearing is of paramount importance in the psychosexual identification of normal human beings, it is necessary to find biologically normal individuals who have been reared as members of the other sex. Obviously, such cross-rearing would usually be related to a peculiar and probably pathological family situation. Diamond (1965) states that the products of such attempts have always reverted to their "proper" chromosomal sex as soon as they were afforded the opportunity to do so. Moreover, examination of the early lives of individuals who manifest a psychosexual identity pattern opposite to that of their chromosomal sex (i.e., transsexuals), reveals little in the way of overt, consistent, or long-term familial imposition of a cross-sex identification. Equally obviously, most attempts to induce cross-sex identification in a normal child would be confounded by the presence of genitalia consistent with the child's chromosomal sex.

Money (1974) has provided information about a case whose bizarre aspects seem more suited to a science fiction story than to scientific annals. The case involves a set of identical twins whose embryonic and fetal development were normally male. In infancy, however, an accident during circumcision resulted in near-total destruction of the tissue of one twin's penis. After much professional and parental agonizing it was decided to reclassify the child as female. This was formally done at the age of 17 months. The sex reassignment was based on the opinion that a child without a penis will be able to function more adequately as a female than as a maimed male. Of course in either case such an individual will be functionally sterile. Female reassignment means surgical and continued hormonal intervention, since the androgen-secreting testes must be removed, exogenous estrogen administered, and a vaginal canal constructed.

These children have been followed extensively through childhood and as they near puberty (Money & Ehrhardt, 1972; Money, 1974, 1976). The ways in which the parents distinguished between this child and her previously identical twin brother are noteworthy. The first items to be changed were clothes and hairdo. The mother reports: "I started dressing her not in dresses but, you know, in little pink slacks and frilly blouses . . . and letting her hair grow . . . I even made all her nightwear into granny gowns and she wears bracelets and hair ribbons" (Money & Ehrhardt, 1972, p. 119). By the age of 4 she is reported as preferring dresses over slacks, taking pride in her long hair, and being much neater and cleaner than her brother. She has been taught to sit while urinating and to be modest about exposing her genital parts (the latter in contrast to her brother, for whom an incident of public urination is described with amusement by the mother). The child has also been encouraged to help her mother with housework, again in contrast to her brother, who "could not care less about it" (p. 121). The "girl" is described as having feminine toy and occupational preferences, while at the age of 5 the boy preferred such "masculine" careers as being a fireman or a policemen. Although it is stated that the "girl" has many tomboyish (a peculiar word to use with reference to this child) traits, she has been encouraged to be less rough and tough than her brother and to be quieter and more "ladylike." The boy is reported as responding by being physically protective of his "sister."

Later reports about these children at age 9 (Money, 1974) suggest that although the feminized twin has been the dominant one since birth, she expresses her "dominance" by being a fussy little mother hen and looking after her brother. "He plays the traditional protective male role, taking up for his sister and fighting on her behalf if she is attacked." (Money, 1974, p. 294). In this pair at least, stereotypically male and female characteristic behaviors appear to be more under the control of socially mediated factors than biological ones. Even in this pair, however, physical characteristics other than the presence or absence of the penis have not remained identical. Presumably owing to the influence of slightly different hormonal factors, even before puberty, the twins are already slightly different in height (he is taller) and growth rate. The full extent of these differences, of course, will not become manifest until puberty, when she is feminized under the influence of exogenous estrogen and he masculinizes as a result of endogenous androgen.

Aside from the medical and ethical aspects of the case, these individuals are of great theoretical interest. If the "female" twin and the two other cases of sex reassignment following injury to the penis reported by Money (1974) continue to maintain a typical female psychosexual gender identity, they provide strong evidence that most of the components of what is considered sexually dimorphic behavior in humans are socially conditioned, and that reversal of sex assignment is possible if it takes place early enough, if there is great consistency about the sex of rearing, and if the external genitalia conform well enough to the sex of assignment. Since it is thus far impossible to surgically reconstruct a functional penis, these generalizations are based on evidence involving change in only one direction—from male to female. These cases, fortunately limited in number as they are, also make us reconsider a number of the labels and categories we use to describe male- and female-characteristic behavior. For example, can the active, assertive behavior of such a feminized chromosomal male be considered tomboyism? If such an individual became sexually attached to a normal male, would "she" be engaging in homosexual behavior? What is the effect of our gender labels on our judgments of physical attractiveness? What about lack of ability to reproduce as a member of either sex? To clinicians at least, a nonfunctional female appears to be preferred over a nonfunctional male. But given the relative status of males and females in our society, how will she feel when she finds out that she could have been a male? Or do these questions point out how questionable our dichotomies are after all?

CROSS-SEX BEHAVIOR: FEMALE TO MALE

Because a partial penis is not able to function like that of normal males, the establishment of male gender identity by either hermaphrodites or apparently anatomically normal female transsexuals would appear to be more difficult than the transition from male to female identity. It has been suggested that more individuals make the transition from male to female than in the opposite direction, but there is little clear evidence in this regard. Adults who decide to pass as members of the opposite sex may range from those who simply dress in that sex's attire in the privacy of their homes to those who undergo extensive cosmetic surgery to make their external structures consonant with those of the sex with which they identify.

Figure 5.9.   The results of surgical and hormonal transformation of a male-to-female transsexual. Note feminization of body contours and posture. (From J. Money. "Prenatal Hormones and Postnatal Socialization in Gender Identity Differentiation," in J. K. Cole and A. Dienstbier (eds.), *Nebraska Symposium on Motivation, 1973* (Lincoln: University of Nebraska Press, 1974). Copyright 1974 by the University of Nebraska Press. Reprinted by permission).

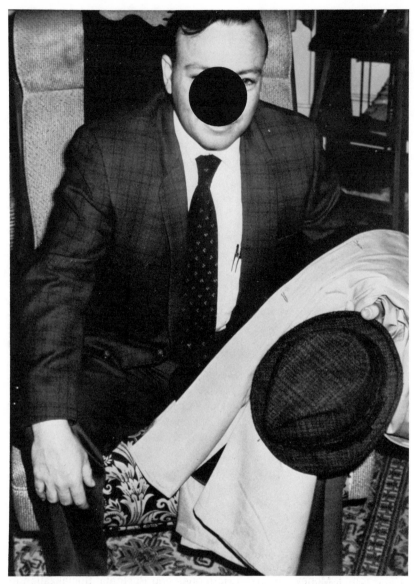

Figure 5.10.   The results of surgical and hormonal transformation of a female-to-male transsexual. Androgen treatment can induce the growth of a beard and body hair. Note also the role of body posture and clothing in our perception of sex. (From J. Money. "Prenatal Hormones and Postnatal Socialization in Gender Identity Differentiation," in J. K. Cole and A. Dienstbier (eds.), *Nebraska Symposium on Motivation, 1973* (Lincoln: University of Nebraska Press, 1974). Copyright 1974 by the University of Nebraska Press. Reprinted by permission.)

Passing as a member of a particular sex seems to be more a matter of attire, hair style, voice, mannerisms and gestures, and dimorphic body language than of any extensive overall physiological change (Figures 5.9 and 5.10). Those who have been investigating the phenomenon of transsexualism point out that there are schools that coach such individuals in how to "pass" (McKenna, personal communication).

It may appear strange that individuals interested in the psychology of women (or of men, for that matter) should be concerned with individuals who seem to be confused about their gender identity. Examination of homosexuals, transsexuals, and the like, however, can tell us much about how gender identity usually develops. For example, we can examine such individuals for evidence supporting biologically determinist theories of sex and gender. We can also determine whether the various components of sex role behavior, including the object of sexual preference, are independent of each other as well as independent of the factors that mediate biological sex. In other words, we are asking questions about the equivalence of biological and psychological sex.

HOMOSEXUALITY AND GENDER IDENTITY

Even the definition of homosexuality is questionable. Our usual definition—an individual whose sexual choice is consistently and compulsively a member of his or her own sex—is not free of value judgments. We do not label heterosexuals as individuals who compulsively seek out members of the opposite sex as their objects of sexual preference. After extensive and painful deliberation the American Psychiatric and the American Psychological Associations recently decided to eliminate homosexuality per se from its definition of behavior pathologies. Thus an individual is no longer considered treatable solely on the basis of sexual preference.

Homosexuals have been examined for almost all the biological determinants of gender that anyone can think of. At one time it was believed that homosexuality was genetically determined, or at least that there was a genetic predisposition for this behavior. This genetic hypothesis was based largely on studies of homosexuality in monozygotic and dizygotic male twins (Kallmann, 1952). In all the pairs of monozygotic twins studied, homosexuality in one twin after adolescence led to a diagnosis of homosexual behavior in the other twin. In over half of the pairs of dizygotic twins examined, however, only one member of the pair showed overt homosexual behavior. Studies of the concordance of a given behavior between pairs of identical versus fraternal twins form the basis for much of the science of human behavioral genetics. In many of these studies, including Kallmann's, genetic interpretations have not been accepted uncritically.

The major objection to genetic interpretations of homosexual behavior is based on the selectivity of this sample. The great majority of the twins studied were schizophrenic as well as homosexual. Moreover, only one of the 85 fathers of the twins had a history of overt homosexual behavior (Ellis, 1963). If the twins' behavior had been genetically programed, one would expect to find a higher incidence of such behavior among their male relatives. Chromosomal analysis of a number of homosexuals has failed to find any chromosomal abnormalities among them (Pare, 1965). And other twin studies have failed to confirm Kallmann's findings. It is also noteworthy that XO individuals rarely show homosexual behavior, while the sexual preference of hermaphrodites appears to be consonant with their sex of rearing more often than with their genetic sex. The sexual preference of XY individuals with the testicular feminizing syndrome also appears to be consonant with their feminine identity rather than with their male chromosome pattern.

Support for a possible hormonal causation of homosexuality is also sparse in the medical and psychological literature. Evidence for hormonal differences between adult homosexual and heterosexual males tends to be unreliable and inconsistent. The homosexual pattern does not appear to be eliminated by administration of testosterone (Kinsey et al., 1953) or by castration. Ellis (1963) points out that male homosexuals are often well-constructed physical specimens with well-developed masculine characteristics. If male homosexuality is related to an endocrine dysfunction, one would expect it to be correlated with physical variation—which it is not.

There is no evidence that excessive amounts of testosterone produce homosexuality in females. In probably the most exhaustive test of this hypothesis, twenty-three adult females who not only had been exposed to excessive androgens prenatally, but had not been treated for their condition in childhood (for at least eight years after birth), as well, were investigated (Ehrhardt, Evers, & Money, 1968). In this group only two individuals had had extensive homosexual contacts and none was exclusively homosexual. None of these individuals was transsexual or wished to have sex change surgery. These data are particularly striking, since in the absence of treatment these individuals probably had masculinized body contours and enlarged, ambiguous clitorises.

Of course it is possible to argue that the hypothesized biological factor underlying homosexuality is so subtle that it is yet to be found. Potential biological determinants could include hormonal potentiation during a critical period of fetal development or a gene that shows its effects only under particular environmental circumstances. There is certainly some evidence that stress, presumably mediated by the large quantities of adrenal hormones produced, can decrease testicular size and sperm count in both animals and humans (Green, 1974). However, we must not confuse biological potency with psychological excitability or libido. In the absence of any strong evidence to the contrary, it appears most parsimonious to suggest that human psychosexual development is extremely sensitive to social and cultural influences in the environment in which that development takes place, and that atypical gender identity, like normal gender identity, is largely a product of learning.

SEXUAL IDENTITY AND BODY BUILD: A NEGLECTED VARIABLE

Evidence that human gender identity is highly malleable does not tell us the bases of gender identity. We are left with the question of whether any biological factors play a role in the gender differentiation of males and females. There are a number of ways in which males and females differ other than in terms of gonadal and genital morphology. Many of these characteristics are related to differential growth and maturation. In fact Tanner (1969), the leading expert on human growth processes, suggests that difference in rate of maturation is in itself a major sexual dimorphism. In this section we will consider some aspects of these growth differences, attempt to determine which of them may be particularly important in the mediation of sexual identity, and try to identify some of the social processes that operate on the basis of these sex differences in biological processes.

As mentioned earlier, the presence of a Y chromosome appears to speed up cell division (Mittwoch, 1973). The embryonic testis is larger than the embryonic ovary at the same fetal age. And in general, male fetuses grow faster than female ones. An interesting countable characteristic that has been used by human geneticists and embryologists to identify various kinds of chromosomal aberrations is dermal ridges (as seen in finger and palm prints). A well-known example of the use of such dermatoglyphics is the "simian crease" (one line crossing the palm rather than several) found in individuals with Down's syndrome. Dermal ridges are laid down in the fetus during the third and fourth months of development and do not change subsequently. They appear to be related to the growth rate of the fetus at that time and are not affected by subsequent uterine or environmental events. The total ridge count is lower in females than in males, and different values have been found for individuals with abnormal numbers of sex chromosomes (Penrose, 1967, 1969; Polani, 1969). The mean ridge count decreases with the addition of more sex chromosomes, but an X has a greater effect than a Y. The count for XO individuals is even higher than that for XYs. The mitotic cycle time of cultured XO cells is shorter than that for XY. The mitotic cycle time of cultured XO cells is also shorter than that for XX cells. Mittwoch (1973) suggests that the ridge count data indicate that in many types of human cells both the X and Y chromosomes slow growth rate, but that the X has a greater effect in this regard than the Y. She suggests that these changes in growth rate may be a function of the nongenic or heterochromatic components of the chromosome.

Hutt (1972) presents a considerable body of information about other biological contributors to sexual dimorphism in humans. On the average, males are larger at birth than females. The calorie intake from the second month on is greater in boys. From infancy to senescence males have a consistently higher basal metabolism than females and have proportionately larger hearts and lungs. Harrison, Weiner, Tanner, and Barnicot (1964), in their book *Human Biology*, state that in all populations women are on the average shorter than men, the magnitude of the difference being between 5 and 8 percent. Although much of this adult height differential is due to the length and timing of the adolescent growth spurt, tables of height and weight (Sobel & Falkner, 1969) suggest that there is a slight average advantage of about 2 percent in favor of males until puberty.

The adolescent spurt of the typical girl occurs two years earlier than that of the boy and is somewhat less marked (Tanner, 1969). In moderately wealthy British children the peak occurs at about age 12 in girls and age 14 in boys. There is a spurt in bone and muscle diameters, which is accompanied in most boys and some girls with a simultaneous fat loss. The boys' muscle development is considerably greater than that of the girls. Naturally, increases in musculature are accompanied by increases in strength. However, this is so much greater for boys in terms of strength per gram of muscle that it may be due to sex-related biochemical differences in muscle cells. The greater muscular development of males appears to be due to stimulation by androgen and may in a sense be considered a secondary sex characteristic, since it is evoked by the same stimulation that produces growth of the pubic and axillary hair and the penis.

Even before puberty boys are, on the average, a little stronger than girls. There are more muscularly built or mesomorphic boys than girls in the population, although the difference is quite small

(Harrison et al., 1964). The differences are not between boys and girls of the same body build but between how many individuals of each body type are likely to be found in either sex. More muscular physiques occur in smaller numbers among girls. There is some slight evidence from the study of XXY and XO individuals that genes on the X chromosome may somewhat inhibit the development of large muscles. You may note from the photograph of the individual with Klinefelter's syndrome (Figure 5.3) that he possesses softer, more rounded contours than are usually considered characteristic of males.

The proportion of fat to body mass is also different for males and females. After the age of 1, girls have more fat than boys (Harrison et al., 1964). At all ages, males are taller than females and have a larger percentage of fat-free body weight (Garn, 1966). Garn suggests that these height and weight differences have their beginnings well before birth. In relative terms, males are mesomorphs and females endomorphs.

THE SOCIAL MEDIATION OF BODY SIZE VARIABLES

Do we have any information that height and weight differences have any effect on human social processes? There is a considerable body of literature showing that body build is a determinant of social status in children. From age 5 through adulthood males and females view the mesomorphic body build as "all things good." Boys in particular associate the mesomorph with an assertive, aggressive pattern of behavior, while ectomorphs are seen as socially submissive (Johnson & Staffieri, 1971). Both boys and girls would prefer to have mesomorphic body builds (Lerner & Korn, 1972; Staffieri, 1972). Endomorphs receive the most negative evaluations from boys and girls. They are seen as most likely to fight, cheat, and worry and to be teased, lonely, lazy, mean, ugly, stupid, and sloppy. These negative associations become particularly relevant when we consider them in light of the body types of males and females in general.

Covert assumptions about body build and gender may be seen to be operative in clinical descriptions of hermaphrodites attempting to "pass" as members of the sex whose body contours they do not possess. Money describes the case of a young man with a micropenis who did well as a boy in childhood and early adolescence. By age 25 he had already established some sort of sex life for himself, but he was greatly depressed by the feeling that he would never look old enough to be a man. He had to stop working as an insurance salesman because clients belittled him as being too young to really have such a job. Since his system was unable to use androgen, he was unable to grow a beard or develop a deep voice. He retained youthful body contours. Money suggests that such an individual would have done better if he had originally been assigned a feminine gender. This case history illustrates the extent to which femininity and immaturity are correlated in our culture.

Changes in body build could be a result as well as a cause of psychological characteristics (Ellis, 1963). For example, girls who wish to repudiate their feminine role could develop a deep voice, male stride, stronger muscles, and so forth through practice. Males who wish to adopt a female role, on the other hand, could stay away from athletics, keep their skins smooth and creamy, and use cosmetics and gestures in ways that would lead people to identify them as having a body build that they do not in fact possess. In other words, gender roles may often be conveyed through "body language" rather than through explicit statements about one's self-identity. Stereotypes about behaviors that are appropriate to particular body builds could also lead some individuals to behave in a manner consistent with others' beliefs about them.

It is not unlikely that the larger body size of males gives them a significant social advantage from childhood:

> The size of the individual after birth is a most conspicuous physical attribute, placing him in relation to his peers and affecting the opinions of his judges. In a culture such as ours that values sheer bigness, greater body size may be an economic as well as a social asset. The taller executive is looked up to both figuratively and literally. In adolescent society, greater body size opens avenues of prestige for the male . . . [Garn, 1966, p. 529]

The parents of short boys and of tall girls are particularly concerned about the ultimate size of their offspring. Biologically based size differences may produce differences in our attitudes toward the cognitive properties of children as well as our attitudes toward their social capabilities. For example, it has been noted that the most important initial advice that can be given to the parents of a dwarfed child in the early years is to remind themselves constantly of the child's chronological age and to treat her or him according to that standard rather than according to his or her height (Drash, 1969). Parents tend to misjudge the age of children with abnormal growth and to treat them inappropriately. Physicians and other professionals who come into contact with these patients also show this tendency.

Both boys and girls with larger lean body mass tend to be advanced in gross motor development, and most measures of "intelligence" are loosely associated with body size during the growing period (Garn, 1966). Of course it is not clear whether such correlations indicate that intellectual and somatic maturity are somehow related or whether one of these variables affects the other. There is some evidence that short children are regarded as less mature by their parents and peers and may even be teased into social and intellectual inadequacy. Correspondingly, taller and/or more physically mature children may be given responsibilities that are advanced for their chronological age, which leads to the accentuation of intellectual and social competence. This hypothesis could account for the finding that children with accelerated maturation from unknown causes have higher-than-expected IQs. It could also account, in part, for some of the intellectual and social inferiority of individuals with Turner's syndrome. In a later chapter we will discuss the way boys and girls treat each other in terms of such socially mediated biological variables as body size and physical attractiveness. Here, however, I wish to stress that physical size is at least as obvious a sexual marker as the external genitalia (especially before puberty, when other secondary sexual characteristics become obvious) and could account for some of the ways in which males and females develop differential role characteristics. The components of the female gender pattern—immaturity, decreased social and intellectual competence, decreased autonomy, decreased dominance, and so on—are maladaptive for any individual in our society, regardless of his or her biological sex. They may be encouraged by physical size differences as much as by any other biological or psychological variable.

Despite the fact that biological sex appears to be a result of a sequence of choices, judgments about an organism's sex are almost always dichotomous. These distinctions are based largely on the presence or absence of a functional penis. Chromosomal males without a penis are labeled as females, while individuals with an enlarged clitoris and fusion of the labial folds are often labeled as males. No one is ever labeled "sex ambiguous." Even essentially neuter individuals who lack any vestige of a functional gonad are labeled as female. All the evidence seems to point to the fact that sex labeling serves a social rather than a biological function. And as one acquires the labels and applies them to oneself one acquires the psychological characteristics that are peculiar to that label's presumed biological determinants.

Chapter 6
The Social Origins of Gender*

Agnes N. O'Connell

It is clear that many people—both now and in the past—believe that sex-characteristic patterns of behavior clearly exist. This view is most strongly developed in theories about personality. Several major theories about personality development stress differences between the sexes. This chapter will review some of these theories and indicate how they have influenced people's thinking about the sexes. Some of the evidence supporting and/or contradicting each view will be presented. Some recent alternative considerations involving androgyny and sex role transcendence will also be reviewed. Two issues need to be resolved: (1) Under what conditions do "masculine" and "feminine" personality patterns manifest themselves? (2) Is the acquisition of an "appropriate" gender identity a positive or necessary condition for males and females, or is a human identity sufficient?

Despite the evidence, reviewed in this and earlier chapters, suggesting that when gender-characteristic patterns of behavior ap-

* Chapter written especially for this book by Agnes N. O'Connell, Department of Psychology, Montclair State College.

pear to exist they seem closely tied to social situations, psychological thinking has been greatly influenced by ideas about biological causality. Part of the reason for the focus on biological factors is a historical one. The first major theorist to take note of the relationship between sex and personality development was Sigmund Freud. Freudian theory has permeated our culture and appears in our literature, in the media, and in our value systems, as well as in our social sciences. And the Freudian theory of gender development is largely a biologically based one with a focus on maturational stages.

THE PSYCHOANALYTIC THEORY OF GENDER IDENTITY DEVELOPMENT

Freud believed that the development of gender took place in a largely predetermined manner by means of a series of stages: oral, anal, phallic, latent, and genital. Each stage was characterized by a concentration of libidinal (sexual) energy in a specific zone of the body. The psychosexual development of females and males was considered to be similar during the first two stages but was thought to diverge during the third or phallic stage (Freud, 1950, 1956, 1965). The child enters this important stage for gender identity between the ages of 3 and 5. During this stage libidinal energy focuses on the genitals.

The Phallic Stage: Boys and Girls

According to Freud (1965), the mother is the first object of love for both boys and girls. As sexual urges increase, the boy's love for his mother becomes incestuous (the Oedipal complex). He views his father as a rival and would like to replace him, but he fears castration by his father as "punishment for inappropriate behavior" (Freud, 1948, p. 189). Aware of the difference in the genitals of a little girl, the boy assumes that the girl's penis has been cut off for some transgression, and this comparison serves to support his fear of castration. This fear of mutilation, or "castration anxiety," acts to repress the boy's sexual desire for his mother and his hostility toward his father. Typically the boy identifies with his father [identification with the aggressor (A. Freud, 1946)] and shares the father's attachment for the mother. The boy's degree of masculinity in later life is determined by the relative strength and success of his identification with his father. The resolution of the Oedipal complex results in the development of the superego.

Although the mother is also the girl's first object of love, Freud (1965) believes that the girl's discovery that she does not have a

Table 6.1 THEORIES ON THE ACQUISITION OF GENDER IDENTITY

PSYCHOANALYTIC (FREUD)	SOCIAL LEARNING (SYNTHESIS)	COGNITIVE DEVELOPMENTAL (KOHLBERG)	SEX ROLE TRANSCENDENCE (REBECCA ET AL.)	ANDROGYNY (BLOCK)
MALE	MALE	MALE	MALE–FEMALE	MALE–FEMALE
1. Desire for mother	1. Attachment to father as major rewarder	1. Cognitive awareness of gender/sex-typed identity	1. Undifferentiated sex role (very young children)	1. Development of gender identity, self-assertion, self-expression, self-interest
2. Fear of father's retaliation (castration anxiety)/identification with father (identification with the aggressor)	2. Identification—modeling of father	2. Modeling of males in general/modeling of father specifically	2. Polarized sex role (present society)	2. Extension of self, self-enhancement
3. Sex-typed identity	3. Sex-typed identity	3. Attachment to father	3. Sex role transcendence (future society)	3. Conformity to external role, development of sex role stereotypes

PSYCHOANALYTIC (FREUD)	SOCIAL LEARNING (SYNTHESIS)	COGNITIVE DEVELOPMENTAL (KOHLBERG)	SEX ROLE TRANSCENDENCE (REBECCA ET AL.)	ANDROGYNY (BLOCK)
FEMALE	**FEMALE**	**FEMALE**		
1. Penis envy/desire for father	1. Attachment to mother as major rewarder	1. Cognitive awareness of gender/ sex-typed identity		4. Examination of self regarding sex role, internalized values
2. Fear of loss of mother's love/ identification with mother (anaclitic identification)	2. Identification– modeling of mother	2. Modeling of females in general/modeling of mother specifically		5. Differentiation of sex role, coping with conflicting masculine–feminine aspects of self
3. Sex-typed identity	3. Sex-typed identity	3. Attachment to mother		6. Achievement of individually defined sex role, integration of both masculine and feminine aspects of self, androgynous sex role definition

SOURCE: From L. Kohlberg, "A Cognitive-Developmental Analysis of Children's Sex Role Concepts and Attitudes," in E. E. Maccoby, ed., *The Development of Sex Differences* (Stanford, Calif.: Stanford University Press, 1966), pp. 82–173; M. Rebecca, R. Hefner, and B. Oleshansky, "A Model of Sex-Role Transcendence," *Journal of Social Issues,* 1976, 32, no. 3, 197–206; and J. H. Block, "Conceptions of Sex Role: Some Cross-Cultural and Longitudinal Perspectives," *American Psychologist,* 28 (1973): 512–526.

penis is a turning point in her growth. She is "mortified by the comparison with the boy's far superior equipment . . . repudiates her love for her mother . . . with the discovery that her mother is castrated" (p. 126). The girl blames her mother for her "deficiency" and transfers her love to her father, who has the organ that she is missing. The girl's desire for a penis is translated into a wish for a baby from her father. "The feminine situation is only established, however, if the wish for a penis is replaced by one for a baby . . ." (Freud, 1965, p. 128). The previously active little girl now becomes passive and receptive.

Freud assumed that for the girl the castration complex precedes the Oedipal complex and does not resolve it, as it does in the boy. Without fear of castration, the chief motive for resolving the Oedipal complex, the girl can remain indefinitely involved in its resolution, a resolution that may never be completely achieved. Freud believed that, as a consequence, the formation of the feminine superego lacks the strength and independence that make it important in our culture—qualities that in males are presumed to form the basis of social law and civilized society. Female identification develops because the girl realizes the impossibility of gratifying her desire for the father and because she fears losing her mother's love (anaclitic identification). (See Table 6.1.) This development is thought to take place at about age 6.

Latency and the Mature Adult

During the later years of childhood, until puberty, Freud assumed that psychosexual development was relatively quiescent. This period was termed the *latency stage*. However, Freud postulated a final stage in which libidinal energy was again focused in the genital area—the *genital stage*. Heterosexual activity with peers becomes important, and substitutes for the unattainable parent are found (Freud, 1930, 1965). The ultimate goal of psychosexual development is mature adulthood, which includes the ability to enter into sexually gratifying love relationships, productive use of one's talents, and relative freedom from pathological conflicts and anxiety (Freud, 1963).

CRITIQUES OF FREUD'S CONCEPTS

Many of Freud's students took issue with his strongly biological theory about the development of gender identity, yet Freud's theory served as the inspiration for many reinterpretations and reformulations. Adler (1954), for example, believed that human beings are primarily social, not sexual, creatures. He argued that "masculine dominance is not a natural thing" (p. 105) but, rather, an outcome of the conflicts among primitive people and the male role of warrior. Women learn quite early that the male is the preferred and privileged member of the family and has the greater social value. Adler emphasized that a girl is born into a biased society that "robs her of her belief in her own value" (p. 110) and undermines her self-confidence so that she is prevented from striving for achievement.

Karen Horney (1926) believed that Freud's theories contained an androcentric bias and that his concepts of female development echoed a little boy's ideas of female anatomy. She told her audiences that she knew just as many men with womb envy as girls with penis envy. She did not see penis envy and castration complex as part of normal female development. In contrast, she proposed a feminine psychology based on lack of confidence and overemphasis on the love relationship (Horney, 1966). Both she and Clara Thompson (1964) took the position that there are no innate or psychological differences between the sexes that could be accounted for strictly by biology. She views the underlying need for security as the basis for behavior. Gender identity then develops in accordance with the limitations set by the culture for females and males. The range of an individual's quest for security and reduction of anxiety is determined by what a particular culture deems appropriate for each sex.

Although Erik Erikson (1963) has offered a psychology sequence that is less constricting than Freud's, he takes a more biologically determinist position than the critics cited previously. His view of gender identity assumes that anatomy "codetermines personality configurations." He finds "inner space," or a woman's ability to bear children, a pervasive force in female identity (Erikson, 1964). His position is based on observations of the miniature play constructions of boys and girls aged 10 through 12. The typical girl's play construction is an interior scene, while the typical boy's construction is an exterior scene involving elaborate walls or façades with protrusions or consisting of high towers. Erikson draws a parallel between the sex differences in the play constructions of children in preadolescence and the internal sex organ of the female and the external organ of the male. Although other interpretations of these findings can be made (e.g., the relationship between internal and external environments and "appropriate" female and male adult roles), Erikson prefers the anatomical analogy.

Although this discussion by no means encompasses all of Freud's students or early critics—Jung (1971), for example, stressed the integration of both the masculine (animus) and feminine (anima) components of personality, a position more consonant with an androgynous viewpoint—it does indicate that his views on sex-specific psychosexual development were by no means generally accepted even in his own time. More recent critiques have stressed an "adult" as well as a male bias in Freud's views. Interpretation of the behavior of young children in sexual terms may be inaccurate, since it is only later that the child will possess knowledge about the genitals and their ultimate role in the sex act (Salzman, 1974). Mary Jane Sherfey (1972) even questions whether the penis is actually primary or whether it does not represent an "exaggerated clitoris."

Examinations of the validity of Freud's theory about psychosexual development have focused on specific concepts such as castration anxiety, penis envy, development of the superego, and identification with the same-sex parent. Sherman's (1971) comprehensive review of the literature on the Freudian view of feminine development concluded that "there is little evidence of castration anxiety in women or of widespread anatomical envy. There is also evidence that males show biological envy of the female sex." She suggests that, for normal female development, "differential sex status positions and preference for the higher male sex-role status" (p. 67) are more important than penis envy.

In one report based on case studies, a male Freudian-oriented therapist describes the clinical experiences that led him to conclude that penis envy is purely a psychological phenomenon and is neither biologically based nor the bedrock of femininity (Moldawsky, 1975):

> When I came upon dream material and associations which led to recognition of feelings of penis envy . . . I was surprised to repeatedly discover that this soon gave way to associations and memories related to maternal deprivation and maternal rejection. It was enticing to me to assume that the deprivation was an expression of Mother's depriving my patient of the penis so that talking of that which was missing was a way of saying that Mother did not provide the missing organ. This never developed into any feeling of conviction for either myself or my patient. The deprivation related to real distance between Mother and daughter and not fantasies of rejection . . . and the thing that was really missing was mother's love and not the penis. "She would have loved me if I'd been a boy" was a stronger root for the penis envy than was the awareness of being different from males and wanting the organ that made the difference. [unnumbered]

In addition, research on moral development (Maccoby & Jacklin, 1974; Oetzel, 1966) and behavioral indexes of adherence to societal laws (e.g., crimes committed) strongly argue against Freud's claims for the superior superego in males (F. Adler, 1975;

Noblit and Burcart, 1973; Sherman, 1971) as an outcome of the resolution of the Oedipal complex. In fact studies on children's preferred parent seem to argue against the Oedipal complex per se. A study of 1626 normal children aged 1 to 12 (Anderson, 1936) found little difference between the sexes in the preferred parent; either the children had no preference or they preferred the mother somewhat more often than the father. A later study of boys and girls aged 3 to 5 also found the mother to be the preferred parent (Piskin, 1960).

IDENTIFICATION AND PSYCHOSEXUAL DEVELOPMENT

The Concept of Identification

The concept of identification would appear to be vital in determining the validity of Freud's theory about sex-specific psychosexual developmental patterns. Much research has concentrated on his postulation that normal personality development depends on identification with the same-sex parent through resolution of the Oedipal complex. Unfortunately the concept of identification is difficult to deal with, since it appears to involve several different definitions. It may refer to (1) behavior—the child acts like the parent; (2) motivation—the child is disposed to act like the parent; or (3) process—the dynamics through which behaviors and motives are learned (Bronfenbrenner, 1960). Some of these usages are susceptible to measurement and some are not. Identification can be examined in terms of an operational definition of behavioral similarity or perceived similarity. Either children and their parents fill out similar tests of personality and comparisons are made between them, or the child responds twice to a questionnaire, once as self and once as parent (Unger & Denmark, 1975). Occasionally a knowledgeable observer fills out the questionnaire for characteristics of both the child and the parents. The responses that are compared to measure the degree of the child's identification with the mother and father are not restricted to those that are directly related to gender role.

The Degree of Identification

While children of both sexes appear to prefer the mother, there is no consistent evidence that they eventually identify more with one parent than with the other. It has been noted that girls are no more similar to their mothers than they are to other women (Helper, 1955; Lazowick, 1955). Other studies have shown that children of both sexes may resemble the maternal parent more than the paternal one.

For example, the anxiety scores (Adams & Sarason, 1963) and authoritarianism scores (Byrne, 1965) of both boys and girls are more closely related to those of their mothers than to those of their fathers. Many theorists believe that both boys and girls form their primary identification with their mother. In boys, this primary identification must be replaced in order for "appropriate" gender identity to develop. A major difference among personality theories depends on the processes through which gender identity is thought to develop and/or shift. While for Freud the process seemed to involve identification through resolution of the Oedipal complex (see Table 6.1), social-learning theorists have stressed reward, punishment, generalization, and the social aspects of gender identity development.

SOCIAL-LEARNING THEORY

Social-learning theorists define identification as a particular kind of imitation, "the spontaneous duplication of a model's complex, integrated pattern of behavior (rather than simple, discrete responses) without specific training or direct reward but based on an intimate relationship between the identifier and the model" (Mussen, 1969, p. 404). Here, as in Freudian theory, identification is considered to be the process by which gender identity is assimilated. It produces relatively stable effects that are resistant to change. This process is facilitated by the child's belief that he or she has some of the model's attributes and feelings (Kagan, 1958).

Processes that Facilitate Identification

Social-learning theory tends to stress the properties of the parents and the nature of the reinforcement processes that serve to facilitate identification. In terms of gender identification, children's perception of similarity between themselves and the parent of the same sex obviously facilitates modeling because they tend to imitate those whom they perceive as similar to themselves (Bandura, 1969). The parents' availability, nurturance, and power over resources and rewards make them the primary models for the development of gender role during the early years of life (Mischel, 1970). (See Table 6.1.)

Two factors that have been extensively investigated in terms of the strength and degree of the child's imitation are (1) the frequency and intensity (or intimacy) of the interactions between the child and the model and (2) the model's control over resources that are valuable to the child. The model may have power because of the ability to reward or nurture the child or because of the ability to threaten or punish. By observing a model's behavior the child may acquire sex-typed responses that are new to his or her behavioral repertoire. The consequences of the model's behavior (either observed or inferred) influence the degree to which the child will model that behavior. A nurturant relationship between observer and model may facilitate modeling but is not essential for it (Bandura & Huston, 1961). Positive consequences are more likely to produce modeling than negative ones (Bandura, Ross, & Ross, 1963b). However, boys and girls are both inclined to model the parent (or adult) whom they perceive to have the most access to valuable resources (Bandura, Ross, & Ross, 1963a). If that parent is male, then females tend to model male behaviors to the extent that cross-sex behavior is tolerated. Indeed, females are more apt to adopt aspects of the male role than males are to adopt aspects of the female role (Brown, 1958; Lynn, 1959). This sex asymmetry may be related to the greater penalty deriving from deviation from the male role as well as its greater reward value.

Sex Role Preference, Adoption, and Identification

Although the child observes and learns the repertoire of both sexes, he or she does not imitate the wide range of characteristics to the same extent. A distinction among sex role preference, adoption, and identification has been suggested that helps clarify this differential imitation (Brown, 1958; Lynn, 1959, 1966, 1969). *Sex role preference* refers to the perception of the behavior of one sex as preferable or more desirable than that of the other sex. It has been measured by asking a respondent if she or he has ever wanted to be a member of the opposite sex or by having the child express his or her preference for objects, pictures, or sex-linked characteristics. *Sex-role adoption* refers to the performance of the behavioral characteristics of one sex or the other. It deals with overt behavior associated with the opposite sex (e.g., the wearing, by a female, of pants, a vest, a shirt, and a tie). Such behavior does not necessarily mean that the person identifies with the role of the other sex. *Identification* refers to internalization of the role of a particular sex as well as to the unconscious reactions that are specific to that role. It is usually measured by projective techniques or by measures of similarity between parent and child. Because of the prestige and privileges associated with the male role, it is not surprising that there is more female-to-male than male-to-female cross-sex preference and adoption. Nevertheless the sexes do not appear to differ in degree of same-sex identification.

Social-Learning Concepts of Gender Role Development

Since there is a great deal of asymmetry between the social rewards for acting like a male and those for acting like a female, one would expect "masculine" behaviors to be more generally adopted than they are. What seems to be crucial for the development of same-sex identification and role self-concept are the different consequences of attempts to engage in sex-typed behaviors for males and females. Social-learning theorists stress that children quickly learn the differential consequences of the same behavior for females and males and therefore perform these behaviors with differing frequencies (Mischel, 1966, 1970).

According to social-learning theory, the process of acquiring gender identity begins at birth with the ascription of a gender label. This labeling initiates a complex set of treatments by significant others that set into motion the process of establishing the attitudes, feelings, and behavior of children of that gender in that particular culture. These roles are reinforced intensively and continuously throughout childhood. The reward (reinforcement of sex-appropriate responses by parents and others) contributes to their repetition or increase in frequency. Conversely, sex-inappropriate responses are likely to result in punishment and therefore are likely to diminish in strength, decrease in frequency, and be extinguished (Mussen, 1969).

In addition to holding that reinforced behavior increases in frequency, social-learning theorists believe that reinforced behavior in one situation will be repeated in other, similar situations and/or environments. This is the learning principle of *generalization*. For example, if a little girl's dependent behavior is rewarded by her mother, she is likely to generalize her behavior from her home and mother to her school and teacher(s).

Evidence from Research

Models of both sexes are present in the lives of both girls and boys. There appears to be little consistent tendency for preschool or school-age children to select same-sex models (Maccoby & Jacklin, 1974). Nevertheless a review of the research on toy and activity preferences indicates that both sexes are sex typed by nursery school age. In fact beginning at about age 4 boys tend to become more sex typed than girls (e.g., they are inclined to reject or avoid sex-inappropriate activities and more inclined to prefer activities that are consonant with their own role).

The evidence also does not indicate that children resemble

their same-sex parent more, nor, indeed, that their personality characteristics are particularly well related to those of their parents. The femininity of girls aged 3 to 6 is unrelated to the femininity of their mothers (Hetherington, 1965), and boys' masculinity is not related to their fathers' masculinity scores (Mussen & Rutherford, 1963). Patterns of sex role preferences of parents and their preschool children (as measured by the IT scale) are not significantly related to each other (Fling & Manosevitz, 1972). In sum, studies do not appear to support the view that children acquire or maintain masculine and/or feminine behavior and interests through modeling of the same sex parent.

There are a number of factors that may account for the lack of relationship between parents' and children's behavior. It is important to keep in mind that masculinity and femininity in young children is qualitatively different from masculinity and femininity in adults (Sears, 1965). The child interprets the behavior he or she sees in accordance with his or her own social and behavioral maturity. Thus children's imitation of masculine or feminine behavior reflects a reprocessing of their observations to make them compatible with their own level of development. Male- or female-characteristic behaviors (e.g., aggression and nurturance, respectively) at age 6 are qualitatively different from male- or female-characteristic behaviors at 16, 26, 36, or 60.

It is also crucial to recognize that measures of identification or imitation based on personality questionnaires primarily assess cultural patterns of behavior that are presumed to be related to gender rather than imitation of particular persons, no matter how important they appear to be in the child's early life (Bandura, 1969). In other words, children may model what they consider to be generally male- or female-specific behaviors rather than particular characteristics of the father or mother. There is ample evidence (discussed in Chapter 7) that children are aware of gender-specific characteristics at a very early age. It is also possible that parents encourage sex typing in children even when they are not aware of doing so. They may even reward gender-characteristic behaviors derived from models other than themselves although they themselves do not practice the behaviors so rewarded. In fact data discussed in the next chapter indicate that much encouragement of sex typing in children emanates from reinforcements by the opposite-sex parent.

A major problem for social-learning theory in general (not just in terms of the modeling of gender-specific behaviors) is how the individual chooses a model to imitate. A variety of models of both sexes are available to children at an early age. Moreover, models of either sex do not practice gender-appropriate behavior exclusively.

Some sex-role-inconsistent behaviors are probably practiced by all of us. What is unclear is when and in what behaviors a child chooses to model her or his same-sex parent.

The quality of the relationship between the child and the parent seems to be important here (Lamb, 1976). Children are not likely to identify with a punitive or rejecting parent of either sex, regardless of perceived sex or other similarities. On the one hand, fathers who are warm, nurturant, and actively involved in childrearing are quite likely to produce masculine sons (Biller, 1969, 1971). On the other, sons from mother-dominant homes are likely to show less identification with their fathers than males from families with a more typical father-dominant pattern (Hetherington, 1965). It is possible that the father's lack of prestige in society as a whole (which is common in such homes) accounts for the son's lack of willingness to identify with him. Close, affectional contact between father and son could, in contrast, foster identification even if the father does not manifest male-characteristic traits directly.

A major variable that is of interest would seem to be the child's perception of the trait as characteristic of the parent rather than its actual degree of appropriateness. Thus if the parent is perceived as a potent source of reinforcement, he or she may serve as a reinforcer of characteristics that are socially attributed to women or men in general but are not possessed by that parent specifically. This kind of focus is more characteristic of cognitive-development theory than of social-learning theory.

COGNITIVE-DEVELOPMENT THEORY

Cognitive-development theory represents a more recent attempt to deal with the issues raised by the development of gender-specific personality patterns. Its major exponent, Kohlberg (1966, 1969), like Freud and Piaget, believes in a predetermined sequence of development in which qualitative changes occur in a hierarchical and invariant order. Kohlberg, however, differs from both Freudian and social-learning theorists in stressing that the child actively structures his or her own experiences and that gender role concepts and values are the outcome of this structuring of information from both physical and social sources. According to Kohlberg's theory, the crucial organizer of gender-related roles, attitudes, and behaviors is the child's self-categorization as a "boy" or "girl." This occurs early in development, generally late in the second year; is irreversible; and is maintained despite the pattern of reinforcements and parental identifications. The child's gender identity finally stabilizes at about age 5 or 6.

Once the child has acquired her or his gender label, she or he comes to positively value behaviors, objects, and attitudes that are consistent with that label. The child may then say, "I am a boy; therefore I want to do boy things; therefore the opportunity to do boy things (and to gain approval for doing them) is rewarding" (Kohlberg, 1966, p. 89). In other words, rewards emanate more from behaving consistently with one's gender label than from reflecting what those in the environment consider gender appropriate. The child selects actively from what is available rather than being a passive recipient of social rewards and sanctions. The child does so in order to receive evaluations that are consistent with maintenance of the appropriate identity.

Kohlberg suggests that the cross-sex preference of girls aged 5 to 8 is a result of their recognition of the occupational, economic, and familial advantages of males. He believes, however, that they eventually find the female adult role attractive enough to merit emulation. Female adults have more competence and power than a child, and certain aspects of the feminine role (e.g., nurturance) may be perceived as "nicer" than some aspects of the masculine role (e.g., aggression). Children's acquisition of sex-characteristic traits is based on similar needs in each sex—needs for control of the environment, for self-esteem, and for achievement. Since, however, different behaviors are prescribed by society, girls acquire the feminine values of attractiveness, goodness, and social approval whereas boys acquire competence, strength, power, and instrumental achievement.

For Kohlberg, identification is an outcome of sex typing and not its antecedent. (See Table 6.1.) The child tends to model those like himself or herself who are high in prestige and competence. "For the boy with masculine interests and values the activities of a male model are more interesting and hence more modeled" (Kohlberg, 1966, p. 129). The boy imitates his father and seeks approval after he recognizes his father's more prestigious position in society. The son's identification with the father progresses from identification with the stereotype of the masculine role to identification with his own father's specific role and personality. Feminine identification requires identification with a female role, which is culturally less prestigious than that of the male. This inequality may account for the initially greater cross-sex preference found in girls.

Kohlberg's theory is essentially a cognitive model that stresses the development of concepts about social roles and events. Cognitive growth is seen as a process "in which basic changes, or qualitative differences, in modes of thinking lead to transformed perceptions of the self and the social world" (Kohlberg, 1966, p. 147).

Cognitively advanced children demonstrate sex role learning earlier than peers of the same age (Kohlberg & Zigler, 1967). They also show same-sex preferences sooner than less cognitively mature children. With increasing cognitive development, however, they emphasize sex differences less than their peers. Such data cast doubt on Freudian conceptions of sex role development and link it more closely with the development of other learned skills. Cognitive-development theory minimizes the role of social reinforcement. The function of social reinforcement here is to serve as "a judgment of normative conformity" or as an "instruction and definition of the right answer" (Kohlberg, 1969, p. 440) by someone more competent than the child. In addition to parental influences, the theory stresses the role of peers and other socializing agents, such as the media, in the development of gender identity.

Recent work lends support to the relationship between cognitive maturity and gender identity. Children 24 months old were able to distinguish between males and females in a variety of roles; at 30 months they could relate the proper gender category to a picture of themselves; and at 36 months they showed a preference for objects and behaviors that was consistent with their gender label (Thompson, 1975). In children aged 3 to 5, high gender constancy and preference for the same-sex model are related (Slaby, 1974). This finding would seem to support Kohlberg's concept of selective attention to same-sex models for imitation. However, further research is needed using this theoretical formulation. And Kohlberg does not adequately define the particular mechanisms for sex role acquisition in females, although he does identify mastery, competence, and self-esteem as relevant variables.

A COMPARISON OF THEORIES OF GENDER IDENTITY ACQUISITION

Psychoanalytic theory assumes that gender role development is primarily a function of maturational biological determinants with some influence of cultural factors. Specifically, it postulates that the child develops gender identity through the resolution of the Oedipal complex and subsequent identification with the same-sex parent.

In contrast to this perspective, social-learning theory contends that a child develops gender identity through reinforcement and generalization of sex-appropriate behavior. These processes include modeling, observational learning, imitation, and/or identification. In this view effective socializing agents (e.g., parents) are extremely important in labeling, rewarding, and instructing the child in sex-appropriate ways.

The cognitive-developmental position, in opposition to other theories, argues that gender identity is an outcome of the child's cognitive structuring of his or her world. The development of feminine or masculine attributes is dependent on the child's emerging cognitive abilities and is limited by his or her current cognitive skills. Psychoanalytic theory stresses biology; social-learning theory, environmental influence; and cognitive-developmental theory, cognitive structuring and maturity. Both the social-learning and cognitive theories stress the importance of salient and positively perceived gender labeling in the acquisition of gender identity. The child positively values (cognitive theory), and is reinforced for (social-learning theory), whatever is consistent with her or his gender and gradually expands her or his repertoire of responses in that direction. Social-learning theory emphasizes external agents (generally parents) as instrumental in the acquisition of gender identity; cognitive theory stresses the role of the child in selecting gender-related behaviors, attitudes, and personality characteristics (i.e., children socialize themselves and are responsible for acquiring the "appropriate" gender identity). According to cognitive theory, the child's gender role responses are stereotypic in the early stages of development but gradually become more personal as he or she matures cognitively.

Part of the problem with all of these theories may be their insistence on the development of unique "masculine" and "feminine" personality patterns. There is no question that most societies define behaviors as consistently characteristic of one sex or the other (as is extensively discussed in Chapter 2), but there is no clear evidence that individuals practice these sex-exclusive patterns. In fact masculine–feminine dimensions of a personality construct have been criticized as artifacts of our methods of personality assessment (Constantinople, 1973). Most of these methods view masculinity–femininity as a unidimensional characteristic such that behaviors that are viewed as feminine are also seen as not masculine, and vice versa. With this construct it is impossible for people to engage in masculine and feminine behaviors at the same time.

There is also a tendency for psychologists to view gender-specific personality patterns as cross-cultural universals. Gender identity, however, is strongly influenced by the culture into which the child is born and raised. The definition of masculinity/femininity varies in Iran and New England, in Asia, Africa, and America just as it has varied over time within the same culture.

NEW APPROACHES TO GENDER-SPECIFIC DEVELOPMENT

Androgyny

A secure sense of one's maleness or femaleness need not depend on the concepts of masculinity or femininity if we all shared the assuredness of the preschooler who silenced the critic who said, "Boys don't play hopscotch" by replying, "I'm a boy and I play hopscotch." The whole repertoire of characteristics and behaviors of human beings may be available to members of either sex. Recently theorists who are interested in the relationship between personality and gender have concerned themselves with the integration of characteristics and behaviors rather than with the masculinity or femininity of those characteristics and behaviors.

The concept of androgyny is not a new one in psychology. Followers of Jung (1953, 1971) are familiar with his concepts of anima (female aspect in males) and animus (male aspect in females) and his belief that the two must be integrated in each of us for the self to be complete. Two noted social psychologists, Sandra Bem and Janet Spence, have recently developed inventories for the empirical measure of individual differences in androgyny. They define androgyny as the possession of a balance between the characteristics that are culturally defined as masculine or feminine. Androgynous people of both biological sexes appear to be more like each other than sex-typed individuals are (Bem, 1975). They are more likely to engage in cross-sex behaviors than sex-typed individuals. In fact sex-typed individuals—masculine men and feminine women—choose same-sex activities even when such choices are not in their best monetary interests (Bem & Lenney, 1976).

Only androgynous subjects display both male-appropriate and female-appropriate behaviors in tasks involving independence and nurturance (Bem, 1975). The androgynous male is competent in both instrumental and expressive domains. He has a broad range of behaviors. He engages in tasks regardless of their stereotypic label if it is in his best monetary interest to do so. He is not easily swayed in his opinions, plays with kittens and human infants, and is sympathetic toward a lonely same-sex transfer student (Bem & Lenney, 1976; Bem, Martyna, & Watson, 1976). In contrast, the feminine male does well only in expressive tasks and the masculine male only in instrumental ones.

Like androgynous males, androgynous females and, to some extent, masculine women can be both expressive and instrumental.

But the feminine women prefers same-sex activities, conforms under pressure, and is not especially nurturant in interaction with either a kitten or a human infant. She is, however, extraordinarily supportive in responding to another woman's loneliness when that support requires a sympathetic listener. Bem suggests that the feminine role inhibits behavior in undefined situations in which the appropriate behavior is not clearly determined and specified. If the situation requires the feminine woman to take the initiative, she does not act even if the situation is conducive to expressing nurturant behavior. The feminine woman does well in situations in which her behavior is clearly defined and in which the outcome will be positive. She prefers to "play it safe."

The restrictiveness of both feminine and masculine roles is well documented; certainly these roles need redefinition to include the full range of human options. A truly androgynous person has a large measure of the characteristics of both sexes (Bem, 1974; Spence, 1975). Bem reports that approximately one-third of the populations she has studied can be classified as androgynous. Perhaps we are closer to this reality than is popularly supposed.

Sex Role Transcendence

The dissatisfaction with masculine/feminine stereotypes and their deviations from reality, the need for a wider range of acceptable human behavior, and the harmful consequences of adherence to masculine/feminine stereotypes make "sex role transcendence" an attractive idea. Meda Rebecca, Robert Hefner, and Barbara Oleshansky (1976) have suggested this new model of sex role development, which consists of three stages. (See Table 6.1.) Stage I is characterized by a global undifferentiated quality very much in the manner described by Piaget, Kohlberg, and others. In this stage the child goes from unawareness of culturally imposed restrictions to a dichotomous awareness of "appropriate" sex roles and sex-typed behaviors. This stage extends from birth to school age. Stage II involves active acceptance of the stereotypic sex role and sex-typed behaviors and rejection of the roles and behavior of the other sex.

Adherence to the appropriate sex role is rewarded and valued in our present society. Stage III goes beyond the present state of society. It involves reorganizing in a personal and unique way that which was learned in stage II; that is, the individual is no longer bound by rigid sex role conformity but is free to express her or his human characteristics without fear of violating stereotypic norms.

In learning the appropriate sex roles and behaviors in stage II, the individual learns the roles and behaviors of both sexes. Therefore with proper reinforcement he or she can call upon the components of either role. This occurs when the individual experiences crises or contradictions that involve role conflict. The transition from stage I to stage II is bolstered by strong societal support. But there are few societal supports for the transition from stage II to stage III. It is a difficult transition to make. Rebecca and her colleagues conceive of stage III as a dynamic process involving continuous conflict and conflict resolution.

The concept of sex role transcendence stresses situational specificity, as does Bem's concept of androgyny. Both deemphasize gender in its usual sense. If an individual has transcended his or her sex role, then assigned gender is not relevant to his or her decision making. Bem (1978) makes this point more succinctly when she recommends that "gender move from figure to ground."

Another stage theory of gender-specific development has been proposed by Jeanne Block (1973). The first two stages are characterized by parental pressures toward socialization. (See Table 6.1.) During the third stage males are discouraged in the warmth–expressiveness domain and females in the domain of aggression. The fourth stage involves examination of self regarding sex roles and internalized values of responsibility and duty. In the fifth stage sex role standards are differentiated. This stage sometimes involves conflict. In the sixth stage integration of both feminine and masculine aspects of the self, the development of an individual sex role definition, and androgyny occur. Not all individuals reach this highest stage. Like Loevinger's (1966, 1970) concept of ego development, on which it is based, Block's theory conceives of development as progressing from an originally undifferentiated state to a highly differentiated state. In Block's sex role theory differentiation is socially determined at first but may be modified later through individual initiative and endeavor. The levels of social development with respect to sex role are conceived of as similar to the varying levels of ego development and moral reasoning. At the higher stages each requires a resynthesis and reintegration of the relationship between the self and society.

Although the formulations of both Block and Rebecca and her associates do not operationalize the mechanism and processes by which gender identity is acquired, they do provide a fresh approach to conceptualizing the socialization process. These approaches are neither bipolar nor unidimensional. According to these theories, conventional sex role standards and accompanying gender identity are intermediary stages in the transcendence of sex role and the acquisition of an androgynous identity.

PERSONALITY AND SOCIETY

Newer theories of sex-related personality development also stress the adaptation of the individual's behavior to the needs of the situation. Only strongly sex-typed people avoid cross-sex behaviors. It is likely that most of us engage in "female-appropriate" and "male-appropriate" behaviors all the time but do not notice this apparent contradiction in either ourselves or others. For example, research by Spence and her associates (Spence, Helmreich, & Stapp, 1974) indicates that there is a weak and unreliable relationship between the degree of sex role stereotyping that people perceive in others and the extent to which they sex type their own characteristics. It seems that androgynous people may be as likely to view others as sex typed as anyone else in our society. Attributions of stereotypic sex roles to others seem to be related to a stronger need for consistency in others than for consistency in ourselves. However, research by Rotter and O'Connell (1978) indicates that androgynous and cross-sexed males and females are significantly more tolerant of ambiguity than sex-typed males and females. Taken together, these studies seem to suggest that we are particularly likely to give ourselves the benefit of the doubt. Thus we may be exaggerating the extent of sex-typed behavior that actually occurs in others; that is, we may be mistaking the stereotype for the reality.

Recent work has also suggested that sex-typed behavior is more likely to occur in ambiguous situations—in which the appropriate behavior is not clear—or in situations in which the structure builds in appropriate roles (e.g., social structures involving helping behavior). In the former case gender-related behaviors presumably reflect a personality characteristic, whereas in the latter sex role behaviors may be emitted by virtually all participants.

It will be necessary to examine more situations in which societal requirements are obscure before we can estimate the extent of actual sex differences in personality characteristics.

The newer theories of sex role identity stress both integration and transcendence and argue persuasively for consideration of the development of a human, rather than a sex-typed, identity. These theories suggest that maleness or femaleness is secondary. They also suggest that concern should shift from the sex role socialization of children to a socialization that encourages and reinforces the potential of the individual child regardless of sex. One's identity would then be a human identity, and maleness or femaleness would neither dictate nor restrict full human potential. The ramifications of living in a society in which human identity is salient remain to be discovered. However, some recent findings on sex role concept (O'Connell, 1977) and sex role identity (O'Connell, 1976) make the ramifications of that yet-to-be-realized eventuality appear most promising.

Chapter 7
Parents and Children:
Sex-by-Sex Interactions

All the theoretical conceptions of how sex differences in personality develop stress in one way or another the role of parents. Thus, according to Freudian theory, sex-characteristic personality patterns develop as a function of psychosexual interactions between children and their same- and opposite-sex parents. In social-learning theory, it is the role of the parents as models and providers of reinforcement that is stressed. And in cognitive-development theory the parents' main function seems to be to serve as a source of labels for the child and her or his behavior. Obviously, therefore, behavioral interactions in the home environment are of great importance in understanding sex differences. Relationships between parents and children are particularly important, since there is considerable evidence that in our society sex differences increase throughout childhood. Even if such differences are largely only self-perceived, self-perceptions of a reality constitute a form of that reality. In this chapter we will examine how a reality concerning sex and gender begins to be constructed.

Societal beliefs about females and males are reflected in parental socialization patterns. The major role of learning in sex-related personality patterns may be demonstrated by the relative ease with which such traits are manipulated by variables such as socioeconomic status, race and ethnicity, the birth position of the child, and his or her individual characteristics, in addition to sex. Situational specificity in the expression of sex-related behaviors may also be stressed.

Our perceptions of sex role socialization practices appear to depend on whether they are studied in the home or in the laboratory, on whether the parents are aware that they are being studied, and on the method used to record the practice itself. Although sex role socialization by parents appears to be modified by many apparently extraneous variables, some clear trends are apparent. The clearest of these seems to be the relationship between parents and their opposite-sex children. Fathers appear to be more important in differentiating the gender-characteristic behaviors of their daughters, and mothers in differentiating those of their sons. Parental effects appear to be present at birth, but increase and change in nature as the child gets older. Processes that operate without the parents' awareness may be more important than their stated child-rearing practices.

SEX PREFERENCES AND SEX STEREOTYPES

Preference for a Male Child

Even the fetus does not exist in a socially neutral environment. Parents have sex preferences and make gender-related attributions well before birth. There still exists in our society a clear preference for male children. Among unmarried college students 90 percent of the males and 78 percent of the females stated that they would prefer a male child if they could have only one child (Hammer, 1970). Among the small number of noncollege adults, 90 percent of the men and 30 percent of the women preferred a son. College-educated women may be more dissatisfied with the female role, and this could account for their high preference for a son rather than a daughter.

Using behavioral rather than attitudinal measures, it has been found that when the first child is a boy the interval before the next child is, on the average, three months longer than it is when the first child is a girl (Westoff, Potter, & Sagi, 1963). A great deal of evidence exists to show that parents in the United States want first a son and then a child of each sex (Pohlman, 1969). Having a girl rather than a boy has been found to be associated with postpartum emotional disorders (Gordon & Gordon, 1967). Women who are pregnant for the first time even dream about male babies twice as often as about female babies (Gillman, 1968).

Sex Stereotypes Begin Before Birth

Parents make predictions about the sex of their unborn babies based on stereotypic notions of masculine and feminine characteristics. If the fetus is active, kicking, and moving a great deal, the mother interprets this to mean that the child is more likely to be a male than a female (Lewis, 1972). It is my impression (anecdotal) that males are also predicted more often than females. Certainly after birth a young infant is identified as a male more readily than as a female (Seavey et al., 1975; Haviland, 1976a). The fact that the sex of unborn children is of great significance to our society is illustrated by the vast number of superstitions designed to inform parents about the sex of their future offspring. Predictions are based on the position in which the baby is carried (high positions, of course, indicate a male) and the amount of nausea felt by the mother as well as on the activity of the fetus.

At birth the first characteristic of the infant that is remarked upon is its sex. Note of its physical health comes a little later. There are many other characteristics of the infant that could be used to describe it, such as its size, its coloring, the presence or absence of hair, and so forth, but its sex remains dominant. Birth announcements proudly proclaim "It's a boy/girl!" rather than "It's a healthy baby!"

Sex-Related Characteristics of the Newborn

There is little evidence that female and male human beings differ much at birth. Newborn males may show somewhat more gross motor activity and somewhat different sleep patterns than females. More noticeable to parents may be the greater average weight of male infants at birth and their greater strength. Newborn males can lift their heads from a prone position at an earlier age than newborn females. Temperament and activity differences may be more important than the child's sex in organizing parental activity. For example, the amount of medication the newborn receives during the birth process affects the degree of parental interaction with the child (Parke, O'Leary, & West, 1972). Maternal interaction with the child increased as medication increased, whereas fathers' interaction decreased. Any explanation of this difference is highly speculative, but it has been suggested that the father prefers an active, alert infant and leaves the task of stimulating the lethargic offspring of a high-medication birth to the mother.

The role of individual differences in infants, whether or not they are sex related, has probably been underestimated. If an infant is unresponsive to holding, cries and fusses excessively, or is late in smiling and looking at the mother's eyes, her feelings of attachment may never develop or may weaken (Robson & Moss, 1970). It has been reported that the parents of premature infants who spend several months in an incubator report difficulty in relating to them once they are in the home. Studies of rhesus monkey mothers indicate that they spend less time cradling "twinned pairs" than mothers rearing single control infants (Deets, 1974). These pairs did not engage in nearly as much interaction with the mother as singly reared infants did. Twin humans may also receive less parental attention.

PARENTAL BEHAVIORS

Fathers and Mothers

Despite the minimal differences between newborn boys and girls, parents treat infants differently depending upon their sex. The frequency of maternal and paternal behaviors directed toward the infant has even been investigated while the mother and child are still in the relatively neutral hospital environment. Fathers appear to be active participants, even in interactions with the newborn child. They are significantly more likely to hold and look at the infant than mothers and to provide physical and auditory stimulation (Parke, 1976). Only in smiling do mothers provide more stimulation than fathers. Interaction with the infant appears to be inhibited by the presence of the spouse. Mother–infant interaction in particular is much higher when the father is not present. The mother is less likely to hold, touch, rock, vocalize to, imitate, or feed her offspring when the father is present. Interestingly enough, parents' behaviors toward the infant when they are alone with it are much more similar than when they interact with it together.

These data may illustrate the mediating effects of social roles within the family even when the only representative of society is another member of the family. Nevertheless other studies also show that the father is an active participant in the socialization of young children. Fathers are unquestionably superior to strangers as elicitors of attachment, but second to mothers at all age levels—10 through 16 months—studied (Cohen & Campos, 1974). When both parents are present the infants approach their mother twice as often as they approach their father. When investigated with each parent alone, they travel to the mother in a shorter time and spend a greater portion of their time with the mother than with the father. The amount of eye contact they are willing to maintain with strangers is greater when the children are near their mothers than when they are near their fathers.

Specific maternal behaviors do not seem to produce or affect attachment behavior. Specific child-training practices associated with feeding or toilet training have not been found to be related to measures of attachment (Schaffer & Emerson, 1964). Whether the mother engages in a great deal of close physical contact with her child or a great deal of eye contact with him or her does not seem to be important. Even the mother's availability and the amount of maternal contact with the child do not appear to be significant factors. Infants seem to attach to adults who respond quickly to their demands and who seek interaction with them. When a relatively unstimulating mother who tends to avoid contact with her child except for routine physical care is combined with an attentive, stimulating father, the child is more likely to form an attachment with the father even though more actual time is spent with the mother.

As we will see later, fathers may be a primary source of their daughters' socialization. One of the reasons researchers may have found sex differences in socialization within the family to be so minimal is the virtual neglect of behaviors involving the father. "In some child development texts, more space is devoted to the infant's relationship to his [sic] toys than to his father" (Cohen & Campos, 1974, p. 146). Fathers as respondents in socialization studies are the focus in only 9 percent of the studies examined, while only 30 percent attempted to examine the socialization practices of both mothers and fathers (Maccoby & Jacklin, 1974). The socialization practices of mothers alone accounted for 49 percent of the studies; the remainder concerned themselves with the responses of teachers or other caretakers.

Sons and Daughters

There is so much in the psychological literature to indicate that sons and daughters are treated differently that it becomes difficult to avoid reiterating the obvious. Without making the request explicit, it is virtually impossible to get parents to provide a neuter environment with respect to sex. An anecdote in a recent child development textbook reveals the frustration of one experimenter who encountered this problem:

> One investigator who was studying sex differences in infancy and did not want her observers to know whether they were watching boys or girls complained that even in the first few days of life some infant girls were brought to the laboratory with pink bows tied to their wisps of hair or taped to their little bald heads. Later when another attempt at concealment of sex was made by asking mothers to dress their infants in overalls, girls appeared in pink and boys in blue overalls, and as the frustrated experimenter said, "Would you believe overalls with ruffles?" [Hetherington & Parke, 1975, pp. 354–355]

This example is somewhat unfair to the mothers, who were not informed that the infants' sex was to be concealed. It also does not illustrate the difficulty that can be encountered when one tries to purchase "unisex" infant's apparel. A psychologist of my acquaintance relates a chilling anecdote about how he and his wife were unable to purchase a woolen cap for their infant after they had overestimated the outdoor temperature. The only remaining caps at the shop were pink, and the proprietor refused to sell one to them for a boy.

Color coding of infants takes place even in the hospital nursery. And parents respond by differentially reacting to their daughters and sons. Within the hospital environment both mothers and fathers touch male newborns more than female newborns (Parke, 1976). Mothers do not make this sex distinction when they were alone with the infant. In the home environment, however, mothers look at and talk to their girl infants more than their boy infants from the third to the twelfth week of the infants' life (Lewis, 1972). During the first three months of life, but not thereafter, boys are touched, held, rocked, and kissed more than girls. After the age of 6 months girls are encouraged to touch and to remain near their mothers more than boys. When children are encouraged to move away (girls at a later age than boys), demands for more socially distant behavior are never as strict for girls as they are for boys. Even among adults same-sex touching is more acceptable for females than for males. Males are not permitted to touch each other except under conditions of great emotional consequence, such as the winning of a major sports event.

Although parents may explicitly deny any intention to distinguish between their sons and daughters, behavioral measures obtained without their awareness tell a different story. One such study graphically demonstrates how sex role socialization can take place without parental awareness. The furnishings and toys of 48 girls and 48 boys under the age of 6 were examined on the assumption that whatever differences were found would indicate parental ideology regarding sex appropriateness (Rheingold & Cook, 1975). It was assumed that children under 6 do not control much of their own toy selection. These children were from a highly selected, highly educated, relatively well-to-do university setting in which one might expect that sex role differentiation would be at a minimum. The investigators found that boys had been given more vehicles, educational art materials, sports equipment, toy animals, vehicle depots, machines, live animals, and military toys. Girls had been provided with more dolls, doll houses, and domestic toys. The rooms of boys were more frequently decorated with animal motifs, while those of girls were decorated with floral motifs, lace, fringes, and ruffles.

The effect of sex on toy selection was not significant for children aged one year or less but became increasingly significant with age. There were no sex differences in the number of books, musical objects, or stuffed animals present in the children's rooms. Boys, however, tended to have more toys than girls at every age. They were also provided with more toys of more different classes than girls were. Sex differences in certain classes of toys were particularly impressive. Summed over age, the number of vehicles for the 48 boys was 375 versus 17 for the 48 girls. No girl's room contained a wagon, boat, kiddie car, motorcycle, snowmobile, or trailer. Conversely, only 8 of the boys' rooms contained a female doll, compared to 41 of the girls' rooms. A majority of the girls' and boys' rooms contained male dolls, and there was no significant difference between them. Thus although both boys and girls were given male dolls, girls were provided with female and baby dolls much more often.

The results of this study indicate the extent to which boys are provided with objects that encourage activities directed away from the home—sports, cars, animals, and the military—while girls are given objects that encourage activities directed toward the home—keeping house and caring for children.

The Effect of Sex-Related Toy and Chore Selection

We do not know how important the role of sex specific toy and chore selection is in the development of sex-related personality patterns. It is intriguing, however, that girls are more frequently assigned tasks that involve domestic and child care responsibilities in other cultures besides our own (Whiting & Edwards, 1973). Boys are more frequently assigned chores that take them away from the immediate home and may involve the care and feeding of animals in association with other boys. These researchers also found that boys who have the task of caring for their younger siblings appear to be less aggressive in encounters with their peers than boys who do not have such responsibilities. Aggression may be generally incompatible with child care. One study done in Kenya found that boys who had to engage in "feminine" work in the home were less aggressive than boys who did "masculine" work (Ember, 1973).

The fantasy play of young children in our own culture appears to reflect sex differences in access to particular roles. Four-year-old girls spent 73 percent of their fantasy activities engaged in domestic activities, as opposed to 31 percent of the boys' fantasy play (Mathews, 1975). Boys modeled adult activities significantly more often than girls. Their fantasy play also took them away from the home more. Nearly 13 percent of the boys' play involved marching bands, parades, and fireworks displays (none of the girls' play was in these categories). Fantasies involving exotic themes such as witches and magic, adventure, spies, ghosts, and wild animals occupied 11 percent of the boys' fantasy time, in contrast to only 1 percent of the girls'.

The relationship between children's fantasy play and adult reality is not clear, but differential toy selection does give children different opportunities to rehearse adult roles. Girls aged 5 or 11 choose family dolls, domestic animals, and furniture as objects of play significantly more frequently than boys of comparable ages (Cramer & Hogan, 1975). The use of blocks to construct sidewalks, roads, buildings, towers, and the like is almost exclusively male. Findings on differential toy selection for children of different sexes emphasize the complete absence of objects of a particular class for one sex or the other. The absence of objects of a particular class prevents children from demonstrating an interest in that class of objects. Thus nurturance and domestic cares become the province of females while adventure and the construction of physical reality become the province of males. As we will see later, covert sex differentiation, as indicated by limited access to certain toys, is amplified by direct reinforcement of sex-specific play behaviors by parents and other caretaking adults.

The programing of children by means of sex-specific toys and games may be done largely without the awareness of the adults involved. In their large-scale study of the toys possessed by girls and boys, Rheingold and Cook (1975) found that almost all the parents involved endorsed sex role equality for their children. Differences in the way they furnish their children's environment may parallel other unconscious forms of sex role socialization:

> The many sex differences found in the contents of the rooms, therefore, do indeed qualify as evidence of differences in parental behavior. It is not parsimonious to assume that one set of principles guides their

behavior in providing their children one setting rather than another, one toy rather than another, and that different sets of principles guide other behaviors. It may therefore be concluded that the differences in how parents furnish the rooms of their boys and girls may well document differences in other classes of their behavior toward their sons and daughters. [Rheingold & Cook, 1975, p. 462]

This form of sex role socialization may also be a reflection of the ideology of other relevant adults such as aunts, uncles, and grandparents.

It may, in fact, be difficult for adults to choose toys that are contrary to societal assumptions about gender appropriateness. A recent study documents the difficulty a group of college students had in getting sales personnel to make nonsexist gift suggestions (Kutner & Levinson, 1978). One young male salesman's response to a request for suggestions for toys for a set of 5-year-old twins (one girl and one boy) who liked to play together was to get the girl a doll family and the boy a building set so that she could play with the dolls while he built the house in which the dolls could live!

Interactions Between the Sexes: Adults and Children

Males—and, in particular, fathers—may be more important agents of sex role socialization than females—or, more specifically, mothers. Fathers rate more behaviors as sex appropriate than mothers do, although both sexes place fewer restrictions on girls' behavior than on boys' (Fagot, 1974). More unmarried college-age men than women rated the behavior of children as young as 18 months of age as sex typed (Fagot, 1973). Roughhouse play, play with transportation toys, and aggressive behavior were characterized as masculine while play with dolls, dressing up, and looking in the mirror were characterized as feminine.

Using a standard instrument, the Child Rearing Practices Report, to collect data on samples of mothers, fathers, and children in six different countries (the United States, England, Finland, Norway, Sweden, and Denmark), Jeanne Block (1978) has reached certain conclusions about similarities and differences in parental child-rearing practices depending on sex. Those conclusions, which are summarized in Table 7.1, represent generalizations based on consensual agreement—cases in which the various participants in the family situation, each parent and the children, agreed on the particular socialization practice in question.

Both mothers and fathers appeared to emphasize achievement and competition more for sons than for daughters. They also encour-

Table 7.1 SUMMARY OF SOCIALIZATION PRACTICES OF MOTHERS AND FATHERS

1. There is evidence for differential socialization of males and females. Twenty-nine percent of the CRPR responses of mothers are significantly sex differentiated. For fathers, 24 percent of the CRPR items revealed significant differences between fathers of boys and fathers of girls.
2. There is evidence that differential socialization emphases of mothers and fathers are reinforcing in many areas; of the total of items showing significant differences, 40 percent show consistent and significant sex-related emphases for both parents.
3. There is evidence that sex differentiation in socialization emphases increases with the age of the child, reaching a maximum during the high school years. This trend is consistent in the data for both mothers and fathers.
4. There is evidence for differential socialization in young adults' perceptions of parental childrearing emphases. For the U.S. sample, 34 percent of the CRPR items describing maternal rearing practices significantly differentiated ($p < .05$) male and female responders. In terms of perceptions of fathers' socialization emphases by students in the United States, 36 percent of the CRPR items were significantly different for male and female responders.
5. There is evidence of cross-cultural continuities in the sex-related socialization patterns as reflected in students' perceptions of parental rearing practices. The data obtained from the student samples, which are both more homogenous within each country and comparable across countries (all college students), are, despite the differences among countries, relatively consistent, powerful, and coherent. Although the method of combining probabilities across the student samples are not applied to these data, it is to be noted that 23 percent of the CRPR items describing mothers yield differences across *three* or more of the six samples that are significant at or beyond the .10 level and are consistent in the direction of difference.

SOURCE: Adapted from J. H. Block, "Another Look at Sex Differentiation in the Socialization Behaviors of Mothers and Fathers," in J. Sherman and F. Denmark, eds., *Psychology of Women: Future Directions of Research* (New York: Psychological Dimensions, 1978).

aged their sons to control their expressions of emotion more than they encouraged their daughters to do so. Parents appear to use physical punishment more in controlling their sons and to emphasize their independence. Fathers appear to be more authoritarian in the rearing of their sons and are less tolerant of aggression directed toward themselves by them. Mothers encourage their sons to conform to external standards of conduct more than they encourage their daughters to do so.

Both parents appear to have a warmer and closer relationship with their daughters. They express greater confidence in their trustworthiness and truthfulness. They expect more "ladylike" behavior, discourage rough-and-tumble games, and expect their daughters to stay clean while playing. Fathers, but not mothers, seem to discourage aggression more in their daughters than in their sons. However, mothers restrict and supervise their daughters more than their sons. Parental warmth, which is an important feature of the mother–daughter relationship, is of even greater significance in the father–daughter one.

Although experimental studies have tended to be lacking in the area of socialization (probably because it is so difficult to set up a naturalistic yet controlled situation involving some form of social control by the parent of the child), fathers' and mothers' behaviors have been found to vary in response to one form of sex-typed behavior—dependency (Osofsky & O'Connell, 1972). The experimenters induced dependent or independent behavior in 4-year-old girls in the presence of the father or mother by giving them either a very easy puzzle (fostering independent behavior) or one that was very difficult to complete (making it likely that the child would seek help and advice from the parent). Unfortunately only girls were used as subjects, so we do not know the effect on parents of similar dependent or independent behaviors in boys.

Both parents interacted more with the child both physically and verbally, and showed more controlling behavior, when she acted in a dependent manner. Fathers were more action oriented; they either helped the child physically or, under some circumstances, withdrew completely. Mothers were less likely to either help the child immediately or leave her entirely on her own. Fathers, but not mothers, positively reinforced their daughters more when they were dependent than when they were independent. Under these laboratory conditions mothers were more likely to encourage independence in their daughters and to resist giving direct help. Despite the fact that the mothers' behavior would seem to reinforce task competence, the girls actually spent more time working on the puzzle with their fathers and more time talking to and seeking attention and support from their mothers. These data suggest that simple social-learning models of sex role socialization may be of limited value, since children receive different information from their fathers than from their mothers. Models of competent versus expressive behavior may be a larger source of information for children in developing their sex roles.

At best, information from the parents seems to be provided on an intermittent reinforcement schedule. In a study using sexually ambiguous children's voices as stimuli in a number of situations involving dependent and autonomous behavior, it was found that fathers were more permissive toward female children in all situations while mothers were more permissive toward male children (Rothbart & Maccoby, 1966). This kind of sex-by-sex interaction could provide some basis for some of the components of child–parent psychosexual attraction hypothesized by Freud. There is some evidence that the degree of sex typing that is regarded as appropriate by parents does affect the extent of sex-typed behavior in their opposite-sex children. A positive correlation has been found between scores for fathers' encouragement of sex typing and their daughters' adoption of behaviors that are stereotypically appropriate to females (Fling & Manosevitz, 1972). The correlation between mothers' encouragement of sex typing and their sons' adoption of male sex-typed behaviors was also positive and approached significance. Although the subject of gender and achievement will be discussed more extensively in Chapter 13, perhaps it should be pointed out here that women who achieve a great deal in nontraditional ways report themselves to have had a warm relationship with a supportive, accepting father and a less good relationship with a rather distant, hostile mother (Anderson, 1973).

VARIABLES AFFECTING SEX ROLE SOCIALIZATION

The Age of the Child

Just as the opposite-sex parent may be a more differentiating reinforcer (as well, perhaps, as a more desirable one) for the child, the forms of behavior that are reinforced probably vary with a wide range of other factors besides the sex of the parent and the child. Obviously, behaviors that are regarded as independent at one age might be regarded as dependent at a subsequent age. For example, riding a tricycle is independent at 4 and presumably dependent at 7 or 8. Sex-related behaviors in children, therefore, may show differences in time sequence rather than absolute differences in content or kind. Such sequential sex-related differences may tell us a great deal about how sex role socialization effects are mediated.

Developmental studies of sex roles using a variety of measures of preferences, adoption of particular aspects of sex roles, or identification with a specific sex role tend to reach the same conclusion. Girls, in general, are less rigidly sex typed than boys. Their degree of sex typing does increase with age, however, especially among working-class girls (Nadelman, 1974). In general, increases in stereotypy of preferences for items that are supposedly appropriate for members of one's own sex increased with age in both sexes, and the effect was greater for working-class children than for middle-class children.

Studies using vocational aspirations as a measure reach the same conclusion. While kindergarten girls state higher occupational aspirations than boys of the same age, this effect is reversed by the fifth grade (Brook, Whiteman, Peisach, & Deutsch, 1974). The change seems to be associated with gender-specific parental aspirations for children. Parents in this study had lower occupational aspirations for their daughters than for their sons. Sex differences in parents' aspirations for their children were particularly marked by the time the children had reached the fifth-grade level in school.

The kinds of control that parents exert upon children change with the child's age. Of particular interest in this context are reports of sex-specific socialization practices. These studies have to be interpreted cautiously, however, since they are largely based on self-report or retrospective data. Through the fourth grade, no sex differences in the perceptions of the parents have been reported. Toward adolescence, females report greater parental acceptance than males (Armentrout & Burger, 1972; Burger, Lamp, & Rogers, 1975), while males report greater control by parents than females and report their mothers as more controlling than their fathers. These data are consistent with those discussed earlier that suggest less rigid sex typing for females during childhood and the operation of major cross-sex child–parent interactions during the socialization process. We do not know, however, whether these effects are associated with sex role socialization in particular.

It could be argued that parental differences in socialization practices are a response to actual differences in the behavior of children of each sex. We discussed in Chapter 4 the minimal number of sex differences that appear to actually exist—especially during childhood. There is evidence, however, that parents do see behavioral differences in their children related to sex. The parents of 10-year-old children report behavioral effects consistent with those reported in studies of sex role stereotyping. Boys are reported as more vigorous, competitive, and quick tempered (Tuddenham, Brooks, & Milkovich, 1974). Girls are reported as neat, fussy, nurturant, noncompetitive, and sensitive. Even if these sex differences do not actually exist, if parents perceive them to exist and act accordingly, they could form the basis for sex differences in socialization.

If maleness does have more status in our society than femaleness, it is reasonable to assume that parents will be more concerned about appropriate sex typing of their sons than of their daughters. Sex differences involving the fear of potential sexual deviance—the "tomboy" versus the "sissy"—are too well known to be more than mentioned here. It may seem quite reasonable to many parents that daughters would prefer to play with and have preference for items belonging to males. These conjectures are consistent with data showing that over the past thirty-five years there has been a gradual shift in preference by females for what were formerly male toys or games (Rosenberg & Sutton-Smith, 1960). This shift represents not sex role convergence but expansion of aspects of the female role. Boys still do not show any greater preference for female play roles.

In sum, data on developmental trends suggest that pressures for appropriate sex typing increase with age—especially for boys. Mothers may be the major agents in the sex role socialization of their sons and are perceived by them as becoming more controlling as they grow older. Females are permitted more latitude in expression of sex role related preferences, although in another chapter we will consider how this changes at adolescence. Since the input from parents of different sexes is likely to be inconsistent, it appears that familial reinforcement of sex typing, at least for the middle class, is intermittent in nature. It is possible, however, that the greater rigidity in male sex typing is due in part to the greater contact between mothers and sons than between fathers and daughters.

Social Class

As mentioned in the preceding section, sex typing varies widely depending on the socioeconomic status of the respondents. Social class is a particularly difficult variable to evaluate psychologically, since it is confounded with educational level, ethnicity, location of the home, and the relationship between the family and society as a whole. Any of these variables (or others not mentioned) might be responsible for the effects of class. Thus class can be considered only as a kind of marker variable—pointing out that something is going on even if we do not know quite what. Social-class effects in sex role socialization are of interest, however, because they exist in great numbers. They point out the limits of considering sex mainly in terms of biological functions.

In sum, lower-class white children appear to be more sex typed than middle- or upper-class children (Nadelman, 1974). Boys of both classes show a more distinct and rigid sex role preference than comparable girls (Hall & Keith, 1964). The bulk of the data indicate that girls are less affected by socioeconomic status than boys are.

A considerable number of studies point out how social-class effects on sex role socialization may take place. Middle-class mothers were more likely to avoid using direct commands with their children and more likely to ask questions or use indirect commands (Zegiob & Forehand, 1975). Lower-class mothers used more direct commands and were more controlling. They appeared more likely to be uninvolved and uncooperative with their daughters. Middle-class fathers have been found to be significantly more nurturant of their sons than lower-class fathers (Jordan, Radin, & Epstein, 1975). No difference in paternal nurturance was found between middle-class and lower-class fathers of girls. Paternal nurturance was also more closely related to a specific characteristic of the boys—verbal intelligence—than to a specific characteristic of the girls. These data are consistent with the idea that less attention is paid to the specific behaviors of girls than to that of boys.

There may be an interaction between the age of the child and the effect of social class on her or his degree of sex typing. Brook and her associates (1974) found that whereas social-class differences in vocational aspirations were stronger among younger children, sex differences were stronger among older children. They suggest that two processes mediate occupational aspirations: an early familial identification and a later, more general acculturation. If they are correct and if these findings hold for other measures of sex typing, they may account for the relatively few studies showing sex differences in young children. What may be being measured is the degree of access to and influence by general societal "norms" about the relative functions and status of males and females.

One intriguing recent study points out that differences in values that change with the age of the children do exist between middle- and lower-class families of preadolescent and adolescent boys (Jacob, Fagin, Perry, & VanDyke, 1975). In this ingenious study the parents of either 11- or 16-year-old boys were asked to first discuss the proverb "A rolling stone gathers no moss" without their son present and then explain it to him. Each family's discussion was evaluated in terms of either a growth interpretation of the proverb (i.e., a positive value was attached to "rolling" and a negative value to "moss," with emphasis on development through mobility, exploration, or striving) or a stability interpretation (i.e., a negative value placed on "rolling" and a positive value on "moss," with emphasis on security through lasting relationships and perserverance as alternatives to rootlessness and lack of security). They found that the growth interpretation was overwhelmingly endorsed by all parents of 11-year-old boys whatever their social class. There were, however, class differences in the interpretations presented to adolescents. Lower-class parents endorsed the growth interpretation. Most upper-middle-class parents reversed this pattern (which had been used for preadolescent boys) and endorsed a stability interpretation.

This study emphasizes that sex roles do not exist in a social vacuum. For the lower middle class, mobility may be viewed as desirable. For upper-class parents, mobility in adolescent boys may be viewed as a threat to their value system. The possibilities of further achievement may seem small, and alternative life styles may be seen as a negative deviation. It would be interesting to see what sort of interpretations were made to adolescent and preadolescent girls, but unfortunately only families with sons were examined.

The relationship between sex roles and social threat is also apparent in the responses of adolescents to a large-scale survey of attitudes toward women's work role (Entwisle & Greenberger, 1972a). Boys were consistently more conservative than girls. Although, in general, adolescents with high IQs tended to be liberal, middle-class boys with high IQs were the least liberal of all the groups surveyed. The greatest difference between girls' and boys' views about women working outside the home occurred among middle-class white adolescents.

Race

In the study just discussed black adolescents were less opposed than whites to women working outside the home. Other studies have shown that black parents have more equivalent vocational aspirations for their sons and daughters than white parents have. In chapter 2 we discussed evidence that sex role stereotyping is less prevalent among black than among white college students or adults. It has also been shown that black males are somewhat more accepting of working wives and mothers than white males are (Axelson, 1970). These data suggest that sex roles are socialized in relation to social reality. Proportionately more married black women than white women work outside the home. In general, the economic status of even the middle-class black family requires two wage earners. Thus the sex roles of black males and females do not appear to be as differentiated, at least in terms of achievement, as those of middle-class white children are. Sex roles also reflect the models children see around them. It is interesting that while both black and white third-grade girls gave fewer sex-stereotyped responses to questions about adults than to questions about their peers, black girls gave less stereotyped responses to questions about adult roles than white girls did (Gold & St. Ange, 1974).

The conclusion that sex roles are related to expectations, which, in turn, are related to social realities, is not invalidated by findings that blacks, in general, perceive themselves to have less control over their environment than whites. Very often there are real external forces that may account for failure. It is notable that fifth-grade black girls were significantly more willing to take credit for their own successes than the standardization sample of middle-class white girls (Garrett & Willoughby, 1972). Among middle-class whites, boys with high IQs are also more willing to accept responsibility for success than girls with comparable IQs (Entwisle & Greenberger, 1972b). These data would seem to indicate that, although the probability of high achievement is limited for blacks in general, limitations are less rigidly stratified by sex than in white middle-class society.

Maternal Employment

While the effect of maternal employment on children will be discussed in Chapter 12, a few studies that show how parental characteristics affect children's sex roles should be discussed here. Kindergarten girls whose mothers are employed full time outside the home show a lower degree of sex typing in their perceptions and interests than the daughters of full-time homemakers (Miller, 1975). They seem to be more aggressive and less passive than other girls and are more likely to be rated by their teachers as boastful and attention seeking. However, the latter category includes behaviors such as speaking out of turn and making unnecessary noises, which could be regarded as assertive rather than aggressive. There was no difference between the groups of girls in self-esteem.

Among children from lower socioeconomic classes full-time employment of the mother has actually been shown to be a positive influence, possibly because the mother is able through her employment to provide material assets for the family (Woods, 1972). Unfortunately these studies seem to be limited to the effect of maternal employment on girls' sex role. We do not know what, if any, effects exist in terms of boys' sex role. Indirectly, there is evidence that maternal employment broadens perceptions of sex roles for both sexes. College students whose mothers are employed full time have been found to have fewer sex role stereotypes than those whose mothers are employed part time or work entirely within the home (Vogel et al., 1970).

Parental Characteristics in Relation to Theories of Socialization

It would be valuable if one could use all this information to test various theories of sex role socialization discussed in the preceding chapter. Unfortunately, few of these theories provide enough operational hypotheses or clear-cut definitions of processes to make testing possible. A few tentative conclusions may be reached. The cross-sex parent provides an important source of reinforcement for sex roles, but it is not clear that this is because of some kind of sexual attraction between parents and opposite-sex children or because reinforcement of sex roles is more consistent between family members of opposite sexes. Parental role models are also clearly important, but why the child chooses one parent over the other as a model is not clear. Probably some of the choice of sex roles is related to perceptions about the parent's relative success or status vis-à-vis the world outside the family. Thus black mothers would be emulated as frequently as black fathers. Social class would have less of an effect on the sex-related behaviors of girls, since their mothers' characteristics vary less in terms of social class than the characteristics of their fathers do.

It is also unclear whether sex role socialization is largely a product of differential reinforcement or whether it takes place mostly through overt and covert labeling. The physical as well as psychological environments provided for children of different sexes are different from the earliest age. Sex typing seems to be very much a matter of cognitive processes in terms of what is or is not deemed appropriate for that particular child. It is intriguing that sex typing increases with age and that Kohlberg and Zigler (1967) find a relationship between sex roles and IQ. Children with higher IQs advance through the various stages of sex role socialization more rapidly than those with lower IQs. These data may indicate that the parental environment does not radically change as the child matures but that her or his perceptions of it are altered. The role of the world outside the home in mediating such changes will be discussed in the next chapter.

Part of our problem in this area may be the willingness to make global judgments about the components of sex roles. For example, it has been found that Latin males have a more stereotyped view of feminine values than non-Latin males (Garcia & Dingman, 1975). They are also, however, more willing to touch or to hug each other than non-Latin males are. Which measure of sex typing we wish to view gives us a different outlook on cultural differences in sex typing in these groups. In other words, there is no necessary relationship between various measures of sex role socialization.

None of the various theories of sex role socialization concern themselves much about the properties of the child. Nevertheless parental pressures act on stimulus persons who possess individualizing characteristics other than sex. While these characteristics of the child may be stimuli for behaviors of others outside the family (and will be discussed as such in later chapters), evidence of differences in sex role socialization as a function of the properties of the child can tell us much about the process.

EFFECTS OF THE CHILD AS A STIMULUS ON PARENTAL SEX ROLE SOCIALIZATION

Birth Position

One of the areas in which sex differences in socialization have been repeatedly demonstrated is that of birth position. From the earliest years firstborn children—especially firstborn sons—are distinguished from their siblings. In the hospital setting fathers touched their firstborn sons more than either later-born boys or neonatal girls of any ordinal position (Parke, 1976). They talked to firstborn boys more than to firstborn girls. Mothers, either alone or in the company of the father, rocked boys more than girls. When the parents were together with the newborn infant, they were more likely to walk with a boy than with a girl, especially if the child was their firstborn.

On the other hand, firstborn females are nursed longer than firstborn males (Thoman, Leiderman, & Olson, 1972). They are talked to more by their mothers than their male counterparts. Fewer sex differences are found with later-born children. These data indicate that first and only boys and girls are probably subjected to more intense sex differentiation than later-born children. And there is consistent evidence that first and only boys and girls are more different from each other than later-born boys and girls are (Sutton-Smith & Rosenberg, 1970; Marks, 1972).

Intellectual Competence

There have been surprisingly few investigations of the effect of the intellectual ability of the child on his or her sex role socialization. Sharp class differences have been found in the relationship between IQ and masculine sex role preference in boys. Upper- and middle-class boys show a positive correlation between intelligence and preference for male-appropriate activities. Among lower-class boys, on the other hand, there is a significant negative association between IQ and preference for a masculine role (Radin, 1972). This effect may be due to such boys' ability to achieve success in the relatively feminine environment of the elementary school, but it may also reflect an unwillingness to model a father who has been relatively unsuccessful in terms of the standards of our society. Boys from families in which the father has been relatively unsuccessful and the mother is dominant within the home do show disruption of male sex role identification (Hetherington, 1965).

The same parental behaviors need not produce the same consequences in girls and boys. Girls' sex role identification is not disrupted in the mother-dominated home. On the other hand, the best predictor of intellectual competence in girls appears to be the social class of her father rather than his paternal nurturance, which is a better predictor of intellectual competence in boys (Jordan, Radin, & Epstein, 1975). Early maternal concern with achievement appears to facilitate boys' early IQ performance but has no effect on that of girls (Moss & Kagan, 1958). We have as yet no information, a priori, about what stimulus properties of the parent as well as of the child will be selected as intense focal points for sex role socialization.

Physical Attractiveness

Recent evidence indicates that the physical attractiveness of the child can mediate sex typing. The value of an attractive personal appearance is more frequently stressed for girls. A pattern of compliment giving has been noted such that girls are more frequently admired for their appearance than boys—especially when they wear dresses rather than pants (Joffe, 1971). Facial beauty is regarded as being more a property of females and young people than of other sex or age groups (Cross & Cross, 1971). Physical attractiveness also interacts with the way sex affects evaluations of children's performance.

Men and women viewed a videotaped interaction between an experimenter and a child who had been made to appear either attractive or unattractive (Dion, 1974). Later the same individuals watched this child perform a picture-matching task and administered penalties based on the child's performance on the task. The same pattern of correct and incorrect responses by the child was presented to all subjects. The subjects were requested to take from one to five pennies away from the child for each error. Female subjects took significantly more pennies from the unattractive boy than from the attractive one. However, they penalized the attractive girl more than the unattractive one. (See Table 7.2.) They did not differentiate between the children on a questionnaire requesting ratings of the child's personality, motivation, or innate ability.

The male subjects did not behaviorally distinguish between the children in terms of either sex or attractiveness. On the questionnaire, however, they showed a generally more positive attitude toward male children. They rated boys as more industrious, friendly, pleasant, and cooperative than girls.

In interactions with adult females attractiveness appears to be an asset for the male child but a liability for the female child. It is possible that attractiveness accentuates sex role expectations for involvement in different types of tasks. Attractive female children

Table 7.2 MEAN NUMBER OF PENNIES WITH-
DRAWN BY FEMALE SUBJECTS

	ATTRACTIVENESS OF CHILD	
SEX OF CHILD	UNATTRACTIVE	ATTRACTIVE
Male	27.80	20.40
Female	25.20	31.10

SOURCE: From K. K. Dion, "Children's Physical Attractiveness and Sex Determinants of Adult Punitiveness,"
Developmental Psychology, 1974, 10, 772–778. Copyright
1974 by the American Psychological Association.

may receive preferential treatment in tasks involving social rather
than cognitive skills. Competence in intellectual tasks may be considered less relevant to an attractive female. It is difficult to conjecture why physical attractiveness would be considered relevant for
an attractive boy. Nevertheless these data do indicate that attractiveness is perceived as somewhat incompatible with intellectual
achievement for girls. Yet girls are encouraged to maximize their
attractiveness.

Physical attractiveness does seem to potentiate the development of social skills by both males and females. More physically
attractive students were rated by their telephone partners as more
socially skillful and likable than less attractive counterparts
(Goldman & Lewis, 1977). It is possible that attractiveness fosters
the differentiation of sex-related personality characteristics by the
fact that it is considered more relevant for females. Parents may be
more willing to perceive females as attractive and to reward them
for "associated" traits. We have no particular evidence that physical
attractiveness mediates sex typing within the home, but we have no
particular reason to believe that it does not do so.

Size and Strength

In Chapter 5 we discussed physical differences in size and strength
as related to sex. It is possible that these differences mediate sex
typing by parents. One anecdote points out the way boys may receive cues about the value of physical strength:

> L. and N. have been arguing over the use of a spade. N. pushes L. and
> L. responds by delivering a solid punch to N's chest. A mother who has
> witnessed the scene says to the observer (within L's hearing), "Did
> you see the punch L. gave N.? He really can take care of himself like a
> man." [Joffe, 1971, p. 470]

Although parental preference for particular body builds in their
children has not been directly investigated, the clinical literature

reports numerous cases of parental concern with tallness in daughters or shortness in sons. In the former case parents have even been willing to subject their daughters to dangerous endocrine manipulation to prevent them from growing "too tall."

It is also not clear whether children's body build has an actual effect on their behaviors as opposed to how their behaviors are perceived by others. Some preliminary investigations in this regard (Unger, unpublished data) lead me to believe that sex-related personality characteristics are affected by body build. For example, boys with ectomorphic (relatively thin and muscleless structures) report the use of more aggressive physical tactics against their peers than mesomorphic (muscular) or endomorphic (fat) boys do. Mesomorphic boys and girls, on the other hand, showed fewer sex differences in power tactics than children in other body build groups. The lack of sex differences was produced by a relatively unexpected effect: Mesomorphic boys were less likely to use aggressive power tactics than other boys, whereas mesomorphic girls were more likely to do so than girls with other body builds. It is not clear how such effects might develop, but they are probably related to both the relative effectiveness with which a child gets her or his way with others and what those others (parents as well as peers) expect on the basis of the stimulus properties of the child.

METHODOLOGICAL ISSUES PECULIAR TO SEX ROLE SOCIALIZATION WITHIN THE FAMILY

Demand Characteristics and Observer Effects

One of the serious issues that have recently emerged in developmental psychology is the question of whether studies done in highly artificial laboratory situations are relevant to what actually happens in natural settings. Whether or not people are aware that they are being observed seems to be particularly important in matters involving sex and sex roles. There is some reason to believe that parents behave differently toward their children when they are being observed than when they are not aware that they are being observed. When a group of researchers observed mother–child interactions during which the mothers were either informed or not informed that they were being observed, they found that the mothers played with their children more, were more positive toward them verbally, and structured their children's activities more during informed observations than during uninformed observations (Zegiob, Arnold, & Forehand, 1975). Mothers were also more willing to use direct controlling techniques to get children to clean up a room during a free-play period (when they may not have been aware that they were observed) than during a period in which they had been requested to work with their children (Zegiob & Forehand, 1975). Lower-class mothers were particularly likely to be uninvolved or uncooperative with their daughters during free-play periods.

These findings indicate that we may be underestimating the extent of the negative aspects of parents' interactions with their children. Certainly children are more likely to be ignored by their mothers when they are unaware that they are being observed by another adult. Sex-asymmetrical effects are less likely to occur during conditions of observation, since our society is ideologically committed to a position of equality of treatment of individuals of any sex—especially children. Although many of the studies reviewed in this chapter indicate that in practice equal treatment does not exist, parents are more likely to try to conform to this ideological norm when they think they are being observed. It is also possible that one of the reasons that more sex-differentiating attitudes and behaviors seem to be found among adult males than among adult females is that the latter are more aware of their function as child socializers and are therefore more likely to attempt to demonstrate sex-blind socialization practices in a laboratory setting. This conjecture remains to be put to an empirical test.

Situational Factors

We must also take into account the fact that parent–child encounters usually take place within the home. Laboratory settings may alter customary responses. For example, it has been found that children protest less when their mother leaves them at home than in the laboratory and that they protest more in the home if she leaves through a door that she rarely uses than if she leaves via her accustomed exit (Littenburg, Tulkin, & Kagan, 1971). Mothers have been found to be less passively attentive and more directive toward their children in the home than in the laboratory (Moustakas, Sigel, & Schalock, 1956). Fathers express more emotion and mothers take a more active part in decision making in the home than in the laboratory (O'Rourke, 1963). It is possible that the laboratory setting makes social roles involving appropriate masculinity and femininity more salient, so that fathers will demonstrate more authority and mothers more nurturance than is usual in the home.

A Multiplicity of Measures

It is important to keep in mind that naturalistic systems such as the family involve a variety of nonverbal and verbal interactions between various participants. Communications involving sex roles (as with communications involving any familial behaviors) may often be contradictory, since they depend on the sex and role of the particular participants. Sex-related behaviors are probably also reinforced intermittently at best. We have no reason to believe that either parent or the children agree on what the socialization practices are within a family. Although this phenomenon does not appear to have been tested recently, an older study found that only 5 out of 24 possible parent–child correlations of socialization practices agreed sufficiently to be statistically significant (Helper, 1958). Similar intrafamilial differences have been found in self-evaluations of the degree of power possessed by various family members. Hence, the investigator's view of family socialization practices may be determined by which family member he or she asks about those practices.

What the experimenter asks or views also makes a difference. For example, Chicano mothers reported large sex differences between their children on nearly twice as many items as Oriental mothers reported (Tuddenham, Brooks, & Milkovich, 1974). We do not know whether these reported sex differences correspond to real differences in Chicano and Oriental children. Nonverbal measures also may not parallel verbal attitude measures. Touching, for example, is permitted to males with a Mediterranean or Latin American background, but these groups make great distinctions between male and female roles on attitude or stereotype questionnaires. Again, these data indicate that various measures of sex role socialization do not always converge. It is also possible that different measures have distinct implications for different ethnic groups even within the general American cultural framework.

The Role of Labels

One of the conceptual confusions that appears to exist in at least some theories of sex role development is the idea that sex role socialization will not have an effect until the child is in some sense aware of his or her own sex. We already know that sex-differentiating childrearing practices begin during the neonatal period. Children may already be conditioned to differential sex-related behaviors before they are aware that there are categories into which they are fitted. It should not be surprising (although it is perhaps chilling) that sex distinctions are present in children at the earliest age at which they are able to communicate them. The child's ability to make gender distinctions does not appear to be related to parental socialization practices (Thompson, 1975). It is more a matter of her or his ability to use language. By the time children are 3 years old they prefer objects and behaviors labeled as appropriate to members of their own sex over those labeled as sex inappropriate. They consistently choose "good" and same-sex objects. There is little difference between boys and girls in the development of concepts about their own and others' sex and gender.

These data suggest that sex differentiation may be more a social than a family matter. We are certainly never justified in the belief that a sex-blind environment exists at any time in a person's life. Children as young as 2 years of age can distinguish between photos of men and women, boys and girls. It is not possible to get them to understand the question before this age. One of the major functions of our socialization process may be not to create sex differences (which are minimal during these early years) but to focus attention on sex as a major cognitive variable. Thus in later years (as we will see in the following chapter) judgments about one's own characteristics as well as those of others cannot help being influenced by sex.

Chapter 8
Sex Role Socialization Outside The Home

Parental pressures for sex role socialization appear to be inconsistent and intermittent. Nevertheless information about appropriate gender labels and sex roles is conveyed slowly. Paralleling the relative ambiguity in sex typing by parents, young children show few consistent sex differences. However, sex differences emerge more consistently by the beginning of the school years and increase throughout adolescence and young adulthood. It is logical, therefore, to look for factors fostering sex typing that exist outside the parental environment. In this chapter we will concern ourselves with the role of peers in the development and maintenance of sex-related differences. Siblings will be viewed as peers, although their interactions take place within the home, because sibling interactions do not appear to be different from interactions between unrelated sets of children. We will consider the way children treat each other in terms of sex and other variables that relate to it. We will look at how sex affects the attributions people make about children's characteristics and behaviors. And finally we will consider how such attributions may be internalized to become gender roles or personality variables.

THE FAMILY AS A STATUS SYSTEM

Children's Perception of Family Structure

In Chapter 3 we discussed how relationships between the sexes could be viewed as status relationships. There is evidence that children view family roles in terms of such status relationships. For example, when boys and girls aged 6–10 were asked to pair statements that might be used in transactions between family members with stick figures portraying familial pairs such as mother–girl, father–boy, mother–father, or girl–boy, they assigned high-power actions to the adult and low-power actions to the child (Emmerich, 1961). (See Table 8.1 for a classification of statements according to relative power and a valence with respect to the other participants' goals.) All of the children assigned more high-power actions to the father figure than to the mother figure. The amount of power attributed to the father increased between the sixth and eighth years. Children did not discriminate between parents in terms of their role functions. The correspondence between younger and female members of the household in attributions of relative powerlessness is noteworthy.

Sibling roles are also perceived on a power dimension. Preadolescent children agreed that the older sibling was more powerful and that the younger sibling showed more resentment and appealed more to the parents for help (Sutton-Smith & Rosenberg, 1968). Most agreement was found on items indicating that firstborns were more bossy and that nonfirstborns engaged in the low-power tactics of going outside the dyad for help, crying, tale telling, and the like.

Table 8.1 CLASSIFICATION OF ITEMS ACCORDING TO RELATIVE POWER AND ATTITUDINAL DIRECTION

HIGH POWER	LOW POWER
POSITIVE ATTITUDE	
1. You can have it.	1. I want it.
2. That's nice. You did what I asked.	2. I'll do what you say.
3. You made that very well.	3. I made it very well.
4. You did what was right.	4. I'll do what is right.
NEGATIVE ATTITUDE	
1. You can't have it.	1. Give me what *I* want.
2. You'd better do as I say.	2. No. I won't do it.
3. You didn't make it very well.	3. I can't make it very well.
4. You did something that is wrong.	4. I'll do something that is wrong.

SOURCE: From W. Emmerich, "Family Role Concepts of Children Ages Six to Ten," *Child Development*, 32 (1961): 609–624. Copyright 1961 by the Society for Research in Child Development. Reprinted by permission.

Of the possible birth order–sex combinations investigated, only a boy with an older sister perceived himself and was perceived by others as not having to seek outside help. Such boys did not indicate the same degree of perceived powerlessness as children in other nonfirst categories. Unlike secondborn girls, these boys reported using bribery, blackmail, breaking things, taking things that did not belong to them, and making their older sibling feel guilty. Only the boy with an older sister did not report needing to seek help from parents, sulking, or pouting. The latter behaviors are considered to be procedures that are used by individuals with a low degree of social power.

Physical power tactics were reported as varying by sex as well as by sibling position. Beating up, belting and hitting, wrestling and chasing were ascribed to boys. Scratching, pinching, and tickling were ascribed to girls. The direct physical power of an older brother over his younger siblings of either sex apparently has a strong effect on them, since they are the only ones who report a high degree of getting angry, shouting, and yelling.

Studies involving retrospective self-reports always carry with them the danger of biases introduced by the subjects' desire to report themselves as behaving in a socially desirable and appropriate manner. However, even among children in kindergarten, secondborns perceive themselves as having less control over the outcomes of social interactions and as having to be more facilitating and agreeable about group goals than eldest children (Bigner, 1974). This study used high- and low-power statements involving goal facilitation or interference similar to those found in Table 8.1. The older sibling was consistently assigned high-power items and the younger one low-power items. Children who had an older male sibling assigned more high-power actions to older siblings than did children who had an older female sibling. Subjects with an older brother also assigned more goal interference actions to males than did those with an older sister. Discrimination of sibling roles by function did not occur, although the author had predicted this finding. At every age group tested—5–13—sex roles were discriminated in terms of a power dimension. Girls made use of this power dimension significantly more frequently than boys.

Children apparently learn about sex roles in terms of a power dimension through their own early experiences in the home environment. Only children made significantly more random assignments of high- and low-power items in terms of both sex and age. Their lack of understanding of the power dimension implicit in sex roles did not change as they grew older and engaged in more outside relationships, although children with siblings increased the amount of power and function attributed to the older sibling as they grew older. Attribution of greatest power to the male reached its peak among 9-year-old children. The ages of 5 through 9 may be particularly salient in the development of sex role concepts based on sibling interactions. Sutton-Smith and Rosenberg (1968) state that

> the accident of birth creates size and ability differences and these no less than size differences in lower species lead to the institution of a pecking order. We may assume the less powerful younger siblings will fight back with all the powers at their command. The younger brother's relative strength when he has only (sic!) an older sister to contend with may be taken as an illustration of this view. Usually, however, younger siblings seem to be content with the exercise of greater power outside their own sibling groups. [p. 70]

The family power structure probably affects other aspects of children's behavior besides the form of power tactics in which they engage. Firstborn males with female second siblings have higher self-esteem than those with male second siblings (Hollender, 1972). Self-esteem was generally lower in females than in males, but there was no differential effect of the sex of the second sibling for females. The effect of the male sibling probably extends beyond behaviors that seem to be directly linked with social power. For example, both male and female children who have an older male sibling show more masculine sex role preferences, as measured by the IT Scale, (a measure of sex role preference discussed in Chapter 6) than singleton children of the same sex (Bigner, 1972). Children with an older female sibling did not differ from singleton children of the same sex. In an extensive review of self-report data from children of many ages and sibling constellations (Sutton-Smith and Rosenberg, 1969), it is suggested that while both males and females may model an opposite-sex sibling in many sex role variables, only females model cognitive variables. These findings may indicate that in our society the male role possesses some reinforcing properties in its own right that may or may not be independent of the power dimension.

We have just summarized the evidence showing comparable power differentials between older and younger siblings and between the male and female sex roles. Where age and sex role conflict in terms of social power, the male sex role seems to take priority so that the younger male sibling has more social power relative to older female siblings than would be expected on the basis of age. The basis for these power hierarchies within the family appears to be the ability to use both physical and psychological power tactics effectively.

Family Status Carried into the Outside World

If peer relationships within the family have such an important influence on aspects of the masculine and feminine sex role, one would expect that children will carry evidence of their place in the power hierarchy with them when they enter the outside world. While birth order effects have been characterized as a phenomenon in search of an explanation (McGurk & Lewis, 1972), evidence of birth order–sex interactions is suggestive. One such study suggests that the interaction of siblings within the home may require later-born children—those with less power than their older siblings—to develop more effective interpersonal skills, with the result that they will be better liked by their peers (Miller & Maruyama, 1976). In this study 1750 grade school children in California were investigated by means of both friendship scales and observations of their play. Later-born children were, indeed, more popular than their early-born peers. Teacher ratings also indicated that later-born children possessed greater social skills. Later-born females were more popular than later-born males. Although we do not know the sex of their older siblings, such younger girls are likely to have to contend with both age-based and sex-based dominance hierarchies within the home. Since only children were not significantly different in popularity from oldest children, the research suggests that the greater popularity of later-born children is due to some positive quality that they possess rather than to the presumed negative social characteristics possessed by firstborns. It is suggestive that firstborns have been found to prefer a hierarchically structured world with unequal distribution of power between parties while later-borns feel more comfortable in a relatively ambiguous situation in which egalitarian interaction with peers is possible (Exner & Sutton-Smith, 1970).

An intriguing similarity between firstborn boys and later-born girls and between firstborn girls and later-born boys may exist. A few relevant findings will be cited here. Teachers rate firstborn females and later-born males as being significantly more strong willed than later-born females and firstborn males (Miller & Maruyama, 1976). There is a higher correlation between scores on a test designed to determine how well someone can manipulate others (Machiavellianism) and school grades for later-born males and firstborn females than for firstborn males and later-born females (Singer, 1964). One could argue that those who may be able to successfully challenge or be challenged within the family hierarchy are more likely to need to learn manipulative strategies than those who are able to use direct physical tactics (firstborn males) or those who have no chance at all (later-born females). Firstborn males and later-born females seem to be more likely to play alone during free play time in kindergarten than later-born males and firstborn females (Laosa & Brophy, 1972).

Although birth order effects become more confusing as one examines older children and/or adults, Sutton-Smith and Rosenberg (1970), in a book, *The Sibling,* devoted to analyzing the effect of familial structure on the individual, note that in two-child families the firstborn male and secondborn female and the firstborn female and secondborn male most closely resemble each other. They suggest that one source of this resemblance in families with opposite-sex children is the strong pressures toward "appropriate" sex role socialization of the eldest child. Hence, the older boy and girl will be the most "masculinized" and "feminized," respectively, and will be less like each other than any other sibling constellation.

At least one recent study shows a sex–birth order relationship in a sex-related personality characteristic consistent with the idea that important sex role socialization effects are affected by peer relationships within the family. Large numbers of undergraduates were interviewed the day after a major California earthquake (Hoyt & Raven, 1973). As would be expected from sex role data, males indicated less anxiety than females and reported that they had engaged in less affiliative behavior following the earthquake (they waited longer before speaking to someone if they were alone). However, firstborn females reported more anxiety than later-born females, whereas firstborn males reported less anxiety than other males. Firstborn males also reported giving more help after the quake. As we saw in Chapter 3, both anxiety and help giving may be related to status. It is difficult to see where sex–birth order differences could arise except by way of interpersonal relations within the family.

PEER GROUP RELATIONSHIPS AND SEX

Group Processes Outside the Home

In Chapter 4 we discussed sex differences in aggression. These appear to be among the most clear-cut of sex-related differences. They appear as early as social play begins—at age 2 or 2½ (Maccoby & Jacklin, 1974). Sex-related differences in aggression exist both in attenuated form, such as mock fighting and aggressive fantasies, and in more overt verbal and physical form. Here we will investigate the facilitation of aggression in males by means of the peer process.

While there is little difference between the ways little boys and girls react when alone in a situation, boys appear to be much more affected by the presence of peers than girls are. The presence of others increases the activity level of all the other boys in a group while having little effect on that of the girls (Maccoby & Jacklin, 1974). Four-year-old boys have been observed to be more aggressive toward their peers as well as toward adults (McGurk & Lewis, 1972). Girls seek more help from adults than from peers and are more obedient to adult instruction. Like girls, later-born children of either sex more often seek adult help and approval. Pairs of 4-year-old boys also play more with a novel toy than they do when alone (Rabinowitz, Moely, Finkel, & McClinton, 1975). Girls spent no more time playing with the toy together than alone.

By the time they reach school age, boys tend to play in large, rather hierarchically structured groups while girls tend to play in smaller groups of two or three. The existence of naturally occurring dominance hierarchies in young children is just beginning to be documented. One study asked children in nursery school through third grade, "Who is toughest?" Nursery school children often answered "me," but by the second and third grades about 70 percent of the children agreed on a dominance hierarchy (Edelson & Omark, 1973). Boys were nominated for the top 40 percent of the positions in the hierarchy, while girls were generally in the bottom 40 percent. Girls agreed with boys on these judgments of peer status, even though they supposedly had low rates of interaction with them at this stage.

In almost every mixed-sex dyad the boy was recognized as the most dominant individual by both children (Freedman, 1972). There was a larger percentage of agreement about boy–boy dyads than about girl–girl pairs. These data are consistent with the idea that dominance and power are more salient to male peer relationships than to female ones. The construction of dominance hierarchies seems to take place during the early school years. Although nursery school children were able to construct a tallness hierarchy and to understand what is meant by being "tough," they were unable to construct a dominance hierarchy. However, dominance hierarchies could be constructed by kindergarten age, and the percentage of agreement about who was dominant increased only slightly from kindergarten through fourth grade.

Other Measures of Peer Status

Social power is not the only dimension on which children order their peer relationships. There are several other dimensions that contribute to social status among children. These dimensions are conceptually distinct, although they may be empirically related. The two dimensions that have received the largest amount of attention are social acceptance or popularity and social or perceived competence. Peer popularity is usually measured in terms of "who likes whom." Such judgments, of course, do not have to be reciprocal. Perceived competence appears to be most validly measured by questions such as "Who is good at doing the things you do at school?" Although there may be a relationship between the child's actual abilities and how they are perceived by other children, actual and subjective competence are not the same thing. A summary of how measures of peer status differentiate children of both sexes as well as what characteristics appear to be more important for one sex or the other is informative. Peer status seems to be closely related to sex-related personality characteristics as well as to sex.

In general, anxious children are less popular with their same-sex peers than nonanxious children (Hill, 1963). Seeking emotional support from or dependence on adults also seems to be negatively related to social acceptance among preschoolers (Moore & Updegraff, 1964). The ability to adapt to the requirements of the group appears to be important for peer popularity at all ages (Moore, 1967). However, conformity with the requirements of the group appears to be more important for the social acceptance of girls than for that of boys (Hartup, 1970). This idea is also supported by the findings that few leaders of groups of children—those who are somewhat more free to violate group norms—are female.

Unfortunately, many studies of the correlates of peer popularity have been done on only one sex, so that we do not know what effect nonconformity in these areas would have on the popularity of members of the sex that was not investigated. Within these limitations, however, peer popularity appears to be related to the possession of stereotypically appropriate sex-related personality characteristics. Popularity and provoked physical aggression have been found to be positively related in fifth- and sixth-grade boys. Rejected male adolescents are characterized as pesty, noisy, conceited, silly—and effeminate—by their male peers (Feinberg, Smith, & Schmidt, 1958). On the other hand, popularity in preschool girls has been found to be associated with the ability to take another girl's viewpoint (Deutsch, 1974). Even as adults, males are expected to disclose less than females. Males who disclose a considerable amount of personal information to another male are liked less (Sermat, 1972).

In perceived competence as in social power, girls receive lower evaluations than boys. In a study involving judgments about one's own and others' ability to perform in a new, unstructured task, first-graders of both sexes rated 80 percent of their female classmates at the median or below, as opposed to 31 percent of their male classmates (Pollis & Doyle, 1972). Judgments about perceived competence were shared by the evaluated individual. There was a high significant correlation ($r = .62$) between the ratings of the group and the ratings children gave themselves. Actually, there was no real difference between boys and girls in task performance. Persistent tendencies to devalue the work of females, similar to the effects found in many studies of adults, have been found among children as young as 10 years of age (Etaugh & Brown, 1975).

Analysis of all the findings on relationships between various components of social status in children available at the time indicates that the correlation between social acceptance and perceived competence is .40; between acceptance and perceived social power, is .60; and between perceived competence and perceived social power, is .30 (Glidewell, Kantor, Smith, & Stringer, 1966). In other words, these relationships indicate that the social acceptance of a child is more closely related to social power than to relative competence. Since we have already seen that social power is more a property of males than of females, we should not be surprised if females are less popular as well.

Sex-Related Characteristics as Status-Related Characteristics

Since females disproportionately occupy the lower positions on status hierarchies among children (no matter how they are measured), it is likely that few of them will engage in behaviors that will alter their perceptions of themselves. For example, girls compete less than boys. When fourth- and fifth-graders compete in a bowling game, only the sharing behavior of boys is affected by manipulations of competition or perceived competence (McGuire & Thomas, 1975). Boys who received feedback that their performance was poorer than that of the child with whom they were asked to share their chips (to be exchanged for prizes later) were least generous. The sharing behavior of girls was unaffected by either competition or assumed competence. Boys, in general, shared significantly less than girls. The results for males seem to have been due to their concern about their potential status. The number of prizes won was dependent on the number of chips; thus relative performance could have become public knowledge at the end of the experiment.

Girls may compete less because they are already aware that their behaviors will not change their relative position among their peers or because competition is perceived as less relevant for them. These two statements may be equivalent. Sex-related personality characteristics may be closely related to expected social rewards for these characteristics. Such an interpretation could help explain sex-related differences in needs and motivations. Males have a higher need for achievement and power because their behaviors in these areas determine their relative social status. Females may have a higher need for affiliation because this is the only area in which they can compete fairly for status. As we have seen, judgments in these dimensions are not independent of each other. Nor, probably, do achievements needs conflict with affiliative ones. Sex-related differences in needs may exist only because sex-related differences in social rewards also exist.

Competition appears to be related to high self-esteem. Pairs of children with high self-esteem are more likely to be competitive than pairs in which only one child or neither child has a high self-concept (Vance & Richmond, 1975). We do not know whether competition produces high self-esteem or is a product of it. We do know, however, that competition appears to foster aggressiveness. Aggression is not viewed as a uniformly negative trait—at least in our society. In fact aggression appears to be rewarded by others and may be rewarding in itself. Although male children who are too highly aggressive are likely to be unpopular (McGuire, 1973), externalization of aggression is associated with positive peer evaluation, especially in lower-class males. Among both American and Guatemalan urban girls and boys, children who internalize aggression and insist on the frustrating situation tend to be rejected by their peers (Adinolfi, Watson, & Klein, 1973). Offering boys high rewards increases their aggression (Rocha & Rogers, 1976). Competition also increases their aggression. In fact among third- to fifth-grade boys winning a competition led to more aggression than losing one (Perry & Perry, 1976).

Aggression may offer intrinsic rewards in itself. We have seen that children who are successful in an aggressive encounter will tend to repeat it, whereas striking back reduces the number of attacks on the victim (Patterson, Littman, & Bricker, 1967). It can be argued (see Chapter 15) that our society fosters an unusual amount of competition and, hence, aggression. But, rewards for competition and aggression are withheld from females.

Males are more willing to use aggressive tactics than females. These tendencies can even outweigh the size advantage that an older sister has over her younger brother. Data from peer interactions both within and outside the family seem to indicate that the use of aggressive tactics among children may have been underestimated. Overt and covert aggression may be used to maintain the relative position of the sexes.

The use of verbal aggression, such as teasing, name calling, and other forms of derogation as they alter perceptions of oneself, has been relatively unexplored by psychologists. Girls are more likely to report being teased or called names than boys. Even as adults they are more subject to verbal denigration, as is indicated by the surveys of linguistic usage and humor cited in Chapter 2. When deceit of the subject was sanctioned by the experimenter, males were more likely to give false feedback to their partners than females, while females were the targets of false feedback significantly more often than males (Mathews & Cooper, 1976). Males lied to females more than was true of any other sex pairing.

Other sex differences in children too may reflect power differences between the sexes. Girls, in general, imitate others more readily than boys. It has been found that individuals of either sex who are low in competence or high in anxiety are more likely to imitate others (Akamatsu & Thelen, 1974). This imitation is particularly likely to occur in situations in which little information concerning appropriate or expected behavior is provided. Highly dependent individuals also model more closely (Geshuri, 1975). Geshuri suggests that the sex differences found in children of preschool age are due to the girls' having been trained to be more aware of the social sanctions that can follow noncompliance with social demands. Girls pay more attention to the cue function of the observed reward for imitation. Their selective attention seems to be mediated by dependency.

We should keep in mind that females may actually be more dependent than males in terms of the social context, for several reasons. They have learned that being liked is more important for them than for males; thus fear of social rejection is a stronger reinforcement for them. In addition, they have learned that males are a more frequent or more potent source of reinforcement. Masculine identification is associated with high self-esteem in females as well as in males (Sears, 1970). Furthermore, females occupy the bottom positions on status hierarchies and are more likely to be the recipients rather than the sources of rewards. Social acceptance, as a reinforcer, is less likely to be under a girl's or her female peers' control. In fact an earlier study showed that girls are significantly more conforming when they are threatened by social rejection than when they are not (Carrigan & Julian, 1966). This difference was not as large for boys.

Social Reality and Actual Reality

An older, but still interesting study attempted to relate children's interpersonal behavior within the classroom to various measures of their social status within the group (Zander & Van Egmond, 1958). Children in a number of classrooms ranging in level from the second to the fifth grade rated each other on perceived social power, attractiveness, academic ability, and ability to "threaten." These children were also put into standardized small problem-solving groups and observed. Finally, teacher evaluations of each child were obtained.

Social power was not highly correlated with actual intelligence in either sex. Boys and girls who were perceived to have high social power were also considered more attractive by their classmates, regardless of intelligence. Girls with greater power were seen as more academically able independently of their intelligence, while boys were described as able only if they were high in both intelligence and power. Boys, but not girls, with high social power were described as more threatening. There was very little difference in the behavior of girls based on their social power or intelligence. Boys, in general, made significantly more demands, made more attempts to influence their peers, and engaged in more aggressive acts. Girls did not display any type of behavior significantly more often than boys.

Boys who were low in both intelligence and power were the only males who were passive in their problem-solving groups. Low–low boys behaved very much like girls. The authors summarize their findings as follows:

> Girls who were high in power and intelligence were little different from those who were low in either of these qualities because, we believe, high social power and intelligence were not needed in order to be the nurturant, obedient or responsible persons required by society. Girls could fulfill these expectations regardless of the amount of power or intelligence they possessed. [Zander & Van Egmond, 1958, p. 266]

What should be stressed here is that individual capacities are unimportant in the fulfillment of the female role. Teachers were able to make fewer distinctions between girls than between boys. Only the higher male status left room for differences in personal achievement.

It should also be stressed that some of these differential perceptions of boys and girls by their peers were as relatively independent of degree of social influence as they were of actual competence. Zander and Van Egmond provided data on the number of influence attempts made within their problem-solving groups by boys and girls who varied in degree of intelligence and social power. The rank order of influence attempts clearly shows the relationship between achievement (social power and intelligence) and

Table 8.2 THE RELATIONSHIP BETWEEN THE TOTAL NUMBER OF INFLUENCE ATTEMPTS, THE PERCENTAGE OF SUCCESSFUL INFLUENCE ATTEMPTS, AND LEVEL OF INTELLIGENCE AND SOCIAL POWER IN BOYS AND GIRLS

GROUP	TOTAL INFLUENCE ATTEMPTS	PERCENT SUCCESSFUL
High intelligence, high power boys	25.55	61%
Low intelligence, high power boys	24.34	56%
High intelligence, low power boys	21.63	55%
High intelligence, high power girls	16.69	58%
Low intelligence, low power boys	16.00	49%
Low intelligence, high power girls	15.96	55%
High intelligence, low power girls	13.57	53%
Low intelligence, low power girls	13.49	41%

SOURCE: From A. Zander and E. Van Egmond, "Relationship of Intelligence and Social Power to the Interpersonal Behavior of Children," *Journal of Educational Psychology*, 1958, 49, 257–268. Copyright 1958 by the American Psychological Association. Reprinted by permission.

the behavior of boys and the lack of such a relationship for girls. (See Table 8.2.) It also shows that there is little relationship between attempted and successful influence attempts. For example, girls who were high in both intelligence and social power were more influential than any other group except comparable boys, yet they showed a smaller number of influence attempts than any male group except those who were low in both intelligence and social power. We are left with the unresolved question of what constitutes effective reinforcement of social power if it is not, as appears from this study, success in the use of one's power to influence.

Other studies have looked at the relationship between the perception of having particular characteristics and particular behaviors in the school environment. The perception of having low status—more than the fact of actually possessing characteristics that are detrimental to school performance—seems to be related to under-utilization of abilities and negative attitudes toward oneself and school (Schmuck, 1962, 1963). An interesting sex difference may exist in the status dimensions that are important for predicting behavior. The performance level of girls was more closely linked to their degree of peer acceptability, while that of the boys was more closely associated with their social power (Schmuck & Van Egmond, 1965). One could interpret this finding as indicating that girls are demoralized more by being disliked than by lacking influence, whereas the reverse is true for boys. These data could link sex differences in need for affiliation or need for power to socialization phenomena. In any case it is important to stress that perceived low status was a more effective predictor of classroom performance than an "actual" characteristic such as IQ.

PEER REINFORCEMENT PHENOMENA

One of the most important functions of groups as opposed to aggregates or conglomerations of individuals is the enforcement of group norms. Stable groups have a set of explicit or implicit norms that are shared by their members. One matter of great interest is how children inform each other about their place in the social framework. The way children reinforce each other for particular kinds of social behaviors is not well understood. One can argue that peer reinforcement phenomena among children are designed to maintain status relationships. Relative status may be measured by the ability of individuals in the group to apply sanctions to other members in cases of nonparticipation in or lack of compliance with group norms. We have some information on whether some individuals are more effective in enforcing group norms than others. Such individuals may be class leaders, are probably high in the dominance hierarchy, and of course are male.

There is considerable evidence that male children control various aspects of social interaction. For example, although both boys and girls (9-year-olds) in a YMCA summer camp were more willing to play with a sex-inappropriate toy after watching someone of their own sex do so, only boys rated the same-sex model as much more attractive than the opposite-sex one (Wolf, 1973). Boys appear to control the preference for same-sex rather than opposite-sex peers. Among fifth-graders, acceptance by girls of boys was positively associated with their acceptance by other boys (Reese, 1962). Although girls who were least accepted by other girls tended to be least accepted by boys, popularity with boys did not differ for girls who were moderately or highly popular with other girls.

Peer reinforcement effects have not been clearly related to the social behaviors of individual children. There is a high relationship between the giving and receiving of positive reinforcements (Charlesworth & Hartup, 1967). Children in nursery school who tended to reinforce a large number of their peers received reinforcement from many children. This is a correlational relationship. We do not know whether children give reinforcements because they are reinforced or vice versa. Boys participated in more give-and-take play in nursery school. Younger girls in particular were less likely to give affection to their peers than older girls or either group of boys. Social acceptance was significantly correlated with the frequency with which a child gave positive reinforcements, but children did not receive more negative reinforcements from disliked peers than from liked peers (Hartup, Glazer, & Charlesworth, 1967). In fact more positive than negative reinforcements were received from both liked and disliked peers.

A reinforcement may have different meanings for two individuals involved in a dyadic interaction. Patterson, Littman, and Bricker (1967) analyzed the behaviors of both the target and the aggressor in aggressive interactions in nursery school. When the target child responded by withdrawing, acquiescing, or crying, the attacker was likely to perform the same aggressive act toward the same victim in subsequent interactions. The victim's low power position appeared to function as a positive reinforcer for the aggressor. Initiators of aggressive encounters are likely to be successful if there is no adult intervention, and it has been estimated that most (as many as 80%) of aggressive incidents are not noticed or are ignored by nursery school staff (Smith & Green, 1975). Boys appeared to have a higher probability of being involved in aggressive encounters than girls, but there was no consistent evidence that adults intervene differentially in boy–boy, boy–girl, or girl–girl encounters.

Regardless of the age group studied, there is a marked tendency for boys to direct reinforcements to boys and girls to girls. In an extensive review of children's peer interactions Hartup (1970), a noted expert in the field, states that "the existence of a sex cleavage in children's peer relations is much too well known to require extensive comment here" (p. 396). Sociometric studies on children as young as 3 years of age provide evidence that children prefer same-sex peers to opposite-sex peers throughout early and middle childhood. This preference appears to reach a peak during preadolescence. There appears to be a relative deprivation of reinforcing stimuli from people of the opposite sex that extends from early in the preschool years (Stevenson, 1965).

Sex cleavage is defined by the frequency with which children have play contacts with same- versus opposite-sex children. Although boys overchoose boys as play companions and girls overchoose girls, sex cleavage is significantly more extreme for boys than for girls (McCandless & Hoyt, 1961). In an observational study of 4-year-old children, the investigators found that boys played with boys for a mean of 114.6 minutes (chance equaled 72.9) while girls played with girls for an average of 82.7 minutes (chance equaled 62.1). Charlesworth and Hartup (1967) also found that boys manifested more gender exclusivity than girls in terms of the number of reinforcements directed toward same- versus opposite-sex peers.

These data suggest that it is males who control the tendency toward same-sex cleavage found among school-age children. Such an interpretation is consistent with the finding that same-race cleavage is stronger among white children than among black children (Morland, 1966). A study done in the New York City area shortly after World War II found gentile children to be more exclusive in their friendship choices than Jewish children in a mixed-religion upper-class private-school setting (Harris & Watson, 1946). It is the group with the higher social status and, presumably, more command of the available resources and reinforcements that mediates in-group exclusivity.

A delightfully informal paper by Kevin Karkau (1974) on sexism in the fourth grade may give us some insights into the dynamics of sexual exclusivity. Karkau found during a period of student teaching in a nontraditional open classroom that boys and girls rarely associated with each other. They did not sit together. They formed two separate lines when they went to other rooms, although the teacher had never asked them to do so. The boys played soccer at recess while the girls skipped rope or played tag. In math lab they played separate math games. They teased each other when someone touched a member of the opposite sex. Although the regular teacher in this classroom did not discriminate on the basis of sex, there was also little encouragement of interactions with a member of the opposite sex.

An analysis of the form and content of teasing is most illuminating. An overemphasis on physical attraction was the main component. People seen talking to members of the opposite sex were said to be "in love" by the girls. Boys noted that touching a girl gave one "cooties" or "girl-touch"—a mysterious quality which could be removed only by saying "no gives." Everyone in the classroom believed privately that talking or touching a member of the opposite sex in itself meant nothing, but they were unable to disregard the group as long as verbal sanctions against interactions were maintained. Lest one think that this is an isolated or exaggerated example, my second-grade daughter, in a relatively structured classroom in an entirely different city, reported a similar phenomenon. While boys are more likely to tease girls, trip them, or chase them about the playground, a boy will run from a girl only if she threatens to kiss him. It is rather frightening to contemplate that a young girl's major source of physical threat to boys is her sexuality.

THE BIOSOCIAL MEDIATION OF STATUS/SEX CHARACTERISTICS

One of the most noteworthy aspects of group structures formed by children is that they develop so rapidly. It has been estimated that they form within a few weeks—perhaps in a few hours—within the elementary school classroom. Despite the rapidity with which they form, hierarchies of social power, perceived competence, and emotional acceptance (Lippitt & Gold, 1959), and patterns of dominance and submission in play (Gellert, 1961), when examined later in the school year show little change from initial peer position. The average correlations between the position at the beginning and at the end of the school year were between .70 and .80. The self-perceptions of children tended to correspond well with their ratings by peers.

Biosocial Bases of Status Hierarchies: Body Build

Since stable hierarchies are constructed so rapidly by children, it is likely that they are based, at least in part, on characteristics that are easily accessible to children. Sex, as opposed to gender, is an obvious cue. However, other cues that are sex related may also be important.

Body build is an obvious indicator of the ability to use force effectively. In the absence of observable handicaps, there is a low positive correlation between general physical fitness and social position in children (Glidewell et al., 1966). Popularity in boys has been correlated with strength and athletic skills (Clarke & Clarke, 1961) and with a mesomorphic body build (Clarke & Greene, 1963). Social adjustment has also been correlated with height in both sexes (Davie, 1972). Physically handicapped children, on the other hand, are significantly less popular with their peers (Centers & Centers, 1963).

There is evidence that children make different attributions based on body build. Boys in particular associate the mesomorph with an assertive, aggressive pattern, while ectomorphs are seen as socially submissive (Johnson & Staffieri, 1971). Both boys and girls would prefer to have mesomorphic body builds (Lerner & Korn, 1972; Staffieri, 1972).

It is not improbable that the body type of male children gives them a significant initial advantage. Later, direct physical force is not usually necessary to maintain status, covert manifestations will do as well. Covert nonverbal behaviors may provide a source of reinforcement for masculine dominance without the awareness of any of the participants. It is noteworthy that females find even verbal, nonphysical confrontations more anxiety provoking than males do (Frodi et al., 1977). Males, but not females, with high social power are seen as more threatening (Zander & Van Egmond, 1958). In fact all males may be seen as quite aggressive by females (Parrott & Saiia, 1972). Females prefer to respond to an aggressive confrontation initiated by another individual in a classroom by ignoring it; males prefer to verbally attack the attacker (Unger, DeMauro, & Imbrognio, unpublished).

Biosocial Bases of Status Hierarchies: Physical Attractiveness

While muscular body builds appear to confer status on males, what characteristics confer status on females? There is a surprising dearth of answers to this question. Most of the studies that can be found seem to indicate negative results (e.g., the expected variables did not relate to group or self-acceptance in females). Thus self-esteem has been found to be related to high masculine role identification for males, but no relationship was found between self-esteem and sex role identification for females (Connell & Johnson, 1970). The self-acceptance of boys seems to be related to their popularity with their peers, but no such relationship has been found for girls (Helper, 1958).

While self-esteem enhances performance in group situations, the relationship is a reciprocal one. Successful group performance also enhances self-esteem (Beker, 1960). It is possible that females are inconsistently reinforced by their peers—sometimes for adopting the male sex role with its properties associated with competence and power—and sometimes for conforming to the feminine stereotype. It is also possible, however, that females are primarily reinforced not for their behaviors but for their appearance. A major variable for understanding female development may be physical attractiveness. This variable fits some of the criteria we applied to body size and structure. It is easily accessible to the observer and subject to stereotypic attributions. Moreover, it may be deemed particularly appropriate for use with females since it requires them only to "be," not to do anything.

Over the past ten years researchers have shown that good-looking people have more social power. Adults are more easily influenced by physically attractive people, like them better, judge them to have more socially desirable personalities, and believe them more likely to be professionally and maritally successful. Beauty is also seen as more relevant to females than to males. (See Chapter 10 for more information in this area.)

Physical attractiveness is relevant to children as young as 3 years of age. They reliably discriminate between photographs of attractive and unattractive male and female peers (that is, attractive or unattractive by adult standards), and they do so in the same direction as adults (Dion, 1973). Attractive children are preferred as

potential friends. They are perceived as being more likely to behave in a socially responsible manner. Unattractive children are
disliked and are perceived as more likely to behave in antisocial
ways. Children make a greater distinction between attractive and
unattractive males than between corresponding females; however,
attractiveness seems to be equally desirable for boys and girls at this
preschool level.

Children also make sex-related personality attributions on the
basis of attractiveness. In general, 4- to 6-year-old children perceive
males to be more aggressive and "scary" than females (Dion &
Berscheid, 1974). Unattractive boys are considered the most aggressive, while attractive girls receive no nominations for aggression.
Unattractive females were named as being more generally fearful
than either unattractive male or attractive female counterparts. Attractive children are generally more popular than their unattractive
peers. Attractive males, however, are more popular than attractive
females.

Children in the fifth and eleventh grades continue to use physical attractiveness as a way of determining interpersonal acceptance
(Cavior & Dokecki, 1973). The importance of physical attractiveness
did not diminish relative to the length of time the person had been
known by the subjects. Academic performance contributed little to
peer popularity. Physical attractiveness accounted for most of the
variance for fifth-grade boys' ranking of girls and boys, for fifth-
grade girls' ranking of boys, and for eleventh-grade boys' ranking of
themselves in terms of popularity. Girls, on the other hand, considered their popularity to be based on the similarity of their attitudes
with those of the rest of the class at both age levels. For the girls
especially, there seems to be a discrepancy between the actual basis
of their social acceptability and what they perceive it to be. Attitude
and behavior seem to be less important than they perceive them to
be.

The physical attractiveness of a child is also a determinant of
adult behavior toward him or her. Teachers evaluated attractive
fifth-graders as more intelligent, more likely to progress further in
school, and more popular with their peers than their unattractive
counterparts (Clifford & Walster, 1973). College-age female subjects penalized an unattractive boy more than an attractive boy and
an attractive girl significantly more than an attractive boy (Dion,
1974). Attractiveness was an asset for the male child, but not for the
female child, in adult females' evaluation of their cognitive
performance.

The data on the effects of physical attractiveness on the peer
relationships of children are somewhat difficult to integrate. For

both sexes physical attractiveness is clearly an asset with peers. However, even among young children some sex-specific attributions seem to be associated with physical attractiveness or the lack of it. Unattractive boys are seen as more aggressive than their peers, and unattractive girls are seen as more fearful. Attractiveness in girls is associated with very low levels of perceived aggression. Since children prefer not to associate with unattractive children, their lack of knowledge about them may make them more likely targets for sex-typed attributions, especially negative ones. Since boys, in general, were more scary to preschoolers, it is possible that attributing lack of aggression to an attractive girl may be considered a compliment. However, a certain level of aggression is necessary for effective functioning in later life, and an attractive female will be penalized if she behaves as passively as others may expect her to do. She will be further handicapped if Dion's demonstration that attractive females are penalized relatively more in a task involving competence is found to be a more general phenomenon.

Relatively little experimental work has been done on the role of physical attractiveness in mediating an individual's behavior. By analogy with data on self-perceptions about social power, competence, and acceptance, we would expect children to have a fairly realistic view of their own attractiveness and to behave in accordance with this self-image. However, the only work in this area seems to have been done in the college classroom. Singer (1964) found that attractive women who were high in Machiavellianism tended to sit in the front of the room, where they could catch the eye of the (presumably male) instructor.

Physical attractiveness may function as a stimulus for the inhibition of aggression. We have already noted that children and females are seen as more attractive than adults and males. The physical basis for these judgments has not yet been explained. One recent suggestion is that the interocular distance is generally greater for females than for males (Haviland, 1976b). This phenomenon may have the effect of making the eyes appear larger and/or more salient. Individuals with such relatively large interocular distances are regarded as "cute"—an appellation that connotes helplessness as well as attractiveness. It is noteworthy that males have been found to be less willing to shock other males in a laboratory setting if the eyes of the victim have been made to appear larger through the use of drugs (Kidd, 1975). People are also less likely to make negative assumptions about attractive individuals. When subjects were asked to choose which of two differentially attractive photos was that of a person with epilepsy, 83 percent chose the less attractive one (Hansson & Duffield, 1976).

THE EFFECTS OF SCHOOL ON PEER RELATIONSHIPS

Children enter the school situation, the first point in development where they must remain members of a stable group of peers, already predisposed toward certain kinds of behavior on the basis of sex. Such predispositions probably emanate from a combination of personality variables, such as aggressiveness; biosocial factors, such as body build and physical attractiveness, and family social-learning history, such as successful use of physical tactics or a history of having them used upon oneself. Children make social judgments about the relative power, competence, and acceptability of others and themselves on the basis of these variables. Social hierarchies are rapidly set up and are relatively impervious to change. Unfortunately all the dimensions of these hierarchies tend to be asymmetrical with respect to sex—girls occupy a disproportionately large portion of the lower positions.

One may ask: What role do the adults in charge of the school situation—the teachers—play in modifying sex inequality in the classroom? Although contradictory data exist, there is evidence that teachers may play a role in fostering sex role inequality. Although female first- and second-grade teachers approved of dependent behaviors more than aggressive ones in a hypothetical child of either sex, dependent girls were liked significantly more than aggressive girls (Levitin & Chananie, 1972). The teachers did not differ in their liking of dependent versus aggressive boys. In a similar vein, when teachers read vignettes about a hypothetical 9-year-old child whose sex, but not behaviors, was varied, boys were generally rated as displaying more leadership, as more active, as more gregarious, and as more accepted by their peers than girls (Rotter, 1967). These data would seem to indicate that violation of sex role stereotypes would be more advantageous for girls than for boys, since masculine characteristics are more useful in later life. Nevertheless the teachers considered orderly, clean, and nondisruptive behavior as the preferred feminine model.

Observational studies of teacher behavior have shown that teachers may encourage dependent behavior in girls (Serbin, O'Leary, Kent, & Tonick, 1973). When the girls were physically close to the teacher, they received greater attention than boys who were close to the teacher. Teachers were more likely to respond to preschool boys when they were aggressive than to girls when they behaved that way. Loud reprimands were more likely to be used on boys. However, loud reprimands tended to maintain the disruptive behavior. Boys who participated in class activities were hugged more and given more detailed instruction than comparable girls.

Studies using a "sex-blind" analysis also indicate that teachers verbally interact more, verbally initiate more, and use more attentional utterances in speech with boys than with girls (Cherry, 1975) (Examples of attentional utterances are *hey, see, now, no, OK*, and the listener's name.) They used more verbal acknowledgments or agreements in speech with girls.

Sex role stereotypes appear to interfere with the teacher's ability to correctly evaluate the behavior of girls. In addition to the previously cited finding that teachers were able to distinguish among the characteristics of individual girls less well than among those of boys, it has been found that correlations between the teacher's ratings on initiation of activities, competence, expression of affection toward other children, and need for approval and the child's actual behavior were all positive for boys but all negative for girls (Staub, 1971). Teachers appear to be responding more to generalized judgments about sex-appropriate behaviors for girls than to such judgments for boys. In any case they appear to be paying little attention to individual differences in the girls' behavior. In fact these negative correlations would indicate that the teachers were actually misperceiving the behaviors of the girls.

INTERACTIONS BETWEEN CHILDREN AND SOCIETY

"Tomboyism"

Since maleness and/or male behaviors are more readily reinforced by both peers and teachers, it is not surprising that during childhood more girls than boys prefer aspects of the opposite sex's role. During childhood, being effective in one's relations appears to be more important than the risk of role-inappropriate behavior. The latitude of permitted behaviors, in this regard, is also much wider for girls than for boys. We have long known that there are many more tomboys than sissies. Even the terms convey different degrees of societal approbation. Tomboys are girls who wear jeans, climb trees, and play baseball. Sissies are defined by the absence of these activities, much the way more "feminine" girls are defined.

Tomboyism may be a more common and "normal" phenomenon than psychologists once believed. In one study involving a retrospective questionnaire given to female college students, junior high school students, and a sample of adult women contacted in a nearby shopping mall, more than half the women reported having been tomboys in childhood (Hyde & Rosenberg, 1974). The percentages ranged from 78 percent of those in a psychology of women course to

51 percent of randomly sampled adult women. Tomboyism seems to be characterized by positive preference for male attire, playmates, and games. Considering the status conferred by our society on maleness relative to femaleness, what is surprising is that so high a percentage of girls do not show such preferences.

What we lack in the research literature is the degree of peer approval conferred on tomboys versus more feminine girls. It is likely, given same-sex exclusivity, that more pressure to conform to appropriate sex roles comes from same-sex peers. If, however, males have more status in the peer hierarchy, tomboys who are accepted as even relatively low-ranking members of mostly male play groups will receive reinforcement for role-inappropriate behavior from the higher-status group. It is likely that the strength of social approval or sanction varies depending on its source.

Sex Roles and Self-Perceptions

It would be interesting to know whether tomboys grow up to be more assertive, effective individuals than girls who are strongly sex typed in preference even in childhood. Certainly the greater involvement of tomboys in athletic activities gives them more practice in competitive, aggressive roles. High affiliative, low-power "feminine" behaviors, on the other hand, may produce a kind of cyclic-feedback situation. Such behavior alters girls' perceptions of themselves; self-labeling increases the extent to which their behaviors diverge from those of males; this divergence fuels sex-different attributions by others, which further alter the ways in which girls view themselves. What may be important initially is not how children behave but what other people notice and reward. Thus both social-learning theory and cognitive-development theory may be partly correct. Social reinforcement may be important for the development of sex-related characteristics, but labeling determines what behaviors will be noticed. The self-labeling of characteristics as well as the attributions of others are of major importance. Self-attributions are particularly difficult for the researcher to define, since they are largely outside the awareness of the individual who holds them. Moreover, they may shift relatively easily in response to social demands.

Because of the social aspects of sex roles, I suspect that it is particularly easy for the researcher to get what he or she wants in this area. For example, it has been found that males observed by a male aggressed more than those observed by a female (Borden, 1975). When the male observer was removed from the situation, the subject's level of aggressiveness more closely matched that set by his opponent. That implicit assumptions about the "demands" of the observer were probably involved was demonstrated by a second experiment. Observers were disguised as members of organizations with explicit values about aggression (either aggressive or pacificist). When the observer with the presumed aggressive values left, subjects decreased their level of aggression. No such effect occurred following the departure of the pacificist observer. Such effects have tempted some to label the psychology of sex roles "the self-fulfilling prophecy."

Correlations between particular kinds of behavior and peer judgments do not tell us anything about causality. It may be just as reasonable to hypothesize that being well liked inspires one to certain behaviors as to hypothesize that those behaviors cause one to be well liked. The interactional nature of socialization phenomena has been omitted from most investigations. If a child is fortunate enough to be strong, well-built, healthy, intelligent, upper-middle class, white, and male, others are likely to respond positively to him. Although we know that there is a positive relationship between the giving and receiving of positive reinforcements, we do not know its causal direction. Perhaps some children are more socially accepted because they possess certain personality characteristics; perhaps they demonstrate such characteristics because they are socially accepted. It is not necessary that socially nonconforming children be rejected. Indifference, rather than active punishment, may be sufficient to control behavior. In any case approval by adults and peers increases self-esteem, self-evaluation, and the perception of control over one's life. Such children will engage in more attempts to control their environment and will probably succeed. Our major problem may be not that few of these children are female but that there are so few at all.

Chapter 9
Around Puberty: Biosocial Aspects of Gender

During the first ten or so years of life there are relatively few physical differences between males and females. This is also the period in which there are the fewest psychological differences between them. As children near puberty, a number of rather massive changes in body structure occur. These structural dimorphisms may be an important factor in increasing the number of psychological and behavioral differences between the sexes. In this chapter we will review what is known about the biological and physiological aspects of puberty. A major issue is whether these effects work directly by way of the central nervous system or via sociocultural patterns of self- and others' perceptions set off by these bodily events. Certain events, such as menstruation, will be discussed in this chapter even though they recur throughout a large part of the woman's lifetime. This is because the earliest psychological adjustments to a characteristic may tell us a great deal about how it continues to be viewed. Phenomena associated with menstruation also show us how the female body and its properties may come to provide a stimulus for expectations about major components of "feminine" behavior—in particular, attributions about inconsistency and instability.

STRUCTURAL DIMORPHISM BEFORE AND AT PUBERTY

Biological and Physical Differences in Childhood

Before adolescence boys are on the average a little stronger than girls (Harrison, Weiner, Tanner, & Barnicot, 1964). This statement does not imply that all boys are a little bit stronger than all girls, only that somewhat more muscularly built or mesomorphic boys than girls are to be found in a given population. From infancy on, males have a consistently higher basal metabolism (which is why they eat more) and proportionately larger hearts and lungs (Hutt, 1972). Size and strength differences between the sexes are usually attributed to the presence of androgen, a hormone that facilitates the production of muscular tissue, in males, but no androgens are found in children of either sex between birth and about 7 years of age (Tanner, 1969). After the age of 7 the adrenal glands manufacture a steadily increasing amount until just before puberty, when the amount of androgens in the bloodstream of both males and females is about one-third of the adult level. There is also a low, roughly constant excretion of estrogenic substances by boys and girls from age 3 to age 7; thereupon it rises in both sexes until adolescence. Hence, any hormonal influence on body structure, as on the nervous system, must be prenatal in origin.

Despite minor differences in bone and muscular structure throughout childhood, those who oppose mixed-sex team sports for children continue to fall back on structural mythologies. They "worry" about girls damaging breasts that aren't even there or having accidents that will call into question their virginity at some later date. It has also been suggested that it is harmful for boys and girls to become too familiar with each other's bodies. All of these arguments take the form of sexualizing heterosexual contacts. They also reduce the opportunities for girls to gain a sense of physical competence and to feel good about what their bodies can do. Institutional approval of same-sex exclusivity can only serve to confirm children's ideas about its appropriateness and eliminate opportunities for sexual mythologies to be disconfirmed. Thus while 60 percent of American girls under the age of 14 mention sports and physical activities as things to do with boys, about the same percentage think that a girl's physical appearance is crucial for her popularity with them (Douvan & Adelson, 1969). They have had little opportunity to explore other alternatives.

Sexual Dimorphism at Puberty

If children are sexually segregated before there are any major physical differences between them, how much more segregation can we expect when the physical and physiological changes associated with puberty begin to take place? A major sexual dimorphism in itself, and the cause of others, is the difference in the timing and relative rate of maturation of males and females. Females are ahead of males in skeletal ossification or "bone age" from fetal life onward (Tanner, 1969). This dimorphism is present in apes and monkeys as well as in rats and mice. It seems to be dependent on the possession of a Y chromosome, since XXY individuals resemble males in this respect while XOs resemble normal girls, at least until puberty.

The term *puberty* is actually a vague and ill-defined one. It refers to a period of rapid growth, changes in the muscle and fat composition of the body, as well as growth of secondary sex characteristics. Each of these events, as well as the sequence of events within each category, varies in timing and ultimate extent by individual as well as by sex. The term *adolescence* has a somewhat precarious social meaning, but it does represent a period of physical change during which the individual can neither be sure what will happen next nor know how permanent any particular development will be.

Some information about between- and within-sex changes at puberty are clear. Although the range of individual variation is large, puberty begins about two years earlier in girls than in boys. The average age at which the peak velocity of physical growth is attained—the so-called adolescent spurt—is about age 12 in well-nourished British girls and about age 14 in comparable boys (Tanner, 1969). The adolescent spurt of girls not only begins earlier but is somewhat less marked. It is at least partly under different hormonal control than growth during childhood. The amount of growth added during the spurt is to some extent independent of the amount of growth that has taken place before. This may add to children's uncertainty during this period, although only 25 percent of the variance in ultimate adult height is accounted for by differences in the adolescent growth apurt.

There are also changes in body composition during adolescence. Boys show a muscle spurt considerably larger than that of girls, while girls put on fat during this period. The increase in musculature is naturally accompanied by an increase in strength. However, the increase in strength per gram of muscle is disproportionately greater in males. This sex-specific difference in strength is believed to be due to the biochemical action of androgens within the muscle cells themselves. The male shoulders and chest develop more in puberty, probably in response to stimulation by testosterone. Stimulation by estrogen increases the width of the hips and pelvic outlet in females. Thus not only the size but the composition and configuration of the body diverge for males and females during puberty.

Researchers have tended to stress the development of secondary sex characteristics as an important component in understanding adolescence. A secondary sex characteristic may be defined as a structure related to reproduction that, while under the control of hormones, does not itself produce hormones. The gonads themselves also mature during puberty, but except in the case of the male testes this is not as obvious as the growth of more secondary characteristics. The sequence of events for males is fairly consistent. First the scrotum and testes become slightly enlarged while the skin of the scrotum is reddened and changed in texture. Later the penis begins to enlarge, with continued scrotal and testicular changes. Pubic hair begins to grow somewhat after penile growth begins, and axillary hair appears on the average two years after the beginning of pubic-hair growth. The growth of facial hair is a relatively late development. In about one-third of all boys studied, some breast enlargement occurs about midway through adolescence.

In girls, the development of the "breast bud" is usually the first sign of puberty. There is a large variation in the age at which this and subsequent events take place. Breast development can begin as early as 8 or as late as 13 years of age. Menarche, the first menstrual period and the most dramatic event in the sequence, is a late stage in the female pubertal sequence. It almost invariably occurs after the peak of the growth spurt. It does not actually signal the onset of ability to reproduce, since there is a year to a year-and-a-half of anovulatory cycles and adolescent sterility, which is found in apes and monkeys as well as in human females. There is no reliable information about a similar period of male sterility. The sequence of changes for females is as follows: breast bud stage (elevation of the breast and papilla as a small mound), further development of the breast and areola, growth of pubic hair, more breast development, and finally, menarche. As in males, axillary hair is a very late development. More important, the amount of breast development is highly variable for girls. Some never go beyond the early-adolescent development of others. Although the amount of breast tissue has no effect on the breast's ability to function during lactation, in our society it has a considerable effect on self- and opposite-sex evaluation of female attractiveness. A discussion of the social implications of breast development will follow, but it is important to remember that the breast size, like penis size, is often used as the single index of female or male sexuality.

The physical differences between men and women are largely due to differences in the timing and intensity of the adolescent spurt. Before it occurs, boys and girls differ in height only by some 2 percent; afterwards they differ by an average of about 8 percent. After adolescence boys are much stronger than girls. Even without taking into consideration changes in internal chemistry due to differential activity of the male and female gonads, it is not difficult to understand why adolescence is a period of great concern with the body. The body and sex-specific differences in its form may mediate a large number of behavioral differences between the sexes.

ADOLESCENT CONCERN WITH THE BODY

As mentioned earlier, there are wide variations in the timing and even the sequence of events during what is termed *puberty*. Young men and women may view such variations less benignly than the professional does. The total time to complete pubertal changes may vary from four to seven years, during which time asynchronies of various parts of the body may be present. The adolescent phase of growth is also unique because of its finality. Adolescents are confronted with the reality of permanent differences. Such differences may also become more noticeable.

It has been known for a long time that adolescents are concerned with physique. In a large-scale study of tenth-graders in a California high school, sex-specific concerns about physique were found, with girls expressing more concern than boys (Frazier & Lisonbee, 1950). Fifty-five percent of the girls expressed concern about their weight compared to 13 percent of the boys. The girls' concern focused on the heaviness of their hips, stomachs, and legs. Although most of the boys and girls thought of themselves as average in height, 49 percent of the girls who perceived themselves as tall expressed concern. Tall boys felt little concern. Although petiteness is supposedly a "feminine" characteristic, 22 percent of the girls who felt that they were short expressed concern about their height. Of course more boys (39%) who felt that they were short worried about it.

A "sex-appropriate" appearance seems to be particularly important to American adolescents. Their ideals of appearance may be quite unrealistic. Males are supposed to be tall, broad shouldered, barrel chested, and narrow-hipped, while females should be slender and busty. "Action-Jackson" and "Barbie" dolls epitomize these physical ideals to preadolescent children. While adolescent boys rarely worry about being tall, tallness bothers girls a great deal (Dwyer & Mayer, 1968). They worry about how they will look together with males, since the cultural ideal is for women to be shorter, Since the female adolescent growth spurt is about two years earlier than that of males, young women are forced to interact with chronologically older males in order to conform to the cultural ideal.

Weight is a more salient worry to adolescent females than height. Current cultural ideals for women, and to a lesser extent for men, link obesity with unattractiveness. Females are supposed to be thinner than males. A study that showed silhouette pictures of different body types to several hundred senior high school students in suburban Boston found that the more ectomorphic silhouette was considered overwhelmingly desirable for girls, whereas a mesomorphic silhouette was considered ideal for boys by a majority of both sexes (Dwyer & Mayer, 1968).

Disturbance over body fatness and overweight is much more widespread during adolescence for girls than for boys. In one high school 28 percent of the boys versus 48 percent of the girls interviewed felt they had a weight problem (Deisher & Mills, 1963). In a recent study of physical characteristics and attitudes toward weight among high school students (Dwyer, Feldman, & Mayer, 1967), about 60 percent of the girls had been on diets by the time they were seniors. Although there was a relationship between actual weight and dieting, 53 percent of those in the below-average fatness category and 27 percent of those in the lean category had been on diets. Lest we decide that their diets accounted for their low weight categories, the researchers found that although only 16 percent of the girls could be currently rated as obese and should have been on diets, 30 percent of the girls were on diets at the time of the study. Although 19 percent of the adolescent boys who were studied were obese, only 24 percent of the males interviewed had ever dieted and only 6 percent of them were currently dieting. The researchers (one of whom was Jean Mayer, a world-famous nutritionist) concluded that boys' weight standards are more in line with medical standards than girls' are.

Self-attributions about fatness also vary with sex. Adolescent girls who were obese perceived their overweight as due to their inability to eat less or to the sins of gluttony and sloth (Bullen, Monello, Cohen, & Mayer, 1963). In fact their obesity seems to be more a matter of an extremely low level of physical activity compared to nonobese girls. Adolescent girls also attribute their overweight to fatness, while boys often attribute it to bone and muscle and may even regard the excess weight as desirable (Huenemann,

Shaping, Hampton, & Mitchell, 1966). Overweight may be seen as a definite advantage in sports such as football and wrestling.

These perceptions may account for sex differences in attempts to lose weight. Girls with real or imaginary weight problems go on a diet; boys prefer increased exercise and activity (Dwyer & Mayer, 1968). Unfortunately musculature is not considered attractive in women and team sports are not considered appropriate adolescent female activities. Many schools have neither the personnel nor the facilities to foster activities that are currently considered appropriate for females (e.g., swimming, tennis, or gymnastics).

While boys seem not to be concerned enough about obesity, girls may be overconcerned. Part of the sex difference may be due to actual differences in the fat component in the female versus the male body. Thus the ideal female physique is further from the physiological norm than the ideal male physique. It is noteworthy that a disorder related to concern about weight—anorexia nervosa—is much more common among female adolescents than among males. The disorder seems most typically to appear early in puberty in a girl who is indeed somewhat overweight. At first her dieting is applauded by family and friends. However, even after she reaches normal and below-average weight she continues to decline food. The disorder is not manifested as a lack of hunger but combines bouts of ravenous appetite with fasting and even forced vomiting and elimination in order to remove the undesired food. Girls who are skeletal in their proportions may continue to perceive themselves as "just right" or even overweight. No one is clear about the etiology of the disease, although it may be associated with resistance to becoming a mature woman (Bruch, 1973). It is associated with delay in the onset of menstruation or discontinuation of menstruation in girls for whom it has already begun. In some ways one may consider this condition to be an exaggerated form of a common female concern. Bruch describes the effects of anorexia as a caricature of what will happen when the common recommendation that reducing will make you slim, beautiful, and happy is taken too literally. Although there are unusual factors in the family environment of girls who manifest the disorder, it may serve as an example of cultural factors causing pathology to take a particular form.

SELF-ACCEPTANCE AND ONE'S APPEARANCE

There is considerable evidence that girls' physical ideal is further from what they perceive to be true about themselves than it is for boys. Boys more often than girls rated their personal appearance as more desirable than that of their peers (Musa & Roach, 1973). More girls than boys rated their appearance as lower than that of their peers. Only 12 percent of the girls desired no change in their appearance. Changes in their weight and figure were more important to girls. Boys were more concerned with changes in their clothing and hair. Perhaps more important, while the researchers found no relationship between self-evaluation of appearance and measures of personal adjustment for boys, they did find such a relationship for girls. Of the girls who were evaluated as being in the low range of personal adjustment, 63 percent rated themselves as below their peers in personal appearance versus 21 percent of those in the high range of personal adjustment.

An exploration of self-concepts in boys and girls in the fourth, sixth, eighth, and tenth grades found that tenth-grade girls had much lower self-concept scores than any other comparison group (Bohan, 1973). Only young married men showed consistency between perceived self and ideal self in a majority of scales (Lyell, 1973). Adolescent males and females and young married women seemed to be equally dissatisfied with themselves, but adult men seem to be able to arrive at a considerable degree of positive self-esteem, which eludes women of all ages.

Dissatisfaction with appearance and the low self-image associated with such dissatisfaction may account for adolescent females' concern with proper attire. Ninth- and twelfth-graders given stories about hypothetical girls who violated the dress norms of the school by wearing mismatched separates, colored socks when white ones were called for or socks when nylons were called for, or expensive clothing with "messy" hair, indicated that they would reject such girls as members of their peer groups (Allen & Eicher, 1973). The most socially elite girls were the most rejecting.

The status of clothing and cosmetic fashions is determined independently of parental evaluation (Kernan, 1973). Younger girls who possess the largest number of "in" items are the most likely to behave independently of their mothers. "Biologically they may be their mothers' daughters; socially, however, they are the compliant shadow of older girls" (p. 349). Sex differences in the relationship between attire and appearance can, of course, be traced back to the earliest years of childhood, when girls are admired for their pretty clothes. Male attire tends to be relatively shapeless and can hide a multitude of "sins."

DEVELOPMENTAL MATURITY AND PEER EVALUATION

There is evidence that body structure affects developmental maturity. Fatness is associated with accelerated growth and advanced maturation in both sexes (Garn & Haskell, 1960). The age of puberty is markedly influenced by body build. The child with an endomorphic build—broad hips and relatively short legs—is likely to mature earlier than average, while ectomorphs mature later (Kraj-Cereck, 1956). In the past century the age of menarche has steadily decreased in the United States and Western Europe. There is reason to believe that this is due to increased nutrition. Menarche is not likely to occur until a critical weight is reached (Frisch & Revelle, 1971). Obviously, slim girls will be the last to reach the criterial weight, while obese girls will reach it faster. If indeed girls with anorexia nervosa are seeking to avoid womanhood, they are going about it the right way.

MENARCHE

By far the most dramatic difference between males and females during puberty is the onset of periodic bleeding. As pointed out earlier, the menarche marks neither the onset of feminine development nor its reproductive culmination. Nevertheless it is an event that is well marked physiologically but is neglected by both the culture generally and psychology specifically. In an attempt to determine the extent of psychology's interest in menstruation, I examined a number of books of readings in adolescent psychology. One might expect this field to be the one that is most concerned with an event which appears first during this time frame. No attempt was made to perform an all-inclusive examination of textbooks in this area. In fact the choice was random and consisted of five books published in 1960, 1969 (two books), 1971, and 1972 that happened to be available in my colleagues' offices when I requested textbooks on the subject of adolescent psychology. None of these volumes contained an article on menstruation in particular. There was, however, a paper by Judith K. Brown entitled "Female Initiation Rites: A Review of the Current Literature" written especially for the textbook *Issues in Adolescent Psychology* edited by Dorothy Rogers (1969). It is noteworthy that this paper concerns itself with the meaning of female pubertal rites in primitive (i.e., not like ours) societies. In fact the policy of "benign neglect" of issues particularly related to being female extends throughout the entire domain defined as adolescent psychology. Of the 158 articles in textbooks edited by males, eight papers were devoted exclusively to males (as indicated by their titles) versus one to females (about the female schizophrenic process). Only one of the books, which was edited by a women, contains articles dealing exclusively with females.

One must ask whether the lack of public discussion of the

menarche and menstruation mirrors actual disinterest in the subject. Do young women fail to react to the onset of such a dramatic periodic change in their bodies simply because we have no institutionalized rite to mark its passage? Or, on the contrary, does the very lack of communication on the subject increase the probability it will have psychological consequences?

Very few studies have examined when and how children learn about menstruation. One of the most extensive studies (Shipman, 1968) indicated that as many as 17 percent of the girls who responded to a questionnaire experienced the onset of their first menstrual period without understanding what was happening to them. This statistic is particularly chilling when one realizes that it is based on data from over 400 women in a university course on marriage. In other words, these were women who were presumably from a relatively high socioeconomic situation and intelligent enough to arrive in a college classroom. These women learned about menstruation from a variety of sources: 58 percent from their mothers or sisters, 23 percent from school and/or reading, and 18 percent from their peers. Whatever the source of information, it does not appear to be entirely accurate. Only 60 percent of female university students seem to be well informed about the facts of menstruation (McCreary-Juhasz, 1967). Information acquired from peers appears to be particularly poor.

Probably more important than the facts of menstruation are the attitudes communicated about it. If a topic is shrouded in secrecy and snickers, it is not surprising that some individuals find it frightening. Shipman found that 10 percent of his respondents reported that they had been shocked or frightened by their menarche. American women appear to be ambivalent about the onset of menstruation. About 50 percent reported being elated, thrilled, or gratified by the phenomenon. As we saw earlier, developmental maturity confers a certain amount of status on a girl. Nevertheless fewer than half the women claimed to have looked forward to menarche. Ten percent had developed negative ideas about it, while another 45 percent accepted it with indifference or resignation.

More dramatic than statistics are some descriptions by women of communications surrounding their first menstrual period (Maddux, 1975): "My mother told me never to tell anyone that I was menstruating . . . always to be careful to hide my tampons and anything else that might 'tell on me.' I really thought that I had done something wrong . . ." "I first mentioned the fact that I was bleeding from 'you know where' one night at the dinner table. I was sent to my room without supper and never mentioned it again until

I went to college and found out that everyone menstruated . . ."
Admittedly, these may be extreme reactions, but certainly there is
a lack of positive associations with menarche in the reminiscences
reported in the psychological literature. The only comparable feeling of fright reported in the literature for males is that occasioned by
the first nocturnal emission or ejaculation. This experience, however, rapidly takes on positive connotations of masculine potency.

HISTORICAL AND CURRENT IDEAS ABOUT MENSTRUATION

Most cultures, including our own, have menstrual taboos of varying
degrees of severity (Stephens, 1961). Until recently women were
believed to be in a particularly vulnerable condition during
menstruation. They were advised to avoid bathing or swimming.
Other superstitions involving menstruation that were prevalent include the belief that green plants would be blighted, milk or other
dairy products curdled, and wine soured by contact with a
menstruating woman, as well as other such "dangers" to living or
once-living things (Maddux, 1975). The similarity between the
characteristics of menstruating women and those of the witches of
traditional fairy tales is quite striking.

The Judeo-Christian tradition has also been responsible for
harsh judgments about menstruating women. It has been suggested
that one of the reasons that women were not permitted to be or-
dained as priests is that they would render the host "unclean" if
they offered mass during menstruation. A similar reason has been
suggested to underlie the former prohibition against women handling the sacred scrolls during Jewish ceremonies. Orthodox
Judaism is still more overt in its segregation of the bleeding woman.
Such women are not permitted to have sexual intercourse with their
husbands until a fixed number of days after bleeding has ceased and
they have been ritually cleansed. Actually, this religious injunction
makes no distinction between the menstruating women and one
who has any sort of "issue of blood." It is interesting that a higher
percentage of women who refrain from intercourse during
menstruation—a behavior that may be considered indicative of acceptance of the menstrual taboo—are found among Jewish and
Catholic women than among Protestant women (Paige, 1973).

A recent examination of American menstrual expressions (Ernster, 1975) graphically illustrates the negative character of this event
for members of our society. Besides collecting a large number of
euphemisms for menstruation (see Table 9.1), the largest class of
which were negative references, Ernster found differences in the

Table 9.1 MENSTRUAL EXPRESSIONS REPORTED BY AMERICAN WOMEN, GROUPED BY CATEGORY

1. Reference to a female visitor, friend, relative, or other person by proper name:
   Aunt Sylvia is visiting me.
   I just got Aunt Susie.
   Aunt Tilly is here.
   Granny's visit.
   I've got my friend.
   My friend is here.
   Mary Lou is visiting.
2. References to a male:
   I've got George.
   Herbie's over or Herbie's visiting.
   Charlie just came to the door.
   I'm going steady with George.
3. Time or cyclic references:
   It's that time again.
   My time of the moon.
   Time of the month.
   Period.
4. Negative references—to illness, inconvenience, distress:
   The curse.
   I've got the misery.
   Under the weather.
   To come sick.
   Being unwell.
   Lady troubles.
   A weeping womb.
   Bride's Barf.
   A tiger is stepping on my toes.
5. References to red or blood:
   Wearing red shoes today.
   Are you a cowboy or an Indian?
6. References to material used during menstruation:
   Ride the white horse.
   To ride the cotton pony.
   Mouse mattresses.
   Saddle blankets.
   Teddy bears.
7. References to nature:
   I'm having flowers.
   Do you have the flowers?
   Mother Nature's gift.
8. References to behavior:
   Off the (gym) floor.
   Observing.
9. Combinations of the above categories:
   Mr. Red (male and red).
   George Monthly (male and time).
   The moon is red (cyclic and red).
   Bloody scourge (blood and negative).
   The red plague (red and negative).
   Ride the horse with the red saddle (material and red).
   My Aunt Flo is coming from Redfield, Pennsylvania (female visitor, blood, and red).
   My aunt from Redwood City (female visitor and red).
   Aunt Flo is taking the slow train to Redlands (female visitor, blood, and red).
   Mother Nature paid me a visit (nature and female visitor).

SOURCE: From V. L. Ernster, "American Menstrual Expressions," *Sex Roles*, 1975, *1*, 3–13. Copyright 1975 by Plenum Press. Reprinted by permission.

kinds of terms used by men and women. While most women used terms like "the curse," more than half the male informants used variants of the term "on the rag." The men interpreted this expression as having deprecatory meaning. The phrase is said to imply lack of attractiveness in personality and even in looks. It is sometimes used by men to describe moodiness, easy anger, or irritability in other men. In one fraternity anyone who did not wish to be disturbed hung on his door a sign bearing the Greek letters O(omega) T(tau) R(rho) (Weideger, 1975).

While menarche may bring with it a sense of admission into adulthood, it also carries with it a dark side, a feeling of periodic uncleanness and unattractiveness. There is an implication of lack of control over one's body and psyche. It is noteworthy that a number of males, friends and partners of women who responded to a menstrual survey, gave condescending responses to the question "Did your attitude toward girls change when you knew about menstruation?" (Weideger, 1975). Their responses included remarks such as "I was glad I didn't have to put up with that and felt sorry for women because they did . . ." "It seemed strange—I didn't understand the physical reasons. I heard it was dirty . . ." "I thought it was messy and repulsive . . ." (p. 164). With male peers like these it is not surprising that women are at best ambivalent about menarche. Their ambivalence is perhaps best epitomized by this statement: "I expected to turn into a beautiful fairy princess—felt ugly when I did not" (p. 159).

MENSTRUATION: THE PHYSIOLOGICAL "TRUTHS"

It would be expected that a cyclic phenomenon such as menstruation should have produced a vast store of folklore, fantasies and superstitions, mingled with a few facts, throughout the course of recorded history. Prior to the eighteenth century, it was believed that menstruation was a device of nature for the periodic excretion of accumulated poisons in women, under the control of the lunar cycle (hence the term *menses*), and in some way essential for the survival of an early embryo. By observation of various animals in estrus, it was erroneously concluded that the production of an egg occured at the time of menstruation, and only as the result of a fruitful coitus. Many of these ancient beliefs are prevalent today among the people of under-developed countries and in the biologically uneducated populace of our own country. [Page, Villee, & Villee, 1972, p. 37]

This passage illustrates the confusion among menstruation, sexuality, and successful reproduction that is still common today. In many ways menstruation is a mysterious phenomenon even among

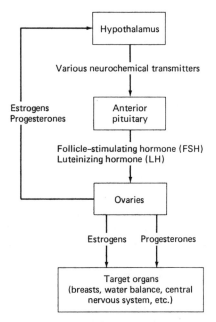

Figure 9.1. The negative-feedback system that controls the menstrual cycle. While more pituitary hormones produce more ovarian hormones, these hormones feed back to the pituitary via the hypothalamus and reduce the flow of ovarian-stimulating hormones.

adult women. Part of its mystery lies in the fact that it is a process that human females do not share with human males and that among other mammals is found only in higher primates. Nevertheless much of the physiological basis of menstruation is well understood and has been for a number of years.

Hormonal Control of the Menstrual Cycle

The ovarian cycle of mammals appears to be almost entirely under endogenous control; that is, it is regulated by the chemical consequences of previous stimulation. Physiologists know it as a negative-feedback system that can be understood largely in terms of the function of three structures: the hypothalamus, the pituitary gland, and the ovaries, with the chemical substances they secrete. (See Figure 9.1.) Under the goad of some still-unknown event, the hypothalamus causes the pituitary to secrete a critical amount of FSH (follicle-stimulating hormone). Although FSH circulates throughout the body by way of the bloodstream, like other endocrine hormones it is particularly likely to affect the parts of the body that contain structures that are sensitive to its chemical message. In the female body this structure, or target organ, is the ovary. Using a microscope one finds two major kinds of internal structures within the ovary—the egg follicle and the corpus luteum—that are actually different stages of the same structure. Under the initial stimulation by FSH one egg usually begins to mature within the human ovary. The level of estrogen, the hormone produced by ovarian cells, begins to rise, but nothing further would happen without the intervention of the other major pituitary gonadotropin, LH (luteinizing hormone). LH is secreted somewhat later in the cycle than FSH and may require a critical amount of FSH to be present in the bloodstream before it is released. It acts to complete the maturation of the egg follicle, which thereupon ruptures, releasing the egg into the passageway between the ovary and the uterus (Garcia, 1975a). The ruptured follicle is known as the corpus luteum and acts as a mini-endocrine gland on its own. Under the stimulation of FSH and LH it produces rising amounts of estrogens and progestogens. The mature and ruptured follicle also produces some androgen.

Estrogens and progestogens have a variety of effects on the female body. Estrogens promote tissue growth in the parts of the body considered illustrative of female secondary sex characteristics, such as the breasts and the pubic axillary hair. In addition, they stimulate growth of the endometrial lining of the uterus and secretion of cervical mucus. They also act on certain centers of bone growth so that the pelvic opening becomes wider under their stimulation. The progestogens mostly act to prepare the uterus for impending implantation by the fertilized egg. The best known of these substances is, of course, progesterone, which may also act to change the water balance within the body. Although the ovaries are the main source of gonadal hormones, estrogens, progestogens, and androgens are secreted by the adrenal glands of both males and females.

In addition to their effects on all parts of the body, the gonadal hormones "feed back" to the hypothalamus and regulate further production of gonadotrophic hormones. If no fertilized egg is deposited in the uterus, the corpus luteum begins to degenerate. As it degenerates, the levels of estrogens and progestogens in the bloodstream decline from their peak. They cease to support the increased vasculization and growth of the uterus that occurred in preparation for pregnancy. When chemical support reaches a sufficiently low level, menstruation, or the sloughing off of this unnecessary tissue, occurs. The relative low level of estrogens and progestogens in the bloodstream also serves as a signal to the hypothalamus to stimulate the production of more FSH, and a new cycle ensues. This is the negative-feedback aspect of the cycle—a low level of gonadal hormones produced by the target gland stimulates an increased production of the hormones (known as trophic or driving hormones) that trigger target gland activity. When target gland activity is at a high level, production of trophic hormone declines, producing the conditions that support the end of one cycle and the start of a new one. If fertilization does take place or if the hypothalamus is "fooled" into thinking it has, either by means of continued gonadal hormones being placed in the bloodstream by "the pill" or through the presence in the uterus of some object (i.e., an IUD), no rise in FSH takes place and the development of a new egg is delayed.

The menstrual cycle has been divided into several phases. The beginning of the cycle is known as the "follicular" phase and consists of the period during which the egg is beginning its development under the prompting of FSH. Estrogen production rises during this period, which encompasses the first fourteen or so days of the human cycle. (See Figure 9.2.) On or about the fourteenth day the egg follicle ruptures and ovulation is said to have taken place. However, it has been said that the only thing that is regular about the human menstrual cycle is its irregularity, so that these statements are only true for a majority of human females a majority of the time. As is well known, those who use the timing of ovulation as their only method of birth control have only slightly less probability of becoming pregnant than those who pay no attention to birth control at all. At the time of ovulation there is an unexplained rise in body temperature that persists until menstruation. This rise of temperature is an accurate barometer of ovulation, but as a method of birth control it is better suited for getting pregnant than avoiding it, since it takes place just about at ovulation and sperm can live for several days in the female body while "waiting for their opportunity."

After ovulation the female enters the "luteal" phase of the cycle. FSH production declines while LH production increases greatly. At about the twenty-fourth day of the cycle, for some unknown reason LH stops being secreted, progesterone production by the corpus luteum declines, and the uterine endometrium or lining having lost its hormonal support, sloughs off. Menstrual bleeding occurs when progesterone reaches its baseline level, but the levels of both estrogens and progesterone have begun to decline precipitously a few days earlier. (See Figure 9.2.) The period of rapid hormonal decrease is often called the premenstrual period, and the entire period of decline (dating from about the twenty-fourth day of the cycle) and menstrual bleeding (about eight days in all) is known

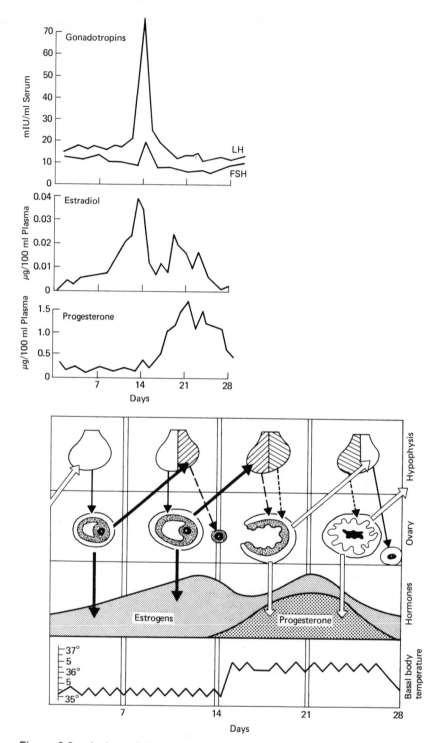

Figure 9.2. A view of the events of a single menstrual cycle. Note the changes in the ovary, in the levels of estrogens and progestogens, and in overall body temperature. Both estrogen and progesterone are at a low ebb when menstruation occurs.

as the paramenstruam. As can be seen from this physiological analysis, menstrual bleeding is a rather unimportant, albeit dramatic, concomitant of cyclic variations in hormonal production.

The Relationship Between the Menstrual and Estrus Cycles

For reasons that are not entirely clear, only human beings and the higher primates menstruate. Among the reasons suggested for this reproductive difference between primates and most other mammals is the relatively longer gestational period of primates and, thus, the greater need for preparation of the uterus. Most mammals do have a period of bleeding during the ovulatory cycle, but it is associated with the ovulatory phase. The behavior of female mammals changes during this period, and the whole phase is known as estrus or "heat." Females of many species, such as cats and dogs, will not accept the sexual advances of males except during this phase and, indeed, are not attractive to them except during this period. The coincidence of ovulation and maximal sexual attractiveness maximizes the probability of successful reproduction, especially for mammals that breed only seasonally. Humans and higher primates, however, are capable of responding sexually at all times of the year and during all phases of the reproductive cycle. In fact Mary Jane Sherfey (1972) has speculated that the development of the menstrual cycle represents an adaptation so that sexual activity can take place at any time. She suggests that the universal responsiveness of the female reinforces the continued presence of the male and his cooperation during the extended period of helplessness of infant primates. She suggests, in other words, that the menstrual cycle is responsible for the development of the family.

Although reproductive behavior in lower mammals is almost entirely dependent on hormones, this is decreasingly true as we ascend the phylogenetic scale (Beach, 1947). Experiential factors become increasingly more important, so that we find that even castration or ovariectomy in sexually experienced humans does not necessarily impair their sexual functioning (Ford & Beach, 1951). If there is any relationship between the menstruation cycle and human sexual activity, it seems to be opposite to that which would be predicted by the estrus cycle. Many more women reach their peak level of sexual arousal around the period of menstruation than during the ovulatory phase (Weideger, 1975). It is the androgens produced by the adrenal glands that affect sexual arousal in women, and production of this hormone also follows a monthly cycle that may or may not be in phase with the menstrual cycle (Money, 1961).

Adrenalectomy often abolishes sexual desire in women, whereas ovariectomy does not.

MENSTRUATION AND PSYCHOLOGY

The one aspect of menstruation that has received a considerable amount of attention from psychologists and psychiatrists is the study of the relationship between cyclic variations in personality and mood and various phases of the menstrual cycle. This area has been particularly subject to "masculinist" biases. For example, until very recently most of the material appeared in medical journals or those devoted to psychosomatic medicine, suggesting at the same time that menstrual changes were abnormal or pathological and that they had their origins in the female "mind." It was almost universally assumed that most women suffered from some of the vast number of negative changes ostensibly associated with menstruation. The level of awareness in the medical literature may be illustrated by the following quotation: ". . . woman's awareness of her inherent disabilities is thought to create added mental and in turn physical changes in the total body response and thus there result problems that concern the physician who must deal with them" (Abramson & Torghele, 1961, p. 223). Mary Parlee (1978) has amply documented the extent and hostile character of myths about menstrual symptomology that have been propagated in the professional literature. She points out that beliefs that women are more irritable, anxious, depressed, tense, and generally more irrational than men during the premenstrual and menstrual phases of the cycle have less scientific support than is generally implied.

Methodological Qualms

Much of the evidence supporting the changes in mood associated with the menstrual cycle has been gathered by means of self-report questionnaires. We have already discussed the way self-reports can generate information based on what people believe to be true about sex-specific characteristics. Few attempts have been made to disguise the nature of the questionnaire. In fact one of the most widely used procedures, the menstrual-distress questionnaire developed by Moos (1968), asks women to rate the severity of their symptoms for both their most recent cycle and the worst cycle they can remember. Even with such an instrument the percentage of women reporting symptomology and the form of the symptoms vary widely.

Premenstrual syndrome is reported by from 25 to 100 percent of subjects. Although most subjects report depression as a common symptom, a small minority report the opposite effect—bursts of energy.

Parlee (1974) has found that when women are asked to report the kind of symptoms and mood changes that women in general experience, they show the same pattern of responses as when they report about themselves. Thus they may be reporting on culturally determined stereotyped information about menstrual symptomology rather than on biologically determined symptoms in their own bodies. There is no convincing evidence that menstrual symptomology is the same in all cultures—as it should be if it is primarily a biologically determined phenomenon. In fact there is little research in this crucial area at all. One review of cross-cultural data on premenstrual tension symptoms (Janiger, Riffenberg, & Kersh, 1972), however, suggests the contrary relationship. Women in different cultures report different constellations of symptoms as the nucleus of a "premenstrual syndrome."

Symptomology is rarely found in a majority of women respondents in any study. There also appears to be a relationship between the personality of the respondent and the number of symptoms noted. There seems to be a high correlation between premenstrual symptoms and neuroticism (Coppen & Kessel, 1963). Women who complain of premenstrual irritability are also more irritable at other times. Recent studies, to be discussed shortly, suggest that some and possibly all women "use" the menstrual cycle to explain bad moods or physical symptoms that are present at other times as well.

A few studies (Gottschalk, Kaplan, Gleser, & Winget, 1962; Ivey & Bardwick, 1968; Paige, 1971) have used less obvious methods to study fluctuations of mood during the menstrual cycle. Their technique involves having women speak for a few minutes on a relatively unstructured topic such as "any memorable life experience." The same women are interviewed during the ovulatory and premenstrual phases of the cycle and may be followed over more than one cycle. Their interviews are scored for manifestations of hostility and anxiety by scorers who are unaware of what phase of the cycle the interview represents. This method seems to show that particular psychological themes are associated with different phases of the cycle. During the ovulatory phase women stress self-satisfaction, competence, and positive feelings toward themselves and others. During the premenstrual phase the same women manifest hostility, anxiety, and depression. Themes of death and mutilation appear frequently during this phase (Ivey & Bardwick, 1968).

A More Social Interpretation of Menstrual Effects

Although these studies offer evidence that mood fluctuates during the menstrual cycle so that negative affect is generally greater just before menstruation than during midcycle, these results should be interpreted cautiously. First, in all of these studies the subjects were aware that they were participating in an examination of menstrual effects. Repeated sampling of the same individuals could also increase the likelihood of their responding in culturally appropriate ways. More important, these studies show nothing about cause-and-effect relationships. Mood changes can be affected by hormonal fluctuations, but they can just as easily be affected by the social implications of body change. There is ample information available to show that blood and periodic bleeding is considered an unpleasant and unattractive characteristic by our culture. Why should women not "welcome" the arrival of such an "unclean" period with depression and hostility?

An extremely interesting study by Karen Paige (1971) provides some evidence that menstrual mood changes are at least partially a product of socially mediated negative attitudes toward bleeding and blood. Paige examined fluctuations of mood in women who were using a variety of different chemical contraceptives containing varying amounts and proportions of estrogen and progesterone. (The type of pill used to some extent controls the degree of menstrual bleeding.) She found that when she contrasted light and heavy bleeders on natural cycles as well as on different hormonal combinations the degree of menstrual bleeding was more closely correlated to the level of premenstrual anxiety than the chemical state of the bloodstream at that time. She suggests that such anxiety may be generated by the need to conceal the fact that one is bleeding and the accompanying degree of psychological and physical restriction this involves. Heavy bleeders are also more likely to restrict their sexual activity at this time than are those who bleed more lightly.

Premenstrual hostility, on the other hand, may be more closely related to metabolic changes within the individual. Paige found that users of a combination contraceptive (which maintains high levels of both estrogen and progesterone throughout the menstrual cycle) did not show cyclic variations in affect similar to those found for women on natural cycles. Their level of hostility, however, was constantly higher than that of women on natural cycles except during the latter's premenstrual phase. Users of sequential contraceptives (15 days of estrogen and followed by 5 days of estrogen and progesterone) showed cycles of affect similar to the natural cycle, except to a much lesser extent.

Fluctuations in hostility may be related to fluctuations in the amount of monoamine oxidase (MAO) present in the body during different phases of the menstrual cycle. MAO fluctuations have been associated with affective changes in emotional disorders similar to those experienced by menstruating women (Luce, 1970). It is also responsible for changes in the distribution of water and salts within the body. Estrogen appears to inhibit the production of MAO, while progesterone increases it. Users of combination contraceptives that have larger amounts of progesterone than sequential contraceptives also have higher MAO levels. The amount of MAO present seems to be correlated to the amount of hostility manifested, whether the increase in progesterone that induces it is endogenous (due to the natural sequence of the menstrual cycle) or exogenous (fed into the bloodstream by one of the chemical contraceptive agents).

We should also be cautious, however, in interpreting these data as evidence of direct chemical causation of hostility in women. Changes in water and salt balance cause changes in the puffiness of tissues and in actual and preceived weight. Every woman who has ever been on a diet (i.e., the majority of women) has noted a rise of several pounds in body weight shortly before and during the premenstrual period. Tissues are also particularly inelastic and may appear flabby during this period. Weight is a very salient characteristic for women, and most are ready to "overperceive" it. Overweight is considered to have very unattractive consequences in terms of heterosexual interpersonal relationships and may have provided a covert cause for hostility in the young college women who were studied. Change in weight may also receive negative conditioning because of its association with the menstrual cycle and may, in part, mediate females' differential sensitivity in this area compared to that of males.

MENSTRUATION AND BEHAVIOR

Other studies have concentrated on the statistical analysis of fluctuations in instances of particular kinds of behavior pathologies in women with the various phases of the menstrual cycle. The eight days of the paramenstruam account for between 45 and 50 percent of the following behaviors among females: admissions to hospitals for acute psychiatric illness or for acute medical surgical problems; violent crimes committed by prisoners; absences due to illness as reported by industrial employees; reports of accidents requiring emergency room treatment (Dalton, 1969). By chance, one would expect 25 percent of these events to occur during this period. Calls involving suicide threats also rise during the menstrual and premenstrual phases of the cycle (Mandell & Mandell, 1967).

Some data suggest that changes in the likelihood of certain kinds of behavior with the menstrual cycle may not be a direct result of acceptance of cultural stereotypes about menstrual symptomology. For example, mothers are more likely to bring their children to a hospital clinic for a relatively minor illness during the paramenstruam than during the midcyle phase (Dalton, 1966). Presumably the mother is unaware of the relationship of the menstrual cycle to her judgments about her child's condition. Rather, her threshold of tolerance is lower during this period and she is more likely to regard the child's condition as serious.

Fluctuations in ability to concentrate have often been cited as responsible for the premenstrual rise in accident rate, as have changes in the ability to react to frustration in accounting for rises in illness, suicide attempts, acts of aggression, and so forth. Periodic chemical instabilities that could influence judgment are often used as a sexist argument in support of the claim that women are not suited to important positions. As Estelle Ramey (1973) has so succinctly put it, "The Devil can quote endocrinology as well as scripture" (p. 237). Although some studies have found evidence of variation in schoolgirls' weekly grades that correlate with phases of the menstrual cycle (Dalton, 1960), the most recent studies (Golub, 1976) find no evidence of fluctuations in intellectual functioning associated with fluctuations in anxiety and depression. Although Golub's subjects were significantly more depressed and anxious premenstrually, their mood change did not impair their cognitive performance. No impairment was found even among subjects who complained of premenstrual difficulties with concentration and performance. These results are consistent with those of Sommer (1973), who suggests that studies that use a subjective measure of behavioral decrement during the premenstrual period are much more likely to demonstrate effects than those that use actual behavioral measures. In other words, women are likely to report their erroneous beliefs even if they don't act on them.

RECENT DEVELOPMENTS IN RESEARCH ON THE MENSTRUAL CYCLE

There has been a recent surge of interest in the psychological concomitants of the menstrual cycle on the part of feminist-oriented researchers. One recent development has been the use of a male "control group." Use of such a group minimizes several methodological weaknesses shared by many of the earlier studies (Parlee, 1973): (1) Subjects are not as likely to be aware that the study is on menstruation and therefore will not rate themselves in accordance with cultural stereotypes. (2) The relative incidence of similar symptomology in a nonmenstruating population can be ascertained. Recent studies have also been reluctant to rely on reminiscence, with its possibility of confusion and exaggeration of symptoms.

The results of menstrual studies using males as a control provide quite different information from that generated by more traditional studies. For example, males are reported to have a somewhat more stable but less pleasant existence than females (Schrader, Wilcoxon, & Sherif, 1975). In daily self-reports they report less positive mood than females, but the frequency of pleasant activities actually engaged in was the same for both sexes. Women experienced changes in pain and water retention associated with the menstrual cycle, but variance in negative mood was accounted for more by their experience of stressful events than by cycle phase. In another study (Garcia, 1975b) a checklist of 18 symptoms or feelings was administered to a large sample of men and women. After subjects had reported on their symptoms, Garcia requested information on the phase of the menstrual cycle and whether the women were using oral contrceptives or not. She found only three significant differences between men and women on a natural cycle. Women reported a higher incidence of cramps, irritability, and numbness of hands than men, but only during the menstrual, rather than the premenstrual, phase of the cycle. It is also interesting to note that the mean incidence of cramps in men is higher than that found among women in midcycle. Moreover, subjects were more likely to attribute their psychological and physiological state to fluctuation of environmental events rather than to the menstrual cycle. Few subjects spontaneously mentioned menstruation as a possible source of their behavior. Women's self-ratings of mood may be more closely related to the day of the week than to the phase of the menstrual cycle (Rossi, 1974).

ATTRIBUTION AND THE MENSTRUAL CYCLE

A few recent studies have used social-psychological theory regarding attributions about the causes of one's own behavior to explain fluctuations of mood during the menstrual cycle. Without going into great detail about attribution theory (about which several books have been written), one of its major points is that people explain their behavior in terms of internal or external sources of control. For example, in one delightfully informal social-psychological study it was found that people who salt their food before eating it explain the behavior in terms of their own personality characteristics ("I like my food salty"), while those who salt it after tasting explain it in terms of external circumstances ("It isn't salty enough" (McGee & Snyder, 1975). The tendency to make internal or external attributions seems to extend beyond the circumstances in which the original behavior was measured. Attribution theory in relation to sex-specific behavior will be discussed more extensively in the chapter on achievement (Chapter 13); however, it has recently been applied to further the understanding of behavior associated with the menstrual cycle.

A group of male and female college students were given information about a hypothetical female student in which the phase of the menstrual cycle (pre- versus postmenstrual) she was in, her mood (positive vs. negative), and the state of her environment (pleasant vs. unpleasant) were varied (Koeske & Koeske, 1975). Subjects were requested to assess mood, personality, and the sources of her behavior (divided 100% among the various categories). Biology was judged important for explaining negative moods that occurred premenstrually. Personality was viewed as being more influential in producing postmenstrual moods. These attributions were made by both women and men. In a sense women are excused for vagaries in their personalities that cannot be accounted for by environmental circumstances when they are entering the menstrual phase of their cycle. Such attributions were used to explain negative but not positive moods. They could enhance negative psychological states associated with menstruation, since they are excusable. At the same time, they could decrease women's self-esteem, since the mood changes are not deemed to be under their control.

It remains to be shown that attributions about the changes associated with the menstrual cycle are used by women to alter their own behavior. In a theoretically interesting, although methodologically complicated, study it has been found that menstruating women who indicated that they had a high level of menstrual symptoms performed better on intellectual tasks following arousal (they were told that the tasks measured ability and that some of the tests would involve electric shocks) than those who had reported a milder level of menstrual symptomology (Rodin, 1976). Arousal had no effect on cognitive performance at midcycle. It has been suggested that women who have a salient and credible attribution for their physiological state may be more capable of avoiding the effects of that state than those who cannot find such a reason for their performance. Predictability may benefit performance either by directly reducing perceived stress or by making individuals work harder in order to overcome an expected decrement in performance. In any case these findings suggest that performance variation due to the menstrual cycle cannot be used to bolster the view that women are less capable than men.

Research on attribution theory and behaviors that previously were regarded as mediated by biological processes has just begun. They indicate that attributions about the negative correlates of menstruation may be used either to enhance or to impair performance, depending on circumstances. The relationship between the severity of menstrual symptomology and behavioral pathology may not be as simple or as one-sided as we once believed. Some suggestive data have been reported in this regard. Women who complained about premenstrual symptoms were less likely to commit suicide during the premenstrual week than those who did not complain (Tonks, Rack, & Rose, 1968). Perhaps the ability to blame one's depression on biology makes it less overwhelmingly threatening than if a source such as personal instability or overpowering situational demands is perceived.

THE MYTH OF FEMALE INSTABILITY

The presumed psychological fluctuations of the menstrual cycle have been used to serve a political purpose—to justify a preferred pattern of social roles for females and males. Women are presumed to be unfit for executive responsibilities because of their susceptibility to "raging hormonal influences." As yet, no major psychological or behavioral effects of raging hormones has been demonstrated on an individual basis. Nor have the biosocial components of affective fluctuations correlated with the menstrual cycle been properly investigated. Theories about the effect of women's reproductive biochemistry on their nonreproductive functions also contain two important fallacies: (1) Statements about hormonal influences imply that biochemical cyclicity associated with menstruation is the only place where biochemistry can produce important psychological effects. (2) Only females show cyclic variations in biochemistry.

Other Human Cycles

Until the late 1940s most endocrinologists assumed that the male body is basically stable and that its normal state is one of constancy

(Unger, 1975). During the 1950s and 1960s, however, it was found that healthy men on a regular sleep schedule show a regular rise and fall of adrenal hormone levels in their blood and urine (Halberg, 1969). This cycle occurred every 24 hours. Twenty-four-hour cycles in various chemical and behavioral measures have been found in virtually every animal and plant species studied. They are called *circadian* rhythms from the Latin *circa dies,* meaning "around a day." It is thought that they represent biological effects due to evolution in a world that changes on a 24-hour cycle. It has been suggested that an organism that is physiologically tuned to the 24-hour oscillation of the planet will have a greater survival value than one that isn't.

Among the measures that show circadian rhythms in humans of both sexes are body temperature, pulse rate, respiration rate, and urine flow rate (Unger, 1975). In rats, clotting time and levels of gamma globulin, the blood fraction that contains a large number of immune antibodies, have been found to fluctuate according to a circadian rhythm. One of the most interesting frontiers of modern medicine is the attempt to determine the relationship between the stresses of illness and operation, the effect of varying dosages of medication, and life or death itself, and the ebb and flow of these circadian tides (Luce, 1970).

Cyclic variations in the release of adrenal hormones appear to be most closely related to mood change. Depressed males show a higher amplitude of change in daily adrenal rhythm than either normal males or females (Curtis, Fogel, McEvoy, & Zarate, 1966). Normal women show a flatter curve than normal men, while depressed women show the least amount of circadian variation. Another study showed phase differences in adrenal rhythms between depressed and healthy people. Healthy people had a peak in the excretions of one of the adrenal hormones around midday; depressed people had their peak excretion in the late afternoon.

The monthly cycle of women may have less conspicuous counterparts in men. Until recently little research had been done in this area, although Luce (1970) notes that Sanctorius, a seventeenth-century physician, weighed healthy men over long periods of time and discovered a monthly weight fluctuation of one to two pounds. Hersey (1931) reported from a year-long study on twenty-five industrial workers who were intellectually and physically normal that long-term variations in mood were characteristic of males as well as females. The men rated themselves daily on an emotional scale and showed mood variations typically ranging from four to nine weeks in periodicity. One young man showed a four- to five-week cycle with a variance no greater than that of the menstrual cycle. During low periods he was indifferent and apathetic at work and at home, and temporarily abandoned his art work. Recently Japanese scientists have reported some success in averting industrial accidents by giving men days off during the period they calculate to be the low point of their mood cycle (Ramey, 1972); however, the male scientific establishment has shown little interest in this work.

It appears likely that rhythmicity is in fact the norm in biological and psychological phenomena. A rhythmic phenomenon associated with sex hormone fluctuation in males has recently been reported (Doering, Brodie, Kraemer, Becker, & Hamburg, 1974). Cyclic variation with an average periodicity of 20 to 22 days has been found in the level of plasma testosterone of 12 of the 20 male subjects studied. The researchers also believe they have found variations in self-perceived mood correlated with these fluctuations in testosterone level. Other researchers have found a relationship between hostility and the amount of testosterone in the bloodstream of healthy young men, although their study examined individual differences rather than variations within an individual (Persky, Smith, & Basu, 1971). The amount of testosterone present is also related to rank in the dominance hierarchy in many primates (Johnson, 1972).

These data are not meant to demonstrate the chemical inconstancy of men or the biological determination of mood states. However, they should serve to put the menstrual cycle in its proper perspective along with the many biological cycles that affect the lives of all of us, male or female. An important unexplored area of research is to determine the relative influence of these various cycles on a given behavior (Parlee, 1978). For example, we have now discussed daily, weekly, and monthly rhythms. Which of these is more important in terms of fluctuation of mood, concentration, or intellectual performance? Is it necessary that the same rhythm contribute equally to all behaviors?

"The Pill" and Biochemical Causality

Considering the large number of American women using birth control pills containing large amounts of synthetic estrogens and progesterones, one could expect large numbers of studies on their psychological effects. After all, here is a chance to see the "raging hormones" in action! Surprisingly, there have been relatively few studies on either the medical or the psychological sequels to ingestion of artificial sex hormones. We have already noted that less cycling of affect but a heightened level of hostility may be involved. Progesterone has been linked to this change in negative affect. Depression has also been linked with pill usage (Kane, Lipton, Krall, & Obrist,

1970; Vaughan, 1970). The two states may in some way be associated with each other. Depression is sometimes considered to result from an inability to express anger. Since aggression is not socially sanctioned for women, it would not be surprising if they converted their hostile feelings into depression.

It is interesting that progesterone, the chemical substance that is considered primarily responsible for this negative affect, is structurally closely related to testosterone, the male hormone associated with aggression. There is some indication that the body can convert one substance into the other rather easily (Page et al., 1972). Thus even biochemical research would indicate that women and men are less different than was previously believed. The role of labeling of biochemically "caused" states also should not be underestimated. One study, for example, has investigated the effect of progesterone in males. There was no significant change in their mood scale during the week of drug dosage, but four of the six men studied spontaneously volunteered the information that they had felt terribly tired on the weekend following progesterone withdrawal, although they did not know the reason (Little, Matta, & Zahn, 1974). The men did not know at what point during the study they would receive progesterone or what its effects would be. These data may indicate that while hormonal factors contribute to our physiological and psychological condition, the way we label this condition may depend on other societal and environmental factors.

THE SOCIAL NATURE OF MENSTRUAL PHENOMENA

The menstrual periods of girls living together in a college dormitory have been found to become synchronized among individuals who have much contact with each other—friends or roommates (McClintock, 1971). Cycle length was also shorter among those who "spent more time" with males. Recent studies indicate that chemical substances reaching the person by means of the sense of smell are responsible for this menstrual synchrony. Pheromonal or exohormonal effects are known to affect the reproductive activities of lower animals. There have been relatively few studies on the sense of smell, since it is regarded as a primitive, rather unimportant sense in humans. It is likely, however, that pheromones represent a relatively unexplored source of variations in human behavior, particularly sexual behavior. For example, the ability to smell "exaltolide," a synthetic hormone with a musklike odor, is found among adult women, in whom it varies with the stage of the menstrual cycle, but rarely among prepubertal girls or men (Bermant & Davidson, 1974).

A combination of pheromonal and social factors could underlie some of the general acceptance of female cyclicity of mood. One recent study failed to find synchrony in the biochemistry of married pairs but did find some evidence of mood synchrony (Clarke-Kudness, 1976). Since we know that female cycle phase can influence sexual activity, this seems to be an obvious area for investigation. Although we do not know its cause, premenstrual tension is more common among older (35- to 45-year-old) women living with a man (Tonks et al., 1968). We do not know whether men (and other women) are aware of the subtle signs that a woman is about to menstruate and how this could affect their assumptions about her behavior. Psychologists have been reluctant to examine how menstruation affects the perceptions of others, probably because it is considered a personal, somewhat secret event. The increase in the number of studies on the social significance of menstruation has coincided with the emergence of a larger number of female researchers.

BIOLOGY AND BEHAVIOR: TOWARD A NEW SYNTHESIS

This chapter makes plain a position that is implicit throughout the book. While no one attempts to deny that biology and chemistry affect behavior, one should not rush to an explanation involving neural causality without considering other possibilities. Biological effects are not limited to one place within the body, even if it is the central nervous system. Endocrine hormones in particular are noteworthy for their broad systemic effects. While the menstrual cycle consists of a number of complex, interacting hormonal changes that affect the central nervous system, it affects all others parts of the body as well. It represents a rather dramatic event, accessible to both the individual and society, with a long history of negative associations in our culture. It would not be meaningful to evaluate menstrual phenomena as though they existed in a "sex-fair" context.

Women share their negative ideas about menstrual bleeding with men. Menstrual symptomology may condition their perceptions about the attractiveness of their bodies and their degree of control over them. Self-attributions involving the association of bad moods and unpleasant physical symptoms during particular periods can both lead to the production of such symptoms and be used as an explanation for them if they occur. In other words, women may respond to real or perceived changes in the body not because their hormones "told them to" but because their behavior is a socially acceptable response to a sex-specific phenomenon. Their behaviors may be reinforced by others, but they may also provide a form of "self-reinforcement." Uncontrolled negative moods can be perceived as threatening. Having an explanation for one's behavior is more satisfactory than not having an explanation. Being periodically permitted a "time out" from the usual consequences of behaviors associated with negative affect may temporarily reduce stress for women. On the other hand, it also fuels long-term perceptions of powerlessness and low self-esteem. It is assumed that the female body is "more likely to betray one." Science and society have combined to provide biological explanations for women's behavior. There is no real evidence, however, that their behaviors are biologically caused to a greater extent than those of men.

Lack of contact between the sexes may exaggerate perceptions about biological differences between them. Also, those differences center on sexuality, which until recently have been taboo for serious scientific scrutiny in our society. The misunderstood link between menstruation and sexuality, in combination with the former's other "unclean" connotations, has also probably contributed to its special character in the differentiation of females from males. There is still some embarrassment when the subject of menstruation is discussed in mixed-sex college classrooms.

Cross-cultural studies are particularly illuminating (and lacking) for the understanding of the social mediation of biological effects. The point is probably best summed up in the following passage by Estelle Ramey, a noted biochemist:

> Males are different biologically from females. They are also different sociologically. Men become United States Presidents and women do not. But then women do become Presidents of Israel and India and Ceylon. Endocrinologists have nothing to contribute to the explanation of these national differences. [1973, p. 244]

Chapter 10
Peers and Pairs

The major context in which heterosexual interpersonal contacts occur is that of sexuality. Same-sex exclusivity is interfered with by the beginning of the dating process. As we will see, however, loving people or being sexually involved with them may not be the same as liking them. Romantic or sexual contact does not seem to reduce cross-sexual lack of understanding.

In this chapter we will examine sex-related differences in perceptions of and attitudes toward contacts with members of the other sex. A number of psychological variables appear to have different meanings for females and males. Some of these variables exist from early childhood, while others seem to emerge only upon presumed sexual maturity. They spring both from biologically based assumptions and from expectations about differential adult sex roles. If anything, institutionalized practices of dating and mating increase sexual asymmetries. For females at least, being a member of a pair is not the same thing as being a peer.

IMPLICATIONS OF ATTRACTIVENESS IN FEMALES AND MALES

Over the past ten years researchers have shown that good-looking people have more social power. Adults are more likely to change their opinions as a function of the communicator's attractiveness (Mills & Aronson, 1965). They like a physically attractive evaluator better (Sigall & Aronson, 1969). They perceive physically attractive people as having more socially desirable personalities and as being more likely to be both professionally and maritally successful (Dion, Berscheid, & Walster, 1972). Physical attractiveness, however, has somewhat different implications for females and males.

Attractiveness as a Predictor of the Other Sex's Behavior

Physical attractiveness is a much more important predictor of the behavior of males toward females than the other way around. A positive relationship between physical attractiveness and dating has been found for females but not for males (Krebs & Adinolfi, 1975). Males remembered a female confederate with whom they had a fleeting contact longer and with greater positive feelings when she was attractive than when she was not (Kleck & Rubenstein, 1975). The perceived attitudinal similarity between themselves and the female partner did not affect how well they remembered her. These male college students revealed two weeks after the encounter that they thought more about the partner during the interim, continued to like her more, and remembered more about her if she was attractive. Unfortunately this study did not consider whether a similar effect of attractive male confederates on females would occur. The lack of an equivalent male "control" group in this and a number of other studies illustrates psychologists' acceptance of society's bias that beauty is a more salient feature in the effect of women on men than in the effect of men on women. Even the term *beauty* seems a little odd when applied to a grown male.

Large-scale studies of dating encounters in a more naturalistic situation—a campus-wide computer match dance—reveal that the good looks of a date are more important to men than to women (Coombs & Kenkel, 1966). Five hundred women and men filled out a questionnaire describing what qualities they wanted in a date. The physical attractiveness of the date was far more important for the men than for the women. Aside from this sex difference in the value of looks, women actually had higher requirements for their dating partners than men. For the women it was important that their dates have good grades, be important "men" on campus, be fashionable, dance well, and be members of the same race and religion as themselves. These characteristics were less important to the men than to the women and less important than the primary feature of the date's "looks."

One would like to believe that the role of physical attractiveness in evaluation decreases as people get to know each other better. Although men and women are more satisfied with a partner with whom they are "matched" by a computer if he or she is attractive (Walster, Aronson, Abrahams, & Rottman, 1966), one might assume that this information is used primarily because it is the only reliable information available. As more information about the partner's personality becomes known, the effect of physical attractiveness on liking should be reduced. This hypothesis was recently tested by having "computer-matched" dating partners go out on a series of five dates (Mathes, 1975). Actually, the pairs were formed so that they combined various levels of attractiveness and anxiety. Although attractive and unattractive subjects were liked equally well during the first encounter, on subsequent encounters attractive subjects were liked significantly more. Increased contact with the partner did not change this effect. In this study physical attractiveness increased the value of both male and female dates to an equal extent.

These data suggest that although physical attractiveness may be given higher priority in the evaluation of females by males, the evaluation of males by females is not immune to the effects of attractiveness. Females are perhaps less willing to admit to being influenced by "superficial" characteristics. Recent studies that evaluate the effect of attractiveness less directly would seem to suggest that this is a possibility. In one such study (Zanna & Pack, 1975) female subjects were asked to describe themselves to a male partner who was either desirable or undesirable and whose stereotype of the ideal woman conformed closely to either a traditional or a nontraditional type. The actual attitudes of these women had been measured on a previous occasion. When the partner was desirable, the women portrayed themselves more in terms of his ideal type as measured by variation from attitude measurements obtained under more neutral conditions. The women also performed better on tests involving intellectual competence when the desirable partner was portrayed as having nonstereotypic views about women. Undesirable partners had no effect on either their attitudes or their behaviors. Since, however, the highly desirable partner was described as a 6-foot, 21-year-old Princeton senior with no girlfriend and the partner with low desirability was described as a 5½-foot, 18-year-old non-Princeton freshman with a girlfriend, it is difficult to determine whether the women's behavior was influenced by the partner's physical attractiveness or his other desirable attributes.

Assumptions About Attractive Individuals

Physical attractiveness may carry with it negative as well as positive connotations. Along with positive character traits, women are more likely to attribute such socially undesirable traits as vanity, egotism, lack of sympathy, and materialism to women who are attractive rather than unattractive (Dermer & Thiel, 1975). Female participants who were not particularly attractive themselves were more likely to view attractive female stimulus persons as less competent parents and as more likely to have a disastrous marriage. They did not view these women as having more attractive personalities. Men are more apprehensive about a date with an attractive woman than about one with an unattractive woman. If they were not sure that a date whom they had selected would select them, college men were more unsure that she would find them acceptable if she was attractive rather than unattractive (Huston, 1973). However, when they were sure that the woman they selected would accept them, they chose the attractive woman more often than the unattractive one.

It has been suggested that physical attractiveness confers a kind of power on women. In one intriguing study 470 pedestrians were observed as they walked past a confederate or confederates positioned at the edge of a sidewalk. Time lapse photography was used to measure how far they deviated from their path to avoid the stimulus person(s). Pedestrians of both sexes stayed further from a man than from a woman, from two persons than from one, and from an attractive woman than from an unattractive one (Dabbs & Stokes, 1975). Beauty, like maleness and number, may be an aspect of power that organizes how people deal with their social and physical environment.

More directly, female subjects are reluctant to ask an attractive confederate for help if she is presumed to be a fellow subject in an experiment (Stokes & Bickman, 1974). When the confederate was unattractive, more subjects asked her for help when they thought she was an experimenter than when they thought she was a fellow subject. This study again suggests that beauty is a form of power, one that interacts with other forms of power such as status. Thus a higher-status individual, an experimenter, is more approachable when she is attractive, and someone of equal status is less approachable when she is attractive. Greater apprehension appears to be aroused by highly attractive women. People are even less willing to reveal much personal information to them (Rubin, 1975). It is as though they fear to put themselves in their power.

The Conferring of Power by Beauty: Sex Asymmetries

If beauty represents a form of power for American women, it is one that is easily transferred by association. In one series of studies men and women were asked to form impressions of a male stimulus person who was presented as either the boyfriend of or unassociated with a female confederate who was made up to appear either attractive or unattractive (Sigall & Landy, 1973). The male stimulus person was evaluated most favorably when he was associated with an attractive woman. It was necessary that a relationship be assumed in order for her attractiveness to affect his evaluations. If the two individuals were presented as simply being together in the same room, no transfer of positive attributes from her to him occurred.

In a second experiment it was found that male subjects were aware of this transfer of beauty as power. They predicted that they would receive more favorable evaluations from raters when they were presented as the boyfriend of an attractive woman and less favorable judgments when they were seen as the boyfriend of an unattractive woman. The presence of an attractive female partner did not enhance perceptions of the male's attractiveness, but it led to more favorable estimates of his character and likability. In other words, the salient feature in the evaluation of females—physical beauty—enhances the evaluation of males not on the same dimension but more in terms of the male's salient feature—the effect he will have on others and on the world. It is as though people are inferring that males must do something well in order to receive such an attractive "prize." (See Figure 10.1.)

In a further investigation of this effect college students of both sexes were given photos of ostensibly married couples who were either similar or dissimilar in level of physical attractiveness (Bar-Tal & Saxe, 1976a). The same photos were presented to other students as unassociated individuals. They found that physical attractiveness was differentially important in the perception of husbands and wives. Female spouses were evaluated independently of the husband's level of attractiveness. Male spouses, especially unattractive males paired with attractive females, were positively affected by the woman's level of attractiveness. Unattractive men married to attractive women were seen as having the highest income and occupational status and the most professional stature, whereas attractive men married to unattractive women rated lowest on these di-

Figure 10.1. The "Jacqueline Kennedy–Aristotle Onassis" effect: Partnership with an attractive woman enhances perceptions of the ability, competence and achievements of a man. (Reprinted by permission of Wide World Photos, Inc., a subsidiary of the Associated Press.)

mensions. Unattractive women married to attractive men did not gain in the estimation of the evaluators.

People may feel a need to explain the association of unattractive and attractive people as marital partners because it violates their notions about equity in relationships. One could almost term this the "Aristotle Onassis–Jackie Kennedy effect." Since feminine beauty is such a valuable commodity, it is assumed that he is giving her other socially valued, material rewards. One might ask why unattractive females don't gain from their association with attractive males. Positive stereotypes associated with attractiveness may be stronger and more unitary for females than for males (Bar-Tal & Saxe, 1976b). Physical attractiveness may serve as a powerful external cue indicating the extent to which a female will successfully fulfill her traditional sex role. Physical attractiveness in males has less of a relationship to their traditional role functions.

In general, the better an individual feels about his or her own attractiveness, the higher he or she evaluates the attractiveness of women (Morse, Gruzen, & Reis, 1976). High self-evaluation in women also predicts their high appreciation of male attractiveness. Surprisingly, however, men with high self-evaluations are less likely to appreciate the attractiveness of other men. It is possible that a high degree of physical attractiveness in a male, a trait so closely associated with the evaluation of females, may decrease his perceived masculinity and power. An intriguing piece of evidence in this regard is a finding that people are much more willing to disclose personal information about themselves to an attractive male experimenter than to a less attractive one, although the opposite relationship exists for women (Rubin, 1975). Self-disclosure and the ability to receive such personal information (empathy) are conceived to be "feminine" characteristics. Male attractiveness might increase perceived similarity to women. However, a number of alternate explanations of these data are equally plausible. It is obvious we need more studies on the effect of physical attractiveness on the evaluation of males. Excuses about the degree of ease (by means of makeup) with which an attractive female can be converted into an unattractive one, as compared to an equivalent male, will no longer serve.

Personality Characteristics of Attractive Males and Females

One of the questions that comes to mind in looking at these findings about the relationship between physical attractiveness and personality attributions is the basis in reality for such beliefs. In other words, does the grain-of-truth hypothesis apply to stereotypes about physical attractiveness? After all, there is a weight of evidence to suggest that attractive and unattractive females, in particular, are treated quite differently by their peers. The former are even more likely to be helped when they are perceived to be in some distress (Athanasiou & Greene, 1973). We have also found that both males and females appear to be made more anxious by attractive females. At times females are even less likely to request their help. And both sexes stay physically farther away from and are less likely to reveal personal information to an attractive woman than to a less attractive woman. While attractive people of both sexes are perceived as brighter, more socially desirable, and more likely to succeed in life, they are also perceived as more egotistical and unsympathetic.

It seems likely that all of these differential attitudes about and behaviors toward more or less attractive people would have an effect on their personalities. However, attractiveness as a mediator of personality characteristics has received very little attention. Attractive people do seem to have higher self-esteem than less attractive individuals (Berscheid, Walster, & Bohrnstedt, 1973). Attractive women who wish to manipulate others may make use of strategies that are dependent on their beauty. One recent study indicates that attractive people of both sexes are rated as more socially skillful by people who have not seen them but have had a telephone conversation with them (Goldman & Lewis, 1977).

There is also some older research on the effect of accelerated physical maturity in males—associated with more mesomorphic body builds and considered more attractive by adults in adolescents—on personality characteristics. Boys who developed early were rated by adults as better groomed (Jones & Bayley, 1950). They did not seem to differ from their less developed peers in terms of group evaluation of popularity, leadership, friendliness, and sense of humor. When, however, the same group was tested at age 33—after differences in physique had virtually disappeared— some intriguing differences emerged. A strong significant correlation of .50 was found between the need to make a "good impression" and skeletal maturity eighteen years earlier (Jones, 1957). There was also a positive correlation between dominance and early maturity. Late maturity, on the other hand, was correlated with flexibility and concern for others as adults. There was some indication that physique-related personality characteristics may also have affected vocational choice. Executives were to be found only among the early-maturing group. None of the late maturers held an important managerial position.

Unfortunately, few studies on the effect of developmental maturity upon girls exist. Developmental maturity may confer prestige among girls in the seventh through ninth grades (Faust, 1960). Developmental maturity among these girls was defined by the age at which they reached menarche. This measure, however, is confounded by height and by the development of more obvious secondary sexual characteristics, such as breast size. It is not clear what characteristic(s) conferred prestige in these girls. In any case they were seen by their peers as more popular, friendly, and assured with adults. Later-maturing girls were seen as quiet, not seeking attention, and avoiding confrontation. Recently a relationship between bust size in adulthood and some personality characteristics has been noted. Women with small breasts who did not seek breast augmentation (used as a control group for those who did) were more likely to score as androgynous on the Bem scale than those with larger busts (Shipley & O'Donnell, 1977). Large-busted women, on the other hand, were more likely to score as feminine in orientation. A strong relationship between body image as a teenager and reported happiness that persists for about the first forty years of a woman's life has been noted in retrospective studies (Berscheid et al., 1973).

Physical attractiveness seems to have both similar and different implications for females and males. While it enhances the ease of some social interactions for individuals of both sexes, it also seems to provoke a certain degree of apprehension in other people. Physically attractive people may respond to this ambivalence by honing their social skills. Physical attractiveness may also make salient some aspects of the feminine stereotype. Thus attractive males may respond by becoming somewhat more self-assertive and self-concerned. Attractive females may become somewhat less interested in objective competence than their less attractive counterparts. Again, this is a question of what sorts of behaviors receive social rewards rather than a matter of all-encompassing personality characteristics.

Physical attractiveness would be less of an issue in the psychology of women if it were not for the information that this characteristic is asymmetrically transferable: Her beauty confers male status characteristics on him. Males appear to be aware of this relationship and offer social rewards based on it. Much of the female concern for appearance may stem from this association. It should also be kept in mind that attractiveness is a difficult variable to quantify because "beauty is so much in the eye of the beholder." In most studies in which attractiveness is ranked, all the photos receive high ratings for attractiveness from some subjects. It seems fair to state, however, that attractiveness is more salient variable for females than for males. In fact fewer individual differences based on this variable may be found for females (when it is looked for) because it represents a social variable that is important in defining the characteristics of females in general.

DATING AND MATING: THE SOCIAL WHIRL

Same-Sex Exclusivity: Changes at Adolescence and Their Implications

Despite the fact that individuals largely travel in same-sex groups throughout childhood and adolescence, information about the social popularity of a peer is somehow communicated between the two sexes. Part of the apparent communication pattern may be that the basis for evaluation of members of each sex is the same regardless of whether a male or a female does the evaluating. Thus boys and girls agree that the most acceptable girls are (in order of importance) good-looking, tidy, friendly, likable, enthusiastic, cheerful, quiet, and interested in dating, (Gronlund & Anderson, 1957). For boys, physical appeal was considered less important than performance characteristics. The most popular boys were named as being active in games and, in fact, received more nominations for this attribute than any characteristic of popular girls. They were also seen as good-looking, tidy, and likable (with these three qualities tied in importance), friendly, cheerful, and able to tell a joke. Similar characteristics for accepted versus rejected boys and girls have been found among sixth- and twelfth-graders, indicating that there is a good deal of consistency between males and females of various ages in terms of evaluative judgments based on gender. What is most important is the nature of the distinctions. The most important characteristic for girls is how they look; for boys it is what they do.

The two sexes show an increase in contact with members of the opposite sex in the period between the sixth and twelfth grades. They are more likely to sit with, play with, and generally associate with opposite-sex peers than adolescents of the same age studied in 1942 (Kuhlen & Houlihan, 1965). Despite this behavioral evidence of increasing contact between the sexes during adolescence, the percentage of children making favorable comments about members of the opposite sex may actually decline in these years, especially among boys (Harris & Tseng, 1957). Using completion of sentence stems such as "Most boys _____" or "Most girls _____," the researchers found that the percentage of boys making favorable responses about girls declined from about 55 percent in the third grade to 42 percent in the twelfth grade while the percentage of favorable comments about other boys remains relatively constant at 60–70 percent. Girls, on the other hand, decrease in favorable comments about other girls from 85 percent in the third grade to 57 percent in the twelfth grade, with a particularly sharp decline in the high school years. Girls showed a generally rather stable percentage (45–50 percent) of comments favorable to boys throughout these years.

These data are quite old and may not reflect recent changes in sex roles. Unfortunately studies on the within- and between-sex evaluations of children and adolescents seem to have gone out of fashion. There is recent evidence, however, that same-sex exclusivity is maintained by boys throughout their high school years. Naturalistic observations of 15- to 16-year-old boys during the school day indicate that 77 percent of their interpersonal interactions are with other males (Newman, 1976). The 23 percent of heterosexual contacts were accounted for by the very few boys who had girlfriends. Same-sex and same-race exclusivity have also been observed recently among elementary school children on cafeteria lines (Willis & Hofmann, 1975).

Romance in Black and White

Despite myths about "teenage romance," intense and intimate relationships with members of the opposite sex may reflect lower family income and lower vocational aspirations as well as personal insecurity. Among a representational sample of high school students, going steady was associated with low socioeconomic status and recent changes in the parent–child relationship (Larson, Spreitzer, & Snyder, 1976). Girls from broken, especially father-absent, homes are particularly likely to become romantically involved and to be married at an earlier age than those from intact homes (Hetherington, 1975).

Among whites at every age (10–17) girls appear to be significantly more heterosexual in their social orientation. They score significantly higher than boys their own age on such issues as wanting to get married and claiming to have had a boyfriend (vs. a girlfriend for boys). The mean scores for white girls in heterosexual orientation was higher than the mean score for boys two years older than themselves (Broderick, 1965). One could argue that these data simply reflect differences in the rate of physical maturation of boys and girls. However, similar sex differences in heterosexual involvement are not always found among black adolescents. In fact in the same study black boys reported more social interactions at ages 13–14 than black girls of the same age. They were more likely to have had a girlfriend and to have begun to date and go steady.

Dating behavior seems to be more closely tied to social than to biological variables. In a study of black and white dating patterns in a Texas high school before and after desegregation (Dickinson, 1975), it was found that black dating behavior changed in the direction of whites' while the behavior of white adolescents changed only slightly over time. The age of the first date declined for blacks from 14.9 years in 1964 to the white average of 13.9 years in 1974. The percentage of blacks reporting going to parties and dances as their primary dating activity also declined, while the percentage who reported "parking" on dates increased to the white level of 75 percent. Dating at the school was intraracial, so any change in social patterns was presumably indirect, perhaps through adoption of the norms of the higher-status group.

The Date as a Social Relationship

It has sometimes been reported that females have somewhat more extensive romantic experiences than males during the high school and college years (Kephart, 1967). A major issue here is the operational definition of romance. If we define romance in terms of heterosexual social contacts, girls do have a greater probability of such contacts in the early years of dating, since the younger female–older male relationship is virtually institutionalized by our society. Boys, however, are more likely to have gone steady than girls of the same age (Larson et al., 1976). Girls, on the other hand, are more likely to report more in the way of romantic fantasies rather than social interactions. They indicate on questionnaires that they have been in love more and kissed when it meant something special (Broderick, 1965). Thus we must distinguish between romantic attitudes and social behaviors.

There is considerable evidence that the date as a social relationship has different connotations for males than for females. An interesting recent study of Australian university students aged 17 through 30 found considerable disharmony between the expectations of males and females, especially among adolescents (Collins, Kennedy, & Francis, 1976). Questioned about the level of intimacy expected at various stages in the dating process, young men expected women to behave more liberally than the women expected to behave. Indeed, men manifest more physical intimacies and expect more permissive behavior than women during the initial stages of dating (Collins, 1974). As commitment between dating pairs increases, the behavior of the women more closely parallels that of the men. It is the female who shifts toward the masculine level of expectation of physical intimacy. Correspondingly, after the teenage years university students appear to agree on the level of intimacy to be expected at various stages of dating. This agreement between the sexes is achieved through a shift in the responses of females toward the level of physical intimacy considered desirable by males.

Progress in a dating relationship appears to be marked by considerable pressure for change in females. McDaniel (1969) attempted to study dating roles and reasons for dating among university women, but seems to have succeeded only examining the way women change their attitudes and behaviors as the relationship with a male becomes more "serious." Girls who were studied in the first stage of random dating tended to be assertive, achievement oriented, autonomous, dominant, and desirous of status. They justified the dating relationship primarily in terms of recreation. When they went steady their behavior shifted to assertive–receptive, and during the final stage—when they were "pinned" or engaged—they became what McDaniel termed wholly receptive: deferential, concerned about helping others, prone to vicariousness, and more anxious. Increasingly their behavior was justified in terms of mate selection and anticipatory socialization. A dating relationship may not progress if the girl fails to manifest the proper role at a particular stage. For example, males were reported to dislike strongly women who are assertive in the later stages of dating.

Whose Date?

If women are forced to conform to male ideals of behavior in order to maintain a steady heterosexual relationship, what are the rewards for doing so? What we need to examine is the function of heterosexual contact, especially as institutionalized by our society in the dating relationship. We need an analysis similar to that done by Jessie Bernard (1972) on "her" versus "his" marriage. Preliminary analysis using this technique suggests that females' rewards from the dating relationship are more in the nature of negative reinforcements than positive ones. For those who are uninformed about operant-conditioning terminology, a negative reinforcement consists of a reward that is reinforcing by its absence; i.e., the organism acts to avoid its presence. Operant conditioners have found that organisms will respond for a long time to avoid such noxious stimuli and will maintain their behavior long after the presence of the noxious stimulus has been terminated. In terms of this analogy, females in our society have been conditioned to perceive that the absence of a male partner after a certain age has highly unpleasant social consequences. They will conform in a variety of ways to avoid this noxious situation.

Her Date

Since the social role for which females are socialized—marriage—is impossible without a male partner, most of the discussion in this area will be reserved for the next chapter. Here we must examine some evidence for the position that "her" date fulfills different requirements than "his." We have already cited the evidence that dating requires a greater shift in attitude and behavior for females than for males. Increased heterosexual contact seems to be accompanied by a decline in liking for members of the same sex for females but not for males. Males continue their group behaviors, whereas females become increasingly isolated from each other by the dating relationship. A sense of "female rivalry" is fostered by the popular media, while at the same time an older unmarried female—a spinster—is portrayed in a variety of unflattering ways. Among many adolescents a girl is expected to give up a prearranged outing with a girlfriend if she is asked for a date. Exclusive contact with other females after the mid-teens is regarded as socially stigmatizing, as a function of lack of choice, or as a source of familial concern about the girl's object of sexual preference.

His Date

Despite the stereotype of the romantic female, females have more stringent requirements for their dates than males do. In a survey of over 1000 college students nearly twice as many men as women said that they were "very easily attracted" to members of the opposite sex (Kephart, 1967). We have also noted the evidence that good looks are the most important criterion in a date for males (Coombs & Kenkel, 1966). Males who were matched with a date by a computer were more attracted by her similarity to him on sexual attitudes, while for females attraction was related to similarity in religious attitudes (Touhey, 1972). Although we are reluctant to admit it, physical intimacy culminating in sexual intercourse may be the most important pressure for heterosexual contact in adolescent males. To paraphrase St. Paul, "It may be better to date than to burn."

Their Date

The acceptance of male parameters of the dating relationship may be facilitated by two factors (1) the differential maturity rate in females and males, and (2) the confusion between maturity of physical appearance and sexual maturity—especially in women. On the average, females mature two years earlier than males. Their secondary sexual characteristics, as well as their height, are equivalent to those of a male two years older. Our society has institutionalized social contact—the "date"—between older boys and younger girls in apparent recognition of these differential rates of maturation. But what effect does contact with intellectually and socially advanced members of the opposite sex have on females? We might assume that it has the effect of highlighting their sexual maturity and, supposedly, their readiness to take on the reproductive role. Chronological status combined with that conferred upon males probably makes females unlikely to deviate from the requirements of the social contract of the date. These factors may both maintain and increase female sexual passivity.

MALE VS. FEMALE SEXUALITY

Male Sexuality

Unlike females, who are socialized to repress their sexuality and to maintain their virginity, the potency of young men is eulogized by our society. Males are expected to "sow their wild oats" whereas "nice" girls do not "give it away." Although there has been some change in attitudes about sexuality in males and females in our society, the double standard still persists. The usual justification for the double standard is physiological differences in male and female sexuality. We will make some comments on those differences later; here we will examine the issue of male sexuality in relation to dating behavior.

Males measure, and indeed may learn, their sexuality with reference to other men (Schwartz, personal communication). In some groups of male adolescents masturbation contests may be held; the winner is the first to ejaculate. A common question following a date is "Did you score?" Males expect more and faster physical intimacies on dates than females do. Their acceptability to their male peers is measured by their degree of sexual experience. Males are much less willing to admit to virginity than females are to admit to not being virgins (G. Rotter, personal communication). In fact college males who attempt aggressive heterosexual behavior, such as forcing coitus on unwilling dating partners, appear to be most influenced by peer pressures to prove their acceptability as males (Kanin, 1967a).

Sexual aggression by males on dates appears to be considerably more common than was previously assumed. In one study of 400 unmarried male college students chosen at random, 23 percent could be classified as sexually aggressive in the dating situation (Kanin, 1967b). In this study aggression was defined by the man's having admitted to attempting coital access with a rejecting female with a degree of physical coercion that elicited an offended response from her. All such acts took place with a date of some sort rather than with a stranger. In a majority of cases the activity was preceded by a rather advanced level of physical intimacy, such as genital "petting." The fact that the women involved reacted with such vehemence, therefore, indicated that the force utilized was at a level that was not expected during normal consensual intimacy.

While 23 percent of the sample may appear to be a small portion of males who date, they probably affect more females than their numbers would suggest. Aggressive males, in contrast to unaggressive males, not only have a larger total number of sexual experiences but also persistently seek new sexual involvements. Males who use physical coercion are also more likely to use exploitive psychological techniques such as attempting to get their date intoxicated, falsely promising marriage, falsely professing love, or threatening to terminate the relationship. Unfortunately those who resort to such devious tactics are also those who are most successful in obtaining a number of sexual experiences.

A majority of 261 female college student respondents to an extensive questionnaire about aspects of sexuality reported that they have encountered some sort of sexual aggression associated with males, to which they reacted with terror, fright, disgust, or anxiety (Shipman, 1968). Twenty-nine percent had encountered an exhibitionist, 27 percent a male who followed them while making obscene gestures or remarks; 23 percent had received an obscene phone call; 31 percent had had an encounter with a man who was overly aggressive in suggesting intercourse; and 35 percent had been with a man whose sexual aggressiveness had to be resisted by force. These data appear to be fairly consistent with those derived from males. In fact when the same questionnaire was given to males 20 percent admitted to persuading a woman to have intercourse against her convictions.

The world as portrayed by pornography, and even some mainstream fiction, glorifies aggressive degradation of the female. Sexuality is defined only in terms of sheer physical activity (Smith, 1976). Although it is highly exaggerated, pornography may represent a covert norm about male–female relationships that is widely disseminated. It could be termed an excellent "capitalist" behavioral indicant, since men spend money on it although they rarely admit to reading it. Analysis of the content of "adults only" paperbacks suggest that they portray a sexual reality that bears a genuine resemblance to that of our own society. Little attention is paid to the physical characteristics of the male, whereas the female is described down to her "last dimple" (Smith, 1976). Unattractive females are referred to negatively, and those over 40 rarely appear. One-third of the sex episodes are accompanied by the use of force in which the initially unwilling female is aroused even though there has been no indication of any particular skill on the part of the male. There is little information on how many men read pornographic literature, but there is evidence that it is a thriving enterprise that supplies small rural towns as well as "sinful" big cities.

Female Sexuality

Western psychology has historically classified women as having a lower sex drive than men. In some of the psychoanalytic literature women have been characterized as masochistic as well as simply passive. Women are seen as slow to be aroused, less interested in sex, and more likely to suffer from various types of sexual inadequacy (Schwartz, 1978). The assumption is that this sex difference is grounded in biology rather than a response to particular cultural prescriptions. It is important to discover, therefore, how much of female sexuality is influenced by cultural context.

Cross-cultural studies of male and female sexual behavior abound; however, they are mainly limited to descriptions of behavior without trying to analyze underlying relationships. Psychologists seem to feel that societies without clothing belong to anthropologists. Analyses of groups within our society indicate that differences in female sexuality are influenced by such nonbiological variables as social class. Less educated women demand less from their men in terms of frequency, number of positions, and variety of sexual practices (Bell, 1974).

Recent evidence indicates little difference between male and female responsiveness (Schwartz, 1978). There is also every indication from the work of Masters and Johnson (1970) that women are quite capable of enjoying sexual activity without being attached to their partner by love, affection, or affiliation. These researchers do give us a picture of sex differences in the length of various phases of the sexual act. Men become sexually excited quickly, peak to climax, and then recede to a nonaroused state. Women, on the other hand, arouse slowly, reach plateau, arouse some more, reach another plateau, and eventually reach climax. Afterwards, however, they do not recede to a state of nonexcitement; under suitable conditions and effective stimulation, many women are capable of multiple orgasms (Masters & Johnson, 1966).

Pepper Schwartz (1978), in her extensive review of the social context of female sexuality, suggests that differences between male and female sexual responsiveness may be a result of adolescent socialization. Sexual experience is a form of masculine validation for men that is completely sanctioned neither by the female partner nor by society. Hence, it is something to be "gotten over with" as quickly as possible. The result is the classic "Wham, bam, thank you ma'am" pattern of intercourse.

Females are socialized not to acknowledge their sexuality and suffer far graver consequences if they are caught indulging it. Young women are judged by their ability to appear sexual and as attractive as possible to men, but are supposed to deliver only as much as the prevailing norms of decency allow. An illicit pregnancy also puts a woman much more at risk than the man involved. Until recently, as well, a woman's virginity was regarded as a commodity to be bargained with in order to obtain a permanent partner. A piece of folk wisdom that prevailed in my not-that-long-ago youth was that "men don't buy what they can borrow." Aware of her stake in the game, it is not surprising that a woman may be slower to be aroused and to be swept away than a man. It is also not surprising that studies showing fewer differences between female and male sexuality than were previously thought to exist have become plentiful since the advent of the pill. Although the pill may be a mixed blessing both physiologically and socially, it does free women who use it from the consequences of an unwanted pregnancy.

THE BASES FOR SEXUAL MISUNDERSTANDING

Given that males have a different concept of the amount of sexual activity expected in the dating situation than females, and that, for whatever reasons, physiological and/or social, the form and length of the pattern of sexual arousal is different in males and females, sexual misunderstandings seem to be almost inevitable. A recent study on the meaning of touch for men and women (Nguyen, Heslin, & Nguyen, 1975) illustrates these difficulties. The researchers tried to find out whether men and women attach similar meanings to a touch applied to equivalent body areas. They questioned 40 male and 40 female undergraduates about the meaning of four varieties of touch—pat, squeeze, brush, and stroke—when applied to various portions of the anatomy by a member of the opposite sex, in terms of their implications of playfulness, warmth/love, friendship/fellowship, sexual desire, and pleasantness. For males, pleasantness, sexual desire, and warmth/love formed a cluster. For females, the more a touch was associated with sexual desire, the less it was considered to imply friendliness, warmth, friendship, and pleasantness. Thus when a close male friend touches a woman in an area that communicates sexual desire to her (her breasts, buttocks, and genital areas), she is unlikely to consider the touch pleasant and indicative of warmth. On the other hand, if she touches him in ways that indicate sexual desire, he interprets the touch as loving, warm, and pleasant as well.

We can see here some of the foundations for sexual misunderstanding. A touch that a male considers friendly may not have at all the same connotation for a woman. She may perceive that she is being touched only for sexual reasons. A friendly touch by a woman, however, may be misinterpreted by her male partner as a sexual come-on. The two sexes don't get much opportunity to talk about it, since discussion of specific sexual issues still tends to be taboo. The opportunities to interact with members of the opposite sex except under circumstances defined as having sexual overtones also may be limited. Thus sexual misunderstandings are not readily noticed or overcome.

American sexual customs and the customary "missionary position" also contribute to sexual misunderstanding. Masters and Johnson have presented extensive evidence that the tissue that is maximally sensitive to erotic stimulation is the female clitoris; the structure that is embryonically analogous to the male penis. They report that there is no such thing as a vaginal orgasm that is distinct from a clitoral one. The clitoris participates fully even when no attempt is made to stimulate it directly.

The issue of the clitoral orgasm has produced a furor apparently well beyond the limits expected by a change in our knowledge of the physiology of sexuality. This is due to the classical Freudian interpretation of female sexuality (Freud, 1931). Freud asserted, on no particular anatomical basis, that women are able to have two types of orgasm—vaginal and clitoral. However, a mature woman—defined as one who accepted her role as childbearer—transfered her sexual response from the clitoris to the vagina. If she was unable to make the transfer, she was considered to have remained immature and frigid. Males, of course, never had to shift from the penis once that had developed as the primary source of eroticism.

Anne Koedt (1970), a founding radical feminist, has attacked Freud as the "father" of the vaginal orgasm and argues that his views have been extremely harmful to women. The accepted "male on top" position, which has the vagina as its target, does not provide as much clitoral stimulation as other positions do. Koedt suggests that men maintain the myth of the vaginal orgasm because the preferred position is maximally stimulating to males and because they want to keep women in their "place."

Freud's concepts of immature and mature female sexuality may have been the source of much feminine anxiety about the question of masturbation. Although adolescents of both sexes are warned about the "dangers" of self-stimulation, the weight of the psychiatric establishment has reinforced the taboo against masturbation in women. It was not so long ago that physicians performed clitorectomies to prevent "self-abuse" (Spitz, 1952). Women rarely talk about masturbation even among themselves. They lack the peer group support for sexual self-exploration that is available to many males. Yet Masters and Johnson have shown that manipulation of the clitoris alone can produce orgasms in many women, and even use this technique to improve orgasmic capacity in "frigid" women. Unfortunately many women are reluctant to request that their male partners perform clitoral manipulation because it seems too much like masturbation.

Serious researchers have been reluctant to deal with taboo topics such as masturbation. They assume that such activity will disappear when the individuals involved engage in more heterosexual acts. However, this appears to be more true for men than for women. Over 90 percent of all men and over 60 percent of all women have masturbated at some time and are more likely to give up the practice out of a sense of shame or disgust than because they derive no pleasure from it. Women who achieve orgasm by means of self-stimulation are more likely to continue to masturbate than those who do not. However, there is some indication that many women prefer intercourse, even without orgasm, over "do it yourself" techniques. Many women enjoy sexual intercourse without orgasm but do not generally enjoy it without a certain amount of touching and kissing throughout the experience (Hite, 1974).

We know little about the role of masturbation in the sexual life of mature women, although there may be a relationship between masturbation, sexual fantasies, and sexual enjoyment (Schwartz, 1978). Drawing upon Barbara Harlton's (1973) studies of the sexual fantasies of women, Schwartz points out that such fantasies are more common among independent, creative women who take an active approach to sexuality. They appear to be correlated with positive and nontraumatic sexual experiences in childhood and adolescence. Fantasy is seen as a reflection of sexual strength, not weakness. The development of rich, exciting fantasies may be assisted by masturbation; hence, female sexual independence may be hampered by limited access to solitary sexual exploration. The areas of both masturbation and sexual fantasy certainly warrant further exploration. They are both areas that women are reluctant to discuss and have been of limited interest to male researchers, who have concentrated on heterosexual sexual experience.

Little serious research has also been done on the meaning of sexual variety for women or men. For example, oral sex is still generally considered somewhat dirty or immature. Genitals—especially female genitals—are regarded as rather nondescript or even ugly. They are regarded as emitting a "fishy" odor and are considered particularly unpleasant during menstruation. Recently the media were full of advertisements for products that disguised the normal odor of the vagina. It was presumably better to smell like a strawberry than like a woman! Gynecology, which appears to be a particularly sexist branch of medicine, even has a stable of "vagina jokes." One of these, for example, involves a man who looks bad but feels good. The consulting physician looks up the symptoms in a book and decides that his problem is that "he is a vagina." We must ask whether an attitude about the ugliness of a particular body part—especially the part that is most specifically female—carries over to a poorer body image in general.

ORGASMIC CAPACITY: ANOTHER DOUBLE BIND?

In some ways the recent emphasis on the female orgasm, although apparently feminist, carries with it some masculinist bias. The emphasis is on the end product—the orgasm—rather than on the mutual enjoyment along the way. Noncoital sex play may sometimes be quite satisfactory for many women. Concentration on the female orgasm puts a burden on the male as well as the female partner. He must "make her enjoy it" for the sake of his own masculine image. She must come to climax or one of them is at fault; either he is not sufficiently skilled or she is not sufficiently liberated.

While this is not to say that sexual exploration and concern for the partner are not important, insufficient attention may have been paid to women whose socialization has not permitted them to express their sexuality freely.

The pain as well as the pleasure of the new sexual freedom for blue-collar wives has recently been explored (Rubin, 1976). She found that more people are engaging in more varieties of sexual behavior than ever before, but they are not necessarily comfortable about it. Every one of the 75 couples she interviewed (50 blue-collar and 25 professional middle-class couples) had stories about problems of sexual adjustment. In particular, working-class wives feel guilty about oral sex and "give in" with little enthusiasm. Cunnilingus is practiced with somewhat less reluctance and greater frequency, possibly because it enables the woman to remain in her classically passive role. Blue-collar women feel that engaging in exotic sexual practices endangers their status as "good girls." They also feel that letting themselves go will be threatening to their husbands, who are, in fact, sending out ambiguous and ambivalent messages. Confrontations also occur about the frequency and meaning of sex. Men equate sex and love, while women are more likely to differentiate between them. Women identify love with communication and self-disclosure, traditional feminine areas that make many men uncomfortable.

While blue-collar families do seem to have more problems involving sexuality than better-educated families, their problems may simply be more overt or magnified rather than different from those of other socioeconomic groups. One interesting point is differences between male and female perceptions of the frequency of sexual activity. In most cases he wants sex more often than she. Therefore it seems to him that they have sex less often than they actually do. To her, it seems that they have sex more often than they actually do.

Demands for performance take a heavy toll on participants of both sexes. We hear less and less about female frigidity (a mythical affliction that implies lack of any sexual feeling whatsoever but classically refers to lack of a vaginal orgasm) and more and more about male impotence (Julty, 1975). Women are told that passivity impairs their husbands' enjoyment, but they are also told that the rising tide of male impotence is due to female sexual assertiveness. Again, women are at fault no matter how they behave.

A similar double bind exists for women and premarital sex. Women have been "liberated" both from the need to be sexually inhibited and from the fear of an unwanted pregnancy. In many groups they are expected to engage in sexual activity without commitment or intimacy. And they have lost their traditional "excuses" for abstaining. An essay by the Lower East Side Women's Liberation Collective (1972) makes clear the point that sexual liberation does not imply liberation from one's sex role:

> The role of women in hip culture is to be all loving—and more to the point—loving of all. The right to be possessive, jealous or hurt is given up with lipstick. Nobody wants to mess with a woman who might get "hung-up." That's not cool. Making demands or being emotionally vulnerable is put down as being either bourgeois or sick. This type of non-monogamy puts social pressure on women to sleep with more than one man—very few men feel responsibility to a woman who is not his possession. The "free" woman is great until she gets pregnant or needs a little emotional or financial support—suddenly she finds that she is not free in the way she thought she was. Not philosophically free, but free like "free beer on St. Patrick's day." [pp. 356–357]

Females who accept male standards of sexual conduct may not find that any change in perception of their sex role has occurred. In fact there has been little exploration of the relationship between sexuality and sex role except in so-called deviant cases involving homosexuality. Sexual freedom and sex role equality may be entirely different developments that have been considered related only because of their mutual association with the new feminist movement. Indeed, recent evidence suggests that there may even be an inverse relationship between certain aspects of sexuality and preference for a more equal sex role.

SEX ROLE AND SEXUAL PREFERENCE: HETEROSEXUAL BODY PREFERENCE

Stereotypic conceptions about the relationship between body build and sexual behavior clearly exist. Women who are "well endowed" by nature are perceived as "sex goddesses," and some, such as Marilyn Monroe, may feel constrained by our cultural expectations to behave in an "appropriate" manner. Since our traditional definition of sexuality has been in terms of a male pattern, the sexuality of female "stars" is usually expressed in terms of a series of affairs involving little in the way of intimacy. In fact women with great natural beauty are perceived not to expect or need intimacy. The dramatically tragic end of a number of great beauties would suggest that once again our stereotypes are misleading.

Nevertheless we still have stereotypes about the relationship between behavior and body build. A relatively unexplored area is stereotypic perceptions of male performance and physique. Hairy arms and chests are considered potent, and large penises are considered more attractive than small ones (Verinis & Roll, 1970). We have already discussed the preference for mesomorphic physiques, but more specific information about the relationship of physique to perceived sexuality is available. Women prefer the parts of the male physique that they consider more potent to be larger (Lerner, 1969). Their preferences appear to be mediated by the performance capacity they attribute to various body builds. A relationship also exists between the kind of physique preferred and women's sex roles (Lavrakas, 1975). Traditionally feminine women preferred traditionally masculine physiques—those embodying a tapering V silhouette with relatively broad shoulders and chest and narrow hips. Less traditional women preferred a more medium male body build.

Although correlations were small, albeit significant, Lavrakas also found that women who had been raised with the relative absence of males (by the mother alone or with more female siblings than male ones) preferred more muscular silhouettes. They, as well as women who espouse more traditional feminine roles, seem to have incorporated the media stereotype into their concept of an ideal male. Since women from homes in which males are lacking tend to marry younger (Hetherington, 1975) and less happily, these data would suggest that marital choice based on physical characteristics may be detrimental.

There is evidence that males, too, reflect their personalities in their body preferences. Wiggins, Wiggins, and Conger (1968) found that men who prefer a large female figure tend to be high on measures of achievement and also to be drinkers. Those who preferred large breasts were likely to be readers of *Playboy* magazine. Those who preferred smaller figures tended to be persevering and from an upper-class background. It is difficult to interpret this information, but it suggests that preference for a traditional sex-appropriate build in members of the opposite sex is associated with more traditional masculine and feminine behavior. Such preference appears to be mediated by assumptions of sexual performance associated with a particular kind of figure. However, even women who have a non-traditional view of women's roles tend to reject body builds that appear unmasculine (Lavrakas, 1975).

Sexual equality should not be confused with sex role equality. Preference for sexually potent masculine and feminine bodies appears to be associated with traditional sex role ideology. Sexually "free hippie" women do not appear to have acquired the freedom of action of their males. Perhaps the best illustration of the lack of relationship between sexuality and other aspects of sex roles is the growth of such movements as "fascinating womanhood," which are designed to seduce men back into their traditional roles. These movements advise women to do everything sexually and nothing ideologically.

WHAT EVER HAPPENED TO ROMANCE?

Romantic Myths and Realities

One would like to believe that the attraction that males and females have for each other contains more positive aspects than the need to avoid being stigmatized as "unpairable" the need to bolster self-esteem by means of an attractive partner, the need to gain status with peers, or physiological needs relieved by sexual activity. An aspect of male–female relationships that is constantly emphasized by the media is the concept of romance. Romance as a factor in marital choice is a curiously American phenomenon. Romantic love as a phenomenon at all is an historically recent development. Rubin (1973), in his book *Liking and Loving*, reminds us that the romantic ideal was conceived by European nobility during the twelfth century in the games of "courtly love."

The essentials of the romantic ideal as portrayed by the media have been ably summarized by Albert Ellis (1954) in his book *The American Sexual Tragedy*. The romantic lover is unrealistic: He overevaluates and fictionalizes the beloved. The love must be described in verbally esthetic terms. As Tolstoy remarked, "Many people's love would be instantly annihilated if they could not speak of it in French." The romantic lover is aggressively individualistic: insisting, utterly, on his own romantic love choice and on an all-but-absolute lack of restraint in that choice. The romantic lover may be more frequently in love with love than with his beloved. He is intensely monogamous *at any one time*, demanding to be loved by the beloved for himself rather than for his position or accomplishments. Sexuality is valued only when it is linked to love. Physical attractiveness is stressed and violent passions are acceptable. Love is sufficient license for any sort of sexual activity, as in the high name of romance any passion can be pursued.

Many social critics have viewed the idea of basing the institution of marriage on romance as a disastrous social experiment. Most societies consider marriage a practical arrangement in which social class and religious similarities between individuals are of greater importance than their mutual attraction. Cross-culturally there is an association between a balanced division of labor by sex and the absence of romantic love as a basis for marriage (Sanday, 1974). We do not know which way this relationship works, if at all. Does the ideal of romantic love help keep women from acquiring power in the public domain? Or does equal participation in other activities give men experience in accepting a more balanced view of male and female relationships?

Recently studies have reported that individuals with low self-esteem have a greater romantic attachment to their partners (Dion & Dion, 1975). In general, women report more romantic attachments. Self-esteem also affects male commitment to female attractiveness, which is one of the components of the romantic ideal. Researchers experimentally altered male college students' self-esteem by informing them that they had performed either well or poorly on a task (Kiesler & Baral, 1970). Subjects later showed more attraction to an attractive female confederate if their self-esteem had been raised and more attraction to a less attractive woman if their self-esteem had been lowered.

The pursuit of the unattainable as a romantic guide appears to suit more selfish needs than has usually been implied. Elaine Walster and her associates (Walster, Walster, Piliavin, & Schmidt, 1973) examined the "playing hard to get" phenomenon in a variety of experimental situations. They found that two components contribute to a women's desirability: (1) how hard the woman is for the male subject to get and (2) how hard she is for other men to get. Selectively hard-to-get women (easy for the subject, but hard for all other men) were preferred to either uniformly hard-to-get women, uniformly easy-to-get women, and women about whom the subject had no information. Hard-to-get women (who had not selected the subject as a potential date) were described as "snotty" or "too picky." The men indicated that they feared that such a popular prestige date might not be enthusiastic about them, might stand them up or otherwise humiliate them in front of their friends, or was likely to be unfriendly, cold, and inflexible in her standards. Dating an easy-to-get woman was also considered a risky business, since she might be hard to get rid of, "get serious," or be so oversexed or overly affectionate in public as to embarrass them. These men also worried about what their friends might say or snicker about when they saw them together. "After all, they would know perfectly well why you were dating her!" (p. 116). In other words, the male romantic ideal combines all the prestige-giving assets of the hard-to-get woman with the warmth, friendliness, and pleasant qualities of the easy-to-get woman. The latter qualities are desirable in a date, but only if they are directed toward the referent male alone. The status-conferring properties of a woman may even be more important than her interpersonal behaviors. In fact one wonders whether the pursuit of an unattainable female (as in the romantic ideal) in itself confers status on a male.

Situational components are also important in the maintenance of romantic relationships between young people. Romances are most likely to break up during a period of separation that is legislated by the school year, such as winter or spring recess and summer vacation (Hill, Rubin, & Peplau, 1976). It is possible that the participants wished to sever the relationship and used these periods as an excuse to weaken their connection. It is also possible that romance is more a matter of convenience than it was previously believed to be.

People sometimes ask, "What is wrong about putting women on a pedestal?" First, it gets very uncomfortable up there. (See Figure 10.2.) Second, it turns women into prizes or possessions to be won rather than people with their own wants and needs. Fairy tales socialize us with the image of the sleeping princess with whose hand goes the kingdom. They fail to take into account the waking woman. We never do quite find out what happens after they all live happily after . . .

Liking and Loving

The major danger of using love as a guide for heterosexual relationships is that liking and loving, although related, are not the same thing (Rubin, 1970). Zick Rubin tested a large number of "emotionally involved" pairs on measuring instruments designed to discriminate "liking" in the sense of friendship from "love" in the sense of emotional involvement. He found that the correlations between scores measuring love of and liking for one's partner were only moderate. Love and liking are more highly related to each other among men than among women (Rubin, 1973). Unsurprisingly, the student pairs reported loving their partners more than their same-sex friends, while the gap between liking for partners and liking for friends was smaller.

OF PEDESTALS AND PIGEONS
By Burton Unger

Women have been put on pedestals for too many years to know about. Now it has always been accepted as truth that putting upon pedestals is a sign of honor, a way of exalting woman's place in the firmament. Why who else gets put upon pedestals but women and historical figures?

Trouble is that most of those historical figures are dead and it is their marble effigies that grace the pedestals. But women are asked, yea required, to mount that platform while still alive. Now marble figures (or granite figures for that matter) can't do much but remain firmly attached to the spot. They can't even avoid marauding pigeons. But for a living, breathing woman, being limited to a pedestal can't be much fun. Think of spending your whole creative life limited to a space about three by four feet in area and waist high above the ground (to my perception most pedestals are about that high, Statue of Liberty's excepted). You can't move around much. You even have to be careful jumping for joy (if you can find any joy) since unless you're a track star you're likely to miss the edge, come down hard and break an ankle. And you can't very well train to be a track star while standing on a pedestal.

Pedestal standing makes communication difficult, too. You've got to shout down at those below and they have to shout up. And your conversation isn't going to be too erudite since it's hard to go to college while standing on a pedestal. Ever try to get through Gibbon while standing in one place? Rodin's "Thinker" is at least sitting on a pedestal, but standing models are to the best of my knowledge unavailable.

There's only one way to get down off a pedestal—that's to be knocked down. It's commonly done to historical figures when new governments rewrite history. And it's commonly done to women when men get sick and tired shouting up to them.

In short, being placed on a pedestal is no honor and no fun—except for those damn pigeons.

Figure 10.2.

A comparison of the love versus liking scores of these male and female dating partners is more informative. The average love scores of men for their girlfriends and of women for their boyfriends were virtually identical. However, women liked their boyfriends significantly more than they were liked in return. Rubin suggests that sex biases in the liking scale (see Table 10.1) involving evaluation of the partner's intelligence, good judgment, and leadership potential produce this effect. Women are more likely to vote for their boyfriend in an election or recommend him for a responsible job than men are to reciprocate in these behaviors for their girlfriend.

One may distinguish between two components of liking: affec-

Table 10.1 ITEMS FROM RUBIN'S LOVE AND LIKING SCALES

LOVE SCALE
4. I would do almost anything for _____.
7. If I were lonely, my first thought would be to seek _____ out.
9. I would forgive _____ for practically anything.
LIKING SCALE
3. I would highly recommend _____ for a responsible job.
9. I think that _____ is one of those people who quickly wins respect.
12. _____ is the sort of person whom I myself would like to be.

SOURCE: Z. Rubin, *Liking and Loving* (New York: Holt, Rinehart and Winston, 1973) p. 216.

tion and respect. Men appear to have affection for their girlfriends but admire them less than they are admired in return. They do not distinguish between characteristics that elicit respect and those that elicit affection in their same-sex friends. In other words, even during a most romantic period the cultural formulas are observed. All the evidence suggests that same-sex "peering" is not the same as opposite-sex "pairing." We might well have entitled this chapter "Lovers and Other Strangers."

Chapter 11
Psychological Issues in Marriage, Housework, and Divorce

One area that has been left almost entirely to sociology is marriage and the family. The rationale for this relative neglect by psychologists has been that marriage is an institution and should be examined by those who are most concerned about the relationship between people and institutions—sociologists. Recent psychological research, however, has indicated that the marital relationship reflects phenomena that are present in unrelated women and men as well. In fact the roles traditionally inherent in being a wife—those of childbearer, childrearer, housekeeper, and sexual and social companion of a husband—are the most salient for the definition of womanhood in our society. Issues relating to children will be discussed in Chapter 12. In this chapter we will concentrate on the effects on men and women of a close dyadic association with a member of the other sex. As we will see, marriage is an asymmetrical institution and, as such, produces more negative effects for women than for men. In this chapter we will examine what these negative effects are, how they are mediated psychologically, and what happens when some of the contractual assumptions of a marriage are violated. Thus we will explore the effect of a relatively "mild" violation, such as the wife's working outside the home, to complete abrogation of the legal contract, such as divorce. This is a chapter in which few lasting conclusions can be reached, since it is evident that attitudes about and customs involving marriage are among the most rapidly changing patterns in our society.

WHO GETS MARRIED AND WHO DOESN'T

Who Marries?

In Chapter 10 we discussed the development of opposite-sex dyads by means of the dating relationship. While by no means everyone dates, nor does dating always start at the same age or go through the same sequence, virtually all Americans marry at some time in their lives. Over 85 percent of American females and a somewhat smaller percentage of males marry. At the moment we will not discuss whether they stay married. Although it is often assumed that no one, especially a woman, remains unmarried through choice, a look at the characteristics of single and married individuals of both sexes is illuminating. In general, women who remain unmarried appear to possess greater physical and mental health and greater economic resources than those who marry. The converse relationship is true for men. We will examine these relationships in some detail. It is important to deal with these data cautiously, however, since they are mostly correlational in nature and it is difficult to determine the causes of the connections between marriage and various sociological and psychological indicators.

Singlehood and Intrapsychic Variables

Although single people have been reported to have more psychiatric disorders than married people, this effect appears to be reversed for women (Gove, 1972). Married men are healthier than never-married men, whereas unmarried women are healthier than married women. The same relationship holds for symptoms of psychological distress such as nervousness, feelings of inertia, and insomnia (Bernard, 1972). Obviously, never-married women are healthier, both psychologically and physically, then never-married men. In other self-report studies single women indicate themselves to be happier than single men, although they report themselves less happy than married women who work outside the home (Shaver & Freedman, 1976). Unmarried women also report that they feel immobilized less than married women (Gurin, Veroff, & Feld, 1960).

Married women score consistently higher than unmarried women on instruments measuring depression, anxiety, phobia, and neurotic tendencies (Knupfer, Clark, & Room, 1966). Unmarried men, on the other hand, are more likely than married men to score as antisocial and as behaving in a morally lax manner.

Singlehood and Achievement

A similar differential relationship between sex and marriage has been found with variables relating to economic and social achievement. Higher levels of intelligence, education, and occupation are associated with singlehood among females (Spreitzer & Riley, 1974). Singlehood among males, however, is associated with poor interpersonal relations with parents and siblings. Successful women are far less likely to marry than their male counterparts. One study found that women scientists and engineers were six times less likely to marry than comparable men.

Preparation for early marriage appears to be associated in females with poorer feelings about the self. Thus women with high self-esteem date more frequently but go steady less often while in college than women with lower self-esteem (Klemer, 1971). Women who adapt to male standards of sexual activity are more likely to be married than those who maintain stricter moral codes (Knupfer et al., 1966). Self-esteem in itself does not appear to be linearly related to marital happinness. Women with either very high or very low self-esteem report less marital happiness than those with an average degree of self-acceptance. The disparity between expectations and reality may be particularly startling to women with high self-esteem. The effects of self-esteem may be confounded with the age of marriage. If low self-esteem, indeed, predicts an early marriage, it probably also predicts a less permanent one as well.

Class Differences and Singlehood

Educational and financial status affects the consequences of remaining single. Individuals from low socioeconomic strata and blue-collar families who remain unmarried are more likely to rely on the family for social contacts and activities and to live in the parental home (Lopata, 1973). When this breaks up, they go to live with siblings and with other close relatives. Marriage may look like a much more desirable alternative to this arrangement for most women.

Educational opportunity provides individuals with a chance to develop concepts about psychological freedom as well as increased scope for independent living. It should therefore not be surprising if more educated women choose alternatives to marriage. It is important to view their behavior as a choice, although it may be affected by male disdain for independent, assertive women. It is such women who skew the statistics about the correlates of remaining single versus being married for women and men. Contrary to popular myth, they appear to be both psychologically and economically able.

The Future of Singlehood

Jessie Bernard (1975a), a noted sociologist and social critic, views the coming decade as a tipping point in our concepts of marriage. The number of women who marry at a young age appears to be declining while the percentage of women with school-age children in the labor force is increasing. She points out that since 1968 more than 50 percent of all white male high school graduates have gone to college. Since college education is related to a positive attitude toward sex role equality in both males and females, it becomes increasingly likely that young women will come into contact with males who have some acceptance of a nontraditional role for women even if they have not had direct access to this idea themselves. Bernard expects the next decade to be a period of rapid change. One change that is already occurring, at least in urban centers, is an increasing number of single people who postpone marriage to relatively older ages. These individuals place considerable strain on societal assumptions about an association between pathology and remaining single.

SOCIETY AND SINGLEHOOD

Stereotypes of the Single Woman and the Psychological Establishment

We have already discussed the general American image of the "spinster" versus the "bachelor." It is important to note, however, that classical clinical psychology and psychiatry have reinforced the notion that failure to marry carries with it evidence of a serious psychological flaw. The "orthodox" view is that it is "well known" that being able to form long-term, close, lasting relationships is a mark of emotional maturity and of a healthy personality. Evidence on the long-term effects of marriage on men and women does not support this view for the latter. Nevertheless unmarried women are susceptible to social judgments about their supposed deficient psyches that may decrease their self-esteem and impair their judgment about themselves and their motives.

Margaret Adams (1976), in her recent book *Single Blessedness,* has discussed the psychological tactics that are used to threaten unmarried women. It is presumed that not being married is *not* due to the woman's choice. Any assertions on her part to the contrary are regarded as rationalizations—intellectual exercises used to deal with a difficult emotional reality. The ultimate tactic is to accuse her of denial, a defense mechanism that is supposedly responsible for all the unresolved conflict and pent-up psychic and sexual energy associated with the stereotype of the single woman.

While we will deal with the role of clinical psychology and psychiatry in supporting social systems that maintain female inferiority in Chapter 14, several of Adams' points are of particular interest here. She points out that such psychological theories define what is essentially a social situation—marriage—in terms of deviance and deficiency. The high premium put on marriage requires that one have a plausible reason to explain singleness. By persuading the individual that his or her socially deviant state will be remedied by marrying, psychological orthodoxy shores up a tottering social system rather than promoting institutional change. It also supports the pervasive but harmful fallacy that there is one psychological norm that embodies good health and social value.

Singlehood and Social Systems

Some of the negative stereotypes about single women in our society may derive from their implied threat to masculine dominance. Their rejection of traditional male protection sets single women up as ready targets for male hostility. Nontraditional single women have been characterized as hostile, aggressive, and castrating. (Traditional ones—or spinsters—are more likely to be characterized as timid.) It should be remembered, however, that they are frequently in situations in which their survival as viable wage earners and as self-respecting individuals depends on their own efforts. Nevertheless we have no objective evidence that never-married women are more assertive than those who do marry, although they do show greater objective achievement.

The traditional social setting also makes survival as a single woman difficult. Much social life, especially in the suburbs, takes place in terms of couples. It is not true, however, that single women have generally fewer social contacts than men. No sex differences in number of friends reported has been found between unmarried men and women (Booth, 1972). Married men, however, report having more friends than married women. The women report more close contact with relatives than men do. Sex differences in number of friends reported after marriage seem to be strongly affected by social class. Blue-collar men and women over 45 report having the same number of close friends, but white-collar men report more than comparable women. This is particularly true if their fathers were white-collar too. These data suggest that marriage, particularly white-collar marriage, is more limiting on women's friendships than on men's. Women are even more likely to identify their husbands' friends as their own closest friends after marriage than men are to accept former close friends of the wife (Babchuk & Bates, 1963). Female friendships, however, do appear to be affectively richer than those of males. They see their friends more, engage in more spontaneous activities with them, and confide in them more than males with the same number of close friends.

WHO MARRIES WHOM?

It is possible that an examination of who marries whom will tell us something about the relative value of marriage for women and men. We have already discussed the fact that virtually all Americans marry at some point in their lifetime. There is evidence that some forms of assortative mating takes place. That is, people tend to select mates who are to some extent similar to themselves. In fact men and women appear to select each other on the basis of physical as well as psychological characteristics. Marital partners have been found to resemble each other in level of physical attractiveness (Murstein, 1972) and in body structure (Vandenburg, 1972). Thin people tend to marry other thin people and plump couples tend to pair. Individuals are also more likely to marry those who are similar to themselves in social-class factors, values, and even geographic contiguity (Rubin, 1973).

While better-educated and more successful women are less likely to marry, those who do are more likely to marry men with a greater degree of occupational success than women with lower amounts of education (Elder, 1969; Taylor & Glenn, 1976). Highly attractive women also make an above-chance percentage of "good" marriages. A good marriage is defined by sociologists in terms of the social status of the mate rather than in terms of the length of the marriage or the personal satisfactions achieved. In terms of the occupational status of their fathers, attractive women tend to marry up. This relationship is most marked among the daughters of manual workers. Attractiveness had little effect on the occupational status of the husbands of women who had high-status fathers. Here it is educational level that relates most to their husbands' occupational prestige (Taylor & Glenn, 1976). Thus in response to the old saw about "whether it is better to be born rich instead of beautiful," these data suggest that either one can enhance a women's marital potential. We know nothing about the value of physical attractiveness in enhancing a man's marital potential (another example of asymmetries in research), but higher socioeconomic status or occupational potential clearly makes him a more desirable marital partner.

WHEN PEOPLE MARRY: THEORIES ABOUT MARRIAGE

Commodity Exchange Theories

Sociologists and social psychologists have tended to view marriage in terms of the exchange of social and material resources. Their basic position is that each partner contributes resources that are valuable to the other and to the family as a whole. The resources that have been examined most carefully are those that are traditionally linked to males, such as income, prestige, and power. Those contributed by the female include her attractiveness and the quality of her performance as a parent, companion, housekeeper, sex partner, and so forth. Although a little attention is now being paid to female contributions in primarily male domains (to be discussed later), no attention is yet being paid to male contributions in primarily female domains. Thus one of the most important texts on husband–wife relationships (Blood & Wolfe, 1960) implies that emotional needs within a marriage are asymmetrical, with the wife needing far more than the husband. They include a number of tables on the therapeutic utilization of the husband after a bad day and a subchapter on rationales for bothering the husband. The book also contains such quotes as "The higher the wife's social status, the more apt she is to turn explicitly to her husband for help in trouble, and the less apt she is to turn her negative feelings against him" (p. 187). No comparable discussion with reference to men's emotional needs is present. For example, what is the role of the special attentions paid to men by their wives and the personal services they provide, such as washing their clothing or buying it, in the positive psychological effects of marriage for men versus its negative effects for women?

Unequal Exchange: Factors Relating to Husband–Wife Power

Marriage has been viewed in terms of an unequal exchange model because the sexes have unequal access to the resources of our society. Sex or services are exchanged for money or status. The more one spouse has control over a particular resource that is considered important or necessary by the other, the greater her or his tolerance of unequal exchange (Safilios-Rothschild, 1976). The greater the gap between the value to the wife of the resources contributed by the husband and the value to the husband of the resources contributed by the wife, the greater the husband's relative power. In sexist societies, including our own, women have little or no access to desirable socioeconomic resources. Thus, their husbands have a great advantage in the determination of family power.

Contribution to the Family Economy

Husband dominance of the family is associated with high-status occupations, occupational prestige, and income (Wolfe, 1959; Blood & Wolfe, 1960). Wives gain power in the family in proportion to their level of education, the number of years they have worked outside the home, and their level of participation in outside activities (Gillespie, 1971). These data are consistent with the hypothesis that power and status outside the family are correlated with power and status within it. When women have an increased opportunity to function outside the home, even in a voluntary capacity, their power within the home increases.

Cross-culturally, there is no evidence that contribution to the family economy, in itself, accounts for the superiority of the male role. Aronoff and Crano (1975) extensively reviewed data from 862 societies and concluded that women do contribute substantially to the family economy—they account for 44 percent of subsistence production. A curvilinear relationship between women's relative contribution to the economy and their relative status in a society appears to exist (Sanday, 1974). When the percentage contributed by women was either very high or very low, female status was low as defined by the women's ability to allocate property beyond the domestic unit, the demand for goods produced by females beyond the family unit, female participation in political life, and membership in female solidarity groups devoted to female political and economic interests. When women contribute an amount equal to that contributed by men, their status is highest. Unfortunately, little in the way of explanation for this rather puzzling relationship has been provided.

Simple resource theory does not appear to be a sufficient explanation of women's relative lack of power within the family. For example, families of recent Cuban immigrants to the Miami area have been examined and it has been found that division of power within the family is affected by both the resources of the family and its ideology (Richmond, 1976). The tradition of male authority is strong among Cubans, and among families where this tradition is held strongly women had little effect on decision making even when they contributed to the family economy to a considerable extent. Women had the highest degree of power within the family when they were economically independent, were younger, and had fewer children. How much money a woman made, rather than her occupational status, also affected her power.

When the ideology of the couple was partialed out, the correlation between the wife's salary and her decision-making power remained significant. The influence of the husband's monetary resources, however, increased tremendously. The men who made the greatest amount of money had the greatest authority within the home, while those who made less exerted less authority. In households where the male holds a high-status position (where it would be difficult in any case for the wife to contribute economic resources equivalent to the husband's high salary), ideology appears to exert a moderating influence on the husband's behavior. Whether or not the wife was working, couples with egalitarian ideologies practiced a more equal division of power within the family than those with male-dominant orientations. However, a two-way interaction between resources and ideology must be considered. It is possible that the wife's access to resources contributes to the development of egalitarian norms.

The power of women within the family also varies as a function of race and socioeconomic status in our society. It appears that the man's position within the family unit is initially dependent on his holding some sort of job (Aldous, 1969a). However, ethnic differences in the relative power of the husband exist that may be dependent on differences in subcultural ideology. Husband power was greatest among oriental couples and least among black couples (Centers, Raven, & Rodriguez, 1971). Having a working wife decreased the husband's decision-making power in black families, but not in white families from the same census tract (Aldous, 1969b). The relationship held even when the data were controlled for family size, income, and the age of the youngest child.

Love as a Power Resource

In addition to demographic variables such as race and class, certain personality variables appear to predict relative power within the family. Both husbands and wives in husband-dominant families have high authoritarianism scores (Centers et al., 1971). Wives in husband-dominant families appear to have a greater need for love and affection than those in wife-dominant families (Wolfe, 1959). If the wife is not seeking emotional support from her husband, she may feel freer to exercise power stemming from other need–resource bases. Of course her exercise of power might lead to a decrease in the love and support she receives.

In a recent paper Constantina Safilios-Rothschild (1976), a leading theorist and researcher on marital roles, has discussed the role of softer, "more feminine" resources, such as love, sex, and companionship, in the distribution of power within the family. She suggests that the spouse who is "less in love" has the advantage in the control of this kind of resource. A wife has an advantage when affectional resources are controlled by her and needed by her husband. It provides her with a basis for control despite her lack of control over socioeconomic resources. It may also serve as a source of actual or perceived equity in the marital relationship (Walster & Walster, 1978).

Love has been almost totally neglected as a variable by social scientists, for several reasons: (1) It is considered to be a vague, subjective feeling that defies operational measurement; (2) it is treated as a constant, since it is assumed that Americans marry for love and remain equally in love throughout the marriage; (3) male researchers are uncomfortable with such a soft, "feminine" variable. Safilios-Rothschild questions each of these assumptions and gives some recent data that she has collected in support of her hypothesis. She asked husbands and wives which spouse each perceived to be more in love. (She considers their perception of reality to be the "reality" that influences their behavior.) She also asked them who makes sacrifices and compromises more. Her hypothesis was supported by the answers supplied by Athenian wives. When the women perceived that their husbands were more in love, they also perceived that they could successfully claim the power to make important and/or infrequent decisions significantly more often then women who perceived that they were more in love than their husbands. When both spouses perceived that they were equally in love, power was shared equally. The resource of love is particularly important to women because of the large number of women who do not have access to a high level of socioeconomic resources.

Power and Children

The wife's ability to control affectional resources may account for some of the findings that are not easily explained by simple exchange theory. For example, the wife's power in the family tends to decline with age and the number of children. Moreover, although the wife who works outside the home receives more assistance (mostly grocery shopping and child care) from her husband than the wife who remains within the home, the financial resources she contributes to the family have only a minimal effect. Surprisingly, it is the wife with fewer children who receives the most help. The husband's power appears to be greatest after the first child is born but is not yet in school. Since it appears that the wife contributes more resources to the marriage in terms of child care during this period, her power ought to increase rather than decrease. It has been suggested that it is the value placed on the resources contributed by each spouse outside the marriage that determines relative power (Heer, 1963). The more power one can exert outside the marriage, the greater the number of attractive alternatives available by which to resist control. Thus even voluntary work that provides no income to the family increases the woman's power within it. The birth of children decreases the power of a woman, since there are few alternatives to her role as principal childrearer in our society. She may also become sexually less attractive during this period, or at least have less time for emotional "stroking" of her mate, thereby further decreasing the resources with which she can "bargain." These data would suggest that attractive women are able to exert greater power, at least during the early years of their marriage, but no studies have yet been done on this issue.

The dynamics of power distribution within a family are probably more closely related to cultural than to biological factors. Here again we find differences between blacks and whites. Powerlessness has been directly related to the number of children in all groups of women in the United States except blacks when age, education, husband's occupation, and family income are controlled (Morris & Sison, 1974). No differences in powerlessness between users and nonusers of contraception were found. Female powerlessness does not seem to increase the number of children, but large numbers of children generate female powerlessness. It is not clear why the same dynamics do not apply to black and white families, although it is possible that the extended family relationships and alternate child care arrangements utilized by many black women may account for the lack of relationship between their power and the number of children they have. However, it should be kept in mind that blacks differ from whites in a variety of ways that relate to sex roles. The relative socioeconomic gap between the two sexes is smaller in blacks; the group as a whole possesses fewer resources; and ideology about sexuality and sex roles appears to be more egalitarian.

IS POWER AN ISSUE IN AMERICAN MARRIAGES?

Some Methodological Concerns

It has long been assumed that the predominant pattern of decision making within the American home is egalitarian. Husbands and wives supposedly dominate in an equal number of representative decision-making areas (Blood & Wolfe, 1960). (See Table 11.1.) One of the major problems in the examination of this area is that wives are much more frequently questioned about the behavior of their families than husbands are (Safilios-Rothschild, 1969). Husbands and wives, however, may disagree radically as to who has more power in the marriage. In one study in the Detroit area Safilios-Rothschild (1969) found that in 55 percent of the sample there was serious disagreement about who was the dominant figure in decision making. In another study (Larson, 1974) only 25 percent of the families studied agreed about their problem-solving processes. Husbands and wives both tended to attribute more power to themselves than to their spouse, but children agreed in assigning more power to their father. It is important to recognize that differential perception of family relationships may be an important aspect of family reality that affects the behavior of all of the family's members.

It is also important to remember that not all decisions made within a family have the same importance. For example, a decision about what job the husband should take is much more important than a decision about how much money the family should spend on food each week. Some decisions are made less often than others, whereas others may require less time and energy to be carried out. Husbands appear to perceive that all "important" decisions are made either by themselves or on an egalitarian basis and to perceive that their wives make the decisions on tasks that are time-consuming and/or repetitive, such as purchasing food or clothing, interacting with relatives and, of course, raising children (Safilios-Rothschild, 1969).

There is evidence that self-report data and data gathered by more direct behavioral observations bear little resemblance to each other. One researcher presented couples with real problems to discuss in areas in which questionnaires answered separately revealed differences between the wife's and the husband's viewpoint (Olson, 1969). No relationship between self-report and behavioral measures of power (whose initial position was eventually jointly agreed upon) was found. Husbands tended to overestimate their actual power and wives to underestimate it. There is more congruence between ac-

Table 11.1   DECISIONS WITHIN THE FAMILY

In every family somebody has to decide such things as where the family will live and so on. Many couples talk such things over first, but the *final* decision often has to be made by the husband or the wife. For instance, who usually makes the final decision about what car to get?

   . . . about whether or not to buy some life insurance?

   . . . about what house or apartment to take?

Who usually makes the final decision about what job your husband should take?

   . . . about whether or not *you* should go to work or quit work?

   . . . about how much money your family can afford to spend per week on food?

   . . . about what doctor to have when someone is sick?

   . . . and, about where to go on a vacation?

Possible answers included:

1. Husband always
2. Husband more of the time
3. Husband and wife exactly the same
4. Wife more than husband
5. Wife always

SOURCE: From R. O. Blood, Jr., and D. M. Wolfe, *Husbands and Wives* (New York: Free Press, 1960) p. 282. Copyright 1960 by the Macmillan Company. Reprinted by permission.

tual and perceived power for wives than for husbands, probably because the women predicted less power for themselves and actually possessed less.

Marital Happiness and Marital Power

Marital partners and potential partners appear to be at least covertly aware that power is an issue in relationships between the sexes. For example, conformity with the partner's perception has been examined in heterosexual couples of varying degrees of acquaintance (Stone, 1973). The judgment involved the autokinetic phenomenon—a situation in which an illusion of movement is generated by a bright light in an otherwise dark room. Groups of individuals usually come to some agreement about the extent of the apparent movement. The extent of this agreement was measured for strangers, strangers who had been told they would like each other, couples who had been dating for a short time, and couples who had been dating over a year or were engaged or married. Both women and men conformed to their partner's judgment, except among the long-term couples. Although all subjects showed the influence of the partner in a subsequent session alone, in the intimate partnerships men conformed less during the session in which they functioned as members of a pair. They may have viewed conformity to their partner's perceptions as a threat to their autonomy or have been afraid that they would be unduly influenced by their intimate partner.

No such effects were found among couples who did not have longstanding relationships. These effects could reflect perceptions about the "legitimate" distribution of authority. Egalitarian or male-dominant patterns are perceived to be the norm in our society. The effectiveness of the decision-making process may be affected by assumptions based on sex roles. Thus blue-collar families have been found to perform better in problem-solving situations when the husband was dominant, while white-collar families performed more effectively when decision making was egalitarian (Tallman & Miller, 1974). It is possible that power structures that are discrepant from normative expectations foster greater family strain. In the white-collar families husbands from egalitarian families had higher self-esteem. There was no relationship between male self-esteem and power distribution in the blue-collar families. The researchers suggest that wives of white-collar husbands can exercise authority only when their husbands are strong enough to allow this. For men who have less self-esteem or are in a weak position in terms of socioeconomic status, the question of who leads the family may be a source of anxiety.

The marital dyad cannot be analyzed in isolation from its sociocultural matrix. Thus it has been reported that families in which the husband is highly dominant are also those that are higher in reported marital happiness and more effective problem solvers (Kolb & Straus, 1974). It appears, however, that in many marriages the wife gains power only through the husband's relative ineffectiveness. Such wife-dominant families are under considerable social as well as economic strain. To the extent to which a family departs from the norms of male dominance, it may come into conflict with other members of society—friends, relatives, employers—and their expectations. In general, working-class families, whatever the familial power distribution, are lower in marital happiness than middle-class families. It is possible that the high satisfaction with marriage in husband-dominant homes may be due to their higher social status and comfortable financial condition. The whole family is better off generally, although we do not know whether the wife and/or husband would be happier under a more egalitarian arrangement. The joint satisfaction of the marital pair does seem to be related to the form as well as the distribution of power within the family (Raven, 1974). Very satisfied couples reported the use of referent power—power based on the goals of the family unit—as a large component of the decision-making process. The few respondents who reported themselves to be very unsatisfied with their marriages indicated that coercive power was used.

SOCIETAL ASSUMPTIONS AND MARITAL RELATIONSHIPS

Male authority in marriage is institutionalized in our society. Although we have removed the word *obey* from "love, honor, and obey" in the marriage ceremony, married women still derive most of their status from that of their husbands. Both husbands and wives pay little attention to the attainments of wives in assessing the social status of a married couple (Felson & Knoke, 1974). This was true despite the fact that in 27 percent of the sample the wives had more education than their husbands and in 42 percent more both spouses were on the same educational level.

In a similar study examining how familial social status is evaluated by individuals outside the dyad, the occupational level and educational attainments of husbands and wives in hypothetical households were varied (Rossi, Sampson, Bose, Jasso, & Passel, 1974). All possible combinations except totally improbable ones (e.g., a female college president married to a janitor) were examined. The investigators found that the husband's occupation counted twice as much toward the household's social standing than his education, no matter what his combination of job and educational level. The husband's characteristics were also twice as important as those of the wife. If a female physician was described as being married to a male lathe operator, the husband's work still had more effect on the perceived status of the family. In deciding the fairness of income, raters thought that the husbands' characteristics were again more important than those of the wives. For example, raters allowed the husband an extra $1000 per additional year of education but gave a comparable wife only $500 before they thought her overpaid. One study, in fact, indicates that the wife's employment actually produces a slight decrease (about 3%) in family status (Nosanchuk, 1972). Even if it was implied that the wife was forced to work by economic pressures (by using descriptions of her that included such phrases as "shops carefully" or "prefers inexpensive entertainment"), no differences in judgment about social status were induced.

Wives who work outside the home may enjoy two sets of status lines: one achieved individually and one derived from their husbands. The wife's achievements may confer status on her personally even though they do not effect judgments about the family. Married female white-collar workers in Finland ranked women in professional occupations higher than the wives of men in comparable occupations (Haavio-Mannila, 1969). Blue-collar women reversed this ranking and seemed to admire a woman's ability to obtain high status in a way that did not entail work. Little work has been done on how people combine statuses to make a global assessment. Small discrepancies between women's achieved and derived statuses may be easily adjusted, but large discrepancies are harder to deal with. A woman with high achieved status who is married to a man from whom she derives a status much lower than that which she has acquired by her own efforts may be considered to have low "erotic rank" (Safilios-Rothschild, 1975). It may be concluded by others that she is not sexy or attractive enough to have obtained a male who is more nearly her equal.

THE WIFE WHO WORKS OUTSIDE THE HOME

Asymmetrical transfer of the husband's occupational and educational status to his wife combined with the fact that she acquires relatively little status from her own accomplishments (which may even detract from judgments about familial position and her own attractiveness) are not likely to provide high motivation for women to work outside the home. Nevertheless an increasing number of women are now employed full or part time. The wife who works outside the home alters the dynamics of the family relationship. These alterations tell us something about how relationships are normatively maintained.

Effects on Wife and Husband

We have already noted that wives who work outside the home report themselves as happier than other women. We have also seen that they appear to gain power relative to their husbands from such employment. Wives who work outside the home also report themselves as more satisfied with their marriages and in more general agreement with their spouses (Burke & Weir, 1976). They felt that they communicated with them more in a variety of areas, and especially in terms of communication of feelings, about sex, and about the spouse's parents. Women who were primarily housewives reported poorer mental and physical health. They reported more feelings of "being in a rut," sickness in their families, and difficulties in communicating with and showing affection for their husbands. The primary area of communication with their husbands was talking about the children.

Surprisingly, despite what would appear to be a better relationship with their wives (and a happier, more satisfied wife at that), the husbands of women who work outside the home reported greater job pressures and expressed greater dissatisfaction with their jobs, marriages, and physical and psychological health than the husbands of homemakers. They were also more concerned about housing problems, feelings of being in a rut, money problems, and increasing difficulties in communicating with and showing affection for their wives. The husbands of homemakers reported more concern with the general world situation and the possibility that their children would not live up to their expectations. The husbands of women working outside the home actually communicated more with their wives and were in greater general agreement with them, even though they perceived themselves to have less marital happiness than the men whose wives did not work outside the home.

Men whose wives work outside the home may be subject to greater stress than men whose wives only work within it. They must participate more in household chores, and the economic benefits that the family derives from the wife's work may not mitigate the difficulties the husband experiences as a result of a dual-career marriage. When the wife works outside the home, the time and energy she can give to the emotional, social, and physical needs of her husband are in shorter supply. Men may have to deal with a diminished sense of self-worth when they are put in an unaccustomed support role. Wives working outside the home, on the other hand, are expanding into a role that has positive value for them. There is little to suggest that men perceive the roles that they fill in dual-career families as contributing to their personal growth and fulfillment. Husbands may accept the situation out of a sense of fair play, wanting to see the wife happy, or resignation to the inevitable rather than for any positive reasons (Bebbington, 1973).

These data must be evaluated cautiously. A number of alternate explanations appear to be equally likely. First, the members of these two-career families were younger and had been married for a shorter time than the members of families in which the woman had remained within the home. It is possible that different reference group norms exist such that younger men expect more personal satisfactions from marriage than older men in longer-established marriages. Second, the sex role ideology of the husbands of women working within versus outside the home has not been explored. It seems likely that men whose wives work outside the home have a less traditional masculine ideology, which is reflected in their behavior. These men communicate more than the husbands of homemakers and worry more about whether or not they are showing affection. They may be more empathetic and self-disclosing than more traditional males. Their responses on the questionnaire may reflect self-report biases in the sense that they are more willing to admit to affective shortcomings and marital problems than the husbands of women who maintain a more traditional homemaking role. Third, the researchers note that the husbands of women who work outside the home earned significantly less income than the husbands in one-career families. While this might have been a function of age, it is also a possible source of dissatisfaction, especially in our society, which tends to measure masculinity by the size of a paycheck. It is possible that their wives worked outside the home in response to real or perceived inadequacy in socioeconomic resources.

I do not wish to deny that dual-career families put a strain on the husband that is not present for the husbands of homemakers. Nor do I wish to suggest that home–career strains must always be shared equally by both sexes, but it is important that sociocultural explanations for phenomena be explored before women are blamed for their husbands' ills.

Sex and the Employed Woman

In addition to the finding that the woman who works outside the home is happier and more satisfied with her marriage, there is also evidence that she is more sexually adventurous. A positive correlation between assertiveness and reported sexual satisfaction has been reported for employed professional women (Whitley & Poulsen, 1975). The more assertive the woman, the more diverse sexual activity she reports. Her sexual satisfaction also increases with age and with the length of the marriage. Interestingly, in light of our previous discussion about the relative importance of the female orgasm, orgasm with intercourse is not the item most heavily affecting the feeling of sexual satisfaction. Activities that most affect sexual satisfaction among these married professional women are, in order of importance, hugging, being held, talking, holding hands, being stroked by a male, bathing with her partner, orgasm with intercourse, and undressing in front of her partner.The women with the highest sexual satisfaction scores included such diverse activities as oral–genital sex for both male and female, more complex (unspecified) undressing techniques, and the use of scents and fantasy.

Married women who are employed outside the home report greater happiness than single women and have fewer psychological problems than homemakers (Shaver & Freedman, 1976). Women with sexual problems, mainly difficulty in reaching orgasm and slowness or inability to be aroused, are less happy in general. Although the question has not been examined directly, it is possible that married women working outside the home have, contrary to popular stereotypes, greater sexual adjustment or capacity to enjoy their sexuality than more traditionally feminine women. The growth and popularity of such movements as Fascinating Womanhood would suggest that more traditional women are concerned about their sexual image. The women who is employed outside the home, since she is more satisfied with herself, seems to have less need to prove herself sexually. In fact recent data indicate that women who work outside the home are less apt to engage in extramarital relationships than wives who are not gainfully employed (Edwards & Booth, 1976). The wife's employment status does not affect the extramarital activity of her husband. However, men's extramarital affairs were increased by their wives' domination of the family. Variables affecting in-marriage and out-of-marriage sexual activity were not highly related to each other. Perceived decrease in the spouse's affection decreased the frequency of coitus for both sexes, but more for men. However, factors that tend to decrease sexual activity in marriage do not appear to lead to increases in sexual activity outside of it. Since women who are employed outside the home report greater satisfaction with their marriage than homemakers, these data imply that the husbands of employed women engage in more frequent and diverse sexual acts. No one has yet noted whether they indeed report themselves to be more sexually satisfied than the husbands of more traditional women.

WHAT'S WRONG WITH BEING A HOUSEWIFE?

Issues involving housewives and housework are among the most divisive in the women's movement today. It is probably no accident that I postponed writing this section of the chapter for about six weeks. It was tempting to dismiss the area as being of major concern only to sociologists. The psychological questions in the area, however, probably strike at the core of questions involving sex-specific behaviors in general and "women's problems" in particular.

What or Who Is a Housewife?

Difficulties in the examination of housewives and housework begin with the definition of the role itself. Although several books have been written exclusively about housewives, they have not produced a completely satisfactory definition of the individuals about whom they are writing. For example, Helena Lopata (1971), in her book *Occupation Housewife*, defines a housewife as the female individual who has the responsibility for running her home, whether she performs the tasks herself or employs others to do so. Thus all housewives are women, although not all women are housewives. In terms of her definition, being a housewife is a nonfamilial role, as opposed to that of wife or mother—although it shares characteristics of these roles.

If, however, being a housewife is not a familial role, is it an employment role? In Britain at least, legal precedent explicitly denies that housework is work because no wages or salary are received for it (Oakley, 1974a). In almost all industrialized countries the housewife as a worker has no right to financial benefits, such as sickness or unemployment benefits, that other workers receive through state insurance systems. The social response to this kind of ambivalent status—neither fish nor fowl, neither supplier of emotional resources nor supplier of material ones—has made the role of housewife a low-status one with which women identify reluctantly. Most of us have heard the defensive comment "I'm just a housewife."

Attitudes Toward Housework

The argument is often advanced that while women enjoy some of the aspects of the role of married female not employed outside the home—primarily some components of their roles as wives and/or mothers—the role of housewife itself is not an enjoyable one. Oakley (1974b) did an intensive analysis of interviews with 40 randomly selected British housewives that has been published in a book entitled *The Sociology of Housework*. She found that 28 of the housewives named housework as the most disliked aspect of the role. The tasks most frequently mentioned as being unpleasant were cleaning, shopping, cooking, washing up, and washing and ironing. When questioned more closely about what it was about these tasks that the housewives found so unpleasant, the majority of her respondents indicated that they involved hard, unsatisfying work. Thirty experienced monotony in housework, and 36 complained of fragmentation. They saw their work as a series of unrelated tasks, none of which required their full attention. Even cooking, which could be creative, was not perceived as being so because of the demands of husbands and children for certain foods at particular times of the day. Oakley notes that housewives share with assembly line workers, the most dissatisfied group of individuals employed outside the home, a similar level of complaints about the monotony, fragmentation, and speed required in their work.

When requested to name the "best thing" about being a

housewife, women cite their autonomy in terms of time. They note, however, that the work must get done even if they can choose, to some extent, the sequence and timing of chores. Autonomy in these terms seems to represent "freedom from" some rigidities of structure rather than "freedom to" structure one's life the way one wishes.

Other criticisms of housework have focused on the lack of rewards. Since much of the work is done in isolation within the home, little in the way of "trade standards" exist. Much of the work, and even the necessity for the work, is self-defined. Clothing must be cleaned periodically, for example, but how often and how intense a cleansing procedure constitutes "cleanliness" remains largely undefined. Many housewives complain of insufficient preparation for this role—one of the few that does not require extensive pre-education. (Home economics or domestic-science courses are often regarded as trivial or somehow demeaning.) It is one of the few positions for which one does not "apply."

The Training of a Housewife

American women enter the role of housewife "sideways," first as an adjunct to the role of wife and later as an adjunct to that of mother. Dating and marriage lead them inevitably to the role for which no similar male counterpart exists. No organized social system tests the woman as a candidate and admits or rejects her on the basis of her skills. In fact one of the major criticisms of the role is that a woman's unique characteristics are considered irrelevant (Bem & Bem, 1970). When a boy is born, it is difficult to predict what he will be doing 25 years later. He will be permitted to fulfill his own unique potential, especially if he is white and middle class. But if the newborn infant is a girl, we can confidently predict how she will be spending her time 25 years later. Her individuality does not have to be considered.

Even an IQ in the genius range does not guarantee that a woman's potential will be expressed. In a famous study of over 1300 men and women whose IQs averaged 151 (Terman & Oden, 1959), 86 percent of the men had achieved prominence in professional and managerial occupations. In contrast, only a minority of the women were even employed at that time. Of those who were employed outside the home, 37 percent were nurses, librarians, social workers, and noncollege teachers. An additional 26 percent were secretaries, stenographers, bookkeepers, and office workers. Only 11 percent were in higher professions such as law, medicine, or college teaching. Even at age 44, long after their children had reached school age, 61 percent of these highly gifted women were full-time homemakers. The homogenization of America's women is the major consequence of society's sex role ideology.

A major focus of debate is whether being a housewife is a freely chosen occupation for women. We may assume that being a wife and, probably, being a mother are to some extent a result of choice, although we have already discussed the fact that marriage as a free choice for women is limited by the degree of social stigma an older unmarried woman endures. The choice of being married and *not* taking responsibility for housekeeping duties appears to be an even greater illusion. Despite the great attention paid in the media to working wives and the changing forms of the American household, the great weight of evidence is that household responsibilities remain primarily in women's hands.

The Distribution of Household Tasks

In a questionnaire answered by 205 housewives, 46 percent reported receiving no help from their husbands in preparing meals while only 10 percent reported receiving regular help from them (Lopata, 1971). Forty-seven percent of the women reported that their husbands never helped in such household tasks as making beds, straightening up, or dusting, and 49 percent received no assistance with laundry or other clothing care. The most common area in which they received assistance was shopping for food. Sometimes, ironically, this was because the woman did not have the use of the family car during the week. Thus she was even more isolated within her home and was prevented from doing the one chore that Oakley's housewives perceived as quite pleasant since it offers an "excuse" for nonfrivolous social contact.

Women who are employed outside the home participate less in household chores and make fewer routine decisions about them, while their husbands participate more and make more decisions. (Hoffman, 1960). Nevertheless even these women have the primary responsibility in task allocation—what we may think of as administrative responsibility for the home. They also spend more time on household chores than their working husbands. Socialist "paradises" do not provide any relief from this sex role specificity in household responsibility. The so-called "time budgets" of 841 working men and women in the Soviet Union were analyzed by an American sociologist, David Mace (1961). Although men and women gave an equal number of hours to their paid work, the division of their time in the performance of household tasks deviated sharply from the concept of equality. The women gave twice as many hours to travel and shopping, and four times as many to domestic work, than the men. This put them four hours behind in the course of each day. Two of these hours were taken out of rest, leisure, and sleep; an hour and a quarter out of self-education; a half-hour out of political activities; and a half-hour out of personal hygiene. They did not specify from what source they drained the final quarter of an hour. Women with older or even grown-up children continued to have much heavier domestic tasks than comparable men. It has been suggested that the Soviet working mother carries the extra burden not of parenthood (since much of the burden of child care is borne outside the home) but of domesticity.

Housework and Psychological Health

Labor-saving devices have not decreased the number of hours spent doing household chores (Vanek, 1974), but they have changed the standards of "excellence" in their performance. We are grimly amused by Mary Hartmann, who worries about "waxy buildup" on her floors. In a sense we may be implicitly responding to the notion that the skills that make one a good housewife may not be the same as those that make one a good wife or mother. In fact they may conflict with interpersonal skills in terms of time. The strongest criticism of housework may be that expressed by Oakley, who states that housework is directly opposed to the possibility of human self-actualization. The same job requirements are imposed on all kinds of women with dissimilar skills and abilities. The housewife cannot get any information about herself from the work she does. There is no possibility of growth or advancement—only a transitory feeling of accomplishment for work that provides little in the way of intellectual challenge. If the housewife receives any recognition from her husband for her labors, she may feel that it is unearned or at least not commensurate with the amount of effort she has expended. Although they report themselves as happy, housewives as a group show more symptoms of stress and are more depressed than any other comparable sex or age group (Radloff, 1975). In Chapter 14 we will discuss the relationship between the gender-specific roles of women and men and their mental health more specifically.

The Politics of Housework

It has been suggested by numerous feminist sociologists that housework is a unique occupational role because those who work at it receive no direct financial reward. It is not completely clear whether housework has such low social status because it is unpaid or that it is not paid because it has such low status. Certainly men have been unwilling to take on more than a small share of domestic tasks, even if their wives are employed outside the home for as many hours as they are themselves. The change in sex roles that has been much heralded in the popular media appears to represent a broadening of roles for only one sex—female. Women are now free to work both within and outside the home. So-called social experiments such as the Israeli *kibbutz* have also demonstrated that males are unwilling to take up the primary role of housework and child-rearing (Hacker, 1975). We cannot consider such experiments in the equalization of gender roles as failures, since they have never actually been carried out. If indeed the role of housewife is danger-ous to one's psychological health, it is not surprising that, no matter how eager one sex is to relinquish it, the other is reluctant to take it on. So far, the role of "househusband" has remained a deviant and suspect one.

Since a certain amount of domestic arrangements appears to be inevitable, it has been suggested that the social status of housework can be increased by paying women a salary for it. Income largely determines status in our society. In addition, control of financial resources might decrease the sense of powerlessness felt by many women who do not work outside the home. Although this idea can lead to many interesting questions and arguments, it is not at all clear whether it would be psychologically helpful to women. Re-ceiving financial payment for work does not resolve the issue of whether that work is satisfying. After all, assembly line workers who are well paid occasionally resort to "sabotage" in order to enliven a psychologically unrewarding existence. And certainly no one eulogizes the high social status of domestic servants!

A more psychologically acceptable solution may be to accept the idea that household tasks are intrinsically uninteresting and unrewarding. Children as young as 9 years of age make this ap-praisal (Hartley, 1961), no matter how often it is explicitly denied in "women's magazines." We must also accept, however, the idea that such tasks are not uniquely the responsibility of one sex or the other. Women do not have a "cleanliness" center in the brain any more than men do. If the household is in disorder, both husband and wife are equally to "blame." Such an analysis suggests that men should not be "thanked" for doing household chores. It also suggests that standards of performance in such chores would probably decrease. But, to borrow a title from a best-selling book about housework, "no one said you had to eat off the floor."

True equality in domestic responsibility may be more of a polit-ical issue than a psychological one. It appears that the value placed on the resources contributed by each spouse outside the marriage determines their relative power within it. The cards are stacked against the women's acquiring outside resources, and thus she may be reluctant to attempt to exert power within her marital situation. Her husband is likely to have a significant advantage in achievement (he is better educated and makes more money); has a greater number of legal rights given to him by marriage; and has an advantage in terms of occupation-related status and esteem. Suburbanization decreases the power of the wife by loosening her ties with relatives and making her more physically isolated and psychologically dependent. Divorce will increase her responsibility for the children and decrease her social status without necessarily increasing her opportunities. It is not surprising that she is reluctant to provoke a confrontation with her husband over housework.

Few researchers bother to ask housewives about anything except their attitudes toward their husbands, their children, or their domestic tasks. In fact a study that I coauthored with Diane Krooth (Unger & Krooth, 1974) on the attitudes of housewives toward success was rejected by several professional journals partly because "examination of this population adds little to psychological knowledge in the area." We found, however, that housewives have considerable hostility toward success in others—whether these others were other females or males. Their hostility was not diminished by participation in volunteer activities of a socially activist nature or by their ideology about the self-actualization of women.

ALTERNATIVES TO MARRIAGE : DIVORCE

Although we have not expanded on this research, it is possible that female hostility and anger may be among the emotional underpinnings of the rapid increase in divorce and separation in our society over the past few decades. Women are, so to speak, voicing their dissatisfaction "with their feet." Numerous sociologists have provided statistics on the changing state of marriage in the United States. Although it has often been suggested that California is not completely typical of the rest of the United States, projections of this state's divorce rates suggest that 3 out of 7 first marriages will end in divorce within 35 years (Schoen, 1975). Couples with the lowest ages at marriage and the largest numbers of children are most likely to seek divorce.

Most adult men (63.1%) and women (57.5%) are married and living with their spouses (Bernard, 1975b). However, the percentage living in some form of nonmarital status, primarily divorce, is increasing. Bernard documents a rise of between 1.5 to 2 percent just in the years between 1970 and 1974. The present rate of divorce is the highest ever recorded in the United States and appears to be still rising (Norton & Glick, 1976).

More divorced women were the heads of households in 1974 than in 1970 (although they do have fewer children in these households). The percentage of women living in nonfamilial households—communes, apartments shared with a female friend, or cohabitation with a male—increased by 40 percent between 1970 and 1974, but still accounts for only 6 percent of all divorced women. Male heads of single-parent households, a small percentage in any event, declined somewhat during this four-year period. The percentage of divorced men who "go home to mother" remains higher than the percentage of divorced women who do so. The evidence points out that divorced men and women are still differentially involved with their children: There are more female heads of single-parent households; fewer women live alone or with their parental family; and fewer live in households composed of unrelated individuals, which are usually not hospitable to children. By contrast, the living arrangements of single women and men are strikingly similar. The overwhelming majority live with relatives; fewer than 10 percent live alone; and still fewer live with nonrelatives. These data would suggest that the social effects of a marriage with children are nonreversible as well as different for women and men.

Causal Factors in Divorce

Very few social scientists have attempted to go beyond the demographic statistics in the analysis of what causes marital breakups. Part of the reason for this apparent neglect of an important area is the reluctance of participants in a divorce to communicate with a researcher during this period of intense social and emotional turmoil, as well as the reluctance of the researcher to "bother" them during a difficult period. Interviews during this period may also be colored by the negative emotions accompanying the act and may not paint a true picture of the preseparation marriage. George Levinger (1976) has recently summarized what we know about the psychological and sociological factors that predict divorce. We will stress those that appear to have sex-specific effects.

The relative income of husband and wife appears to have a complex effect on the probability of divorce. While higher family income makes divorce more unlikely, high earnings by the woman are positively correlated with the probability of divorce. Thus wives with incomes independent of their husband's earnings are less likely to be tied to their marriage. Higher family income probably also accounts for the finding that marriages in which the husband has a high level of education are also more likely to endure.

Demographic similarities between husband and wife also predict marital durability. Thus religious, educational, and age similarities all play a role. There are also differences between dyads of the same religious affiliation. Jewish couples have the least instability, followed by Catholics, with Protestants having the highest divorce rate. Couples indicating no religious affiliation, however, have the highest divorce rates of all. Mixed religious affiliation was more predictive of divorce, with some intriguing sex-specific effects. In both the United States and Holland, marriages in which the wife belonged to the more rigid religious sect were much more likely to endure than when the husband belonged to a comparable group and his wife did not. It has been suggested that religion provides a greater barrier to divorce for women than for men. Possible explanations for this effect include concern for the religious upbringing of the children and/or greater religious belief among women.

With the length of the marriage controlled, childless couples generally have higher separation rates than couples with children. In fact unsatisfied married couples often report their children as their only or greatest source of gratification (Luckey & Bain, 1970). As we will see in the next chapter, however, children actually place a great psychological burden and much financial stress on a marriage. Since this burden of child care will probably remain hers whether or not she remains married, the stress of children probably does not make it more likely that the wife will terminate the marriage. The likelihood of termination is probably a result of one or the other partner's decision that life outside the marital relationship will probably be more pleasant, or at least less unpleasant, than life within it. The wife's alternate options are particularly important, since the wife is the plaintiff in over 70 percent of American divorce actions. Although the husband's actions often precipitate the break, the end of the wife's ability to tolerate the situation appears to determine whether and when a divorce will occur. (Goode, 1956).

The Sequelae of Divorce

In our society the women's status is much more diminished by divorce than that of her ex-husband. Women are less likely to remarry after a divorce than men, and their earning capacity is usually considerably lower. Thus a woman may break the marital tie more readily if she is in a position to support herself adequately outside of the relationship. However, a woman is very unlikely to find herself in such a financial position after a number of years of marriage. She probably married younger than her husband and has fewer years of education than he. Even if she worked for some time in the early years of the marriage, her skills may be rusty and her references obsolete. She will also probably have custody of the children, so that she must fit her work into her plans for child care. It is extremely likely, therefore, that divorce, particularly for women who are accustomed to a relatively high income, will result in a considerable loss of financial resources.

Not only is the divorced woman deprived of economic resources; she is deprived of social support as well. Fewer divorced women than married women contact or receive help from their (former) spouse's relatives (Anspach, 1976). Their children also have less social contact with the paternal kin following a divorce. This is related to their degree of contact with their absent father, who provides the necessary link with his relatives. We do not fully understand the effect on either the children or their primary caretaker, the divorced mother, of the absence of resources provided by the kin network.

Very little is known about the lives of divorced mothers who have not remarried. Although she has been separated from the role of wife, the divorced woman has not been separated from the role of mother. There are no limits to the expectations about her availability to respond to the needs of her children. Thus while many women opt out of marriage, few opt out of motherhood. In addition to the lack of customary economic and social support systems, the divorced mother now has complete responsibility for the household chores. Her personal needs, those of the children, and household and economic responsibilities must be traded off against each other in view of her limited free time (Feldberg & Kohen, 1976). A major complaint of divorced mothers is difficulty in scheduling activities involving child care, housework, household repairs, and maintenance (Brown, Feldberg, Fox, & Kohen, 1976).

The divorced mother also faces stigma as a result of her divorced status and discrimination against her as the female head of a household (Brandwein, Brown, & Fox, 1974). She may have difficulty getting credit, be treated as financially irresponsible, and be regarded as "fair game" sexually. The divorced father is often seen as doing something special and praiseworthy when he takes care of his children while she is seen as just doing her job when she does so, even when she is employed full time (George & Wilding, 1972). It is not surprising that large-scale studies show that divorced women are more depressed than still-married and never-married women of comparable ages (Radloff, 1975). Both men and women, paradoxically, may be desolate at the absence of a spouse whom they can no longer respect or love (Weiss, 1976). Becoming detached from the absent spouse may involve a difficult period of adjustment.

The Benefits of Divorce

Although the price of independence is high, a woman may receive real benefits from separation from her husband. A number of divorced women mention freedom from restrictive domestic routines and an opportunity to mold the parent–child relationship without the interference of their spouse (Brandwein et al., 1974). They also mention an increased sense of personal autonomy and competence. Despite their reduced economic resources, they may benefit from having all the resources subject to their own control. They also feel more in control of their own time. Only 4 of the 30 women interviewed (all of whom had been living without a husband for at least a year) were seriously interested in remarriage. However, they did not reject long-term relationships with men on their own terms. The majority, in fact, reported that their sexual lives were more enjoyable now than they had been when they were married.

There is some evidence that divorce may not necessarily reduce the economic condition of women. One study has indicated that previously married women can gain greater economic rewards with respect to their occupational status than never-married women with greater labor force continuity (Hudis, 1976). Since they have overcome the handicap of their reduced work experience, these data suggest that marital-status differences in earnings are due to more than simply the "lost-seniority" cost of marriage. The salaries of previously married women are less affected by number of children than the salaries of women working at comparable jobs who are still married. Thus divorced women appear to have reordered their financial and familial priorities. Their higher salaries may be a reflection of greater assertiveness, greater access to alternate job opportunities (they are less tied to a specific geographic area than still-married women), or greater reluctance to trade off other attractive aspects of a job (e.g., working hours or commuting distance) for its financial rewards.

A Word of Caution

We must be cautious about inferring causal effects from correlational data. Statistics like those just discussed may be a reflection of the relative readiness to seek a divorce of women whose qualifications for employment are less affected by absence from the job market than the qualifications of other women. We must also note that the probability, and probably the opportunity, for remarriage declines more steeply with age for women than for men (Levinger, 1976). Living alone or as the head of a household may be more desirable for younger divorced women than for older ones. In an analogous examination of widowhood, Helena Lopata (1973) found that while among widows under 40 two-thirds or more agreed with the statement "I like living alone," by age 55 half or less agreed with this statement. Since divorce is often followed by loss of friends, some kin, social ties (usually based on mixed-sex couples, except in a few highly select localities), and the like, most divorced women would probably benefit from some sort of support network. Nevertheless divorce should not be viewed as an unmitigated disaster but as an increasingly common shift in the social contract that may be either a cause or an effect of our changing social mores.

FUTURE TRENDS

In this chapter marriage has been discussed in terms of traditional forms—a monogamous heterosexual arrangement that involves setting up a nuclear household on a presumably permanent basis. As has been suggested, this form appears to support traditionally socialized masculine and feminine roles. Divorce, however, has become an ever-increasing reality in our social system. New social structures, such as serial monogamy, communal households, and contractually "equal" dyadic arrangements, appear to be evolving to meet needs that traditional forms cannot. It is possibly premature to postulate the psychological effects of various nontraditional social structures. All but a few social scientists have ignored the area, partly because alternate structures are viewed as illegitimate and impermanent. From the work that has been done, however, it appears that psychological changes occur among all participants in alternate structures (Kanter, 1973). Some of these changes may be viewed as negative by society as a whole, but it is difficult to determine whether these effects are a by-product of a particular alternate structure or a function of living within a system that is defined as deviant by society.

It is fairly clear that the evolution of alternate structures seems to be in response to negative evaluations of the traditional marital system. For example, college students who live together do so partly because they perceive their parents' marriages to have been unhappy (Clatworthy, 1975). Behavioral changes in each sex appear to be taking place as both women and men recognize that they are likely to be "nonmarried" during some period of their adult lives. The changes that we call women's liberation may be a cause or an effect of that recognition.

Chapter 12
Parenthood: Options and Necessities

Until now we have not discussed the effects of the usual concomitant of marriage in our society—children. In this chapter we will focus on the effects of children on the people who have them—their parents of both sexes. We will ask questions such as Why do people wish or not wish to have children? What is the relationship between childbearing and childrearing? and How do the properties of the child affect the behaviors of the parent? We will also examine the longstanding notion of "maternal instinct" and the process of "blaming the mother." What do we really know about the effects of the mother's employment outside the home on the child? And lastly, what are the long-term effects of parenthood?

MOTIVES FOR AND AGAINST HAVING A CHILD

Cross-Cultural Considerations

It is important to distinguish between motives for having a child in our society as opposed to motives in other societies—especially in less developed, more traditional societies. In the latter, children are necessary as a source of family income, as a mechanism for passing on the family property and way of life, and in some groups as a form of personal immortality. In many of these societies a high birthrate is perceived as essential because of the high risk of infant mortality. Four or five children may have to be borne, and more conceived, for two to live to adulthood. In the absence of social-security benefits, these children may represent the only form of economic security the aging parents possess. In such societies it is difficult to limit the rate of childbearing despite the great need for population control.

The best predictor of fertility limitation in developing countries seems to be the attitude toward modern science and medicine (Miller & Inkeles, 1974). Experience with modern institutions such as factories and schools has little effect unless it is accompanied by high approval of science and technology. High economic level as measured by the amount of consumer goods possessed does not by itself predict the use of birth control. This relationship between the acceptance of one aspect of modernity and limitation of births may be mediated by very practical considerations. If one believes that science and medicine can deal with one's problems, one may feel that it is not necessary to have many children for a few to grow up. Nevertheless attitudes change more slowly than societies, so that there is a considerable lag between the development of better medical conditions and limitation of family size.

Attitudes toward having children in our society also appear to reflect a lag between social necessities and personal expectancies. Americans of both sexes continue to accept the value of having several children. The most commonly reported figure for preferred or ideal family size tends to hover around 3.2 children (Blake, 1967; Pohlman, 1969), although in actual practice married couples appear to have averaged about two children in the past few years. Even among college students 84 percent stated that they wanted to have two to four children (Russo & Stadler, 1971). The social premium of children is underlined by our tendency to refer to "childless" couples rather than "child-free" ones, as has been suggested by some proponents of zero population growth.

Individual and Sex-Related Differences in Reasons for and against Having Children

What is striking about studies examining motives for having a child is the great individual variation. No one motive has particularly great importance across individuals, although there are some interesting sex differences between motives (Kirchner, Seaver, Vegega, & Straw, 1976). The five most important reasons stated by women for having a child were (in declining order) experiencing love and life's fuller meaning, opportunity for personal growth, stimulation and feeling of pride, acting as a sculptor (to make someone in own image), and experiencing the birth process. The five most important reasons stated by men were fun (to do and enjoy things with a child), experiencing love and life's fuller meaning, acting as a sculptor, partnership benefits (bringing spouse and self closer together), and the desire to be needed and loved. It is interesting that men regard having fun as a reason for having a child much more than women do. Having fun is a behavior that is more likely to occur with an older child than with a young infant.

Women and men also differ somewhat in their reasons for not having a child. Women are concerned with (in declining order) financial considerations, education and career interference, dangers of childbirth and possibility of a defective child, population concerns, and (tied for fifth place) emotional immaturity and a pessimistic world view. Men, on the other hand, are most concerned about the dangers of childbirth (independent of concerns about a defective child), financial considerations, discomforts of childbearing, possibility of a defective child, and job interference. It appears as though men focus their objections to childbearing more on the event itself and its immediate consequences while women are more concerned about the long-term pressures of childrearing. This is, of course, consonant with the role of each sex in the childrearing process.

Correlates of the Desire for Few or No Children

It is only recently that psychologists have concerned themselves with women who express a preference for remaining childless or having only one child. One such study examined 20 female college students who expressed a desire to remain childless compared with a group that was matched with them in many ways but wished to have children (Houseknecht, 1976). Women who expressed a desire to remain childless were significantly more likely to have come from a mother-dominant family, to have achieved more psychological distance from their family during adolescence, and to be more individualistic than those who desired children. They were also more aware of alternatives to motherhood than those who wanted children. Interestingly, although women who wished to remain childless were more aware of the disadvantages of childbearing than those who desired children, there was considerable consensus among groups that childlessness provided more freedom from responsibility (89% of the "desire childlessness" sample vs. 48% of the "desire children" group acknowledged this point). There was no particular advantage in having children that was seen to be a gain by most of the women who anticipated parenthood.

The women who desired no children were more inclined to identify with the women's movement. They were significantly more confident that the women's movement would positively affect their lives (48% vs. 19%) as well as the lives of the next generation of women (44% vs. 19%). Thus the women's movement could have provided a group with which to identify whether or not the respondents were actually members of some kind of feminist organization. Women who desired no children emphasized life goals involving success in vocational and other nonfamilial roles to a much greater extent than females who desired children. They were also more likely to reject or be uncertain about marriage. It is quite possible that the same factors that cause individuals to deviate from societal norms prescribing children also make them more likely to be nonconforming with respect to marital status (Veevers, 1971).

A number of other studies have found that plans for future labor force participation reduce the fertility expectations of women. In a study of 3589 women in their mid-20s a woman's plans to participate in the labor force when she was 35 were found to have a substantial effect on the total number of children she planned to bear in her lifetime (Waite & Stolzenberg, 1976). This relationship held both for never-married and for currently married women even when the husband's income and his attitude toward women's participation in the labor force were taken into account. Reduced birth intentions were highly correlated with an egalitarian position on sex roles.

The woman's rejection of traditional sex role norms was a more powerful predictor of her expected work behavior than men's views in this area (Scanzoni, 1976). Women consistently expected to work more than men expected their wives to work. Women who seek individualistic rewards must reduce family "costs." Men who are amenable to women's aspirations seem to be amenable to child reduction, but may be more indifferent to the matter.

There is also suggestive evidence that women who want only one child are more involved in nonfamilial roles than those who prefer more children (Beckman, 1976). Although the differences were not significant, women who wanted an only child also were somewhat more likely to be employed full time and to have been employed for a larger portion of the time since marriage. It is difficult to make generalizations about these women, since they represent a very small percentage of the women sampled (3 percent, or 18 of the 583 women surveyed). Eighty-four percent of the women who currently had one child desired and planned to have at least one additional child before the end of their childbearing years. Most of the reasons they gave for having another child were essentially altruistic—to please their husbands or provide companionship for their child. They were also more likely to mention their desire for a boy than women with two or more children who desired at least one more child.

A variety of internal and external factors may affect decisions about whether or not to have a child. An all-or-none model of decision making in childbearing is probably not useful. Role-innovative women may not necessarily reject "core" female roles as wife and mother, although they do expect to postpone marriage and to have fewer children than more traditional women (Tangri, 1972). The data on the relationship between attitudes toward participation in the work force and childbearing and the actual statistics showing a decline of childbirths below the zero population growth point would seem to indicate that a major social change is taking place, with fewer women engaged in childrearing for fewer years in their lives. Nevertheless evidence exists that there is still considerable social pressure on women to bear a child.

Social Norms and Childlessness

There is a societal norm against childlessness and one-child families (Thompson, 1974). Deliberate childlessness is viewed as a sign of psychological maladjustment (Pohlman, 1969). Negative stereotypes about both the childless woman and the mother of only one child include characterization of the woman as neurotic, selfish, and otherwise maladjusted (Rainwater, 1965). Only children are also the objects of negative stereotypes—they are considered generally maladjusted and socially inadequate (Thompson, 1974). Only children are regarded as self-centered and self-willed, attention seeking and dependent on others, temperamental and anxious, generally unhappy and unlikable. There is no evidence that only children actually possess such characteristics.

In the United States a "moral imperative" may persist concerning repeated reproduction. "One should—or must—have *children;* a *child* will not be sufficient" (Thompson, 1974, p. 96). Complicated sociological models about decision making in childbearing exist; however, what is important here is the recognition that having a child may not be as much a matter of individual decision making as we think. Strong normative pressures decrease the probability of making a negative decision. I am reminded of some friends who voluntarily postponed childbearing until relatively late in their marriage. The pressures on them to conform were so great that they spread it about that they had fertility problems rather than "admit" that they did not yet wish to have a child. It is difficult, of course, to determine how common such behavior is. Implicit acceptance of such norms may also, of course, influence the responses that individuals make to questionnaires about reasons for and against having a child.

FAMILY PLANNING

It would be erroneous to assume, moreover, that every pregnancy is a planned one. In fact it has been estimated that 22 percent of the births that occurred between 1960 and 1965 were unwanted by one spouse and 17 percent by both (Bumpass & Westoff, 1970). These figures probably underestimate the percentage of unwanted pregnancies, since they do not take into account infants born to women who are not living with their husbands or those born out of wedlock.

Contraception and Family Planning

Accidental pregnancies are attributable to a number of causes: nonavailability of effective contraceptives or abortion, their cost or geographic distance, lack of contraceptive knowledge or skill, resistance to regular contraceptive use because of intrinsic aversiveness or because side effects are perceived to be possible, and unpredictability regarding time, place, or partner in intercourse (Wiest & Squier, 1974). There is surprisingly little correct knowledge about reproduction and contraception among American teenagers. Even teenagers with some college and those of high socioeconomic status scored little over 50 percent in a test of total knowledge in these areas (Reichelt & Werley, 1975). Females had nearly twice as much information about birth control than males, but still answered only slightly more than one-third of the questions correctly. Sexually experienced teenagers were not significantly better informed than those who had not had intercourse. Misinformation about all forms of birth control was common. (See Table 12.1.)

Although it has been estimated that there are more than 3.3 million unmarried women aged 15–19 who are sexually active and at risk of unwanted pregnancy (Dryfoos, 1975), many of these women are reluctant to use contraceptive measures regularly. The most frequently given answer to the question of why they did not want to use birth control was that they were afraid that it would lessen the pleasure of intercourse (Reichelt, 1976). Other answers

Table 12.1   PERCENT DISTRIBUTION OF RESPONSES OF TEENAGERS TO STATEMENTS ON CONTRACEPTION, REPRODUCTION, AND ABORTION, BY QUESTIONNAIRE ITEM, 1973 (N = 1,190)

QUESTIONNAIRE ITEM[a]	PERCENT, BY TYPE OF RESPONSE		
	CORRECT	INCORRECT	DON'T KNOW
ORALS			
The pill must be stopped every year for three months (F)	32	4	64
The pill is generally dangerous to use (F)	65	5	30
The pill may be taken along with other medications without decreasing its effectiveness (T)	31	8	61
The pill may be taken by a girl who uses alcohol and/or drugs (T)	33	13	54
The pill may not be taken if the woman has a history of certain illnesses (T)	39	4	57
The pill is the most effective method of birth control (T)	72	6	22
IUDS			
The IUD is inserted before each act of intercourse (making love) (F)	39	14	47
The IUD cannot be felt by the man or woman during intercourse (T)	37	7	56
The IUD is the second most effective method of birth control (T)	29	6	65
The IUD usually works best if the uterus (womb) has been stretched by a previous pregnancy (T)	20	7	73
DIAPHRAGM			
The diaphragm must be worn at all times (F)	40	14	47
A diaphragm should be used only after having been fitted for it by a doctor (T)	55	5	40
The effectiveness of the diaphragm is increased when used with a cream or jelly (T)	34	6	61
The diaphragm cannot be felt by either the man or woman when properly in place (T)	44	3	53

Table 12.1 *Continued*

QUESTIONNAIRE ITEM[a]	PERCENT, BY TYPE OF RESPONSE		
	CORRECT	INCORRECT	DON'T KNOW
CONDOM (RUBBER)			
A rubber should be tested before use (T)	55	14	31
Rubbers break easily (F)	19	48	33
The rubber should be held around the base of the man's penis when withdrawn (T)	48	5	48
SPERMICIDES (FOAMS, CREAMS, JELLIES)			
They should be inserted just *before each* intercourse (T)	68	6	26
They work by killing sperm (T)	63	5	32
They can be bought without a prescription in any drugstore (T)	67	6	27
When used with a rubber, they are a highly effective birth control method (T)	41	11	48
They should be washed out with a douche immediately after intercourse (F)	16	26	58
MISCELLANEOUS METHODS			
Rhythm is a highly effective method of birth control (F)	49	6	45
Withdrawal (pulling out) is a highly effective birth control method (F)	61	11	28
Douching after intercourse is a highly effective birth control method (F)	58	7	35
REPRODUCTION			
Menstruation (monthly period) is a clearing of the uterus to prepare again for possible pregnancy (T)	74	9	16
A woman's fertile time (when she is most likely to become pregnant) covers the middle of the interval between her menstrual periods (T)	64	10	27
A girl can get pregnant the first time she has intercourse (T)	76	12	12
Sperm can live in the female's reproductive system for about 72 hours (three days) (T)	43	17	40

Table 12.1 *Continued*

	PERCENT, BY TYPE OF RESPONSE		
QUESTIONNAIRE ITEM[a]	CORRECT	INCORRECT	DON'T KNOW
If a woman does not have an orgasm (climax) during intercourse, she can't get pregnant (F)	70	6	24
ABORTION			
An abortion can be done safely and easily by a doctor during the first 12 weeks of pregnancy (T)	81	5	14
Having an abortion will make the woman sterile (unable to have children in the future) (F)	87	3	10
Anyone can tell if a girl has had an abortion (F)	85	1	14

SOURCE: From P. A. Reichelt and H. H. Werley, "Contraception, Abortion, and Veneral Disease: Teenagers' Knowledge and the Effect of Education," *Family Planning Perspectives*, 1975, 7, 83–88. Copyright 1975 by the Planned Parenthood Federation of America. Reprinted by permission.
[a] Correct answer in this and following tables is shown in parentheses following each statement. T = True; F = False.
NOTE: Percents may not add to 100 because of rounding.

given included not wanting to plan to have sex, being afraid that sex would become a routine thing, and being afraid that contraception would be detrimental to health. Other sexually active young women deny the possibility that they could become pregnant.

Almost everyone complains about every form of contraception. Various methods are said to be messy, inconvenient, or awkward, or they can be felt (foam, condoms, or diaphragms). They may be painful or cause bleeding (IUD), are felt to be responsible for nausea or weight gain, and require daily remembering (the pill) (Bardwick, 1973). The pill has also been implicated in the medical problems of many women who use it. Although people appear to be most satisfied with tubal ligation and vasectomy (Wiest & Janke, 1974), irreversible sterilization cannot be used as a contraceptive for child spacing. One scientist's fantasy about a nonaversive contraceptive includes the following properties: It would produce a mild euphoria, function as an aphrodisiac, and have no immediate or long-range negative consequences (de Nevers, 1971). Despite the new brightly colored and shaped condoms of Japanese manufacture, no one has yet invented a contraceptive that is fun to use.

The use of birth control methods, therefore, is due more to the desire to avoid the negative effects of a pregnancy than for intrinsic rewards. Since women bear more of the consequences of pregnancy, it is not surprising that they are both more informed about and more willing to use contraceptive measures than men. From the evidence of behavior (actually having fewer children), it is probable that women who have nontraditional attitudes are either more willing to use birth control measures or more competent in their use.

Personal Power and Birth Control

One would assume that women who have a sense of control over their lives would also exert effective control over their bodies in terms of childbearing. Although this relationship has not been tested directly, there appears to be a negative relationship between sex role liberalism and sexual activity in adolescent females (Grote, 1976). Teenagers who were sexually active held more conservative or stereotypical sex role attitudes than those who remained virgins. The virgins appeared to be more mature, in the sense of integration of their identities, than young women who were sexually active at an early age.

Even if a sense of powerlessness does not lead to early sexual activity and/or nonuse of contraception, high fertility does appear to generate a sense of lack of control in some females. Thus while no differences in perceived powerlessness was found between users and nonusers of contraception among low-income black and white married women living in both Guam and the United States, white women with large numbers of children perceived themselves to have less power (Morris & Sison, 1974). A relationship between high powerlessness and large family size has also been found among Catholics but not among Protestants (Groat & Neal, 1967). The differences may be due to differential bases for high fertility between groups. For example, among Catholics contraception is proscribed. Hence, large numbers of children are not a matter of choice on the part of the woman.

When Contraception Fails: Abortion

It has been argued that the number of children a woman reports wanting may be more closely related to the number she expects to have rather than to her own desires (Wiest & Squier, 1974). Thus the fact that a higher percentage of poor women state that they "want" many children may be interpreted as acceptance of their relative lack of control over their own reproduction. Recent data show that it is poor women who have benefited most from liberalized abortion laws; the birthrate drop is sharpest at the lowest economic level (Tietze, 1973).

It would be absurd and irresponsible to argue that abortion is a medically defensible and ethically desirable form of birth control. Nevertheless it is important to examine the impact of the abortion experience on women. There are few facts to support the idea that abortions are destructive to the female psyche. A recent extensive review of the literature concerning psychological reactions to thera-peutic abortion concluded that the evidence indicating that women experienced favorable consequences is stronger than data indicat-ing negative consequences (Shusterman, 1976). Studies of abortion on request indicate that such requests tend to come from young unmarried women who are not in a social position to bear and care for a child. They either were not aware of or not concerned about the possibility of pregnancy at the time of intercourse or suffered a contraceptive failure. The psychological consequences of abortion on request appear to be mostly benign.

There is no empirical evidence to support the notion that any woman who wants an abortion is mentally ill. A woman's emotional symptoms after an abortion may be more a function of her overall mental health than of the interruption of her pregnancy. The pre-disposing factors that can increase the likelihood of postabortion psychological problems include (1) a history of repeated abortions, (2) a previous history of psychiatric or psychological problems, (3) an unresolved state of denial, (4) failure to use contraception, (5) unassertive behavior with respect to contraception (6) strict reli-gious or family values, (7) the absence of any supportive relation-ships, and (8) an unstable relationship with the boyfriend (Freiberg & Bridwell, 1976). The most favorable outcomes of abortion in early-adolescent girls occurred when the girl made the decision herself and her parents, caretaking personnel, and society showed a helping rather than critical and punitive attitude (Perez-Reyes & Falk, 1973). When the individuals around them were helpful, the girls experienced the crisis and operation as helpful in the "growing-up" process.

The development of negative aftereffects, such as guilt or de-pression, may be dependent on the attitude of the medical staff and clinic toward the aborting women (Shusterman, 1976). Negative effects are more likely to develop when the medical environment is not supportive. Moreover, no studies have compared the psycholog-ical effects with those of an appropriate control group—women with unwanted pregnancies who bear the child anyway.

PREGNANCY AS A PSYCHOPHYSIOLOGICAL EVENT

Assuming that the woman decides or is forced to bear a child, the next set of events that should be considered is pregnancy rather than the act of childbearing that terminates it. At first glance one would think that a body of material relating to the psychological concomitants of pregnancy should exist that is at least as large as the literature on the psychosocial determinants of who gets pregnant and when. Surprisingly, however, there has been virtually no research on pregnancy as a psychological event. The little that has been done has been based either on the psychoanalytic model, which is not empirical and focuses on the "pathological" nature of the woman who resents her pregnancy, or on the medical model, which treats pregnancy as a "benign" illness. It may not be to the point here to raise the issue of this incredible hiatus in our exploration of the human psyche when other, apparently far less important areas have been extensively explored by psychologists. I suggest that this neglect may be a result of a process of cultural and professional inurement; that is, women are supposed to get pregnant, it is their lot, why make a fuss about it? In fact it has been suggested that there are more studies of the husbands of pregnant women than of the pregnant women themselves. One such study, for example (Hartman & Nicolay, 1966), focused on the acting-out behavior that occurs among men who have a history of being violent when their wives become pregnant.

The Medical Model of Pregnancy

The medical model of pregnancy views it as a period of increased physical and psychological vulnerability that, in some women or under certain stresses, can result in severe emotional problems, "psychogenic" physical complications, or even psychotic breakdowns (Parlee, 1978). Researchers can either view the psychological state as a reflection of the physiological facts of pregnancy or take a more interactional view—that while the physiological facts of pregnancy increase psychological vulnerability, the extent to which a woman will succumb to stress is largely a matter of her individual history and present circumstances. The focus has been on individual differences (probably owing to the use of a medical model), so that in the literature on pregnancy we rarely find generalizations about what "women" experience, despite similar, but more frequent, generalizations in the literature on menstruation. This is surprising, since the hormonal changes that occur during pregnancy are much larger than those of the menstrual cycle.

The Hormonal Characteristics of Pregnancy

The biochemical interrelationships of pregnancy are not totally known. If, however, the egg is fertilized, the pituitary continues its release of luteinizing hormone. The corpus luteum, therefore, does not degenerate but increases in size and secretes even larger quantities of progesterone and other progestogens. Later in pregnancy the placenta takes over as the chief source of progestogen production, with the overall level of this hormone being maintained many times above the level of nonpregnant women until childbirth. The progesterone level at the termination of pregnancy is more than nine times the peak level during the luteal phase of the menstrual cycle. The estrogen level is also much higher than its peak level at the time of ovulation. The level of both hormones in the bloodstream drops precipitously after birth. (See Figure 12.1.)

Besides major changes in levels of gonadal hormones, researchers have found alterations in the levels of substances that may be associated with the way the central nervous system functions. The level of norepinephrine, a neurotransmitter, is lower during pregnancy, while there is an increase in the secretion of adrenal cortical hormones associated with stress (Treadway, Kane, Jarrahi-Zadeh, & Lipton, 1969). Treadway and his associates have done one of the few studies that followed pregnant women through pregnancy and the postpartum period, utilizing both biochemical and psychological measures. In addition to the physiological changes noted earlier, they found that pregnant women were significantly more hypochrondriacal than control hospitalized nonpregnant women. They were more concerned about their health and body functions and more depressed than the controls. They scored themselves as being more easily startled. Both pregnant and postpartum women had significantly increased social-introversion scores, indicating increased interest in self. Surprisingly, the pregnant women also had decreased scores in feminine orientation. No cognitive differences between pregnant and nonpregnant women were found.

The Relationship Between Chemicals and Behavior

The researchers found a statistically significant correlation of .76 between the reduced norepinephrine levels and increased depression scores in these pregnant women. Norepinephrine has been associated with depression in nonpregnant humans. Progesterone may be the substance that is responsible for the decrease of norepinephrine in the body. Progesterone has been shown to have depressant effects on the central nervous system. Biochemical

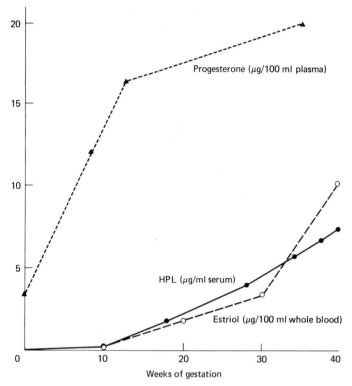

Figure 12.1. The enormous rise of estrogens and progestogens during the course of a pregnancy. Levels of both hormones drop precipitously during the first few days after birth.

changes linked to gonadal hormone functions could increase susceptibility to affective disorders in women during both the pregnancy and postpartum periods.

Although there have been few careful examinations of the relationship between gonadal hormones and mood during pregnancy, it is possible to consider data on the psychological effects of oral contraceptives as somewhat analogous in this regard. The substances in these pills mimic the activities of estrogen and progesterone during early pregnancy. Uterine tissue continues to proliferate, and widespread effects on the entire organism have been described. Many of the so-called side effects of the pill are similar to the symptoms of early pregnancy: nausea, weight gain, fluid retention, headache, loss of interest in sex, and so on (Herzberg & Coppen, 1970).

Of more interest in this context is the relationship between this synthetic state of "a little bit of pregnancy" and mood state—especially depression. A number of researchers have reported an increase in negative affect in women on the pill, although they have suggested that it is correlated with neuroticism or negative affect during the prepill period as well. Probably the most important study in this area was done by Karen Paige (1971). She found that the level of hostility—as measured by content analysis of verbal statements—was related to the amount of progesterone in the pill used. Women who used pills that contained a larger amount of progesterone showed higher levels of verbal hostility compared to other pill users. Hostility, moreover, did not fluctuate cyclically the way it did in women on sequential pills (which use estrogen and then progesterone only toward the end of the cycle) or women on normal, non-chemically manipulated cycles.

Some physical symptomology during pregnancy appears to be related to high levels of gonadal hormones. Obstetricians appear to agree that the mild nausea and vomiting of early pregnancy is probably due to rapidly changing hormone levels. Taste thresholds may also change during pregnancy and play a role in the unusual food cravings found in some women. Medical investigators, however, seem to be willing to accept intrapsychic explanations for pregnancy symptoms even when the weight of scientific explanation suggests that biological causes are more likely (Lennane & Lennane, 1973). For example, some psychoanalysts have suggested that a woman who vomits is attempting to reject her fetus. Pregnant women are also blamed for their anxiety about weight gain, although much of this concern about their weight may reflect the anxiety of their physicians. In one report "unrealistic" concern over eating and obesity was regarded by physicians as a problem. Yet analysis of the procedures used by the staff of that prenatal clinic indicated that pregnant women were either lectured severely or approved of exceedingly, depending on the amount of weight they had gained (Parlee, 1978).

TOWARD A BIOSOCIAL THEORY OF PREGNANCY

In sum, there is some evidence of a connection between the chemical state of the body and the psychology of pregnancy. However, negative effects of pregnancy on mood can be explained by a variety of psychosocial factors as well. It is possible that some psychological effects are due to "labeling." For example, as was mentioned earlier, progesterone injections produced a sensation of fatigue in male volunteers during the weekend after the injections ceased (Little et al., 1974). None of these subjects knew what substance they were receiving or what effects it was supposed to have on them. A number of studies that are well known to social psychologists indicate that if an individual is physiologically aroused, the form his or her behavior takes depends on cognitive judgments about the situation (Schachter, 1964). These cognitive judgments depend, to some extent, on socialized expectations about the situation. Although the area has not been studied systematically by psychologists, there is an enormous weight of subjective and anecdotal evidence indicating that the state of pregnancy induces assumptions about both internal state and interpersonal behavior.

It is rather strange that psychologists have virtually ignored the role of the social as opposed to hormonal changes accompanying pregnancy. In previous chapters we have discussed the great importance attached to slimness and attractiveness in women. Pregnancy may be viewed as the increasing loss of this desirable state. It should not be surprising that pregnant women feel less feminine or that they react with depression or hostility without the added nudge given to these states by the rising level of gonadal hormones. Obviously, the past history of a woman with regard to these external variables will influence her behavior during pregnancy, as will her circumstances during pregnancy and her anticipation of the consequences of childbirth. Biochemical factors could act by way of the central nervous system, but they could also alter behavior by way of level of body comfort, self-image, and actual appearance.

The pregnant woman can be viewed as one who lacks control over her body. Changes will occur no matter what she does or does not do. Pregnancy may represent a period during which helplessness is learned or enforced. In our society at least, pregnant women are considered incapable of functioning, and until recently insurance laws forcibly prevented them from functioning. In the nineteenth century and even in the early twentieth century pregnant women were expected to remain secluded within the home. Recent "pop" evolutionary theorists have focused upon the helplessness of the parturient female in the wild. If she comes to view herself merely as a vessel for the forthcoming generation, it would be surprising if she did not express some depressed feelings. Our major contribution here would be to view this depression as a generalized product of our culture rather than the responsibility of the defective psyches of some or most women.

A recent intriguing experiment by two social psychologists, Shelley Taylor and Ellen Langer (1977), illustrates the way the "typical" behavior of pregnant women may be socialized in our society. These researchers used two female stimulus persons who alternated between being apparently pregnant (by means of a false stomach) or carrying a large box the same size as the presumptive pregnancy. These individuals entered small apartment house elevators and noted the average distance other occupants stood from them. Individuals of both sexes preferred to stand next to the nonpregnant confederate. Men, however, avoided the "pregnant" woman much more than women did. She was also stared at more, so much so that both confederates experienced discomfort when simulating pregnancy. The following is an account of an extreme avoidance reaction that occurred during the study:

> A large curious dog was wrenched away from the pregnant confederate by his master so abruptly and so far that he spent the remainder of the ride sitting on the feet of the nonpregnant experimenter, a fact completely unnoticed by his owner, who was still apologizing to the pregnant experimenter. [Taylor & Langer, p. 30]

In another part of the study subjects were given an opportunity to interact in a laboratory situation with either a pregnant or a nonpregnant confederate. Women preferred the pregnant woman more when she had been passive during a group discussion than when she had been assertive during it. However, they preferred not to have any future interactions with the passive pregnant woman. As in the public situation, subjects of both sexes spent a considerable amount of time furtively staring at her stomach.

It may be suggested that social encouragement of pregnant women to withdraw from their usual activities makes them a statistically rare or novel sight. Social reactions to novelty can include both unwarranted attention to the novel characteristic and avoidance of the unusual individual. Both responses operate to make the individual uncomfortable in society, which further increases her novelty or social deviance. Expectations about passive behavior in pregnant women may magnify their social isolation during this period. Feelings of and responses to lack of control may also be fueled by this social isolation.

THE EVENT OF CHILDBIRTH

Childbirth, too, is not a neutral social or psychological event. Many of the customary procedures surrounding birth in the United States are highly unusual and do not necessarily appear to be in the best interests of either the mother or the baby. Birth is experienced lying down and in many cases strapped down, drugged, shaved, purged, and psychologically isolated to a degree that is virtually unknown in other parts of the world (Lomas, 1964; Tennov, 1973).

In the United States women are also routinely taught that they will need relief from pain during normal delivery. It is noteworthy that men, but not women, rank the dangers of childbirth as the primary reason for not having a child. Men, of course, dominate the obstetrical profession. Such aspects of "normal" hospital practice as an unfamiliar environment, the presence of strangers, and being moved from one room to another late in labor have been shown to adversely affect labor in human and subhuman species (Newton, 1970). Hospital practices may also increase the risk to the child as compared to birth at home attended by a midwife (Mehl, 1977). The increased risk may be produced either directly by the physician's practices or by the greater anxiety they engender in women.

It has been argued that these procedures are warranted for better management of complications that may occur at birth. The complications, however, form a low percentage of total births and are often predictable before labor begins. A quotation from a police training manual on "emergency" childbirth written by a physician may be illuminating here: "In over 95 percent of the cases of emergency childbirth, though the emergency attendant will be overwhelmed with gratitude and widely praised as a hero, he can smile within himself at the knowledge that his simple task could have been performed by any bright eight year old" (Tennov & Hirsch, 1973).

Women tend to report repeated negative experiences associated with childbirth as it is ritualized in American hospitals. Some of these experiences are described in popular critical looks at current obstetrical practices, such as *Our Bodies, Our Selves, The Great American Birth Rite,* and *Immaculate Deception.* More objective studies of childbirth indicate that while childbirth training is not necessary to minimize pain or tension during childbirth, women who are trained rarely show great pain (Standley, 1976). When the mother and father talk often during the course of labor about the woman's well-being and about topics that are unrelated to the childbirth, the woman is less likely to be in pain. It is difficult to generalize from these observations, since women who seek training for childbirth are a self-selected population. It is possible that the increased sense of personal control acquired through such training, as well as the element of personal choice involved in selection of the birth environment, may alleviate anxiety independently of the physiological effect of such practices. Certainly isolation from social contact during labor increases a woman's fear and tension and may contribute to more negative feelings about the birth experience even if it does not actually prolong it or make it more painful.

Despite the objections of the medical profession, which appears to believe that the average woman is not informed enough to judge the quality of her medical care, the movement toward nurse–midwives, drugless deliveries, and even home births seems to be growing (Woolfolk & Woolfolk, 1975). In some ways the struggle for self-determination in childbirth parallels the struggle for reproductive self-determination in general. It may be seen to transcend the issue of personal choice and to be a matter of politics. Women's struggle for control over their own bodies, in terms of bearing children at all, has been the focus of an extensive social revolution that is not yet completely successful even in the United States (Gordon, 1976). Issues involving childbearing, one of the most specifically female functions, appear to be particularly subject to rigid societal concern. Control of the childbirth environment illustrates the way social institutions can decrease the power of women. Perceived helplessness accompanies this real lack of control and enhances it. The view of birth as a natural event, rather than in terms of a medical model, could prove quite beneficial to many women, and to their families as well.

THE POSTPARTUM PERIOD

The postpartum period is the only part of pregnancy that has received considerable attention in the psychological and psychiatric literature. We have discussed the nature of the biochemical factors that may put women at risk in an earlier part of this chapter. The early postpartum period is often characterized as one involving great mood swings or depression. Researchers, however, even disagree about what symptoms constitute a depressive state and how long the postpartum period is defined to be. Many of the studies found in the literature lack control groups, use inappropriate selection procedures (e.g., all women who seek or are referred for psychiatric assistance following the birth of a child), or use retrospective analyses. It is clear that a woman who is depressed will describe her early experiences in terms that are colored by her low affective tone. Thus we have little clear information on the actual incidence of depression in the population of mothers of newborns or what antecedent intrapsychic variables might predict such depression. In particular, the present circumstances of the birth and the familial situation have been almost completely ignored.

Postpartum Depression: Intrapsychic Variables

As yet, no researcher has been able to predict the kinds of variables that predispose particular women to severe postpartum reactions. Increasing age and number of children may have an effect, but the evidence is inconclusive. The failure to predict such major psychic reactions on the basis of personality characteristics or psychological history would seem to indicate that the relevant variables are not to be found here. Psychoanalytic interpretations would lead one to conclude that nearly all mothers show some unconscious rejection of the role, but such a universal "truth" does not assist us in understanding individual reactions. There is some evidence that women who are younger members of their own families are at somewhat more risk (Melges, 1968). Postpartum psychotic reactions may reflect the absence of adequate mothering during the woman's own childhood. However, there is no evidence relating to inadequate mothering among new mothers who do not show severe depressive reactions. Not only does personal history not adequately predict the possibility of a postpartum reaction, but psychiatric treatment of the afflicted individual does not seem to be particularly effective. Melges, for example, notes a 44 percent recurrence rate.

Postpartum Depression: Social Variables

One can view the birth of a child as a point of transition in the life cycle—particularly for the mother, who bears the major responsibility for the care and well-being of the child. It is possible that the ambivalence or hostility that many women express following childbirth represents hostility not toward the child but toward certain activities that are culturally defined as part of the "mother" role. It is important to distinguish between the activities of childbearing and childrearing. The arrival of the first child, in particular, can be viewed·as a crisis event requiring the reorganization of the family as a social system—reassignment of roles, shifting of status, and reorientation of values (LeMasters, 1957). Of the 46 couples interviewed (selected as modern young parents), 83 percent reported an extensive or severe crisis accompanying the arrival of the first child. The crisis pattern occurred whether the marriage was evaluated as "good" (89 percent) or poor. The large majority of these couples were rated as above average in personality adjustment.

These couples seem to have romanticized parenthood. One mother said, "We knew where babies came from, but not what they were like." The problems the mothers reported included loss of sleep, chronic tiredness or exhaustion, extensive confinement to the home and cutting off of social contacts, giving up the satisfactions and income of outside employment, additional housework, guilt, and a decline in standards for housekeeping and personal appearance. The fathers agreed with most of these complaints, but added decline in the sexual responsiveness of the wife, economic pressures, and interference with their social life. The eight mothers with professional training all experienced a severe crisis. For them, two major adjustments had to be made simultaneously: giving up an occupation that had deep significance for them and assuming the role of mother for the first time. Dyer (1963), Douglas (1968), and others have all noted an association between a previous career outside the home and postpartum depression in women who chose to become "full-time" mothers, but none of these authors comments extensively on it or explores it further. We know from other contexts, however, the relationship between life crises and decreased mental health (Dohrenwend, 1973a).

Parenthood appears to be a more severe life crisis for women than for men (Hobbs, 1965). In Hobbs' randomly sampled group of lower-middle-class Protestant couples, 60 percent of the women complained of feeling "edgy" or emotionally upset. Three-quarters of the parents of both sexes complained of being upset by the interruption of routine habits—especially sleep. However, the majority of the respondents reported positive reactions to the child. Income affected the degree of crisis reaction by the fathers but not by the mothers, suggesting that the males viewed their relationship to the infant primarily as an economic one.

Recent Western culture, and American culture especially, is relatively unique in having as the norm a small nuclear family, with few enforceable obligations resting on the other kin. This nuclear family is both highly mobile and easily fragmented. Particularly new is the combination of crowding and isolation (e.g., a nuclear family crowded into a few small rooms, coexisting with a socially isolated, housebound mother) (Seiden, 1976a). Contemporary American society is distinctly unusual in relying far more heavily on the mother for primary child care, with relatively little participation by older children, husbands, or other kin.

Children appear to detract from marital satisfaction (Hicks & Platt, 1970). There are sharp differences in reported satisfaction with life as a whole between young, married, childless women (89% satisfied) and married women with young children (65% satisfied) (Campbell, Converse, & Rodgers, 1976). Indicators of psychological stress were greatest for both men and women during the early parental life stage. Women as a group exceeded men in self-reported overall life satisfaction when they had remained unmarried or were married but had no children. There is a clear contrast between the traditional belief that women require marriage and children for psychological fulfillment more than men do and objective questionnaires evaluating the state of mental health.

Women with young children have particularly high rates of depression. Community surveys in London found depression in 26–40 percent of women with young children (Brown, Bhrolchain, & Harris, 1975). The highest rate was found in working-class women with a child under age 6. Depressed women appear to have fewer material and social resources than comparable groups of nondepressed women. Four vulnerability factors seem to predispose a woman to develop depression: (1) lack of a confiding relationship with her husband or boyfriend, (2) not going to work, (3) having lost her own mother before the age of 11, and (4) having three or more children under 14 (Brown, Harris, & Peto, 1973).

It has been suggested that a major cause of this depression is the isolation of the woman within her home and without adult companionship. Day care centers that are well run and employ adults who have chosen child care as their work have found that about six hours of direct child care per day is an optimal maximum (Seiden, 1976a). Full-time homemakers significantly exceed this level. By contrast, one study found that a sample of middle-class husbands spent less than one minute per day in direct contact with their infants (Bronfenbrenner, 1974). Many women are further isolated by being the heads of single-parent households. It has been estimated that by the time they reach 18, 35 to 45 percent of all American children will have spent an average of five years in a single-parent home (Bane, 1976).

Children are probably disruptive even of marriages that remain intact. One intriguing observational study looked at the behavior of 440 adult couples, with or without accompanying children, in a variety of public places (Rosenblatt, 1974). Couples with children touched, talked, and smiled at each other less often. They may experience reduced reward levels and less adequate communication. A moving book by Judy Sullivan (1974), a "runaway" mother, recounts her experiences: "I geared my life completely to Kathleen's. I got up when she got up and ate when she was hungry. All my bodily functions were attuned to those of other people . . . There was no guarantee I could finish a letter to Glenda uninterrupted, or even go to the bathroom by myself" (p. 101).

Child Abuse

Although only a very small fraction of parents react to these disruptions of their lives by abusing their children, the incidence of child abuse is rising faster than the amount of publicity given to it in the media. A review of the number of murder victims aged 0 to 1 year of age supplied by the FBI indicates that infanticides have increased steadily in the years 1969 through 1975 (G. Rotter, personal communication). It has been suggested that there is something about parental relations with young, subsocial children that leads some parents to abuse them. Abusive parents often complain that they hit the child because they could not toilet train the child, get the child to stop crying, or get the child to obey commands (Gelles, 1973). Abuse is clearly not a rational response to difficulties with infants; however, there is no agreement as to whether abusive parents have psychopathic disorders. Researchers have also been unable to pinpoint the personality traits that characterize the disorder. Some sociological variables do seem to be predictive of child abuse. Child abusers are characteristically of low socioeconomic status (Gil, 1971) as well as having lower educational, occupational, and income levels than the general population (Galdston, 1965). The fathers are frequently unemployed or working part time. The new child creates stress and may interfere with occupational or educational plans. He or she is frequently the product of an unwanted pregnancy (Bennie & Sclare, 1969).

Contrary to most data on aggressive behaviors, mothers engage in child abuse more than fathers. While mothers have more opportunity to do so since they are alone with the child more, children may also threaten the mother's esteem and identity more than the father's. Since the responsibility for controling and rearing the child is primarily in the mother's hands, it should not be surprising that she is more ready to overreact when her demands are frustrated. Very young children are the most unable to comply with socialization demands and are the most vulnerable to abuse. The abused child is usually the youngest or only one. Responsibility for many children also increases stress. More abuse is found in families with four or more children (Gil, 1971). There is evidence that social support systems can decrease the amount of child abuse.

Social Support and Childrearing

While no one suggests that child abuse is a reasonable or probable response to the frustrations encountered in childrearing, it is suggestive that similar social-psychological variables affect both the expression of negative affect and the acting out of it. Women, because of their social isolation, their primary responsibility for childrearing, and their lack of a sense of control over themselves, are more vulnerable to the life stress of children than comparable men. Positive social supports or alternative forms of life satisfaction have much to do with how women cope with the stresses associated with childbearing and childrearing (Nuckolls, Cassel, & Kaplan, 1972). Even ten weeks of two-hour discussions exploring issues of family life enabled eight women from a low socioeconomic bracket to significantly change their appraisal about how much control they had over their own lives (Croft & Gluck, 1976). These women had previously been troubled by the discrepancy between the responsibility they were ceded for the home and child compared to their involvement with the rest of the world.

There is nothing to suggest that the social aspects of becoming a mother have been the subject of much research. There is considerable evidence that recent mothers are subject to both biological and psychological stress. It seems reasonable to take the position that the variables that mediate negative affect, especially depression, may have a strong sociocultural component. For the American woman the stresses associated with childbirth and childrearing are enhanced by the relative isolation of the nuclear family, the sole responsibility of the mother for the care and discipline of the child, and the contrast between this responsibility and the woman's sense of lack of control over many of the events leading up to childbirth. No one salient positive rationale for the presence of children appears to exist, whereas a large number of births appear to be accidental in nature. Stressful life events appear to have more deleterious effects on people who feel helpless to anticipate or control them than on those who feel they can (Schmale, 1972). Children will continue to have a deleterious effect on the mental health and marriages of their parents—particularly their mothers—as long as support networks that decrease isolation and enhance a sense of personal control do not exist in large numbers. Above all, depressive and hostile responses to children must be recognized as a cultural phenomenon rather than as a product of the rejecting psyches of women.

BLAMING THE MOTHER

Blaming the Victim

Since mothers have the greatest amount of responsibility for rearing their children, it probably should be expected that they are blamed more than fathers if something goes wrong. One study examined the attitudes of male and female college students toward parental responsibility for the psychological problems of children (Kellerman, 1974). The students read case histories of boys, girls, or children whose sex was unspecified, case histories similar to actual cases found in the clinical literature. They were told to assume that 100 percent of the blame for the disorders belonged to the parents and to divide the total blame between the father and the mother. Five psychological disorders were thought to be more the responsibility of the father: excessive aggression or acting out (fathers received 62.2% of the blame), passivity (53.2%), rebellion against authority (62.3%), school failure in math and science (54.6%), and athletic incompetence (57.8%). Five psychological problems were thought to be more the responsibility of the mother: problems of emotional-ity, especially tantrums (mothers received 60.8% of the blame), emotional coldness (53.5%), dependent behavior, particularly thumb sucking (67.5%), school failure in English (53.5%), and obe-sity (69.3%). Five psychological problems that were conceptualized by the researchers as neutral were also blamed more on the mother: asthma, stuttering, tics, enuresis (for which the mother received 57.8% of the blame), and mental retardation.

Not only are psychological problems that are stereotypically attributed to females more frequently considered to be a product of the mother's defective rearing practices, but psychological prob-lems that are more likely to have biological causes, such as mental retardation, are her fault too. Female subjects were no more willing to excuse the mother than males. In fact female college students tended to blame the father less for his children's disorders than male students did. Subjects in general blamed the fathers less for girls' disorders than for the psychological problems of boys.

Although this study by Kellerman is the only one that provides empirical support for the notion that greater maternal responsibility for the children leads to greater maternal blame, the popular media offer a wealth of materials designed to feed mothers' guilt. A recent article in the Newark *Star Ledger* headlined "MD outlines reasons for child accidents," which proved to be a summary of a nationally distributed booklet, exemplifies this technique of "blaming the vic-tim." Among the circumstances noted as those under which acci-dents are most likely to occur are (1) during an illness in the family or during the pregnancy or menstruation of the mother; (2) recent substitution of the person caring for the child; (3) illness or death of other family members, taking most of the mother's attention; (4) mother too rushed or busy (Saturday is the worst accident day, par-ticularly between 3 P.M. and 6 P.M.). Although friction between fam-ily members and moving or vacations are also noted as potential danger points, the article betrays almost complete neglect of the idea that anyone else—even the father—can be responsible for the care and safety of the child. Saturday—usually a day off for the father—is specifically referred as a time of great danger, with the mother's responsibility stressed. Mother, apparently, is not sup-posed to have any time off.

The Response to Motherhood: Growing Older

As it is now structured, the mother role seems to be highly guilt producing for women. When children do not meet their parent's expectations, or when social climates change so that the young adult does not behave as the older generation would like them to, it is the mother who is likely to see this as her fault (Lazarre, 1976; McBride, 1973). Older women in their 40s and 50s are particularly vulnerable to depressive feelings (Bart, 1970). In fact their syndrome of un-realistic fears, loneliness, crying bouts, and so forth has been chris-tened "Mama Portnoy's complaint." Other psychologists and sociologists have labeled the phenomenon the "empty-nest syn-drome." It is considered to be related to the arrival at adulthood of the youngest child and the woman's sense that she is no longer needed by her family. Depressive reactions are more common among women in ethnic groups that traditionally put a great premium on motherhood and the family (e.g., Jews and Italian Americans).

While depression in the middle years is common among women, mourning the departure from home of the children proba-bly is not. A widely cited survey by Ann Landers indicated that 70 percent of her female readers would not have had a child if they could do it again. Of course this group could have selected itself, so that only the most dissatisfied mothers responded. In any case childlessness appears to enhance the perceived quality of life, whereas mothers whose children have left home may be happier than those whose children remain.

The natural conclusion of such findings is not that childrearing ought to be abandoned in the name of mental health but that the roles and values associated with traditional motherhood need to be examined. Womanhood is not necessarily the same as motherhood. Nor does the timetable for bearing and rearing children and work-ing outside the home need to be the same for everyone. An impor-tant research priority is the woman who bears and cares for her children and then reenters the academic and job market in her mid-dle years, in contradistinction to the more typical career woman pattern, which postpones childbearing until a career has been established.

Adult women in continuing-education programs form an impor-tant source population for understanding the relationship between traditional sex roles and mental health. They appear to emerge from such programs with a highly positive self-image (Astin, 1976). Their most important self-ratings were in the areas of independence, in-tellectual self-confidence, and leadership ability. Few of their hus-bands and children under 18 consider their emerging autonomy detrimental to the family. In fact they applauded the woman's deci-sion as increasing the well-being of the family economically and enhancing her growth as a person. Sex role stereotypes may operate to make women more sensitive to their responsibilities as the pri-mary parent than either their husbands or children perceive neces-sary in terms of actual physical or psychological support services.

MATERNAL EMPLOYMENT

The popular notion that the mother is responsible and deserving of blame for all aspects of her children's behavior probably reaches its highest peak in "myths of the working mother." The absence of the mother from the home is perceived to produce delinquency and neuroticism. A "good mother" devotes her full time and energy to her children. But what actually is the relationship between maternal employment and children's characteristics? Is the working–nonworking dichotomy adequate or useful for explaining the effects of maternal employment? We must investigate historical, cross-cultural, and cross-species evidence that may be relevant for an understanding of the mother–child relationship. In particular, we need to examine what happens to the child's behavior when the relationship with the female parent is not quite as "one-to-one" as the ideal presented by some of the professional as well as the popular literature on childrearing.

A number of critical surveys of the childrearing literature have appeared over the years (Stolz, 1960; Wallston, 1973; Hoffman, 1974). The author of one early critical review (Stolz, 1960) concluded that "one can say almost anything one desires about children of employed mothers and support the statement by some research study" (p. 772). This conclusion does not seem to have lost any validity from the research of the past decade and a half. It is still possible to damn the woman who works outside the home or exonerate her, depending on which study one wishes to use as evidence.

When a variety of studies support a variety of conclusions, it is usually because the conceptualization of either the independent or dependent variable is not clear. In the case of the employed mother, operational definitions of both kinds of variables appear to be faulty. In particular, making a distinction between mothers who do or do not work outside the home obscures a number of variables that have been shown in one study or another to be of some importance in mediating the effects of maternal employment on the child. It is especially important in this regard to distinguish between the effects of maternal separation and maternal deprivation.

Does Separation Equal Deprivation?

Major "evidence" for the belief that it is essential for young children to have a mother at home is the literature on the harmful effects of maternal deprivation (see Yarrow, 1964 for a summary of this literature). While there is no doubt that maternal deprivation has severe emotional and cognitive effects on the child, there is no reason to regard these data as analogous to the experience of a child whose mother works outside the home. Most of the studies of maternal deprivation have been done on institutionalized children whose mothers were virtually totally unavailable. Moreover, the staff at such institutions was often inadequate and unable to provide sufficient contact with the children. There is little evidence to support the idea that cognitive impairment results when the mother is absent part of the time. It has been noted, in fact, that Bowlby, the English psychologist who has provided much of the data on the effects of maternal deprivation, studied the children of working mothers cared for in day nurseries as a control and found these children to be normal (Yudkin & Holme, 1963). He distinguished between children who are separated for part of the day and those who are extensively deprived, and appeared to imply that partial separation is harmless.

A more important distinction may be between supervised and unsupervised children. Few researchers, however, have concerned themselves with the distinction. One study of fifth-grade children attending school in a black ghetto area (Woods, 1972) actually found that children whose mothers worked at home or who were away part of the time did less well than those whose mothers were employed full time. The latter mothers provided economic assets for the family that may have enhanced rather than detracted from the mother–child relationship. Mothers who worked full time were evaluated as providing more supervision, and it was lack of supervision rather than maternal employment that appeared to contribute to the poorer cognitive development found in some of these children.

Stable substitute care also appears to be an important variable. As could be predicted, children with unstable care (more than two substitute mothers over a two-year period) do less well than those with stable care (Moore, 1969). Children with exclusive maternal care were found to be more dependent, more conforming, and less aggressive than those who had been cared by people other than their mothers. One can argue about the relative balance between the needs of the individual and those of society. But if our aim is to provide independent, autonomous adults, substitute care may actually be more desirable. These data also indicate that the psychological problems of children whose mothers are absent some of the time may be due as much to the unstable nature of the family situation as to maternal deprivation, since unstable homes tended to produce unstable substitute child care arrangements.

The Employed Mother as a Role Model

The mother who works outside the home differs from her nonemployed counterpart in several major ways. First, the working mother provides a different role model than the nonemployed mother. The daughters of employed mothers show fewer stereotypes about the feminine role than the daughters of mothers who do not work outside the home (Hoffman, 1974a). Daughters of employed mothers saw women as more competent and effective, while their sons saw men as warm and expressive. These perceptions probably reflect the children's experience with their parents' sharing of both work and parental roles. The daughters of women who work outside the home score lower on traditional femininity scales. This is a problem only if we view traditional femininity as mentally healthy. The motivation to model a working mother was also stronger. Adolescent daughters of women who work outside the home were more likely to name their mother as the person they most admire and resemble.

The adolescent daughters of employed mothers have also been found to be relatively independent, autonomous, and active. They show higher and more unconventional aspirations. Maternal employment, however, may have some drawbacks. The kindergarten daughters of employed mothers were more likely to rate themselves as likely to get into a fight than girls whose mothers did not work outside the home (Miller, 1975). This could be because their mothers present a more aggressive, less passive model or because they permit more expressions of aggression. Their teachers rated these girls as being more likely to boast about their exploits and more attention seeking. As we have seen in other contexts, such behaviors are stereotypically male and may reflect the girls' less feminine role orientation. Teachers' ratings may also reflect their own stereotypic notions about appropriate male and female behavior. It would be questionable to assume that the teachers were unaware of the mothers' employment status, and their ratings may have been influenced by their opinions about the suitability of outside employment for mothers of such relatively young children.

Maternal employment may lower the son's esteem for the father as the person he most admires (Hoffman, 1974a). There is no clear evidence, however, that it produces lower occupational aspirations. College students, male or female, whose mothers were employed outside the home held less traditional stereotypes about both sexes (Vogel, Broverman, Broverman, Clarkson & Rosenkrantz, 1970). These data tend to confirm the view that sex role perceptions, and probably behaviors as well, are affected by the actual parental role behaviors to which children are exposed.

Employment and the Mother's Emotional State

Employed mothers tend to have a different relationship with their children than mothers who do not work outside the home. The former tend to stress independence in their school-age children, although this is less true for highly educated mothers and those who enjoy their work (Hoffman, 1974a). Satisfactory work experiences for women may enhance their guilt about not being "good mothers," and they may avoid pushing their children into maturity, stressing the nurturant aspects of their role to make up for their absence at work. Mothers who worked for personal satisfaction showed more guilt and more negative attitudes toward the effects of maternal employment than those who worked for financial reasons (Spargo, 1968). The children of working mothers who liked work report that they were less inconvenienced by having to do household tasks than the children of mothers who did not work outside the home (Hoffman, 1963). However, they also reported receiving more positive affect from their mothers. Both groups of children—those whose mothers liked work and those whose mothers did not work outside the home—were better off than those whose mothers disliked their work. The latter group was much more likely to be subjected to strict disciplinary methods. These data indicate that mothers are in another "double bind" with regard to the effect of their employment on their children. It appears to be OK to work but not OK to like it too much.

Deleterious effects on marriage satisfaction are more likely to exist if the woman is not doing what she wants (whether in outside employment or as a homemaker) or if the spouses disagree on what she should be doing (Orden & Bradburn, 1969). In a survey of couples with young children in which both the husband and the wife approved of the wife's work status, there was no difference in reported satisfaction between employed-wife couples and housewife couples (Thomopoulos & Huyck, 1976). However, employed mothers did report significantly less satisfaction with their personal activities than housewives (their husbands were also somewhat less satisfied). The major problem encountered was "not enough time" (identified by 70% of the employed mothers as a difficulty). Nearly half reported increased fatigue but did not perceive the combination of employment and family as "too much work" or unduly restricting opportunities for entertaining or socializing.

One-third of the respondents reported that employment helped make them "better mothers," and only a very few felt that working caused child neglect. Fifteen percent of the women were dissatisfied with their child care arrangements, and one-third felt that they neglected their housework. Only 20 percent of the husbands perceived that this neglect of housework was a problem.

These data on the attitudes of employed mothers can be contrasted with the attitudes of gifted family-oriented women

(Birnbaum, 1975). The study contrasted distinguished alumnae of a prestigious institution some 15 to 25 years following graduation. It included homemakers, married professionals with children, and single professionals. Of the three groups, the homemakers had the lowest self-esteem and sense of personal competence, even including child care and social skills. These women felt least attractive, expressed more concern over self-identity issues, and often indicated feelings of loneliness. While the professional women most frequently mentioned time as a problem, the homemakers mentioned missing a sense of challenge and involvement. They insisted on an altruistic model of maternity: "You have to neglect yourself for them"; "She must subordinate her life to theirs . . . put what is best for them ahead of pleasure for herself"; "Her needs must become secondary to the more immediate demands of a child, the result is maturity, the reward—love" (p. 407). What comes through is the need of the woman for her children rather than the opposite. Her children make her feel important, valuable, and complete. Married professionals, on the other hand, admit their irritations with the untidiness, demands, and interruptions of children. They worry about affiliative inadequacy—whether they are close enough to their children or too self-preoccupied. Despite their ready protestations of guilt, however, no difference in self-esteem and self-gratification between married and single professional women was found. Given the striking contrast to the low self-evaluation of similarly gifted homemakers, Birnbaum questions whether we can in good conscience continue to raise girls to seek their primary gratification within the family.

Family Dynamics and Economic Variables

There has been relatively little work on the question of whether the mother who is employed outside the home actually does neglect her child—particularly her school-age child. Lois Hoffman (1974) concludes that the working mother, especially in the middle class, makes a deliberate attempt to compensate the child for her employment. The dissatisfied mother, whether or not she is employed outside the home, is likely to provide less adequate mothering. The idea that the school-age child whose mother is employed suffers emotional deprivation has not been supported. However, the absence of negative effects does not mean that the mother's employment is an irrelevant variable; rather, it means that mothers may have been sufficiently concerned to counterbalance any negative effects. It is also possible that the variable of interest is not employment per se but the woman's attitude toward herself, her family, and what she is doing. We have already pointed out the possible negative effects of parental friction about what the woman is doing. It has also been found that in families in which the father is absent periodically there is increased marital discord when he is present as well as greater enforcement of maternal discipline (Marsella, Dubanoski, & Mohs, 1974).

The power structure of the husband–wife relationship almost certainly has effects on the behavior of the child. It is also most certain that maternal employment alters these family relationships. Yet we have little information on how alteration of traditional role relationships alters parent–child dynamics. We are also handicapped in this area by our assumptions about "normal" husband/father dominance of the home. Thus many researchers have assumed the Moynihan (1965) position that the black family is significantly more disturbed because it is dominated by the mother. While an examination of the evidence for matriarchial structure in the black family is beyond the scope of this chapter, it is important to evaluate how our biases about normative structures can affect empirical research. Black families differ from predominant white middle-class families in a number of other ways besides ostensive female dominance. For example, they are more likely to be poor and discriminated against in a variety of covert and overt ways.

Examination of white middle-class families with an adolescent son reveals that the child gains influence at the expense of the mother (Jacob, 1974). In group discussion situations all the mothers were more influential than their 11-year-old sons. Seven of the eleven 16-year-old sons, however, were more influential than their mothers. The mother was least influential family member in over half of the families with adolescent sons. "In brief, the power struggle in middle-class families seems to involve mother and son vying for 'second place,' with fathers being relatively secure as the most powerful family member" (p. 9). Lower-class fathers lost relatively more influence than middle-class fathers when interacting with a 16-year-old son. Total family disagreement was also greater in lower-class than middle-class families, so that the mothers did not gain power relative to their husbands (they also lost some power relative to their sons). Sex-characteristic distributions of power may be upset as a function of the relative powerlessness of the family as a whole. Unfortunately no information is given on the employment status of the mother.

It appears that we need more examinations of discipline encounters within the home. Martin Hoffman (1975) suggests that the parent and child have a disciplinary encounter every six to nine minutes and that the parent "wins" 65–75 percent of the time.

While he does not specify the sex of the parent, one can suppose that it is the mother, since she is the only parent who is likely to be around to interact at such frequent intervals. Most of these encounters are initiated by the parent because of the child's "misbehavior." It is important to find out what effect maternal employment has on discipline of the child either directly or by way of alteration of husband–wife power relationships. There is evidence that the father's absence influences the mother's discipline (Hoffman, 1971), but how does the substitute father act in the mother's absence? An examination of the permanent absence of divorce indicates that, at least temporarily, discipline encounters between the child and the mother increase and those between the child and the father decrease (Hetherington, Cox, & Cox, 1975).

ALTERNATE PARENTAL MODELS

Father Power

As more and more mothers work outside the home, one would expect to find more and more fathers engaged in nurturant roles. As feminist psychologists have increasingly concerned themselves with the issues related to alternatives to traditionally female roles, notably work and achievement, feminist-oriented male psychologists have concerned themselves with an alternative to the traditional work-oriented male role—namely, the male as parent. A number of articles and books supportive of effective fathering have appeared (Biller & Meredith, 1974; Lynn, 1974). These books stress both the individual and social benefits of the father as caretaking parent. It is noted, for example, that males who are frequently exposed to their children become more involved with them. Contact with an intact family situation makes it more likely that individuals will maintain intact marriages themselves. These male social critics are particularly concerned with the way nurturance and maternalism are viewed as synonymous. They suggest that fathers can grow through their interactions with their children and need to learn to use their affective capacities just as women need to learn to use their competence capacities. They are very much part of the movement that suggests that all traits are human and need to be exercised.

Societal Structures for Child Care Alternatives

Much of the information on the effects of child care outside of the nuclear family has been collected in the Israeli *kibbutz*. Unfortunately the evidence is subject to differing interpretations depending on the bias of the researcher. The results have also tended to be overgeneralized. The structure of the *kibbutz* is not the same in every study. In some *kibbutzim,* for example, children live in children's homes rather than with their parents, although the mother participates a great deal in the care of the young infant. In others, nuclear family arrangements exist and child care is more in the form of day care. The use of alternate models for child care is not necessarily indicative of any large-scale change in sex role ideology. For many residents of *kibbutzim,* attitudes toward appropriate roles for women and men are essentially similar to those that are traditionally associated with respondents from the United States (Mednick, 1975).

There is no evidence that experiments with multiple mothering within the *kibbutz* have had any long-range deleterious effects on personality development (Rabin, 1965). Intellectual deficits have not been found either (Spiro, 1965). *Kibbutz* children have been found to be less competitive than urban Israeli children (Shapira & Madsen, 1969). They have been found to be healthy, intelligent, generous, and shy, but warm (Rabkin & Rabkin, 1969). There has been no sign of an emotional disturbance that one might expect from a violation of our ideal mother–child relationship.

Fewer studies of the day care environment have been done. Studies of adequately staffed day care facilities indicate that they may actually be beneficial to the child's development. One study of lower- and middle-class children between 6 months and 4 years old attending a day care center designed to provide an enriched environment found gains in development, while a nonintervention group showed a decline (Caldwell & Smith, 1970). There was no difference in adjustment between those who had entered day care before or after the age of 3. Three- and 4-year-old children who have had a considerable amount of day care seem to be less distressed about absence from their mothers than children without day care experience (Moskowitz & Schwartz, 1976). However, the effects of day care seem to be affected by the sex of the child. Males seem to be more consistently affected than females. Males who had had a considerable amount of day care experience were more aggressive and independent than males who had had exclusive maternal care. The latter were more anxious for adult approval and less assertive (Moore, 1975).

It is important to remember that, in the United States at least, child care has been instituted primarily during periods when it was desirable to increase the number of women in the labor force. Centers were established during the Depression and during World War

II, when women were needed in heavy construction (Wallston & Citron, 1972). Their rapid closing immediately after the war clearly showed that these centers were intended primarily to facilitate production, not to benefit children or free mothers to develop their potential in other areas. Multiple parenting in other cultures has not been adequately explored. Full-time mothering is an extravagance that has not been affordable in most historical eras or, as yet, in many parts of the world. Mothers have usually been so busy dealing with the economic realities of subsistence that they have had little time to entertain the children. Elder siblings or aged relatives often provide most of the necessary child care. In fact Margaret Mead (1954) has condemned the overemphasis on the importance of the tie between a child and her or his biological mother and the insistence that any separation is damaging. "On the contrary, cross-cultural studies suggest that adjustment is most facilitated if the child is cared for by many warm friendly people" (p. 477).

SOME CRITIQUES OF THE CONCEPT OF MATERNITY

The Infant as a Stimulus

The idea that mothers are primarily responsible for their offspring's deficits has produced much guilt in women. There is no evidence that females are uniquely responsive to the needs of infants. There is evidence that infants of many species have some characteristics and behaviors that facilitate the attachment of adults to them. (See Figure 12.2.) When situational factors are taken into account, both male and female college students are equally willing to admit being attracted to the photo of a "cute" human or monkey infant (Berman, Cooper, Mansfield, Shields, & Abplanalp, 1975). Observation of humans observing sleeping infants indicate that most react to a smile by smiling themselves (Minard, personal communication).

If an infant is unresponsive to holding, cries or fusses excessively, and is late in smiling and looking at the mother's eyes, her feeling of attachment may never develop or may weaken (Robson & Moss, 1970). We can view the process of social attachment as an adaptive characteristic among primates, with their long period of infant helplessness. There are parallel mechanisms exerted by the behavior of the young on adult primates (Harper, 1971). Just because the stimuli are unlearned, however, we should not be led to suppose that adult reactions to such stimuli have no learned components. Our cultural mechanisms are designed to enhance the mother's attachment to her child and to minimize the degree of attachment of the father. Early contact between mother and infant

Figure 12.2. Two "cute" infant apes that do *not* elicit a female ecstasy response. (Reprinted by permission of Phyllis Berman, Ph.D.)

(earlier than is possible under usual hospital routines) has been associated with increased mother–child interactions a month later as compared to those of a control group of mothers who had the usual amount of contact permitted by hospitals (Klaus, Jerauld, Kreger, McAlpine, Stefta, & Kennell, 1972). Differences between these two groups of mothers in their behavior toward their children were still present two years later (Kennell, 1975). It is not clear whether this research relates to purely maternal attachments or whether "paternal" attachment could take place if it were permitted to do so. It has been suggested that the total exclusion of husband and siblings from contact with the infant during the days immediately after birth may adversely affect other family bonds as well (Seiden, 1976a).

The direction of effects from parents (especially mothers) to children needs to be reanalyzed. Thus while most children may possess the equipment to elicit attachment in their caretakers, some children may lack these mechanisms. Autistic children, for example, have been characterized as being irresponsive to interpersonal stimuli from the earliest age. One would not expect their parents to be particularly attached to them. However, the child's deviance might not be a response to the parents' irresponsiveness. The properties of the child at or near birth may be as important a predictor of his or her ultimate psychological destiny as the properties of the parents.

Temperamental characteristics that may have a strong genetic component may be important in mediating the caretaker's response to the child. For example, difficulty in acquiring regular habits and low fastidiousness in young children appears to be predictive of later psychiatric disorders (Graham, Rutter, & George, 1973). There was no strong relationship, however, between the degree of disturbance of the mother and the degree of disturbance of the child. Reactions to particular characteristics of the child seemed to be more important than the particular properties of the caretaker. Lack of insight into caretaker–child interactions may be responsible for many findings indicating that some maternal or nurturant practice appears to have had little effect on subsequent development. Little note has been made of such nil findings. Relatively little attention has been paid even to such large-scale studies as the one of 3101 men that found few effects of maternal employment or any other background or family structure variable in adulthood (Schooler, 1972). It is difficult to estimate how many "negative" findings are never published.

The Animal Model: What Can Monkeys Tell Us?

Researchers who seek to bolster traditional concepts of male and female roles stress that nurturant behavior is more common to female mammals than to male mammals. No single behavior, however, appears to be the exclusive property of one sex or the other. Even in the rat—where neither males nor females are noteworthy for their degree of nurturance—maternal behavior has been induced in the male rat by injections of small amounts of testosterone into the brain (Fisher, 1956). The care of young among primates appears to require a considerable degree of learning as well as some experience with a normal social environment (Harlow, 1971). Female monkeys reared under socially isolated conditions are likely to brutalize their infants, although their behavior becomes less bizarre when they are given more experience with young monkeys. On the other hand, male rhesus monkeys can learn to accept a month-old infant and rear it in the absence of the mother (Redican & Mitchell, 1972). Males appear to be initially more hostile to the overtures of young monkeys than comparable inexperienced females are. Within 15 minutes, nevertheless, 5 out of 15 preadolescent males showed various forms of "maternal" behavior directed toward a one-month-old rhesus infant (Chamove, Harlow, & Mitchell, 1967).

A wide range of paternalistic behaviors are found in primates, depending on the species studied (Mitchell, 1969). At one extreme is the male bush baby, who is never found with the female and young in his natural habitat and in the laboratory may kill and eat infants. At the other extreme is the male lemur, who lives in a compatible family group. Adult males may sometimes crowd around infants soon after birth, try to groom them and will hold and cuddle them while the mother eats. In one new-world monkey, the titi monkey, the male holds and carries the infant most of the time except when it is nursing (Mason, 1966).

The primate species that exhibits the greatest degree of sexual dimorphism is the baboon. In this species male care of the young seems to be limited to protecting the whole colony from predation. It is noteworthy that this is the primate species that also shows the greatest degree of male–female dimorphism in physical size and strength. It has been suggested that the degree of male dominance in primates varies with the harshness of the environment (Russell & Russell, 1971). Thus sexual differentiation is minimal, absent, or even reversed among species that live high in the trees, have few enemies, and have a plentiful food supply, such as titis and gibbons. By contrast, male dominance and aggression are maximal among species that spend much of their time on the ground in hostile environments, such as the Hamadryas baboon.

Primate infants also vary in terms of how much they suffer from the effects of maternal separation. For some macaques birth is a social event. These young receive a great deal of stimulation from a number of sources—both male and female (Harth, 1977). Rhesus monkeys, in contrast, have a close mother–infant bond, and no one adopts an abandoned infant. Harth suggests that we cannot generalize from monkeys to people or even from monkeys to monkeys.

The major problem here is which primate species do we wish to regard as an analog of human behavior? We are humans, and the social relations of animals, even if they were not species specific, have no relevance for the problems of human ethics and society (Gross, 1974). Do we really want to take the Hamadryas baboon as our social and ethical model?

How Behavioral Science Defines the Maternal Role

The acceptance of the maternal role by social scientists has been harmful to women. When one reads the literature on mother–infant interactions it is necessary to keep in mind the following questions (Wortis, 1971):

1. Is it a biological fact that in the human species the mother is the most capable person to socialize the infant?
2. Is it a biological fact that the human newborn seeks out the mother (rather than the father) or a female (rather than a male) as the figure to which it naturally relates best, needs most, and attaches itself to socially?
3. Socially, what criteria should we employ to define whether it is beneficial for the infant to form a strong bond of attachment to one woman?
4. Is it beneficial for the mother to assume the principal responsibility for the care and socialization of the young child?

Although there has been a resurgence of interest in naturalistic observation of parent–child relationships in various primate species, including our own, these descriptive studies have not been free of bias. Wortis notes that ethology has long been linked with instinct theory, which emphasizes the biological predisposition of many psychological characteristics. There is considerable evidence that human women, like female primates, need experience in learning how to care for infants. And there is clear evidence from the literature on brutality toward children that not all mothers "instinctively" love their children. As noted earlier, there is also clear evidence that what the child does or does not do affects how readily the caretaker will become attached to him or her. The infant helps the adult develop appropriate responses that will bring about the satisfaction of its needs. There is no evidence to deny and considerable cross-cultural evidence to support the idea that many adult or subadult individuals can assist in serving and supporting the child. The assumption that only women can perform the mothering function adequately is a cheap way for society to keep women quiet without seriously considering their grievances or improving their position. Alternate forms of child care such as day care will have no effect on the generalized societal attitude that the socialization of children is the responsibility of women unless the alternate forms are staffed by men as well as women. A sexual division of labor still persists in the *kibbutzim*—only women work as nurses and infants' teachers. Having other women take care of one's children does not change the issue of a need for social change. When evidence on the "myth of motherhood" is carefully investigated it appears that we are confusing a cultural norm with a biological truth. Isolated, intense contact between infant and mother may have a profound effect on the infant's personality, but by what criteria do we suggest that the effect is a good one? On the contrary, there is much more to suggest that everyone in the family—mother, father, and children—benefits from an extension of psychological roles.

Chapter 13
Achievement: Descriptions and Explanations

While the parental role is considered the most salient for females, the role of material support of the family is considered the most salient for males. Psychology has fostered this dichotomy by utilizing males almost exclusively in research on achievement, just as nurturant characteristics have almost always been examined in terms of a female "norm." In this chapter we will look at some of the facts on differential male and female achievement and examine the nature of the explanations for such differences. Psychological explanations have tended to concentrate on (1) intrapsychic processes—the idea that males and females have different needs and fears; (2) social processes—the idea that achievement and achievement situations have a different meaning for females and males; and (3) institutional processes—the way our society measures and rewards achievement differently for males and females. Some evidence from the world of work will be examined to show that all three processes operate to reduce the probability of identical female and male achievement levels. Finally, we will discuss how social science defines achievement, myths about creative and achieving women, male models of success, and how concern with achievement affects other characteristics of human beings.

ACHIEVEMENT: SOME OF THE REALITIES

The term *achievement* has been used so loosely and has so many applications that it seems valuable to begin with some sort of definition of the term as well as an explanation of what will be included and excluded in a consideration of achievement. Achievement as it will be discussed here refers to the evaluation of performance against some standard of excellence (Unger & Denmark, 1975). While it is quite clear that women may achieve a great deal in terms of their homes and families, it is also quite clear that only vague standards for excellent performance exist in these areas. Criteria exist only for failure. In terms of some standard of excellence, data exist only for achievement in the occupational and academic spheres (Mednick, Tangri, & Hoffman, 1975). It is in relation to these areas that society makes judgments about the differential nature of male and female needs and about differential female and male behaviors, and, in the process, produces differential opportunities for achievement on the basis of sex. Thus it is in the context of the academic and occupational world that achievement will be discussed.

Women in the Work Force: Some Statistics

It is also necessary to distinguish between achievement and work. Work has always been part of many women's lives. In the years of World War II, for example, society's need for labor facilitated the entry into the labor force of large numbers of women, independent of their age and marital status (Astin, 1978). A particularly dramatic increase in work force participation has occurred among married women with young children since the 1940s. In recent years employment has changed from a minority phenomenon to a majority one in this group (Laws, 1978). The woman worker is not the exception. Thirty-seven percent of all workers are women, whereas in 1968, 41.6 percent of all women were employed. Over half of all married women are employed, and their median age in 1968 was 40. Wives working outside the home are estimated to contribute between 35 and 40 percent of the total family income, and they often do not have a "choice" as to whether or not they will engage in paid employment. Two-thirds of women working full time, year round had annual incomes below $5,000 (as compared with less than 25 percent of men). The median income for female-headed households in 1969 was $4,000 (as compared with $11,600 for all families with children under 18). While more women have entered the work force since 1969, relative economic conditions have remained unchanged. It has been estimated that half the families below the poverty line in America would move out of that category if women received equal pay.

Women who work outside the home are concentrated in a narrow range of occupations. Eighty-five percent of all working women are found in low-level white-collar or service occupations. Twenty-five percent are secretaries, saleswomen, domestics, and elementary school teachers. If we include nurses, waitresses, and bookkeepers, we have categorized more than one-third of all women workers. In fact the major historical change in women workers has been the move from private household employment to office work (Ridley & Jaffe, 1975). In 1900, one out of every 3 women who were employed in a nonagricultural occupation was a private household worker (e.g., a domestic). By 1970, only one out of 25 was so employed. In 1900, one out of 20 employed women was an office worker; by 1970, more than one out of every 3 employed women were engaged in this kind of activity. Some feminists might dispute that this represents much of a change, since many office workers today function as domestic adjuncts to men.

In the past 70 years the proportion of women employed in professional occupations has only increased from one in ten to one in six. Although, overall, the occupational structures of men and women workers have tended to approach each other since 1900, on the basis of the rate of past change it has been estimated that it will require 130 more years before women and men hold similar jobs. Thus if present trends continue, perfect equality of the sexes in occupations can be expected by the year 2100.

Relative Achievement: Relative Earnings

Disparities between the sexes are particularly marked in terms of earning power. For year-round, full-time workers, the female median is 58 percent of the male's (Kreps, 1971). The sex-related difference in earnings of full-time workers has, moreover, been increasing—in 1956 the female median was 63 percent of the male's. A further decline has been documented in the years through 1973.

Part of the explanation for sex differences in earnings has been the specialization of the labor force into male and female jobs (Kreps, 1971). Many of the occupational groups in which women are heavily concentrated pay low wages while requiring higher-than-average educational achievement. The median number of years of school completed by males and females in these occupations is higher than the median of the total male labor force; yet the median income for both women and men in these female-dominated occupations is lower than the median for the total male labor force (Oppenheimer, 1968). Her table (see Table 13.1) clearly illustrates the relationship between relative income and educational requirements of various occupations in terms of the proportion of women to men to be found in them. Higher levels of education do not pay off for either sex in these "female" occupations, which employ 71 percent of all women in professional and technical work, 98 percent of all women in clerical jobs, and 42 percent of all female workers.

When men and women working in the same occupations are compared, women still make a lower wage than men. The median income of women as a percent of that received by comparable men in 1970 ranged from a low of 42.8 percent for sales workers to a high of 66.7 percent for professional and technical workers (Astin, 1978). The lower salaries of women are not attributable to a lower level of achievement. Indeed, while occupational and educational achievements of women have kept pace with men's in recent years and have even exceeded male means, the ratio of female to male earnings has continued to decline (Featherman & Hauser, 1976). Men derive greater benefits from their social origin, education, and occupational standing, even among people with statistically equivalent work experiences and current level of labor force participation. Featherman and Hauser suggest that sexual discrimination accounted for 84 percent of the earnings gap between men and women in 1973.

High levels of achievement in women do not necessarily predict their occupational success in comparison to males. For example, the vocational achievements of over 600 male and female members of Phi Beta Kappa compared with the achievements of the general population of female and male college graduates has recently been examined (Vaughter, Ginorio, & Trilling, 1977). While Phi Beta Kappa women were significantly more likely to be found in high-prestige occupations than college women in general, they did not differ from college men in general in their vocational achievements. Phi Beta Kappa men and college men did not differ in their representation in high-prestige occupations, but both were represented significantly more often than Phi Beta Kappa women. Moreover, the single occupational category in which Phi Beta Kappa women significantly exceeded comparable men was college teaching—a job that combines the need for high academic attainment with low financial reward. Thus the superiority of the achievements of Phi Beta

Table 13.1   RELATIVE INCOME AND EDUCATIONAL STANDING OF
SELECTED OCCUPATIONS, 1960[a]

OCCUPATION	RATIO OF MEDIAN NUMBER OF SCHOOL YEARS COMPLETED IN OCCUPATION TO MEDIAN FOR TOTAL MALE LABOR FORCE[b]		RATIO OF 1959 MEDIAN INCOME IN OCCUPATION TO MEDIAN FOR TOTAL MALE LABOR FORCE[c]	
	MALE	FEMALE	MALE	FEMALE
Total	1.00	1.09	1.00	0.59
PROFESSIONAL WORKERS				
Dancers and dancing teachers	1.12	1.12	0.83	0.61
Dietitians and nutritionists	1.14	1.19	0.76	0.68
Librarians	1.50	1.46	1.01	0.77
Musicians and music teachers	1.34	1.33	1.03	0.29
Nurses	1.17	1.19	0.84	0.71
Recreation and group workers	1.36	1.32	1.00	0.78
Social and welfare workers	1.49	1.48	1.04	0.87
Religious workers	1.47	1.21	0.77	0.49
Elementary teachers	1.53	1.48	1.03	0.85
Teachers, n.e.c.	1.48	1.45	1.10	0.74
Therapists and healers	1.48	1.45	0.97	0.83
CLERICAL WORKERS				
Library attendants and assistants	1.23	1.18	0.55	0.54
Physician and dentist office attendants	1.12	1.12	0.68	0.53
Bank tellers	1.14	1.12	0.84	0.63
Bookkeepers	1.14	1.12	0.89	0.64
File clerks	1.12	1.10	0.75	0.59
Office-machine operators	1.13	1.12	0.96	0.68
Payroll and timekeeping clerks	1.13	1.12	1.00	0.73
Receptionists	1.13	1.13	0.77	0.57
Secretaries	1.15	1.14	1.05	0.71
Stenographers	1.14	1.14	1.02	0.70
Typists	1.13	1.13	0.80	0.64
Telephone operators	1.11	1.10	1.07	0.67
Cashiers	1.08	1.08	0.78	0.53
Clerical workers, n.e.c.	1.12	1.12	0.99	0.66
SALES WORKERS				
Demonstrators	1.08	1.09	—[d]	0.50
Hucksters and peddlers	0.92	1.09	0.82	0.16

SOURCE: *1960 Census of Population: Occupational Characteristics*, Subject Report
PC(2)-7A. Tables 9 and 28. Also from V. K. Oppenheimer, "The Sex-Labeling of
Jobs," *Industrial Relations*, 1968, 7, 219–234. Copyright 1968 by the Institute of
Industrial Relations.
[a] Includes occupations in which at least 51 percent of the workers were female and
where the median school years completed was greater than 11.1—the median for the
total male experienced civilian labor force.
[b] Experienced civilian labor force.
[c] Wage and salary workers in the experienced civilian labor force who worked 50–52
weeks in 1959.
[d] Base not large enough to compute a median.

Kappa women is definable and recognizable only when their achievements are compared to those of people of the same sex and only in terms of occupational prestige rather than financial reward. The point may be made more succinctly by noting that the female college graduate can expect to be paid at approximately the rate of a male high school dropout (Laws, 1978).

DIFFERENTIAL ACCESS TO THE MEANS FOR ACHIEVEMENT

The preceding analysis suggests that the focus of action should move from making training and education more accessible to women to ensuring that they receive the rewards for their achievements. Nevertheless there is considerable evidence that women have a more limited access to the means for achievement than men do. While females receive better grades than males through the high school years, they are less likely to go to college than men are. Socioeconomic status, for example, penalizes women more than men. Two-thirds of high-ability, low-socioeconomic-status males go to college, whereas half of comparable females do so (Folger, Astin, & Bayer, 1970).

Men of more average ability are also more likely to be welcomed by colleges than comparable women. One study sent applications for admission to a random sample of 240 colleges in all parts of the United States (Walster, Cleary, & Clifford, 1971). The applications were identical except for sex and race and ability level (which varied among applicants from high to medium to low). At the low ability level there was a significant sex-by-ability interaction; males were preferred over females. This effect tended to disappear at the higher levels, although when all levels of ability were taken into account the sex difference approached significance ($p < .06$). Contrary to expectations, blacks were not accepted any more frequently than whites, regardless of ability level. Black women were treated the same way white women were. In other words, a woman can expect an objective "sex-blind" evaluation of her abilities only when they are exceptional.

Women are also less likely to be accepted into postgraduate programs than men and they are far less likely to receive financial support for their studies (Ekstrom, 1972). Thus it should not be surprising that they drop out of advanced-degree programs at a higher rate than men. This issue will be discussed further in Chapter 15 in relation to gender and institutional processes. It is important to note here that the evidence in this area indicates that women's achievements are not as well related to social outcomes as those of comparable men. There is much evidence showing that American colleges do not reward achievement in comparable ways for women and men (Roby, 1973). Competent women receive less financial and social support and are frequently counseled to seek less demanding careers. The higher the academic degree, the less likely women are to receive it (Kutner & Brogan, 1976). One possible effect of institutional biases against aspiring women is that women perceive that they have fewer options available to them at any given time. Thus they are more likely to focus on options outside of educational and occupational settings in making career decisions, and their vocational aspirations lack continuity compared with those of men.

THE SEARCH FOR AN INTRAPSYCHIC EXPLANATION

Although these data suggest that institutional processes may account for major differences in achievement between women and men (women simply have less to gain from achievement), social science has focused on personality variables as a major source of explanations for these differences. Personality variables are frequently conceived of as relatively stable dispositions that generalize across situations. As we saw in Chapter 6, they may be conceived to have a strong biological component or be the product of early socialization events. Among the personality measures that have been used to explain differences between male and female achievement are (1) need for achievement, (2) internal versus external locus of control, (3) self-attributions about the causes of success and failure, and (4) fear of success—the most popular current intrapsychic explanation. The applicability of each personality variable to sex differences in achievement will be reviewed briefly here, as well as alternative social-psychological explanations for such sex differences.

Need for Achievement

Need for achievement is frequently measured by a projective technique involving the stimuli from the Thematic Apperception Test (TAT). Subjects are shown rather vague pictures of people interacting and are asked to tell stories suggested by the pictures. McClelland and his associates (McClelland, Atkinson, Clark, & Lowell, 1953) developed this procedure, scoring their subjects' stories for achievement themes and relating their scores to their level of achievement in subsequent competitive achievement situations. Scores on projective tests of need for achievement among females, however, were not able to predict their behavior in subsequent achievement situations. These researchers' response to the inability of their measure to predict the behavior of half of the human race was a single footnote in an immense tome on the subject. It is perhaps characteristic of the masculinist bias of that period that further studies on American females were omitted in favor of studies of Japanese and Indian males.

To say that projective measures of achievement motivation in females do not correlate with their achievement efforts or with their academic or intellectual performance is not the same as saying that females have a lower need for achievement than males (Entwisle, 1972). In fact the matter is much less simple than one might suppose. For example, both males and females give more achievement-related responses to pictures with men in them (Veroff, Wilcox, & Atkinson, 1953). It appears probable that both sexes see achievement and success as male traits. Achievement areas are defined by sex role (Stein & Bailey, 1973). Children appear to learn cultural sex role definitions of achievement areas by early elementary school age. Children from the second through twelfth grades consider social, verbal, and artistic skills feminine and mechanical, spatial, and athletic skills masculine. Math was also considered masculine by adolescents, but not by younger children (Stein, 1971; Stein & Smithells, 1969). Children of low socioeconomic status were more affected by sex typing of achievement areas than children from higher socioeconomic strata.

Other researchers have looked to women with different levels of achievement motivation in order to understand the phenomena that underlie sex-related differences in this area. In another examination of responses to male and female stimuli, it has been noted that female achievers had higher achievement scores for female pictures than male pictures, but underachievers attributed higher achievements to male stimuli (Lesser, Krawitz, & Packard, 1963). Female achievers are able to see women as achievers too. It is also noteworthy that women students at all-female colleges had higher need for achievement scores than those attending coeducational colleges (French & Lesser, 1964). In an all-female school the conflict between femininity and competence may be less salient. On the other hand, women who select an all-female school may be more concerned with achievement needs. For example, Radcliffe alumnae gave much higher levels of achievement imagery than a nationwide sample of women (Baruch, 1967). It is possible, of course, that self-selection and the experience of finding that competitive striving is not incompatible with affiliation needs may both operate to enhance the expression of desire for achievement among these women.

Still other researchers have concentrated on differential male and female expectations about successful achievement as an explanation for why need for achievement explains less about female behavior than about male. Virginia Crandall (1969), using a variety of different intellectual tasks as well as a wide range of age groups, found that females did not approach new tasks with as much confidence as males, even when their past intellectual performance had been better. Females also continually estimated their future academic performance at a lower level than would be warranted by their past performance, whereas males consistently predicted better performance than in the past. Males and females also extracted different information from cues about their performance. When they received some cues that told them they were capable and others that told them they were not, females focused on the negative aspects of the feedback and males on the positive aspects. There were no major differences in the way the two sexes assimilated laboratory task situations, but there appeared to be a real difference in the way they derived their expectancies from contradictory life–school situations. As was discussed in a previous chapter, the school environment appears to discriminate the individual characteristics of boys much more readily than those of girls. A recent study notes that the probability of success in school work is determined by the individual's knowledge of her or his own relative ability (Gjesme, 1973). In traditional classrooms, where ability is heterogeneous, only girls with high ability receive enough information about their capacities to have their achievement-related motives strongly aroused.

Internal vs. External Locus of Control

Information on the relationship between the expectation of success and need for achievement appears to be closely associated with recent work on internal versus external locus of control. An internal locus of control appears to be associated with the belief that one is responsible for one's actions and that there is a causal relationship between one's actions and their outcomes. An external locus of control, on the other hand, appears to reflect the belief that one is not in control of one's destiny and that individual outcomes are a result of unstable, chance variables such as luck. A number of studies have examined the relationship between sex and locus of control. In general, males appear to have a more internal locus of control than females, especially from adolescence onward (Marks, 1972).

Researchers have found cultural and subcultural effects on the relationship between sex and locus of control. An examination of college students in five countries showed that while females in general had a higher belief in external control of their lives than males, belief in externality varied from country to country. In order of decreasing externality were Sweden, Japan, Australia, the United States, and New Zealand (McGinnies, Nordholm, Ward, & Bhanthumnavin, 1974). Among younger children, from the second through the sixth grades, only Spanish-American girls gave significantly more external responses than comparable boys (Gruen, Korte, & Baum, 1974). In the black population in fact, sex differences were reversed, with girls significantly more internal than comparable boys.

It has been suggested that individual differences in locus of control reflect real differences in opportunities to control the results of one's behavior. In this regard it is noteworthy that older children make more internal responses than younger children and affluent children make more internal responses than disadvantaged children of the same age (Gruen et al., 1974). White American children make more internal responses than either black or Spanish-American children. Expectancies about the consequences of one's behavior affected the performance of these children—their grade point average—but not measures of IQ or social desirability.

A power–helplessness factor contributes most to variability in internal–external scores among young children (Nowicki & Duke, 1974). This factor deals with making people and things do what you want them to do. A sample question is "When you do something wrong is there little you can do to make it right again?" Children who report that their parents used more punishing and controlling types of behaviors have been found to have greater expectations of control by powerful others (Levenson, 1973). For females especially, internality is related negatively to maternal protectiveness.

Other recent work has concentrated on the relationship between beliefs about personal control and performance characteristics. The children who persist least in intellectual tasks are those who take the least responsibility for outcomes (Dweck & Reppucci, 1973). Children who persist in the face of failure place less stress on the presence or absence of ability and more on the role of effort in determining behavioral outcomes. Dweck and Reppucci found that boys showed more of this characteristic than girls. There is considerable evidence that this sex difference is accounted for less by biological variables than by social processes. Early success induces skill orientation toward a task (Langer & Roth, 1975). Subjects who initially did well on a purely chance task rated themselves better at predicting outcomes, overremembered past successes, and expected more future successes. Subjects who cause their own outcomes and know beforehand what they hope to obtain also perceive themselves to have more control over the outcome, more choice over what that outcome will be, and more responsibility for the outcome (Wortman, 1975).

Individuals of either sex who fail to show persistence in performance may be affected by both long-term socialization practices, as reflected in their personality dynamics, and the short-term consequences of their achievement-related behaviors. Martin Seligman has elucidated a phenomenon found in both animals and human beings called learned helplessness. Individuals who are exposed to either a series of insoluble problems or inescapable punishment are less likely to solve a subsequent series of solvable problems (Hiroto & Seligman, 1975). Exposure to such conditions engenders expectancies that responding is independent of reinforcement. The generality of the process suggests that learned helplessness is an induced "trait" rather than a personality dimension.

Individuals who manifest an external rather than an internal locus of control may be more affected by conditions that induce learned helplessness than more internal subjects. Although both internal and external subjects performed more poorly on tasks requiring problem-solving strategies following exposure to nonsoluble problems, only external individuals showed helplessness effects in subsequent non-problem-solving tasks (Cohen, Rothbart, & Phillips, 1976). People with a high external locus of control tended to be perceptibly slower in a color-naming task as well as having difficulty in cognitive coping strategies. Carol Dweck (1975) has explored techniques for dealing with children who show learned helplessness effects in problem-solving situations. She finds that in these children simple exposure to success experiences alone are not sufficient to prevent severe deterioration in performance after failure. When, on the other hand, the children were trained to take responsibility for failure and to attribute it to their lack of effort, performance levels were maintained or improved. Thus cognitive restructuring as well as objective success in performing intellectual tasks appears to be required.

Recent evidence about locus of control in general and concepts about the consequences to be expected from one's behavior in particular appear to be especially relevant to thinking about differences in female versus male achievement. It can be argued that females are socialized to make less connection between their behavior and its consequences. Indeed, society may make less connection between behavioral contingencies and reinforcements for females than for males. This interpretation is given support by the variety of findings indicating that women may show more self-confidence in achievement situations than men when clear feedback about their actual performance is provided (Lenney, 1977).

Attributions About the Causes of Success and Failure

Recently psychologists have attempted to analyze sex differences in achievement situations within the framework of attribution theory. In addition to expectations about the results of their performance, people tend to make judgments about why particular events occur. These casual attributions may be distinguished on an internal–external dimension. Ability and effort are causes originating within the subject, while task difficulty or luck are causes within the environment or external to the individual (Frieze, Fisher, McHugh, & Valle, 1978). Causal attributions may also be categorized by their stability. Ability and task difficulty are stable causes, while effort and luck are relatively unstable. The stability of a cause may affect the expectation of a change in one's performance. If an individual regards the cause to be stable, little change can be expected. If, on the other hand, unstable causes are seen as the reason for the particular level of performance, the possibility of change at any time must be acknowledged.

Attribution theorists hypothesize that many people have well-established patterns of making causal attributions. Theoretically, maximum self-esteem would be associated with a tendency to make internal, stable attributions for successful performance and external or unstable attributions for failure. There is considerable evidence that the attributional patterns for men and women differ from each other. Women are more likely than men to attribute success to luck and failure to lack of ability. This self-derogatory pattern has been found to exist, in part, in grade school girls (Nicholls, 1975). Failure was attributed to lack of ability to a greater extent than success was attributed to high ability. Adult women, too, are more likely than men to attribute failure to lack of ability (McMahon, 1972). The two sexes, in fact, select achievement situations in terms of these attributional tendencies when they are given the opportunity to do so. In a combined field and laboratory study, it was noted that males at a fair tended to select games of skill significantly more often than females and to persist longer at such games (Deaux, White, & Farris, 1975). In an analogous laboratory experiment, males again showed a preference for games involving skill, both in terms of choice and in the amount of time they persisted in such games. Females preferred to play games in which luck was the determinant. While these women and men did not differ in their expectation of success in luck games, the women did have a higher expectation of success than in skill games, which may dispose them to make that choice. Men, in contrast, had higher expectations for skill games than for luck games. Although neither success in the skill games for males and females nor success in the luck games for males affected their satisfaction, females' satisfaction was affected by their success in luck games. Luck appears to be a more potent force in female behavior than in male behavior.

Other studies also find a general pattern of externality in females (Frieze et al., 1978). Females are more likely than males to rate tasks as easier in both success and failure conditions and to make greater use of luck attributions for success and failure. By employing either of these patterns women reduce the value of their successes and take less responsibility for them. They may also tend to feel less pride about their successes or shame about their failures. This form of internal processing would lead women to experience little joy or pain in achievement situations. It is noteworthy that such processes are also found in other low-power groups. For example, white fifth-graders judged that ability and effort (internal causes) were relatively more important for their performance than task difficulty or luck (external attributions) (Friend & Neale, 1972). The reverse was true for black children.

It is important to remember that the differences being discussed are not in terms of self-concepts about ability and effort but in terms of evaluation of the importance of ability and effort as an explanation for the person's performance. As long ago as 1962, Crandall and her associates (Crandall, Katkovsky, & Preston, 1962) indicated that the importance children placed on intellectual achievement predicted performance for boys but not for girls. Boys' stated expectations of intellectual success were positively associated with their achievement efforts, while the expectations of girls were either negatively or nonsignificantly related to their performance behaviors. Girls had little sense of responsibility in intellectual situations. The cognitive structure and inferences that girls and boys make with reference to achievement may precondition the kinds of behaviors they bring with them to achievement situations. Boys who are given instructions that a task is solvable by means of skill persist longer than their counterparts in a chance condition (Altshuler & Kassinove, 1975). Moreover, they persist at a level that is consistent with their previous level of reinforcement. Under chance conditions it is the girls who persist longer.

Fear of Success

The final intrapsychic process that has been hypothesized to account for the inability of psychologists to validly predict the achievement behavior of females is fear of success. This process was given wide circulation through the work of Matina Horner, currently president of Radcliffe College. The concept was based on work done for her doctoral dissertation in 1968 and was an attempt to explain why females who score high in need for achievement often fail to perform well when exposed to competitive achievement situations. Horner (1972) hypothesized that women who have high achievement aspirations often deny such aspirations, since they see femininity and achievement as incompatible with each other. She also suggested that fear of the consequences of success would be more characteristic of the high-ability woman engaged in competitive achievement activities, since for her success may actually be within her grasp and her fears of the results of such success are aroused by participation in competitive activities. She tested her theories by exposing male and female students to verbal leads that pictured a high level of accomplishment in a mixed-sex competitive situation. Ninety females in the original study responded to the lead "After first-term finals, Anne finds herself at the top of her medical-school class." The males in her sample received the same information, but with the name John instead of Anne. The stories they related in response to the cue were evaluated for the presence or absence of fear of success imagery.

In Horner's original study 9.1 percent of the males versus 65.5 percent of the females gave responses that were indicative of fear of success. In subsequent studies Horner noted that fear of success imagery increased in girls from junior high school through college, whereas the percentage of males who showed such imagery remained relatively unchanged. Female responses to stimuli portraying a successful woman tended to characterize her as physically impaired or unattractive, unliked, unlikable, and unhappy, or denied that she could ever have had such success at all. Unusual excellence in women was clearly associated with loss of femininity, social rejection, personal or societal destruction, or some combination of these problems. (See Table 13.2.) Horner also found that young women who were high in fear of success tended to show poorer performance in a competitive achievement situation, while women who gave few negative images to the cue, like men, improved their performance under competition. Women who were high in fear of success also viewed doing well in competition as less important to them than those who were low in anxiety about success.

Horner's results are particularly important because they indicate that women who have the greatest objective probability of success are the ones who are most likely to feel conflict about the social consequences of such success. In other studies (Horner, 1970)

Table 13.2 SAMPLE RESPONSES TO CUES INVOLVING SUCCESS

CUE: JO ANN IS GRADUATING FROM MEDICAL SCHOOL AND IS AT THE TOP OF HER CLASS

RESPONSES FROM FEMALES WHO ARE *LOW* IN FEAR OF SUCCESS

"Her big day had come. The frustrations, sleepless nights, and many endless problems were finally starting to take some meaning. The future held promise. . . ."

"She is very aggressive and has to be. She has fought all the way and will continue. After specializing in further study, she will be successful, in monetary terms at least. . . ."

"She is now deciding where she'll be able to get a job as a woman. Since she had attained high honors she is sure that she will be able to get any position that she tries for. . . ."

RESPONSES FROM FEMALES SCORED AS *HIGH* IN FEAR OF SUCCESS

"Joanne after graduation will practice in a 20 story office building where she will be a number among the 40,000 others around her; no one will be interested if she was first or last in her graduating class."

. . . "Joanne's life took a radical turn for the worse. On dates, young men would ask her about her work and when she told them she was a doctor, they would ask her to examine them. Joanne would not comply with their requests, and she found herself alone and dejected. . . ."

. . . "At first, her life is a success. She has a happy marriage and 3 children. After a few years, the marriage breaks up. Her husband is getting involved with too many things and Joanne just stays home with the kids. . . ."

"She is guaranteed a job on the medical staff of one of the top hospitals in the country. She loves her work and is extremely happy especially because next week is her 7th birthday."

. . . "On the day of her graduation she was killed by a car when she was crossing the street. I guess she didn't have as much control of her future as she thought."

SOURCE: From a survey by Nancy Pollack, Margaret Rosenberg, and Rita Folkman for a course in the psychology of women, Montclair State College, May 1974.

Horner points out that Radcliffe women who were high in fear of success were most likely to alter their career aspirations in traditionally feminine directions during their college years. They were either not dating at all or dating men who did not approve of "career women." On the other hand, women who were either low in fear of success or persisting in competitive striving despite their anxieties were dating men who were not threatened by female success and, in fact, encouraged it. Horner also notes that women who were high in fear of success were more likely to become involved in drugs and/or to drop out of college. Anxiety generated by violation of sex role boundaries seems to predispose women to engage in behaviors that result in a reduction of achievement aspirations. Such behaviors may not appear to reflect direct choice but may be an indirect manipulation of others or the environment so that the woman perceives herself to have no other options. Comments by girls who are high in fear of success who were dating nonsupportive males include the following:

> He thinks it's ridiculous for me to go to graduate school or law school.
>
> He says I can be happy as a housewife and I just need to get a liberal arts education.
>
> He wants a wife who will be a mother fulltime until the kids are grown. [Horner, 1970]

Some Limitations on Fear of Success

Since Matina Horner's conceptualization of fear-of-success motivation became widely known, more than 200 studies on the subject have appeared either in the research literature or as oral presentations at psychological conventions. It has become clear that such a motivation is not as common among women as Horner's work would suggest, that it can appear in selected male groups, and most important, that it is not as an all-inclusive explanation of women's lower achievement performance relative to men as had first been presumed. A number of factors that apparently interact with fear of success will be briefly summarized here.

1. Sex role orientation may be an important determinant of whether women show fear of success. Nontraditionally oriented students generated fewer success-avoidant responses than moderate or traditionally oriented students (O'Leary & Hammack, 1975). Nontraditional students were also more affected by the achievement context of the cue (e.g., they gave few success-avoidant responses to cues involving domestic or artistic competition and more to cues portraying achievement in a vocational–academic context). Traditional women have a high level of success-avoidant themes to all cues regardless of situational context. Traditional sex role attitudes seem to have a greater impact than fear of success on women's achievements both in the laboratory and in daily life (Peplau, 1976a). Women with traditional attitudes perform significantly better on a verbal task when working as a team with their boyfriend than when working in individual competition against their boyfriend, whereas nontraditional women showed an opposite pattern. Their projected fear of success did not vary depending on whether they were competing or cooperating with their boyfriend, but there is some evidence that women who combine traditionalism and high fear of success may be most affected by variation in achievement settings. Sex role traditionalism, but not fear of success, moreover, was associated with significantly lower career aspirations, lower SAT verbal scores, and lower self-ratings of "intelligence."

2. Not all studies find differences in fear of success between males and females. Extensive reviews in this regard have been published by Tresemer (1976, 1977) and Zuckerman and Wheeler (1975). Sex differences in fear of success are particularly unlikely to occur during the early school years (Condry & Dyer, 1976a), although girls may reduce their academic striving during the period when they show no differences from boys in fear-of-success motivation. At least one developmental study (Kimball & Leahy, 1976) indicated that fear of success rose in both sexes from the fourth through the tenth grade and then dropped from the tenth to the twelfth grade. Changes in fear of success may be related to the development of affiliation motives that occur during the junior high school years.

3. The motive appears to be more likely to be aroused by certain specific situational and competitive contexts. Females in a high school secretarial course showed lower fear of success imagery than females in a college preparatory course (Kimball & Leahy, 1976). Women in a college preparatory program did have higher scores than comparable males. Women are more likely to give avoidance-of-success responses to cues portraying female success in a nontraditional context (Tresemer, 1976). A study of fear of success in 91 college-age dating couples found that while there was no direct relationship between the woman's fear of success and any of seven measures of her boyfriend's sex role attitudes, there was a tendency for women who were high in fear of success to anticipate problems in their relationship due to differences in intelligence or to their own desire for independence (Peplau, 1976b). While boyfriends do not affect the strength of a woman's underlying motivations, they may arouse them in specific situations.

4. Expression of sex-related conflicts about achievement appear to be facilitated by extensive contacts of females with members of the opposite sex. For example, fear-of-success responses were more frequent among women in coeducational schools than among those who attended all-female ones (Winchel, Fenner, & Shaver, 1974). Women with high fear of success performed better when competing against a woman on a feminine task and on tasks described as feminine (Makosky, 1976). Women who showed no fear of success did better when competing against a man on a masculine task and on tasks described as masculine. Women who had high fear of success rated a home and family as more important and a professional career as less important than women who manifested no fear of success. They also viewed themselves as less feminine than women with no fear of success. These data again suggest that it is the threat of the consequences of social deviance that enhance the expression of fears about achievement found in these women (Lock-

heed, 1975). Males, on the other hand, who are rated as high in fear of success are more likely to portray high achievement as not worth the effort (Hoffman, 1974b).

5. Fear of success is not always found where one expects it. An examination of women managers in the field found little evidence of fear of success among these highly achieving women (Wood & Greenfield, 1976). Black women are also less likely to show fear of success than white women (Weston & Mednick, 1970).

6. Probably the most potent critique of the concept is that fear of success is not always associated with decrements in performance in achievement situations. No relationship between fear of success and gender role orientation was found in a study of 100 female honors students (Depner & O'Leary, 1976). Fear-of-success scores predict a very limited amount of women's behavior (as little as 5%) (Peplau, 1976b). Women who are high in fear of success tend to deprecate women generally, not only in achievement situations. It would be interesting to find out what such women say about women who are portrayed as being less achieving than in conventional tests for fear of success.

7. It has been suggested by a number of researchers that fear of success represents the expression of a culturally based "norm" about the expected consequences of female achievement in a nontraditional context (Monahan, Kuhn, & Shaver, 1974). These researchers asked 120 10- to 16-year-old boys and girls to respond to male or female cues in a complete "fear-of-success" design. In support of a cultural-belief interpretation, they found that both sexes gave more negative responses to a cue portraying female success. Recently Shaver (1976) has suggested that if Horner had used a story portraying a superlatively beautiful woman rather than a highly successful one she might have developed a concept about the "fear of beauty." In other words, he suggests that women may not fear success so much as they harbor negative stereotypes about people who are more fortunately endowed than they are in any characteristic. Of course the expression of negative stereotypes is not the property of any one sex or any other group.

Negative imagery about female success is common among males. One study presented 576 people with a TAT cue about a high-achieving college student as part of a large attitude survey conducted in the Detroit area in the summer of 1973 (Moore, 1974). The respondents represented a probability sample of the economic, racial, and geographic population characteristics of the greater Detroit metropolitan area. Subjects told stories to one of two cues: Either "Anne" or "John" has just graduated at the top of her or his college class. This large-scale demographic study found a number of interesting relationships: The highest percent of fear-of-success stories (50%) were elicited from white males speaking of "Anne," while the lowest percent (23%) were produced by black females speaking of "John." Fear of success imagery showed a steady increase as education increased among white males speaking of "Anne," whereas a slight decline appeared among white males who received the "John" cue. White females speaking of "Anne" were most likely to tell fear-of-success stories when they themselves were extremely well educated. There was also an overall tendency among blacks for fear of success to be more common among the better educated, with 47 percent of respondents who were educated beyond high school telling fear-of-success stories compared to 25 percent of those with less education. A parallel effect was found in men and women of both races in terms of level of occupational status.

Younger people were more likely to evidence fear of success than older people. Overall, then, respondents who are young, well educated, and employed in professional occupations tend most often to indicate fear of success in their stories about "Anne." Fear-of-success stories about "John," on the other hand, are told more often by males with less education and lower-status jobs. Fear of success was also related to some attitudinal characteristics in women. Women with fear of success are less likely to say that they would work if they didn't need the money. Women who are currently married or have never been married are less likely to fear success than women whose marriages have been broken by separation, divorce, or death. Fear of success appears to be particularly well related to the amount of money a married woman earns relative to her husband's income. When the wife earns no money, 27 percent of the wives tell fear-of-success stories. When she earns one-tenth to under six-tenths of the family income, 42 percent tell fear-of-success stories. When she earns six-tenths or more of the family income, then 61 percent tell fear-of-success stories. Fear of success is also positively correlated with large family size among white, but not black, women. Women who both fear success and hold traditional attitudes about the woman's role are significantly different from other women. They have significantly more children than other women, even when religion and family income are controlled.

These data suggest that well-defined relationships exist between the probability of conflict with—or as—a successful woman and the production of fearful, hostile responses to cues involving successful women. Fear of success may be viewed less as a personality variable and more as evidence of an objective evaluation of the probable social consequences of superior female achievement. The role of significant males in a woman's environment may be particularly important in arousing her feelings of conflict.

We may also ask why need for achievement and fear of success has become such an important issue in social psychology today. Depner and O'Leary (1976) suggest that the use of these variables as the most salient ones for explaining women's reluctance to assume nontraditional roles represents an example of the American fascination with the myth that a person can accomplish anything for which he or she strives. Shaver (1976) suggests that changing values about women's role in society have created more conflict and increased the probability that women will express their fears when given an opportunity to do so. Thus some researchers have found, paradoxically, that women who favor the women's movement and have more liberal or radical political beliefs are more likely to express fear of success than more traditional women (Caballero, Giles, & Shaver, 1975). Black militant women are also more apt to express fear of success than women who espouse less militant attitudes (Puryear & Mednick, 1974). These data appear to conflict with the majority of studies that show a negative relationship between fear of success and nontraditional attitudes towards sex roles. It is not clear what such exceptions indicate about the concept, except that it is more labile and more interrelated with other variables than first appeared.

The current emphasis on fear of success as a variable may also represent a way of blaming the victim. More attention has been paid to this concept in the popular media than any other recent psychological construct. A recent survey of materials cited in textbooks of social psychology indicated that reference to Horner's work is one of the few points of similarity among different textbooks. Stress on this concept has political significance. If lower need for achievement or higher fear of success is primarily responsible for lower female achievement as compared to male achievement, the onus for change is on women who manifest such "undesirable" personality characteristics. It will not be necessary for society to change its patterns of rewards and punishments. If any change in the social situation is warranted, childhood socialization practices are indited, ensuring that change will be slow if it comes at all.

Intrapsychic Variables in Males

One must also ask why the focus of most of these studies has been the female, sometimes with a male comparison group. Don't males have fears as well? A recent study suggests that the tendency of males to attribute their failures to luck may reflect a greater degree of fear of failure than is found in females (Levine, Reis, Sue, & Turner, 1976). Differences between male and female attributional biases may be due to greater defensiveness in males, who find failure more distressing to them. Fear of failure could account for the greater male tendency to predict higher grades than would be warranted by their grade point averages (Vaughter, Gubernick, Matossian, & Haslett, 1974). One could suggest that rather than having lower aspirations, women are simply making more realistic appraisals. Males, on the other hand, are comforming to the stereotypic masculine sex role, which mandates that they appear self-confident, not to say boastful, in achievement contexts.

THE SOCIAL DEFINITION OF ACHIEVEMENT AS MALE

A variety of different studies indicate that members of both sexes view achievement as a male characteristic. Males are even the more salient evaluators of competence for both sexes. One recent study revealed that the failure of the male partner to reward or punish according to social expectations involving achievement detracted from subsequent performance (Argote, Fisher, McDonald, & O'Neal, 1976). Both females and males who were rejected by him following success or accepted following failure performed less well on a subsequent task than subjects who were accepted following success or rejected after failure. Approval or punishment by a female partner had little effect on subsequent performance.

Recent research has documented the existence of a number of subtle markers of societal biases against success by women. Much of this information has been generated through the creative efforts of one researcher, Kay Deaux. In a series of studies she and her students have elucidated the nature of social judgments about causes of success and failure in males and females. They find (Deaux & Emswiller, 1974) that when males and females evaluate the performance of either a male or a female stimulus person who performed in an above-average manner on either a male- or a female-related task, they perceived that the males were, in general, more skillful than the females. Performance by a male on a masculine task was seen to be more the product of his skill, whereas an equivalent performance by a female on the same task was seen to be influenced more by luck. Contrary to their prediction, the reverse did not hold for performance on feminine tasks. Instead, the performance of males and females on the feminine task was evaluated as being equivalent. Performance on the masculine task, moreover, was seen as better than equivalent performance on the feminine task. Males and females shared these biases equally. (See Figure 13.1.)

The evidence points to a cognitive link between success and

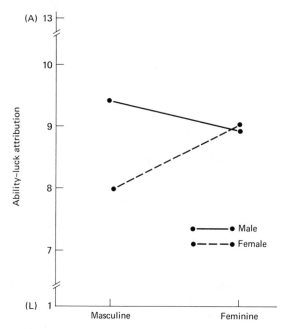

Figure 13.1.   Ability–luck attributions as a function of sex of task and performer. The most skill is assumed when males perform well on a masculine task. Female performance on such a task is seen to be more a matter of luck. Less different assumptions are made about performance on a feminine task. (From K. Deaux and T. Emswiller, "Explanations of Successful Performance on Sex-Linked Tasks: What Is Skill for the Male Is Luck for the Female," *Journal of Personality and Social Psychology,* 1974, *29,* 80–85. Copyright 1974 by the American Psychological Association. Reprinted by permission.)

maleness. Females are, in fact, overrated for performing well in a situation that is culturally defined as male (Taynor & Deaux, 1973). Students given information that a stimulus person (male or female) had performed well (by being quick-thinking and cool-headed) in an emergency (an armed robbery), thereby enabling the police to capture the criminal, perceive a woman who performed well in this situation as having performed better than a man in a similar context. Males in such a situation were rated as having exerted less effort than a comparable woman. Thus it appears that in this situation evaluation bias favors the female. The stimulus situation differs, however, from those usually used to examine evaluation bias. It is transitory in nature; it is unlikely to occur; and the outcome of the performance is explicit, minimizing the need for subjects to make additional assumptions. It may be the very exceptional nature of the situation and the implied lack of continuity that led subjects to reward the female's behavior more positively than that of the male. After all, he only did "what he was supposed to do."

Even children try to explain the unexpected outcomes of female achievement performance by unstable causes—luck or a particularly intense amount of effort. In a developmental study of 40 males and 40 females at each of four grade levels—fifth, eighth, eleventh, and college—a female stimulus person who was described as succeeding in mechanics had her success attributed less to ability than a comparable male stimulus person (Etaugh & Brown, 1975). Effort was used more often to explain her success. Female failure on a mechanical task—which was expected—was more frequently attributed to lack of ability than male failure was. There were no significant sex-of-subject or age differences. Thus differential biases about male and female performance appear to be well established in both boys and girls by the fifth grade.

How females and males perform in the stylistic sense is also a component in differential judgments about their performance. Performance of a masculine task in a logical, assertive manner was rated more favorably and assigned a greater reward than performance of the same task in a feminine manner (Taynor & Deaux, 1975). On the feminine task, behavior done in a sensitive, intuitive mode was rated more favorably on the performance measure. In contrast to the masculine mode, however, the feminine mode was not allocated greater reward, even though the actor was liked better when he or she dealt with a child in a feminine mode.

THE CHASTISEMENT OF MALE FAILURE

It has been suggested that males are evaluated along a broader range than females (Deaux & Taynor, 1973). They appear to be considered more competent at the positive end of a scale of performance, but suffer greater devaluation under conditions of low competence. Female subjects persistently downgrade unsuccessful males as contrasted to successful males and downgrade successful females in comparison with unsuccessful females (Feather & Simon, 1975). Females are evaluated more positively and seen as more powerful if they fail. Causal attributions about males and females ranged from global judgments about the individuals to rather trivial assumptions about their behavior following success or failure. An example of a trivial attribution is that males were rated as more likely to throw a wild party after success and females more likely to do so after failure.

While failure is deleterious to a male's self-evaluation, success by other men may be threatening to him as well. Highly competent men who make a single blunder during an interview (spill coffee on themselves) are preferred by other men over equally competent men who do not take a pratfall, and over incompetent men regardless of whether they have made a mistake (Deaux, 1972). This effect operates only for males judging males. Men and women appear to be less tolerant of error when judging members of the opposite sex. It should be noted, however, that competent individuals were preferred over less competent ones in every experimental condition.

THE PENALTIES FOR FEMALE SUCCESS

The Social Rejection of Competent Women

At the same time that males are lauded for success and penalized for failure, females who manifest "too" competent behavior appear to suffer a variety of social penalties. Although their original study (Spence & Helmreich, 1973) seemed to indicate that competent women were evaluated as positively as competent men, some later results seem to indicate that this effect is not as clear-cut as was first supposed. Recently Spence and her associates have found that when males and females are given an opportunity to respond to a portrait of a competent person (in a videotape interview) by means of a projective technique (a series of TAT-type questions about the stimulus person) before answering objective questions about her or him, only feminist women continued to prefer the masculine competent woman to the feminine competent one (Spence, Helmreich, & Stapp, 1975b). Other groups of subjects reversed their ratings. Spence and her coresearchers suggest that use of the TAT format may have forced subjects to consider the stimulus persons more actively and thus elicited less superficial reactions than the objective questionnaire items did on their own.

Males appear to like the competent woman only when they observe her performance and are not involved in an interaction with her (Hagen & Kahn, 1975). Both males and females were more likely to exclude a competent woman from their group than a competent man, and more likely to include an incompetent woman than an incompetent man. Although competent women were not discriminated against on a leadership measure, it was clear that a social atmosphere conducive to low performance by women was established. These results could be interpreted in terms of ethnocentric behavior; ingroup members (men) attempt to maintain self-esteem and high rewards at the expense of an outgroup (women).

Devaluation and rejection of women seems to occur most

strongly under conditions in which competent women openly adopt competitive orientations and reject female roles and behavior (Shaffer & Wegley, 1974). In this investigation male and female college students read descriptions of a highly successful female student who was viewed by her college instructors as having great potential for a successful career in her chosen field. Two characteristics of this fictitious individual—her degree of success orientation and her preference for masculine or feminine sex roles—were varied. She appeared either to be strongly oriented toward success or not oriented in this direction, and seemed to prefer either traditional feminine roles or competitive, masculine ones. Both male and female students rated the competent woman as less attractive as a work partner when she combined high success orientation with a preference for masculine roles. They seemed to be highly threatened by such an aggressive, achievement-oriented female and devalued her strongly when she showed such a pattern. Either characteristic by itself also produced devaluation, but not as strongly.

Although men report more favorable attitudes toward women in recent years, their behavior toward them does not appear to have changed. Men like a competent woman only from a distance. These discriminatory behaviors toward competent women appear during both brief confrontations and longstanding relationships. When college students were asked whether they would be willing to serve as student contacts for high school students applying for admission to the university, they volunteered to spend more time helping a female applicant if she wanted to become a librarian than if she wanted to become an engineer (Appleton & Gurwitz, 1976). In contrast, they volunteered to spend more time helping a male applicant when he wanted to become an engineer than when he wanted to become a librarian. The results were the same whether the volunteer activity involved time spent in interviews, telephone conversations, or letter writing. The amount of personal contact involved did not affect the preference for assisting those whose career aspirations were "appropriate" for members of their sex.

The Social Context of Competition

Girls who had traditional attitudes about women's roles and feared success performed less well when competing against their boyfriends than they did when joining them to compete against others (Pleck, 1976). These women may have been taking their cue from the men with whom they were emotionally involved, since Pleck also found that the men who gave threatened or hostile responses to stories of achievement by women also increased their performance when competing against their girlfriends as contrasted to competing with them against others. Losing in a competition with a female may be particularly destructive to the masculine image of some males. Following competition with a member of the opposite sex, males who failed estimated that their partners would view them as less masculine than males who succeeded would (Murphy-Berman, 1976). Initial statements about success may increase boys' persistence on subsequent tasks but decrease that of girls (Dweck & Gilliard, 1975). These data can be explained by the presumption that successful performance is inconsistent with the traditional feminine role. Since success does not occur unobtrusively, it may increase the anxiety level of females. Failure, of course, is more anxiety provoking for males.

Sex-related achievement differences can reflect the social context of the achievement situation. Male–female interpersonal transactions enhance the feminine sex role. Thus males competing against males and females against females take more credit for success than they give the successful opponent and blame themselves less for failure than they blame their opponent (Stephan, Rosenfield, & Stephan, 1976). Females competing against males do not make such attributions. The male opponent is given more credit for success and less for failure than the female opponent.

Individuals appear to prefer to compete against same-sex reference groups. When they are given a choice of which sex to compete against, virtually all of them first choose a same-sex reference group (Zanna, Goethals, & Hill, 1975). When they are given information that an opposite-sex group excelled in the task, both sexes switched to the standard setter for the second comparison. Although no sex differences were found in this study, we are reminded that in the real world women are much more frequently involved in activities in which males set standards than the other way around. Thus women are more often required to compare themselves with members of the opposite sex than men are. It has also been found that positive information regarding the performance of same-sex others can result in higher performance goals in some settings (Stake, 1976a). Females are at a double disadvantage because they have limited access to female achievers and must compare themselves to the opposite sex—the male model—in order to determine the extent of their achievements. Females are probably uncertain about the applicability of male standards of achievement to them, and this uncertainty could account for the limitation of goals by many females. In at least one study feedback about a high probability of success eliminated traditional sex differences in level of aspiration (Stake, 1976b).

The Dynamics of Sex-Appropriate and -Inappropriate Tasks

We have known for a long time that some tasks are considered to be appropriate for males and others for females. Researchers are now beginning to explore how the sex appropriateness of a task affects performance in it. Sex-inappropriate tasks appear to offer lower rewards. Both sexes tend to describe themselves as less wise when they succeed at a sex-inappropriate task or fail at a sex-appropriate one (Libow & Mogy, 1976). Women, more than men, attribute their success less to ability and see themselves as doing less well when they succeed at a sex-inappropriate task. Subtle, self-deprecatory effects may be operative here. Women report not only less pride after a successful performance but also slightly more shame (Fontaine, 1976). These data indicate not that women care less about their achievements but that they are ambivalent about their implications. These findings become particularly important when we take into account the fact that achievement in general is defined as a male domain.

THE DEVELOPMENT OF GENDER-SPECIFIC ATTITUDES TOWARD ACHIEVEMENT

One of the most noteworthy aspects of gender-specific attitudes toward aspiration and achievement is the early age at which they appear. Differences in vocational aspirations have been reported in children as young as 3 and 4 years old. The most common vocational aspirations of these little girls are "nurse," "teacher," or "mommy." Boys state many more vocational options. Preschool children also differentiate among tasks and objects by means of stereotypic male/female distinctions (Verner & Wesse, 1965).

Sex-Related Differential Aspirations

Suggestive evidence that girls perceive their options to be more limited than those of boys by the first few years of elementary school has been provided by a study by William Looft (1971). He questioned first- and second-graders in a Catholic parochial school in two steps: (1) "What would you like to be when you grow up?" and (2) "Now what do you think you *really* will do when you grow-up?" These questions represented an attempt to separate wanting from expectation. In response to question 1 the 33 boys nominated 18 different occupations. The most frequent were football player (9) and policeman (4). Other choices included doctor, dentist, scientist, pilot, and astronaut. The 33 girls nominated only 8 different occupations. In fact 25 girls named either nurse (14) or teacher (11) as their first choice. Other choices included mother, stewardess, and sales clerk. Only one girl wanted to be a doctor.

In response to the second question 23 boys shifted their initial response to another vocation that is perceived as desirable, but only 14 girls did so. These findings suggest that from an early age girls perceive themselves to have fewer career options than boys and also perceive a lower possibility of change in these opportunities. This very early limitation of vocational aspirations is probably most poignantly captured in the response of the single girl who initially expressed a desire to be a doctor. When questioned further she commented "I'll probably have to be something else—maybe a store lady" (Looft, p. 366).

It has sometimes been suggested that girls simply express more realistic goals than comparable boys. There is no evidence that such a pattern is found cross-culturally. In an appraisal of the realism of self-evaluation and school achievement in eight countries, no consistent overall tendency for one sex to be more realistic than the other has been found (Peck, 1972). In the United States, nevertheless, clear sex differences in patterns of behavior involving achievement develop early. For example, by the fourth and fifth grades boys consistently choose more difficult tasks than girls when given an opportunity to choose between tasks of varying difficulty (Veroff & Peele, 1969). An inverse relationship between the occupations to which they aspire and the status of these occupations has been found for girls, but not for boys (Barnett, 1975). This negative correlation increases as the girls near adolescence.

Parental Attitudes and Achievement

The relationship between the aspirations of children and their parents was discussed in Chapter 7. The same-sex parent seems to be particularly important in determining occupational aspirations. Fathers have been found to be more traditional than mothers in the expectations they hold for their sons; mothers are more traditional than fathers in the expectations they hold for their daughters; and the parents of sons are more traditional in their vocational preferences than the parents of daughters (Thornburg & Weeks, 1975). In this study the 5-year-olds had not yet accepted the values of their parents.

The effect of parental values may extend beyond what may narrowly be defined as an achievement area. For example, even in the fourth grade boys score higher than girls on tests of political information (Greenstein, 1961). They are better able to think of a news story, to prefer national to local news, and to name a public figure as a person whom they would like to emulate. All the children were more likely to name their father rather than their mother as an appropriate source of voting advice. Awareness of politics appears to develop as an area of male specialization during childhood. Aside from the obvious implications of this development, it provides another example of the narrower options for interests and careers for females as defined by the socialization process.

Mother's Employment and Female Achievement

That parental values and attitudes strongly affect the probability of female achievement is amply illustrated by data on the effect of the mother's employment on the career aspirations and achievements of her daughters. For example, women who showed a tendency to devalue female competence were more likely to have had a mother who did not work outside the home (Baruch, 1972). This pattern existed even among upper-middle-class females enrolled at Swarthmore, a college noted for its rigorous intellectual standards. College women who perceive themselves as competent, on the other hand, had mothers whose own self-perceptions were high and who placed significantly more value on traits related to independence, assertiveness, and achievement (Baruch, 1976). In this group there were no effects of maternal employment. Girls who were rated as having a high perception of their own competence in the fifth and tenth grades had higher career aspirations and desired fewer children.

The mother's employment status may play a role later on. The daughters of employed mothers were more likely to graduate in an honors curriculum than those whose mothers did not work outside the home (Marecek, 1976). They were also more likely to have chosen a career by the time they graduated and more likely to have made plans for graduate school. They expected to postpone marriage and childbearing longer and in fact were more likely to have already entered graduate school than women who had graduated with them but whose mothers were not employed. We have little information on what dynamics influenced these differences between graduates of the same elite institution. It is noteworthy, however, that while all these women reported that their mothers wished them to complete college and become employed, employed mothers were more likely to hope that their daughters would have professional careers rather than full-time jobs.

The sex role ideology of the woman herself also influenced

career aspirations and planning. Women with conservative sex role ideology were less likely to attend graduate school and more likely to be married than more liberal women. However, the family backgrounds of these conservative women also differed. The aspirations and expectations of both parents for their daughter were lower; they were more disapproving of employment for women with children; and their mothers had less power within the family than the mothers of less traditional women. It is difficult to determine which factors, or how many, had influenced their career aspirations. It is noteworthy, however, that the parents of adolescent females have been reported to be more influential in their later attainments than the parents of adolescent males (Featherman & Hauser, 1976). Maternal education in particular has a greater effect on the school achievement of young women than it does on that of young men (Alexander & Eckland, 1974). The friends of adolescent males, on the other hand, are more influential than the friends of adolescent females.

THE SUCCESSFUL WOMAN: WHO IS SHE?

Measures of women's drives and needs do not appear to predict their level of performance and achievement. There also seems to be little relationship between a woman's achievements and her intellectual ability. The question remains, Who is the successful woman? Success is defined here in terms of material achievement, financial rewards, and social recognition. We must remember that we are thereby using a "male model" of success. We will leave for the moment the issue of whether male models of behavior are ultimately the best patterns for human beings. However, it is indicative of our society that no other model of successful performance has yet been provided.

Research on the successful woman seems to be divided into two major methodologies. One type selects a large number of women, usually in college; distinguishes them in terms of some criteria such as academic performance, role innovation, or vocational aspiration; and attempts to determine the antecedents and correlates of their behaviors in comparison to women who follow a more "feminine" course. The other technique concentrates on a smaller group of women who have already been classified as successful in terms of our society's definition of success and attempts to distinguish their personality characteristics and social development from those of less successful women. In these studies the comparison group may be "comparable" men or less successful women in the same profession rather than women who are not employed outside the home at all. Since each technique asks somewhat different questions and produces somewhat different information, we will discuss results of the two kinds of studies separately.

Correlates of Nontraditional Career Aspirations

Probably the most intensive study of the characteristics of women who aspire to succes in fields that are not traditionally associated with feminine aspirations was conducted by Sandra Tangri (1972). She examined 200 women students at the University of Michigan with a wide variety of psychological measures. She also intensively investigated their past and present familial relationships and the kind or quality of their relationships with family and friends. She found that, contrary to previous indications, women who aspired to male-dominated professions did not show any evidence of having identified more with their fathers than with their mothers. In fact more educated mothers, particularly those who were themselves in male-dominated professions, seem to have been taken as role models by their daughters. There was also no evidence that these women made innovative career plans because of difficulty attracting members of the opposite sex. They had as many romantic and casual relationships with men as more traditional women did. Their commitment to careers was greater than that of women planning to enter more feminine professions, even during the college years. Their decision to continue, therefore, cannot be considered as having been made by default when other alternatives failed.

Tangri also found that women who were role innovators were more autonomous, individualistic, and internally motivated than traditional women. They also expressed more doubts about their ability to succeed and about their identity. She interprets these doubts as indicating realistic apprehension about the actual difficulty of their chosen field and about the social context in which women must achieve. Although these women found some support for their aspirations from faculty in their major field and from female college friends, support from a tolerant or supportive boyfriend appears to be more important in this stage of life. Their aspirations may also have been facilitated by social relationships with older males—teaching assistants or graduate students—in the same field.

Women who choose a high-status, nontraditional career have, possibly, lower affiliative needs than women who are interested in more traditional pursuits (Trigg & Perlman, 1976). As in Tangri's study, they are more likely to have a boyfriend who is supportive and tolerant of their nontraditional aspirations. Rather than assume, however, that a key male determines their relatively unusual career decisions, it is possible to believe that their association with a male who is positive toward women's achievements is a result of their career aspirations. Suggestively, as compared to more traditional women, women who aspire to careers in male-dominated fields (1) consider being married and having children to be less important, (2) consider nontraditional careers to be compatible with the satisfaction of social and marital needs, and (3) consider the attitudes of significant others to be favorable toward nontraditional careers. Thus they may select males who agree with their aspirations. Males who do not agree cannot maintain relationships with such women.

Plans for marriage seem to be a highly negative predictor of significant female achievement. While women's career patterns could not be predicted from data available at the time they entered college, they were predictable from data collected five years later. The most significant data were related to the marital situation. Women who had a high-to-moderate or unusual amount of vocational experience either had not yet married or, if they were married (about half of the members of these groups), had the fewest children (Wolfson, 1976). Since their youngest child was younger than those of women had worked little or not at all, it is likely that they married later than women who had little vocational experience. Those who had little or no vocational experience following college professed themselves to be happiest in their marriage. It is noteworthy that their husbands earned considerably larger salaries than the husbands of women with more extensive vocational experience.

Marital plans are a much more major determinant of the educational aspirations of high school girls than of those of high school boys (Bayer, 1969). It has been estimated that the direct effects of marriage intentions account for 21 percent of the variation in the educational plans of girls versus only 8 percent of the variation in those of boys. In their senior year virtually all high school girls expect to be homemakers at some time in their lives (Turner, 1964). Only 48 percent of the girls expected a lifetime career as well. During adolescence, girls appear to suffer a decline in intellectual ability (as measured by IQ points) while boys experience a mean gain (Campbell & McKain, 1974). A survey of women who decline versus those who may be classified as "nondecliners" found that decliners rated themselves as significantly less active than nondecliners and also had less need to control others than young women who did not decline. There was also a greater tendency for women who did not decline to have less need to be included by others and to rate a job as being for both men and women. Decline in intellectual abilities of adolescent women may be sociological in nature.

Young women who declined saw themselves as closer to the passive, nonassertive ideal than young women who did not decline. "Since part of that ideal is not to be smarter than the men, it would appear that young women who decline are again fitting themselves to the feminine ideal by ignoring or not using their abilities" (Campbell & McKain, 1974, p. 6). The result of acceptance of the traditional feminine personality ideal appears even in a relatively objective, nonspecific measure such as IQ.

One innovative attempt to determine the characteristics of outstanding women involved an intensive analysis of twelve women who had been unusually successful in science (Kundsin, 1973). These women had been named by colleagues of both sexes as very competent scientists who had made significant contributions to their chosen fields. Those who arranged for them to be studied were particularly interested in women who were married and had children as well as participating in a meaningful career. Each of these unusual women wrote extensive life histories, which were analyzed and evaluated by experts from a variety of fields. Although they were by no means typical of most women (or of most men), the sources of their strengths and motivation as well as the personal problems they encountered tell us much about the nature of the successful woman.

Of particular interest to us here are the results of an analysis of psychological determinants in these twelve outstanding women done by Jane Anderson (1973), a psychiatrist at Harvard Medical School. Anderson found that the most important psychological determinant that enabled these women to perform so successfully was their capacity to cope emotionally with being reacted to as a deviant. One, a physicist, relates the following experience: "During my first year of graduate school, what seemed to me like an infinite number of professors, teaching assistants and colleagues, none of whom were women, told me that women can't think analytically and therefore I must be husband hunting" (p. 185). Another, a chemist, says, "I did experience a great deal of guilt leaving my children to go to work, most of it, I now realize, brought on by comments of nonworking mothers, such as those at nursery school: 'Don't you think you're ruining your children's lives?' " (p. 186). A third, an architect, remarks, "When I chose my way, I never thought that my sex made me different. It was not until I came to the United States that I realized that from a mundane architect, I was transformed into a pioneer" (p. 186).

These women were able to function autonomously to an unusual degree despite lack of sympathy from those around them. There is considerable evidence that their early family environment was highly supportive and facilitory. Both male and female role models for achievement appear to have been readily accessible. Nine of their fathers and seven of their mothers were rated as being supportive of their high aspirations, and only one parent was rated as being negative toward them. These women may also have been assisted by their birth position within the family. Half were first children, and more than half had only one sibling. Interestingly, they have on the average more children than the families into which they were born. They evaluate their marriages as satisfying— although for several it is their second marriage that is the happy one. Thus they appear to be functioning effectively in all areas of their lives. Anderson suggests that it was the early facilitory familial environment that enabled these women to successfully combine a complex set of professional and family responsibilities.

The pressures on American women not to achieve are longer lasting than was once believed. Although we are sensitive to the effects of early socialization, we have paid little attention to later dangers to the female self-image (Epstein, 1973). Women lawyers, for example, are just as likely to drop out at the peak of their careers as at the start. Women are constantly being urged to ask, "Am I doing the right thing?" Occupational success never comes out as the right answer to this question. Women are asked to demonstrate competence in a variety of roles in order to be deemed successes.

> Occupational excellence is not sufficient for them to be considered really successful. In exchange for this multirole achievement, women are permitted to perform somewhat less than men in their occupational roles and still be considered a success ("for a woman"). Men, on the other hand, must succeed or fail primarily on the basis of occupational achievement. They get few extra credits for being good husbands and fathers. [Epstein, 1973, p. 65]

Creativity and Social Influences

Highly creative women are another excellent source of information on the factors that hinder or facilitate women in the quest for achievement. This area has been relatively neglected—partially because, according to many male scholars, women are not creative. This conclusion was reached mainly by dealing with creativity in science (in which few women have excelled for a variety of sociocultural reasons); by ignoring the results of creativity tests of grade school children, which showed no difference between males and females; and by defining areas in which women create (e.g., in the domestic sphere) as not being creative at all (Helson, 1978). Although there have been almost no great artists from the aristocracy, we do not conclude from this that men of the aristocracy lack creative ability. Instead we infer that their duties and way of life preclude dedication to the career of an artist (Nochlin cited by Helson, 1978). That has certainly been true of most women.

Most researchers who deal with the creative process, however, have argued that the scarcity of creative women has its source in women's psychology (e.g., certain traits possessed by the creative person conflict with those generally attributed to women). The assumptions behind Helson's work, on the other hand, are that there are creative women, that they probably resemble creative men in essential respects but might differ in others, and that cultural factors certainly work to their disadvantage. Although in her earlier studies (Helson, 1966, 1967) she found that creative women were not rare—accounting for about 15 to 20 percent of a college class—her more recent work on unusually creative women mathematicians and writers of children's fantasy is perhaps more exciting. She concentrated on these two fields, distinct as they appear to be, because there are still claims that women are deficient in symbolic originality, in manipulating and organizing symbol patterns so that new structures emerge. In both mathematics and literary fantasy a creative contribution is a work of symbolic originality.

Helson and her staff mingled with a group of women mathematicians who varied between average and high degrees of creativity for a week (Helson, 1978). They found that a number of characteristics were positively associated with high creativity in this group of women. They tended to think in unusual ways, tended to be rebellious and nonconforming, genuinely valued intellectual and cognitive matters, and were self-dramatizing, with fluctuating moods. One could contrast this picture of the creative women with the traditional stereotypic portrait of femininity. Creative women appear to be less involved in social roles and interpersonal relationships than comparable less creative women in their own field, and more invested in their own inner life and autonomy.

The characteristics of highly creative women do not appear to be compatible with the feminine role as usually assumed. It is not surprising, therefore, that very creative men were found to be more buoyant and self-assured than comparable women. These men were also much more likely to be respected men at the top of their field than women with an equivalent level of ability and performance. Such recognition no doubt adds to their feelings of self-worth and -esteem.

The most striking difference between unusually creative women and their female peers in the same fields is the unusual commitment of the former to their creative goals. The highly creative women restricted their lives to a few things about which they cared a great deal. The comparison women spent more time on teaching, administration, and community or political activities. They expressed interest in a wide variety of leisure activities. The result of the highly creative women's sacrifices was not "domination of the field." There was more congruence between their work and the demands and rewards of the environment for the men than there was for either highly or less highly creative women. Helson stresses that we need to distinguish between creative style and output. Why should one publish a great deal when there is little or no reward for doing so?

Although most of us are not unusually talented, work on women who achieve a great deal points out many of the contradictions between achievement as it is usually defined and gender as it is usually defined. Highly achieving women must be concerned about their own needs to a degree that is not acceptable according to the usual definition of the female sex role. They may be "able to get away with it" if they prove to be highly competent, but judgments of them will be very harsh on the way up. Such women must either possess or develop traits that allow them to resist societal judgments about their mental health, happiness, and social skills. There does not appear to be a point in the life span at which such social judgments cannot be internalized and longstanding careers abandoned.

High achievement may not be compatible with the development of other humane characteristics for either men or women. Highly achieving people are not necessarily likable or unselfish. In fact if they were thoroughly satisfied with "things the way they are" they probably would not be trying to change them. On the other hand, achievement at any level produces satisfaction. The contradiction between femaleness and achievement places women in yet another multiple bind. They are socialized to deny the possibilities of achievement; their achievements are not defined as such and are not recognized; and yet, achievement is one of the few ways by which one can acquire status in this society. Any achievement by a woman may occur at the cost of divergence from the "ideal" female sex role. Thus it is not surprising that women feel conflict about achievement or that it remains a major source of role strain. However, it would be fallacious to assume that the strains will go away as the woman becomes more competent or takes on more of the male model of achievement behavior. Role reversal in this area will place women in a dilemma that many men are now beginning to recognize: living to work as opposed to working to live. This issue must be considered in any appraisal of sex and achievement.

Chapter 14
Sex and Mental Health

In the past few decades women appear to have surpassed men as the sex with the larger number of emotional and mental-health problems. The kinds of disorders, as well as their incidence, appear to vary by sex. In this chapter we will discuss how sex-related issues affect the expression of mental illness. Effects include both the form "atypical" behaviors take and how they are evaluated socially. We will also discuss another form of the "double bind" for women. As we will see, while women may be readily labeled as "ill" for engaging in "male-appropriate" behaviors, they may also become "ill" simply by no longer fitting the ideal female "model"—young, attractive, sexually responsive, and so forth. Thus aging and/or the menopause may be more serious social crises for women than for men. Psychology defines mental health for women and men in sex-specific ways. Treatments for departure from mental health are also different. Many feminist critiques of theory and practice in clinical psychology exist. We will examine the ways in which feminist critiques have affected research and treatment in this area.

SEX AND MENTAL ILLNESS

There is considerable evidence that females exceed males in incidence of various forms of mental illness. In one review of previous studies that used different methods of estimating the percentage of mentally ill men and women in different areas of the country over a period of about 15 years, all 17 community health surveys conducted since World War II found more women than men to be mentally ill (Gove & Tudor, 1973). Mental illness was defined in a general sense (e.g., as a disorder that involves personal discomfort and/or mental disorganization that is not caused by an organic or toxic condition.) Various methods of estimation produced similar sex differentials in incidence. Women outnumber men in rate of first admission to a psychiatric hospital by 1.4 : 1. More women than men receive psychiatric care in general hospitals in the United States for both functional psychoses (1.44 : 1) and neuroses (1.89 : 1). More women than men are involved in psychiatric outcare, and a larger percentage have contacts with psychiatrists in private practice. Women are also more likely to be treated for emotional and psychosomatic disorders by private practitioners than men are.

The higher probability that women will be treated for mental illness seems to be a recent phenomenon in the United States, postdating World War II. Before then, more men than women with psychiatric disorders were admitted to mental hospitals. Moreover, more recent surveys of relative incidence are likely to show a higher rate for women than for men, whereas the converse is true of earlier studies. The sex difference in incidence seems to be relatively independent of both race and age. Among both blacks and whites and younger and older individuals, females exceed males in psychiatric symptomology (Chesler, 1971). (See Table 14.1 for a breakdown of symptoms by age and sex.)

Table 14.1 (a) SYMPTOM RATES BY SEX

SYMPTOM	MALE	FEMALE
Nervous breakdown	3.2	6.0
Felt impending nervous breakdown	7.7	17.8
Nervousness	47.2	73.2
Inertia	16.9	33.1
Insomnia	24.1	40.9
Trembling hands	6.9	10.6
Nightmares	6.9	12.3
Perspiring hands	17.0	22.2
Fainting	17.5	30.4
Headaches	13.8	27.5
Dizziness	6.9	10.3
Heart palpitations	3.6	5.7

SOURCE: From a National Institutes of Mental Health study.

Table 14.1 (b) PERCENTAGE INCIDENCE OF DIAGNOSTIC CLASSIFICATION IN PSYCHIATRIC FACILITIES, BY SEX: 1966–1968

DIAGNOSTIC CLASSIFICATION	GENERAL HOSPITALS			OUTPATIENT CLINICS			PRIVATE HOSPITALS			STATE AND COUNTY HOSPITALS		
	TOTAL NO. OF PATIENTS	WOMEN	MEN	TOTAL NO. OF PATIENTS	WOMEN	MEN	TOTAL NO. OF PATIENTS	WOMEN	MEN	TOTAL NO. OF PATIENTS	WOMEN	MEN
THE "FEMALE DISEASES"												
Psychotic depressive	30,743	69%	31%	5,453	73%	27%	7,140	73%	27%	6,058	68%	32%
Manic depressive	28,232	64%	36%	8,411	67%	33%	7,579	66%	34%	36,694	69%	31%
Psychoneurotic	378,289	70%	30%	156,525	68%	32%	61,241	66%	34%	20,159	64%	36%
Psychophysiological	27,562	67%	33%	5,317	59%	41%	858	64%	36%	547	63%	37%
Psychotic	262,961	64%	36%	143,092	62%	38%	57,882	66%	34%	636,195	54%	46%
Schizophrenic	158,689	61%	39%	116,088	60%	40%	32,548	63%	37%	546,237	51%	49%
Paranoid	59,718	57%	43%	38,030	57%	43%	10,418	67%	33%	191,309	53%	47%
Drug intoxication (poison)	20,229	60%	40%	831	56%	44%	1,103	58%	42%	1,508	48%	52%
THE "MALE DISEASES"												
Alcohol addiction	69,183	25%	75%	20,564	22%	78%	9,487	29%	71%	18,168	18%	82%
Alcohol intoxication	52,087	27%	73%	3,907	30%	70%	6,054	27%	73%	37,943	25%	75%
Drug addiction	11,004	36%	64%	3,622	24%	76%	1,643	45%	55%	3,081	23%	77%
Personality disorders	143,142	40%	60%	169,239	44%	56%	21,717	41%	59%	44,064	23%	77%

SOURCE: From P. Chesler, *Women and Madness* (Garden City, N.Y.: Doubleday, 1972).

Although females exceed males in number of symptoms, there is evidence that the kinds of symptoms exhibited differ by sex. It has been suggested that while male symptomology appears to reflect destructive hostility and/or pathological self-indulgence, female symptomology tends to be harsh, self-critical, self-depriving, and often self-destructive (Phillips, 1964). Female patients are more often found to be depressed, perplexed, suffering from suicidal thoughts, or making actual suicide attempts (Chesler, 1971). Male patients are more assaultive than females and more likely to act out impulses such as robbery, rape, and homosexuality (Zigler & Phillips, 1960). Women report higher rates of nervousness, insomnia, trembling hands, nightmares, fainting, and headaches. They report more disturbance in general adjustment, self-perception, and ability to function in marital and parental roles than men. These sex differences are most marked at younger age levels.

The most impressive sex differences in clinical symptomology is associated with the diagnosis of depression. The ratio of women diagnosed as having overt clinical depression to men suffering from these symptoms may be as high as 2 or 3 to 1 (Seiden, 1976b). Superficially, depression appears to be an exaggeration of normal sadness. Depressed individuals describe their emotional state in highly negative terms, may have a sad facial expression, and may experience loss of appetite, insomnia, and fatigue. Other symptoms include stooped posture, slow speech, indecisiveness, hopelessness, feelings of inadequacy, guilt, loss of interest and motivation, and a tendency to become fatigued easily.

Women are more likely than men to report symptoms of depression even when their symptoms do not reach clinical levels. It is unlikely that this sex difference is wholly biological in origin, since it is found only among married individuals. In a large-scale survey of a representative "normal" population, Radloff (1975) found that married women consistently reported more depression than married men of comparable age, education, income, and number of children. Among unmarried individuals, women may actually report less depression than men. Combining work and marriage does not appear to be harmful to women—although it has not yet been shown to be particularly beneficial in terms of depressive symptomology. Housewives and women who work outside the home do not show consistently different depression scores. Among clinically depressed women, however, some symptoms are less severe in those who work outside the home than in those whose work is primarily within it (Weissman & Paykel, 1974).

Environmental factors related to marital and parental roles appear to be more important in determining the degree of nonclinical depression than biologically based sex differences. Divorced or separated females are more depressed than divorced or separated males (Radloff, 1974). For both sexes, those with children were more depressed than those who were not. The younger the children, the higher the depression score. Although we discussed the advent of a child as a crisis situation in Chapter 12, it should be emphasized that some negative effects of children on affect or general mood appear to persist long after the neonatal period. It is not surprising that these effects will be most persistent and dominant in the sex that bears the primary responsibility for the care of the children. It is particularly noteworthy in this regard—despite popular myths— that never-married women who were the heads of households (i.e., living alone rather than as dependent daughters or sisters) and had incomes of $12,000 per year or more reported the lowest depression scores of any marital category, including married men.

EXPLANATIONS OF SEX-SPECIFIC EMOTIONAL PROBLEMS

Only recently have analyses of emotional problems that stress environmental and social determinants had any impact on the psychiatric and psychological world. Data showing the relationship among sex roles, marital status, and mental illness in post-World War II industrial societies have tended to cast doubt on biological explanations. In general, married women have higher rates of mental disorder than married men. In contrast, single, divorced, or widowed women tend to have somewhat lower rates (except, possibly, for depression) than their male counterparts (Gove, 1972). Explanations based on supposedly different personality characteristics for men and women have also become more questionable. Later in this chapter we will discuss institutionalized biases in the evaluation and diagnosis of female versus male "symptomology." Here it will suffice to make the general point that personality or intrapsychic explanations of emotional disorders tend to be based on retrospective reports and that there is little evidence to support the concept of, for example, a "depressive personality." Studies successfully predicting the onset of an emotional disorder of any type have been notably lacking in the professional literature.

Recent explanations have concentrated on such determinants as exaggeration of the "normal" sex role (Chesler, 1972), role conflicts (Powell & Reznikoff, 1976), controllable versus uncontrollable life change (Dohrenwend, 1973a), and learned helplessness (Radloff, 1975, 1976). Actually, all of these explanations may relate to the lower status of females in our society and the perceived and real lack of power that may accompany low status (Unger, 1978). Since each of these analyses stresses different aspects of female power-lessness and provides different supporting evidence, each will be discussed separately in some depth.

Exaggeration of the Female Role

The most extensive discussion of sex differences in the origin of emotional disorders is Phyllis Chesler's critique of the relationship between women and the mental-health establishment, entitled *Women and Madness* (1972). Symptoms of emotional illness may involve either extreme acceptance or rejection of "normal" sex roles:

> What we consider "madness," whether it appears in women or in men, is either the acting out of the devalued female role or the total or partial rejection of one's sex role stereotype. Women who fully act out the conditioned female role are clinically viewed as "neurotic" or "psy-chotic." When and if they are hospitalized it is for predominantly fe-male behaviors such as "depression," "suicide attempts," "anxiety neuroses," "paranoia," or "promiscuity." [p. 56]

Women who violate sex role stereotypes are more likely to be classified as schizophrenic, as are men who behave in a stereotypi-cally feminine manner—passive, dependent, sexually and physi-cally fearful and inactive. (Men who act out the masculine role—aggressive, dominant, physically and sexually powerful—are less likely to be hospitalized for psychiatric illness, especially if they are married. Men who act out the male role—but are too young, poor, or black—are usually incarcerated as "criminals" or "sociopaths." Chesler suggests that they are punished for stealing what more powerful men in our society can "buy.") A double bind exists for women—they cannot be perceived as a healthy woman and a healthy adult at the same time. Behaviors that are reinforced as feminine are considered to have lower social desirability and there-fore are less compatible with a good self-image than masculine be-haviors. Women who engage in more socially desirable masculine behaviors, however, deviate from sex-appropriate roles and may well be censured or punished. Chesler suggests that it is this double bind that accounts for the higher incidence of female emotional disorders or, more strongly, that this patriarchal definition of "femi-ninity" quite literally "drives women mad."

Role Conflict

As one might imagine, empirical investigations of Chesler's hy-potheses are difficult to conceive. In more operational terms, it has been argued that it is the incompatibility between the roles that women are called upon to play (in contrast to the essential similarity of most male roles) that is the source of their greater susceptibility to emotional problems. In one attempt to investigate the relationship between role conflict and symptoms of mental illness, over 250 graduates of Wellesley College (an elite women's institution) were studied (Powell & Reznikoff, 1976). The researchers found that neither employment status nor need for achievement related to symptom scores in these women. However, women with a contemporary sex role orientation (as opposed to a more traditional role orientation) had higher symptom scores, as did members of the class 10 years out of college in contrast to those who had graduated 25 years before.

While this study provides support for the recency of the high incidence of emotional disorders among women, it tells us little about its cause. Contemporary sex role orientation, which stresses autonomy and self-fulfillment, might be to blame. The women in this study who showed the greatest behavioral commitment to an autonomous role—women with doctoral degrees—had more symptoms than any other women who were employed full time outside the home. When their income was considered, however, the results were reversed. Women earning over $20,000 per year had the fewest symptoms. Thus the contrast between commitment to a nonfamilial role and the material results of such commitment might be the "culprit" responsible for high symptomology, rather than contemporary sex role orientation itself.

The percentage of women with four or more symptoms of emotional distress was particularly high among full-time employed women with preschool and school-age children. This research, combined with similar relationships found with depression scores, suggests that role strain rather than role conflict may be producing emotional distress. Obviously, even with child care arrangements women with small children who are engaged in full-time employment have limited time in which to engage in all their necessary tasks and roles. Nevertheless college women consider such a combination more desirable than any other combination of familial and employment roles (Alpert, Richardson, Perlmutter, & Shutzer, 1976).

We are also not sure about the relative contribution of role strain to symptomology as compared with other sources of emotional distress among women. Social isolation seems to be especially productive of feelings of low self-worth. For example, it has been reported that among full-time homemakers the amount of time spent watching TV is positively correlated to feelings of worthlessness and the number of hours reportedly spent with young children is associated with feelings of loneliness (Shaver & Freedman, 1976). Even housewives who report themselves as happy as wives working outside the home also report more anxiety and worry (46% vs. 28), more loneliness (44% vs. 26%), more feelings of worthlessness (41% vs. 24%), as well as more love for their husbands than they are loved in return.

Control over Stressful Life Events

Recently attempts have been made to link symptoms of emotional distress with environmental events (Dohrenwend, 1973b; Dohrenwend, Krasnoff, Askenasy, & Dohrenwend, in press). Life changes in themselves rather than the desirability or undesirability of the changes appears to be an important determinant of clinical symptomology. Barbara Dohrenwend and her associates have surveyed large populations using checklists involving both positive and negative changes in one's life. They find that the number of life changes reported is related to the symptom level reported and that this relationship holds independent of the sex, social class, age, or ethnicity of the individuals studied.

Table 14.2 provides an illustrative list of events that involve life change (Dohrenwend et al., in press). These are events for which a probability sample of judges (who varied in social class, ethnicity, and sex) generally agreed about the magnitude of the life change involved. The magnitude of each event was judged against a standard of 500 assigned to marriage. Some of these events were ranked differently by males and females. In particular, females were more likely to judge events involving marriage and childbirth as being of greater magnitude than male judges felt them to be.

In addition to variations in perception of the extent of change that a particular event will cause in one's life, variations in the number of stressful life events to which people are exposed have also been found. Dohrenwend (1973a) finds that people of low social status are disproportionately exposed to stressful life events. Those in low socioeconomic strata are exposed to more life changes than those in higher socioeconomic strata. Women are exposed to more life changes than men. The contrast between the sexes is particularly marked when all events versus events over which the person has no control are compared. Since women have a larger life change score than men even when events that are not under their own control are taken into account, one cannot argue that women are simply more likely to put themselves into crisis situations than men. Also, women are not less able to predict future life events than men (Dohrenwend, 1973a).

Table 14.2 MEAN JUDGMENTS OF THE MAGNITUDE OF VARIOUS LIFE EVENTS AS RATED BY A PROBABILITY SAMPLE OF JUDGES WHO VARIED IN SOCIAL CLASS, ETHNICITY, AND SEX[a]

EVENT	DESIRABILITY	MEAN MAGNITUDE OF LIFE CHANGE	RANK OF DEGREE OF CHANGE
SCHOOL			
1. Started school or a training program after not going to school for a long time	+	340	59.5
2. Changed schools or training programs	?	257	88
3. Graduated from school or training program	+	323	68
4. Had problems in school or training program	—	268	86
6. Did not graduate from school or training program	—	300	71.5
WORK			
7. Started work for the first time	+	386	44
8. Returned to work after not working for a long time	?	348	54
9. Changed jobs for a better one	+	472	46
10. Changed jobs for a worse one	—	359	69.5
13. Demoted at work	—	379	53
14. *Not* promoted at work	—	345	78
15. Conditions at work got worse	—	316	57
16. Promoted	+	374	50
17. Had significant success at work	+	350	56
18. Conditions at work improved	+	318	63.5
19. Laid off	—	325	59.5
20. Fired	—	407	40

389

Table 14.2 *Continued*

EVENT	DESIRABILITY	MEAN MAGNITUDE OF LIFE CHANGE	RANK OF DEGREE OF CHANGE
21. Started a business or profession	+	471	33
22. Expanded business or professional practice	+	478	35
23. Took on a greatly increased work load	?	289	74
24. Suffered a business loss or failure	−	510	30
25. Sharply reduced work load	?	245	89.5
26. Retired	?	461	31
27. Stopped working (*not* retirement) for an extended period	?	456	48.5
LOVE AND MARRIAGE			
28. Became engaged	+	409	57
29. Engagement was broken	−	309* (males = 234) (females = 333)	81
30. Married	+ +	standard	22
31. Started a love affair	+	381	65.5
32. Relations with spouse changed for the worse, without separation or divorce	−	526	9.5
34. Divorce	−	633	5
35. Relations with spouse changed for the better	+ +	520	18
36. Married couple got together after separation	+ +	558	14
37. Marital infidelity	−	558* (males = 586) (females = 449)	17
38. Trouble with in-laws	−	310	80
39. Spouse died	−	821 (no consensual agreement)	2

EVENT	DESIRABILITY	MEAN MAGNITUDE OF LIFE CHANGE	RANK OF DEGREE OF CHANGE
HAVING CHILDREN			
40. Became pregnant	?	419	32
41. Birth of a first child	+	577	6
42. Birth of a second or later child	?	448	26
43. Abortion	−	370	42.5
44. Miscarriage or stillbirth	−	457* (males = 374) (females = 619)	19
46. Child died	−	1036	1
47. Adopted a child	+	458	27
FAMILY			
49. New person moved into the household	?	297	71.5
50. Person moved out of the household	?	333	79
51. Someone stayed on in the household after he or she was expected to leave	−	285	76
52. Serious family argument other than with spouse	−	262	92.5
54. Family member other than spouse or child died	−	463* (males = 415) (females = 551)	25
RESIDENCE			
56. Moved to a worse residence or neighborhood	−	463	39
57. Moved to a residence or neighborhood the same as the last one	?	241	89.5
58. Unable to move after expecting to be able to move	−	308	73
59. Built a home or had one built	+	548	29

Table 14.2 *Continued*

EVENT	DESIRABILITY	MEAN MAGNITUDE OF LIFE CHANGE	RANK OF DEGREE OF CHANGE
60. Remodeled a home	+	314	65.5
61. Lost a home through a disaster	−	580	12.5
CRIME AND LEGAL MATTERS			
62. Assaulted	−	383* (males = 276) (females = 472)	52
63. Robbed	−	314	63.5
65. Involved in a lawsuit	−	408	37
66. Accused of something for which a person could be sent to jail	−	489	15
68. Arrested	−	475	21
69. Went to jail	−	566	4
71. Convicted of a crime	−	539	8
72. Acquitted of a crime	+	468	24
73. Released from jail	+	497	11
FINANCES			
75. Took out a mortgage	?	320	77
76. Started buying a car or other large purchase on the installment plan	+	264	91
77. Foreclosure of a mortgage or loan	−	460	41
79. Took a cut in wage or salary without a demotion	−	396* (males = 334) (females = 443)	45
81. Went on welfare	?	422	34
82. Went off welfare	+	352	61
85. Had financial improvement not related to work	+	517	36

EVENT	DESIRABILITY	MEAN MAGNITUDE OF LIFE CHANGE	RANK OF DEGREE OF CHANGE
SOCIAL ACTIVITIES			
86. Increased religious, neighborhood, or other organizational activities	+	274	84
87. Took a vacation	+	273	82
91. Acquired a pet	+	163	102
92. Pet died	−	196* (males = 153) (females = 267)	100
93. Made new friends	+	247	94
95. Close friend died	−	457	23
MISCELLANEOUS			
96. Entered the armed services	?	406	55
97. Left the armed services	?	360* (males = 328) (females = 464)	42.5
HEALTH			
99. Physical health improved	+	562	28
100. Physical illness	−	668	3
101. Injury	−	560	12.5

SOURCE: From Dohrenwend et al. "Exemplification of a Method for Scaling Life Events: The PERI Life Events Scale." *Journal of Health and Social Behavior*, in press.

*All items listed either showed consensual agreement among judges or varied according to the status of the judges. Items marked with an asterisk showed significant sex differences. The magnitude of the estimated life change was judged against a standard of 500 assigned to marriage.

Women's higher symptom levels may be a reflection of their higher exposure to stressful life events. Instability is productive of a high level of individual distress. Women are particularly affected by events that they cannot control, suggesting that their psychological distress is associated with lack of power to control their own lives. Women are also more sensitive to changes in the life events of others (Dohrenwend, 1976), which may further increase the demands on their emotional resources as compared to those of men.

Learned Helplessness

Recently those who are interested in the etiology of mental illness in general and in the origin of differential rates of risk for women and men in particular have focused more intensively on issues related to power and control. They are interested in a process that Seligman (1974, 1975) has named *learned helplessness*. Seligman's original research was on dogs placed in situations in which no response could help them avoid an electric shock. When they were subsequently placed in situations in which a particular response could prevent a shock, they remained apathetic and failed to perform the necessary action. One could say that their experience in uncontrollable situations had led them to form a habit of being helpless in dealing with the world. Animals who had not been exposed to environments in which their behaviors had no effect readily learned to avoid an electric shock.

Both animals and human beings will show deficits in their performance following exposure to situations in which none of their behaviors produce the desired result (Maier & Seligman, 1976). The behavioral characteristics described following exposure to these kinds of "no win" situations resembles the state known as depression to an astonishing degree (Miller & Seligman, 1975, 1976). Individuals not only fail to perform adequately but restructure their appraisal of the situation in a manner that supports their expectation that they will be unable to succeed. A particularly noteworthy aspect of these findings is that randomly chosen males will respond in a similarly depressed fashion after being exposed to insoluble problems (Klein, Fencil-Morse, & Seligman, 1976). These data suggest that depression—a behavior considered more characteristic of females than of males—may be a response to situations that are structured so that no behavior produces a significant amount of reinforcement. We could also characterize such situations as "double binds." What must be stressed here is that these phenomena seem to be the usual result of particular social processes and will produce their effects on most individuals—regardless of sex—who are exposed to them. Females, of course, are more likely to be exposed to them than males.

It is not even necessary that the individual really have been subject to uncontrollable forces in order to become depressed. It is only necessary that the individual believe that "nothing you can do will matter" (Beck, 1974). Beck suggests that women may have a culturally induced tendency to see themselves as powerless (Beck & Greenberg, 1974). We have seen in previous chapters that females confer more power on males than they do on themselves. Many female children are taught that their personal worth and survival depend not on their effective response to life situations but on physical beauty and attractiveness to men—factors over which they have little direct control. Parental and institutional supervision both restrict their alternatives and shield them from the consequences of whatever disapproved alternatives they do choose to pursue. "Perhaps women, like dogs who have learned that their own behavior is unrelated to their subsequent welfare, lose their ability to respond effectively and to learn that responding produces relief" (Beck & Greenberg, 1974, pp. 120–121). Thus even in situations where their own behavior could ameliorate their circumstances, women may persist in interpreting individual events in terms of their own helplessness and lack of power rather than selecting from an uncensored set of interpretations. Such an interpretation of events will lead to passivity. The passivity and the depressed affect that accompanies it may then be interpreted as confirming the perceived helplessness. Such women are bound more by internalized cultural expectations than by specific obstacles to their happiness and success. Beck claims to have achieved a considerable degree of success with such patients by using behavioral methods that lead to reduction of their distortion of reality. Such methods include calling attention to stereotyped themes in thinking; exposure of misconceptions, prejudices, and even superstitions; and emphasis on the fact that a variety of areas of gratification exist.

Dorothy Tennov (1975), a noted critic of the psychodynamic approach to psychotherapy, stresses intervention techniques that teach the patient how to deal with the environment as well as how to restructure cognitions about it. She cites several case studies showing that the production of positive results by her own efforts, even in a relatively minor area of functioning, has produced major changes in a woman's perception of her situation. While it is too early to determine which method of therapy is most effective, it is noteworthy that all of these intervention techniques stress the learning of autonomy—the idea that situations can be changed by one's own behavior—rather than focusing on personality "inadequacies" that originate from either biological or early familial circumstances.

Actual Lack of Power as a Consideration in Symptomology

We must be careful in discussing the higher female risk of all degrees of emotional disorder not to fall into the trap of "blaming the victim." It is not that females have "weaker" psyches than males but that females are exposed to a larger variety of situations that teach helplessness than men are. Lenore Radloff (1976) ably summarizes these "teaching aids": (1) the characteristics of the feminine stereotype, (2) differential treatment of daughters and sons, (3) differential evaluation of female and male performance, and (4) differential attitudes toward the meaning of success and failure for females and males. Women do, indeed, have less control over their environment than men. In terms of both the family and the occupational world as social institutions they are actively discriminated against. Learned helplessness, in such circumstances, may even be viewed as protective.

SOCIAL BLAME AND SOCIAL ADJUSTMENT

Women are assisted in their inability to cope by popular conceptions of the relationship between gender and mental illness. In men such illness is looked upon as a feminine characteristic to be shunned (Phillips, 1964). Not long ago a vice-presidential nominee, Thomas Eagleton, was forced to resign as a candidate because it was revealed that he had been treated for emotional problems some years before. On the other hand, a man who publicly announces that he does not know what it means to be sick and "toughs it out" may improve his masculine image. Women appear to reject mentally ill males who seek help more strongly than females with identical behavioral descriptions. Unfortunately no data have been provided for male subjects.

Other studies demonstrate that both males and females evaluate symptomology associated with emotional stress differently depending on the sex of the stimulus person. The effects are complicated by an interrelationship with the nature of the supposed disorder as well as the supposed situational factors precipitating the symptom. In one study (Coie, Pennington, & Buckley, 1974) the kind of situational stress to which the stimulus individual (male or female) had purportedly been exposed was varied as shown in Table

14.3. The investigators also described four behavioral reactions to these stressful situations; each intended to portray a moderately deviant behavior that might be categorized as aggression, social withdrawal, somatic complaints, or cognitive dissociation. (See Table 14.3.) Subjects were requested to rate how deviant or disturbed they felt the portrayed behavior to be and to evaluate the appropriateness and helpfulness of eight different remediation suggestions. The courses of action suggested varied from letting the person cope with the problem in his or her own way through urging the person to seek professional counseling or therapy to getting the person to admit herself or himself for psychiatric treatment at a hospital. In toto, 288 male and 288 female undergraduates served as subjects in this study.

Since the study is a very complex one with many significant effects, only effects that are sex specific will be stressed here. Although female subjects saw counseling for remediation of socially unacceptable behavioral episodes as more advisable than male subjects saw it to be, both sexes agreed about the relationship between sex role and responses to situational stress. In the context of pressure regarding competence, the help of a psychiatrist or psychologist was viewed as less appropriate for a male than for a female. On the other hand, hospitalization was regarded as more appropriate for a male than for a female who showed a pathogenic behavior pattern in the context of rejection by a fiancé. Perceptions about appropriate treatment appear to relate to how visibly the behavior deviates from sex role expectations rather than to the pathology of the behavior from a mental-health point of view. Thus these college students apparently perceived pressure for competence as a greater excuse for deviant behavior in males and interpersonal rejection as a greater excuse for deviant behavior in females. Given identical behavioral reactions, males who respond strongly to interpersonal rejection and females who respond strongly to a threat to personal competence are judged to be more in need of treatment than their opposite-sex counterparts, who conform more clearly to sex role stereotypes.

The form of the behavioral response to stress is also subject to sex-specific expectations. Greater pathology was attributed to females for aggressive behavior than to males, whereas greater pathology was attributed to males for somatic complaints than to females (Coie et al., 1974). A similar effect of sex role stereotypes on student evaluations of psychiatric patients has been demonstrated in a recent study by Zeldow (1976). When hypothetical female patients expressed attitudes or preferences that are conventionally associated with the masculine sex role, male judges evaluated them as

Table 14.3 STIMULUS MATERIALS USED IN STUDY ON THE
ATTRIBUTION OF PSYCHOLOGICAL DISORDERS

The three different kinds of situational stress that were used in the stories
included accounts of rejection from a potential career choice, interpersonal rejection, and the pressure of a test of competency. These three
were written to apply to the college student circumstance and are as
follows:

[*Medical school rejection*] Jerry has just received letters from all three of
the medical schools to which he applied and they all three rejected
him. This was a severe blow to him as he had very much counted on
starting medical school next year.

[*Interpersonal rejection*] Larry's fiancée told him that she was breaking
their engagement. This came as a real surprise to him since they had
been going together for several years.

[*Competency pressure*] Bob has been preparing for a demanding oral
exam in a senior seminar in his major. The exam, which will take
place in one week, is being given by three professors, each of whose
recommendation Bob needs for his application to graduate school.

Four behavioral reactions to these stressful situations were described; each
was intended to portray moderately deviant behavior in the form that
follows:

[*Aggression*] Lately he has been somewhat touchy and verbally abusive
with his friends. On his way down to lunch the other day, a stranger
accidentally brushed past him. [Story figure] turned suddenly and
deliberately pushed the person down the stairs, so that the other man
fell and hurt himself.

[*Social withdrawal*] [Story figure] has been keeping to his room for the
last few weeks, coming out only for occasional meals which he eats
alone. He has seriously neglected his personal appearance and
avoids contact with all of his old friends.

[*Somatic complaints*] For a week now, [story figure] has had severe mi-
graine headaches and has been so nauseous that he cannot eat. In
addition, sometimes his heart pounds rapidly and his breath is short.

more disturbed than if they uttered a comparable sex-neutral statement or one that was associated with the feminine stereotype. Negative evaluations were made even though none of the statements
were necessarily indicative of psychopathology and they did not
produce such consequences when supposedly uttered by male patients. The important implication of these findings as well as of
some of those to be discussed shortly is that the behaviors involved
are not inherently disturbed, but acquire that property because of
the social category of the individual who engages in them.

When Stereotypes Hurt

Behaviors reflecting sex role reversals are more likely to be punished than the same behaviors produced by a person of the "appro-

Table 14.3 *Continued*

[*Cognitive dissociation*] For the past week, [story figure] has experienced blank spells in which he didn't know what was going on around him. One time, he found himself several blocks from campus and had no idea how he had gotten there.

Think about Jerry as if he were a friend of yours and you wanted to do what would be best for him. Evaluate the following suggestions according to your estimation of how appropriate and helpful each course of action would be:

a. You would try to let Jerry cope with his problems on his own rather than interfere. [no advice]

b. You would strongly urge Jerry to see a physician. [physician]

c. You would advise Jerry to get away for awhile and get some rest and enjoy a change of pace. [get away]

d. You would suggest that Jerry get some counseling from either a clergyman, a dean, or similar type of counselor. [counselor]

e. You would strongly urge that Jerry get personal therapy from a professional psychologist or psychiatrist. [mental health professional]

f. You would try to get Jerry to admit himself for inpatient psychiatric treatment at a hospital. [hospital]

g. You would talk with Jerry about his problem, helping him to see that things are really not as bad as they seem, helping him to focus on the positive aspects of the situation. [rationalization]

h. You would actively engage in trying to help Jerry solve his problem, helping him to discover some new solution that he had not seen as yet. [look for new solutions]

SOURCE: From J. D. Coie et al., "Effects of Situational Stress and Sex Roles on the Attribution of Psychological Disorder," *Journal of Consulting and Clinical Psychology*, 1974, 42, 559–568. Copyright 1974 by the American Psychological Association. Reprinted by permission.

priate" sex. Jeanne Marecek and her associates (Marecek, 1974; Costrich, Feinstein, Kidder, Marecek, & Pascale, 1975) performed a series of studies on responses to dependent or aggressive communications. They prepared booklets of psychotherapy vignettes including some that represented expressions of dependence on the therapist and some that represented expressions of aggression toward the therapist. Each vignette also included a description of the patient in terms of sex and age. As usual, there were two forms of each vignette, identical except for the stated sex of the patient. The researchers found that dependent men were liked significantly less than dependent women and were judged to have more serious problems. Aggressive communications produced more negative reactions when the communicator was a woman rather than a man. There was a trend for the aggressive woman to be more disliked than her male counterpart, and she was regarded as having significantly more serious problems. Both male and female subjects agreed in their assessments (Marecek, 1974). For both sexes violators of sex role norms were regarded as having more serious emotional problems.

In further studies in this area (Costrich et al., 1975) the researchers found that penalties for sex role reversals were administered more strongly by male subjects. The more submissive a male was rated to be, the less popular he was. There was no relationship between a female's level of submissiveness and her popularity. Although aggression was penalized in both sexes, the aggressive woman and the passive man were both seen as having greater need of therapy. The more dominant a male was seen to be, the less he was perceived to need therapy. For females, perceived dominance was positively correlated with need for therapy.

These studies suggest that it is not possible for women and men to manifest identical behaviors. A more specific analysis of aggressive behavior supports this statement (Rose, 1975). The components of aggressive behavior were analyzed and found to be characterized by high levels of loudness and inflection in speech and a high degree of body involvement in gestures. Male and female judges did not differ in their assessments of what physical measures enabled them to make distinctions along a continuum of behavior ranging from subassertive through assertive to aggressive. However, when confronted with scenes in which similar actions were performed by females and males (controlled by equalizing the levels of five physical measures), raters considered female reactions more aggressive than those of males. Their ratings were consistent with their belief that males should be more assertive in interpersonal confrontations.

In an earlier chapter we discussed evidence that aggressive behavior is more easily tolerated in male children than in female children. Recent evidence suggests, moreover, that socialized inhibition of aggression in females can take place even for individuals who have physiological problems that may predispose them toward behavior that is characterized by lack of control. It has been found that variation within the nonclinical range of physical anomalies associated with Down's syndrome (smaller-than-normal head circumference, epicanthal folds in non-Mongolian populations, malformed ears, furrowed tongue, a single transverse palmar crease, etc.) is associated with behavioral abnormalities in young males (Waldrop & Goering, 1971). Boys with a higher number of anomalies were found to be fast moving, impulsive, and clumsy compared with the attentive, controlled, and well-coordinated behavior of boys with few anomalies. No such effect had been found for girls. Recently, however, the presence of multiple minor physical anomalies has been found to be associated with inhibited, fearful, and socially ill-at-ease behavior in elementary school girls (Waldrop, Bell, & Goering, 1976). Their most salient characteristic appears to be nonsociability (not speaking or being spoken to and not being liked by peers) in comparison to the hyperactivity that is the most salient characteristic of boys with a high number of anomalies. These sex differences may be due to sex-specific socialization processes. More aggressive behavior is tolerated for males but is punished in females. This conclusion is consistent with data on preschoolers showing that girls with anomalies have problems of both over- and undercontrol. Nondisruptive, excessively inhibited girls, however, receive little attention.

Dependency and Agoraphobia

While aggression is punished in females, dependency is reinforced. Dependency in females has been found to be rewarded in a laboratory situation (Gruder & Cook, 1971). It is more difficult to show how dependent behaviors constitute a specific mental-health problem, since these are behaviors that may be rewarded rather than punished by society. We have a control problem here because women who are overly passive are much less likely to be regarded as in need of therapeutic treatment and less likely to be so treated (thus not showing up in our statistics) than aggressive women. One indicative piece of evidence comes from the analysis of certain behavioral syndromes in terms of sex. Agoraphobia, which may be defined as fear of going out of one's home and of unenclosed spaces and/or travel, is much more common among women than among men (Fodor, 1974). On the average, 84 percent of such cases are female, and agoraphobics account for more than half of patients with phobic disorders. The average age of onset is the mid-20s, and 80 percent of the patients are married. Their personalities are described as dependent, anxious, and shy, and their families are described as overprotective and close (Marks, 1970). They are found in all geographic areas and at every socioeconomic level.

In many ways the agoraphobic female can be considered an extreme product of female sex role socialization. Girls are not encouraged to master their fears or to reduce their dependence on their families. Agoraphobia often develops after marriage in women who feel trapped by their situation. They may be responding not to the marriage per se but to feelings of being dominated, with no outlet for self-assertion (Fodor, 1974). Even the most independent women may hang onto a few phobic symptoms such as fear of driving, riding bikes, or skating in order to preserve a last remnant of dependency. Erika Jong's book *Fear of Flying* eloquently documents the conflict between a woman's need for autonomy and her fears about loss of femininity if she does not permit herself to be dominated.

The "Battered-Woman Syndrome"

Dependency and agoraphobia may contribute to the relatively high percentage of married women who are beaten and brutalized by their husbands. While we tend to think of wife beating as a lower-class phenomenon, there is increasing evidence that many middle-class and upper-class women are beaten (Straus, 1977b). It is hard to estimate their numbers since they are more reluctant to seek the help of social services than poorer women, perhaps because they fear public exposure more or because they are less aware of the existence of such services. Women who are beaten often come from families in which they saw their own mothers beaten. They characteristically report great emotional dependence on their abusive partners and/or great fear of how the world outside the home will treat them. They often lack or perceive themselves to lack the skills necessary to obtain paid employment outside the home. Frequently their spouses have instigated or enhanced these fears.

Until recently no social services existed that were designed to assist battered women. Assaults within the family were not treated as criminal matters. Just as a wife could until recently legally be raped by her husband, so could she legally be beaten by him. One experiment staged within the confines of a public restaurant clearly demonstrates the perception of "the marriage license as a hitting license" (Straus, 1975). A male and a female confederate staged an argument in a restaurant that culminated in the woman's being slapped. During the course of the argument it was made clear either that the couple were unacquainted or that they were husband and wife. When the woman indicated that she did not know the man who hit her, many spectators came to her assistance. When they appeared to be married, however, nearly all observers remained uninvolved.

DRUG ABUSE AND THE FEMININE ROLE

Social pressure for passivity may account for sex-specific patterns of drug use among women and men. Although fewer females than males appear to become alcoholics, the incidence of alcoholism among women is masked by the fact that they drink more at home. Many women alcoholics are able to minimally maintain their homes and families. They are less likely to aggress against social institutions than alcoholic men. An alcoholic woman appears to be punishing herself in a manner compatible with traditional female roles. Her alcoholism isolates her while at the same time justifying her rejection of and by others (Gomberg, 1974). It is noteworthy that alcoholic women do not reject femininity but, on the contrary, tend to overemphasize and overvalue the wife–mother role. They marry to the same extent as women in the general population, and there are far fewer single, unmarried women drinkers than married or formerly married ones. Alcoholic women have been reported to prefer significantly more children than control subjects (Wilsnack, 1973).

Abuse of psychoactive drugs is a more frequent problem among women than simple alcoholism. More women than men use psychoactive drugs—especially psychoactive drugs prescribed by physicians. Women visit physicians more often than men, but they also receive more drugs than they make visits (Fidell, 1973). They make 58 percent of the visits to physicians and receive 67 percent of the prescriptions for psychoactive drugs. They are the most heavy users of barbiturates, sedatives, relaxants, major and minor tranquilizers, antidepressants, pep pills, diet pills, noncontrolled narcotics, and analgesics. Men are the major users of marijuana/hashish, LSD, the inhalants, methedrine, and heroin. Most of the drugs that are overused by males can be classified as excitatory, whereas "female" drugs of abuse depress and desensitize the central nervous system. It has been estimated that somewhere between 45 and 50 percent of women over 30 have used mood-modifying or psychoactive drugs (Linn & Davis, 1971; Mellinger, Balter, & Manheimer, 1971). Women are heavily involved with drug use, but their usage appears legitimate because they tend to obtain drugs legally by prescription from a physician. Legality, however, does not alter the potentially harmful physiological and/or social effects of drug use. Furthermore, people who obtain drugs from physicians tend to use them longer and more consistently (Mellinger et al., 1971).

Why do women use tranquilizing drugs in disproportionate numbers? Even if we do not take personality variables into account, women as a group appear to be perceived as much more likely targets for mood-depressing substances than men. For example, sex stereotypes pervade the drug advertisements in leading medical journals (Prather & Fidell, 1975). Among the effects found in the analysis of the contents of drug advertisements over a five-year period were the following:

1. A strong tendency to associate psychoactive drugs with female patients.
2. Nonpsychoactive drug advertisements usually show a male

as the patient. Fidell (1973) finds this particularly insidious because it indicates that real illnesses are experienced by men while mental problems are shown by women.

3. The symptoms listed for male and female users of psychoactive drugs are significantly different. Males are usually depicted as presenting specific and work-related symptoms, whereas women are shown to complain of diffuse anxiety, tension, and depression. In a more recent study Fidell (1977) notes that there is little consistency between the physical or mental symptoms reported by women patients and the kind of psychotropic drug prescribed, raising even more serious questions about the abuse of these drugs.

In drug advertisements men are portrayed in a greater variety of contexts and ages. Women are more often shown as difficult patients for whom mood-modifying drugs are recommended. One description of a specific drug ad may be illuminating. A before-and-after technique is used. The woman is shown performing a tedious housecleaning job—mopping floors or washing a large number of dishes. She is portrayed as severely depressed. In the "after" portion of the ad, after she has taken the drug being advertised, she is seen happy and smiling, with spotless kitchen and dishes. Robert Seidenberg, a noted psychiatrist, has criticized such advertising as leading to a number of false impressions (Seidenberg, 1971). It presents the view that difficulty with or reluctance to do housework may be a sign of mental illness. It suggests that it is medically sound to prescribe drugs to overcome possible resentment toward one's role in life. It deflects the observer from other feasible alternatives for this woman.

Another technique in drug advertising is to show the bothersome patient who repeatedly visits the physician's office. The ad notes the need of the drug for a woman who presents vague "functional" symptoms. The same woman with the same look of distress is pictured over and over. Such an advertisement contributes to an image of "oneness" among the symptoms of all women. It depicts the woman as a complainer with no real reason for her mental distress and suggests that the use of this psychoactive substance will fulfill the dual purpose of relieving her psychosomatic symptoms and keeping her out of the doctor's office.

Although the idea that there is a chemical solution to all problems is not limited to the female patient, there is considerable evidence that psychoactive drug "overkill" is a greater problem for women. Physicians share the stereotypes of our society. Males in our society are more likely to be viewed as "really" sick. When physicians are asked to describe "the typical complaining patient," 72 percent spontaneously referred to a woman whereas only 4 percent referred spontaneously to a man (Cooperstock, 1971). Physicians excuse their willingness to give tranquilizers to a housewife by saying that she can always take a nap and need not be mentally alert anyway (Prather & Fidell, 1975). A considerably higher percentage judged daily use of librium by a housewife as legitimate as contrasted with comparable usage by a student (Linn, 1971). Physicians' attitudes in this regard seem to reflect a widespread view that women's social roles can be fulfilled by anyone with a small degree of mental competence. Thus, depriving women of some degree of capability by means of psychoactive drugs is not seen to constitute a "problem" for society.

In a large-scale review of medical practices in the United States, Linda Fidell (1978) points out that stereotypes about female patients probably lead physicians to make psychogenic diagnoses of their symptoms more frequently than they do for comparable symptoms presented by men. Such differential diagnostic practices probably stem more from medical training practices than from real differences in physical or mental health between women and men. It should be noted, too, that these medical practices merely reflect more general cultural attitudes toward illness and gender.

THE SOCIAL DEFINITION OF MENTAL ILLNESS

Sociologists and some psychologists have long been aware that illness is not an objective fact perceived, reacted to, and reported similarly by members of all subcultures. In some circles all illnesses are suspected of being psychosomatic. It is possible that some women have learned to label their symptoms in psychogenic terms. For example, women who present themselves for treatment to the psychiatric service of a hospital are more likely to be urban, to have been born in an urban area of the country, to be Jewish, to have gone to college, to have husbands who are professionals, and, in general, to have higher social status than women who present themselves for treatment to a neurological service (supposedly for more purely medical complaints) and are eventually classified as having a psychiatric disorder (Bart, 1968). In other words, at a somewhat higher level of sophistication women self-classify their behaviors as psychogenic rather than physiological in origin.

The medical profession has a long history of labeling female symptomology in psychogenic terms. In the nineteenth century it was fashionable for middle- and upper-class women to faint or to remain in bed for long periods for vague, ill-defined illnesses. However, fainting is no longer regarded as a sign of femininity. *Hysteria* is another term that was used to label "female" complaints. In fact the term is derived from the Greek word for womb and was not considered appropriate to describe the behaviors of males. "In its evaluation of women as patients, the American medical profession defines all adult women as sick on the basis of their reproductive functions, which in current medical ideology, can only be managed with professional expertise" (Lorber, 1975, p. 98). Pregnancy and menopause have been defined as diseases, menstruation as a chronic disorder, and childbirth as a surgical event (Ehrenreich & English, 1973). Primary dysmennorhea, nausea of pregnancy, and labor pains are commonly thought by the medical profession to be caused or exaggerated by psychological factors and are minimized, derided, and treated inadequately or punitively (Lennane & Lennane, 1973). All of these states may readily have physiological bases, and it is just as accurate to argue that a woman's physical state is responsible for her anxiety and apprehension as it is to argue that her psyche is responsible for her physical condition.

Gynecologists are recognized as our society's official specialists on women, yet an examination of 27 general gynecology textbooks published since 1943 revealed a persistent bias toward greater concern with the patient's husband than with the patient herself (Scully & Bart, 1973). Gynecology texts also claim legitimacy for statements about the female psyche as well as the female body. Scully and Bart cite statements such as "An important feature of sex desire in the man is the urge to dominate the woman and subjugate her to his will; in the woman acquiescence to the masterful takes a high place" or "The traits that compose the core of the female personality are feminine narcissism, masochism and passivity." These statements were culled from books published as recently as 1971.

Menopause is also viewed in psychogenic terms. The prevailing view of psychoanalytically conditioned physicians is that menopause is a time of mortification, with a woman's service to her species finished (Parlee, 1978). In contradistinction to male psychology, female psychology is seen as being dependent on biology. This thinking has influenced the therapy offered for menopausal symptoms. Physiological symptoms may be treated psychologically, while psychological treatment is designed to merely gain acceptance of biological loss. In recent years estrogens have been touted as a "magic pill" designed to retain a woman's youth, attractiveness, and sexual capacity. There is little or no recognition that women may be able to function as mature human beings following menopause. A symposium on menopause sponsored by the National Institutes of Health had twenty-five participants, all of whom were male. The only statement on the psychology of menopause to appear in the summary was the undocumented view of one of the participants that menopausal women are "a caricature of their younger selves at their emotional worst." "It sometimes seems as if the only thing worse than being subjected to the raging hormonal influences of the menstrual cycle is to have these influences subside" (Parlee, 1976, p. 5).

Negative attitudes toward postmenopausal women provide a classic case of blaming the victim. When women come to doctors for help with their reproductive activities, they are blamed for their own physical and mental state. Nevertheless there is some evidence to suggest that menopausal symptomology is as much a product of society as it is of biology. Very few Indian women of the Rajput class show any effect of menopause other than menstrual-cycle change—there is no depression, dizziness, or physical incapacitation (Flint, 1975). The researcher suggests that this is because in this society menopause results in an improvement in social role—the end of female seclusion and the ability to participate in public life. In our culture, on the other hand, menopause is a time of punishment rather than reward. The woman has lost her youth without any compensating gain in status. The "menopausal syndrome" appears to be a phenomenon largely limited to Western European and American women. In fact one intriguing finding indicates that West African women increased in number of subjective menopausal symptoms in direct relation to the amount of contact they had with European women (Cherry, 1976).

The relationship between female reproductive physiology and psychological symptomology appears to be as old as the idea of psychogenic causation itself. It is not surprising, therefore, that control over one's own body has become a major issue for feminists. In the nineteenth century, clitorectomies were frequently prescribed as a treatment for female mania or oversexuality (Spitz, 1952). Today, "prophylactic" hysterectomies probably rank as the supreme example of women's willingness to submit to male judgments about their physiological functions. A womb, however—even after childbearing—should be no more superfluous than an appendix. In this regard it should be noted that surgery, like gynecology, has one of the lowest percentages of female practitioners in the field of medicine.

PSYCHOTHERAPY

The Psychotherapeutic Establishment

The mental-health profession is also a predominantly male institution. Far more men than women are psychiatrists or clinical psychologists. In social work, the lowest-status helping profession, the sex distribution may be more nearly equal or even reversed. Far more women than men function as clients or patients. It has been charged that traditional psychotherapy functions in a manner that supports female submission to male authority (Chesler, 1972). Men are the experts and women are the patients who need to be helped. Women reveal their intimate problems, while their male therapists are taught to remain impersonal and emotionally uninvolved. Psychotherapy isolates women from each other; it emphasizes individual rather than collective solutions to problems. Psychotherapy offers a socially approved mechanism for expressing anxiety, fear, and anger. At the same time, it may defuse these emotions by enabling the stresses that produced them to be relabeled in personal rather than social terms. The demand for change remains with the woman—not with the social situation. Accordingly, Chesler regards traditional psychotherapy as a patriarchal institution—one that contributes to female oppression.

Traditional Ideology and Its Critique

Psychotherapists cannot be criticized for ignoring women. In fact until recently psychoanalysts were the only people interested in behavior who paid any significant attention to women. Scholars since the time of Freud have focused on biological rather than social or cultural reasons for women's inferior status. Although Freud's observations did not have any scientific basis, his views have had an impact not only on therapists and mental-health workers but on twentieth-century thought in general. Among the concepts emanating from Freud's "anatomy is destiny" position that have been particularly detrimental to women are the following: (1) Females envy the anatomical equipment of the male—this is called penis envy; (2) because females do not have to resolve an Oedipal conflict they develop less powerful superegos and therefore have less advanced moral development than males; (3) clitoral masturbation is male, and abolition of clitoral sexuality is necessary before a woman can attain full femininity—the role of wife and mother.

It is very easy to criticize Freud's ideas about women, and many such critiques have appeared in recent years. What is probably less often recognized is that many "neo-Freudians" and even less traditionally psychoanalytic theorists have also held views that are detrimental to women. Erik Erikson (1964), for example, also defines women in terms of their relationship to men. Although he believes that the anatomical distinction that accounts for personality differences between women and men is the possession of a "productive inner body space" rather than the lack of a penis, he sees a woman's identity as defined not simply by the man she marries but by the man or men by whom she would like to be sought. Even Erich Fromm (1956), a theorist who emphasizes the importance of the social and cultural milieu in personal growth, defines personality in sex-typed terms. He characterizes masculinity as defined by the properties of penetration, activity, adventurousness, and discipline. Femininity, on the other hand, is seen as productive, receptive, realistic, enduring, and maternal.

It has been pointed out that most ideas about women have been formulated by men and accepted by women. Even many of the women students of Freud differed with him more on the issue of the anatomical basis of female sexuality than on the equally important issue of a female personality distinct from that of the male. Issues having to do with personality were discussed in Chapter 6. Here it should only be noted that traditional therapeutic conceptions about female versus male characteristics are suspiciously like the sex role stereotypes shared by many people in our culture.

Recent critics of Freudian-derived views of females and femininity have concentrated in two major camps. There are those who believe that males and females do indeed have distinctly different personalities, although they disagree about the causes of such differences. Some theorists have reversed the rationales and suggested that males envy the productive capacity of females (Wolman, 1975). In a more sociocultural vein, others believe that most women are "mad" or intensely angry because they have attempted to conform to the behavioral standards devised for them by men (Chesler, 1972; Mundy, 1975). Another group of therapists, mostly defining themselves as feminists of one orientation or another, have stressed the essential similarity between the personalities of males and females. The concept of an androgynous personality—that males and females possess traits that are characteristic of both sexes—is also discussed more fully in Chapter 6.

Psychotherapy: Who and How

The major ideological differences among therapists have created equally major issues relating to who should treat whom and with what methods. Positions on these questions range from "Any qualified therapists can treat any patient" through "Women are best treated by women therapists" to "Traditional psychotherapeutic treatment is not effective for anyone—particularly women." Although these issues are complex and difficult to view dispassionately, they do lead to a number of questions that can be studied, although not necessarily resolved, by research. One basic question is that of whether the impact of treatment is affected by the ideology of the therapist.

There is some suggestive evidence that the judgments of mental-health professionals regarding the appropriateness of certain behaviors and certain treatments may be affected both by the sex of the therapist and by her or his ideology. One study presented seventy-one professional counselors with bogus clinical profiles varying in the client's politics and sex (Abramowitz, Abramowitz, Jackson, & Gomes, 1973). Greater psychological maladjustment was attributed to women leaning toward the "left" than to comparable men, but only by ideologically more conservative examiners. Men were allowed a wider range of permissible behaviors than women. Julia Sherman and her associates (Sherman, Koufacos, & Kenworthy, 1978) found that women clinical practitioners who responded to their questionnaire were both more informed about the psychology of women and less biased in their views about women than male respondents. At a rate of more than two males to one female, respondents did *not* think that (1) male therapists tend to keep women in therapy longer than females or (2) people tend to regard women as incompetent until proven otherwise and vice versa for men. Also at a rate of more than two males to one female, respondents believed that (3) it is better for women with young children to be at home and (4) decisions about marriage or its continuation should be considered an important goal for women in therapy. Male therapists appeared to be particularly uninformed in the area of the "psychology of female bodily functioning."

A surprisingly high percentage of clinicians of both sexes agreed with a number of statements that seem questionable on the basis of the research literature. Fifty-seven percent of all respondents thought that acceptance of one's sex role is necessary for mental health. Forty-one percent thought that the cure of "frigidity" was an important goal of therapy. Forty-six percent did not think it was easier for a woman to relate to a female therapist (significantly more men than women held this view). Also interesting was the finding that 4 percent of the respondents (with another 2 percent neither agreeing or disagreeing) agreed with the statement that "sexual intimacy with a client might be helpful to her."

Scores on the Machiavellianism scale—a test designed to measure individuals' willingness to manipulate others—appear related to attitudes about clients and therapy (Marecek, 1975). Although Maracek studied only a relatively small group, 43 male and 12 female clinicians who were members of the American Psychological Association, she found that among male therapists Machiavellianism was linked to a preference for treating women clients. There was no relationship between Machiavellianism and preference for women clients among female therapists. Machiavellians of both sexes were more likely to favor the use of placebo drug treatments and the coercion of individuals into treatment. They were also more likely to feel that control over their client was important. The issue of control and power in psychotherapy is of more than academic interest, since therapists with a strong control orientation were more likely to feel that sex was permitted in therapy in more circumstances than therapists who were less concerned about control. Marecek's data suggest that some power-oriented therapists may seek female clients and may respond to them in not altogether therapeutic ways.

Psychoanalytically oriented theorists have been the most consistently negative in their treatment of women (Tennov, 1975). There is no direct evidence that treatment by a therapist with a Freudian view of the psychological world is any more harmful than treatment by any traditional therapist. However, it has been demonstrated that therapists view their patients as becoming healthier as their values become more similar to those of the therapist (Welkowitz, Cohen, & Ortmeyer, 1967). Younger therapists are less likely to express traditional views of women than older male therapists, while women therapists appear to be the most egalitarian of all (Goldberg as cited in Tanney & Birk, 1976). Current evidence indicates that both male and female therapists are becoming more egalitarian (Fabrikant, 1974; Gomes & Abramowitz, 1976). Thus it may be more important to know the therapist's ideology (his or her age may provide a cue) than his or her sex.

Female vs. Male Therapists

Research on the impact of pairing client and counselor on the basis of sex gives equivocal results. Nevertheless there is evidence that the sex of the therapist may have an effect. While this may be due simply to the fact that women therapists view women more favorably, it cannot be dismissed as an artifact at this time. Women appear to prefer to talk to women counselors about personal–social problems, although they may prefer males for vocational counseling (Tanney & Birk, 1976). When patients are assigned randomly to male or female counselors, fewer patients remain with female-led groups, but those who do report themselves to be more satisfied (Gould, 1975). In general, patients rate therapy sessions with female therapists as more satisfying than sessions with male therapists (Howard, Orlinsky, & Hill, 1970). Female subjects paired with female counselors produced more discussion of feelings than mixed-sex dyads (Hill, 1975). However, neither counselor sex nor client sex has been found to be a significant predictor of counseling outcome (Scher, 1975).

One of the great difficulties in this area is the question of how to evaluate the outcome of psychotherapy. Some critics of traditional psychotherapy stress that therapy as it is traditionally conceived may have a "cure" rate no higher than the rate that would result from leaving the patient alone (Tennov, 1975). Since this is not an area that is sex specific per se (although it has more meaning for women than for men, since women comprise the bulk of the patient–client population), we will not go into this issue in any depth. Of more interest in the context of this book are the issues related to the counseling of women.

Sex-Specific Problems and Counseling

We have provided ample evidence that feminine roles carry an elevated risk of psychological disorder, with more traditional roles (e.g., that of housewife) correspondingly more hazardous. While there are few psychological disorders that are exclusively male or female, the risks of specific disorders differ greatly for women and men. Men and women are at high risk for psychological disorders that dovetail with masculine and feminine stereotypes, respectively (Marecek, 1975). Women are at heightened risk for disorders involving low self-esteem, passivity, guilt, depression, and social withdrawal. Men are at heightened risk for disorders involving antisocial behavior, aggression, violence, impulsiveness, and psychopathy. "Masculine" symptoms have two characteristics that contrast with "feminine" symptoms. First, they involve behaviors directed against others rather than against the self. Second, they involve an active orientation rather than a passive one.

Low self-esteem is a particularly critical problem for females. Male self-esteem seems to be related to degree of identification with the male sex role (Connell & Johnson, 1970). Among adolescents highly male-identified males had the highest self-esteem scores, followed by both high- and low-male-identified females, while the lowest self-esteem scores were those of males with low male sex role identification. There was no difference between the self-esteem scores of girls who identify with the male role (sex-inappropriate identification) and those of girls who do not (sex-appropriate identification). The male sex role appears to have reward value in itself whether it is adopted by a male or by a female.

Sibling status, established by birth position, also appears to be a source of self-esteem for males but not for females. Firstborn boys have higher self-esteem than later-born males, although no such effect exists for girls (Hollender, 1972). For all firstborns, self-esteem was lower in females than in males regardless of the sex of the second sibling. High self-derogation scores among adult females are associated with retrospective reports of having received less attention from parents than siblings received (Kaplan & Pokorny, 1972). Males with high self-derogation report more poor peer pressure from outside the family.

Females with low self-esteem appear to gain less from their accomplishments. For males, a low course grade was associated with lower self-esteem; for females, a high course grade was associated with lower self-esteem (Hollender, 1972). Low self-esteem is also associated with an external locus of control—feeling that one's fate is in others' rather than one's own hands. Women with a strong external locus of control tend to recall having had little control over their lives during the early childhood years (Bryant & Trockel, 1976). They are less likely to aspire to innovative occupations. They project that their real, as opposed to their ideal, occupation will be traditional in nature (Burlin, 1976). Low self-esteem is, therefore, closely associated with problems of achievement, autonomy, and self-assertion. Problems encountered in the counseling of males, in contrast, are more likely to be related to difficulty in expressing emotions, withholding aggression, and coping with stresses associated with social expectations of male success.

There appears to be a contradiction between data indicating that females are more likely to develop disorders that involve exaggeration of the feminine role and data indicating that females are judged as more severely ill when they deviate from that role. This apparent contradiction makes sense, however, if we consider the frequency and severity of symptoms of illness as separate issues. Thus females are most likely to show symptoms of excessive sex role socialization, but when they violate sex-appropriate roles they are seen to be more severely ill. A similar argument can be made for males.

The arenas of life in which women encounter problems are different than those in which men encounter problems. A recent issue of *The Counseling Psychologist* devoted to the issues encountered in counseling women suggests that areas in which women frequently require therapeutic intervention tend to be associated with either uniquely female biological processes or the feminine roles of wife and mother. Biological areas in which intervention models are discussed include the counseling of victims of rape and unwanted pregnancies (Freiberg & Bridwell, 1976) and the counseling of mastectomy patients (Schain, 1976). An area that could have been included but was not is the counseling of aging and menopausal women.

Many problems for which women seek counseling center on concern with loss of youth and attractiveness, which is equated with loss of femininity. We may regard aging and events connected with this inevitable process as forms of psychopathology that are socially defined as "problems" for the "afflicted" individuals. For example, young people in our society perceive that older people lose competence, power, and even social acceptability (O'Connell & Rotter, 1977). Men drop more precipitously in these categories than women, who were never perceived to possess these characteristics to a great extent at any period in their lives.

While it may be better to be a woman than to be aged in our society, the greater readiness of women to seek counseling, as well as their greater life expectancy, makes it more likely that a therapist will encounter female clients seeking assistance because of stresses associated with aging. Again, as in many areas discussed in this book, the problems encountered may be due not to the biological processes themselves but to the interpretation that socialization in our culture places upon them.

ALTERNATIVES TO TRADITIONAL PSYCHOTHERAPY

C-R Groups

There is more disagreement about the question of how women should be helped. Some feminist therapists, such as Annette Brodsky (1973) and Barbara Kirsh (1974), suggest that consciousness-raising (C-R) groups provide a model for therapy with women. Brodsky suggests a number of rationales for the use of the consciousness-raising group: (1) Such groups are not associated with the medical model, which implies that women's characteristic responses to stress are indicative of illness and/or abnormality; (2) women have been encouraged to conform and to be passive, whereas the C-R group offers a way of sharing common experiences in the absence of an expert male or female therapist; (3) C-R groups start with the assumption that the environment rather than biological factors or intrapsychic dynamics plays a major role in the difficulties of individuals. Such groups often assist in the redefining of goals and the reshaping of behaviors. One difficulty with the groups is the difficulty many women encounter when they attempt to transfer their new-found behaviors to life outside the group. Others outside the group may not respond as positively to the change. It is easy for an individual to become angry with employers, lovers, and old friends who respond in a male-chauvinistic, stereotyped manner. Such behavior may provoke a backlash from those who are threatened by the change.

Assertiveness Training

Assertiveness training has also been suggested as a solution for women who need to acquire new social skills in order to enhance their growth as people. Assertive behavior may be defined as "interpersonal behavior in which a person stands up for her legitimate rights in such a way that the rights of others are not violated" (Jakubowski-Spector, 1973, p. 76). It is intended to communicate respect rather than deference for the other person. Another individual's behavior, rather than his or her person, is attacked. Jakubowski-Spector provides a number of examples that may serve to distinguish an assertive response from an aggressive response in the same situation. (See Table 14.4.) She suggests that an important part of assertiveness training is helping the person build a personal belief system that supports and justifies her acting assertively. It is not simply building up a repertory of responses. The client must be convinced that she will be happier if she appropriately exercises her rights and that nonassertion is harmful in the long run. Behavioral rehearsal is often helpful in allaying anxieties about acting assertively.

Feminist Therapy

Feminist therapy represents an outgrowth of the philosophy of the women's movement as applied to the adjustment of women—and others—as people. It makes use of the techniques discussed earlier as well as many other procedures. In fact the only thing that all feminist therapists may have in common is their eclecticism. Jean Holroyd (1976) has assembled a number of principles that appear to synthesize feminist views on counseling women. (See Table 14.5.)

Another definition of a feminist therapist is provided by Susan Herman (1974). A feminist therapist is a person who understands and supports the drive for female equality. Such a therapist recognizes the need for personal support if a woman is to expand beyond her currently defined roles and the opposition that is encountered from husbands and families as expansion is tried. A client–patient is approached on an equal basis—person to person as opposed to expert–student or parent–child. *All* areas brought up by the client are explored, with a focus on growth and expansion. No one model

Table 14.4 DISTINGUISHING BETWEEN AGGRESSIVE AND ASSERTIVE RESPONSES

In each of the following examples, the first response given is aggressive and the second is assertive.

COMPLAINING ABOUT THE UNSATISFACTORY NATURE OF LOVE-MAKING

"Bill, you're really inadequate as a lover. If this is how our sex life is going to be, we might as well forget it right now. I could get more satisfaction doing it myself."

"Bill, I'd like to talk about how we could act differently in sex so that I could get greater satisfaction. For one thing, I think you really need to slow down a lot so that I could start tuning into my own sensations."

REFUSING A ROOMMATE'S REQUEST TO BORROW CLOTHES

"Absolutely not! I've had enough of your leeching clothes off of me."

"I'm sorry, but the last time you borrowed my sweater you were careless with it and really got it dirty. I don't want to loan you any more of my clothes."

REFUSING TO TYPE TERM PAPERS FOR A BOYFRIEND

"Where in the hell do you get off asking me to type your papers? What do you think I am—some sort of slave?"

"I think that it's about time that I told you how I feel when you constantly ask me to type your papers. I'm getting irritated, and I feel like I'm being taken for granted when you assume that I'll type for you. I hate typing and I think that you're asking too much when you expect me to do that for you. Please don't ask me to type any more."

REPRIMANDING ONE'S CHILDREN

"You kids are so sloppy . . . sometimes I hate you. You've got to be the worst kids in the whole city! If I had known motherhood was going to be like this, I would never have had any kids at all!"

"Listen, I feel as though I'm being taken advantage of when you are this sloppy in cleaning up after yourselves. I can't enjoy myself with you in the evening when I have to spend all that extra time cleaning up after your mess. This is a problem that must be solved. What are your ideas?"

REFUSING A REQUEST TO BABYSIT

"No thanks! You couldn't pay me enough to babysit for your kids. Why don't you stay home once in a while?"

"Beth, I'm sorry but I feel too tired to babysit after working all day. I hope that you can find someone else."

SOURCE: From P. Jakubowski-Spector, "Facilitating Growth Through Assertive Training," *The Counseling Psychologist*, 1973, *4*, 75–86.

of a healthy person (or two, for that matter!) is held. A multifaceted model of health encompassing many life styles and personality differences for both men and women is envisioned. The stress is on self-nurturance (as opposed to pressures for women to be more concerned about the needs of others), self-definition, and self-validation. In all of these statements I would prefer not to focus on the sex of the feminist therapist. It seems that it is neither necessary

Table 14.5 PRINCIPLES FOR THE COUNSELING OF WOMEN

1. There is an abundance of conflicting information about women, much of it generated to support someone's research hypothesis, clinical theory, or political stance. Psychologically and biologically there is no "typical" woman and often not even a "type" of response pattern. Your client's self-report should be respected above all.
2. Relate to your client as a person valued in her own right rather than focusing on her wife-role, mother-role, feminist identity, or whether she looks and acts like what you think a woman should be.
3. Share your attitudes about woman's role, so that both of you are aware of your relative positions. This assumes social awareness on your part—not just self-awareness but where you fit into the overall system of shifting values. If your client has experienced more consciousness raising than you have, at least that is somewhat better than when both of you are "blind" to the issues.
4. Recognize that society's ambivalence about sexuality and about woman's role may cause your client a lot of confusion and personal grief. Discourage her from claiming problems which are someone else's (frigidity vs. premature ejaculation; vocational incompetence vs. unjust occupational restrictions). On the other hand, reinforce her for taking responsibility, for actively seeking solutions, for changing the system which constrains her, and for not taking the role of the victim. In considering her struggle to know herself or give up symptoms, "listen with the fourth ear" for evidence of the subtle pull of her environment, the social pressures large and small which impinge on her decisions.
5. Women's groups (consciousness-raising or otherwise) permit formation of new identifications with other women who view themselves as competent and provide mutual support as women undergo rapid social changes, especially for the female client who has not experienced belonging to a group of other women. Female therapists may or may not be beneficial as models, depending on their level of consciousness and whether they are similar enough to the client to permit identification.
6. Supplement therapy with specific training to counteract deficiencies in socialization skills due to sex-role stereotyping during the developmental period: assertion training, desensitization of achievement fears, vocational guidance, and the like. It would almost seem to be poor practice not to advise the new sex therapies for women with sexual dysfunction by referral to an appropriate clinic if necessary (with or without continuing therapy).

SOURCE: From J. Holroyd, "Psychotherapy and Women's Liberation," *The Counseling Psychologist*, 1976, 6, 22–28.

nor sufficient to be a woman to be a feminist therapist. It is not necessary to be a woman to be a client of one, either.

Androgyny and Therapy

Studies by Sandra Bem, cited in Chapter 6, suggest that the androgynous personality is more adaptive to the requirements of a situation than personalities in which either masculine or feminine characteristics predominate. A number of feminist therapists have seized upon the implications of androgyny for clinical practice.

> I have no doubt that androgyny will become a well-worn concept in our profession. It is indeed a normalizing concept. I personally find it refreshing: I have in the course of my time been called many things, ranging from accusations of penis envy to possession of physiological anomalies and hormonal imbalances. But never have I been so fortunate as to be called androgynous. Whether I am in fact androgynous or not is not the problem—it is just that there has never been a momentary pause while someone considered the possibility that I might be androgynous, and it might even be a good thing for me to be.. . . . [Kenworthy & Kirlin, 1976, p. 8]

There are, however, a number of cautions to consider before we embrace androgyny as the basis of sound mental health for all. First, although it is important to understand that both men and women may express both sex-"appropriate" and sex-"inappropriate" traits and still remain healthy, functioning human beings, being androgynous does not automatically enable one to select the situation in which a particular behavior is appropriate. In other words, someone—male or female—must be able to recognize when nurturance or assertion is a valid self-enhancing behavior. What we may need is behaviors that combine what are generally regarded as dualistic states (Kaplan, 1979). However, we are hampered by our language in recognizing that such hybrid characteristics as "anger tempered by warmth" or "dependency tempered by assertiveness" can exist. We do have linguistic precedent in this regard, since the category "passive–aggressive" denotes an easily identifiable category of behavior. Kaplan suggests that there may be an infinite number of other logical possibilities awaiting our conceptualization, such as "rational sensitivity," "compassionate ambition," "tender forcefulness," and "gentle dominance."

Second, we have discussed extensively the pervasiveness of sex role stereotypes and of sexist thinking such that it appears virtually impossible for females and males to be perceived as engaging in identical behaviors. Thus while a woman may perceive that she is being assertive or a man that he is being nurturant, significant others may perceive them as, respectively, aggressive and passive–effeminate. If a man has gained a sufficient number of "idiosyncrasy credits" in other ways, he may be permitted, like Roosevelt Greer, to engage in needlepoint. Females who engage in "masculine" assertive and achievement-related behaviors, however, may have difficulty persuading others that they are "feminine" in other contexts—for example, that they are happy, loving wives and mothers. Androgyny may in fact have smaller payoffs for women than for men.

Third, it is important to remember that "masculine" and "feminine" traits do not possess the same value in our culture. Male-typed traits are regarded as more socially desirable and have higher status than female-typed traits. "Masculine" traits may well be more enhancing to one's self-esteem. It may be difficult for individuals of either sex to reach a flexible balance for themselves in view of the unbalanced pressures from cultural norms. "Feminine" traits may be virtuous, but virtue is not yet its own reward. Therapists are often confronted with the problem of curing a perfectly admirable person of a perfectly "acceptable" and equally dreadful case of virtue (Kenworthy & Kirlin, 1976).

Fourth, it is important to understand that androgynous models may not assist women in adjusting to and fulfilling traditional roles.

> A woman who, while working with her therapist, develops or mobilizes her capacity for self-reliance, analysis, assertiveness, and a host of other latent traits, may very well also begin to yearn for a more complex medium than Dr. Seuss, a more challenging preoccupation than P.T.A. She may want to return to work or go to school. This self-reliant behavior may make her a better role model for her children, but we can't ignore the possibility it will also result in the greatest threat of all to Peoria—a "broken" marriage. [Kenworthy & Kirlin, p. 6]

Fifth, we are faced with the problem of whether androgynous behaviors on the part of individuals can change the position of women in society as it exists today. "Women and social systems" is the major focus of the next chapter. It is clear that we do not know how individual behavior affects social structures. Androgyny, of itself, may remedy nothing. It cannot serve as a substitute for social change or as a palliative to a skewed tradition. Nevertheless it may be viewed as a proximate tool in a resistant context. It may be viewed as a concept that assists the individual in normalizing attitudes about his or her maladjusted behavior. Thus it may assist society in constructing less distressed human beings.

Chapter 15
Sexism: Institutional and Institutionalized

In the preceding chapter we noted the peculiar vulnerability of females to emotional disorders. It was suggested that sex asymmetries in the degree of emotional symptomology is a function of the different social assumptions about roles and norms of behavior for the sexes. In this chapter we will examine in some detail the way our society fosters sex inequality. Since these mechanisms are largely institutional, they operate largely independently of the attitudes toward sex roles of the individuals participating in them. They involve the unconscious assumptions of members of society about other members of society. Sexist practices may be documented in our society as a whole; in specific institutions within it, such as the work world, academia, or our educational and marital arrangements; and in terms of individual behaviors toward others in these institutional contexts. In the latter case distinctions can be made between institutional practices and individual ones. We could term individual sexist behaviors and attitudes in institutional settings *institutionalized sexist practices*. And in that category we will review what we know about the personalized management of behavioral norms and deviance therefrom. The chapter represents an attempt to synthesize sociological and psychological knowledge—to see how societal mechanisms are reflected in the behaviors of the members of that society.

GENERAL SOCIOCULTURAL ATTITUDES

Unfortunately it is very easy to document sexist practices in our society. An examination of our social institutions reveals an almost universal sexist bias—prejudice toward and discrimination against people who happen to belong to one particular group, namely, females. As noted earlier, there appears to be a general preference in our society for male children. There is also evidence that male children receive more rewards in our society. Examination of the educational system also reveals greater concern for males. For example, much more research has been done on the causes and cures of dyslexia—a reading disfunction that appears much more frequently in males—than on mathematical "dysfunctions" that are more frequently found in females. The male-oriented content of elementary school readers has been defended on the basis of greater male disinterest in reading (Stacey, Bereaud, & Daniels, 1974), but few attempts have been made to feminize the content of arithmetic texts. In Chapter 2 we documented the extent of sex role stereotypes in both children's and adult media. Each of these examples indicates the greater importance attached to males and male behavior in our society.

It may be argued that sex role inequality is greater in the United States than it is in many other industrialized Western countries. Studies directly measuring negative attitudes toward male–female equality show more negative responses among Americans and Canadians than among Germans, Norwegians, or residents of the British Isles (Luckey & Nass, 1969). For example, in response to the question "Do you support the idea that individuals and society function best if masculine and feminine roles in life remain essentially different though equal?" 86.5 percent of the U.S. residents said yes. The figures were 91 percent for Canadians versus 67 percent, 58 percent, and 45.5 percent for Britain, Germany, and Norway, respectively. European men and women agreed with each other more than North American men and women and were more sure that there should be equal education for the sexes. The largest discrepancies between the responses of women and men were found in the United States.

Nearly twice as many men from the United States and Canada (60%) as European men thought that many bright girls consciously downgrade their career ambitions for fear that they might hurt their chances for marriage. More European than North American women (28% vs. 15%) believed that they could live happily unmarried. American males were also more likely to endorse the double standard for sexual relationships than males from other countries. The discrepancy between the sexes among Americans in this belief was larger than that found for any other question or sample. Spence and Helmreich (1972) have also found that there is greater disagreement among men and women in the United States on questions relating to social mores than on those relating to purely economic matters.

Differences Between the Attitudes of Women and Men

Several studies have indicated that men and women in this country have very different attitudes toward traditional and nontraditional sex roles. In one large-scale study of people in New York City, it was found that although social class, race, age, and the like were all related to attitudes about sex roles, the major determinant was the sex of the respondent (Yorburg & Arafat, 1975). Significant differences between the sexes persisted throughout all other categories and in almost every item on the questionnaire. Men consistently opted for less sex role equality than women, although most people did indicate that they preferred more equality than currently exists.

Attitudes Toward Sex Roles and Other Demographic Variables

Single women who have not yet had direct experience in the traditional female role appear to be more likely to idealize it than married women (Travis, 1976). They tend to see marriage and children as the most important life experiences for a woman, to have lower career commitments, and to plan to alter their career plans significantly in order to accommodate children. Education appears to alter women's attitudes in this regard. College seniors are more liberal about sex roles than women in lower grades (Stein & Weston, 1976). Students in business and education were more conservative than those in other majors.

Attitudes Toward Sex Roles and Personality Characteristics

Negative attitudes toward women appear to be related to defensiveness in either sex (Albright & Chang, 1976). Independently of defensiveness, males were again found to be, in general, more negative than females. More dogmatic individuals of either sex also support feminism less, with the effect somewhat stronger for males (Whitehead & Tawes, 1976). Older and less educated women are also less supportive. Neither age nor education level had any effect on males' attitudes toward feminism. One study has indicated that males who are strongly antifeminist have lower self-esteem than more egalitarian males (Miller, 1974), while another researcher has noted that negative attitudes toward females seem to exist almost universally independently of other characteristics of the males studied (Goldberg, 1974). He suggests that this misogyny represents a social judgment rather than individual attitudinal differences among the males studied.

Both nonfeminist and conservative sexual attitudes independently correlate with antihomosexual attitudes (Minnigerode, 1976). Antihomosexual individuals had more stereotyped attitudes toward women and defined acceptable heterosexual behaviors more narrowly. The degree of psychological androgyny that they themselves possessed had no effect on their attitudes.

Expression of negative attitudes toward nontraditional roles for women may actually be an optimistic picture of the extent of sexism in our society. For example, Carol Tavris (1973), in a large-scale survey of readers of *Psychology Today*, a magazine designed to attract well-educated, affluent, liberal readers, found that although most of the males in her sample endorsed "women's liberation," few indicated that they contributed in any real way to the liberation of any particular woman. They indicated that the major share of household tasks were still the responsibility of their female partner. In a survey of male undergraduates at Columbia University it was found that they endorsed a woman's participation in a career only if it did not interfere with her "other" activities—caring for husband and family (Komarovsky, 1973).

SEXISM AND OUR SOCIETY: WHY?

Sexual Power

It is easier to document the widespread existence of sexist attitudes in our society than to explain why they exist. One intriguing theory links male power with concern for male genitalia (Eichler, 1975). In a survey of a number of primitive societies a positive correlation was found between male superiority and concern with the protection and covering of the male genitals. This connection explains why a self-assertive feminist might be labeled a "ball breaker" or a "castrating bitch." The most recent overt connection between power and male sexual fears in modern society involves attributions about increases in male impotence. Some psychiatrists (Ginsberg, Frosch, & Shapiro, 1972) believe this "new impotence" is explained by the new sexual demands wives make on their husbands. They see men as increasingly concerned with the question "Will I have to maintain an erection in order to maintain a relationship?" Queries such as "Who is sex for?" and "Who will call the shots?" indicate that dissemination of information about women's capacity for multiple orgasms has threatened men.

It is possible to link this male sexual fear with other sexually taboo areas such as those involving blood and menstruation. The widespread misperceptions and prohibitions surrounding menstruation were discussed in Chapter 9. It is noteworthy that "menstrual taboos are unusual in that they appear to reflect hardly any solicitude for the safety of the menstruating woman herself" (Stephens, 1961, p. 95). Such taboos are not simply by-products of primitive societies. A recent survey indicates that about 50 percent of American men and women subscribe to the practice of sexual abstention during menstruation (Paige, 1977). Observance of this custom is strongly associated with traditional attitudes toward sex roles and marriage.

One can argue that our tradition reflects great concern with sexual control by all-powerful others. Analysis of the psychological themes of fairy tales reveals many portraits of domineering parents (particularly female) and rejected children. Andrea Dworkin (1974), in her poetic book *Woman Hating,* discusses many of the roles women play in Western fairy tales, and their implications. In particular, females are especially desirable when they are asleep. "Good" men are all too likely to fall under the power of a powerful female and harm their children. "The good woman must be possessed. The bad woman must be killed, or punished. Both must be nullified" (Dworkin, 1974, p. 48).

Social Power

One can also argue that the prevalence of sexism in our society is related to our societal concern with competition and aggressiveness. Children in the United States are more likely to be rivalrous than their Mexican peers (Kagan & Madsen, 1972a). In one study children were permitted to take marbles from the top or bottom half of the left or right side of a choice card. (See Figure 15.1.) The card contained rivalrous and nonrivalrous choices. For example, if the child chose from the right side of card 1 (the rivalrous condition), she or he might take two marbles, leaving one for the opponent. If she or

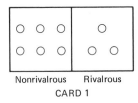   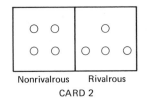

Figure 15.1. Example of the stimuli used to measure rivalry in children. The child can choose either the right or left half of the card. If he or she chooses the left side, each participant (the subject and the alleged opponent) will receive three marbles. If the right side is chosen, the child gets two marbles, leaving one for the opponent. Thus, the right side is the rivalrous choice—the child gives up an absolute gain in order to gain relative to the opponent. (From S. Kagan and M. C. Madsen, "Rivalry in Anglo-American and Mexican Children of Two Ages," *Journal of Personality and Social Psychology*, 1972, *24*, 214–220. Copyright 1972 by the American Psychological Association. Reprinted by permission.)

he chose from the left side, three marbles would be gained, leaving three for the opponent (the nonrivalrous choice). Hence, the child would have to give up an absolute gain in order to gain relative to the partner. Anglo-American children made significantly more rivalrous choices than Mexican children, and these cultural differences tended to increase with age. More Anglo-American boys than girls were rivalrous, although there was no sex difference for the Mexican children. With increasing age, an increasing percentage of Anglo-American boys always acted to lower the outcome of their partner, and they were even willing to take a loss in absolute gains to do so. Rivalry appears to be a value for which the Anglo-American male, in particular, is willing to sacrifice. These results parallel findings by the same researchers on interpersonal conflict. While Mexican children avoid conflict, Anglo-American children enter conflict even when doing so would be irrational in terms of their own goals (Kagan & Madsen, 1972b).

Violence and Sexual Rigidity

Aggressiveness (if it does not become too great) is valued in males in our society. Across societies, there appears to be a positive relationship between the degree of sexual rigidity (and inequality) and the level of aggressiveness present in that society (McConahay & McConahay, 1977). We do not know the direction of causality in this relationship. Violence may generate more rigid and unequal sex roles in an effort to defend against aggression. Or excessive aggression may generate strains that foster rigidity in sex roles. In any case both violence and sex role inequality are high in the United States relative to other industrialized nations. These cross-cultural data indicate that the connection is not fortuitous.

The same study also indicates that there is no relationship between sexual permissiveness within a society and the amount of violence in which its members engage. As discussed in Chapter 10, these data support the lack of relationship between sexual liberalness and sex role liberation. It is likely that negative attitudes toward women's nontraditional activities reflect fear of a loss of social more than sexual power. As noted in Chapter 13, men who express the most negative attitudes about women's successes are those who have the most to lose in competition with them. This issue will be raised later in terms of social mechanisms for the control of threatening groups.

RAPE AND POWER

Rape and social attitudes toward rape represent an area where concerns about sexual and social power come together. Thus it may well serve as an area in which the mechanisms by which sex roles are institutionalized in our society can be better understood. Rape may be a manifestation of irrational male fear of women. Such powerful fear of women has been christened the "Coatlicue complex" after the Aztec mother of the gods—the goddess of the earth and of death (Sherman, 1975). She is often represented with human hearts strung about her neck and with a skirt of writhing serpents. The goddess Kali of India, with her necklace of human skulls, is similar. These goddesses may symbolize the power of life and death that each mother holds over her infant. Many rapists have highly passive attitudes toward their mothers, although they express violent, aggressive impulses against other women.

It is becoming increasingly clear that rape is primarily a crime of violence and not one of sex; that is, the motivation is primarily to hurt, dominate, and degrade women, not to satisfy sexual desire. Although careful empirical studies of the motivations of large numbers of men who rape are lacking, there is some evidence that convicted sex offenders do not constitute a group that is significantly more disturbed than males who commit other violent crimes (Griffin, 1971). More than 50 percent of all rapes committed by a single individual are planned and involve individuals who are at least somewhat acquainted with each other (Amir, 1971).

The incidence of rape may be determined in part by the ideology of a group or individual about the nature of human sexuality and the place of women (Sherman, 1975). Whether or not a man rapes may depend more on his opportunities than on his motivations. For example, researchers found an increase in rapes in Toronto during a long bus strike during which women hitched rides in the absence of public transportation (Geller, 1977). Susan Brownmiller (1975) has amply documented the enormous number of rapes committed by so-called normal men during periods of warfare. Men are rarely raped even under conditions of tremendous social upheaval. Janeway (1974), however, does point out that under prison conditions it is the weak, low-status male who is raped.

Feminists have indicted rape as a social vehicle for keeping "women in their place." A widely quoted anecdote in this regard concerns Golda Meier when she was prime minister of Israel. Her predominantly male cabinet, concerned about the rapidly rising number of rapes in Tel Aviv, suggested a curfew for the women of that city. Meier is said to have responded, "Why not a curfew for the men? They are the ones doing the raping!"

Social Attitude Toward Rape

Rape has often been viewed as the responsibility of the victim. She is thought to have been seductive or blamed for being in the wrong place at the wrong time. It is interesting, therefore, that the social institution that is structured for heterosexual contact in our society—the date—is very likely to put the woman in the wrong place at the wrong time. Seduction based on the use of psychological or physical force is quite common among dating couples (Schultz, 1976). Nevertheless rapists are much more likely to be prosecuted if they rape someone who is old or is otherwise considered unattractive.

The rape victim is more likely to be faulted the more respectable she is deemed to be (Jones & Aronson, 1973). College students reading case reports of rape trials faulted the victim more when she was married or a virgin (most respectable) than when she was a divorcee. They also sentenced the defendant to a longer imprisonment for the rape of a married woman than for the rape of a divorcee. Women were just as severe in attributing fault to the victim as men were. There was no significant difference in the degree of fault attributed to a victim between cases in which the rape was actual and those in which the rape was an attempt. The characteristics of the victim apparently wholly determined how much she was blamed for the crime.

It has been said that rape is the only crime for which the victim is on trial. She becomes the victim not only of physical assault but also of a set of negative attitudes imposed upon her by society.

Somehow the woman must have done, said, or worn something to precipitate the rape. It is noteworthy that a recent study has indicated that males view females as being more causally responsible for rape than females do (Selby, Calhoun, & Brock, 1977).

Internalization of Social Attitudes

Women respond to these generalized beliefs about rape by feeling guilty, ashamed, and responsible for being raped (Adleman, 1976). They may continue to refer to themselves as rape victims rather than as women, wives, sociologists, or what have you for many months after they are raped. Women who are raped are reported to experience an intense feeling of loss of control, autonomy, power, and self-esteem. Rape is, indeed, "the ultimate intrusion into the inner space of a person" (Bard & Ellison, 1974).

The experience of being raped may be particularly destructive of a woman's relationships with males (Schultz, 1975). She no longer trusts her companions or her environment. Victims may stop dressing attractively, sleep only with the lights on, go places only in groups, or begin carrying weapons. The most severe dysfunctions appear to occur when the victim was intimate with the rapist before the attack. This, of course, increases her culpability in the eyes of society (and perhaps herself) and confirms her perception that the world is a threatening and untrustworthy place.

Rape as a Form of Social Control

Until modern times rape was treated legally as a crime against property—the property of the woman's father or husband (Dworkin, 1976). Men are not perceived as either physically or sexually assaulting their wives. Although few men are prosecuted for rape, young females are especially likely to be imprisoned for "sexual delinquency" (Brodsky, 1973). Fear of sexual assault may be used to maintain tighter control over female conduct than over male conduct. As Goffman (1963a) has pointed out in this regard, standards of formality in dress are different for males and females in our society. A man who appears in public with hair tousled, tie loosened, and a cigarette in his lips seems less offensive than a woman similarly arrayed. Informality in women seems to be more readily seen as a license for sexual abuse by males.

SEXISM IN THE WORK WORLD

Although sexist attitudes and discrimination against women does not take such drastic forms in most social institutions, there is reason

"OKAY, SO YOU KNOW A LOT MORE THAN ME. TELL YA WHAT I'M GONNA DO...WHEN I GET OLDER, I'LL HIRE YOU AS MY *SECKATARY!*"

Figure 15.2. ("Dennis the Menace," by Hank Ketcham, © 1976 Field Newspaper Syndicate T.M.R.)

to believe that women are also "out of place" in the work world and suffer social penalties for this "disobedience" with social norms. A variety of negative stereotypes about women in the work force exist. Working women are seen as less committed to their careers, less concerned about the financial rewards of their jobs (and, conversely, more interested in their social rewards), and more likely to leave their jobs than comparable men (Laws, 1978). They are viewed as fitting the managerial model less than comparable men (Schein, 1973; Strache, 1976). (See Figure 15.2.)

Subtle as well as obvious sex role inequalities exist. For example, male supervisors are seen as more effective than females when they reward their subordinates whereas relationships between

Table 15.1 PROBLEMS OF FAMILY–JOB CONFLICT

1. *Travel:* This incident involved evaluation of an applicant for a position requiring extensive travel. It consisted of the following memorandum:

MEMORANDUM TO: Executive Vice President
FROM: Corporate Recruiting Office

Pursuant to our recent discussion with you about the need to recruit a purchasing manager for the new operation, we have developed a set of brief job specifications and have located some candidates who may be suitable for the opening. Will you please review the attached resume and give us your evaluation?

JOB REQUIREMENTS FOR PURCHASING MANAGER

The major responsibilities of the new purchasing manager will be to purchase fabrics, materials, and clothing accessories (buttons, belts, buckles, zippers, etc.) for the production of finished goods.

For the most part, the purchasing manager will have to travel around the country visiting wholesalers and attending conventions and showings. The person hired for this position should have a knowledge of the quality of raw materials, and the ability to establish a "fair" price for goods purchased in large quantities. The person selected for this position will have to travel at least twenty days each month.

RESUME

NAME: Mrs. Karen Wood
POSITION APPLIED FOR: Purchasing Manager
AGE: 35   PLACE OF BIRTH: Cleveland, Ohio
MARITAL STATUS: Married, four children ages 11, 8, 7, and 4
EDUCATION: B.S. in Business Administration, The Ohio State University
RELEVANT WORK EXPERIENCE: One year as purchasing trainee, Campbell Textile, Inc.
    Ten years experience in various retail clothing stores, in sales, buying and general management.
INTERVIEWER'S REMARKS: Good personal appearance, seems earnest and convincing.
    Good recommendations from previous employers.

2. *Moving:* This incident depicted a conflict between professional careers of husband and wife. It consisted of the following memorandum:

MEMORANDUM TO: Executive Vice President
FROM: Joseph Schmidt, Computer Operations

As you know, Rachael Cooper is a computer operator in my section. She has played a key role in computerizing our inventory system. Recently, Rachael's husband was offered a very attractive managerial position with a large retail organization on the West Coast. They are seriously considering the move. I told Rachael that she has a very bright future with our organization and it would be a shame for her to pull out just as we are expanding our operations. I sure would hate to lose her now. What do you think we should do about the situation?

3. *Promotion:* This incident depicted a conflict between job demands and family responsibilities. It consisted of the following memorandum:

Table 15.1   *Continued*

MEMORANDUM TO: Executive Vice President
FROM: Mark Taylor—Corporate Personnel Office
SUBJECT: Promotion of Margaret Adams
We are at the point where we must make a decision on the promotion of Margaret Adams of our personnel staff. Margaret is one of the most competent employees in the corporate personnel office and I am convinced that she is capable of handling even more responsibility as Bennett Division Personnel Director. However, I am not altogether certain that she is willing to subordinate time with her family to time on the job, to the extent that may be required with Bennett. I have had the opportunity to explore with her the general problem of family life. She believes that her first duty is to her family, and she should manage her time accordingly. This viewpoint has not affected her performance in the past, but it could be a problem in the more demanding role as head of Personnel with the Bennett Division. What do you think we should do?

4. *Child Care:* This incident depicted a situation of conflict between career demands and child-care responsibilities. The memorandum was as follows:

MEMORANDUM TO: Executive Vice President
FROM: Richard Bell, Accounting Manager
SUBJECT: Request for Leave of Absence
Ralph Brown, an accountant in the main office has requested one month's leave beginning next week. He has already taken his vacation this year. He wants the leave in order to take care of his three young children. The day care arrangements the Browns had made for the period covered by this request suddenly fell through, and they have been unable to make other arrangements satisfying their high standards. Ralph's wife is principal of the junior high school and she cannot possibly get time off during the next month.

The problem is that Ralph is the only person experienced in handling the "cost" section in the accounting department. We would either have to transfer an accountant with the same experience from the Richardson Division or else train a replacement for only one month's work. I have urged Ralph to reconsider this request, but he insists on going ahead with it.

I have also checked with the legal department and we do not have to hold the position open for Ralph if he insists on taking the whole month off. I would appreciate if you could give me your decision on this as soon as possible.

SOURCE: From B. Rosen et al., "Dual-Career Marital Adjustment: Potential Effects of Discriminatory Managerial Attitudes," *Journal of Marriage and the Family*, 37, (1975):565–572, Copyright 1975 by the National Council on Family Relations, Reprinted by permission.

supervisors and subordinates of opposite sexes are seen ·as most effective when their transactions are conducted in a friendly–dependent style (Rosen & Jerdee, 1973). Undergraduate business majors are particularly likely to evaluate female applicants as unsuitable for "demanding" managerial positions (Rosen & Jerdee,

1974a). Real male administrators (95 bank managers) have also been shown to discriminate against female employees in simulated personnel decisions involving promotion, development, and supervision (Rosen & Jerdee, 1974b). A young, highly promotable female was preferred only slightly more than an older, unpromotable male. Women, on the other hand, were more likely to be discriminated "for" in personnel decisions involving a leave of absence in order to care for young children. Both pro- and anti-female personnel decisions reveal attitudes about the limits of sex roles for men and women alike.

When problems of family–job conflict are depicted and the sex of the employee involved is manipulated (see Table 15.1), managers express less confidence in the ability of women to balance home and career responsibilities (Rosen, Jerdee, & Prestwich, 1975). They do not expect that a career woman's husband should sacrifice for the sake of his wife's career. More specifically, positions involving travel were viewed as more appropriate for the married man than for the married woman; women were expected to move to foster their husbands' acquisition of a better job, but not vice versa; women more than men were expected to attend social functions dictated by business to assist their spouses' careers; and women who noted that "my first duty is to my family" were evaluated less favorably than men who make the same statement.

Discrimination against women in the work world appears to be closely related to certain kinds of challenging jobs, particularly those involving high demands for interpersonal aggressiveness and decisive action or potential home–career conflicts (Rosen & Jerdee, 1975b). Females will *not* be treated like males when job requirements are perceived to conflict with presumed social and family requirements. In contrast, women's performance may be evaluated more highly than men's when the job that is being evaluated is a low-level, unskilled one (Hamner, Kim, Baird, & Bigoness, 1974). Women are perceived as operating under considerably more internal and external constraints than men, and they may be penalized if they violate expectations about these constraints.

THE DUAL-CAREER FAMILY

While we discussed some aspects of the dual-career family in Chapter 11, this kind of relationship is particularly relevant for understanding the difficulties involved in resolving perceived sex role conflicts in our society. It is important for our understanding of the interaction between sex and social institutions. A dual-career family can be defined as a social unit in which both husband and wife hold jobs that are highly salient to their identity, have a developmental sequence (i.e., represent a ladder of advancement), and require a high degree of commitment (Rapoport & Rapoport, 1971). Such a family unit is distinguished from the "two-earner" family, which is characterized by gainful but not necessarily permanent or meaningful employment of the wife.

Even dual-career families—in which the woman is engaged in a career that is highly fulfilling to her—do not provide a model of sex role equality. Studies of such families indicate that the higher the husband's occupational prestige, the greater the demands to migrate and the greater the opportunity for employment in his field that may be found elsewhere (Duncan & Perrucci, 1976). Men with high occupational prestige, therefore, are very likely to move out of state. The relative "fullness" of the wife's work role, however, as measured by her occupational prestige and relative contribution to the family income, does not affect the family's migration probability. Nor do her opportunities for employment elsewhere. In fact interstate migration reduced the probability of continued employment among women who were employed before the move.

Empirical studies of dual-career couples have concentrated on couples in which wife and husband are both employed in a college setting, for a number of reasons: (1) Men and women in the same academic field are likely to meet in graduate school and to marry; (2) college teaching is the profession with the largest percentage of women employed full time; (3) college teachers are likely to indicate that they believe in sexually egalitarian work–marriage arrangements. Nevertheless examination of dual-career couples shows us something about the limitations posed by societal mechanisms that affect the sexes unequally.

In one study of psychologist pairs (Bryson, Bryson, Licht, & Licht, 1976) it was found that males (whether or not they were married to a psychologist) were more likely to be employed than either psychologist wives or control females. The psychologist wives of psychologists were more likely than any other group to be unemployed (husbands, 1%; wives, 10.6%; male controls, 2.7%; female controls, 4.8%). Their husbands were found to be the most productive group in terms of books and papers published or presented. The wives exceeded female controls (psychologists not married to a man in the same field) in all categories and were essentially similar to male controls. Nevertheless they earned substantially less than these males and less than female controls, despite their greater professional productivity. Geographic restrictions on their employment appear to account for this difference.

While there were major institutional restrictions on hiring a husband and wife in the same field, differential assumptions about the relative value of the husband's and wife's careers and unequal division of responsibility for domestic activities also played a role in the unequal professional development of these couples. Wives indicated that they were more willing to make sacrifices for their husbands' careers than they expected their husbands to make for them. The wives also appeared to place more restrictions on themselves than their husbands might expect them to. More husbands claimed that they would accept another position only if their wives received a satisfactory offer than the wives, in reality, expected.

The only stereotypically female activity for which professional wives did not bear an absolute majority of responsibility was housecleaning, but this was because outside help was employed rather than because their husbands shared the responsibility. Husbands, in contrast, had majority responsibility for only one activity—household repairs. Males who were not married to women in psychology did not differ from these dual-career husbands in degree of responsibility for household chores. Data on responsibility for domestic chores seem to be similar for other professional women, such as physicians. (See Figure 15.3.) One should also note the differences between the kinds of household tasks for which men and women had majority responsibility. The tasks for which women are primarily responsible are repetitive and time-consuming and cannot easily be put off. Household repairs, on the other hand, may require a single major effort that can be put off.

Professional wives reported less satisfaction with their careers than any other group in all categories except the opportunity to interact with colleagues, in which the female controls reported the least satisfaction. Married female controls were also less satisfied with their freedom to pursue long-term career goals and with their treatment by administrators as professionals similar in competence to their husbands. The researchers suggest that some dissatisfaction stems from the constraints imposed by marriage rather than from being a member of a professional pair. Nevertheless it is interesting that husbands in dual-career families in which both members of the couple are in the same profession appear to gain relative to men who are not married to women in the same profession, while their wives loss relative to control women.

Exploration of the mechanisms that lead to such inequities in career development suggest that job seeking in such dual-career families may be more in the nature of a forced choice, despite egalitarian intentions (Wallston, Foster, & Berger, 1978). Often only one job was available when the final choice had to be made. Institutional constraints appear to be a major impediment to egalitarian job

75% of Women Physicians In Detroit Survey Report They Do Housework, Too

DETROIT, Oct. 29 (AP)—Three of four women physicians surveyed in the Detroit area said they took care of all their families' cooking, shopping, child care and money management in addition to their patients' health.

The survey, reported in the current Journal of the American Medical Association, also indicated that the women physicians earned less than their male counterparts and rarely held high-status positions in their profession.

Dr. Marilyn Heins of the Wayne State University School of Medicine and Sue Smock of the school's Center for Urban Studies surveyed 87 Detroit-area women who had been trained as doctors.

Two-thirds of the women said, however, that they had domestic help one or two days a week to assist with laundry and cleaning chores. The remaining third said they did all their own housework.

The average family income among women doctors, most of whom have working husbands, was lower than the average family income of male doctors, few of whom had working wives, the study said. Forty-three percent of the women doctors are married to doctors.

"I don't think there's any question that there is sex discrimination in medicine," Dr. Heins said.

She said the survey findings contradicted an assumption held by some medical educators that training women for the profession was a waste of time because they tended to leave to care for their families.

The study indicated that 84 percent of the women were doing medical work and 90 percent were working full-time at some job.

The researchers said only 7 percent were not working for reasons related to sex. The others not working were physically disabled or had retired.

Figure 15.3. (Reprinted by permission of the Associated Press.)

attainment by dual-career couples. Many respondents reported that a job was extremely difficult to find and that the job market was the major reason for not getting better jobs. The women in these couples were more likely to perceive sex-discriminatory policies than the men. In in-depth interviews about the job-seeking experiences of 15 dual-career couples, 61 percent of the husbands obtained their job first (Berger, Foster, & Wallston, 1975). Twice as many women as men (82% vs. 40%) said that they would opt for a nontraditional job-seeking strategy the next time they looked for jobs. It was clear from the interviews that the whole job-seeking experience had placed a great deal of stress on the marriage. The dilemma that is specific to dual-career couples is that the person who is closest to you—your spouse—is also the person who is standing in the way of your career.

WOMEN AS PROFESSIONALS

Institutional barriers impede the advancement of women even when they are not married to a man in the same field. Although substantial numbers of women become college teachers (37% of all faculty members under 30 are women), many of these women are aware of a lack of relationship between performance and rewards in institutions of higher education. In one large-scale survey of college faculty members all over the country, 68 percent of the women agreed and 60 percent of the men disagreed with the statement "There is no way to determine what is the 'best' academically. 'Meritocracy' is a smokescreen behind which faculty have hidden in promoting discriminatory practices" (Ladd & Lipset, 1976).

A number of findings support these women's perceptions that sexual inequities exist between men and women employed at institutions of higher education. For example, in 1973 the Task Force on the Status of Women in Psychology reported that although women account for 25 percent or more of the doctorates currently awarded in psychology and about the same percentage of members of the American Psychological Association, they (1) form a disproportionately small fraction of those employed by high-status institutions, (2) are most frequently found in low (instructor–assistant professor) academic ranks, (3) have lower salaries than comparable men even when rank and number of years of employment are equated, (4) account for an extremely small fraction of those administering programs or supervising graduate training, and (5) are less often found in regular tenure track appointments as opposed to part-time quasi-positions.

Barriers to Sex-Equal Achievement in Academia

It is frequently stated that the reason women do not rise in academia is because they do not deserve to do so (i.e., they do not fulfill the requirements of academic positions as well as men do). It is stressed, in particular, that women do less research than men. Most of the sex-specific inequities cited earlier are attributed to this single factor. In fact elitism is often stated as a *prima facie* rationale for maintaining the sexual status quo (Robinson, 1973).

While it may have been true in the past that academic women published less than academic men (Bernard, 1964), recent research indicates that some women Ph.D.'s may be outpublishing comparable men (Loeb & Ferber, 1973). Moreover, it is not useful to state that women publish less because they are women. If we hope to move closer to psychological explanations of scholarly productivity, we must be able to predict or explain why particular individuals of any sex publish less than others.

A task force of the American Psychological Association's Division 35 (Psychology of Women) has been examining some of the structural and internal barriers to women doing research (O'Connell, Alpert, Richardson, Ruble, Rotter, & Unger, 1978). For example, a variety of training barriers to women doing research exist (N. Rotter, 1977). Women's research contributions have remained largely invisible to the psychological world partly because of the convention of using initials rather than names when research is cited. Since research is perceived to be a "male" enterprise, women are not as likely as men to develop role models for doing research. Since the overall percentage of women Ph.D.'s employed by universities is 15.9 percent (and this percentage decreases for higher-status institutions and graduate programs), women are also not as likely to encounter female role models as professors during their tenure as students. Women are also especially unlikely to be found in the psychological fields that are most traditionally research oriented (experimental, physiological, or social psychology).

Reinforcement for research activities comes partly in the form of recognition through publication and paper presentation. In her survey of graduate students in the Southeast, Brodsky (1974) reports equal encouragement for males and females to publish research and present papers. However, males (41%) more frequently reported that they were offered authorship for research participation than females (19%). The involvement of individuals in research may also be influenced by rehearsal of their role as researchers. In a sample of job applicants for a position in social psychology, males more than females (77.8% vs. 66.7%) held research assistantships, while the reverse held for teaching assistantships (McNeel, McKillip, Di-Miceli, Van Tuinen, Reid, & Barrett, 1975). The sex difference for research assistantships increased when the quality of the graduate department was taken into account. Females from less highly rated departments reported much less frequent holding of research assistantships (41%) compared to the other three groups combined (62%). If the woman as researcher contradicts the stereotyped role of women, many graduate departments may unconsciously be biased in their assignment of assistantships. There is evidence that undergraduate psychology students view the competent female researcher as less feminine than her incompetent counterpart (Piacente, 1974). It remains to be proven whether their professional mentors feel the same way.

Females more than males are likely to perceive sex discrimination in the attitudes of faculty members (Brodsky, 1974; Freeman, 1975). When one looks at the types of encouragement received from faculty, males report more invitations than females to accompany faculty on professional trips, more offers of authorship for research participation, and more encouragement to meet scholars outside the department. On occasion such discrimination can take more overt form. An analysis of the contents of letters of recommendation to graduate school found that those describing a female applicant were more likely to focus on her physical and personality characteristics, in contrast to her performance capabilities (Lunneborg & Lillie, 1973). Letters describing presumably comparable males focused more on objective achievement.

Women describe discouragement of their professional aspirations much more frequently than men do. Women frequently report that the seriousness of their career plans is questioned by faculty (Freeman, 1975). Male students report receiving more positive encouragement from significant others than female students do. Jo Freeman suggests that it is possible for a graduate school to discriminate against women without really trying. She has formulated the "null environment hypothesis" in this regard. An academic situation that neither encourages nor discourages students of either sex becomes inherently discriminatory against women because it fails to take into account the differentiating socialization environments from which women and men come. Because females have been socialized to expect low achievement from themselves and to rely on sources external to themselves for their self-esteem, women need to be actively encouraged. Women report, however, not the presence of negative feedback about their progress and performance but the failure of institutions or professors to respond to them at all.

The Relationship Between Achievement and Reward

While the evidence that women are always less productive than men is unclear, the evidence that they receive fewer scholarly or financial rewards for their productivity is much clearer. Several studies examining the relationship among sex, various indexes of faculty productivity, and rewards within the academic system find that publication is a more significant predictor of academic rank and salary for males than for females (Astin & Bayer, 1973; Loeb & Ferber, 1973). Men who publish advance more rapidly than women with the same rate of publication. "Sex is a better predictor of rank than such factors as number of years since completion of education, number of years employed at present institution, or number of books published" (Astin & Bayer, 1973, p. 339). In turn, rank predicts salary and tenure.

Different factors predict professional success for women and men. The type of institution where the individual got his or her degree and where he or she teaches is a more important predictor of advancement for men than for women. Number of children contributes to success for men but restricts it for women. For women, advancement is enhanced by being single or divorced (although never being married is better), teaching at smaller public institutions, and teaching in the health fields. As in many other areas (cf. Alexander & Eckland, 1974), standards for performance by women are less relevant to their advancement than standards for performance by men. Women may be correct in their assumption that their advancement is often due to luck.

Access to Formal and Informal Academic Networks

Much advancement in the professional world comes through access to formal and informal networks. Predominantly male faculties in graduate and professional schools are reluctant to accept female students as protégées (Epstein, 1970; Schwartz & Lever, 1973). Part of their reluctance may be due to concern with potential sexualization of the relationship as perceived by faculty wives, but male mentors may also be concerned that their research goals will not be forwarded by female junior associates. Because they lack male sponsors, women are not as likely to be recruited into professional networks as are men.

Psychology as a social institution is a male enterprise. The percentage of women editors and consulting editors of journals sponsored by the American Psychological Association is considerably smaller than the percentage of women members of the Association (Tennov, 1975). Women are not even represented as editors as often as one would expect from their numbers as authors (Teghtsoonian, 1974). When men and women do collaborative research the male is more frequently the senior author. Even in areas in which women outnumber men (such as child or school psychology), men are more likely to be the authors of articles found in both prestigious handbooks and popular magazines about psychology. This process appears to be similar to that of using males, almost exclusively, as the voice-over in radio and TV commercials. Males are assumed to have greater credibility as experts.

Recruitment into collegial networks seems to be based on subjective criteria. Men do the selecting, and they select other men. Women involve themselves in professional organizations in their scholarly disciplines less than men and hold a smaller number of decision-making positions within them (Morlock, 1973). Since perceived competence in a discipline is often related to visibility, the relative absence of women produces circular effects. Women see less reward for getting involved, fail to be drawn in, and perpetuate the relative lack of women for another academic generation.

A variety of informal mechanisms may be used to exclude women from the "male club." Women Ph.D.'s who are full-time contributors to their profession may be denied many informal signs of belonging and recognition.

> These women report that even on such daily activities as finding someone to have lunch or take a coffee break with, or finding someone with whom she can chew over an idea, or on larger issues such as finding a partner with whom she can share a research interest, the women Ph.D. has a special and lower status. [Simon, Clark, & Galway, 1967, p. 236]

Women are less secure about their status and less willing to protest being left out (White, 1970). They are more likely than men to attribute their exclusion to personal rather than sociocultural reasons. However, recent informal discussions within organizations such as the Association for Women in Psychology indicates that such exclusion has been encountered by almost every women professional.

THE SOCIALIZATION OF STATUS INEQUALITY

Women have been relatively unwilling to protest their exclusion from professional networks, for a number of reasons. First, since they have remained rather isolated from each other both within and between institutions (partly because of their small numbers), they may be unaware of the actual extent of institutional discrimination. In one study of a major academic institution it was found that women faculty members perceived a much smaller amount of sex discrimination than the actual data would appear to warrant (Liss, 1975). Within departments, women tended to state categorically that there was no sex discrimination although statistical data documented inequities of salary, promotion, rank, and tenure based on sex. Such women may have internalized the academic norm that merit is the basis of academic status. Qualities of intelligence, reason, objectivity, professionalism, and justice are associated with scholarship. Since personnel decisions are confidential, a kind of "pluralistic ignorance" prevails. It is noteworthy that the women who appear to be least discriminated against, those who are highest in the academic hierarchy, perceive the most discrimination. These women have access to more information than the majority of those at the lowest rungs of the academic ladder.

While lack of knowledge that sexism is a social rather than a personal event probably accounts for the unwillingness of many professional women to acknowledge sex discrimination, some women professionals seem to identify completely with the male viewpoint. Women who have achieved good jobs and social success but show no sympathy for younger women working toward such goals or with the current women's movement have been dubbed "queen bees" (Staines, Tavris, & Jayaratne, 1974). Women who deny the social realities of women's inequality tend to fall into two main categories in terms of psychological processes (Keiffer & Cullen, 1974). They either deny that membership in a particular sexual category is relevant to professional life or aggressively attack women because lack of professional achievement is their own fault. An example of a comment by a woman in the former category is the following:

> What forms of discrimination that exist in psychology tend to be so subtle and of such a nature, in my opinion, that it is a waste of time and psychic energy to schedule symposia, develop questionnaires, and in other ways make formal issue of the matter. A more appropriate procedure is for individual women to ignore the question of sex in a feminist sense and to go about their business of becoming reasonable human beings and competent contributors to their profession. [Keiffer & Cullen, 1974, pp. 26–27]

One comment, which revealed self-hate as well as aggression, seemed to be particularly poignant:

The young should be willing to grow before they reap rewards of
growth . . . If he shoots the arrow straighter than I do—more power to
him. He does it. For myself, I'll carry my little bottle of painkillers and
I'll have my uses too. [Keiffer & Cullen, 1974, p. 29]

Although only 24 out of 209 responses to this survey could be
classified as unfavorable, they tended to come from women who had
succeeded and were functioning as "academic gatekeepers." An
academic gatekeeper is a person who occupies a decision-making
position that determines who will enter a system and/or whether
they will move up in it. A few token women may be used as
gatekeepers to keep other women out (Epstein, 1970). Judith Laws
(1975) has provided a model for how such token women might be
produced. She characterizes American society as a gender–class
system wherein tokenism represents a form of interclass mobility.
Two role partners, "sponsor" and "token," are needed to sustain
tokenism; the token is a member of the inferior class and the sponsor
a member of the dominant class. Although the woman is technically
qualified and has sufficient credentials for participation, she is an
outsider. It is the sponsor who assumes the major responsibility for
socializing her into the specific niche reserved for her. Sex role
pressures are communicated powerfully in the relationship between sponsor and token.

Women who are likely to become tokens have a history of close
relationships with members of the dominant group. They are
trained toward attributes that characterize the dominant group, and
they adopt its standards. The process is likely to occur in the professions, since they are dominated by men, as are all the training procedures by which one enters these professions. In terms of material
rewards, men have more to offer women within them than most
women do. Both token and sponsor agree that the token is unusually
competent. Assertion of the token's excellence bolsters the premise
of meritocracy on which the academic reward system is supposedly
based. Thus the token is likely to perceive that her exceptionalism
justifies her inclusion in the dominant class and that she has escaped
her membership in the inferior one.

As mentioned earlier, however, the perceptions of members of
two groups may not agree with each other. For the sponsor, as well
as for most of those of either class with whom the token comes into
contact, her sex is the salient status. Her status as colleague may be
important to the sponsor, but her sex may be a more important problem for him than for her. He may attempt to resolve the conflict by
encouraging her to resolve her "role conflicts" in favor of gender
rather than occupational role. This is done by means of differential

expectations and assumptions about the share of family responsibilities and their priority in the life of a *female* professional. She
may be encouraged to function as the subordinate member of a
dual-career pair or as a kind of collegial "assistant." Thus her interpersonal stresses will be minimal until she leaves the protective
training environment, where such discipleship is considered appropriate for both male and female students.

Special niches may be reserved for tokens. They may be assigned the task of screening female applicants. When they discredit
the claims of exceptionalism of other aspirants, their own claims to
exceptionalism are enhanced. Rejection of female aspirants can be
justified in terms of the high standards and superior attributes of the
dominant class. The "openness" of the system can also be demonstrated by the fact that it is a woman who is performing such
gatekeeping functions. Having a woman function as gatekeeper also
maintains the beliefs that professions are meritocracies, that membership is achieved not ascribed; that the group's high standards are
legitimate in terms of its exclusivity, and that excellence is
rewarded.

WOMAN AS DEVIANT

Laws suggests that professional boundaries are maintained in terms
of informal interpersonal mechanisms more than formal ones. It is
clear that women in professional occupations are viewed as "out of
place" in terms of status relationships. For example, the perceived
status and desirability of male-dominated professions such as medicine and law went down when subjects were given the information
that increasing numbers of women would be entering them,
whereas evaluation of a female-dominated profession such as nursing or elementary school education went up when they believed
that more men would be entering these fields (Touhey, 1974a, b).

Behavior toward women when they step out of place appears to
be similar to behavior toward other individuals who bear a
"stigma." Goffman (1963b) has defined a stigma as a characteristic
that can create a situation in which "an individual who might have
been received easily in orderly social intercourse possesses a trait
that can obtrude itself upon attention and turn those of us whom he
meets away from him, breaking the claim that his other attributes
have upon us (p. 5)." Recently feminist scholars have begun to
analyze the relationships between men and women and between
women and society in terms of sex as a social stigma or woman as
deviant.

We must be cautious in the application of the term *deviant* to

Figure 15.4.   The social and changing definition of deviance. ("Doonesbury," by G. B. Trudeau, © 1976 Universal Press Syndicate.)

women, since it can be defined in two distinct senses. The term is commonly used by sociologists to refer to individuals whose behavior violates our institutionalized expectations and who are liable to societal sanctions for their violation (Bell, 1971). By this definition social deviants may be mental patients, criminals, drug addicts, and so forth. Institutions such as the law or medicine provide for their sanction. Another way of looking at social deviance, however, has been developed in the work of Erving Goffman and his students. In their view deviance is not a property inherent in any particular behavior. It is a property conferred upon that behavior by people who are threatened, embarrassed, or made to feel uncomfortable by it. This concept of deviance stresses the unofficial, informal, face-to-face interpersonal regulation in which people routinely engage. It is a form of deviance to which women may be particularly liable by virtue of their subordinate position within social systems.

This form of social deviance is not limited to women. Goffman (1963b) reminds us that we are all stigmatized at times. Being normal and being stigmatized are not two distinct categories but, rather, depend on the perspective of others. (See Figure 15.4.) Of course some groups and people suffer more than others, but this perspective forces us to pay attention to something that we might otherwise overlook: "that we engage every day in extraordinarily powerful, consequential, and often painful interpersonal negotiations about what is or is not acceptable and about what our respective places are in a world that provides less and less guidance and certainty about such matters" (Millman, 1975, pp. 271–272). Millman points out that when we study interpersonal government we enter a level of analysis that is especially important for understanding the experiences of women, for when individuals do not have official titles, formal positions, or other safeguards to cover and protect them, unofficial and informal interpersonal gestures and maneuvers take on greater importance. Being snubbed or ignored has greater meaning and consequence when one is at the bottom of the social hierarchy.

THE SOCIAL CONTROL OF FEMALE DEVIANCE

Application of the Definition

Unlike some other groups, women are not always perceived as stigmatized individuals. Global denigration of females as females is not often found. Women are likely to be derogated when they step out of the inferior position they are expected to occupy within a social system. They are particularly likely to be penalized if they assert their independence or competence. A clever stem story developed by Martha Kent (1974) may illustrate this point. She asked students to complete an incident involving humiliation and bystander participation:

> As a second year student in medicine, Jane (John) discovered a new method for measuring blood pressure. She (He) demonstrates her (his) technique to one of her (his) classes. Someone comments "You sure think you're good . . ."

Kent found that the stories did not contain a single instance of someone coming to Jane's rescue, while in stories with a male protagonist other students and the teacher are portrayed as having intervened in behalf of John.

Other studies have shown that gifted girls are viewed much more negatively than girls of average ability by their peers and are judged significantly less favorably than similarly gifted boys (Solano, 1976). The adjectives most frequently selected as describing them were aggressive and unfavorable ones such as *aloof, bossy, careless, conceited, snobbish, showoff, dull, apathetic, self-centered,* and *fickle*. These were much more negative than the unfavorable adjectives used to describe gifted boys. Even more frightening in this regard are the results of a second study by the same researcher on the evaluations of gifted boys and girls by educators before and after they became familiar with them. Educators who were unfamiliar with gifted boys perceived them as argumentative, opinionated, impatient, and having narrow interests. However, those who were familiar with such boys did not select any unfavorable adjective frequently enough to meet a 25-percent criterion. In judgments about gifted girls, in contrast, familiarity did not make any difference in ratings on the favorable scale. Moreover, the familiar educators were significantly more negative on the unfavorable scale than the unfamiliar ones. Thus for gifted girls, but not gifted boys, negative attitudes appeared to develop on the basis of personal contact. Both their peers and their superiors harbored negative feelings about gifted girls, although they had no objection to boys with the same degree of talent.

Negative attitudes toward competence in women appear to be more common in mathematics and the physical sciences. In a pioneering study in this area the attitudes toward women members of a number of academic departments in a small liberal-arts college were measured (McGuigan & Olive, 1976). Members of the chemistry and mathematics departments, more so than other departments, viewed women's roles as those of mother and homemaker. Members of the chemistry and biology departments also viewed women as less intelligent than men. Although these departments did not differ from departments oriented toward the social sciences in their attitudes on the education of women, subtle inferences may be communicated to their students. Data showing that people of both sexes view mathematics as a male domain have been discussed elsewhere. It is noteworthy that many gifted girls who have the aptitude for higher mathematics self-select themselves out of math courses in high school and college (Ernest, 1975; Haven, 1972). In choosing not to take such courses women may not be aware that they are also eliminating themselves from many careers in which knowledge of mathematics is a prerequisite. Males appear to be more aware that such courses are necessary to their future occupational plans (Ernest, 1975).

Dealing with the Deviant Female in a Group Setting

Several recent studies illustrate the way a competent female may be dealt with as a deviant by members of our society. A series of laboratory studies were designed to investigate the effect of sex on the violation of procedural norms in a group setting (Wahrman & Pugh, 1972, 1974). A male or female confederate violated procedural rules in a problem-solving situation early in, in the middle of, late in, or never in a series of trials. Early nonconformity by a male confederate led to increased influence and desirability as a co-worker, although the nonconformist was also disliked more than one who went along with the group. The earlier the female confederate violated the procedural rules, the less she influenced the group and the more disliked and less desirable as a co-worker she became. The best liked of all confederates was the conforming female. A competent performance on the part of the nonconforming female had no effect on her acceptance by these otherwise all-male groups. Competent nonconforming females were preferred less than incompetent non-conforming males—even though the group as a whole gained from competent performance.

The role of the lone woman in small groups designed to facilitate interpersonal communication has also been examined (Wolman & Frank, 1975). All participants were of equal status. They were, in fact, peer groups of graduate students or psychiatric residents who participated in these groups as part of their professional training. In five of the six groups studied, the lone woman became a deviant or isolated member of the group. In one group she was able to acquire low-status regular membership.

Wolman and Frank provide an illuminating description of the techniques used by male groups to deal with a woman who is "out of place." They found that when the group members started to interact, women were not allowed to compete freely for status. Attempts by a woman to influence the group were ignored, while similar attempts made subsequently by a man were heeded and credited to him. A woman who persisted in trying to influence the group after having been ignored received either coordinated reaction against her or further instances of no reaction. Men labeled assertiveness as bitchiness or manipulation, and appeared to be more threatened by competition with a woman than by competition with each other. When a woman showed feelings or advocated their expression, emotionality became identified with feminine behavior. The sex of the female was either virtually ignored or joked about. When the women tried to escape their role as isolates or deviants by increasing their number of interactions with others, they were increasingly ignored:

> Many coping mechanisms carry sex-role labels in our culture. If she acted friendly, she was thought to be flirting. If she acted weak, the men tried to infantilize her, treating her as a "little sister" rather than a peer. If she apologized for alienating the group, she was seen as a submissive woman knowing her place. If she asked for help, she earned a "needy female" label. If she became angry, or tried to point out rationally what the group process was doing to her, she was seen as competitive, in a bitchy, unfeminine way. "Feminine" coping mechanisms increased her perceived differences, "masculine" ones threatened the men so that they isolated her even more. Any internal ambivalence about her sexual role was rekindled by these labels, and increased her anxiety, which increased her coping behavior, which further increased her deviance! [Wolman & Frank, 1975, p. 168]

Men who affiliated with the single woman in these groups risked being identified with her and sharing her deviance. Since they had been led to expect that the professions were a male sanctuary, the men presumably resented the presence of a woman and acted to prevent her becoming a regular member so that they could have an almost all-male group. The women tended to give up their efforts after a while, becoming depressed instead. One could almost consider them group casualties. The single characteristic that these women shared and that was presumably the rationale for group hostility was the fact of being female.

A number of social mechanisms operate to decrease female participation in group processes:

1. Ignore her contributions to the group. Systematic ignoring of female subjects' participation in a conversation has been found to greatly reduce their participation (Geller, Goodstein, Silver, & Sternberg, 1974). Instead of leaving or getting angry, the subjects reacted by evaluating themselves and the female confederates less favorably than individuals who had not been ignored.
2. Foster dependency and then help her. While subjects will help a partner who has asked for help, they also describe her as relatively unattractive (Lerner & Lichtman, 1968).
3. Label her use of "masculine" behaviors as deviant. When a woman acted as an "expert," unlike a man, she was not seen as becoming more competent (Johnson, 1974). Even when she attempted to manipulate others by acting helpless she was seen as "pushy."
4. "Sexualize" the conduct of the female "offender." Much female "misbehavior" has been explained by sexuality: "She did it all for love!" (Millman, 1975). Restriction of female activity is often suggested as a solution to the problem of sexual assault, although restriction of private property is not considered a serious solution to the problem of mugging and burglary.

There is ample evidence that women have reason to fear being labeled as social deviants and becoming the recipients of sanctions by members of the dominant group—men. In fact the single most important and widely confirmed generalization about social groups is that they form norms for the behavior of their members (Argyle, 1969). Deviates from the group make norms more explicit and show other members what happens to those who break them. Those who are lowest in the group in terms of perceived value are most vulnerable to social manipulations within the group. The most frightening aspect of such within-group interactions is that they appear with such great regularity when women enter almost all-male groups and that, because such women are relatively socially isolated, group effects are seen as reactions to the personality and behavior of the individual rather than as more general social processes.

It has even been suggested that fear of success in women may actually be a function of fear of becoming a social deviant. In one study of this effect college students were given cues about "Ann in medical school" that defined her attendance as either deviant or typical (Lockheed, 1975). In the former case all of Ann's classmates were portrayed as males, whereas in the latter case half of her classmates were female. When the activity was described as typical for both sexes, no differences between males and females were found in the number of negative responses to Ann's successes. When, however, her behavior was described as atypical for women, nearly twice as many men as women reported negative consequences of her successful behavior. The men were especially likely to attribute her success to use of her sexuality. The media accounts of the "conversion" of Patti Hearst is an everyday illustration of the view that women's deviant behaviors are accounted for by their sexuality (Millman, 1975).

Individual Responses to Social Control

As noted earlier, the two major techniques by which stigmatized individuals are controlled within social groups is by deviance labels and/or group unresponsiveness. Silence as a social sanction appears to be more recognizable to women than to men (Unger, DeMauro, & Imbrognio, unpublished). Members of both sexes, however, are aware that an unresponsive environment impairs their freedom of expression. In a questionnaire mailed to a substantial number of university students, the students noted that although no one actively prevented them from speaking, no one listened, understood, or cared (Turner, 1973). Unresponsiveness may be a particularly effective method of social control because the failure to respond reduces the chance of an encounter in which the challenger could seek removal of the sanction. It is also difficult to classify as a reward or a punishment. Turner notes that "people who feel a distinct sense of oppression identify unequivocal sanctions; people whose condition is ambiguous are unable either to identify sanctions used against them or to feel entirely free, and therefore see an unresponsive system as the sanction impairing their freedom" (p. 11).

Unresponsiveness as a sanction may also erode the boundary between lack of freedom and powerlessness. Women who are ignored by other women view themselves as well as those who apply the sanction less favorably than those whose contributions are attended to (Geller et al., 1974). In transactional-analysis terms, Julia

Sherman (1976) views women as living by a "women's script." If a woman violates the script without social support, she is likely to feel uneasy, anxious, and/or depressed. Unresponsive environments are also likely to produce learned helplessness and/or depression.

The Creation of the "Deviant's" Behavior: Self-Fulfilling Prophecies

Perceptions of social deviance can be conveyed by means of either verbal labels or nonverbal gestures. Gestures connoting dominance and submission, intimacy and social distance were discussed extensively in Chapter 3. Indicants of women as deviant are similar to those directed toward other stigmatized individuals—the physically disabled, the mentally impaired, or those with unusual sexual preferences. Recent evidence indicates that verbal and nonverbal behaviors connoting deviant or stigmatized status (e.g., greater physical distances in interpersonal transactions, less intimate eye contact, colder tones of voice, etc.) can function to create the behaviors expected of the stigmatized individual. The perceiver's behavior acts to create a self-fulfilling prophecy of the behavior of the target individual. Such prophecies appear to operate in a wide variety of situations.

In one study white male subjects interviewed a black and a white applicant for a position (the applicant was actually a confederate) while their behavior was observed closely through a one-way mirror (Word, Zanna, & Cooper, 1974). The confederates were trained to behave in a standardized manner during the interview. The white interviewers placed their chairs significantly farther from the black applicants and showed significantly less "total immediacy" in terms of body orientation and eye contact. They also ended the interviews with the blacks sooner and made more speech errors. In a subsequent study confederates posed as experimenters and were trained to exhibit either immediate or nonimmediate behaviors toward naive white applicants. The applicants reciprocated the degree of intimacy of the interviewer. Moreover, those who were interviewed with the less immediate technique performed more poorly during the interview and showed less composure during the interview, as evaluated by judges who were not aware of the conditions existing during it.

More recently a similar study has indicated the existence of self-fulfilling prophecies in terms of physical attractiveness (Snyder, Tanke, & Berscheid, 1977). Male "perceivers" interacted with female "targets" whom they believed to be either physically attractive or unattractive. Although the males' perceptions were unknown to the females with whom they interacted, the targets who were perceived to be physically attractive came to behave in a more friendly, sociable, and likable manner than those who were perceived to be less physically attractive. In a sense the perceivers created their own information as well as processing it.

Women are more vulnerable to interpersonal rejection from men than from other women. They report lower self-esteem when severe failure in competition is due to the actions of an alleged male opponent than to those of a female one (Dion, 1975). They are, however, less likely to interpret their failure as reflecting personally on them if they perceive it as due to prejudice against women as compared to women who believe that they have an unprejudiced opponent.

The Internalization of Status Inferiority

It has long been suggested that women and blacks, as members of socially stigmatized groups, share a number of characteristics (Myrdal, 1944; Hacker, 1951). (See Table 15.2 for a summary of black–female comparisons). It may be particularly noteworthy that both groups have been characterized as more emotional and sensitive. We may translate this behavior as an awareness of social nuance—a characteristic that is of some value to members of groups that are particularly liable to social sanctions for violation of appropriate norms of behavior.

Members of socially inferior groups are also vulnerable to feelings of low self-worth. Women even value their bodies less than men in strict financial terms (Plutchik, Conte, Baker, & Weiner, 1973). When asked to "write down the amount of money you would ask in compensation for each part of your body that was lost," female college students thought their eyes were worthy of a median dollar value of $20,000 compared to the $50,000 estimate by males. Men over 65 placed a value of $25,000 on their eyes versus $10,000 for women of comparable age. Women have been taught to demand less for their bodies, as they have for their services.

A similar case for a relationship between low status and other "feminine" characteristics such as anxiety, conformity, or dependency can also be argued. These personality traits may be a result of ongoing interpersonal transactions as well as a result of long-term socialization phenomena. Cynthia Epstein (1973) points out that while we are sensitive to the effects of early socialization, we have paid little attention to continuing threats to female autonomy. For example, in a study of women lawyers she found that they were just as likely to drop out at the peak of their careers as at the start.

Table 15.2 CASTELIKE STATUS OF WOMEN AND NEGROES

NEGROES	WOMEN
1. HIGH SOCIAL VISIBILITY	
a. Skin color, other "racial" characteristics	a. Secondary sex characteristics
b. (Sometimes) distinctive dress—bandana, flashy clothes	b. Distinctive dress, skirts, etc.
2. ASCRIBED ATTRIBUTES	
a. Inferior intelligence, smaller brain, less convoluted, scarcity of geniuses	a. ditto
b. More free in instinctual gratifications. More emotional, "primitive" and childlike. Imagined sexual prowess envied.	b. Irresponsible, inconsistent, emotionally unstable. Lack strong super-ego. Women as "temptresses."
c. Common stereotype "inferior"	c. "Weaker"
3. RATIONALIZATION OF STATUS	
a. Thought all right in his place	a. Woman's place is in the home
b. Myth of contented Negro	b. Myth of contented woman—"feminine" woman is happy in subordinate role
4. ACCOMMODATION ATTITUDES	
a. Supplicatory whining intonation of voice	a. Rising inflection, smiles, laughs, downward glances
b. Deferential manner	b. Flattering manner
c. Concealment of real feelings	c. "Feminine wiles"
d. Outwit "white folks"	d. Outwit "menfolk"
e. Careful study of points at which dominant group is susceptible to influence	e. ditto
f. Fake appeals for directives; show of ignorance	f. Appearance of helplessness
5. DISCRIMINATIONS	
a. Limitations on education—should fit "place" in society	a. ditto
b. Confined to traditional jobs—barred from supervisory positions. Their competition feared. No family precedents for new aspirations.	b. ditto
c. Deprived of political importance	c. ditto
d. Social and professional segregation	d. ditto
e. More vulnerable to criticism	e. e.g., conduct in bars
6. SIMILAR PROBLEMS	
a. Roles not clearly defined, but in flux as result of social change. Conflict between achieved status and ascribed status.	

SOURCE: From H. M. Hacker, "Women as a Minority Group," *Social Forces,* 1951, *30*, 60–69. Copyright by University of North Carolina Press. Reprinted by permission.

Women are constantly being urged to ask "Am I doing the right thing?" Occupational success never comes out as the positive answer to this question.

SOCIETAL EFFECTS OF JUDGMENTS ABOUT FEMALE DEVIANCE

Perhaps the major source of judgments about female deviance is perceived violations of the sanctity of the family. As noted earlier, in our discussion of women in the work world, women are most likely to be discriminated against when their aspirations are perceived to conflict with the presumed needs of their families. It is noteworthy in this regard that women who return to the work force after having separated or been divorced from their husbands receive higher salaries than comparable still-married women with greater labor force continuity (Hudis, 1976). These data could be interpreted in several ways—for example, one gets paid what one demands—but they suggest that some sex-discriminatory effects may be mediated by assumptions about constraints on married women's behavior. In fact women are most likely to be penalized for great success in a nontraditional area when they are portrayed as succeeding in spite of role overload from familial responsibilities (Bremer & Wittig, 1977).

The Institutionalization of Sex-Specific Work–Family Assumptions

Although occupational and familial roles are not necessarily incompatible, it is difficult for women to demonstrate their lack of relationship. For example, replaceability on jobs is defined by institutional fiat rather than by a definition based on actual task requirements (Coser & Rokoff, 1971). In the below-college educational establishment absenteeism is institutionalized by the provision of a substitute teacher. Yet everyone expects that the substitute will be ineffective, that students will be hostile, and that very little learning will take place. In contrast, the norm in hospital internships and residencies is irreplaceability, even though all physicians in training are required to be familiar with all patients. Replaceability is inversely related to the status of the occupation. And there is a strong tendency for people to see high-status occupations as dominated by males (Dwyer, Salbod, & Bedell, 1978). In fact, only one stereotypically feminine occupation—nurse—received a rating of 5 in a perceived status scale ranging from 1 (low prestige) to 7 (high).

People even see a high relationship between happiness and success for individuals in sex-appropriate occupations (Feather, 1975). And we are all familiar with the relationship between occupational status and the actual percentage of women in that occupation.

In addition, higher-status occupations are expected to make demands on their occupants more frequently—demands that will cause disruption in their lives. There is a paradox between the attitude that women are unacceptable in positions in which family commitments might cause disruption and the attitude that some disruptions are to be taken for granted in high-status occupations. In fact those who are employed in high-status positions are often congratulated for bringing honor to their organizations by being wanted elsewhere. Our famous colleagues probably cancel their classes more often than less notable colleagues; nevertheless they are often rewarded by their institution for deviation from strict adherence to its demands (Coser, 1966). When individuals in insecure status positions (e.g., women) desire flexibility, they may be perceived as having taken for themselves a freedom to which they have no right. This perception is partly due to the fact that family responsibilities convey no status in our society.

A term that is rarely used by psychologists may be useful here. The important issue appears to be the *legitimacy* of the individual's behavior. Since the woman's occupational status is never quite legitimate, she cannot risk the same behaviors as a man in the same position. The distinction between power and culturally legitimate authority—between the ability to carry out one's goals and the recognition that it is right to do so—is crucial to the understanding of the role of sex in society (Rosaldo, 1974). Characteristic asymmetries in the status of men and women may be due to the distinction between domestic and public spheres of activity. Women are granted neither the time nor the social distance necessary for legitimate authority owing to the nature of household tasks. A woman who is outside of her role as wife and mother is both illegitimate and wrong. For example, a witch may be defined as a woman who possesses real power but exists outside of the male-defined social structure.

Among societies in which the greatest distinction between public and private spheres of activity exist, efforts by women to achieve power or authority are regarded as disruptive (Collier, 1974). Women are seen as being able to obtain power only by breaking up domestic units (e.g., parent–child, husband–wife relationships). Such conflicts may be dismissed by anthropologists as well as psychologists as mere "domestic conflicts." Women are expected to exert power by indirect means—through the men with whom they are allied. Domestic power, however, is not translatable for them into social power or a position in the public sphere (Sacks, 1974).

The Societal Function of Status Inequalities

How is it that social position is assigned on grounds other than performance capability? It has been suggested that power and status are alternate modes of obtaining benefits from others (Kemper, 1974). Individuals who can obtain benefits by coercive means will attempt to convert a power relationship into a status relationship so that the benefits obtained will be given voluntarily. When those who have less power accept the legitimacy of receiving lesser rewards for participation in social life, the possibility of performance competition or an out-and-out struggle in which there is a victor and a vanquished is decreased. Use of ascriptive as opposed to achieved social categories has sometimes been described as an "economical" societal mechanism. It is cheap, however, only for those in the higher categories on the scale. It is definitely not cheap for those in the lower categories, who pay a large intrapsychic price for the ease with which decisions about differential rewards are made.

Studies of our society suggest that men will try to seize power from other men when there is any opportunity to do so. In one study, for example, the apparent self-confidence of a more senior male colleague was varied (Mulder, Veen, Hijzen, & Jansen, 1973). Subjects were more ready to reduce the power distance between themselves and that colleague when he was perceived to lack confidence. The exercise of power appears to enhance the self-esteem of both males and females (Johnson, 1974; Raven & Kruglanski, 1970). The form of power exerted seems to be related to the subject's expectation of success in its use. Thus when men believe that they will be successful in influencing another male worker who is of lower status than themselves, they use milder forms of influence such as personal persuasion (Goodstadt & Hjelle, 1973). When they believe that they will be unable to influence him, they use harsher forms of coercive power.

It may be possible to synthesize these data in terms of sex by suggesting that whereas men fear competition with women, women fear conflict with men. This distinction is due to their different social realities—as seen from the top or the bottom of a single status hierarchy. A formulation such as this views the position of women not as a unique phenomenon in terms of the psychology of attitudes, stereotypes, and motivations, but from the more sociological perspective of social power and access to resources. Sex may be viewed in terms of social mechanisms for personal control.

The Prospect for Status Equalization of the Sexes

The dimensions that come closest to being regarded as bases for status systems within societies are wealth, power, and prestige. We have discussed at length how women have unequal access to all three dimensions. The question that is of interest here is how personal characteristics (e.g., achievements) can modify institutionalized sex inequalities. Unfortunately, little empirical, as opposed to theoretical, work has been done in this area. However, analogies may be made with other groups who are also subject to ascribed status inferiority, for example, blacks and the young.

Using age as the status variable, it has been found that inequity can be reduced when members of the higher-status group are exposed to an increasing number of status unequals who possess characteristics that contradict status expectations (Freese & Cohen, 1973; Freese, 1974). These characteristics must be similar to those required for performance in tasks worked on by members of both groups as a whole. Unless, however, the expectations for competence held by both the low- and high-status groups are treated, the high-status group will continue to dominate (Cohen & Roper, 1973). By analogy, treating the expectations and behaviors of women alone may be ineffective in changing their position in the social system.

In our society there appears to be a zero-sum view of power and status. If one group goes "up," it is assumed that another group will go "down." Sex differences may be irretrievably entangled with power differences. "As always, the world belongs to the powerful" (Janeway, 1974). It is the weak who are the second sex. The equation of weakness and femininity may underlie a great deal of masculine reaction to a redefinition of women's role. Such a shift requires a resynthesis not only of sex relations but of power relations too. Equality may be seen not as "A woman is as good as I am" but as "I'm no better than she is" (Janeway, 1974, p. 197).

Although most males in our society probably do not particularly want power (which confers responsibility, may make one disliked, and may not be seen as leading to any clear reward), they are allied by sex with those who do have power. The effect of closing the male–female split may increase awareness of the gap between the powerful and the weak. Men may cooperate in the social mechanisms that keep women down because in that way maleness gives them psychological protection. Thus they are the "setters of the norms"—not the "deviants."

We are all—male and female—victims of socialization in the unconscious assumptions of our society. It would be wrong to use this kind of political analysis to apologize for the treatment of any person. Such explanations, however, show us how unequal treatment of members of various groups can survive without being challenged. It remains to be seen what happens to such institutionalized phenomena as recognition of their existence becomes more widespread and part of our individual awareness as human beings.

Chapter 16
Making Connections

Looking at sex and gender from a different perspective in some ways raises more questions than it answers. Nevertheless it appears that we are learning some of the proper questions to ask. Some consistent themes seem to reappear in different areas. These themes involve reevaluation of when sex differences appear, explanation of sex-characteristic behavior in a situational rather than an intrapsychic context, investigation of how biological variables operate within a social context to produce sex-characteristic behaviors, and concern with the way definitions of appropriate feminine behavior seem "inevitably" to lead to double binds for women.

From this new perspective gender may be viewed as a self-fulfilling prophecy based on the expectations of others for "normal" sex-appropriate behavior. These expectations are often internalized by the individuals themselves, thereby becoming difficult to distinguish from personality characteristics. From this new perspective it is impossible to evaluate sex differentiation without consideration of the needs of society. Maleness and femaleness must be evaluated in terms of their different places in a social hierarchy. In many situations social processes are asymmetrical with respect to sex, with males representing the group with the greater amount of legitimate social and physical power. The power to enforce one's demands may have been underestimated as a basis for sex role differentiation.

The social mechanisms used to enforce sex-role-characteristic behavior are not different from those used to control behavior in other socially powerless groups. A number of mechanisms that enforce sex-different behavior will be reviewed in this chapter. Possibly the most important aspect of this "new view" is that sex forms an important stimulus base for role distinctions in our society. As with other ascribed bases for social roles, it is assumed that biology explains the role differentiation. Social determinants, however, seem to be much more important. Major changes in sex-specific assumptions will not occur until this "hidden agenda" of societal necessity is examined more openly.

SEX DIFFERENCES

People look for explanations and predictabilities in their own and others' behavior. Psychologists share this tendency with everyone else. A major source of both common sense and psychological explanation has been in terms of sex and sex-related (gender) characteristics. An increasing amount of research indicates, however, that actual sex differences in behavior appear inconsistently and in relatively few areas. Sex differences are most likely to occur in group situations in which the social context defines sex-characteristic behavior as socially desirable behavior.

Even when the behavior of males and females is objectively identical, it is not evaluated in the same way. Female behavior is not perceived to have the same psychological base as that of males. Females' behavior is perceived to require more intrapsychic or biological explanations than the equivalent behavior of males. When situational factors are taken into account, they are more likely to be explained by unstable causes such as an unusual amount of effort or luck. In addition, the male role appears to be more clearly defined than the female role. Thus people find it easier to assign cause for the behavior of males.

Sex-specific personality characteristics appear to represent characteristics that are rewarded differentially in our society. It is important to understand societal mechanisms for reward and punishment in order to evaluate the meaning of sex differences. For example, it is assumed that women have a greater need for affiliation than men whereas men have a greater need for achievement. However, we all need to be loved. Males, in contrast to females, have since childhood been rewarded with love for their achievements:

> Of course men don't seem to need approval for achievement, because
> by the time they have gotten to their college years, they have been
> approved of and indeed loved to pieces for their successful achieve-
> ment endeavors; nor does it ever stop. After a while people start to pay
> them. [Mednick, 1978, p. 85]

Many of the behavioral differences between the sexes have
been perceived to be based on so-called biological universals.
While it is true that, biologically, only females can bear children,
much of their social inferiority seem to be based on activities connected with childrearing. When women function in the world outside the home, they are penalized by perceptions about their lack of
commitment and/or mobility due to familial responsibilities. The
women themselves may select career options that are limited by
these perceptions about relative parental responsibility. Role strain
rather than role incompatibility appears to be the major issue for
women attempting to function effectively both within and outside
the home (Hall, 1972; Alpert & Richardson, 1977).

Males can enjoy being parents too. We seem to have based our
ideas about "built-in" maternal personality characteristics around
social systems that are rather specific to this society. Thus we find
that responsiveness toward infants is enhanced by early contact
with them; that child care may lead to the increase in males of some
behaviors that are considered female-specific, such as lowered aggression; in other words, many sex-related behaviors may not be as
much a product of prenatal potentiation or early socialization as we
used to believe. A more situational analysis might explain rather
curious and, as yet, un-followed-up findings such as the one that
notes that fathers who have sons but no daughters have a more
feminine sexual identification than fathers who have daughters but
no sons (Lansky, 1964). Since it is difficult to understand how feminine identification could produce male offspring, this finding suggests that sex-related characteristics are subject to change even in
adulthood.

THE STIMULUS BASES OF SEX DIFFERENCES

It appears that psychology shares with the general population the
assumption that many more sex differences exist than have been
consistently shown to exist. Part of the reason for these assumptions
is the tendency to conceptualize the sexes as a dichotomy. Splitting
the psychological world in two in terms of biology leads to a concentration on means rather than on variability. That is, in almost all
behaviors studied, females and males cluster on two overlapping
distributions (see Figure 16.1), with a greater amount of overlap

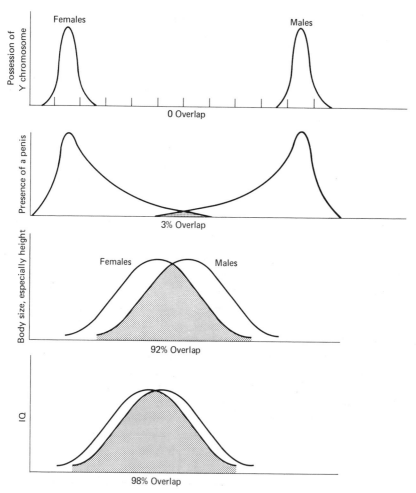

Figure 16.1. A frequency distribution of some characteristics related to sex. The frequencies are idealized to illustrate the range of possible overlap in supposedly sexually dimorphic characteristics.

between members of each group than there are differences between them.

There is ample evidence that perceptually there are two sexes. People use sex as a major variable for differentiating between individuals even when this information is relatively useless, statistically, for doing so. As a stimulus variable, sex controls judgments about mental adjustment, academic and creative achievement, and attitudes and values. The sexes are never so much alike as when they are agreeing about their differences.

Assumptions about differences between males and females may represent a triumph of form over content. One interesting account of the problems of a genetic male with a deficiency of testosterone in being accepted as a mature adult may be illuminating:

> For this man, the account to be settled was not whether he could or could not have some kind of a sex life, as is so often the case. He had already established that he could. His unsettled account was whether he could ever look old enough. At 25 he got a job as an insurance salesman. Clients ridiculed and belittled him as though he were a boy of 16 or 17 pretending to be a salesman and had no business trying to con them. He had to quit. There was nothing he could do to look more mature. Because his system was unable to use androgen, his face could not grow a beard, he could not get a masculine, adult-looking skin texture, his voice did not deepen fully, and his body shape remained too youthful. He would look like a kid forever. [Money, 1974, p. 266]

In many ways descriptions of this man resemble descriptions of young women, and many of the latter can describe similar difficulty being taken seriously in the job world. One recent study provided college students with extensive descriptions of a situation involving a job interview in which the two forms differed only in whether the stimulus person was consistently described as a woman or as a girl (Brannon, unpublished). The girl was viewed as being significantly less suitable for a managerial job than the woman. If she was hired, the subjects perceived that the difference between a girl and a woman was about $6000 in annual salary.

There seems to be a complex interaction between the way a woman looks and how her behaviors are evaluated. Thus the woman who successfully adopts certain male roles while retaining her "womanliness" is considered more attractive than women who manifest the same characteristics but have more masculine characteristics (Kristal, Sanders, Spence, & Helmreich, 1975). While female professors as a group are not evaluated as significantly poorer teachers than male professors in a real-life evaluation situation, women who were viewed as difficult graders received lower evaluations as teachers than women who were viewed as easier graders (Unger, 1977a). No such relationship existed for male professors. These data may indicate something about the processes by which sex role stereotyping leads to sexism. Women are not expected to be professors, certainly not demanding ones. Those who do not conform to their students' expectations about nurturant femininity may receive lower evaluations of their teaching effectiveness than they deserve. If faculty retention is based on such criteria (as it increasingly is), subtle evaluational bias may ensure that the women who remain as college teachers will be less strong, less effective by objective standards, and less likely to cause problems for their male colleagues.

It is difficult to document how often evaluations that are assumed to be based on performance are affected by surface characteristics. A recent comment about Bella Abzug that appeared in *New York* Magazine (Brenner, 1977) would suggest that the problem is not limited to academia: "If Bella had the same politics, but looked like Mary Lindsay, she could be president,' one of her detractors told me" (p. 59). This can pose quite a problem for women who assume that they are being judged on their behavior. And there is evidence that females do not always recognize the difference between the way they think they are being judged and the way they are judged.

THE "DOUBLE BIND" AND ITS IMPLICATIONS

Discrepancies between the way women are judged by others and the way they think they are judged easily set women up for "double-bind" situations. This kind of situation could more colloquially be phrased the "damned if you do, damned if you don't" problem. Double binds for women have been noted in a variety of contexts. Perhaps the best-publicized example is noted in the work of Matina Horner (1972) on fear of success. Women who show a great deal of achievement in an academic or occupational context may be viewed as lacking femininity or in some way deviant from the feminine norm. Both men and women indicate that they believe that women are "unsexed" by success. Men, in contrast, are "unsexed" by failure.

Other examples of "double binds" include the seeming incompatibility between the mentally healthy adult and the mentally healthy female. If there are basic incompatibilities between the definitions of appropriate female behavior and appropriate adult behavior in a wide variety of areas, it is obviously impossible for any one woman to meet both sets of standards. It puts her at greater risk of breakdowns in "mental health" and sets her up for yet another "classic" bind—"blaming the victim" (Ryan, 1971). A member of a socially powerless group who manifests behavior that is defined as being somehow undesirable may be viewed as responsible for that behavior. Thus any change in that behavior is the responsibility of the individual rather than of society. The origins of the behavior are perceived as safely in the past or in biology—beyond the need for any effective social change.

SEX-APPROPRIATE BEHAVIORS AS SELF-FULFILLING PROPHECIES

Behaviors that are defined as appropriate for females tend to be ineffective and immature, whereas those defined as appropriate for males are deemed effective and mature. Females who identify themselves as sex typed display a catalog of deficiencies that makes for dismal reading (Bem, 1978). They do not willingly engage in cross-sex behaviors; they report themselves as discomfited when required to do so; they yield readily to group pressure for conformity; they do not initiate play with a kitten; and they do not distinguish themselves in the most traditional of all female behaviors, the nurturance of a human infant. The major effect of femininity that is not tempered by a sufficient number of male-typed characteristics seems to be the inhibition of any behavior at all in situations in which "appropriate" behaviors are ambiguous and unspecified. Passivity appears to be a major feature of the behavior of the woman who has "bought" the feminine stereotype. It is noteworthy, however, that such women account for a minority of the women studied by Bem and her associates.

People appear to manifest the behaviors that others expect of them even when they are not explicitly given information about what the people with whom they interact perceive. Thus we find that women who are labeled attractive come to behave in a sociable manner consistent with the stereotype of physical attractiveness although they are unaware of that perception in male partners with whom they had no face-to-face interaction. Similarly, nonverbal signals of hostility and/or coldness produce poorer performance at an interview of an individual to whom such gestures are directed.

It appears that women are the targets of such signals when they engage in behaviors that are perceived to be "out of place" for them. Thus pregnant women are perceived to be more socially acceptable when they are passive, and inordinate achievement by women is seen to be more socially unacceptable if they do so while simultaneously engaging in a parental role than when they succeed outside of a marital relationship. If female out-of-role behaviors are not actively punished, they are likely to be virtually ignored. Teachers are more aware of individual differences between boys than between girls and are better able to correctly predict their behaviors. Only exceptionally bright girls are allowed enough room for high accomplishment in the classroom.

While active behaviors are discouraged in females, being rather than doing is rewarded. Physical attractiveness is a more salient variable in judgments about females than in judgments about males. Moreover, judgments about a woman's attractiveness transfer to evaluations of her male partner whereas the opposite relationship does not exist. Males, of course, can transfer their social status and occupational prestige to their wives. It is not surprising, therefore, that females come to value their appearance more than males do. For example, disorders of weight control such as anorexia nervosa and bulimia are found almost exclusively in females (Boskind-Lodahl, 1976).

THE SOCIAL MEDIATION OF SEX-RELATED CHARACTERISTICS

Threat vs. Fear

In some ways women and men do not inhabit the same society. One can view their position in terms of relative status. Males, in general, possess higher status than females. Any attempt by women to attain male status may be viewed by men as a threat to their social power. Women, conversely, may fear to step out of place. The use of covert and overt means of coercion to maintain the sexual status quo may be more common than is usually assumed. Battered wives have received considerable attention in the media lately. It has been estimated by a sociologist who is considered one of the leading experts in the field that violence between family members may be at least as common as love (Straus, 1974). The same sociologist has also estimated that less than 5 percent of all wife beatings are due to purely individual problems involving inability to control aggression (Straus, 1977a). Instead, he suggests that general cultural norms permit marital violence. In fact about 25 percent of the women who responded to a nationally representative questionnaire stated that marital violence was either necessary, normal, or good. Thirty-one percent of the male respondents also made one of these statements (Straus, 1977b).

Violence is often precipitated when the woman departs even minimally from passive, accepting behavior. Such violence, of course, also decreases the probability that she will assert herself again. The probability that the woman in such a marital situation will be physically attacked during pregnancy is quite high (Gelles, 1975). Pregnancy further decreases her options for leaving the marriage. It is incredible how much ill-treatment many women tolerate without removing themselves from the situation. Many of them have become so passive that they do not realize that such an option even exists.

Direct force and social-power manipulations maintain sexual inequalities among children within a family, too. Younger children are less powerful than older ones, except in the case of a younger brother with an older sister. Outside the family, boys with high social power are seen as "threatening" by other children. In general, only males form dominance hierarchies, but when females are evaluated as part of such hierarchies, they usually fall in the lower half.

The basis for social status among children appears to be the same as that for adults, although children may be more direct and overt in their social manipulations. Boys report that they are the givers and receivers of more high-power social manipulations than girls are (Unger, unpublished). These behaviors, however, seem to be influenced by body build. Mesomorphic children—those with the muscular physiques considered most desirable by other children—are more like each other than girls and boys of other builds. Mesomorphic boys use fewer high-power tactics than other boys, whereas mesomorphic girls use more. These effects may be due to a relationship between ascribed status and the ability to use physical force effectively. High-status boys may have less need to use physical tactics, whereas girls who can do so may use such tactics to raise their status within the group. The fact that identical physical characteristics may produce opposite behaviors in the two sexes may be a reflection of their differing initial positions in the social system.

Sexual threat may also be a basis for maintaining inequality between the sexes. Cross-sex relationships in childhood are socially suspect and may be ridiculed by the peer group. Young females are particularly likely to be institutionalized for "crimes" such as running away from home or engaging in "illicit" sexual activity. By legal definition it is difficult for a married woman to be raped by her husband. Those who are raped by someone else are often subject to social condemnation and the assumption that they brought on the rape by behaving provocatively. Rape may provide a rationale for women's remaining within their "natural environment"—the safety of the home. We are learning more and more about the sexual harassment that many women endure when they work outside the home.

The Social Construction of Sex Roles

Sex-characteristic behaviors are most likely to occur when the sexes interact with each other. For example, women are less likely than men to emerge as leaders of mixed-sex groups (Lockheed & Hall,

1976). In fact after receiving feedback about effective performance on a leadership task female leaders actually decreased in influence whereas male leaders maintained their level of effectiveness. In this situation sex-stereotypic assumptions about how females should behave decreased the performance of the women in out-of-role positions.

Females appear to be more concerned about the perceptions of males than males about the perceptions of females. They seem to feel that males would like them to have more feminine characteristics than they themselves feel are desirable (Deutsch & Gilbert, 1976). During the dating process, which may be viewed as a training ground for future adult roles, females alter their behavior more than their male partners do.

Female concern about male judgments may represent "legitimate" anxiety. For example, many studies have found that males are more negative to high levels of female achievement than women who are supposedly afraid of female success (Condry & Dyer, 1976b). Males are also more affected by the sex composition of the group in which the woman is achieving that success; that is, they are less ready to penalize her for success in a group with a 50–50 sex composition than in one in which women are a small minority. Women's fear of success may be a fear of their male partners' sanctions (Peplau, 1976b). This fear may have a very real basis. Men who have a high fear of female competence appear to accelerate their performance when competing with females and show a greater desire to avoid future interaction with them than other males do (Pleck, 1976). We do not yet know how widespread this fear of female competence is or from what it springs. It does seem related, however, to the actual probability of competition with a female. The largest percentage of men responding negatively to a cue portraying female success in a large-scale multiracial sample were white middle-class males with a college education (Moore, 1974).

The Microprocesses of Social Control

In recent years a number of processes by which social control is exerted through definitions of sex and gender have been elucidated.

1. *Under some conditions simply being a female can act as a social stigma and evoke group sanctions.* These conditions usually involve some sort of competition in the male world. Ambition is more likely to be labeled aggression in women, and assertive behaviors can generate negative responses. Women are permitted to wield power only if they do it indirectly. Overt social sanctions against

high female status appear more frequently late in the maturation process. This is the period of life when the female is seen as sexually receptive, and it is at this point that her normative adjunctive familial role becomes salient. Out-of-role behavior is especially liable to presumptions about deviance in matters of sexual preference. Sex role stereotypes exist concerning the deviant sexuality of "overage" tomboys, those who remain voluntarily single, and those who are "excessively" concerned about their careers.

It is important to remember that male deviance may also be controlled in this manner. The label of homosexual as well as that of lesbian effectively threatens those who lag in their acceptance of the proper sex role. Fear of gender-inconsistent behavior may be more common to both sexes than fear of success. For example, male nurses are as likely to be stigmatized by society as female doctors (Cherry & Deaux, 1975).

It is also important to remember that social mechanisms for the control of deviance are the same no matter what groups are labeled deviant. People are likely to use more distant modes of social interaction with such diverse groups as blacks, homosexuals, the physically disabled, or pregnant women. None of these groups are expected to assert themselves or to assume leadership positions. These groups also share some intrapsychic characteristics—most specifically, the expectation of having little control over their lives.

2. *A major mechanism of social control is the unresponsive environment.* Under most conditions less attention is paid to the behaviors of females than to those of males, and they are less individualized by those around them. Males are both more likely to be rewarded for their successes and more like to be punished for their failure than females (Deaux & Taynor, 1973). Young females are penalized for violation of sex roles less often than young males (Feinman, 1977). In a variety of situations females receive fewer rewards in terms of both subjective evaluations and objective success than males engaged in identical activities. An unresponsive environment is similar to the kind of environment that produces learned helplessness—in both cases the individual receives no feedback about the effectiveness of his or her behavior. In retraining children with low school achievement (i.e., those who fail to persist in performing school tasks), it is not enough to simply provide them with success experiences (Dweck, 1975). They must also be taught to take responsibility for their failures in order for retraining to have a positive effect. Little has yet been found out about the relationship between one's perception of ability to control the environment and the actual degree to which one does so. However, blacks, His-

panics, and other relatively powerless groups in our society appear to share females' expectations about low personal control.

3. *People may be quite unaware of the ways in which their behaviors are controlled in terms of their sex.* Women who achieve a great deal may focus on their achievements although the men around them remain more responsive to their sex (Laws, 1975). Touching, for example, appears to have very different connotations for men and women, with men regarding a touch as a gesture of affection and women viewing it as a possible sexual threat. This sex difference, of course, can easily be a function of their relative positions sexually and socially. This differential position also mediates the way one interprets being crowded. Women are made more anxious by being crowded under mixed-sex conditions than men are. Again, this may be a function of their reality, since when people have no choice about whether or not to violate the personal space of another (e.g., when they must reach the floor selection panel of an elevator) men are more likely to violate the space of a female than to violate that of a male (Buchanan, Juhnke, & Goldman, 1976). Henley and Freeman (1975) make this point more succinctly when they note that "what is habitual is often seen as desirable."

4. *Characteristics that are socialized as appropriate for each sex may be used to mediate further sex role differentiation.* Both boys and girls used closer interpersonal distances in moving around silhouettes of peers described as outgoing and intelligent (Guardo, 1976). Boys, however, used larger distances than girls from peers described as being affected by feelings or apprehensive. Girls distanced the figures more when the peers were described as assertive. It should be noted that these sex-discriminating characteristics are those that are stereotypically considered more appropriate for members of the opposite sex. In a similar vein, it has been found that people will disclose more to men who are considered physically attractive. Physical attractiveness may lead to expectations about "feminine" behavior, just as physical size and strength may produce expectations about "masculine" behavior. This kind of attribution process will usually lead to sexual differentiation, since females are more likely to be labeled pretty and males to be labeled strong.

Biological variables that have social significance may be particularly important in the covert mediation of sex roles. We have noted the effect of body build and physical attractiveness in a number of contexts and are now becoming aware of even more subtle variations. Thus bust size contributes to feminine sex typing in some women (Shipley & O'Donnell, 1977), and a recent finding by one of my students, Mary Kalchbrenner (1978), indicates that there is a significant negative correlation between height and feminine sex typing on the Bem androgyny scale for people of both sexes. This relationship means that shorter people rate themselves as having more "feminine" characteristics. It is not clear how this relationship is mediated, but it is likely to be related to attributions about relative powerlessness based on relative size.

5. *Variability in female socialization may be mediated by the way different women construct their social reality as well as by actual differences in that social reality.* Judith Laws has christened this phenomenon the Radcliffe syndrome. It consists of a woman selecting a supportive male as a partner or spouse and then proclaiming that he is responsible for her nontraditional success. It is difficult to decide whether this is a positive or a negative mechanism. The woman has avoided some social control of her aspirations and defused some views of her deviance, since she has a "normal" relationship with a male. On the other hand, she abdicates responsibility for her own behavior and may provide an nonutilitarian role model, since the supply of such supportive males is small. Males who support an aspiring woman who is viewed as deviant by other males may risk being labeled deviant themselves (Wolman & Frank, 1975), but it is unclear how commonly this mechanism operates in everyday life and in long-term partnerships. In any case there is evidence that women who aspire to nontraditional careers (e.g., math and science) are more likely to believe that the significant men in their lives are positive about the idea that women can perform in the business and professional world without jeopardizing their marriages, family, or femininity (Hawley, 1972). Would-be teachers are more likely to offer justifications for a sexual division of labor.

6. *The extent to which sex-specific behaviors have been controlled by assumptions about social desirability has probably been underestimated.* Sex-characteristic behaviors are more likely to occur in a group context than when the individual is alone (Kidder et al., 1977). It does not appear necessary that the individuals involved engage in any kind of interpersonal transaction with each other. Assumptions about what others believe seem to be sufficient to induce social-desirability effects. In some ways it appears that the presence of other individuals enhances the demand characteristics of sex. The subject tries to give other people what she or he thinks they want. A similar pattern has recently been demonstrated in terms of race. Solitary white bystanders help black and white victims equally. When, however, others are believed to be present, blacks were helped less than whites (Gaertner & Dovidio, 1977).

In a sense people engage in a kind of social game in which

everyone knows the rules although they are never made explicit. It is difficult to disguise the stimulus properties of sex. Thus people may conjecture what behaviors are desirable on the basis of the sex of either the experimenters, cosubjects, or real or hypothetical observers. The sex composition of a group, as well as whether or not the behavior occurs within a group context, is probably a variable of some importance. Certainly almost all-male groups seem to manifest an inordinate amount of masculine solidarity. As yet, however, no one has explicitly varied the ideological framework of the group (e.g., feminist or sexist) to see what effect this has on various sex-characteristic behaviors.

7. *Assumptions about sex and gender are often mediated by differential perceptions about the biological properties of females and males.* A number of biological assumptions can be noted:

1. Female psychology is more dependent on biology than male psychology.
2. Psychological characteristics that are affected by biological properties are more irreversible than other psychological characteristics whose biological bases are unknown.
3. Critical periods exist during which sex-characteristic properties are more salient. Menstruation, pregnancy, and the menopause are examples of this kind of "special" condition.
4. Conditions that have a strong biological basis in women are assumed to have no analog in men; therefore male control groups are not appropriate for studying the psychological events associated with these biological events.
5. Last, and possibly most important, behavioral characteristics associated with biological events are assumed to occur by way of direct central-nervous-system regulation. Social perceptions and cognitions relating to these events are presumed to have little effect on behaviors associated with them.

Although each of these ideas has been proven false under some conditions, much research in psychology is based on one or more of these implicit assumptions. These assumptions lead to the further assumption of a psychology that is "unique" to women.

Many biologically based assumptions can be destroyed by a focus on other cultures, classes other than the middle class, or races other than the white one. Within our own society there appear to be fewer differences between the sexes and less sex role stereotyping among blacks than among whites. This similarity may be related to the greater between-sex similarity in occupational and familial roles for black women and men. While both sexes have been limited in their occupational roles, the difference between the two is relatively less than it is for white women and men (Treiman & Terrell, 1975).

> By dint of necessity, she [the black woman] has had to be adequate and independent. And though she has been lonely, embittered, I think, and uncherished, at least she has not had to contend with an image of dependency, passivity and incompetence. She does not view herself in such a manner, nor, interestingly, does her mate. [Gump, 1978]

Little work has been done on cross-racial effects related to critical "biological" points, but it is intriguing that black women do not report as great a sense of powerlessness with an increasing number of children as white women do. Black child care systems are structured to provide more care outside the nuclear family. It is difficult to support a biological interpretation of effects that exist as sex differences in one racial group and as sex similarities in another.

Although it sometimes seems that anthropologists have a monopoly on cultures other than industrialized Western ones, there is evidence from other societies that biologically related events do not have the same characteristics in all cultures. Thus menstrual symptomology is different in India from such symptomology in the United States (Parlee, 1978), and so is menopausal behavior. Although biology may put a stress on the system, the behaviors that accompany a biologically based state may frequently be a product of social conditioning.

8. *Relevant biological variables may operate outside the body—by way of social cognitive effects—rather than as direct effects on the central nervous system.* We have explored the role of size, shape, and physical attractiveness in social perceptions. A new biological variable that requires attention is the growth process itself. Individuals differ widely in the rate at which they grow and mature. One recent study found that, regardless of sex, early maturers scored better on verbal tasks than on spatial ones whereas late maturers scored better on spatial tasks than on verbal ones (Waber, 1976). Sex differences were, of themselves, not significant, although the largest cognitive differences were found between early-maturing girls and late-maturing boys. Another study has shown that somatic variables are related to spatial ability in females (Peterson, 1976). By the age of 18 spatial ability was significantly related to masculine appearance in overall body shape and pubic-hair development.

Although these researchers have suggested that chromosomal and/or hormonal factors are responsible for these relationships, it may be more parsimonious to consider the role of the social mediation of body build. Spatial ability is a stereotypically male skill, and more physically androgynous women might be expected to excel in it. Although this hypothesis is conjectural, it should be explored before we again assume that some unknown biological mechanism is operating somewhere inside the central nervous system. What needs to be explored here is the relationship between physical and psychological androgyny.

9. *It is important not to confuse personality change with social change.* Just because people become more androgynous does not necessarily indicate that they will become more tolerant of the androgyny of others. In fact, Spence and Helmreich (1978) indicate that there is little relationship between an individual's score on an androgyny scale and score on an instrument designed to measure attitudes about sex-role equality. Androgyny may be a more limited predictor of psycho-sexual flexibility than it first appeared. For example, some of my students (Kurland & Wirth, 1978) have found no relationship between androgyny and the tendency of college men and women to perceive that more attractive women will be more involved in traditional rather than radical campus political organizations or will have more traditional occupational goals. Similarly, the attitudes towards feminism of both women and men had no effect on the extent to which they viewed attractive males as being supportive or unsupportive of the women's movement (Kupecky & Hilderbrand, 1979).

It appears that androgyny may even be more acceptable for males than for females. Nontraditional males are viewed more positively than sex-typed males by today's college students (O'Leary & Donoghue, 1978). A man who cried was not viewed as less masculine than a man who became angry in response to an identical provocation (Kahn, 1979). A male or female who cried and a male who became angry were equally acceptable when viewed on videotape by college students. The expression of anger by a woman, however, was viewed less positively. Only males devalued an angry woman. The picture that emerges from this research is that men may feel free to permit other men to behave in a nontraditional manner but may deny women this freedom when it becomes too threatening.

ALL THE SEXES?

Since sex forms one of the major bases for social stratification in our society, it seems extraordinarily important to clarify our bases for identifying an individual as a member of a particular sex. Nevertheless review of the many biological and psychosocial indicators mentioned in this regard reveals that no one indicator uniquely defines sex. Disconsonance with respect to genetic, endocrine, somatic, internally socialized, and environmental (the perceptions and assumptions of others) components seems to be very common. In fact biological "determinants" of sex-specific behaviors seem to be so weak in human beings that it takes intensive socialization through adulthood for them to become manifest. And these sex-specific characteristics have a way of disappearing in social contexts in which they are not perceived as desirable.

One can argue that our society depends on role allocation in terms of familial and outside-the-home occupational responsibilities. Sexual categories provide a convenient basis for such role allocation. Dichotomizing people in terms of sex and then attaching gender-specific labels to behaviors that are in line with the sex label is a way of putting people in the needed slots. Individual differences in talent, motivation, and desire are irrelevant to this societal function. One of the important purposes of a "new" psychology of sex and gender is to examine how independent these various aspects of sex are when they serve individual rather than social needs.

TOWARD A SYSTEMS APPROACH TO SEX AND GENDER

It is instructive to look at some of the things we are learning about the socialization of female gender in terms of a behaviorist analysis. Males, of course, control the reinforcements, with the assistance of women after they have been suitably socialized. Reinforcements are defined in terms of status, power, and money and are the commodities in which males already have an initial advantage. Affiliation, security, and love are more appropriate reinforcers for women, but they do not allow them to "buy into" general societal games. Many women are unaware that differential reinforcements exist, and those who do are conditioned to believe that traditional male reinforcers are somehow less moral and not to be used in connection with women.

One can also argue that traditional female reinforcers may not always take the form of positive rewards but can be forms of negative reinforcement, that is, rewards whose absence causes anxiety and an increase in behaviors designed to reacquire them. Thus it could be argued that females engage in appropriate feminine activity not to acquire male attention and affection but because the absence of male attention and affection causes them to fear social isolation and judgments about their deviance. In other words, they engage in stereotypically feminine behavior in order to avoid the anxieties that are generated when they do not engage in such behavior. Studies of such avoidance schedules in animals indicate that they are maintained by fewer applications of reinforcement than positively reinforced schedules and are much more difficult to extinguish.

It is also possible to analyze in some detail the nature of the reinforcement schedules by which female behavior may be socialized. Not only are extinction and avoidance used more in female socialization than in male socialization, but many female behaviors are controlled by what might be termed a variable time schedule. In contrast to either response or interval schedules, variable time schedules are not dependent on the individual's making a particular response. Rewards seemingly appear erratically and do not reflect what the individual does. It is easy under these conditions for the organism to devise superstitions explaining the relationship between themselves and the environment (people do not like to believe they exist in a noncausative world). Females' focus on their appearance, attire, and other components of external identity could be a response to this apparently random process of reinforcement. Of course such a mechanism is difficult to identify, since some reinforcement does take place and a rationale for it can always be found at the time.

While this kind of analysis provides no new data of itself, it does tie together a lot of apparently unrelated information. It explains the greater probability of anxiety for females as well as the greater probability of depression. It explains why women engage in a great deal of behavior that does not seem to please them. It explains why they involve themselves in relationships that do not enhance their self-esteem. It is because they are more uncomfortable when they are not engaging in such behaviors than when they are. It also explains why women in general feel that they are less in control of their persons than men. Control by direct positive reinforcement is much more likely to generate feedback that informs the subject as to what behavior is valuable for reinforcement. Avoidance-controlled behavior, on the other hand, generates diffuse anxiety about all behaviors except the one correct one. The individual may indeed be largely unaware of when the behavior that postpones the inevitable punishment was performed.

Unresponsive environments are particularly likely to generate diffuse hostility and depression. They are also difficult to deal with, since no overt sanction can be acted on. Such environments can be maintained for a long time without our awareness, since reinforcing events do not take place frequently. In fact reinforcement is defined by the absence of acutely painful events.

It is also unnecessary that the environment function this way all the time. It has long been known that intermittent reinforcement is a more effective method of behavioral control than continual reinforcement. We are also unclear as to when the individual's perception of the reinforcing consequences of his or her behavior becomes almost as effective as the actual reinforcement itself. The relationship between expectation and attribution in the control of behavior has just recently begun to be explored.

Recognition of these mechanisms (whether they are phrased in behaviorist terminology or not) may have to precede effective techniques for social and personal change. First, the definition of what is an effective reinforcer of human behavior must be dealt with. One can question whether love and companionship are not just as important human needs as status and power. Second, one has to deal with who has control of the reinforcements and why. Little effective change will take place as long as people assume that a male-defined and/or male-designated reward is somehow better. Women need to feel free to offer affiliation to other women (and men to other men) without fear of the label "homosexual." Third, we must realize that the schedules that are generally in force in our society are different for women than for men. Thus we may assume that the social world is sex biased, a priori, unless proven otherwise.

Another way of looking at how sex influences behavior is to view sex-related processes in the context of specific organizations and within society as an organization. This kind of approach is very closely related to sociological thinking. The kinds of questions that are generated by such an approach include (1) How do sexist biases and assumptions permeate our social institutions? (2) Why is our society sexist? (3) What is the relationship between sexism and other aspects of a society? (4) What benefits do societies derive from sexism? (5) How are these benefits transfered to particular individuals so that they maintain behaviors that uphold sexist norms? This last question is the one that is most directly relevant to psychologists.

Evidence that sexist assumptions permeate our society in language, the communications media, social institutions such as marriage and child care arrangements, and so forth has been presented throughout this book. It is important to get beyond the relatively simple demonstration that sexism exists to show the mechanisms by which it is transmitted. A series of exploratory studies by Virginia O'Leary and her colleagues (Hansen, O'Leary, & Stonner, 1976) may show something about the underlying nature of the cognitive processes involved. These investigators presented subjects with statements such as "Mary laughs at the comedian" and asked them to rank order the information that would be important in determining why she had laughed. They were given information related to the distinctiveness, consensus, and consistency of the stimulus person's behavior and were asked to evaluate how important or unimportant such information was in making their decision about the causes of the behavior. They found that access to information about the stimulus person was more important when the behaviors were performed by a woman than when they were performed by a man. Both sexes considered knowing something about the distinctiveness and consistency of the behavior (which behavior does not matter— all the behaviors judged showed the same effect) more important for understanding why women behaved the way they did than for understanding why men did so. The authors interpret these results in terms of the fact that the male role is more clearly defined than the female role. Thus people find it easier to assign cause for the behavior of males. Since females are perceived as more inconsistent and unstable, people look for explanations of their behavior within the female personality. These findings may indicate that the vagueness of females' roles as they are currently constructed by our society may help perpetuate the myth that female personalities are uniquely suited for such roles.

Female roles within particular institutions in our society are characterized by lack of clear definition. It is hard to measure what explicit achievements make one a good homemaker, good mother, or a good secretary. On the other hand, it is difficult to perform abominably in such roles. Thus women receive very little feedback about how to make their performance more adequate. Interestingly, the most ambiguous situations are those in which sex is most central as a predictor of behavior. Both in terms of self-definitions of role-appropriate behavior, as in Bem's sex-role typology, and in terms of the way people perceive others, people stereotype most when they have the least information.

Many of the other questions asked earlier are beyond the scope of the psychologist and may best be left to the sociologist and anthropologist. It is the responsibility of the psychologist, however, to try to understand how social mechanisms are interpreted and transmitted by individuals. It is obvious that sexism as it now exists is advantageous for males, since it minimizes competition and ensures a large supply of underpaid and interchangeable work units both within and outside the home. An analysis may be made largely in terms of power, which is the province of political science, but it would be trivial to politicize all interpersonal transactions. Those who are interested in the psychology of women are beginning to realize that it is necessary to analyze processes, not people, in terms of sex. For example, many women never put themselves in any danger of social sanctions because they remain within the home and act out the traditional feminine role. Is their behavior reinforced only by the need to avoid unpleasant outcomes? Or does vicarious reinforcement play a role? What societal function does ridicule of aspiring women serve in preventing women from taking such women as role models? And in fact, since none of us remains within our appropriate roles all of the time, how does society decide when sanctions are necessary? Questions like these indicate the need for psychology to look at the surroundings and systemic connections of a behavior before attempting to explain it.

POTENTIAL FEMINIST PITFALLS

While feminists are not very happy with the world as it is, it is easy to fall into the trap of believing that it is satisfactory for most males. Investigators have concentrated on the limitations of the female role as it is now laid out, but there are advantages to that role, too. First, many men do not have high occupational aspirations and do not feel fulfilled by their on-the-job activities. Many occupations that are defined as male appropriate are dull, require hard physical labor and/or repetitive activities, and offer few opportunities for choice within the job framework or advancement to a new framework. To be fair, it should be noted that men in general do define themselves in terms of their occupational status, and removal from such status due to unemployment or retirement is a common source of male depression.

Since women are rarely permitted to define themselves in terms of occupational status, they are freer to offer a number of role definitions of themselves. While each of these roles may offer more limited satisfactions, they do have some satisfactions to offer. This consideration may be behind the rather mysterious findings that continue to reappear to the effect that women report themselves as happier than men although they are less satisfied with their lives. Housework and care of husband and children offer some autonomy and freedom for growth that may be denied to males in lower socio-economic strata. Many women suffer from relative rather than absolute deprivation. Thus it is reasonable that the women's-liberation movement is more powerful among women with middle- and upper-class husbands. These women are also those who are most likely to suffer from the role strains associated with attempting to function effectively in a multitude of roles.

The parental role may offer a considerable amount of power as well. It is also ideally suited to meet affiliative needs, which the occupational world ignores. Thus there has been a movement toward the idea of "fathering" among feminist males who are concerned with the incompatibility between achievement and personal happiness for men as well as for women. Some of the traits that women develop in response to the parental role would be valuable for society as a whole. For example, women in general seem to be more tolerant and cooperative than men.

It is important for feminists to avoid labeling traditional women as deviant. No one should have to apologize for being a homemaker. The major consideration is that social roles should be assumed through choice and individual talent and inclination rather than biological inevitability. Some men make better "mothers" than some women, just as some women have acquired characteristics that are very valuable for childrearing. We should also not assume that because a woman is engaged in full-time childrearing there is nothing else she can do or nothing else she will do in the future. Exploration of a variety of models of adult life development is important. It is not clear whether it is better in terms of individual fulfillment to have a career and then have children or vice versa, or not to have children at all. We must find out, in addition, how social mechanisms operate to facilitate or inhibit the function of particular life styles (e.g., communes, role-reversals, non-zero-sum marriages, etc.).

People are infinitely variable. It is easy to make simplistic generalizations in this area, since it is remarkable how many social relationships are altered by the addition of sex to the equation. It is clear, however, that there are many exceptions to all rules. It is important to study the exceptions—women and men who appear to be invulnerable to the social influences around them. When are people able to define themselves independently of the way others define them? What is the role of what one thinks one does? How much does our perception of reality create that reality?

It is important to study the areas in which women have been neglected or in which their treatment has been biased, but one should not make a fetish about the quasi-religious, unique properties of women. Menstruation may function socially in the same way that the common cold does. Processes, not people, must become the focus; sex, not the sexes. Perhaps at some point I could retitle this book *None of the Sexes*.

Afterword
Specific Notes for
Specific People

FOR THE STUDENT

Psychology of women is not for someone who wants all the answers. It is very much in a state of flux. Because the area is still in its infancy, it provides an excellent illustration of how subjects are carved out of a discipline by means of redefinition, new perspectives, and new questions that generate further questions. Those who are involved in this area are some of the most enthusiastic people in psychology. In fact one writer who surveyed various areas of psychology in terms of careers for young women noted that some of the most interesting women in the country are involved in it (McHugh, 1976).

I do not believe that this area is a sidetrack from or irrelevant to psychology as a whole. Although at the moment most of its energy seems to be concentrated on revising traditional conceptions of femininity and femaleness, some evidence of increased contact between the psychology of women and the rest of psychology exists. First, more men are entering the field and doing research in the area—my courses on the subject usually consist about 20 percent of men. Second, concepts developed in the area are affecting the field of psychology in general. One survey of references in social-psychology textbooks found that the most frequently cited study was that by Matina Horner on fear of success.

The field is also one of the easiest for students to become involved in. One can become an affiliate member of the Division of the Psychology of Women of the American Psychological Association for a small sum of money and receive a newsletter that is issued regularly. An organization, the Association for Women in Psychology, is open to undergraduate and graduate students and offers inexpensive accommodations at almost all major psychological conventions. These organizations provide an opportunity to find out about the problems and joys of the professional psychologist before one has committed oneself. It is also easier to understand academic issues as one becomes more involved in them.

For students who care to pursue graduate study in the psychology of women, graduate programs on the master's and doctoral levels are becoming available. Caution is advised in investing in graduate training in this area, however, because it is not yet quite legitimate in the view of professional psychology. For example, few ads are found in *The Monitor*, the official newspaper of the American Psychological Association, for people with a specialty in the psychology of women. Suggesting an alternative seems like a "cop-out," but thorough training in an additional area of psychology would not be ill advised. Probably the most useful and relevant areas are social psychology, developmental psychology, or clinical and counseling psychology. However, almost all areas of psychology have aspects that are relevant to the study of women.

The area should not be considered a ghetto suitable only for women. As sex, not the sexes, becomes more and more the focus of study, information acquired in this area will appear more relevant for men as well as women. Already information on parenting and alternate marriage arrangements has been utilized by feminist males. Questions about the male model of the occupational world are worth consideration by males as well as by females. It is clear that any sizable change in the social system will involve all the sexes.

FOR THE TEACHER

Although it is true in all fields, this is an area in which it is especially true that one learns as one teaches. As one questions the hierarchical control in many areas that are male dominated, the dynamics of the classroom system with its "expert" and its "novices" may also come into question. I have no simple answers with which to confront this problem except that one should keep an open mind and accept personal experience as another form of data to be discussed and evaluated. On the other hand, it is easy to fall into the trap of having the course become a "consciousness-raising session." I have tried to provide enough empirical data so that this is unlikely to occur. I also feel that it is unfair to students to be in a graded course in which subjectivity is the valid response. Some instructors have reported much success with "auxiliary" consciousness-raising techniques such as out-of-class exercises or special sessions put aside for experiential relations. Sue Cox (1976), in her book of readings *Female Psychology: The Emerging Self*, has provided a variety of exercises that may be illuminating and useful.

There are a large number of films on women available, and some of them have been reviewed in the *Psychology of Women Quarterly*. As yet, there has been little development of curriculum materials and aids at the college level. Some materials developed for high schools might be useful and are available from the Training Institute for Sex Desegregation at Douglass College of Rutgers University. A new game called Access will soon be on the market and might provide a useful learning device. Some other games on sex roles are currently available, but most of them are simplistic or too limited in scope (Greenblatt & Baily, 1978).

It is important in the classroom to go beyond the relatively simple documentation of sexist effects and examine the mechanisms that underlie such effects. Almost any area of psychology can be used, and almost any theoretical perspective can be of service. It is easy to generate individual and class projects by starting with the premise that "it has long been known that . . ." is probably wrong. It is also easy to generate projects by perceiving that there are no content areas that should be taboo to psychologists. The area lends itself to interdisciplinary projects, and I have found that some exciting ones were generated by means of slides, interviews with particular groups or people with whom students have had access, as well as more conventional research techniques. I have also found that students are willing to spend more time on projects than in most other areas, and provision should be made for independent research after the conclusion of the course if the students wish to take their projects further.

Perhaps the most exciting and depressing aspect of the course is the fact that it generates a great deal of enthusiasm and consciousness raising (not necessarily deliberate) among its participants. You will find male colleagues complaining about indoctrination when your students raise questions in their courses. And you will find students returning for periodic "fixes" after having been in a less supportive atmosphere for a while. You might have to make provision for more advanced seminars (e.g., on research methods) if your institution permits. It might also be interesting to explore the development of an alternate course—the psychology of men—if there are receptive male faculty members available.

FOR THE COUNSELOR

I feel less comfortable about making suggestions in this area since I am untrained in the issues. Everyone who teaches courses in the psychology of women, however, is eventually sought out for advice and asked to make recommendations about specific student problems. The fact that the problems are socially derived rather than personal does not make them less painful for the person. I think the issue of whether to seek a female or a male therapist (if this seems necessary) is less important than stressing the harmful effect of doctrinaire assumptions. Both female and male students need to learn to be "good consumers" of psychological information so that they can choose their sources of assistance with the hope of maximal effectiveness. It seems clear that they should understand the ideological assumptions of any counselor before beginning a therapeutic relationship. They should be aware, moreover, that change is possible at any point in their lives.

It is also important for the counselor to impress on students the fact that change in the person does not automatically imply change in their social system or in society. In some sense behavior is what others perceive and define it to be. If a person becomes more assertive and others perceive her or him as aggressive, that behavior may be penalized by others. It is important that one learns to define behavior independently of the judgments of others, but it is also important that one acquire a reference group that will enable him or her to appraise realistically the results of one's behaviors. A critical mass or ratio of people who have changed their behavior may often be necessary for social change to take place.

People should also be made aware that they exist in a series of "contractual" relationships with other people. These others have some right to expect that these contracts will be fulfilled. Thus teachers have a right to expect acceptable work from their students, and spouses have certain expectations about social arrangements between the pair. While these arrangements can and may be unilaterally abrogated, people should be aware of the consequences of these actions. It may be helpful to explore the advantages and disadvantages of a given course of action before it is carried out. It may also be valuable for people to explore what psychological and material resources are under their own control. As has been stated before, personal control may be the single most major issue in the psychology of women.

FOR THE RESEARCHER

It is obvious from the materials supplied in this book that information in this area is being accumulated at an ever-increasing rate. More sources for publication of feminist research seem to be opening up daily. In fact this information explosion provides one of the greatest problems for research in the area. It is difficult to tell what is trivial from what is to be centrally important. Theories that organize and synthesize materials over a large content area are largely missing.

There are a few guidelines that may be helpful to the would-be feminist researcher:

1. Reiteration of proof that sexism exists is trivial unless an unusual new population is available.
2. Proving that old procedures examined only with male subjects do or do not work with females is also not terribly exciting unless some theoretical position stands or falls on the work.
3. It is advisable to examine the data base from psychology as it existed before the advent of psychology of women to see what is relevant or useful.
4. It is unwise to assume that many psychological processes are unique to women. Male control groups should be used, and if possible, it would be important to examine a phenomenon by means of people of both sexes who are high or low in the relevant variable.
5. Whenever possible, information should be integrated with material gathered in areas distinct from the psychology of women.

Aside from the fact that I believe these points to be good research practice, they help serve another purpose—the legitimization of research in this area. In the past year several leading feminist scholars have been denied tenure at major institutions. One leading female scholar, Jo Freeman, was not hired at several institutions because her work was not "general" enough. Work can be dismissed as trivial if it is not of interest to male scholarship. Of course excuses can always be found to show that work that is politically questionable is academically questionable as well, but there is no reason to make it easy to do so.

FOR THE PROFESSIONAL

There are some encouraging signs that sex and gender are becoming more legitimate areas for psychology as a profession. In 1973 Division 35 (The Psychology of Women) of the American Psychological Association was established. By January 1976 it had 1222 members, making it one of the largest as well as one of the fastest-growing divisions of APA (Unger, O'Leary, & Fabian, 1976). The purposes of division 35 are

> to promote the research and study of women, including both biological and socio-cultural determinants of behavior. To encourage the integration of information about women with the current psychological knowledge and beliefs in order to apply gained knowledge to the society and its institutions.

As might be anticipated, the majority (97%) of APA members who have expressed agreement with these goals by joining Division 35 are women.

An analysis of the characteristics of about 50 percent of the membership of Division 35 has been conducted (Unger et al., 1976). We found that the majority of members are young and are in the more traditionally feminine areas of concentration within psychology (e.g., clinical, counseling, education, and developmental). More than half are employed in academic institutions. An analysis of the small number of males who belong to this division seems to indicate something about the mechanisms of informal academic networks. Almost all these men are at institutions in which one or more female members of Division 35 are employed. These data would indicate that personal recruitment is the major vehicle by which individuals are induced to involve themselves in organizations in which they may not perceive themselves as compatible with or desirable to the rest of the membership.

One of the first presidents of Division 35, Florence Denmark (1977), has recently documented some organizational developments that have occurred since the organization came into being. A journal called *The Psychology of Women Quarterly* has been published, and for the first time the *Annual Review of Psychology* contained a review of topics in the psychology of women (Mednick & Weissman, 1975). In 1975, too, the first conference on new directions for research on women was held, funded by the National Institute of Mental Health and the Ford Foundation, and a book on its findings was compiled (Sherman & Denmark, 1978). In addition to the appearance of other cross-disciplinary journals on sex and gender (e.g., *Sex Roles* and *Signs*), more "mainstream" journals appear to be increasing the percentage of women on editorial boards, and more papers relevant to women seem to be appearing in them (Denmark, 1977). It is also heartening that for the first time a researcher who is concerned primarily with issues relevant to women, Sandra Bem, received a prestigious award as a prominant young researcher from the American Psychological Association, and that a book on the social relationships of women and men by Kay Deaux (1976) was a runner-up for a national media award by that organization. Although Division 35 cannot be credited for all these achievements, it is enlightening that the development and growth of the organization is coincident with the increasing visibility and recognition of women in psychology.

A more recent survey of the membership of Division 35 indicates that the number of courses entitled "The Psychology of Women" is increasing rapidly (Mednick, 1978). Members reported that 191 such courses are listed in their college catalogues as compared to 36 courses noted in a survey made by the Task Force on the Status of Women in Psychology (1973). As the number of such courses grows, they should increase the legitimacy of the area for both women and men. Several independent studies (Ruble & Croke, 1974; Olive & McGuigan, 1975) have shown that courses in psychology of women stimulate favorable attitude change among their participants. This attitude change may ultimately smooth the way for change in societal structures and ease the process of personal adjustment to cultural and institutional change.

The greater involvement and visibility of women in psychology and psychology of women should produce a cumulative effect. At the very least it should provide a large number of female role models for professional involvement in the field. Elizabeth Douvan (1976), in the first presidential address to the division on the psychology of women, has pointed out the importance of role models in professional identification. She notes that the proliferation of cigars and beards during the clinical-training process suggests that identification with noted figures in the area is taking place. Less humorously, she notes that the greater impact of women in the field will alter its thought processes as well as its personal style. We may expect a shift away from the objectification and depersonalization of people as well as an increased concern with feelings and growth of the self.

There is some danger that the study of women will be ghettoized. Changes in scholarly thinking are not readily accepted if they represent ideas about women put forth by women. Women scholars do not, in general, have sufficient prestige to alter their fields. For example, I find it particularly intriguing that while a number of textbooks on the psychology of women have appeared in recent years, only a very few have appeared in hardcover editions. Developmental-psychology textbooks, in contrast, routinely appear in hardcover editions. This difference may represent covert assumptions about the legitimacy of the area. Softcover editions may more readily be used as "accessory" texts in more "substantial" areas such as social or clinical psychology.

At the risk of angering some radical feminists, I do not believe the future of this field lies in a psychology of women. What we are really saying is that some processes are more likely to occur to some people because of some social mechanisms. Some physiological mechanisms may be involved as well, but we will be unable to find out much about these until sex-blind environments generally exist. And if we are really successful—both politically and psychologically—the psychology of women, as a separate field, may put itself out of business one day.

References

Abramowitz, S. I., Abramowitz, C. V., Jackson, C., & Gomes, B. "The Politics of Clinical Judgment: What Nonliberal Examiners Infer About Women Who Don't Stifle Themselves." *Journal of Consulting and Clinical Psychology*, 1973, *41*, 385–391.

Abramson, M., & Torghele, J. R. "Weight, Temperature Changes, and Psychosomatic Symptomatology in Relation to the Menstrual Cycle." *American Journal of Obstetrics and Gynecology*, 1961, *81*, 223–232.

Adams, E. B., & Sarason, I. G. "Relations Between Anxiety in Children and Their Parents." *Child Development*, 1963, *34*, 237–246.

Adams, M. *Single Blessedness*. New York: Basic Books, 1976.

Adinolfi, A. A., Watson, R. I., Jr., & Klein, R. E. "Aggressive Reactions to Frustration in Urban Guatemalan Children: The Effects of Sex and Social Class." *Journal of Personality and Social Psychology*, 1973, *25*, 227–233.

Adleman, C. S. "Psychological Intervention into the Crisis of Rape." In E. C. Viano, ed. *Victims & Society*. Washington, D.C.: Visage Press, 1976.

Adler, A. *Understanding Human Nature*. Greenwich, Conn.: Fawcett Premier, 1954.

Adler, F. *Sisters in Crime: The Rise of the New Female Criminal*. New York: McGraw-Hill, 1975.

Aiello, J. R., & Aiello, T. D. "The Development of Personal Space: Proxemic Behavior of Children Six Through Sixteen." *Human Ecology*, 1974, *2*, 177–189.

Akamatsu, T. J., & Thelen, M. H. "A Review of the Literature on Observer Characteristics and Imitation." *Developmental Psychology*, 1974, *10*, 38–47.

Albright, D. G., & Chang, A. F. "An Examination of How One's Attitudes Toward Women are Reflected in One's Defensiveness and Self-esteem." *Sex Roles*, 1976, *2*, 195–198.

Aldous, J. "Wives' Employment Status and Lower-class Men as Husbands–Fathers: Support for the Moynihan Thesis." *Journal of Marriage and the Family*, 1969a, *31*, 469–476.

Aldous, J. "Occupational Characteristics and Males' Role Performance in the Family." *Journal of Marriage and the Family*, 1969b, *31*, 707–712.

Alexander, K. L., & Eckland, B. K. "Sex Differences in the Educational Attainment Process." *American Sociological Review*, 1974, *39*, 668–682.

Alkire, A. A., Collum, M. E., Kaswan, J., & Love, L. R. "Information Exchange and Accuracy of Verbal Communication Under Social Power Conditions." *Journal of Personality and Social Psychology*, 1968, *9*, 301–308.

Allen, C. D., & Eicher, J. B. "Adolescent Girls' Acceptance and Rejection Based on Appearance." *Adolescence*, 1973, *8*, 125–138.

Allen, V. L., & Newtson, D. "Development of Conformity and Independence." *Journal of Personality and Social Psychology*, 1972, *22*, 18–30.

Alpert, J. L. "Sex as a Subject Versus Sex as a Stimulus Variable: Discussion." Paper presented at the meeting of the Eastern Psychological Association, Boston, April 1977.

Alpert, J. L., & Gibbons, J. "Sex-Role Stereotyping in Statistics Textbooks." Paper presented at the meeting of the Eastern Psychological Association, New York City, April 1976.

Alpert, J. L., & Richardson, M. S. "Internal Barriers to Women Doing Research." Paper prepared for the Task Force on Women Doing Research. Division 35 of the American Psychological Association, March 1977.

Alpert, J. L., Richardson, M. S., Perlmutter, B., & Shutzer, T. "Women's and Men's Perceptions of Single and Multiple Roles." Paper presented at the meeting of the American Psychological Association, Washington, D.C., 1976.

Altshuler, R., & Kassinove, H. "The Effects of Skill and Chance Instructional Sets, Schedule of Reinforcement, and Sex on Children's Temporal Persistence." *Child Development*, 1975, *46*, 258–262.

Amir, M. *Patterns in Forcible Rape.* Chicago: University of Chicago Press, 1971.

Anderson, J. E. *The Young Child in the Home.* Englewood Cliffs, N.J.: Prentice-Hall, 1936.

Anderson, J. V. Psychological Determinants. In R. B. Kundsin, ed. *Successful Women in the Sciences: An Analysis of Determinants.* New York: New York Academy of Sciences, 1973.

Anspach, D. F. "Kinship and Divorce." *Journal of Marriage and the Family*, 1976, *38*, 323–330.

Appleton, H. L., & Gurwitz, S. B. Willingness to Help as Determined by the Sex-Role Appropriateness of the Helpseeker's Career Goals." *Sex Roles*, 1976, *2*, 321–330.

Argote, L. M., Fisher, J. E., McDonald, P. J., & O'Neal, E. C. "Competitiveness in Males and in Females: Situational Determinants of Fear of Success Behavior." *Sex Roles*, 1976, *2*, 295–303.

Argyle, M. *Social Interaction*. New York: Atherton Press, 1969.

Armentrout, J. A., & Burger, G. K. "Children's Reports of Parental Child-Rearing Behavior at Five Grade Levels." *Developmental Psychology*, 1972, *7*, 44–48.

Arms, S. *Immaculate Deception: A New Look at Women and Childbirth in America*. Boston: Houghton Mifflin, 1975.

Aronoff, J., & Crano, W. D. "A Re-examination of the Cross-cultural Principles of Task Segregation and Sex Role Differentiation in the Family." *American Sociological Review*, 1975, *40*, 12–20.

Astin, H. S. "The Role of Continuing Education in the Development of Adult Women." *The Counseling Psychologist*, 1976, *6*, 55–60.

Astin, H. S. "Women and Work." In J. Sherman & F. Denmark, eds. *Psychology of Women: Future Directions of Research*. New York: Psychological Dimensions, 1978.

Astin, H. S., & Bayer, A. E. "Sex Discrimination in Academe." In A. S. Rossi & A. Calderwood, eds. *Academic Women on the Move*. New York: Russell Sage, 1973.

Athanasiou, R., & Greene, P. "Physical Attractiveness and Helping Behavior." Paper presented at the meeting of the American Psychological Association, Montreal, August 1973.

Axelson, L. J. "The Working Wife: Differences in Perception Among Negro and White Males." *Journal of Marriage and the Family*, 1970, *32*, 457–464.

Babchuk, N., & Bates, A. P. "The Primary Relations of Middle-Class Couples: A Study in Male Dominance. *American Sociological Review*, 1963, *28*, 377–384.

Babladelis, G. "The Psychology of Women." Invited address, University of Hawaii, Department of Psychology, May 3, 1977.

Bales, R. F. "Task Roles and Social Roles in Problem Solving Groups." In I. D. Steiner & M. Fishbein, eds. *Current Studies in Social Psychology*. New York: Holt, 1965.

Bandura, A. "Influence of Models' Reinforcement Contingencies on the Acquisition of Imitative Responses." *Journal of Personality and Social Psychology*, 1965, *1*, 589–595.

Bandura, A. "Social-Learning Theory of Identificatory Processes." In A. D. Goslin, ed. *Handbook of Socialization Theory and Research*. Chicago: Rand McNally, 1969, pp. 213–262.

Bandura, A., & Huston, A. C. "Identification as a Process of Incidental Learning." *Journal of Abnormal and Social Psychology*, 1961, *63*, 311–318.

Bandura, A., Ross, D., & Ross, S. A. "Imitation of Film-Mediated Aggressive Models." *Journal of Abnormal and Social Psychology*, 1963a, 66, 3–11.

Bandura, A., Ross, D., & Ross, S. A. "A Comparative Test of the Status Envy, Social Power, and Secondary Reinforcement Theories of Identificatory Learning." *Journal of Abnormal and Social Psychology*, 1963b, 67, 529–534.

Bane, M. "Marital Disruption and the Lives of Children." *Journal of Social Issues*, 1976, 32, 103–117.

Bard, M., & Ellison, K. "Crisis Intervention and Investigation of Forcible Rape." *The Police Chief*, May 1974, pp. 68–72.

Bardwick, J. M. "Psychological Factors in the Acceptance and Use of Oral Contraceptives." In J. T. Fawcett, ed. *Psychological Perspectives on Population*. New York: Basic Books, 1973.

Barnett, R. C. "Sex Differences and Age Trends in Occupational Preference and Occupational Prestige. *Journal of Counseling Psychology*, 1975, 22, 35–38.

Bart, P. B. "Social Structure and Vocabularies of Discomfort: What Happened to Female Hysteria?" *Journal of Health and Social Behavior*, 1968, 9, 188–193.

Bart, P. "Mother Portnoy's Complaint." *Transaction*, 1970, 8, 69–74.

Bar-Tal, D., & Saxe, L. "Perceptions of Similarly and Dissimilarly Attractive Couples and Individuals." *Journal of Personality and Social Psychology*, 1976a, 33, 772–781.

Bar-Tal, D., & Saxe, L. "Physical Attractiveness and Its Relationship to Sex Role Stereotyping." *Sex Roles*, 1976b, 2, 123–133.

Baruch, G. K. "Maternal Influences upon College Women's Attitude Toward Women and Work." *Developmental Psychology*, 1972, 6, 32–37.

Baruch, G. K. "Girls Who Perceive Themselves as Competent: Some Antecedents and Correlates." *Psychology of Women Quarterly*, 1976, 1, 38–49.

Baruch, R. "The Achievement Motive in Women: Implications for Career Development." *Journal of Personality and Social Psychology*, 1967, 5, 260–267.

Bayer, A. E. "Marriage Plans and Educational Aspirations." *American Journal of Sociology*, 1969, 75, 239–244.

Beach, F. A. "A Review of Physiological and Psychological Studies of Sexual Behavior in Mammals." *Physiological Review*, 1947, 27, 240–307.

Beach, F. A. "Factors Involved in the Control of Mounting Behavior by Female Mammals." In M. Diamond, ed. *Reproduction and Sexual Behavior*. Bloomington: University of Indiana Press, 1968.

Bebbington, A. C. "The Function of Stress in the Establishment of the Dual-Career Family." *Journal of Marriage and the Family*, 1973, 35, 530–537.

Beck, A. T. "The Development of Depression: A Cognitive Model." In R. J. Friedman & M. M. Katz, eds. *The Psychology of Depression: Contemporary Theory and Research*. Washington D.C.: V. H. Winston, 1974.

Beck, A. T., & Greenberg, R. L. "Cognitive Therapy with Depressed

Women." In V. Franks & V. Burtle, eds. *Women in Therapy*. New York: Brunner/Mazel, 1974.

Beckman, L. J. "Values of Parenthood Among Women Who Want an Only Child." Paper presented at the meeting of the American Psychological Association, Washington D.C., September 1976.

Beekman, S. "Sex Differences in Nonverbal Behavior." Unpublished Ph.D. dissertation, 1974. Cited in S. Weitz. "Sex Differences in Nonverbal Communication." *Sex Roles*, 1976, *2*, 175–184.

Beker, J. "The Influence of School Camping on the Self-concepts and Social Relationships of Sixth Grade Children." *Journal of Educational Psychology*, 1960, *51*, 352–356.

Bell, R. R. *Social Deviance*. Homewood, Ill.: Dorsey Press, 1971.

Bell, R. R. "Female Sexual Satisfaction as Related to Levels of Education." In L. Gross, ed. *Sexual Behavior*. Flushing, N.Y.: Spectrum, 1974.

Bem, S. L. "The Measurement of Psychological Androgyny." *Journal of Consulting and Clinical Psychology*, 1974, *42*, 155–162.

Bem, S. L. "Sex Role Adaptability: One Consequence of Psychological Androgyny." *Journal of Personality and Social Psychology*, 1975, *31*, 634–643.

Bem, S. L. "Beyond Androgyny: Some Presumptuous Prescriptions for a Liberated Sexual Identity." In J. Sherman & F. L. Denmark, eds. *Psychology of Women: Future Directions of Research*. New York: Psychological Dimensions, 1978.

Bem, S. L., & Bem, D. J. "Training the Woman to Know Her Place: The Power of a Nonconscious Ideology." In D. J. Bem, ed. *Beliefs, Attitudes, and Human Affairs*. Belmont, Calif. Brooks/Cole, 1970.

Bem, S. L., & Lenney, E. "Sex Typing and the Avoidance of Cross-sex Behavior." *Journal of Personality and Social Psychology*, 1976, *33*, 48–54.

Bem, S. L., Martyna, W., & Watson, C. "Sex Typing and Androgyny: Further Explorations of the Expressive Domain." *Journal of Personality and Social Psychology*, 1976, *34*, 1016–1023.

Bennie, E., & Sclare, A. "The Battered Child Syndrome." *American Journal of Psychiatry*, 1969, *125*, 975–979.

Berger, J., Cohen, B. P., & Zelditch, M., Jr. "Status Characteristics and Social Interaction." *American Sociological Review*, 1972, *37*, 241–255.

Berger, M., Foster, M., & Wallston, B. S. "Dual-Career Couples: Job Seeking Strategies and Family Structure." Paper presented at the meeting of the American Psychological Association, Chicago, September 1975.

Berman, P. W., Cooper, P., Mansfield, P., Shields, S., & Abplanalp, J. "Sex Differences in Attraction to Infants: When Do They Occur?" *Sex Roles*, 1975, *1*, 311–318.

Bermant, G., & Davidson, J. M. *Biological Bases of Sexual Behavior*. New York: Harper & Row, 1974.

Bernard, J. *Academic Women*. University Park: Pennsylvania State University Press, 1964.

Bernard, J. *The Future of Marriage*. New York: World, 1972.

Bernard, J. *Women, Wives, Mothers: Values and Options.* Chicago: Atherton-Aldine, 1975a.

Bernard, J. "Note on Changing Life Styles, 1970–1974." *Journal of Marriage and the Family,* 1975b, *37,* 582–593.

Bernstein, M. D. & Russo, N. F. "The History of Psychology Revisited: Or, Up With Our Foremothers." *American Psychologist,* 1974, *29,* 130–134.

Berscheid, E., Walster, E., & Bohrnstedt, G. "The Happy American Body: A Survey Report." *Psychology Today,* Mar. 1973, 119–131.

Bigner, J. J. "Sibling Influence on Sex-Role Preference of Young Children." *Journal of Genetic Psychology,* 1972, *121,* 271–282.

Bigner, J. J. "Second Borns' Discrimination of Sibling Role Concepts." *Developmental Psychology,* 1974, *10,* 564–573.

Biller, H. B. "Father Dominance and Sex-Role Development in Kindergarten Age Boys." *Developmental Psychology,* 1969, *1,* 87–94.

Biller, H. B. *Father, Child and Sex Role: Paternal Determinants of Personality Development.* Lexington, Mass.: Heath-Lexington, 1971.

Biller, H. B., & Meredith, D. *Father Power.* New York: McKay, 1974.

Birnbaum, J. A. "Life Patterns and Self Esteem in Gifted Family Oriented and Career Committed Women." In M. T. S. Mednick, S. S. Tangri, & L. W. Hoffman, eds. *Women and Achievement.* Washington D.C.: Hemisphere, 1975.

Black, T. E., & Higbee, K. L. "Effects of Power, Threat, and Sex on Exploitation." *Journal of Personality and Social Psychology,* 1973, *27,* 382–388.

Blade, M., & Watson, W. S. "Increase in Spatial Visualization Test Scores during Engineering Study." *Psychological Monographs,* 1955, *69* (12, Whole no. 397).

Blake, J. "Family Size in the 1960's: A Baffling Fad?" *Eugenics Quarterly,* 1967, *14,* 60–74.

Block, J. H. "Conceptions of Sex Role: Some Cross-Cultural and Longitudinal Perspectives." *American Psychologist,* 1973, *28,* 512–526.

Block, J. H. "Debatable Conclusions About Sex Differences." *Contemporary Psychology,* 1976, *21,* 517–522.

Block, J. H. "Another Look at Sex Differentiation in the Socialization Behaviors of Mothers and Fathers." In J. Sherman & F. Denmark, eds. *Psychology of Women: Future Directions of Research.* New York: Psychological Dimensions, 1978.

Blood, R. O., Jr., & Wolfe, D. M. *Husbands and Wives.* New York: Free Press, 1960.

Bock, D. R., & Kolakowski, D. "Further Evidence of Sex-Linked Major-Gene Influence on Human Spatial Visualizing Ability." *American Journal of Human Genetics,* 1973, *25,* 1–14.

Bohan, J. S. "Age and Sex Differences in Self Concept." *Adolescence,* 1973, *8,* 379–384.

Booth, A. "Sex and Social Participation." *American Sociological Review,* 1972, *37,* 183–192.

Borden, R. J. "Witnessed Aggression: Influence of an Observer's Sex and

Values on Aggressive Responding." *Journal of Personality and Social Psychology*, 1975, *31*, 567–573.

Boskind-Lodahl, M. "Cinderella's Stepsisters: A Feminist Perspective on Anorexia Nervosa and Bulimia." *Signs*, 1976, *2*, 342–356.

Boston Women's Health Book Collective. *Our Bodies, Our Selves*. New York: Simon & Schuster, 1976.

Brandwein, R. A., Brown, C. A., & Fox, E. M. "Women and Children Last: The Social Situation of Divorced Mothers and Their Families." *Journal of Marriage and the Family*, 1974, *36*, 498–514.

Brannon, R. Unpublished paper, 1977.

Bremer, T. H., & Wittig, M. A. "Fear of Success: A Personality Trait or a Response to Occupational Deviance and Role Overload?" Paper presented at the meeting of the American Psychological Association, San Francisco, August 1977.

Brenner, M. "What Makes Bella Run?" *New York*, June 20, 1977, pp. 54–64.

Broderick, C. B. "Social Heterosexual Development Among Urban Negroes and Whites." *Journal of Marriage and the Family*, 1965, *27*, 200–203.

Brodsky, A. "The Consciousness-Raising Group as a Model for Therapy with Women." *Psychotherapy: Theory, Research, and Practice*, 1973, *10*, 24–29.

Brodsky, A. "Special Problems of Women in Prison." Paper presented at Conference on Corrections, Florida League of Women Voters, Gainesville, Florida, October 1973.

Brodsky, A. "Status of Women in the Psychological Community in the Southeast: Women as Graduate Students." *American Psychologist*, 1974, *29*, 523–526.

Bronfenbrenner, U. "Freudian Theories of Identification and Their Derivatives." *Child Development*, 1960, *31*, 15–40.

Bronfenbrenner, U. *American Families: Trends and Pressures*. Washington D.C.: GPO, 1974.

Brook, J., Whiteman, M., Peisach, E., & Deutsch, M. "Aspiration Levels of and for Children: Age, Sex, Race, and Socioeconomic Correlates." *Journal of Genetic Psychology*, 1974, *124*, 3–16.

Broverman, D. M., Klaiber, E. L., Kobayashi, Y., & Vogel, W. "Roles of Activation and Inhibition in Sex Differences in Cognitive Abilities." *Psychological Review*, 1968, *75*, 23–50.

Broverman, I. K., Broverman, D. M., Clarkson, F. E., Rosenkrantz, P. S., & Vogel, S. R. "Sex-Role Stereotypes and Clinical Judgments of Mental Health." *Journal of Consulting and Clinical Psychology*, 1970, *34*, 1–7.

Broverman, I. K., Vogel, S. R., Broverman, D. M., Clarkson, F. E., & Rosenkrantz, P. S. "Sex-Role Stereotypes: A Current Appraisal." *Journal of Social Issues*, 1972, *28*, 59–78.

Brown, C. A., Feldberg, R., Fox, E. M. & Kohen, J. "Divorce: Chance of a New Lifetime." *Journal of Social Issues*, 1976, *32*, 119–133.

Brown, D. G. "Sex-Role Development in a Changing Culture." *Psychological Bulletin*, 1958, *55*, 232–242.

Brown, G. W., Bhrolchain, M. N., & Harris, T. "Social Class and Psychiatric

Disturbance Among Women in an Urban Population." *Sociology,* 1975, *9,* 225–254.

Brown, G. W., Harris, T. O., & Peto, S. "Life Events and Psychiatric Disorders—2. Nature of Causal Link." *Psychological Medicine,* 1973, *3,* 159–176.

Brown, R., & Gilman, A. "The Pronouns of Power and Solidarity." In T. A. Sebeck, ed. *Style in Language.* Cambridge, Mass.: Technology Press, 1960.

Brownmiller, S. *Against Our Will: Men, Women, and Rape.* New York: Simon & Schuster, 1975.

Bruch, H. *Eating Disorders.* New York: Basic Books, 1973.

Bryant, B. K., & Trockel, J. F. "Personal History of Psychological Stress Related to Locus of Control Orientation Among College Women." *Journal of Consulting and Clinical Psychology,* 1976, *44,* 266–271.

Bryson, R. B., Bryson, J. B., Licht, M. H., & Licht, B. G. "The Professional Pair: Husband and Wife Psychologists." *American Psychologist,* 1976, *31,* 10–16.

Buchanan, D. R., Juhnke, R., & Goldman, M. "Violation of Personal Space as a Function of Sex." *Journal of Social Psychology,* 1976, *99,* 187–192.

Bugental, D. E., Love, L. R., & Gianetto, R. M. "Perfidious Feminine Faces." *Journal of Personality and Social Psychology,* 1971, *17,* 314–318.

Bullen, B. A., Monello, L. F., Cohen, H., & Mayer, J. "Attitudes Toward Physical Activity, Food, and Family in Obese and Nonobese Adolescent Girls." *American Journal of Clinical Nutrition,* 1963, *12,* 1–11.

Bumpass, L. L., & Westoff, C. F. "Unwanted Births and U.S. Population Growth." *Family Planning Perspectives,* 1970, *2,* 9–11.

Burger, G. K., Lamp, R. E., & Rogers, D. "Developmental Trends in Children's Perceptions of Parental Child-Rearing Behavior." *Developmental Psychology,* 1975, *11,* 391.

Burke, R. J., & Weir, T. "Relationship of Wives' Employment Status to Husband, Wife, and Pair Satisfaction and Performance." *Journal of Marriage and the Family,* 1976, *38,* 279–287.

Burlin, F. D. "Locus of Control and Female Occupational Aspiration." *Journal of Counseling Psychology,* 1976, *23,* 126–129.

Busby, L. J. "Sex-role Research on the Mass Media." *Journal of Communication,* 1975, Autumn, 107–131.

Byrne, D. Parental Antecedents of Authoritarianism." *Journal of Personality and Social Psychology,* 1965, *1,* 369–373.

Caballero, C. M., Giles, P., & Shaver, P. "Sex-role Traditionalism and Fear of Success." *Sex Roles,* 1975, *1,* 319–326.

Caldwell, B. M., & Smith, L. E. "Day Care For the Very Young—Prime Opportunity for Primary Prevention." *American Journal of Public Health,* 1970, *60,* 690–697.

Campbell, A., Converse, P. E., & Rodgers, W. L. *The Quality of American Life: Perceptions, Evaluations, and Satisfaction.* New York: Russell Sage Foundation, 1976.

Campbell, P. B., & McKain, A. E. "Intellectual Decline and the Adolescent

Woman." Paper presented at the meeting of the American Psychological Association, New Orleans, August 1974.

Carlson, E. R., & Carlson, R. "Male and Female Subjects in Personality Research." *Journal of Abnormal and Social Psychology*, 1961, *61*, 482–483.

Carrigan, W. C., & Julian, J. W. "Sex and Birth-Order Differences in Conformity as a Function of Need Affiliation Arousal." *Journal of Personality and Social Psychology*, 1966, *3*, 479–483.

Cavior, N., & Dokecki, P. R. "Physical Attractiveness, Perceived Attitude Similarity, and Academic Achievement as Contributors to Interpersonal Attraction Among Adolescents." *Developmental Psychology*, 1973, *9*, 44–54.

Centers, L., & Centers, R. "Peer Group Attitudes Toward the Amputee Child." *Journal of Social Psychology*, 1963, *61*, 127–132.

Centers, R., Raven, B. H., & Rodriguez, A. "Conjugal Power Structure: A Reexamination." *American Sociological Review*, 1971, *36*, 264–278.

Chamove, A., Harlow, H. F., & Mitchell, G. "Sex Differences in the Infant-Directed Behavior of Preadolescent Rhesus Monkeys." *Child Development*, 1967, *38*, 329–335.

Charlesworth, R., & Hartup, W. W. "Positive Social Reinforcement in the Nursery School Peer Group." *Child Development*, 1967, *38*, 993–1002.

Cherry, F., & Deaux, K. "Fear of Success Versus Fear of Gender-Inconsistent Behavior: A Sex Similarity." Paper presented at the meeting of the Midwestern Psychological Association, Chicago, May 1975.

Cherry, L. "The Preschool Teacher–Child Dyad: Sex Differences in Verbal Interaction." *Child Development*, 1975, *46*, 532–535.

Cherry, S. H. *The Menopause Myth*. New York: Ballantine Books, 1976.

Chesler, P. "Women Psychiatric and Psychotherapeutic Patients." *Journal of Marriage and the Family*, 1971, *33*, 746–759.

Chesler, P. *Women and Madness*. Garden City, N.Y.: Doubleday, 1972.

Clarke, H. H., & Clarke, D. H. "Social Status and Mental Health of Boys as Related to Their Maturity, Structural, and Strength Characteristics." *Research Quarterly of the American Association of Health and Physical Education*, 1961, *32*, 326–334.

Clarke, H. H., & Greene, W. H. Relationships Between Personal–Social Measures Applied to Ten-Year-Old Boys." *Research Quarterly of the American Association of Health and Physical Education*, 1963, *34*, 288–298.

Clarke-Kudness, D. "Metanephrine and Normetanephrine Levels and Affective States of Male/Female Couples During the Menstrual Cycle." Unpublished master's dissertation, Montclair State College, 1976.

Clatworthy, N. M. "Living Together." In N. Glazer-Malbin, ed. *Old Family/New Family*. New York: Van Nostrand, 1975.

Clifford, M. M., & Walster, E. "The Effect of Physical Attractiveness on Teacher Expectations." *Sociology of Education*, 1973, *46*, 248–258.

Cohen, E. G., & Roper, S. S. "Modification of Interracial Interaction Disability: An Application of Status Characteristic Theory." *American Sociological Review*, 1973, *37*, 643–657.

Cohen, L. J., & Campos, J. J. "Father, Mother, and Stranger as Elicitors of Attachment Behaviors in Infancy." *Developmental Psychology*, 1974, *10*, 146–154.

Cohen, S., Rothbart, M., & Phillips, S. "Locus of Control and the Generality of Learned Helplessness in Humans." *Journal of Personality and Social Psychology*, 1976, *34*, 1049–1056.

Coie, J. D., Pennington, B. F., & Buckley, H. H. "Effects of Situational Stress and Sex Roles on the Attribution of Psychological Disorder." *Journal of Consulting and Clinical Psychology*, 1974, *42*, 559–568.

Collier, J. F. "Women in Politics." In M. Z. Rosaldo & L. Lamphere eds. *Women, Culture and Society*. Stanford, Calif.: Stanford University Press, 1974.

Collins, J. K. "Adolescent Dating Intimacy: Norms and Peer Expectations." *Journal of Youth and Adolescence*, 1974, *3*, 317–327.

Collins, J. K., Kennedy, J. R., & Francis, R. D. "Insights into a Dating Partner's Expectations of How Behavior Should Ensue During the Courtship Process." *Journal of Marriage and the Family*. 1976, *38*, 373–378.

Condry, J. C., & Dyer, S. L. "Behavioral and Fantasy Measures of Fear of Success in Children." Paper presented at the meeting of the Eastern Psychological Association, New York City, April 1976a.

Condry, J. C., & Dyer, S. L. "Fear of Success: Attribution of Cause to the Victim." *Journal of Social Issues*, 1976b, *32*, 63–83.

Connell, D. M., & Johnson, J. E. "Relationship Between Sex-Role Identification and Self-Esteem in Early Adolescents." *Developmental Psychology*, 1970, *3*, 268.

Constantinople, A. "Masculinity–Femininity: An Exception to a Famous Dictum?" *Psychological Bulletin*, 1973, *80*, 389–407.

Coombs, R. H., & Kenkel, W. F. "Sex Differences in Dating Aspirations and Satisfaction with Computer-Selected Partners." *Journal of Marriage and the Family*, 1966, *28*, 62–66.

Cooperstock, R. "Sex Differences in the Use of Mood-Modifying Drugs: An Explanatory Model." *Journal of Health and Social Behavior*, 1971, *12*, 238–244.

Coppen, A., & Kessel, N. "Menstruation and Personality." *British Journal of Psychiatry*, 1963, *109*, 711–721.

Coser, R. L. "Role Distance, Sociological Ambivalence and Transitional Status Systems." *American Journal of Sociology*, 1966, *72*, 173–187.

Coser, R. L., & Rokoff, G. "Women in the Occupational World: Social Disruption and Conflict." *Social Problems*, 1971, *18*, 535–554.

Costrich, N., Feinstein, J., Kidder, L., Maracek, J., & Pascale, L. "When Stereotypes Hurt: Three Studies of Penalties for Sex-Role Reversals." *Journal of Experimental Social Psychology*, 1975, *11*, 520–530.

Cox, S. *Female Psychology: The Emerging Self*. Chicago: Science Research Associates, 1976.

Cramer, P., & Hogan, K. A. "Sex Differences in Verbal and Play Fantasy." *Developmental Psychology*, 1975, *11*, 145–154.

Crandall, V. C. "Sex Differences in Expectancy of Intellectual and Academic Reinforcement." In C. P. Smith, ed. *Achievement-Related Motives.* New York: Russell Sage, 1969.

Crandall, V. J., Katkovsky, W., & Preston, A. "Motivational and Ability Determinants of Young Children's Achievement Behaviors." *Child Development,* 1962, *33,* 643–661.

Croft, R. G. F., & Gluck, P. G. "Attitude Changes in a Behaviorally Oriented Mother Discussion Group." Paper presented at the meeting of the American Psychological Association, Washington, D.C., September 1976.

Cross, J. F., & Cross, J. "Age, Sex, Race, and the Perception of Facial Beauty." *Developmental Psychology,* 1971, 5, 433–439.

Curtis, G. C., Fogel, M. L., McEvoy, D., & Zarate, C. "The Effect of Sustained Effort on the Diurnal Rhythms of Adrenal Cortical Activity." *Psychosomatic Medicine,* 1966, *28,* 696–713.

Dabbs, J. M., Jr. & Stokes, N. A., III. "Beauty is Power: The Use of Space on the Sidewalk." *Sociometry,* 1975, *38,* 551–557.

Dalton, K. "Effect of Menstruation on Schoolgirls' Weekly Work." *British Medical Journal,* 1960, 326–328.

Dalton, K. "The Influence of Mother's Menstruation on her Child." *Proceedings of the Royal Society of Medicine,* 1966, *59,* 1014–1016.

Dalton, K. *The Menstrual Cycle.* New York: Pantheon Books, 1969.

David, D., & Brannon, R., eds. *The Forty-nine Percent Majority: The Male Sex Role.* Reading, Mass.: Addison-Wesley, 1976.

Davie, R. "Socio-biological Influences on Children's Development." In F. J. Monks, W. W. Hartup, & J. deWit, eds. *Determinants of Behavioral Development.* New York: Academic Press, 1972.

Deaux, K. "Honking at the Intersection: A Replication and Extension." *Journal of Social Psychology,* 1971, *84,* 159–160.

Deaux, K. "To Err Is Humanizing, but Sex Makes a Difference." *Representative Research in Social Psychology,* 1972, *3,* 20–28.

Deaux, K. *The Behavior of Women and Men.* Belmont, Calif.: Brooks/Cole, 1976.

Deaux, K., & Emswiller, T. "Explanations of Successful Performance on Sex-Linked Tasks: What Is Skill for the Male is Luck for the Female." *Journal of Personality and Social Psychology,* 1974, *29,* 80–85.

Deaux, K., & Taynor, J. "Evaluation of Male and Female Ability: Bias Works Both Ways." *Psychological Reports,* 1973, *32,* 261–262.

Deaux, K., White, L., & Farris, E. "Skill Versus Luck: Field and Laboratory Studies of Male and Female Preferences." *Journal of Personality and Social Psychology,* 1975, *32,* 629–636.

Deets, A. C. "Age-Mate or Twin Sibling: Effects on Interactions Between Monkey Mothers and Infants." *Developmental Psychology,* 1974, *10,* 748–763.

DeFleur, M. L. "Occupational Roles as Portrayed on Television." *Public Opinion Quarterly,* 1964, *28,* 57–74.

Deisher, R. W., & Mills, C. A. "The Adolescent Looks at His Health and Medical Care." *American Journal of Public Health,* 1963, *53,* 1928–1936.

Dengerink, H. A., & Myers, J. D. "The Effects of Failure and Depression on Subsequent Aggression." *Journal of Personality and Social Psychology*, 1977, *35*, 88–96.

de Nevers, N. "Another Approach to Population Control?" *Bulletin of Atomic Scientists*, 1971, *27*, 34.

Denmark, F. L. "The Psychology of Women: An Overview of an Emerging Field." *Personality and Social Psychology Bulletin*, 1977, *3*, 356–367.

Depner, C. E., & O'Leary, V. E. "Understanding Female Careerism: Fear of Success and New Directions." *Sex Roles*, 1976, *2*, 259–268.

Dermer, M., & Thiel, D. L. "When Beauty May Fail." *Journal of Personality and Social Psychology*, 1975, *31*, 1168–1176.

Deutsch, C. J., & Gilbert, L. A. "Sex Role Stereotypes: Effect on Perceptions of Self and Others and on Personal Adjustment." *Journal of Counseling Psychology*, 1976, *23*, 373–379.

Deutsch, F. Observational and Sociometric Measures of Peer Popularity and Their Relationship to Egocentric Communication in Female Preschoolers." *Developmental Psychology*, 1974, *10*, 745–747.

Deutsch, F. "Effects of Sex of Subject and Story Character on Preschoolers' Perceptions of Affective Responses and Intrapersonal Behavior in Story Sequences." *Developmental Psychology*, 1975, *11*, 112–113.

Diamond, M. A. "A Critical Evaluation of the Ontogeny of Human Sexual Behavior." *Quarterly Review of Biology*, 1965, *40*, 147–175.

Diamond, M. A. "Genetic–Endocrine Interactions and Human Psychosexuality." In M. Diamond, ed. *Perspectives in Reproduction and Sexual Behavior*. Bloomington: University of Indiana Press, 1968.

Dickinson, G. E. "Dating Behavior of Black and White Adolescents Before and After Segregation." *Journal of Marriage and the Family*, 1975, *37*, 602–608.

Dion, K. K. "Young Children's Stereotyping of Facial Attractiveness." *Developmental Psychology*, 1973, *9*, 183–188.

Dion, K. K. "Children's Physical Attractiveness and Sex Determinants of Adult Punitiveness." *Developmental Psychology*, 1974, *10*, 772–778.

Dion, K. K., & Berscheid, E. "Physical Attractiveness and Peer Perception Among Children." *Sociometry*, 1974, *37*, 1–12.

Dion, K. K., Berscheid, E., & Walster, E. "What Is Beautiful Is Good." *Journal of Personality and Social Psychology*, 1972, *24*, 285–290.

Dion, K. K., & Dion, K. L. "Self-esteem and Romantic Love." *Journal of Personality*, 1975, *43*, 39–57.

Dion, K. L. "Women's Reactions to Discrimination from Members of the Same or Opposite Sex." *Journal of Research in Personality*, 1975, *9*, 294–306.

Dion, K. L., & Dion, K. K. "The Honi Phenomenon Revisited: Factors Underlying the Resistance to Perceptual Distortion of One's Partner." *Journal of Personality and Social Psychology*, 1976, *33*, 170–177.

Doering, C. H., Brodie, H. K. H., Kraemer, H., Becker, H., & Hamburg, D. A. "Plasma Testosterone Levels and Psychologic Measures in Men over a 2-Month Period." In R. C. Friedman, R. M. Richard, & R. L. V. Weil, eds. *Sex Differences in Behavior*. New York: Wiley, 1974.

Dohrenwend, B. S. "Social Status and Stressful Life Events." *Journal of Personality and Social Psychology*, 1973a, *28*, 225–236.

Dohrenwend, B. S. "Life Events as Stressors: A Methodological Inquiry." *Journal of Health and Social Behavior*, 1973b, *14*, 167–175.

Dohrenwend, B. S. "Anticipation and Control of Stressful Life Events: An Exploratory Analysis." Paper presented at the meeting of the Eastern Psychological Association, New York City, April 1976.

Dohrenwend, B. S., Krasnoff, L., Askenasy, A. R., & Dohrenwend, B. P. "Exemplification of a Method for Scaling Life Events: The PERI Life Events Scale." *Journal of Health and Social Behavior*, in press.

Doob, A. N., & Gross, A. E. "Status of Frustrator as an Inhibitor of Horn-Honking Responses." *Journal of Social Psychology*, 1968, *76*, 213–218.

Douglas, G. "Some Disorders of the Puerperium." *Journal of Psychosomatic Research*, 1968, *12*, 101–106.

Douvan, E. "The Role of Models in Women's Professional Development." *Psychology of Women Quarterly*, 1976, *2*, 5–20.

Douvan, E., & Adelson, J. "American Dating Patterns." In D. Rogers, ed. *Issues in Adolescent Psychology*. Englewood Cliffs, N.J.: Prentice-Hall, 1969.

Drash, P. W. "Psychologic Counseling: Dwarfism." In L. I. Gardner, ed. *Endocrine and Genetic Diseases of Childhood*. Philadelphia: W. B. Saunders, 1969.

Dryfoos, J. C. "Women Who Need and Receive Family Planning Services: Estimates at Mid-decade." *Family Planning Perspectives*, 1975, *7*, 172–179.

Duncan, R. P., & Perrucci, C. C. "Dual Occupation Families and Migration." *American Sociological Review*, 1976, *41*, 252–261.

Dweck, C. S. "The Role of Expectations and Attributions in the Alleviation of Learned Helplessness." *Journal of Personality and Social Psychology*, 1975, *31*, 674–685.

Dweck, C. S., & Gilliard, D. "Expectancy Statements as Determinants of Reactions to Failure: Sex Differences in Persistence and Expectancy Change." *Journal of Personality and Social Psychology*, 1975, *32*, 1077–1084.

Dweck, C. S., & Reppucci, N. D. "Learned Helplessness and Reinforcement Responsibility in Children." *Journal of Personality and Social Psychology*, 1973, *25*, 109–116.

Dworkin, A. *Woman Hating*. New York: E. P. Dutton, 1974.

Dworkin, A. *Our Blood*. New York: Harper & Row, 1976.

Dwyer, C. A. "Children's Sex Role Standards and Sex Role Identification and Their Relationship to Achievement." Unpublished doctoral dissertation, University of California at Berkeley, 1973.

Dwyer, D., Salbod, S., & Bedell, P. "Stereotyping Occupations According to Prestige and Sex-Role Dimensions." Paper presented at the meeting of the Eastern Psychological Association, Washington, D. C., April 1978.

Dwyer, J., Feldman, J. J., & Mayer, J. "Adolescent Dieters: Who Are They? Physical Characteristics, Attitudes, and Dieting Practices of Adolescent Girls." *American Journal of Clinical Nutrition*, 1967, *20*, 1045–1056.

Dwyer, J., & Mayer, J. "Psychological Effects of Variations in Physical Appearance During Adolescence." *Adolescence*, 1968, *3*, 353–380.

Dyer, E. D. "Parenthood as Crisis: A Re-study." *Marriage and Family Living*, 1963, *25*, 196–201.

Eagly, A. H. "Sex Differences in Influenceability." *Psychological Bulletin*, 1978, *85*, 86–116.

Eberts, E. H., & Lepper, M. R. "Individual Consistency in the Proxemic Behavior of Preschool Children." *Journal of Personality and Social Psychology*, 1975, *32*, 841–849.

Edelson, M. S., & Omark, D. R. "Dominance Hierarchies in Young Children." *Social Science Information*, 1973, *12*, 1.

Edney, J. J., & Jordan-Edney, N. L. "Territorial Spacing on a Beach." *Sociometry*, 1974, *37*, 92–104.

Edwards, J. N., & Booth, A. "Sexual Behavior In and Out of Marriage: An Assessment of Correlates." *Journal of Marriage and the Family*, 1976, *38*, 73–81.

Ehrenreich, B., & English, D. *Complaints and Disorders*. Westbury, N.Y.: Feminist Press, 1973.

Ehrhardt, A., Evers, K., & Money, J. "Influence of Androgen and Some Aspects of Sexually Dimorphic Behavior in Women with the Late-Treated Adrenogenital Syndrome." *Johns Hopkins Medical Journal*, 1968, *123*, 115–122.

Eichler, M. "Power and Sexual Fear in Primitive Societies." *Journal of Marriage and the Family*, 1975, *37*, 917–926.

Ekstrom, R. B. "Barriers to Women's Participation in Post-secondary Education: A Review of the Literature." Paper presented at the meeting of the American Psychological Association, Honolulu, September 1972.

Elder, G. H., Jr. "Appearance and Education in Marriage Mobility." *American Sociological Review*, 1969, *34*, 519–533.

Ellis, A. *The American Sexual Tragedy*. New York: Twayne Publications, 1954.

Ellis, A. "Constitutional Factors in Homosexuality: A Reexamination of the Evidence." In H. G. Beigel, ed. *Advances in Sex Research*. New York: Harper & Row, 1963.

Ember, C. R. "Feminine Task Assignment and the Social Behavior of Boys." *Ethos*, 1973, *1*, 424–439.

Emmerich, W. "Family Role Concepts of Children Ages Six to Ten." *Child Development*, 1961, *32*, 609–624.

Entwisle, D. R. "To Dispel Fantasies About Fantasy-Based Measures of Achievement Motivation." *Psychological Bulletin*, 1972, *77*, 377–391.

Entwisle, D. R., & Greenberger, E. "Adolescents' Views of Women's Work Role." *American Journal of Orthopsychiatry*, 1972a, *42*, 648–656.

Entwisle, D. R., & Greenberger, E. "Questions About Social Class, Internality–Externality, and Test Anxiety." *Developmental Psychology*, 1972b, *7*, 218.

Epstein, C. F. *Woman's Place.* Berkeley: University of California Press, 1970.

Epstein, C. F. "Bringing Women In: Rewards, Punishments, and the Structure of Achievement." *Annals of the New York Academy of Sciences,* 1973, *208,* 62–70.

Erikson, E. H. *Childhood and Society.* Canada: Norton, 1963.

Erikson, E. H. "Inner and Outer Space: Reflections on Womanhood." *Daedalus,* 1964, *93,* 582–606.

Ernest, J. "Mathematics and Sex." Unpublished manuscript, Mathematics Department, University of California, Santa Barbara, 1975. Cited in A. N. O'Connell et al. "Gender-Specific Barriers to Research in Psychology," *Catalog of Selected Documents in Psychology,* 8, 1978, 80.

Ernster, V. L. "American Menstrual Expressions." *Sex Roles,* 1975, *1,* 3–13.

Etaugh, C., & Brown, B. "Perceiving the Causes of Success and Failure of Male and Female Performers." *Developmental Psychology,* 1975, *11,* 103.

Exline, R. V. "Explorations in the Process of Personal Perception: Visual Interaction in Relation to Competition, Sex and Need for Affiliation." *Journal of Personality,* 1963, *31,* 1–20.

Exline, R. V., Gray, D., & Schuette, D. "Visual Behavior in a Dyad as Affected by Interview Context and Sex of Respondent." *Journal of Personality and Social Psychology,* 1965, *1,* 201–209.

Exner, J., & Sutton-Smith, B. "Birth-Order and Hierarchical Versus Innovative Role Requirements." *Journal of Personality,* 1970, *38,* 581–587.

Fabrikant, B. "The Psychotherapist and the Female Patient: Perceptions, Misperceptions and Change." In V. Franks & V. Burtle, eds. *Women in Therapy.* New York: Bruner/Mazel, 1974.

Fagot, B. I. "Sex-Related Stereotyping of Toddlers' Behaviors." *Developmental Psychology,* 1973, *9,* 429.

Fagot, B. I. "Sex Differences in Toddlers' Behavior and Parental Reaction." *Developmental Psychology,* 1974, *10,* 554–558.

Falbo, T. "Sex Role Typing and Sex in the Use of and Susceptibility to Influence." Manuscript submitted for publication, 1976.

Fallon, B. J., & Hollander, E. P. "Sex Role Stereotyping in Leadership: A Study of Undergraduate Discussion Groups." Paper presented at the meeting of the American Psychological Association, Washington D.C., September 1976.

Faust, M. S. "Developmental Maturity as a Determinant of Prestige of Adolescent Girls." *Child Development,* 1960, *31,* 173–184.

Feather, N. T. "Positive and Negative Reactions to Male and Female Success and Failure in Relation to the Perceived Status and Sex-Typed Appropriateness of Occupations." *Journal of Personality and Social Psychology,* 1975, *31,* 536–548.

Feather, N. T., & Simon, J. G. "Reactions to Male and Female Success and Failure in Sex-Linked Occupations: Impressions of Personality, Causal Attributions and Perceived Likelihood of Different Consequences." *Journal of Personality and Social Psychology,* 1975, *31,* 20–31.

Featherman, D. L., & Hauser, R. M. "Sexual Inequalities and Socioeconomic Achievement in the United States: 1962–1973." *American Sociological Review*, 1976, *41*, 462–483.

Federbush, M. "The Sex Problems of School Math Books." In J. Stacey, S. Bereaud, & J. Daniels, eds. *And Jill Came Tumbling After: Sexism in American Education*. New York: Dell, 1974.

Feinberg, M. R., Smith, M., & Schmidt, R. "An Analysis of Expressions Used by Adolescents of Varying Economic Levels to Describe Accepted and Rejected Peers." *Journal of Genetic Psychology*, 1958, 93, 133–148.

Feinman, S. "Why is Cross-Sex Role Behavior More Approved For Girls Than Boys?" Manuscript submitted for publication, 1977.

Feldberg, R., & Kohen, J. "Family Life in an Anti-family Setting: A Critique of Marriage and Divorce." *Family Coordinator*, 1976, *25*, 151–159.

Feldman-Summers, S., & Kiesler, S. B. "Those Who Are Number Two Try Harder: The Effect of Sex on Attributions of Causality." *Journal of Personality and Social Psychology*, 1974, *30*, 846–855.

Felson, M., & Knoke, D. "Social Status and the Married Woman." *Journal of Marriage and the Family*, 1974, *36*, 516–521.

Fernberger, S. W. "Persistence of Stereotypes Concerning Sex Differences." *Journal of Abnormal and Social Psychology*, 1948, *43*, 97–101.

Fidell, L. S. "Empirical Verification of Sex Discrimination in Hiring Practices in Psychology." *American Psychologist*, 1970, *25*, 1094–1098.

Fidell, L. S. "Put Her Down on Drugs: Prescribed Drug Usage in Women." Paper presented at the Western Psychological Association, Anaheim, California, April 1973.

Fidell, L. S. "Psychotropic Drug Use by Women: Health, Attitudinal, Personality and Demographic Correlates." Paper presented at the meeting of the American Psychological Association, San Francisco, August 1977.

Fidell, L. S. "Sex Role Stereotypes and the American Physician." *Psychology of Women Quarterly*, 1978, in press.

Finz, S. D., & Waters, J. "An Analysis of Sex Role Stereotyping in Daytime Television Serials." Paper presented at the meeting of the American Psychological Association, Washington D.C., September 1976.

Fishelson, L. "Protogynous Sex Reversal in the Fish *Anthias squamipinnis* Regulated by the Presence or Absence of a Male Fish." *Nature*, 1970, *227*, 90–91.

Fisher, A. E. "Maternal and Sexual Behavior Induced by Intracranial Chemical Stimulation." *Science*, 1956, *124*, 228–229.

Fisher, J. D., & Byrne, D. "Too Close For Comfort: Sex Differences in Response to Invasions of Personal Space." *Journal of Personality and Social Psychology*, 1975, *32*, 15–21.

Fling, S., & Manosevitz, M. "Sex Typing in Nursery School Children's Play Interests." *Developmental Psychology*, 1972, 7, 146–152.

Flint, M. "The Menopause: Reward or Punishment?" *Psychosomatics*, 1975, *16*, 161–163.

Fodor, I. G. "The Phobic Syndrome in Women: Implications for Treatment." In V. Franks & V. Burtle, eds. *Women in Therapy*. New York: Bruner/Mazel, 1974.

Folger, J. K., Astin, H. S., & Bayer, A. E. *Human Resources and Higher Education*. New York: Russell Sage, 1970.

Fontaine, C. M. "Cognitive and Self-Reward Patterns in an Achievement Situation as a Function of Task Outcome, Sex, and Achievement Motivation." Paper presented at the meeting of the Eastern Psychological Association, New York City, April 1976.

Ford, C. S., & Beach, F. A. *Patterns of Sexual Behavior*. New York: Harper Colophon Books, 1951.

Forssman, H. "The Medical Implications of Sex Chromosome Aberrations." *British Journal of Psychiatry*, 1970, *117*, 353–363.

Franzwa, H. H. "Female Roles in Women's Magazine Fiction, 1940–1970." In R. K. Unger & F. L. Denmark, eds. *Woman: Dependent or Independent Variable?* New York: Psychological Dimensions, 1975.

Frazier, A., & Lisonbee, L. K. "Adolescent Concerns with Physique." *School Review*, 1950, *58*, 397–405.

Freedman, D. G. "Genetic Variations on the Hominid Theme: Individual, Sex, and Ethnic Differences." In F. J. Monks, W. W. Hartup, & J. deWit, eds. *Determinants of Behavioral Development*. New York: Academic Press, 1972.

Freeman, J. "How to Discriminate Against Women Without Really Trying." In J. Freeman, ed. *Women: A Feminist Perspective*. Palo Alto, Calif.: Mayfield, 1975.

Freese, L. "Conditions for Status Equality in Informal Task Groups." *Sociometry*, 1974, *37*, 174–188.

Freese, L., & Cohen, B. P. "Eliminating Status Generalization." *Sociometry*, 1973, *36*, 177–193.

Freiberg, P., & Bridwell, M. W. "An Intervention Model for Rape and Unwanted Pregnancy." *The Counseling Psychologist*, 1976, *6*, 50–53.

French, G., & Lesser, G. S. "Some Characteristics of the Achievement Motive in Women." *Journal of Abnormal and Social Psychology*, 1964, *68*, 119–128.

French, J. R. P., Jr., & Raven, B. "The Bases of Social Power." In D. Cartwright, ed. *Studies in Social Power*. Ann Arbor: University of Michigan Press, 1959.

Freud, A. *The Ego and Mechanisms of Defense*. New York: International Universities Press, 1946.

Freud, S. *Three Contributions to the Theory of Sex*. New York: Nervous & Mental Disease Publishing Co., 1930.

Freud, S. "Some Psychological Consequences of the Anatomical Distinction Between the Sexes." In *Collected Papers*, vol. V. London: Hogarth, 1948, pp. 186–197.

Freud, S. "Female Sexuality." In *Collected Papers*, vol. V. London: Hogarth, 1950.

Freud, S. "The Passing of the Oedipus-Complex." In E. Jones, ed. *Collected Papers*, vol. II. London: Hogarth, 1956.

Freud, S. "Female Sexuality." In J. Strachey, ed. *Collected Works, 1931*. London: Hogarth Press, 1961.

Freud, S. "Introductory Lectures on Psychoanalysis." In *Collected Papers Vols. XV and XVI*. London: Hogarth, 1963.

Freud, S. *New Introductory Lectures on Psychoanalysis*. New York: Norton, 1965.

Friedrich, L. K., & Stein, A. H. "Prosocial Television and Young Children: The Effects of Verbal Labeling and Role Playing on Learning and Behavior." *Child Development*, 1975, *46*, 27–38.

Friend, R. M., & Neale, J. M. "Children's Perception of Success and Failure: An Attributional Analysis of the Effects of Race and Social Class." *Developmental Psychology*, 1972, 7, 124–128.

Frieze, I. H., Fisher, J., McHugh, M. C., & Valle, V. A. "Attributing the Causes of Success and Failure: Internal and External Barriers to Achievement in Women." In J. Sherman & F. Denmark, eds. *Psychology of Women: Future Directions of Research*. New York: Psychological Dimensions, 1978.

Frisch, R. E., & Revelle, R. "Height and Weight at Menarche and a Hypothesis of Menarche." *Archives of Diseases in Childhood*, 1971, *46*, 695.

Frodi, A., Macaulay, J., & Thome, P. R. "Are Women Always Less Aggressive Than Men?" *Psychological Bulletin*, 1977, *84*, 634–660.

Fromm, E. *The Art of Loving*. New York: Harper & Row, 1956.

Fromme, D. K., & Beam, D. C. "Dominance and Sex Differences in Nonverbal Responses to Differential Eye Contact." *Journal of Research in Personality*, 1974, 8, 76–87.

Frueh, T., & McGhee, P. E. "Traditional Sex Role Development and Amount of Time Spent Watching Television." *Developmental Psychology*, 1975, *11*, 109.

Fry, A. M., & Willis, F. N. "Invasion of Personal Space as a Function of the Age of the Invader." *Psychological Record*, 1971, *21*, 385–389.

Gaertner, S. L., & Dovidio, J. F. "The Subtlety of White Racism, Arousal, and Helping Behavior." *Journal of Personality and Social Psychology*, 1977, *35*, 691–707.

Galdston, R. "Observations of Children Who Have Been Physically Abused by Their Parents." *American Journal of Psychiatry*, 1965, *122*, 440–443.

Garcia, M. "Hormonal Interaction, Menstruation, and the Oral Contraceptives." In R. K. Unger & F. L. Denmark, eds. *Woman: Dependent or Independent Variable?* New York: Psychological Dimensions, 1975a.

Garcia, M. "Fluctuations of Mood in the Menstrual Cycle *Not* Confirmed." Paper presented at the meeting of the Eastern Psychological Association, New York City, April 1975b.

Garcia, M., & Dingman, J. A. "Sex-Role Stereotypes Among Latinos: They Only Work One Way." Paper presented at the meeting of the American Psychological Association. Chicago, August 1975.

Garn, S. M. "Body Size and Its Implications." In L. W. Hoffman & M. L.

Hoffman, eds. *Review of Child Development Research*, vol. 2. New York: Russell Sage, 1966.

Garn, S. M., & Haskell, J. A. "Fat Thickness and Developmental Status in Childhood and Adolescence." *American Journal of Diseases of Children*, 1960, *99*, 746–751.

Garrett, A. M., & Willoughby, R. H. "Personal Orientation and Reactions to Success and Failure in Urban Black Children." *Developmental Psychology*, 1972, *7*, 92.

Geller, D. M., Goodstein, L., Silver, M., & Sternberg, W. C. "On Being Ignored: The Effects of Violations of Implicit Rules of Social Interaction." *Sociometry*, 1974, *37*, 541–556.

Geller, S. H. "Female Sexual Offenses: Innocent Victim or Temptress?" Paper presented at the meeting of the Eastern Psychological Association, Boston, April 1977.

Gellert, E. "Stability and Fluctuation in the Power Relationships of Young Children." *Journal of Abnormal and Social Psychology*, 1961, *62*, 8–15.

Gelles, R. J. "Child Abuse as Psychopathology: A Sociological Critique and Reformulation." *American Journal of Orthopsychiatry*, 1973, *43*, 611–621.

Gelles, R. J. "Violence and Pregnancy: A Note on the Extent of the Problem and Needed Services." *The Family Coordinator*, 1975, *24*, 81–86.

George, V., & Wilding, P. *Motherless Families.* London: Routledge & Kegan Paul, 1972.

Gerbner, G. "Violence in Television Drama: Trends and Symbolic Functions." In G. A. Comstock & E. A. Rubinstein, eds. *Television and Social Behavior.* Washington, D.C., GPO, 1972.

Geshuri, Y. "Discriminative Observational Learning: Effects of Observed Reward and Dependency." *Child Development*, 1975, *46*, 550–554.

Gil, D. "Violence Against Children." *Journal of Marriage and the Family*, 1971, *33*, 637–657.

Gillespie, D. "Who Has the Power? The Marital Struggle." *Journal of Marriage and the Family*, 1971, *33*, 445–458.

Gillman, R. D. "The Dreams of Pregnant Women and Maternal Adaptation." *American Journal of Orthopsychiatry*, 1968, *38*, 688–692.

Ginsberg, G. L., Frosch, W. A., & Shapiro, T. "The New Impotence." *Archives of General Psychiatry*, 1972, *26*, 218–220.

Gjesme, T. "Achievement-Related Motives and School Performance for Girls." *Journal of Personality and Social Psychology*, 1973, *26*, 131–136.

Glidewell, J. C., Kantor, M. B., Smith, L. M., & Stringer, L. A. "Socialization and Social Structure in the Classroom." In L. W. Hoffman & M. L. Hoffman, eds. *Review of Child Development Research*, vol. 2. New York: Russell Sage, 1966.

Goffman, E. "The Nature of Deference and Demeanor." *American Anthropologist*, 1956, *58*, 473–502.

Goffman, E. *Behavior in Public Places.* New York: Free Press, 1963a.

Goffman, E. *Stigma.* Englewood Cliffs, N.J.: Prentice-Hall, 1963b.

Gold, A. R., & St. Ange, M. C. "Development of Sex Role Stereotypes in

Black and White Elementary School Girls." *Developmental Psychology*, 1974, *10*, 461.

Goldberg, P. A. "Are Women Prejudiced Against Women?" *Transaction*, April 1968, pp. 28–30.

Goldberg, P. A. "Prejudice Toward Women: Some Personality Correlates." *International Journal of Group Tensions*, 1974, *4*, 53–63.

Goldberg, P. A., Gottesdiener, M., & Abramson, P. R. "Another Put-down of Women? Perceived Attractiveness as a Function of Support for the Feminist Movement." *Journal of Personality and Social Psychology*, 1975, *32*, 113–115.

Goldfoot, D. A., Feder, H. H., & Goy, R. W. "Development of Bisexuality in the Male Rat Treated Neonatally with Androstenedione." *Journal of Comparative and Physiological Psychology*, 1969, *67*, 41–45.

Goldman, W., & Lewis, P. "Beautiful is good: Evidence That the Physically Attractive Are More Socially Skillful." *Journal of Experimental Social Psychology*, 1977, *13*, 125–130.

Goldstein, A. G., & Chance, J. E. "Effects of Practice on Sex-Related Differences in Performance on Embedded Figures." *Psychonomic Science*, 1965, *3*, 361–362.

Golub, S. "The Effect of Premenstrual Anxiety and Depression on Cognitive Function." *Journal of Personality and Social Psychology*, 1976, *34*, 99–104.

Gomberg, E. A. "Women and Alcoholism." In V. Franks & V. Burtle, eds. *Women in Therapy*. New York: Bruner/Mazel, 1974.

Gomes, B., & Abramowitz, S. I. "Sex-Related Patient and Therapist Effects on Clinical Judgment." *Sex Roles*, 1976, *2*, 1–13.

Goode, W. J. *After Divorce*. New York: Free Press, 1956.

Goodstadt, B. E., & Hjelle, L. A. "Power to the Powerless: Locus of Control and the Use of Power." *Journal of Personality and Social Psychology*, 1973, *27*, 190–196.

Gordon, L. *Woman's Body, Woman's Right: A Social History of Birth Control in America*. New York: Grossman, 1976.

Gordon, R. E., & Gordon, K. K. "Factors in Postpartum Emotional Adjustment." *American Journal of Orthopsychiatry*, 1967, *37*, 359–360.

Gottschalk, L. A., Kaplan, S. M., Gleser, C., & Winget, C. M. "Variations in Magnitude of Emotion: A Method Applied to Anxiety and Hostility During Phases of the Menstrual Cycle." *Psychosomatic Medicine*, 1962, *24*, 300–311.

Gould, L. "Responses to Women in Authority and Leadership." Paper presented at the symposium "Women in Politics," Adelphi University, Garden City, N.Y., September 1975.

Gove, W. R. "The Relationship Between Sex Roles, Marital Status, and Mental Illness." *Social Forces*, 1972, *51*, 34–44.

Gove, W. R., & Tudor, J. "Adult Sex Roles and Mental Illness." *American Journal of Sociology*, 1973, *78*, 812–835.

Goy, R. W. "Early Hormonal Influences on the Development of Sexual and Sex-Related Behavior." In F. O. Schmitt, ed. *The Neurosciences: Second Study Program*. New York: Rockefeller University Press, 1970.

Grady, K. "Androgyny Reconsidered." Paper presented at the meeting of the Eastern Psychological Association, New York City, April 1975.

Grady, K. "The Belief in Sex Differences." Paper presented at the meeting of the Eastern Psychological Association, Boston, April, 1977.

Graham, A. "The Making of a Nonsexist Dictionary." In B. Thorne & N. Henley, eds. *Language and Sex: Difference and Dominance.* Rowley, Mass.: Newbury House, 1975.

Graham, P., Rutter, M., & George, S. "Temperamental Characteristics as Predictors of Behavior Disorders in Children." *American Journal of Orthopsychiatry,* 1973, *43,* 328–339.

Green, R. *Sexual Identity Conflict in Children and Adults.* New York: Basic Books, 1974.

Greenblatt, C. S. & Baily, J. G. "Sex Role Games." *Signs,* 1978, *3,* 622–637.

Greenstein, F. I. "Sex-Related Political Differences in Childhood." *Journal of Politics,* 1961, *23,* 353–371.

Griffin, S. "Rape: The All-American Crime." *Ramparts,* 1971, *10,* 26–35.

Groat, H. T., & Neal, A. G. "Social Psychological Correlates of Urban Fertility." *American Sociological Review,* 1967, *36,* 945–959.

Gronlund, N. E., & Anderson, L. "Personality Characteristics of Socially Accepted, Socially Neglected, and Socially Rejected Junior High School Pupils." *Educational Administration and Supervision,* 1957, *43,* 329–338.

Gross, C. G. "Biology and Pop-biology: Sex and Sexism." In E. Tobach, ed. *The Four Horsemen: Racism, Sexism, Militarism and Social Darwinism.* New York: Behavioral Publications, 1974.

Grote, B. H. "Psychosexual Development and the Problem of Illegitimacy." Paper presented at the meeting of the American Psychological Association, Washington, D.C., September, 1976.

Gruder, C. L., & Cook, T. D. "Sex, Dependency, and Helping." *Journal of Personality and Social Psychology,* 1971, *19,* 290–294.

Gruen, G. E., Korte, J. R., & Baum, J. R. "Group Measure of Locus of Control." *Developmental Psychology,* 1974, *10,* 683–686.

Grusec, J. E. "Demand Characteristics of the Modeling Experiment: Altruism as a Function of Age and Aggression." *Journal of Personality and Social Psychology,* 1972, *22,* 139–148.

Guardo, C. J. "Personal Space, Sex Differences and Interpersonal Attraction." *Journal of Personality,* 1976, *92,* 9–14.

Gump, J. P. "Reality and Myth: Employment and Sex Role Ideology in Black Women." In J. Sherman & F. Denmark, eds. *Psychology of Women: Future Directions of Research.* New York: Psychological Dimensions, 1978.

Gurin, G., Veroff, J., & Feld, S. *Americans View Their Mental Health.* New York: Basic Books, 1960.

Haavio-Mannila, E. "Some Consequences of Women's Emancipation." *Journal of Marriage and the Family,* 1969, *31,* 123–134.

Hacker, H. M. "Women as a Minority Group." *Social Forces,* 1951, *30,* 60–69.

Hacker, H. M. *The Social Roles of Women and Men: A Sociological Ap-*

proach. New York: Harper & Row, 1975.

Hagen, R. I., & Kahn, A. "Discrimination Against Competent Women." *Journal of Applied Social Psychology*, 1975, 5, 362–376.

Halberg, F. "Chronobiology." *Annual Review of Physiology*, 1969, *31*, 675–725.

Hall, D. L. "Social Implications of the Scientific Study of Sex." Paper presented at the symposium "The Scholar and the Feminist IV," Barnard College, April 23, 1977.

Hall, D. T. "A Model of Coping with Role Conflict: The Role Behavior of College Educated Women." *Administrative Science Quarterly*, 1972, *17*, 471–485.

Hall, M., & Keith, R. A. "Sex-Role Preference Among Children of Upper and Lower Social Class." *Journal of Social Psychology*, 1964, *62*, 101–110.

Hammer, M. "Preference for a Male Child: Cultural Factor." *Journal of Individual Psychology*, 1970, *26*, 54–56.

Hamner, W. C., Kim, J. S., Baird, L., & Bigoness, W. J. "Race and Sex as Determinants of Ratings by Potential Employers in a Simulated Work-Sampling Task." *Journal of Applied Psychology*, 1974, *59*, 705–711.

Hansen, R. D., O'Leary, V. E., & Stonner, D. M. "Causal Information: What Do Perceivers Want to Know? Paper presented at the meeting of the Midwestern Psychological Assocation, Chicago, May 1976.

Hansson, R. C., & Duffield, B. J. "Physical Attractiveness and the Attribution of Epilepsy." *Journal of Social Psychology*, 1976, *99*, 233–240.

Harlow, H. F. *Learning to Love*. San Francisco: Albion, 1971.

Harlton, B. E. "The Sexual Fantasies of Women." *Psychology Today*, March 1973, pp. 39–48.

Harper, L. "The Young as a Source of Stimuli Controlling Caretaker Behavior." *Developmental Psychology*, 1971, *4*, 73–88.

Harper, L. V., & Sanders, K. M. "Preschool Children's Use of Space: Sex Differences in Outdoor Play." *Developmental Psychology*, 1975, *11*, 119.

Harris, A., & Watson, G. "Are Jewish or Gentile Children More Clannish?" *Journal of Social Psychology*, 1946, *24*, 71–76.

Harris, D. B., & Tseng, S. C. "Children's Attitudes Toward Peers and Parents as Revealed by Sentence Completions." *Child Development*, 1957, *28*, 401–411.

Harris, M. B. "Instigators and Inhibitors of Aggression in a Field Experiment." *Journal of Social Psychology*, 1976, *98*, 27–38.

Harris, M. B., & Bays, G. "Altruism and Sex Roles." *Psychological Reports*, 1973, *32*, 1002.

Harris, S. "Influence of Subject and Experimenter Sex in Psychological Research." *Journal of Consulting and Clinical Psychology*, 1971, *37*, 291–294.

Harrison, G. A., Weiner, J. S., Tanner, J. M., & Barnicot, N. A. *Human Biology*. New York: Oxford University Press, 1964.

Harth, M. "What Do Monkeys Tell Us About Bringing Up Baby?" Paper presented at the conference "Childbearing," Ramapo College, Mahwah, N.J., February 1977.

Hartley, R. E. "Current Patterns in Sex Roles: Children's Perspectives." *Journal of National Association of Women's Deans and Counselors,* 1961, *25,* 3–13.

Hartmen, A. A., & Nicolay, R. C. "Sexually Deviant Behavior in Expectant Fathers." *Journal of Abnormal Psychology,* 1966, *71,* 232–234.

Hartup, W. W. "Peer Interaction and Social Organization. In P. H. Mussen, ed. *Manual of Child Psychology,* 3d ed. New York: Wiley, 1970.

Hartup, W. W., Glazer, J. A., & Charlesworth, R. "Peer Reinforcement and Sociometric Status." *Child Development,* 1967, *38,* 1017–1024.

Harvey, O. J. "An Experimental Approach to the Study of Status Relations in Informal Groups." *American Sociological Review,* 1953, *18,* 357–367.

Haugen, E. " 'Sexism' and the Norwegian Language." Paper presented at the meeting of the Society for the Advancement of Scandinavian Study. (Cited in Thorne & Henley, op. cit.)

Haven, E. W. "Factors Associated with the Selection of Advanced Academic Mathematic Courses by Girls in High Schools." *Research Bulletin, 72:12.* Princeton: N.J.: Educational Testing Service, 1972.

Haviland, J. M. "Sex-Related Pragmatics in Infants' Nonverbal Communication." Paper presented at the meeting of the Eastern Psychological Association, New York City, April 1976a.

Haviland, J. M. Sex Differences in the Presentation and Perception of the Face." Paper presented at the meeting of the Eastern Psychological Association, New York City, April 1976b.

Hawley, P. "Perceptions of Male Models of Femininity Related to Career Choice." *Journal of Counseling Psychology,* 1972, *19,* 308–313.

Heer, D. M. "The Measurement and Bases of Family Power: An Overview." *Marriage and Family Living,* 1963, *25,* 133–139.

Helper, M. M. "Learning Theory and Self-concept." *Journal of Abnormal and Social Psychology,* 1955, *51,* 184–194.

Helper, M. M. "Parental Evaluations of Children and Children's Self-evaluations." *Journal of Abnormal and Social Psychology,* 1958, *56,* 190–194.

Helson, R. "Personality of Women with Imaginative and Artistic Interests: The Role of Masculinity, Originality, and Other Characteristics in Their Creativity." *Journal of Personality,* 1966, *34,* 1–25.

Helson, R. "Sex Differences in Creative Style." *Journal of Personality,* 1967, *35,* 214–233.

Helson, R. "Creativity in Women." In J. Sherman & F. Denmark, eds. *Psychology of Women: Future Directions of Research.* New York: Psychological Dimensions, 1978.

Henley, N. M. "Status and Sex: Some Touching Observations." *Bulletin of the Psychonomic Society,* 1973, *2,* 91–93.

Henley, N. M., & Freeman, J. The Sexual Politics of Interpersonal Behavior. In J. Freeman, ed. *Women: A Feminist Perspective.* Palo Alto, Calif.: Mayfield, 1975.

Herman, S. J. "Feminist Issues in Psychotherapy." Paper presented at the symposium "Woman: Scholar and Advocate," Montclair State College, N.J., May 1974.

Hersey, P. "Emotional Cycles of Man." *Journal of Mental Science*, 1931, 77, 151–169.

Herzberg, B. N., & Coppen, A. "Changes in Psychological Symptoms in Women Taking Oral Contraceptives." *British Journal of Psychiatric Medicine*, 1970, *116*, 161–164.

Hetherington, E. M. "A Developmental Study of the Effects of Sex of the Dominant Parent on Sex-Role Preference, Identification, and Imitation in Children." *Journal of Personality and Social Psychology*, 1965, *2*, 188–194.

Hetherington, E. M. Commentary at conference "Future Research on Women," Madison, Wisc., June 1975.

Hetherington, E. M., Cox, M., & Cox, R. "Beyond Father Absence: Conceptualization of Effects of Divorce." Paper presented at the meeting of the Society for Research in Child Development, Denver, April 1975.

Hetherington, E. M., & Parke, R. D. *Child Psychology: A Contemporary Viewpoint.* New York: McGraw-Hill, 1975.

Hicks, M., & Platt, M. "Marital Happiness and Stability: A Review of the Research in the 60's." *Journal of Marriage and the Family*, 1970, *32*, 553–574.

Hill, C. E. "Sex of Client and Sex and Experience Level of Counselor." *Journal of Counseling Psychology*, 1975, *22*, 6–11.

Hill, C. T., Rubin, Z., & Peplau, L. A. "Breakups Before Marriage: The End of 103 Affairs." *Journal of Social Issues*, 1976, *32*, 147–168.

Hill, K. T. "Relation of Test Anxiety, Defensiveness, and Intelligence to Sociometric Status." *Child Development*, 1963, *34*, 767–776.

Hiroto, D. S., & Seligman, M. E. P. "Generality of Learned Helplessness in Man." *Journal of Personality and Social Psychology*, 1975, *31*, 311–327.

Hite, S. The Hite Report: A Nationwide Study on Female Sexuality. New York: Macmillan, 1976.

Hobbs, D., Jr. "Parenthood as a Crisis: A Third Study." *Marriage and Family Living*, 1965, *27*, 367–372.

Hoffman, L. R. "Group Problem Solving." In L. Berkowitz, ed. *Advances in Experimental Social Psychology*, vol. 2. New York: Academic Press, 1965.

Hoffman, L. R., & Maier, N. R. F. "Social Factors Influencing Problem Solving in Women." *Journal of Personality and Social Psychology*, 1966, *4*, 382–390.

Hoffman, L. W. "Parental Power Relations and the Division of Household Tasks." *Marriage and Family Living*, 1960, *22*, 27–35.

Hoffman, L. W. "Mother's Enjoyment of Work and Effects on the Child." In F. I. Nye & L. W. Hoffman, eds. *The Employed Mother in America.* Chicago: Rand McNally, 1963.

Hoffman, L. W. "Effects of Maternal Employment on the Child—A Review of the Research." *Developmental Psychology*, 1974, *10*, 204–228.

Hoffman, L. W. "Fear of Success in Males and Females: 1965 and 1971." *Journal of Consulting and Clinical Psychology,* 1974b, *42,* 353–358.

Hoffman, M. L. "Father Absence and Conscience Development." *Developmental Psychology,* 1971, *4,* 400–406.

Hoffman, M. L. "Moral Internalization, Parental Power, and the Nature of Parent–Child Interaction." *Developmental Psychology,* 1975, *11,* 228–239.

Hollender, J. "Sex Differences in Sources of Social Self-esteem." *Journal of Consulting and Clinical Psychology,* 1972, 38, 343–347.

Holmes, D. S., & Jorgenson, B. W. "Do Personality and Social Psychologists Study Men More Than Women?" *Representative Research in Social Psychology,* 1971, *2,* 71–76.

Holroyd, J. "Psychotherapy and Women's Liberation." *The Counseling Psychologist,* 1976, 6, 22–28.

Hooker, E. "Male Homosexuality in the Rorschach." *Journal of Projective Techniques,* 1957, *21,* 18–31.

Horner, M. S. "The Motive to Avoid Success and Changing Aspirations of College Women." In *Women on Campus 1970: A Symposium.* Ann Arbor, Mich.: Center for Continuing Education of Women, 1970.

Horner, M. S. "Toward an Understanding of Achievement-Related Conflicts in Women." *Journal of Social Issues,* 1972, *28,* 157–176.

Horney, K. "The Flight from Womanhood." *International Journal of Psychoanalysis,* 1926, 7, 324–339.

Horney, K. *New Ways in Psychoanalysis.* New York: Norton, 1966.

Houseknecht, S. K. "A Social Psychological Model of Voluntary Childlessness." Paper presented at the meeting of the American Psychological Association, Washington, D.C., September 1976.

Howard, K. I., Orlinsky, D. W., & Hill, J. A. "Patients' Satisfaction in Psychotherapy as a Function of Patient–Therapist Pairings." *Psychotherapy: Theory, Research and Practice,* 1970, 7, 130–134.

Howard, W., & Crano, W. D. "Effects of Sex, Conversation, Location, and Size of Observer Group on Bystander Intervention in a High Risk Situation." *Sociometry,* 1974, *37,* 491–507.

Hoyt, M. F., & Raven, B. H. "Birth Order and the 1971 Los Angeles Earthquake." *Journal of Personality and Social Psychology,* 1973, *28,* 123–128.

Hrycenko, I., & Minton, H. L. "Internal–External Control, Power Position, and Satisfaction in Task-Oriented Groups." *Journal of Personality and Social Psychology,* 1974, *30,* 871–878.

Hsia, D. Y. *Human Developmental Genetics.* Chicago: Year Book Medical Publishers, 1968.

Hudis, P. M. "Commitment to Work and to Family: Marital-Status Differences in Women's Earnings." *Journal of Marriage and the Family,* 1976, *38,* 267–278.

Huenemann, R. L., Shaping, L. R., Hampton, M. C., & Mitchell, B. W. "A Longitudinal Study of Gross Body Composition and Body Conformation and Association with Food and Activity in a Teen-age Population: Views of Teen-age Subjects on Body Conformation, Food, and Activity." *American Journal of Clinical Nutrition,* 1966, *18,* 323–338.

Hurwitz, J. I., Zander, A. F., & Hymovitch, B. "Some Effects of Power on the Relations Among Group Members." In D. Cartwright & A. Zander, eds. *Group Dynamics,* New York: Harper & Row, 1968.

Huston, T. L. "Ambiguity of Acceptance, Social Desirability, and Dating Choice." *Journal of Experimental Social Psychology,* 1973, *9,* 32–42.

Hutt, C. "Sexual Dimorphism: Its Significance in Human Development." In F. J. Monks, W. W. Hartup, & J. deWit, eds. *Determinants of Behavioral Development.* New York: Academic Press, 1972.

Hyde, J. S., & Rosenberg, B. G. "Tomboyism: Implications for Theories of Female Development." Paper presented at the meeting of the Western Psychological Association, San Francisco, April 1974.

Ivey, M. E., & Bardwick, J. M. "Patterns of Affective Fluctuation in the Menstrual Cycle." *Psychosomatic Medicine,* 1968, *30,* 336–345.

Jacob, T. "Patterns of Family Conflict and Dominance as a Function of Child Age and Social Class." *Developmental Psychology,* 1974, *10,* 1–12.

Jacob, T., Fagin, R., Perry, J., & VanDyke, R. A. "Social Class, Child Age, and Parental Socialization Values." *Developmental Psychology,* 1975, *11,* 393.

Jacobs, P. A., Brenton, M., Melville, M. M., Brittain, R. P., & McClemont, W. F. "Aggressive Behavior, Mental Subnormality, and the XYY Male. *Nature,* 1965, *208,* 1351–1353.

Jakubowski-Spector, P. "Facilitating the Growth of Women Through Assertive Training." *The Counseling Psychologist,* 1973, *4,* 75–86.

Janeway, E. *Between Myth and Morning: Women Awakening.* New York: William Morrow, 1974.

Janiger, O., Riffenburg, R., & Kersh, R. "Cross-cultural Study of Premenstrual Symptoms." *Psychosomatics,* 1972, *13,* 226–235.

Jennings, S. A. "Effects of Sex Typing in Children's Stories on Preference and Recall." *Child Development,* 1975, *46,* 220–223.

Jens, K. S. "Situational Factors Affecting Sex Differences in Small Group Behavior." Paper presented at the meeting of the American Psychological Association, Washington, D.C., September 1976.

Jensen, A. "How Much Can We Boost IQ and Scholastic Attainment?" *Harvard Educational Review,* 1969, *39,* 1–123.

Joffe, C. "Sex Role Socialization and the Nursery School: As the Twig is Bent." *Journal of Marriage and the Family,* 1971, *33,* 467–475.

Joffe, C. "As the Twig is Bent." In J. Stacey, S. Bereaud, & J. Daniels, eds. *And Jill Came Tumbling After: Sexism in American Education.* New York: Dell, 1974.

Johnson, D. W., & Ahlegren, A. "Relationship Between Student Attitudes About Cooperation and Competition and Attitudes Toward Schooling." *Journal of Educational Psychology,* 1976, *68,* 92–102.

Johnson, P. "Social Power and Sex Role Stereotypes." Paper presented at the meeting of the Western Psychological Association, San Francisco, May, 1974.

Johnson, P. S., & Staffieri, J. R. "Stereotypic Affective Properties of Personal Names and Somatotypes in Children." *Developmental Psychology,* 1971, *5,* 176.

Johnson, R. *Aggression in Man and Animals*. Philadelphia: Saunders, 1972.

Jones, C., & Aronson, E. "Attribution of Fault to a Rape Victim as a Function of Respectability of the Victim." *Journal of Personality and Social Psychology*, 1973, *26*, 415–420.

Jones, M. C. "The Later Careers of Boys Who Were Early- or Late-Maturing." *Child Development*, 1957, *28*, 113–128.

Jones, M. C., & Bayley, N. "Physical Maturing Among Boys as Related to Behavior." *Journal of Educational Psychology*, 1950, *41*, 129–148.

Jong, E. *Fear of Flying*. New York: Holt, Rinehart & Winston, 1973.

Jordan, B. E., Radin, N., & Epstein, A. "Paternal Behavior and Intellectual Functioning in Preschool Boys and Girls." *Developmental Psychology*, 1975, *11*, 407–408.

Jost, A. "Hormonal Factors in the Development of the Male Genital System." In E. Rosenberg & C. A. Paulsen, eds. *The Human Testis*. New York: Plenum, 1970a.

Jost, A. "Hormonal Factors in Sex Differentiation." *Philosophical Transactions of the Royal Society of London*, 1970b, *B259*, 119–130.

Jost, A., Jones, H. W., & Scott, W. W., eds. *Hermaphroditism, Genital Anomalies and Related Endocrine Disorders*, 2d ed. Baltimore, Williams & Wilkins, 1969.

Julty, S. *MSP* Male Sexual Performance*. New York: Dell, 1975.

Jung, C. G. "Anima and Animus." In *Two Essays on Analytical Psychology: Collected Works of C. G. Jung*, vol. 7. New York: Bollinger Foundation, 1953, pp. 186–209.

Jung, C. G. *The Portable Jung*, ed. J. Campbell New York: Viking, 1971.

Kagan, J. "The Concept of Identification." *Psychological Review*, 1958, *65*, 296–305.

Kagan, J. "Emergent Themes in Human Development." *American Scientist*, 1976, *64*, 186–196.

Kagan, J., & Moss, H. A. *Birth to Maturity*. New York: Wiley, 1962.

Kagan, S., & Madsen, M. C. "Experimental Analyses of Cooperation and Competition of Anglo-American and Mexican Children." *Developmental Psychology*, 1972a, *6*, 49–59.

Kagan, S., & Madsen, M. C. "Rivalry in Anglo-American and Mexican Children of Two Ages." *Journal of Personality and Social Psychology*, 1972b, *24*, 214–220.

Kahn, A. "Latitudes of Emotional Expressions in Women and Men." Paper submitted for the meeting of the American Psychological Association, New York City, September 1979.

Kahn, A., & McGaughey, T. A. "Distance and Liking: When Moving Close Produces Increased Liking." *Sociometry*, 1977, *40*, 138–144.

Kalchbrenner, M. "Blaming the Mother as a Function of Maternal Employment and Degree of Sex Typing." Unpublished master's thesis, Montclair State College, N.J., 1978.

Kallmann, F. J. "Comparative Twin Study on the Genetic Aspects of Male Homosexuality." *Journal of Nervous and Mental Diseases*, 1952, *115*, 283–298.

Kane, F. J., Jr., Lipton, M. A., Krall, A. R., & Obrist, P. A. "Psychoendocrine

Study of Oral Contraceptive Agents." *American Journal of Psychiatry,* 1970, *127,* 443–450.

Kanin, E. J. "An Examination of Sexual Aggression as a Response to Sexual Frustration." *Journal of Marriage and the Family,* 1967a, *29,* 428–433.

Kanin, E. J. "Reference Groups and Sex Conduct Norm Violations." *Sociological Quarterly,* 1967b, *8,* 495–504.

Kaplan, A. G. "Clarifying the Concept of Androgyny: Implications for Therapy." *Psychology of Women Quarterly,* 1979, in press.

Kaplan, H. B., & Pokorny, A. D. "Sex-related Correlates of Adult Self-Derogation: Reports of Childhood Experiences." Developmental Psychology, 1972, *6,* 536.

Kanter, E. "Sex Differences in Cue Observations and Inferences in Person Perception." Paper presented at the meeting of the Eastern Psychological Association, Boston, April 1977.

Kanter, R. M. *Communes: Creating and Managing the Collective Life.* New York: Harper & Row, 1973.

Karkau, K. "Sexism in the Fourth Grade." Paper printed by KNOW Inc., Pittsburgh, 1974.

Keasey, C. B., & Tomlinson-Keasey, C. I. "Social Influence in a High-Ego-Involvement Situation: A Field Study of Petition Signing. Paper presented at the meeting of the Eastern Psychological Association, New York City, April, 1971.

Keiffer, M. G., & Cullen, D. M. "Women Who discriminate Against Other Women: The Process of Denial." *International Journal of Group Tensions,* 1974, *4,* 21–33.

Kellerman, J. "Sex Role Stereotypes and Attitudes Toward Parental Blame for the Psychological Problems of Children." *Journal of Consulting and Clinical Psychology,* 1974, *42,* 153–154.

Kemper, T. D. "On the Nature and Purpose of Ascription." *American Sociological Review,* 1974, *39,* 844–853.

Kennell, J. H. "Discussion of Early Human Interaction." Third Annual Conference on Psychosomatic Obstetrics and Gynecology, Philadelphia, 1975.

Kent, M. "Higher Education and Gender Role Socialization." Paper presented to the American Association of University Women, Washington D.C., 1974.

Kenworthy, J. A. & Kirlin, M. C. "Androgyny in Psychotherapy: But Will it Sell in Peoria?" Paper presented at the meeting of the American Psychological Association, Washington D.C., September 1976.

Kenworthy, J. A., Koufacos, C., & Sherman, J. "Women and therapy: A Survey of Attitudes and Information." Paper presented at the meeting of the American Psychological Association, Washington D.C., September 1976.

Keogh, B. K. "Pattern Copying Under Three Conditions of an Expanded Spatial Field. *Developmental Psychology,* 1971, *4,* 25–31.

Kephart, W. "Some Correlates of Romantic Love." *Journal of Marriage and the Family,* 1967, *29,* 470–479.

Kernan, J. B. "Her Mother's Daughter? The Case of Clothing and Cosmetic Fashions." *Adolescence*, 1973, *8*, 343–350.

Kessler, S. J. & McKenna, W. *Gender: An Ethnomethodological Approach.* New York: Wiley, 1978.

Kidd, R. F. "Pupil size, Eye Contact, and Instrumental Aggression." *Perceptual and Motor Skills*, 1975, *41*, 538.

Kidder, L. H., Bellettirie, G., & Cohn, E. S. "Secret Ambitions and Public Performance: The Effects of Anonymity on Reward Allocations made by Men and Women." *Journal of Experimental Social Psychology*, 1977, *13*, 70–80.

Kiesler, S. B. "Actuarial Prejudice Toward Women and Its Implications." *Journal of Applied Social Psychology*, 1975, 5, 201–216.

Kiesler, S. B., & Baral, R. L. "The Search for a Romantic Partner: The Effects of Self-esteem and Physical Attractiveness on Romantic Behavior. In K. J. Gergen & D. Marlowe, eds. *Personality and Social Behavior.* Reading, Mass.: Addison-Wesley, 1970.

Kimball, B., & Leahy, R. L. "Fear of Success in Males and Females: Effects of Developmental Level and Sex-Linked Course of Study." *Sex Roles*, 1976, *2*, 273–281.

Kinsey, A. C., Pomeroy, W. B., Martin, C. E., & Gebhard, R. *Sexual Behavior in the Human Female.* Philadelphia: Saunders, 1953.

Kinzel, A. S. "Body-Buffer Zone in Violent Prisoners." *American Journal of Psychiatry*, 1970, *127*, 59–64.

Kirchner, E. P. "The Fight Question: A Mirror of Differential Socialization and Instance of Discrimination Against Little Boys." *Developmental Psychology*, 1974, *10*, 300.

Kirchner, E. P., Seaver, W. B., Vegega, M. E., & Straw, M. K. "Motives For and Against Having a Child." Paper presented at the meeting of the American Psychological Association, Washington, D.C., September 1976.

Kirkpatrick, C. "The Construction of a Belief Pattern Scale for Measuring Attitudes Toward Feminism." *Journal of Social Psychology*, 1936, 7, 421–437.

Kirsh, B. "Consciousness-Raising Groups as Therapy for Women." In V. Franks & V. Burtle, eds. *Women in Therapy.* New York: Bruner/Mazel, 1974.

Kitay, P. M. "A Comparison of the Sexes in Their Attitudes and Beliefs About Women: A Study of Prestige Groups." *Sociometry*, 1940, 3, 399–407.

Klaus, M. H., Jerauld, R., Kreger, N. C., McAlpine, W., Stefta, M., & Kennell, J. H. "Maternal Attachment: Importance of the First Postpartum Days." *New England Journal of Medicine*, 1972, *286*, 460–463.

Kleck, R. E., & Rubenstein, C. "Physical Attractiveness, Perceived Attitudinal Similarity, and Interpresonal Attraction in an Opposite-Sex Encounter." *Journal of Personality and Social Psychology*, 1975, *31*, 107–114.

Klein, D. C., Fencil-Morse, E., & Seligman, M. E. P. "Learned Helplessness, Depression, and the Attribution of Failure." *Journal of Personality and Social Psychology*, 1976, *33*, 508–516.

Klemer, R. H. "Self-esteem and College Dating Experience as Factors in Mate Selection and Marital Happiness: A Longitudinal Study." *Journal of Marriage and the Family*, 1971, *33*, 183–187.

Knupfer, G., Clark, W., & Room, R. "The Mental Health of the Unmarried." *American Journal of Psychiatry*, 1966, *122*, 841–851.

Koedt, A. "The Myth of the Vaginal Orgasm." Pittsburgh, KNOW, 1970.

Koen, F. "Codability of Complex Stimuli: Three Modes of Representation." *Journal of Personality and Social Psychology*, 1966, *3*, 435–441.

Koeske, R. K., & Koeske, G. F. "An Attributional Approach to Moods and the Menstrual Cycle." *Journal of Personality and Social Psychology*, 1975, *31*, 473–478.

Kohlberg, L. "A Cognitive-Developmental Analysis of Children's Sex Role Concepts and Attitudes." In E. E. Maccoby, ed. *The Development of Sex Differences*. Stanford, Calif.: Stanford University Press, 1966, pp. 82–173.

Kohlberg, L. "Stage and Sequence: The Cognitive Developmental Approach to Socialization. In D. A. Goslin, ed. *Handbook of Socialization Theory and Research*. Chicago: Rand McNally, 1969, pp. 347–480.

Kohlberg, L., & Zigler, E. "The Impact of Cognitive Maturity on the Development of Sex-Role Attitudes in the Years 4 to 8." *Genetic Psychology Monographs*, 1967, *75*, 89–165.

Kolb, T. M., & Straus, M. A. "Marital Power and Marital Happiness in Relation to Problem Solving Ability." *Journal of Marriage and the Family*, 1974, *36*, 756–766.

Komarovsky, M. "Cultural Contradictions and Sex Roles: The Masculine Case." *American Journal of Sociology*, 1973, *78*, 873–884.

Koslin, B. L., Haarlow, R. N., Karlins, M., & Pargament, R. "Predicting Group Status from Members' Cognitions." *Sociometry*, 1968, *31*, 64–75.

Kralj-Cereck, L. "The Influence of Food, Body Build, and Social Origin on the Age of Menarche." *Human Biology*, 1956, *28*, 393–406.

Krebs, D. L. "Altruism: An Examination of the Concept and a Review of the Literature." *Psychological Bulletin*, 1970, *73*, 258–302.

Krebs, D., & Adinolfi, A. A. "Physical Attractiveness, Social Relations, and Personality Style." *Journal of Personality and Social Psychology*, 1975, *31*, 245–253.

Kreps, J. *Sex in the Marketplace: American Women at Work*. Baltimore: Johns Hopkins Press, 1971.

Kristal, J., Sanders, D., Spence, J. T., & Helmreich, R. "Inferences About the Femininity of Competent Women and Their Implications for Likability." *Sex Roles*, 1975, *1*, 33–40.

Krooth, R. S. Personal communication, 1975.

Kuhlen, R. G., & Houlihan, N. B. "Adolescent Heterosexual Interest in 1942 and 1963." *Child Development*, 1965, *36*, 1049–1052.

Kundsin, R. B., ed. "Successful Women in the Sciences: An Analysis of

Determinants." *Annals of the New York Academy of Sciences*, 1973, *208*.

Kupecky, I., & Hilderbrand, M. "The Relationship Between Physical Attractiveness in Males and Their Perceived Support of the Feminist Movement." Paper presented at the meeting of the American Psychological Association, New York City, September, 1979.

Kurland, L., & Wirth, D. Unpublished manuscript, Montclair State College, 1978.

Kutner, N. G., & Brogan, D. An Investigation of Sex-Related Slang Vocabulary and Sex-Role Orientation Among Male and Female University Students." *Journal of Marriage and the Family*, 1974, *36*, 474–484.

Kutner, N. G., & Brogan, D. "Sources of Sex Discrimination in Educational Systems: A Conceptual Analysis." *Psychology of Women Quarterly*, 1976, *1*, 50–69.

Kutner, N. G., & Levinson, R. M. "The Toy Salesperson: A Voice for Change in Sex-Role Stereotypes?" *Sex Roles*, 1978, *4*, 1–7.

Labov, W. "The Linguistic Consequences of Being a Lame." *Language in Society*, 1973, *2*, 81–115.

Ladd, E. C., Jr., & Lipset, S. M. "Sex Differences in Academe." *The Chronicle of Higher Education*, May 10, 1976, p. 18.

Lakoff, R. *Language and Woman's Place*. New York: Harper Colophon Books, 1975.

Lamb, M. E., ed. *The Role of the Father in Child Development*. New York: Wiley, 1976.

Langer, E. J., & Roth, J. "Heads I Win, Tails It's Chance: The Illusion of Control as a Function of the Sequence of Outcomes in a Purely Chance Task." *Journal of Personality and Social Psychology*, 1975, *32*, 951–955.

Lansky, L. M. "The Family Structure Also Affects the Model: Sex-Role Identification in Parents of Preschool Children." *Merrill-Palmer Quarterly*, 1964, *10*, 39–50.

Laosa, L., & Brophy, J. "Effects of Sex and Birth Order on Sex-Role Development and Intelligence in Kindergarten Children." *Developmental Psychology*, 1972, *6*, 409–415.

Larson, D. L., Spreitzer, E. A., & Snyder, E. E. "Social Factors in the Frequency of Romantic Involvement Among Adolescents." *Adolescence*, 1976, *11*, 7–12.

Larson, L. E. "System and Subsystem Perception of Family Roles." *Journal of Marriage and the Family*, 1974, *36*, 123–138.

Larwood, L., O'Neal, E., & Brennan, P. "Increasing the Physical Aggressiveness of Women." *Journal of Social Psychology*, 1977, *101*, 97–101.

Latané, B., & Dabbs, J. M., Jr. "Sex, Group Size and Helping in Three Cities." *Sociometry*, 1975, *38*, 180–194.

Lavrakas, P. J. "Female Preferences for Male Physiques." *Journal of Research in Personality*, 1975, *9*, 324–334.

Laws, J. L. "The Psychology of Tokenism: An Analysis." *Sex Roles*, 1975, *1*, 51–67.

Laws, J. L. "Work Motivation and Work Behavior of Women: New Perspectives. In J. Sherman & F. Denmark, eds. *Psychology of Women: Future Directions of Research.* New York: Psychological Dimensions, 1978.

Lazarre, J. *The Mother Knot.* New York: McGraw-Hill, 1976.

Lazowick, L. M. "On the Nature of Identification." *Journal of Abnormal and Social Psychology,* 1955, *51,* 175–183.

Lehrke, R. "A Theory of X-Linkage of Major Intellectual Traits." *American Journal of Mental Deficiency,* 1972, *76,* 611–619.

Leibman, N. "The Effects of Sex and Race Norms on Personal Space." *Environment and Behavior,* 1970, *2,* 208–246.

LeMasters, E. E. "Parenthood as Crisis." *Marriage and Family Living,* 1957, *19,* 352–355.

Lennane, M. B., & Lennane, R. J. "Alleged Psychogenic Disorders in Women—A Possible Manifestation of Sexual Prejudice." *New England Journal of Medicine,* 1973, *288,* 288–292.

Lenney, E. "Women's Self-confidence in Achievement Settings." *Psychological Bulletin,* 1977, *84,* 1–13.

Lerner, M. J., & Lichtman, R. R. "Effects of Perceived Norms on Attitudes and Altruistic Behavior Toward a Dependent Other." *Journal of Personality and Social Psychology,* 1968, *9,* 226–232.

Lerner, R. M. "Some Female Stereotypes of Male Body Build–Behavior Relations." *Perceptual and Motor Skills,* 1969, *28,* 363–366.

Lerner, R. M., & Korn, S. J. "The Development of Body-Build Stereotypes in Males." *Child Development,* 1972, *43,* 908–920.

Lesser, G. S., Krawitz, R. N., & Packard, R. "Experimental Arousal of Achievement Motivation in Adolescent Girls." *Journal of Abnormal and Social Psychology,* 1963, *66,* 59–66.

Levenson, H. "Perceived Parental Antecedents of Internal Powerful Others and Chance Locus of Control Orientations." *Developmental Psychology,* 1973, *9,* 268–274.

Levine, R., Reis, H. T., Sue, E., & Turner, G. "Fear of Failure in Males: A More Salient Factor Than Fear of Success in Females?" *Sex Roles,* 1976, *2,* 389–398.

Levinger, G. "A Social Psychological Perspective on Marital Dissolution." *Journal of Social Issues,* 1976, *32,* 21–47.

Levinson, B. M. "Wechsler M–F Index." *Journal of General Psychology,* 1963, *69,* 217–220.

Levitin, T. A., & Chananie, J. D. "Responses of Female Primary School Teachers to Sex-Typed Behaviors in Male and Female Children." *Child Development,* 1972, *43,* 1309–1316.

Levy, B. "Do Schools Sell Girls Short?" In J. Stacey et al., eds. *And Jill Came Tumbling After: Sexism in American Education.* New York: Dell, 1974.

Lewis, M. "Parents and Children: Sex Role Development." *The School Review,* 1972, *80,* 229–240.

Libow, J. A., & Mogy, R. B. "Task Self-appropriateness and Sex Differences in Self-attribution for Performance." Paper presented at the meeting of the American Psychological Association, Washington, D.C., September 1976.

Linn, L. "Physician Characteristics and Attitudes Toward Legitimate Use of Psychotherapeutic Drugs." *Journal of Health and Social Behavior,* 1971, *12,* 132–140.

Linn, L., & Davis, M. "The Use of Psychotherapeutic Drugs by Middle Aged Women." *Journal of Health and Social Behavior,* 1971, *12,* 331–340.

Lippitt, R., & Gold, M. "Classroom Social structure as a Mental Health Problem." *Journal of Social Issues,* 1959, *15,* 40–49.

Lippman, W. *Public Opinion.* New York: Harcourt, 1922.

Lirtzman, S. I., & Wahba, M. A. "Determinants of Coalitional Behavior of Men and Women: Sex Roles or Situational Requirements." *Journal of Applied Psychology,* 1972, *56,* 406–411.

Liss, L. "Why Academic Women Do Not Revolt: Implications for Affirmative Action." *Sex Roles,* 1975, *1,* 209–223.

Littenburg, R., Tulkin, S., & Kagan, J. "Cognitive Components of Separation Anxiety." *Developmental Psychology,* 1971, *4,* 387–388.

Little, B. C., Matta, R. J., & Zahn, T. P. "Physiological and Psychological Effects of Progesterone in Man." *Journal of Nervous and Mental Disease,* 1974, *159,* 256–262.

Lockheed, M. E. "Female Motive to Avoid Success: A Psychological Barrier or a Response to Deviancy?" *Sex Roles,* 1975, *1,* 41–50.

Lockheed, M. E., & Hall, K. P. "Conceptualizing Sex as a Status Characteristic: Applications to Leadership Training Strategies." *Journal of Social Issues,* 1976, *32,* 111–124.

Loeb, J. W., & Ferber, M. A. "Representation, Performance, and the Status of Women on the Faculty of the Urbana-Champaign Campus of the University of Illinois." In A. S. Rossi & A. Calderwood, eds. *Academic Women on the Move.* New York: Russell Sage, 1973.

Loevinger, J. "The Meaning and Measurement of Ego Development." *American Psychologist,* 1966, *21,* 195–206.

Loevinger, J., & Wessler, R. *Measuring Ego Development,* vol. 1. San Francisco: Jossey-Bass, 1970.

Lomas, P. "Childbirth Ritual." *New Society,* December 1964, *31.*

Looft, W. R. "Sex Differences in the Expression of Vocational Aspirations by Elementary School Children." *Developmental Psychology,* 1971, *5,* 366.

Lopata, H. Z. *Occupation Housewife.* New York: Oxford University Press, 1971.

Lopata, H. Z. *Widowhood in an American City.* Cambridge: Schenkman, 1973.

Lorber, J. "Women and Medical Sociology: Invisible Professionals and Ubiquitous Patients." In M. Millman & R. M. Kanter, eds. *Another Voice: Feminist Perspectives on Social Life and Social Science.* Garden City, N.Y.: Anchor-Press, 1975.

Lott, D. F., & Sommer, R. "Seating Arrangements and Status." *Journal of Personality and Social Psychology,* 1967, *7,* 90–95.

Lower East Side Women's Liberation Collective. "Love is Just a Four-

Letter Word." In W. Martin, ed. *The American Sisterhood.* New York: Harper & Row, 1972.

Luce, G. G. *Biological Rhythms in Psychiatry and Medicine.* Chevy Chase, Md.: U.S. Department of Health, Education and Welfare, 1970.

Luckey, E. B., & Bain, J. K. "Children: A Factor in Marital Satisfaction." *Journal of Marriage and the Family,* 1970, *32,* 43–44.

Luckey, E. B., & Nass, G. D. "A Comparison of Sexual Attitudes and Behavior in an International Sample." *Journal of Marriage and the Family,* 1969, *31,* 364–379.

Lunneborg, P., & Lillie, C. "Sexism in Graduate Admissions: The Letter of Recommendation." *American Psychologist,* 1973, *28,* 188–189.

Lyell, R. G. "Adolescent and Adult Self-esteem as Related to Cultural Values." *Adolescence,* 1973, *8,* 85–92.

Lynn, D. B. "A Note on Sex Differences in the Development of Masculine and Feminine Identification." *Psychological Review,* 1959, *66,* 126–135.

Lynn, D. B. "The Process of Learning Parental and Sex-Role Identification." *Journal of Marriage and the Family,* 1966, *23,* 446–470.

Lynn, D. B. *Parental and Sex Role Identification: A Theoretical Formulation.* Berkeley, Calif.: McCutchan, 1969.

Lynn, D. B. *The Father: His Role in Child Development.* Monterey, Calif.: Wadsworth, 1974.

Lyon, M. F. "Gene Action in the X-Chromosome of the Mouse." *Nature,* 1961, *190,* 372–373.

Maccoby, E. E. "The Development of Stimulus Selection." In J. P. Hill, ed. *Minnesota Symposium on Child Development,* 1969, *3,* 68–98.

Maccoby, E. E., & Jacklin, C. N. *The Psychology of Sex Differences.* Stanford, Calif.: Stanford University Press, 1974.

Mace, D. "The Employed Mother in the USSR." *Marriage and Family Living,* 1961, *23,* 330–333.

Maddux, H. C. *Menstruation.* New Canaan, Conn.: Tobey, 1975.

Mahoney, E. R. "Compensatory Reactions to Spatial Immediacy." *Sociometry,* 1974, *37,* 423–431.

Maier, S. F., & Seligman, M. E. P. "Learned Helplessness: Theory and Evidence." *Journal of Experimental Psychology,* 1976, *105,* 3–46.

Makosky, V. P. "Sex-Role Compatibility of Task and of Competitor, and Fear of Success as Variables Affecting Women's Performance." *Sex Roles,* 1976, *2,* 237–248.

Mandell, A. J., & Mandell, M. P. "Suicide and the Menstrual Cycle." *Journal of the American Medical Association,* 1967, *200,* 792–793.

Marecek, J. "When Stereotypes Hurt: Responses to Dependent and Aggressive Communications." Paper presented at the meeting of the Eastern Psychological Association, Philadelphia, April 1974.

Marecek, J. "Power and Women's Psychological Disorders: Preliminary Observations." Paper presented at the meeting of the Eastern Psychological Association, New York City, April 1975.

Marecek, J. "Predictors of Women's Career Attainment: A Longitudinal

Study." Paper presented at the meeting of the Eastern Psychological Association, New York City, April 1976.

Marks, E. "Sex, Birth Order, and Beliefs About Personal Power." *Developmental Psychology,* 1972, 6, 184.

Marks, I. "Agoraphobic Syndrome: Phobic Anxiety State." *Archives of General Psychiatry,* 1970, 23, 538–553.

Marsella, A. J., Dubanoski, R. A., & Mohs, K. "The Effects of Father Presence and Absence upon Maternal Attitudes." *Journal of Genetic Psychology,* 1974, 125, 257–263.

Marshall, J. E., & Heslin, R. "Boys and Girls Together: Sexual Composition and the Effect of Density and Group Size on Cohesiveness." *Journal of Personality and Social Psychology,* 1975, 31, 952–961.

Mason, W. A. "Social Organization of the South American Monkey *Callicebus moloch:* A Preliminary Report." *Tulane Studies in Zoology,* 1966, 13, 23–28.

Masters, W., & Johnson, V. *Human Sexual Response.* Boston: Little, Brown, 1966.

Masters, W., & Johnson, V. *Human Sexual Inadequacy.* Boston: Little, Brown, 1970.

Mathes, E. W. "The Effects of Physical Attractiveness and Anxiety on Heterosexual Attraction over a Series of Five Encounters." *Journal of Marriage and the Family,* 1975, 37, 769–773.

Matthews, K. E., Jr., & Cooper, S. "Deceit as a Function of Sex of Subject and Target Person." *Sex Roles,* 1976, 2, 29–38.

Mathews, W. S. "Sex Differences in the Fantasy Play of Young Children." Paper presented at the meeting of the New Jersey Psychological Association, Somerset, May 1975.

McBride, A. *The Growth and Development of Mothers.* New York: Harper & Row, 1973.

McCandless, B. R., & Hoyt, J. M. "Sex, Ethnicity, and Play Preferences of Preschool Children." *Journal of Abnormal and Social Psychology,* 1961, 62, 683–685.

McClelland, D. C. *The Achieving Society.* New York: Van Nostrand, 1961.

McClelland, D. C. "Wanted: A New Self-image for Women." In R. J. Lifton, ed. *The Woman in America.* Boston: Beacon, 1964.

McClelland, D. C., Atkinson, J. W., Clark, R. A., & Lowell, E. L. *The Achievement Motive.* Englewood Cliffs, N.J.: Prentice-Hall, 1953.

McClintock, M. K. "Menstrual Synchrony and Suppression." *Nature,* 1971, 229, 244–245.

McConahay, S. A., & McConahay, J. B. "Sexual Permissiveness, Sex-Role Rigidity, and Violence Across Cultures." *Journal of Social Issues,* 1977, 33, 134–143.

McCreary-Juhasz, A. "How Accurate are Student Evaluations of the Extent of Their Knowledge of Human Sexuality?" *Journal of School Health,* 1967, 37, 409–412.

McDaniel, C. O., Jr. "Dating Roles and Reasons for Dating." *Journal of Marriage and the Family,* 1969, 31, 97–107.

McGee, M. G., & Snyder, M. "Attribution and Behavior: Two Field Studies." *Journal of Personality and Social Psychology*, 1975, *32*, 185–190.

McGinnies, E., Nordholm, L. A., Ward, C. D., & Bhanthumnavin, D. L. "Sex and Cultural Differences in Perceived Locus of Control Among Students in Five Countries." *Journal of Consulting and Clinical Psychology*. 1974, *42*, 451–455.

McGuigan, D. I., & Olive, H. "Faculty Attitudes Towards Women." Paper presented at the meeting of the New Jersey Psychological Association, Union, May 1976.

McGuire, J. M. "Aggression and Sociometric Status with Preschool Children." *Sociometry*, 1973, *36*, 542–549.

McGuire, J. M., & Thomas, M. H. "Effects of Sex, Competence, and Competition on Sharing Behavior in Children." *Journal of Personality and Social Psychology*, 1975, *32*, 490–494.

McGurk, H., & Lewis, M. "Birth Order: A Phenomenon in Search of an Explanation." *Developmental Psychology*, 1972, *7*, 366.

McHugh, M. *Psychology and the New Woman*. New York: Franklin Watts, 1976.

McKee, J. P., & Sheriffs, A. C. "The Differential Evaluation of Males and Females." *Journal of Personality*, 1957, *25*, 356–371.

McKee, J. P., & Sherriffs, A. C. "Men's and Women's Beliefs, Ideals and Self-Concepts." *American Journal of Sociology*, 1959, *64*, 356–363.

McKenna, W. Personal communication, 1975.

McKenna, W., & Kessler, S. J. "Experimental Design as a Source of Sex Bias in Social Psychology." *Sex Roles*, 1977, *3*, 117–128.

McKusick, V. A. *Human Genetics*. Englewood Cliffs, N.J.: Prentice-Hall, 1964.

McMahon, I. D. "Sex Differences in the Expectancy of Success as a Function of Task." Paper presented at the meeting of the Eastern Psychological Association, Washington, D.C., April 1972.

McNeel, S. P., McKillip, J., DiMiceli, A. J., Van Tuinen, M., Reid, E., & Barrett, G. "Social Psychology Job Applications: Normative Information and the Question of Sexism." *Personality and Social Psychology Bulletin*, 1975, *1*, 570–574.

Mead, M. "Some Theoretical Considerations on the Problem of Mother–Child Separation." *American Journal of Orthopsychiatry*, 1954, *24*, 471–483.

Mednick, M. T. S. "Social Change and Sex-Role Inertia: The Case of the Kibbutz." In M. T. S. Mednick, S. S. Tangri, & L. W. Hoffman, eds. *Women and Achievement: Social and Motivational Analyses*. Washington, D.C.: Hemisphere, 1975.

Mednick, M. T. S. "Comment on 'Review Essay: Psychology.'" *Signs*, 1976, *1*, 763–770.

Mednick, M. T. S. "Psychology of Women: Research Issues and Trends." *Annals of the New York Academy of Sciences*, 1978, *309*, 77–92.

Mednick, M. T. S. "Now We are Four: What Should We Be When We Grow Up?" *Psychology of Women Quarterly*, 1978, *2*, 123–138.

Mednick, M. T. S., Tangri, S. S., & Hoffman, L. W., eds. *Women and Achievement: Social and Motivational Analyses.* Washington, D.C.: Hemisphere, 1975.

Mednick, M. T. S., & Weissman, H. J. "The Psychology of Women— Selected Topics." *Annual Review of Psychology*, 1975, *26*, 1–18.

Mehl, L. "Homebirth: How Safe an Alternative?" Paper presented at conference "Childbearing," Ramapo College, Mahwah, N.J., February 1977.

Mehrabian, A. "Relationship of Attitude to Seated Posture, Orientation, and Distance." *Journal of Personality and Social Psychology*, 1968, *10*, 26–30.

Melges, F. T. "Postpartum Psychiatric Syndromes." *Psychosomatic Medicine*, 1968, *30*, 95–108.

Mellinger, G. D., Balter, M. B., & Manheimer, D. I. "Patterns of Psychotherapeutic Drug Use Among Adults in San Francisco." *Archives of General Psychiatry*, 1971, *25*, 385–394.

Mendelsohn, G. A., Griswald, B. B., & Anderson, M. L. "Individual Differences in Anagram-Solving Ability." *Psychological Reports*, 1966, *2*, 429–439.

Miller, K. A., & Inkeles, A. "Modernity and Acceptance of Family Limitation in Four Developing Countries." *Journal of Social Issues*, 1974, *30*, 167–188.

Miller, N., & Maruyama, G. "Ordinal Position and Peer Popularity." *Journal of Personality and Social Psychology*, 1976, *33*, 123–131.

Miller, S. M. "Effect of Maternal Employment on Sex Role Perception, Interests and Self Esteem in Kindergarten Girls." *Developmental Psychology*, 1975, *11*, 405–406.

Miller, T. W. "Male Attitudes Toward Women's Rights as a Function of Their Level of Self-esteem." *International Journal of Group Tensions*, 1974, *4*, 35–44.

Miller, W. R., & Seligman, M. E. P. "Depression and Learned Helplessness in Man." *Journal of Abnormal Psychology*, 1975, *84*, 228–238.

Miller, W. R., & Seligman, M. E. P. "Learned Helplessness, Depression, and the Perception of Reinforcement." *Behavior Research and Therapy*, 1976, *14*, 7–17.

Millman, M. "She Did it All for Love: A Feminist View of the Sociology of Deviance." In M. Millman & R. M. Kanter, eds. *Another Voice: Feminist Perspectives on Social Life and Social Science.* Garden City, N.Y.: Anchor Books, 1975.

Mills, J., & Aronson, E. "Opinion Change as a Function of the Communicator's Attractiveness and Desire to Influence." *Journal of Personality and Social Psychology*, 1965, *1*, 173–177.

Minard, J. Personal communication, March 1976.

Minnigerode, F. A. "Attitudes Toward Homosexuality: Feminist Attitudes and Sexual Conservatism." *Sex Roles*, 1976, *2*, 347–352.

Miransky, J., Mulvey, A., & Grady, K. "A Non-verbal Measure of Dominance." Paper presented at the meeting of the American Psychological

Association, Washington, D.C., September 1976.

Mischel, W. "A Social-Learning View of Sex Differences in Behavior." In E. Maccoby, ed. *The Development of Sex Differences.* Stanford, Calif.: Stanford University Press, 1966.

Mischel, W. "Sex-Typing and Socialization." In P. H. Mussen, ed. *Carmichael's Manual of Child Psychology.* New York: Wiley, 1970.

Mitchell, G. D. "Paternalistic Behavior in Primates." *Psychological Bulletin,* 1969, *71,* 399–417.

Mittwoch, U. *Genetics of Sex Differentiation.* New York: Academic Press, 1973.

Moldawsky, S. "A Freudian Looks at Freud and Femininity." Paper presented at the meeting of the American Psychological Association, Chicago, September 1975.

Monahan, L., Kuhn, D., & Shaver, P. "Intrapsychic Versus Cultural Explanations of the 'Fear of Success' Motive." *Journal of Personality and Social Psychology,* 1974, *29,* 60–64.

Money, J. "Sex Hormones and Other Variables in Human Eroticism." In W. C. Young, ed. *Sex and Internal Secretions.* Baltimore: Williams & Wilkins, 1961.

Money, J. "Intellectual Functioning in Childhood Endocrinopathies and Related Cytogenetic Disorders." In L. T. Gardner, ed. *Endocrine and Genetic Diseases of Childhood.* Philadelphia: W. B. Saunders, 1969.

Money, J. "Sexually Dimorphis Behavior, Normal and Abnormal." In N. Kretchmer & D. N. Walcher, eds. *Environmental Influences on Genetic Expression.* Washington, D.C.: USGPO, 1971.

Money, J. "Prenatal Hormones and Postnatal Socialization in Gender Identity Differentiation. In J. K. Cole & R. Dienstbier, eds. *Nebraska Symposium on Motivation 1973.* Lincoln: University of Nebraska Press, 1974.

Money, J. "Gender and Disorders of Eroticism." Paper presented at the meeting of the Eastern Psychological Association, New York City, April 1976.

Money, J., & Ehrhardt, A. *Man and Woman, Boy and Girl.* Baltimore: Johns Hopkins University Press, 1972.

Money, J., Hampson, J. G., & Hampson, J. L. "Imprinting and the Establishment of Gender Role." *Archives of Neurology and Psychiatry,* 1957, *77,* 333–336.

Moore, J. C., Jr., Johnson, E. B., & Arnold, M. S. C. "Status Congruence and Equity in Restricted Communication Networks." *Sociometry,* 1972, *35,* 519–537.

Moore, K. A. "Fear of Success: The Distribution, Correlates, Reliability and Consequences for Fertility of Fear of Success Among Respondents in a Metropolitan Survey Population." CRSO Working Paper no. 111, Center for Research on Social Organization, University of Michigan, August 1974.

Moore, S. G. "Correlates of Peer Acceptance in Nursery School Children." In W. W. Hartup & N. L. Smothergill, eds. *The Young Child.* Washington, D.C.: National Association for the Education of Young Children, 1967.

Moore, S. G., & Updegraff, R. "Sociometric Status of Preschool Children as Related to Age, Sex, Nurturance-Giving, and Dependence." *Child Development*, 1964, *35*, 519–524.

Moore, T. W. "Stress in Normal Childhood." *Human Relations*, 1969, *22*, 235–250.

Moore, T. W. "Exclusive Early Mothering and Its Alternatives: The Outcome to Adolescence." *Scandinavian Journal of Psychology*, 1975, *16*, 255–272.

Moos, R. H. "The Development of a Menstrual Distress Questionnaire." *Psychosomatic Medicine*, 1968, *30*, 853–867.

Morland, J. K. "A Comparison of Race Awareness in Northern and Southern Children." *American Journal of Orthopsychiatry*, 1966, *36*, 22–31.

Morlock, L. "Discipline Variation in the Status of Academic Women." In A. S. Rossi & A. Calderwood, eds. *Academic Women on the Move*. New York: Russell Sage, 1973.

Morris, N. M., & Sison, B. S. "Correlates of Female Powerlessness: Parity, Methods of Birth Control, Pregnancy." *Journal of Marriage and the Family*, 1974, *36*, 708–712.

Morse, S. J., Gruzen, J., & Reis, H. "The 'eye of the beholder': A Neglected Variable in the Study of Physical Attractiveness?" *Journal of Personality*, 1976, *44*, 209–225.

Moskowitz, D. S., & Schwartz, J. C. "Effect of Day Care Experience on Three-Year-Old Children's Attachment Behavior." Paper presented at the meeting of the Eastern Psychological Association, New York City, April 1976.

Moss, H. A., & Kagan, J. "Maternal Influences on Early IQ Scores." *Psychological Reports*, 1958, *4*, 655–661.

Mossip, C. E., & Unger, R. K. "The Perception of Asymmetrical Faces: Maturational and Environmental Factors." Paper submitted for publication, 1977.

Moustakas, C. E., Sigel, I. E., & Schalock, N. D. "An Objective Method for the Measurement and Analysis of Child–Adult Interaction." *Child Development*, 1956, *27*, 109–134.

Moynihan, D. P. *The Negro Family*. Washington, D.C.: Office of Public Planning and Research, United States Department of Labor, 1975.

Mulder, M., Veen, P., Hijzen, T., & Jansen, P. "On Power Equalization: A Behavioral Example of Power-Distance Reduction." *Journal of Personality and Social Psychology*, 1973, *26*, 151–158.

Mundy, J. "Women in Rage: A Psychological Look at the Helpless Heroine." In R. K. Unger & F. L. Denmark, eds. *Woman: Dependent or Independent Variable?* New York: Psychological Dimensions, 1975.

Murphy-Berman, V. "Effects of Success and Failure on Perceptions of Gender Identity." *Sex Roles*, 1976, *2*, 367–374.

Murstein, B. I. "Physical Attractiveness and Marital Choice." *Journal of Personality and Social Psychology*, 1972, *22*, 8–12.

Musa, K. E., & Roach, M. E. "Adolescent Appearance and Self Concept." *Adolescence*, 1973, 8, 385–394.

Mussen, P. H. "Early Sex-Role Development." In D. A. Goslin, ed. *Handbook of Socialization Theory and Research*. Chicago: Rand McNally, 1969, pp. 707–732.

Mussen, P. H., & Rutherford, E. "Parent–Child Relations and Parental Personality in Relation to Young Children's Sex-Role Preferences." *Child Development*, 1963, 34, 589–607.

Myrdal, G. "A Parallel to the Negro Problem." In G. Myrdal. *An American Dilemma*. New York: Harper & Row, 1944.

Nadelman, L. "Sex Identity in American Children: Memory, Knowledge and Preference Tests." *Developmental Psychology*, 1974, 10, 413–417.

Nash, S. C. "The Relationship Among Sex-Role Stereotyping, Sex-Role Preference, and the Sex Difference in Spatial Visualization." *Sex Roles*, 1975, 1, 15–32.

Nemeth, C., & Wachtler, J. "Creating the Perceptions of Consistency and Confidence: A Necessary Condition for Minority Influence." *Sociometry*, 1974, 37, 529–540.

Nesbitt, P. D., & Steven, G. "Personal Space and Stimulus Intensity in a Southern California Amusement Park." *Sociometry*, 1974, 37, 105–115.

Newman, B. M. "The Study of Interpersonal Behavior in Adolescence." *Adolescence*, 1976, 11, 127–142.

Newton, N. "The Effect of Psychological Environment on Childbirth: Combined Cross-Cultural and Experimental Approach." *Journal of Cross-Cultural Psychology*, 1970, 1, 85–90.

Nguyen, T., Heslin, R., & Nguyen, M. L. "The Meanings of Touch: Sex Differences." *Journal of Communication*, 1975, 25, 92–103.

Nicholls, J. "Causal Attributions and Other Achievement Related Cognitions: Effects of Task, Outcome, Attainment Value and Sex." *Journal of Personality and Social Psychology*, 1975, 31, 379–389.

Nielsen, J. M., & Doyle, P. T. "Sex-Role Stereotypes of Feminists and Nonfeminists." *Sex Roles*, 1975, 1, 83–95.

Nisbett, R. E., & Gurwitz, S. B. "Weight, Sex, and the Eating Behavior of Human Newborns." *Journal of Comparative and Physiological Psychology*, 1970, 73, 245–253.

Noblit, G., & Burcart, J. "Crime and Women in America: Some Preliminary Trends of a Decade (1960–70)." Paper presented at the meeting of the Pacific Sociological Association, Spring 1973.

Norton, A. J., & Glick, P. C. "Marital Instability: Past, Present, and Future." *Journal of Social Issues*, 1976, 32, 5–20.

Norum, G. A., Russo, N. J., & Sommer, R. "Seating Patterns and Group Task." *Psychology in the Schools*, 1967, 4, 276–280.

Nosanchuk, T. A. "The Vignette as an Experimental Approach to the Study of Social Status: An Exploratory Study." *Social Science Research*, 1972, 1, 107–120.

Nowicki, S., Jr., & Duke, M. P. "A Preschool and Primary Internal–External Control Scale." *Developmental Psychology*, 1974, 10, 874–880.

Nuckolls, K. B., Cassel, J., & Kaplan, B. A. "Psychosocial Assets, Life Crises, and the Prognosis of Pregnancy." *American Journal of Epidemiology,* 1972, 95, 431–441.

Oakley, A. *The Sociology of Housework.* New York: Pantheon, 1974a.

Oakley, A. *Woman's Work: The Housewife Past and Present.* New York: Pantheon, 1974b.

O'Connell, A. N. "The Relationship Between Life Style and Identity Synthesis and Resynthesis in Traditional, Neotraditional, and Nontraditional Women." *Journal of Personality,* 1976, 44, 675–688.

O'Connell, A. N. "The Decision to Return to College: Role Concepts, Personality, Attitudes, and Significant Others." *Sex Roles,* 1977, 3 (3), 229–240.

O'Connell, A. N., Alpert, J. L., Richardson, M. S., Rotter, N. G., Ruble, D. N., & Unger, R. K. "Gender-specific barriers to research in psychology." *Catalog of Selected Documents in Psychology,* 1978, 8, 80.

O'Connell, A., & Rotter, N. "The Influence of Stimulus Age and Sex on Person Perception." Paper presented at the meeting of the Eastern Psychological Association, Boston, April 1977.

Oetzel, R. M. "Annotated Bibliography and Classified Summary of Research in Sex Differences." In E. Maccoby, ed. *The Development of Sex Differences.* Stanford, Calif.: Stanford University Press, 1966.

O'Leary, V. E. & Donoghue, J. M. "Latitudes of Masculinity: Reactions to Sex-Role Deviance in Men." *Journal of Social Issues,* 1978, 34, 17–28.

O'Leary, V. E., & Hammack, B. "Sex-Role Orientation and Achievement Context as Determinants of the Motive to Avoid Success." *Sex Roles,* 1975, 1, 225–234.

O'Leary, V. E., & Harrison, A. O. "Sex-Role Stereotypes as a Function of Race and Sex." Paper presented at the meeting of the American Psychological Association, Chicago, September 1975.

Olive, H., & McGuigan, D. I. "Attitude Change in Students Following a Course in the Personality Development of Women." Paper presented at the meeting of the New Jersey Psychological Association, Somerset, May 1975.

Olson, D. H. "The Measurement of Family Power by Self-Report and Behavioral Measures." *Journal of Marriage and the Family,* 1969, 31, 545–550.

Oppenheimer, V. K. "The Sex-Labeling of Jobs." *Industrial Relations,* 1968, 7, 219–234.

Orden, S. R., & Bradburn, N. M. "Working Wives and Marriage Happiness." *American Journal of Sociology,* 1969, 74, 392–402.

O'Rourke, J. F. "Field and Laboratory: The Decision Making Behavior of Family Groups in Two Experimental Conditions." *Sociometry,* 1963, 26, 422–435.

Osofsky, J. D., & O'Connell, E. J. "Parent–Child Interaction: Daughters' Effects upon Mothers' and Fathers' Behaviors." *Developmental Psychology,* 1972, 7, 157–168.

Page, E. W., Villee, C. A., & Villee, D. B. *Human Reproduction.* Philadelphia: W. B. Saunders, 1972.

Paige, K. E. "Effects of Oral Contraceptives on Affective Fluctuations Associated with the Menstrual Cycle." *Psychosomatic Medicine*, 1971, *33*, 515–537.

Paige, K. E. "Women Learn to Sing the Menstrual Blues." *Psychology Today*, 1973, *7*, 41–46.

Paige, K. E. "Sexual Pollution: Reproductive Sex Taboos in American Society." *Journal of Social Issues*, 1977, *33*, 144–165.

Pare, C. M. B. "Etiology of Homosexuality: Genetic and Chromosomal Aspects." In J. Marmor, ed. *Sexual Inversion*. New York: Basic Books, 1965.

Parke, R. D. "Family Interaction in the Newborn Period: Some Findings, Some Observations, and Some Unresolved Issues." In K. Riegel & J. Meacham, eds. *The Developing Individual in a Changing World*, vol. 2. The Hague: Mouton, 1976.

Parke, R. D., O'Leary, S. E., & West, S. "Mother–Father–Newborn Interaction: Effects of Maternal Medication, Labor, and Sex of Infant." *Proceedings, 80th Annual Convention of the American Psychological Association*, 1972, pp. 85–86.

Parlee, M. B. "The Premenstrual Syndrome." *Psychological Bulletin*, 1973, *80*, 454–465.

Parlee, M. B. "Stereotypic Beliefs About Menstruation: A Methodological Note on the Moos Menstrual Distress Questionnaire and Some New Data." *Psychosomatic Medicine*, 1974, *36*, 229–240.

Parlee, M. B. "Review Essay: Psychology." *Signs*, 1975, *1*, 119–138.

Parlee, M. B. "Sex Differences in Perceptual Field Dependence: A Look at Some Data Embedded in Theory." Manuscript submitted for publication, 1976a.

Parlee, M. B. "Psychological Aspects of the Climacteric in Women." Paper presented at the meeting of the Eastern Psychological Association, New York City, April 1976b.

Parlee, M. B. "Psychological Aspects of Menstruation, Childbirth, and Menopause: An Overview with Suggestions for Further Research." In J. Sherman & F. L. Denmark, eds. *Psychology of Women: Future Directions of Research*. New York: Psychological Dimensions, 1978.

Parrott, G. L., & Saiia, S. "Heterosexual Perception: In Black and White." *Proceedings, 80th Annual Convention of the American Psychological Association*, 1972, *7*, 289–290.

Payer, M. E. "Is Traditional Scholarship Value Free? Toward a Critical Theory." Paper presented at the symposium "The Scholar and the Feminist IV," Barnard College, April 23, 1977.

Patterson, G. R., Littman, R. A., & Bricker, W. "Assertive Behavior in Children: A Step Toward a Theory of Aggression." *Monographs of the Society for Research in Child Development*, 1967, *32*, no. 113.

Peck, R. F. "Realism of Self-appraisal and School Achievement in Eight Countries." In F. J. Monks, W. W. Hartup, & J. deWitt, eds. *Determinants of Behavioral Development*. New York: Academic Press, 1972.

Pedersen, D. M., Shinedling, M. M., & Johnson, D. L. "Effects of Sex of

Examiner and Subject on Children's Quantitative Test Performance." *Journal of Personality and Social Psychology,* 1968, *10,* 251–254.

Penrose, L. S. "Finger-Print Pattern and the Sex Chromosomes." *Lancet,* 1967, *i,* 298–300.

Penrose, L. S. "Dermatoglyphics." *Scientific American,* 1969, *221,* 72–83.

Peplau, L. A. "Impact of Fear of Success and Sex-Role Attitudes on Women's Competitive Achievement." *Journal of Personality and Social Psychology,* 1976a, *34,* 561–568.

Peplau, L. A. "Fear of Success in Dating Couples." *Sex Roles,* 1976b, *2,* 249–258.

Perez-Reyes, M. G., & Falk, R. "Follow-up After Therapeutic Abortion in Early Adolescence." *Archives of General Psychiatry,* 1973, *28,* 120–126.

Perry, D. G., & Perry, L. C. "A Note on the Effects of Prior Anger Arousal and Winning or Losing a Competition on Aggressive Behavior in Boys." *Journal of Child Psychology and Psychiatry and Allied Disciplines,* 1976, *17,* 145–149.

Persky, H., Smith, K. D., & Basu, G. K. "Relation of Psychologic Measures of Aggression and Hostility to Testosterone Production in Man." *Psychosomatic Medicine,* 1971, *33,* 515–537.

Petersen, A. C. "Physical Androgyny and Cognitive Functioning." Paper presented at the meeting of the American Psychological Association, Washington, D.C., September 1976.

Pheterson, G. I., Kiesler, S. B., & Goldberg, P. A. "Evaluation of the Performance of Women as a Function of Their Sex, Achievement, and Personal History." *Journal of Personality and Social Psychology,* 1971, *19,* 114–118.

Phillips, D. "Rejection of the Mentally Ill: The Influence of Behavior and Sex." *American Sociological Review,* 1964, *29,* 679–687.

Piacente, B. "Status of Women in the Psychological Community of the Southeast: Women as Experimenters." *American Psychologist,* 1974, *29,* 526–529.

Piliavin, J. A. "On Feminine Self-presentation in Groups." In J. I. Roberts, ed. *Beyond Intellectual Sexism.* New York: McKay, 1976.

Pilisuk, M., Skolnick, P., & Overstreet, E. "Predicting Cooperation from the Two Sexes in a Conflict Situation." *Journal of Personality and Social Psychology,* 1968, *10,* 35–43.

Piskin, V. "Psychosexual Development in Terms of Object and Role Preferences." *Journal of Clinical Psychology* 1960, *16,* 238–240.

Pleck, J. H., & Sawyer, J. *Men and Masculinity.* Englewood Cliffs, N.J.: Prentice-Hall, 1974.

Pleck, J. H. "Male Threat from Female Competence: An Experimental Study in College Dating Couples." *Journal of Consulting and Clinical Psychology,* 1976, *44,* 608–613.

Plutchik, R., Conte, H., Baker, M., & Weiner, U. R. "Studies of Body Image to Dollar Values of Body Parts." *Journal of Gerontology,* 1973, *27,* 89–91.

Pohlman, E. *The Psychology of Birth Planning.* Cambridge, Mass.: Schenkman, 1969.

Polani, P. E. "Abnormal Sex Chromosomes and Mental Disorder." *Nature,* 1969, *223,* 680–686.

Polani, P. E. "Chromosome Phenotypes—Sex Chromosomes." In F. C. Fraser & V. A. McKusick, eds. *Congenital Malformations.* Amsterdam: Excerpta Medica, 1970.

Pollis, N. P., & Doyle, D. C. "Sex Role, Status, and Perceived Competence Among First-Graders." *Perceptual and Motor Skills,* 1972, *34,* 235–238.

Post, B., & Hetherington, E. M. "Sex Differences in the Use of Proximity and Eye Contact in Judgments of Affiliation in Preschool Children." *Developmental Psychology,* 1974, *10,* 881–889.

Powell, B., & Reznikoff, M. "Role Conflict and Symptoms of Psychological Distress in College-Educated Women." *Journal of Consulting and Clinical Psychology,* 1976, *44,* 473–479.

Prather, J., & Fidell, L. S. "Sex Differences in the Content and Style of Medical Advertisements." *Social Science and Medicine,* 1975, *9,* 23–26.

Prescott, S., & Foster, K. "Why Researchers Don't Study Women." Paper presented at the meeting of the American Psychological Association, New Orleans, August 1974.

Purycar, G. R. & Mednick, M. S. "Black Militancy, Affective Attachment, and the Fear of Success in Black College Women." *Journal of Consulting and Clinical Psychology,* 1974, *42,* 263–266.

Rabin, A. I. *Growing Up in the Kibbutz.* New York: Springer, 1965.

Rabinowitz, F. M., Moely, B. E., Finkel, N., & McClinton, S. "The Effect of Toy Novelty and Social Interaction on the Exploratory Behavior of Preschool Children." *Child Development,* 1975, *46,* 286–289.

Rabkin, L. Y., & Rabkin, K. "Children of the Kibbutz." *Psychology Today,* 1969, *3,* 40.

Radin, N. "Father–Child Interaction and the Intellectual Functioning of Four-Year-Old Boys." *Developmental Psychology,* 1972, *6,* 353–361.

Radloff, L. "Sex Differences in Mental Health: The Effects of Marital and Occupational Status." Paper presented at the meeting of the American Public Health Association, 1974.

Radloff, L. S. "Sex Differences in Depression: The Effects of Occupation and Marital Status." *Sex Roles,* 1975, *1,* 249–265.

Radloff, L. S. "Sex Roles, Power and Depression." Paper presented at the Pioneers for Century III Conference, Cincinnati, April 1976.

Rainwater, L. *Family Design: Marital Sexuality, Family Size, and Contraception.* Chicago: Aldine, 1965.

Ramey, E. "Men's Cycles." *Ms.,* January 1972.

Ramey, E. "Sex Hormones and Executive Ability." *Annals of the New York Academy of Sciences,* 1973, *208,* 237–245.

Rapoport, R., & Rapoport, R. *Dual-Career Families.* Baltimore: Penquin Books, 1971.

Ratcliffe, S., Stewart, A. L., Melville, M. M., Jacobs, P. A., & Keay, A. J. "Chromosome Studies on 3500 Newborn Male Infants." *Lancet,* 1970, *i,* 121–122.

Raven, B. H. "Power Relations in Home and School." Paper presented at the meeting of the Western Psychological Association, San Francisco, May 1974.

Raven, B. H., & Kruglanski, A. W. "Conflict and Power." In P. Swingle, ed. *The Structure of Conflict.* New York: Academic Press, 1970.

Raymond, B. J., & Unger, R. K. "The Apparel Oft Proclaims the Man: Cooperation with Deviant and Conventional Youths." *Journal of Social Psychology,* 1972, *87,* 75–82.

Rebecca, M., Hefner, R., & Oleshansky, B. "A Model of Sex-Role Transcendence." *Journal of Social Issues,* 1976, *32,* 197–206.

Redican, W. K., & Mitchell, G. "Male Parental Behavior in Adult Rhesus Monkeys." Paper presented at the meeting of the Western Psychological Association, Portland, Ore., April 1972.

Reese, H. W. "Sociometric Choices of the Same and Opposite Sex in Late Childhood." *Merrill-Palmer Quarterly,* 1962, *8,* 173–174.

Reichelt, P. A. "Psychosexual Background of Female Adolescents Seeking Contraceptive Assistance." Paper presented at the American Psychological Association, Washington D.C., September, 1976.

Reichelt, P. A., & Werley, H. H. "Contraception, Abortion and Veneral Disease: Teenagers' Knowledge and the Effect of Education." *Family Planning Perspectives,* 1975, *7,* 83–88.

Renne, K. S., & Allen, P. C. "Gender and the Ritual of the Door." *Sex Roles,* 1976, *2,* 167–174.

Rheingold, H. L., & Cook, K. V. "The Contents of Boys' and Girls' Rooms as an Index of Parents' Behavior." *Child Development,* 1975, *46,* 459–463.

Richardson, J. T., Dugan, J. R., Gray, L. N., & Mayhew, B. H., Jr. "Expert Power: A Behavioral Interpretation." *Sociometry,* 1973, *36,* 302–324.

Richmond, M. L. "Beyond Resource Theory: Another Look at Factors Enabling Women to Affect Family Interaction." *Journal of Marriage and the Family,* 1976, *38,* 257–266.

Ridley, J. C., & Jaffe, A. J. "A Brief Note on Occupational Differentiation by Sex in the United States, 1900 to 1970." *The New York Statistician,* 1975, *27,* 17–19.

Roby, P. "Institutional Barriers to Women Students in Higher Education." In A. S. Rossi & A. Calderwood, eds. *Academic Women on the Move.* New York: Russell Sage, 1973.

Robinson, L. H. "Institutional Variation in the Status of Academic Women." In A. S. Rossi & A. Calderwood, eds. *Academic Women on the Move.* New York: Russell Sage, 1973.

Robson, K. S., & Moss, H. A. "Patterns and Determinants of Maternal Attachment." *Journal of Pediatrics,* 1970, *77,* 976–985.

Rocha, F. F., & Rogers, R. W. "Ares and Babbitt in the Classroom: Effects of Competition and Reward on Children's Aggression." *Journal of Personality and Social Psychology,* 1976, *33,* 588–593.

Rodin, J. "Menstruation, Reattribution, and Competence." *Journal of Personality and Social Psychology*, 1976, *33*, 345–353.

Rogers, D. ed. *Issues in Adolescent Psychology*. Englewood Cliffs, N.J.: Prentice-Hall, 1969.

Rosaldo, M. Z. "Woman, Culture and Society: A Theoretical Overview." In M. Z. Rosaldo & L. Lamphere, eds. *Woman, Culture and Society*. Palo Alto, Calif.: Stanford University Press, 1974.

Rose, S. A., Blank, M., & Spalter, I. "Situational Specificity of Behavior in Young Children." *Child Development*, 1975, *46*, 464–469.

Rose, Y. J. "Defining Assertive, Subassertive, and Aggressive Behavior as a Function of Loudness, Latency, Content, Sex, Gestures, and Inflection." Unpublished Ph.D. dissertation, Fordham University, 1975.

Rosen, B., & Jerdee, T. H. "The Influence of Sex-Role Stereotypes on Evaluations of Male and Female Supervisory Behavior." *Journal of Applied Psychology*, 1973, *57*, 44–48.

Rosen, B., & Jerdee, T. H. "Effects of Applicant's Sex and Difficulty of Job on Evaluations of Candidates for Managerial Positions." *Journal of Applied Psychology*, 1974a, *59*, 511–512.

Rosen, B., & Jerdee, T. H. "Influence of Sex Role Stereotypes on Personnel Decisions." *Journal of Applied Psychology*, 1974b, *59*, 9–14.

Rosen, B., & Jerdee, T. H. "Effects of Employee's Sex and Threatening Versus Pleading Appeals on Managerial Evaluations of Grievances." *Journal of Applied Psychology*, 1975, *60*, 442–445.

Rosen, B., Jerdee, T. H., & Prestwich, T. L. "Dual-Career Marital Adjustment: Potential Effects of Disciminatory Managerial Attitudes." *Journal of Marriage and the Family*, 1975, *37*, 565–572.

Rosenberg, B. G., & Sutton-Smith, B. "A Revised Conception of Masculine–Feminine Differences in Play Activities." *Journal of Genetic Psychology*, 1960, *96*, 165–170.

Rosenblatt, P. C. "Behavior in Public Places: Comparison of Couples Accompanied and Unaccompanied by Children." *Journal of Marriage and the Family*, 1974, *36*, 750–755.

Rosenkrantz, P. S., Vogel, S. R., Bee, H., Broverman, I. K., & Broverman, D. M. "Sex-Role Stereotypes and Self Concepts in College Students." *Journal of Consulting and Clinical Psychology*, 1968, *32*, 287–295.

Rossi, A. "Physiological and Social Rhythms: The Study of Human Cyclicity." Lecture delivered to the American Psychiatric Association, Detroit, May 1974.

Rossi, P., Sampson, W., Bose, C., Jasso, G., & Passel, J. "Measuring Household Social Standing." *Social Science Research*, 1974, *3*, 169–190.

Rothbart, M. K., & Maccoby, E. E. "Parents' Differential Reactions to Sons and Daughters." *Journal of Personality and Social Psychology*, 1966, *4*, 237–243.

Rotter, G. S. "The Effect of Sex Identification upon Teacher Evaluation of Pupils." Paper presented at the meeting of the Eastern Psychological Association, Boston, April 1967.

Rotter, G. S. Personal communication, February 1977.

Rotter, N. G. "Effects of Worker Sex upon Perceived Committment and Merited Salary." Paper presented at the meeting of the American Psychological Association, Washington, D.C., September 1976.

Rotter, N. G. "Tripping up from Girl to Colleague: Training Barriers to Women Doing Research." Paper presented to the Task Force on Women Doing Research, Division 35 of the American Psychological Association, March 1977.

Rotter, N. G., & O'Connell, A. N. "Are Sex-Role Orientation, Cognitive Style and Tolerance for Ambiguity Related?" Paper presented at the meeting of the Eastern Psychological Association, Washington, D.C., April 1978.

Rubin, J. Z., Provenzano, F. J., & Luria, Z. "The Eye of the Beholder: Parents' Views on Sex of Newborns." *American Journal of Orthopsychiatry*, 1974, *44*, 512–519.

Rubin, L. B. "The Marriage Bed." *Psychology Today*, August 1976, *10*, 44–50, 91–92.

Rubin, Z. "Do American Women Marry Up?" *American Sociological Review*, 1968, *33*, 750–760.

Rubin, Z. "Measurement of Romantic Love." *Journal of Personality and Social Psychology*, 1970, *16*, 265–273.

Rubin, Z. *Liking and Loving*. New York: Holt, 1973.

Rubin, Z. "Disclosing Oneself to a Stranger: Reciprocity and Its Limits." *Journal of Experimental Social Psychology*, 1975, *11*, 233–260.

Ruble, D. N., & Croke, J. H. "Attitude Maintenance Factors: Their Structure and Changeability. Paper presented at the meeting of the Eastern Psychological Association, Philadelphia, April 1974.

Ruble, D. N., & Higgins, E. T. "Effects of Group Sex Compositions on Self-presentation and Sex-Typing." *Journal of Social Issues*, 1976, *32*, 125–132.

Rumenik, D. K., Capasso, D. R., & Hendrick, C. "Experimenter Sex Effects in Behavioral Research." *Psychological Bulletin*, 1977, *84*, 852–877.

Russell, C., & Russell, W. M. S. "Primate Male Behavior and Its Human Analogues." *Impact of Science on Society*, 1971, *21*, 63–74.

Russo, N. F., & Stradler, M. "College Students and Family Planning: Sex and Religious Influences." Paper presented at the meeting of the American Psychological Association, Washington, D.C., September 1971.

Ryan, W. *Blaming the Victim*. New York: Vintage Books, 1971.

Saario, T. N., Jacklin, C. N., & Tittle, C. K. "Sex Role Stereotyping in the Public Schools." *Harvard Educational Review*, 1973, *43*, 386–416.

Sacks, K. "Engels Revisited: Women, the Organization of Production and Private Property." In M. Z. Rosaldo & L. Lamphere, eds. *Women, Culture and Society*. Palo Alto, Calif.: Stanford University Press, 1974.

Safilios-Rothschild, C. "Family Sociology or Wives' Family Sociology? A Cross-Cultural Examination of Decision Making." *Journal of Marriage and the Family*, 1969, *31*, 290–301.

Salifios-Rothschild, C. "Family and Stratification: Some Macrosociological Observations and Hypotheses." *Journal of Marriage and the Family*, 1975, *37*, 855–860.

Safilios-Rothschild, C. "A Macro-and Micro-examination of Family Power and Love: An Exchange Model." *Journal of Marriage and the Family,* 1976, *38,* 355–362.

Salzman, L. "Psychology of the Female: A New Look." In J. B. Miller, ed. *Psychoanalysis and Women.* Baltimore: Penguin, 1974, pp. 202–220.

Sanday, P. R. "Female Status in the Public Domain. In M. Z. Rosaldo & L. Lamphere, eds. *Woman, Culture and Society.* Stanford, Calif.: Stanford University Press, 1974.

Scanzoni, J. "Sex Role Change and Influences on Birth Intentions." *Journal of Marriage and the Family,* 1976, *38,* 43–58.

Schachter, S. "The Interaction of Cognitive and Physiological Determinants of Emotional State." In L. Berkowitz, ed. *Advances in Experimental Social Psychology,* vol. I. New York: Academic Press, 1964.

Schaffer, H. R., & Emerson, P. E. "The Development of Social Attachments in Infancy." *Monographs of the Society for Research in Child Development,* 1964, *29,* 5–77.

Schain, W. S. "Psychosocial Issues in Counseling Mastectomy Patients." *The Counseling Psychologist,* 1976, *6,* 45–49.

Schein, V. E. "The Relationship Between Sex Role Stereotypes and Requisite Management Characteristics." *Journal of Applied Psychology,* 1973, *57,* 95–100.

Scher, M. "Verbal Activity, Sex, Counselor Experience, and Success in Counseling." *Journal of Counseling Psychology,* 1975, *22,* 97–101.

Schettino, A. P., & Borden, R. J. "Sex Differences in Response to Naturalistic Crowding: Affective Reactions to Group Size and Group Density." *Personality and Social Psychology Bulletin,* 1976, *2,* 67–70.

Schilling, K. M., & Jacobi, M. "Attribution of Menstrual Distress." Paper presented at the meeting of the American Psychological Association, San Francisco, August 1977.

Schlegel, R. J., & Gardner, L. I. "Ambiguous and Abnormal Genitalia in Infants: Differential Diagnosis and Clinical Management." In L. I. Gardner, ed. *Endocrine and Genetic Diseases of Childhood.* Philadelphia: W. B. Saunders, 1969.

Schmale, A. H. "Giving Up as a Final Common Pathway to Changes in Health." *Advances in Psychosomatic Medicine,* 1972, *8,* 20–40.

Schneider, J. W., & Hacker, S. L. "Sex Role Imagery and the Use of the Generic 'Man' in Introductory Texts." *American Sociologist,* 1973, *8,* 12–18.

Schmuck, R. A. "Sociometric Status and Utilization of Academic Abilities." *Merrill-Palmer Quarterly,* 1962, *8,* 165–172.

Schmuck, R. A. "Some Relationships of Peer Liking Patterns in the Classroom to Pupil Attitudes and Achievement." *School Review,* 1963, *71,* 337–359.

Schmuck, R. A., & Van Egmond, E. "Sex Differences in the Relationships of Interpersonal Perceptions to Academic Performance." *Psychology in the Schools,* 1965, *2,* 32–40.

Schoen, R. "California Divorce Rates by Age at First Marriage and Duration of First Marriage." *Journal of Marriage and the Family*, 1975, 37, 548–555.

Schooler. C. "Childhood Family Structure and Adult Characteristics." *Sociometry*, 1972, 35, 255–269.

Schrader, S. L., Wilcoxon, L. A., & Sherif, C. W. "Daily Self Reports on Activities, Life Events, Moods, and Somatic Changes During the Menstrual Cycle." Paper given at the meeting of the Eastern Psychological Association, New York City, April 1975.

Schultz, L. G. "The Control of Campus Rape: An Overview of Individual Tactics and Environmental Design." Paper presented at the meeting of the American Psychological Association, Washington, D.C., September 1976.

Schultz, M. R. "The Semantic Derogation of Women." In B. Thorne & N. Henley, eds. *Language and Sex: Difference and Dominance*. Rowley, Mass: Newbury House, 1975.

Schwartz, P. Personal communication, May 1975.

Schwartz, P. "The Social Psychology of Female Sexuality." In J. Sherman & F. L. Denmark, eds. *Psychology of Women: Future Directions of Research*. New York: Psychological Dimensions, 1978.

Schwartz, P., & Lever, J. "Women in the Male World of Higher Education." In A. S. Rossi & A. Calderwood, eds. *Academic Women on the Move*. New York: Russell Sage, 1973.

Scully, D., & Bart, P. "A Funny Thing Happened on the Way to the Orifice: Women in Gynecology Textbooks." *American Journal of Sociology*, 1973, 78, 1045–1050.

Sears, R. R. "Development of Gender Role." In F. Beach, ed. *Sex and Behavior*. New York: Wiley, 1965.

Sears, R. R. "Relation of Early Socialization Experiences to Self-Concepts and Gender Role in Middle Childhood." *Child Development*, 1970, 41, 267–289.

Seavey, C. A., Katz, P. A., & Zalk, S. R. "Baby X: The Effect of Gender Labels on Adult Responses to Infants." *Sex Roles*, 1975, 1, 103–110.

Seiden, A. M. "Overview: Research on the Psychology of Women. I. Gender Differences and Sexual and Reproductive Life." *The American Journal of Psychiatry*, 1976a, 133, 995–1007.

Seiden, A. M. "Overview: Research on the Psychology of Women. II. Women in Families, Work, and Psychotherapy." *The American Journal of Psychiatry*, 1976b, 133, 1111–1123.

Seidenberg, R. "Advertising and Abuse of Drugs." *New England Journal of Medicine*, 1971, 284, 789–790.

Selby, J. W., Calhoun, L. G., & Brock, T. A. "Sex Differences in the Social Perception of Rape Victims." *Personality and Social Psychology Bulletin*, 1977, 3, 412–415.

Seligman, M. E. P. "Depression and Learned Helplessness." In R. J. Friedman & M. M. Katz, eds. *The Psychology of Depression: Contemporary Theory and Research*. Washington, D.C.: V. H. Winston, 1974.

Seligman, M. E. P. *Helplessness: On Depression, Development and Death*. San Francisco: W. H. Freeman, 1975.

Serbin, L. A., O'Leary, D. K., Kent, R. N., & Tonick, J. J. "A Comparison of Teacher Response to the Preacademic and Problem Behavior of Boys and Girls." *Child Development*, 1973, *44*, 796–804.

Sermat, V. "The Effect of Some Dimensions of Verbal Communication on Self-disclosure, Liking and Sexual Attraction." Paper presented at the meeting of the American Psychological Association, Honolulu, September 1972.

Shaffer, D. R., & Wegley, C. "Success Orientation and Sex Role Congruence as Determinants of the Attractiveness of Competent Women." *Journal of Personality*, 1974, *42*, 586–600.

Shaffer, J. W. "Masculinity–Femininity and Other Personality Traits in Gonadal Aplasia (Turner's Syndrome)." In H. G. Beigel, ed. *Advances in Sex Research*. New York: Harper & Row, 1963.

Shapira, A., & Madsen, M. C. Cooperative and Competitive Behavior of Kibbutz and Urban Children in Israel. *Child Development*, 1969, *40*, 609–617.

Shaver, P. "Questions Concerning Fear of Success and Its Conceptual Relatives." *Sex Roles*, 1976, *2*, 305–320.

Shaver, P., & Freedman, J. "Your Pursuit of Happiness." *Psychology Today*, 1976, *10*, 26–32.

Sherfey, M. J. *The Nature and Evolution of Female Sexuality*. New York: Random House, 1972.

Sherif, M., & Sherif, C. W. *Social Psychology*. New York: Harper & Row, 1969.

Sherriffs, A. C., & Jarrett, R. F. "Sex Differences in Attitudes About Sex Differences." *Journal of Psychology*, 1953, *35*, 161–168.

Sheriffs, A. C., & McKee, J. P. "Qualitative Aspects of Beliefs About Men and Women." *Journal of Personality*, 1957, *25*, 451–467.

Sherman, J. A. "Problem of Sex Differences in Space Perception and Aspects of Intellectual Functioning." *Psychological Review*, 1967, *74*, 290–299.

Sherman, J. A. *On the Psychology of Women: A Survey of Empirical Studies*. Springfield, Ill.: Charles C. Thomas, 1971.

Sherman, J. "The Coatlicue Complex: A Source of Irrational Responses Against Women." *Transactional Analysis Journal*, 1975, *5*, 188–192.

Sherman, J. "Social Values, Femininity, and the Development of Female Competence." *Journal of Social Issues*, 1976, *32*, 181–195.

Sherman, J., & Denmark, F., eds. *Psychology of Women: Future Directions of Research*. New York: Psychological Dimensions, 1978.

Sherman, J., Koufacos, C., & Kenworthy, J. A. "Therapists: Their Attitudes and Information about Women." *Psychology of Women Quarterly*, 1978, *2*, 299–313.

Sherman, R. C., & Smith, F. "Sex Differences in Cue-Dependency as a Function of Socialization Environment." *Perception and Motor Skills*, 1967, *24*, 599–602.

Shields, S. A. "The Psychology of Women: An Historical Analysis." Paper presented at the meeting of the American Psychological Association, New Orleans, September 1974.

Shields, S. A. "Functionalism, Darwinism, and the Psychology of Women: A Study in Social Myth." *American Psychologist,* 1975a, *30,* 739–754.

Shields, S. A. "Ms. Pilgrim's Progress: The Contribution of Leta Stetter Hollingworth to the Psychology of Women." *American Psychologist,* 1975b, *30,* 852–857.

Shinedling, M. M., & Pedersen, D. M. "Effects of Sex of Teacher and Student on Children's Gain in Quantitative and Verbal Performance." *Journal of Psychology,* 1970, *76,* 79–84.

Shipley, R. H., & O'Donnell, J. M. "Personality Correlates of Bust Size and Desire for Breast Augmentation." Paper presented at the meeting of the American Psychological Association, San Francisco, Calif., August 1977.

Shipman, G. "The Psychodynamics of Sex Education." *Family Coordinator,* 1968, *17,* 3–12.

Shusterman, L. R. "The Psychosocial Factors of the Abortion Experience: A Critical Review." *Psychology of Women Quarterly,* 1976, *1,* 79–106.

Sigall, H., & Aronson, E. "Liking for an Evaluator as a Function of Her Physical Attractiveness and the Nature of the Evaluations." *Journal of Experimental Social Psychology,* 1969, *5,* 93–100.

Sigall, H., & Landy, D. "Radiating Beauty: Effects of Having a Physically Attractive Partner on Person Perception." *Journal of Personality and Social Psychology,* 1973, *28,* 218–224.

Siiter, R., & Unger, R. K. "Ethnic Differences in Sex-Role Stereotypes." Paper presented at the meeting of the American Psychological Association, Chicago, September 1975.

Siiter, R., & Unger, R. K. "Sex-Typing Versus Sex-Role Stereotyping: It All Depends on Your Reference Group." Paper presented at the meeting of the Eastern Psychological Association, Washington, D.C., April 1978.

Siiter, R., & Unger, R. K. "Sex Role Stereotypes, Sex Typing, and Self Typing: Some Considerations About Reference Groups." Manuscript submitted for publication, 1979.

Simon, R. J., Clark, S. M., & Galway, K. "The Woman Ph.D.: A Recent Profile." *Social Problems,* 1967, *15,* 221–236.

Singer, J. E. "The Use of Manipulative Strategies: Machiavellianism and Attractiveness." *Sociometry,* 1964, *27,* 128–150.

Slaby, R. G. Personal communication on gender constancy and model selection. Cited in E. E. Maccoby & C. N. Jacklin, eds. *The Psychology of Sex Differences.* Stanford, Calif.: Stanford University Press, 1974.

Smith, D. D. "The Social Content of Pornography." *Journal of Communication,* 1976, *26,* 16–24.

Smith, P. K., & Green, M. "Aggressive Behavior in English Nurseries and Play Groups: Sex Differences and Response of Adults." *Child Development,* 1975, *46,* 211–214.

Snyder, M., Tanke, E. D., & Berscheid, E. "Social Perception and Interpersonal Behavior: On the Self-fulfilling Nature of Social Stereotypes." *Journal of Personality and Social Psychology,* 1977, *35,* 656–666.

Sobel, E. H., & Falkner, F. "Normal and Abnormal Growth Patterns of the Newlyborn and the Preadolescent." In L. I. Gardner, ed. *Endocrine and Genetic Diseases of Childhood.* Philadelphia: W. B. Saunders, 1969.

Solano, C. H. "Teacher and Pupil Stereotypes of Gifted Boys and Girls." Paper presented at the meeting of the American Psychological Association, Washington, D.C., September 1976.

Sommer, B. "The Effect of Menstruation on Cognitive and Perceptual–Motor Behavior: A Review." *Psychosomatic Medicine,* 1973, *35,* 515–534.

Sommer, R. *Personal Space.* Englewood Cliffs, N.J.: Prentice-Hall, 1969.

Spargo, C. J. "Attitudes of Mothers Using Day Care Centers Toward Their Employment." Unpublished master's thesis, University of Wisconsin, Madison, 1968. Cited in B. Wallston. "The Effects of Maternal Employment on Children." *Journal of Child Psychology and Psychiatry,* 1973, *14,* 81–95.

Spence, J. T., & Helmreich, R. "The Attitudes Toward Women Scale: An Objective Instrument to Measure Attitudes Toward the Rights and Roles of Women in Contemporary Society." *JSAS Catalog of Selected Documents in Psychology,* 1972, *2,* 66.

Spence, J. T. & Helmreich, R. *Masculinity and Femininity: Their Psychological Dimensions, Correlates, and Antecedents.* Austin, Tex.: University of Texas Press, 1978.

Spence, J. T., Helmreich, R., & Stapp, J. "The Personal Attributes Questionnaire: A Measure of Sex Role Stereotypes and Masculinity–Femininity." *JSAS Catalog of Selected Documents in Psychology,* 1974, *4,* 43.

Spence, J. T., Helmreich, R., & Stapp, J. "Ratings of Self and Peers on Sex Role Attributes and Their Relation to Self-esteem and Conceptions of Masculinity and Femininity." *Journal of Personality and Social Psychology,* 1975a, *32,* 29–39.

Spence, J. T., Helmreich, R., & Stapp, J. "Likability, Sex-Role Congruence of Interest, and Competence: It All Depends on How You Ask." *Journal of Applied Social Psychology,* 1975b, *5,* 93–109.

Spiro, M. E. *Children of the Kibbutz.* New York: Schocken, 1965.

Spitz, R. A. "Authority and Masturbation: Some Remarks on a Bibliographical Investigation." *The Psychoanalytic Quarterly,* 1952, *21,* 490–527.

Spreitzer, E., & Riley, L. E. "Factors Associated with Singlehood." *Journal of Marriage and the Family,* 1974, *36,* 533–542.

Stacey, J., Bereaud, S., & Daniels, J., eds. *And Jill Came Tumbling After: Sexism in American Education.* New York: Dell, 1974.

Staffieri, J. R. "Body Build and Behavioral Expectancies in Young Females." *Developmental Psychology,* 1972, *6,* 125–127.

Stafford, R. E. "Sex Differences in Spatial Visualization as Evidence of Sex-Linked Inheritance." *Perceptual Motor Skills,* 1961, *13,* 428.

Staines, G., Tavris, C., & Jayaratne, T. E. "The Queen Bee Syndrome." *Psychology Today,* January 1974, *7,* 55–60.

Stake, J. E. "The Effect of Information Regarding Sex Group Performance Norms on Goal-Setting in Males and Females." *Sex Roles,* 1976a, *2,* 23–28.

Stake, J. E. "Effect of Probability of Forthcoming Success on Sex Differences in Goal Setting: A Test of the Fear of Success Hypothesis." *Journal of Consulting and Clinical Psychology*, 1976b, *44*, 444–448.

Standley, K. "Observational Data on the Psychological Experience of Childbirth." Paper presented at the meeting of the American Psychological Association, Washington, D.C., September 1976.

Starer, R., & Denmark, F. "Discrimination Against Aspiring Women." *International Journal of Group Tensions*, 1974, *4*, 65–70.

Staub, E. "A Child in Distress: The Influence of Nurturance and Modeling on Children's Attempts to Help." *Developmental Psychology*, 1971, *5*, 124–132.

Stein, A. H. "The Effects of Sex-Role Standards for Achievement and Sex-Role Preference on Three Determinants of Achievement Motivation." *Developmental Psychology*, 1971, *4*, 219–231.

Stein, A. H., & Bailey, M. M. "The Socialization of Achievement Orientation in Females." *Psychological Bulletin*, 1973, *80*, 345–366.

Stein, A. H., & Smithells, J. "Age and Sex Differences in Children's Sex-Role Standards About Achievement." *Developmental Psychology*, 1969, *1*, 252–259.

Stein, S. L., & Weston, L. C. "Attitudes Toward Women Among Female College Students." *Sex Roles*, 1976, *2*, 199–202.

Stempfel, R. S., Jr. "Abnormalities of Sexual Differentiation." In L. I. Gardner, ed. *Endocrine and Genetic Diseases of Childhood*. Philadelphia: W. B. Saunders, 1969.

Stephan, W. G., Rosenfield, D., & Stephan, C. "Egotism in Males and Females." *Journal of Personality and Social Psychology*, 1976, *34*, 1161–1167.

Stephens, W. N. "A Cross-Cultural Study of Menstrual Taboos." *Genetic Psychology Monographs*, 1961, *64*, 385–416.

Stern, J. J. "Neonatal Castration, Androstenedione, and the Mating Behavior of the Male Rat." *Journal of Comparative and Physiological Psychology*, 1969, *69*, 608–612.

Sternglanz, S. H., & Serbin, L. A. "Sex Role Stereotyping in Children's Television Programs." *Developmental Psychology*, 1974, *10*, 710–715.

Stevenson, H. W. "Social Reinforcement of Children's Behavior." In L. P. Lipsitt & C. C. Spiker, eds. *Advances in Child Development and Behavior*. New York: Academic Press, 1965.

Stokes, S. J., & Bickman, L. "The Effect of the Physical Attractiveness and Role of the Helper on Help Seeking." *Journal of Applied Social Psychology*, 1974, *4*, 286–294.

Stolz, L. M. "Effects of Maternal Employment on Children: Evidence from Research." *Child Development*, 1960, *31*, 749–782.

Stone, W. F. "Patterns of Conformity in Couples Varying in Intimacy." *Journal of Personality and Social Psychology*, 1973, *27*, 413–418.

Strache, K. "Personality Characteristics of Men and Women Administrators: Actual vs. Perceived." Paper presented at the meeting of the American Psychological Association, Washington, D.C., September 1976.

Straus, M. A. "Cultural and Social Organizational Influence on Violence Between Family Members." In R. Prince & D. Barrier, eds. *Configura-*

tions: Biological and Cultural Factors in Sexuality and Family Life. Lexington, Mass.: D.C. Heath, 1974.

Straus, M. A. "The Marriage License as a Hitting License: Social Instigation of Physical Aggression in the Family." Paper presented at the meeting of the American Psychological Association, Chicago, September 1975.

Straus, M. A. "A Sociological Perspective on the Prevention and Treatment of Wife-Beating." In M. Roy, ed. *Battered Women.* New York: Van Nostrand-Reinhold, 1977a.

Straus, M. A. "Normative and Behavioral Aspects of Violence Between Spouses: Preliminary Data on a Nationally Representative USA Sample." Paper presented at the Conference on Violence in Canadian Society, March 15, 1977b.

Sundstrom, E., & Sundstrom, M. G. "Personal Space Invasions: What Happens when the Invader asks Permission? *Environmental Psychology and Nonverbal Behavior,* 1977, *2,* 76–82.

Sutton-Smith, B., & Rosenberg, B. G. "Sibling Consensus on Power Tactics." *Journal of Genetic Psychology,* 1968, *112,* 63–72.

Sutton-Smith, B., & Rosenberg, B. G. "Modeling and Reactive Components of Sibling Interaction." In J. P. Hill, ed. *Minnesota Symposia on Child Psychology,* vol. 3. Minneapolis: University of Minnesota Press, 1969.

Sutton-Smith, B., & Rosenberg, B. G. *The Sibling.* New York: Holt, 1970.

Sullivan, J. *Mama Doesn't Live Here Anymore.* New York: Arthur Fields Books, 1974.

Tallman, I., & Miller, G. "Class Differences in Family Problem Solving: The Effects of Verbal Ability, Hierarchical Structure and Role Expectations." *Sociometry,* 1974, *37,* 13–37.

Tangri, S. S. "Determinants of Occupational Role Innovation Among College Women." *Journal of Social Issues,* 1972, *28,* 177–199.

Tanner, J. M. "Growth and Endocrinology of the Adolescent." In L. I. Gardner, ed. *Endocrine and Genetic Diseases of Childhood.* Philadelphia: W. B. Saunders, 1969.

Tanney, M. F., & Birk, J. M. "Women Counselors for Women Clients? A Review of the Research." *The Counseling Psychologist,* 1976, *6,* 28–32.

Task Force on the Status of Women in Psychology. Report. *American Psychologist,* 1973, *28,* 611–616.

Tavris, C. "Who Like Women's Liberation—And Why: The Case of the Unliberated Liberals." *Journal of Social Issues,* 1973, *29,* 175–198.

Taylor, P. A., & Glenn, N. D. "The Utility of Education and Attractiveness for Female Status Attainment Through Marriage." *American Sociological Review,* 1976, *41,* 484–498.

Taylor, S. E., & Langer, E. J. "Pregnancy: A Social Stigma?" *Sex Roles,* 1977, *3,* 27–35.

Taylor, S. P., & Epstein, S. "Aggression as a Function of the Interaction of the Sex of the Aggressor and the Sex of the Victim." *Journal of Personality,* 1967, *35,* 474–486.

Taynor, J., & Deaux, K. "When Women Are More Deserving Than Men:

Equity, Attribution, and Perceived Sex Differences." *Journal of Personality and Social Psychology,* 1973, *28,* 360–367.

Taynor, J., & Deaux, K. "Equity and Perceived Sex Differences: Role Behavior as Defined by the Task, the Mode, and the Actor." *Journal of Personality and Social Psychology,* 1975, *32,* 381–390.

Tedeschi, J., Lesnick, S., & Gahagan, J. "Feedback and "Washout" Effects in the Prisoner's Dilemma Game." *Journal of Personality and Social Psychology,* 1968, *10,* 31–34.

Teghtsoonian, M. "Distribution by Sex of Authors and Editors of Psychological Journals, 1970–1972." Are There Enough Women Editors?" *American Psychologist,* 1974, *29,* 262–269.

Tennov, D. "The Relationship Between Obstetrical Procedures and Perinatal Anoxia." *Journal of Clinical Child Psychology,* 1973, *2,* 20–22.

Tennov, D. *Psychotherapy: The Hazardous Cure.* New York: Abelard-Schuman, 1975.

Tennov, D., & Hirsch, L. G., eds. *Proceedings of the First International Childbirth Conference.* Stamford, Conn.: New Moon Publications, 1973.

Terman, L. M., & Oden, M. *The Gifted Group at Mid-life.* Stanford, Calif.: Stanford University Press, 1959.

Tessler, R. C., & Schwartz, S. H. "Help Seeking, Self-esteem, and Achievement Motivation: An Attributional Analysis." *Journal of Personality and Social Psychology,* 1972, *21,* 318–326.

Thoman, E. B., Leiderman, P. H., & Olson, J. P. "Neonate–Mother Interaction During Breast Feeding." *Developmental Psychology,* 1972, *6,* 110–118.

Thomopoulos, E., & Huyck, M. H. "Love and Labor: Maternal Work Status and Family Relationships." Paper presented at the meeting of the American Psychological Association, Washington, D.C., September 1976.

Thompson, C. M. *On Women,* ed. M. R. Green. New York: New American Library, 1964.

Thompson, S. K. "Gender Labels and Early Sex Role Development." *Child Development,* 1975, *46,* 339–347.

Thompson, V. D. "Family Size: Implicit Policies and Assumed Psychological Outcomes." *Journal of Social Issues,* 1974, *30,* 93–124.

Thornburg, K. R., & Weeks, M. O. "Vocational Role Expectations of Five-Year-Old Children and Their Parents." *Sex Roles,* 1975, *1,* 395–396.

Thorne, B., & Henley, N. "Difference and Dominance: An Overview of Language, Gender, and Society." In B. Thorne & N. Henley, eds. *Language and Sex: Difference and Dominance.* Rowley, Mass.: Newbury House, 1975.

Tietze, C. "Two Years' Experience with a Liberal Abortion Law: Its Impact on Fertility Trends in New York City." *Family Planning Perspectives,* 1973, *5,* 36–41.

Tobach, E. "Some Evolutionary Aspects of Human Gender." *American Journal of Orthopsychiatry,* 1971, *41,* 710–715.

Tonks, C. M., Rack, L., & Rose, G. R. "Attempted Suicide and the Menstrual Cycle." *Journal of Psychosomatic Research*, 1968, *11*, 319–323.

Touhey, J. C. "Comparison of Two Dimensions of Attitude Similarity on Heterosexual Attraction." *Journal of Personality and Social Psychology*, 1972, *23*, 8–10.

Touhey, J. C. "Effects of Additional Women Professionals on Ratings of Occupational Prestige and Desirability." *Journal of Personality and Social Psychology*, 1974a, *29*, 86–89.

Touhey, J. C. "Effects of Additional Men on Prestige and Desirability of Occupations Typically Performed by Women." *Journal of Applied Social Psychology*, 1974b, *4*, 330–335.

Travis, C. B. "Women's Liberation Among Two Samples of Young Women." *Psychology of Women Quarterly*, 1976, *1*, 189–199.

Treadway, C. R., Kane, F. J., Jr., Jarrahi-Zadeh, A., & Lipton, M. A. A Psychoendocrine Study of Pregnancy and Puerperium." *American Journal of Psychiatry*, 1969, *125*, 1380–1386.

Treiman, D. J., & Terrell, K. "Sex and the Process of Status Attainment: A Comparison of Working Women and Men." *American Sociological Review*, 1975, *40*, 174–200.

Tresemer, D. "The Cumulative Record of Research on "Fear of Success." *Sex Roles*, 1976, *2*, 217–236.

Tresemer, D. *Fear of Success.* New York: Plenum Press, 1977.

Trigg, L. J., & Perlman, D. "Social Influences on Women's Pursuit of a Nontraditional Career." *Psychology of Women Quarterly*, 1976, *1*, 138–150.

Trudgill, P. "Sex, Covert Prestige and Linguistic Change in the Urban British English of Norwich." *Language in Society*, 1972, *1*, 179–195.

Tuddenham, R. D., Brooks, J., & Milkovich, L. "Mothers' Reports of Behavior of Ten-Year-Olds: Relationships with Sex, Ethnicity, and Mother's Education." *Developmental Psychology*, 1974, *10*, 959–995.

Turner, R. H. "Some Aspects of Women's Ambition." *American Journal of Sociology*, 1964, *70*, 271–285.

Turner, R. H. "Unresponsiveness as a Social Sanction." *Sociometry*, 1973, *36*, 1–19.

Unger, R. K. "The Case for Human Cycles." In R. K. Unger & F. L. Denmark, eds. *Woman: Dependent or Independent Variable?* New York: Psychological Dimensions, 1975.

Unger, R. K. "Male Is Greater Than Female: The Socialization of Status Inequality." *The Counseling Psychologist*, 1976, *6*, 2–9.

Unger, R. K. "The Politics of Gender: A Review of Relevant Literature." In J. Sherman & F. Denmark, eds. *Psychology of Women: Future Directions of Research.* New York: Psychological Dimensions, 1978.

Unger, R. K. "The Student Teacher Evaluation Form as an Instrument of Sexism." Paper presented at the meeting of the American Psychological Association, San Francisco, August 1977a.

Unger, R. K. "Body Structure and Social Power Tactics in Children. Unpublished data, 1977b.

Unger, R. K. "The Rediscovery of Gender." Paper presented at the meeting of the Eastern Psychological Association, Boston, April 1977c.

Unger, R. K., DeMauro, D., & Imbrognio, L. "Sex Differences in Aggression? It All Depends on How You Ask." Manuscript submitted for publication, 1976.

Unger, R. K., & Denmark, F., eds. *Woman: Dependent or Independent Variable?* New York: Psychological Dimensions, 1975.

Unger, R. K., & Krooth, D. M. "Female Role Perception and Attitudes Toward Competence as Related to Activism in Housewives." Paper presented at the meeting of the American Psychological Association, New Orleans, 1974.

Unger, R. K., O'Leary, V. E., & Fabian, S. "Membership Characteristics of the Division of the Psychology of Women of the American Psychological Association." Report to Division 35 of the American Psychological Association, December 1976.

Unger, R. K., Raymond, B. J., & Levine, S. M. "Are Women a Minority Group? Sometimes!" *International Journal of Group Tensions*, 1974, *4*, 71–81.

Unger, R. K., & Siiter, R. "Sex-Role Stereotypes: The Weight of a "Grain of Truth." In R. K. Unger, ed. *Sex Role Stereotypes Revisited: Psychological Approaches to Women's Studies.* New York: Harper & Row, 1975.

Vance, J. J., & Richmond, B. O. "Cooperative and Competitive Behavior as a Function of Self-esteem." *Psychology in the Schools*, 1975, *12*, 225–229.

Vandenberg, S. G. "Assortative Mating, or Who Marries Whom?" *Behavioral Genetics*, 1972, *2*, 127–157.

Vandenberg, S. G., & Kuse, A. R. "Spatial Ability: A Critical Review of the Sex-Linked Major Gene Hypothesis." In M. A. Wittig & A. C. Peterson, eds. *Sex-Related Differences in Cognitive Functioning: Developmental Issues.* New York: Academic Press, 1978.

Vanek, J. "Time Spent in Housework." *Scientific American*, November 1974, *231*, 116–120.

van Tienhoven, A. "Endocrinology of Reproduction in Birds." In W. C. Young, ed. *Sex and Internal Secretions*, 3d ed., London: Balliere, Tindall & Cox, 1961.

Vaughan, P. *The Pill on Trial.* London: Weidenfeld & Nicolson, 1970.

Vaughter, R. M. "Review Essay: Psychology." *Signs*, 1976, *2*, 120–146.

Vaughter, R. M., Ginorio, A. B., & Trilling, B. A. "The Failure of Trait Theories to Predict Success." *Signs*, 1977, *3*, 664–674.

Vaughter, R. M., Gubernick, D., Matossian, J., & Haslett, B. "Sex Differences in Academic Expectations and Achievement." Paper presented at the meeting of the American Psychological Association, New Orleans, August 1974.

Veevers, J. E. "The Violation of Fertility Mores: Voluntary Childlessness and Deviant Behavior." In C. Boydell, C. Grindstaff, & P. Whitehead, eds. *Deviant Behavior and Societal Reaction.* Toronto: Holt, 1971.

Verinis, J. S., & Roll, S. "Primary and Secondary Male Characteristics: The

Hairiness and Large Penis Stereotypes." *Psychological Reports,* 1970, 26, 123–126.

Verner, A., & Wesse, A. "The Preschool Child's Perception of Adult Sex-Linked Objects." *Journal of Home Economics,* 1965, 57, 49–54.

Veroff, J., & Peele, S. "Initial Effects of Desegregation on the Achievement Motivation of Negro Elementary School Children." *Journal of Social Issues,* 1969, 25, 71–91.

Veroff, J., Wilcox, S., & Atkinson, J. W. "The Achievement Motive in High School and College Age Women." *Journal of Abnormal and Social Psychology,* 1953, 43, 108–119.

Vinacke, W. E., & Gullickson, G. R. "Age and Sex Differences in the Formation of Coalitions." *Child Development,* 1964, 35, 1217–1231.

Vogel, S. R., Broverman, I. K., Broverman, D. M., Clarkson, F. E., & Rosenkrantz, P. S. "Maternal Employment and Perception of Sex-Roles Among College Students." *Developmental Psychology,* 1970, 3, 384–391.

Waber, D. P. "Sex Differences in Cognition: A Function of Maturation Rate?" *Science,* 1976, 192, 572–574.

Wahrman, R., & Pugh, M. D. "Competence and Conformity: Another Look at Hollander's Study." *Sociometry,* 1972, 35, 376–386.

Wahrman, R., & Pugh, M. D. "Sex, Nonconformity and Influence." *Sociometry,* 1974, 37, 137–147.

Waite, L. J., & Stolzenberg, R. M. "Intended Childbearing and Labor Force Participation of Young Women: Insights from Nonrecursive Models." *American Sociological Review,* 1976, 41, 235–252.

Waldrop, M. F., Bell, R. Q., & Goering, J. D. "Minor Physical Anomalies and Inhibited Behavior in Elementary School Girls." *Journal of Child Psychology and Psychiatry,* 1976, 17, 113–122.

Waldrop, M. F., & Goering, J. D. "Hyperactivity and Minor Physical Anomalies in Elementary School Children." *American Journal of Orthopsychiatry,* 1971, 41, 602–607.

Walker, J. W., & Borden, R. J. "Sex, Status, and the Invasion of Shared Space." *Representative Research in Social Psychology,* 1976, 1, 28–34.

Wallston, B. "The Effects of Maternal Employment on Children." *Journal of Child Psychology and Psychiatry,* 1973, 14, 81–95.

Wallston, B., & Citron, M. "The Myth of the Working Mother." Pittsburgh: KNOW reprint, 1972.

Wallston, B. S., Foster, M. A., & Berger, M. "I Will Follow Him: Myth, Reality, or Forced Choice—Job-Seeking Experiences of Dual-Career Couples." *Psychology of Women Quarterly,* 1978, 3, 9–21.

Walstedt, J. J. "A Content Analysis of Sexual Discrimination in Children's Literature." In R. K. Unger, ed. *Sex-Role Stereotypes Revisited.* New York: Harper & Row, 1975.

Walster, E., Aronson, V., Abrahams, D., & Rottman, L. "The Importance of Physical Attractiveness in Dating Behavior." *Journal of Personality and Social Psychology,* 1966, 4, 508–516.

Walster, E., Cleary, T., & Clifford, M. M. "The Effect of Race and Sex on

College Admission." Paper presented at the meeting of the Eastern Psychological Association, New York City, April 1971.

Walster, E., & Walster, G. W. *A New Look at Love.* Reading, Mass.: Addison-Wesley, 1978.

Walster, E., Walster, G. W., Piliavin, J., & Schmidt, L. "Playing Hard to Get": Understanding an Elusive Phenomenon. *Journal of Personality and Social Psychology,* 1973, *26,* 113–121.

Walum, L. R. "The Changing Door Ceremony: Notes on the Operation of Sex Roles in Everyday Life." *Urban Life and Culture,* 1974, *2,* 506–515.

Ward, I. "Prenatal Stress Feminizes and Demasculinizes the Behavior of Males." *Science,* 1972, *175,* 82–84.

Weideger, P. *Menstruation and Menopause.* New York: Knopf, 1975.

Weiss, R. S. "The Emotional Impact of Marital Separation." *Journal of Social Issues,* 1976, *32,* 135–145.

Weissman, M. M., & Paykel, E. A. *The Depressed Woman.* Chicago: University of Chicago Press, 1974.

Weisstein, N. *Kinder, Kuche, Kirche as Scientific Law: Psychology Constructs the Female.* Boston: New England Free Press, 1968.

Weitz, S. "Sex Differences in Nonverbal Communication." *Sex Roles,* 1976, *2,* 175–184.

Weitzman, L., Eifler, D., Hokada, E., & Ross, C. "Sex-Role Socialization in Picture Books for Preschool Children." *American Journal of Sociology,* 1972, *77,* 1125–1150.

Welkowitz, J., Cohen, J., & Ortmeyer, D. "Value System Similarity: Investigation of Patient–Therapist Dyads." *Journal of Consulting Psychology,* 1967, *31,* 548–551.

Westoff, C. F., Potter, R. G., Jr., & Sagi, P. C. *The Third Child.* Princeton, N.J.: Princeton University Press, 1963.

Weston, P. J., & Mednick, M. T. S. "Race, Social Class, and the Motive to Avoid Success in Women." *Journal of Cross-Cultural Psychology,* 1970, *1,* 283–291.

White, M. S. "Women in the Professions: Psychological and Social Barriers to Women in Science." *Science,* 1970, *170,* 413–416.

Whitehead, G. I. III, & Tawes, S. L. "Dogmatism, Age, and Educational Level as Correlates of Feminism for Males and Females." *Sex Roles,* 1976, *2,* 401–405.

Whiting, B. B., & Edwards, C. P. "A Cross-Cultural Analysis of Sex Differences in the Behavior of Children Aged Three Through Eleven." *Journal of Social Psychology,* 1973, *91,* 171–188.

Whitley, M. P., & Poulsen, S. B. "Assertiveness and Sexual Satisfaction in Employed Professional Women." *Journal of Marriage and the Family,* 1975, *37,* 573–581.

Wiest, W. M., & Janke, L. D. "A Methodological Critique of Research on Psychological Effects of Vasectomy." *Psychosomatic Medicine,* 1974, *36,* 438–449.

Wiest, W. M., & Squier, L. H. "Incentives and Reinforcement: A Behavioral Approach to Fertility." *Journal of Social Issues,* 1974, *30,* 235–263.

Wiggins, J. S., Wiggins, N., & Conger, J. "Correlates of Heterosexual Somatic Preference." *Journal of Personality and Social Psychology*, 1968, *10*, 82–90.

Wiley, M. G. "Sex Roles in Games." *Sociometry*, 1973, *36*, 526–541.

Willis, F., & Hofman, G. "Development of Tactile Patterns in Relation to Age, Sex, and Race." *Developmental Psychology*, 1975, *11*, 866.

Wilsnack, S. C. "Sex-Role Identity in Female Alcoholism." *Journal of Abnormal Psychology*, 1973, *82*, 253–261.

Wilson, E. O. *Sociobiology*, Cambridge: Harvard University Press, 1975.

Winchel, R., Fenner, D., & Shaver, P. "Impact of Coeducation on Fear of Success Imagery." *Journal of Educational Psychology*, 1974, *66*, 726–730.

Witkin, H. A. "The Nature and Importance of Individual Differences in Perception." *Journal of Personality*, 1949, *18*, 145–170.

Witkin, H. A. "A Cognitive-Style Approach to Cross-Cultural Research." *International Journal of Psychology*, 1967, *2*, 233–250.

Witkin, H. A., Birnbaum, J., Lomonaco, S., Lehr, S., & Herman, J. L. "Cognitive Patterning in Congenitally Totally Blind Children." *Child Development*, 1968, *39*, 768–786.

Witkin, H. A., Dyk, R. B., Faterson, H. F., Goodenough, D. R., & Karp, S. A. *Psychological Differentiation: Studies of Development.* New York: Wiley, 1962.

Wittig, M. A. "Sex Differences in Intellectual Functioning: How Much of a Difference Do Genes Make? *Sex Roles*, 1976, *2*, 63–74.

Wolf, T. M. "Effects of Live-Modeled Sex-Inappropriate Play Behavior in a Naturalistic Setting." *Developmental Psychology*, 1973, *9*, 120–123.

Wolfe, D. M. "Power and Authority in the Family." In D. Cartwright, ed. *Studies in Social Power.* Ann Arbor, Mich.: Institute for Social Research, 1959.

Wolff, E., & Wolff, E. "The Effects of Castration on Bird Embryos." *Journal of Experimental Zoology*, 1951, *116*, 59–97.

Wolfson, K. P. "Career Development Patterns of College Women." *Journal of Counseling Psychology*, 1976, *23*, 119–125.

Wolman, B. B. "Between Men and Women." In R. K. Unger & F. L. Denmark, eds. *Women: Dependent or Independent Variable:* New York: Psychological Dimensions, 1975.

Wolman, C., & Frank, H. "The Solo Woman in a Professional Peer Group." *American Journal of Orthopsychiatry*, 1975, *45*, 164–171.

Women on Words and Images. *Dick and Jane as Victims.* Princeton, N.J., 1972.

Women on Words and Images. *Channeling Children: Sex Stereotyping on Prime Time TV.* Princeton, N.J., 1975.

Wood, M. M., & Greenfield, S. T. "Women Managers and Fear of Success: A Study in the Field." *Sex Roles*, 1976, *2*, 375–388.

Woods, M. B. "The Unsupervised Child of the Working Mother." *Developmental Psychology*, 1972, *6*, 14–25.

Woolfolk, W., & Woolfolk, J. *The Great American Birth Rite.* New York: Dial Press, 1975.

Word, C. O., Zanna, M. P., & Cooper, J. "The Nonverbal Mediation of Self-fulfilling Prophecies in Interracial Interaction." *Journal of Experimental Social Psychology,* 1974, *10,* 109–120.

Wortis, R. P. "The Acceptance of the Concept of the Maternal Role by Behavioral Scientists: Its Effects on Women." *American Journal of Orthopsychiatry,* 1971, *41,* 733–746.

Wortman, C. B. "Some Determinants of Perceived Control." *Journal of Personality and Social Psychology,* 1975, *31,* 282–294.

Yamamoto, T. "Sex Differentiation." In W. S. Hoar & D. J. Randall, eds. *Fish Physiology,* vol. 3. New York: Academic Press, 1969.

Yarrow, L. J. "Separation from Parents During Early Childhood." In M. L. Hoffman & L. W. Hoffman, eds. *Review of Child Development Research,* vol. I. New York: Russell Sage, 1964.

Yorburg, B., & Arafat, I. "Current Sex Role Conceptions and Conflict." *Sex Roles,* 1975, *1,* 135–146.

Young, D. M., Beier, E. G., Beier, P., & Barton, C. "Is Chivalry Dead?" *Journal of Communication,* 1975, *25,* 57–64.

Yudkin, S., & Holme, A. *Working Mothers and Their Children.* London: Michael Joseph, 1963.

Zander, A., & Van Egmond, E. "Relationship of Intelligence and Social Power to the Interpersonal Behavior of Children." *Journal of Educational Psychology,* 1958, *49,* 257–268.

Zanna, M. P., Goethals, G. R., & Hill, J. F. "Evaluating a Sex-Related Ability: Social Comparison with Similar Others and Standard Setters." *Journal of Experimental Social Psychology,* 1975, *11,* 86–93.

Zanna, M. P., & Pack, S. J. "On the Self-fulfilling Nature of Apparent Sex Differences in Behavior." *Journal of Experimental Social Psychology,* 1975, *11,* 583–591.

Zegiob, L. E., Arnold, S., & Forehand, R. "An Examination of Observer Effects in Parent–Child Interactions." *Child Development,* 1975, *46,* 509–512.

Zegiob, L. E., & Forehand, R. "Maternal Interactive Behavior as a Function of Race, Socioeconomic Status, and Sex of the Child." *Child Development,* 1975, *46,* 564–568.

Zeldow, P. B. "Effects of Nonpathological Sex Role Stereotypes on Student Evaluations of Psychiatric Patients." *Journal of Consulting and Clinical Psychology,* 1976, *44,* 304.

Zigler, E., & Phillips, L. "Social Effectiveness and Symptomatic Behaviors. *Journal of Abnormal and Social Psychology,* 1960, *61,* 231–238.

Zimbardo, P. G., & Meadow, W. "Sexism Springs Eternal in the Reader's Digest." Paper presented at the meeting of the Western Psychological Association, San Francisco, May 1974.

Zuckerman, M., & Wheeler, L. "To Dispel Fantasies About the Fantasy-Based Measure of Fear of Success." *Psychological Bulletin,* 1975, *82,* 932–946.

Author Index

Subject Index

Abortion, 315
Achievement, 345–380. *See also* Achievement motivation; Fear of success
  as characteristic of males, 28, 31, 352, 365
  definition of, 346
  familial correlates of, 373, 374, 378, 439
  low self esteem and, 413
  rewards for, 439
  sex context of, 249, 365–367, 371
Achievement motivation, 78, 84, 351–353. *See also* Thematic apperception test (TAT)
Activity level
  sex comparisons of, 86
  sex role stereotypes about, 27, 29, 43
  and weight control, 221–222
Adolescence. *See also* Menstruation; Puberty
  concern about appearance, 220–223
  effects of social class, 181–182
  growth spurt in 141–143, 218
Adrenogenital syndrome, 122–125
Affiliation, 58, 77, 375. *See also* Attraction; Friendship; Peers
Age. *See also* Maturation
  as a status variable, 193–195
  effect on sex differences, 85–86
  and responses to "fear of success" cues, 361, 363
  and sex-typing, 178–180
Aging. *See also* Menopause; Widowhood
  attitudes toward, 33, 49–50, 414
  and motherhood, 330
  and social status, 406–407
Aggression, 58, 63, 208. *See also* Competition; Power; Rape; Testosterone
  and maternal employment, 333
  and personal space, 56
  research bias in study of, 4, 6
  sex comparisons of, 66–67, 86, 197–198, 201–202
  and sex-role rigidity, 425–426
  sex-role socialization of, 67, 173–174, 177, 199, 206, 210
  social rewards and punishments of, 199, 206, 399–400
  and the Y chromosome, 115
Agoraphobia, 401
Alcoholism, 403
American Psychological Association. *See also* Psychology of women

  division 35 (Psychology of women), 437, 481, 485–486
  male bias in, 439–440
  task force on the status of women in psychology, 436, 486
  women in psychology, 7–9
Androgens, 110, 233. *See also* Testosterone
Androgyny, 13–14, 22, 146. *See also* Femininity; Masculinity
  behavioral correlates of, 36, 162–163, 165, 473
  and external appearance, 254–255, 470
  and mental health, 417–419, 473
Anorexia Nervosa, 222, 465
Anxiety, 43, 58, 61, 98, 208, 475
  birth position and, 197
  and the menstrual cycle, 235–236
  and peer rejection, 199
  and physical attractiveness of a dating partner, 249–250, 253
  sex comparisons of, 86
Assertiveness, 21, 74, 400. *See also* Aggression
  effects on male and female sexuality, 268, 292
  training, 415
Assortative mating, 280
Attire, 56
  and help-giving, 70–71
  in sex role socialization, 135–139, 172, 186
Attitudes. *See also* Norms; Stereotypes
  influence on by desirable others, 249–250, 258–260
  about sex roles, 422–423
Attraction, 210, 247–274 (passim). *See also* Dating; Love; Peers
Attributions
  about achievement, 37–39, 356–357, 366–368, 371
  about fetal behavior, 27–28
  and maternal blame, 328–329
  about the menstrual cycle, 239–241
Autism, 341

Barr body, 111
"Battered Women Syndrome," 402
Beauty. *See* Physical attractiveness
Biological cycles, 84, 239, 241–243
Biological explanations. *See also* Socio-biology
  of homosexuality, 139–140

Neonates. *See* Infants
Nonconscious assumptions, 80, 175–176, 469.
    See also Nonverbal communication;
    Sexism
Nontraditional women, 375–376, 387, 473. *See also* Achievement; Creativity; Singlehood
    familial relationships, 308–309
    and fear of success, 360
    relationship with parents, 178
Nonverbal communication, 55–61, 78, 80, 464.
    See also Dominance; Eye contact; Personal space; Power; Smiling; Status;
    Touching
    and stigmatized individuals, 450–451
Norms, 62–63, 73, 77. *See also* Group processes; Social deviance; Stigma
    and female achievement, 362–364
    and social deviance, 448–449
NOW. *See also* Women's liberation
    analysis of children's readers, 43
    analysis of TV programs, 46
Nuclear family, 12–13, 325–326, 339. *See also*
    Parenthood
Nurturance, 31, 179

Obesity, 221–222. *See also* Body build; Weight
Occupations. *See also* Achievement; Sex role socialization; Work
    in dual-career couples, 433
    sex comparisons of preferences for, 135, 179, 371–372
    status and sex segregation within, 348–350, 453–454
    success in relation to effort, 439
Oral contraceptives. *See* Birth control pills
Organismic variables, 3, 16, 21
Orgasm, 265, 267–268, 292. *See also* Sexuality
Ovaries, 107–109, 111, 230–233. *See also* Estrogen; Menstrual cycle; Progesterone

Parenthood, 305–344 (passim). *See also* Children; Fathers; Mothers
Parents. *See also* Sex role socialization
    agreement on child-rearing practices, 170–171, 175–178
    children's perceptions of, 80
    as models, 158
    and opposite sex children, 153, 168, 178
Passivity, 21, 43, 150, 400, 465
Peers, 247–274 (passim). *See also* Attraction;
    Friendship; Status hierarchies
    correlates of popularity with, 256
    influence on achievement, 374
    same sex cleavage, 205–207, 255–257
Peer status, 198–205. *See also* Body build;
    Physical attractiveness
Penis, 114, 122, 125, 126, 143, 145, 265. *See also* Sexual differentiation
    castration anxiety, 147
Penis envy, 150, 152, 408. *See also* Freud;
    Superego
Perception. *See also* Sex role stereotypes; Stereotypes
    differences between family members, 267–268, 273–274, 286–287

differences between self and others , 19, 200
    effect of social relationships on, 97–98, 287–288
Personal appearance, 34, 49, 223, 469–470. *See also* Body build; Physical attractiveness
Personal control. *See* Control
Personality. *See also* Androgyny; Femininity;
    Masculinity (and specific traits)
    authoritarianism and husband power, 283
    physical correlates of, 254
    and popularity with peers, 199–202
    sex typing of, 146, 161
Personal space. 56–57, 61–63, 172, 469. *See also* Dominance; Nonverbal communication
Physical attractiveness, 45, 209–211. *See also* Body build; Self-fulfilling prophecy
    and attribution of sex typed characteristics, 186–187, 210, 211, 252–255
    and couple formation, 248–250, 280
    and menstruation, 245
    and power, 250–253
    stereotypes about, 71–72, 210–211, 250, 253
Physical strength, 45, 187. *See also* Sex role stereotypes; Sexual dimorphism
Pituitary, 229. *See also* FSH; Hypothalamus;
    LH; Menstrual cycle
Play, 47, 151, 174. *See also* Toys
Pornography, 262. *See also* Aggression; Rape
Postpartum period, 323–326. *See also*
    Childbearing; Depression; Parenthood
Power, 53–80 (passim). *See also* Status
    children's use of, 193–197, 203–204
    exploitation and retaliation, 65
    and locus of control, 354–355, 357
    in marriage, 282–283, 287–289, 301, 336–337
    media representation of, 47–48
    and modeling, 154–155
    and rape, 427
    and self-esteem, 456
    sex typing of, 71–75, 80
    and the social system, 449–450, 454–455, 466
Pregnancy, 21, 263, 316–323. *See also* Abortion; Childbearing; Contraception; Medical model; Postpartum period
    unplanned, 310, 327
Prejudice against women, 33, 34, 36–39, 451.
    See also Evaluation bias; Misogyny; Sex discrimination; Sexism
Premenstrual syndrome, 22, 235–237
Primates, 58, 170, 342–343
Problem solving, 18, 75
Professional networks, 439–440, 485
Progesterone, 230–232. *See also* Birth control pills; Pregnancy
    and negative mood, 243–244
Psychoanalysis, 319. *See also* Freud; Mental illness; Psychotherapy
Psychological research. *See also* Science, Sex bias; Sexism
    guidelines for, 484
    methodological issues in, 86, 94–96, 234–237, 239, 335–336, 343–344